*Be Centered in Christ
and Not in Self*

Be Centered in Christ and Not in Self

The Missionary Society of Saint Columban:
The North American Story (1918–2018)

Angelyn Dries, OSF

Library of Congress Control Number: 2017911012
ISBN: Hardcover   978-1-5434-3620-4
                 Softcover   978-1-5434-3621-1
                 eBook   978-1-5434-3622-8

Print information available on the last page.

Rev. date: 07/25/2017

To order additional copies of this book, contact:
Xlibris
1-888-795-4274
www.Xlibris.com
Orders@Xlibris.com
762848

CONTENTS

PREFACE

From our foundation in 1918, the focus of the endeavors of the Missionary Society of St. Columban has been to "go out to all the world and proclaim the Good News." At the outset, evangelization in China was the priority. Then, over the succeeding decades, we expanded our outreach to several other countries in Asia, Oceania, and Latin America. However, as becomes abundantly clear in the pages of this book, these accomplishments were made possible only because of the dedication and generosity of those who tended the home fires. Their lives may not have been as adventurous as those of missionaries in distant lands, but their challenges were just as real. Moreover, they understood that their contribution to God's mission was inspired by the same Spirit who hovers over the entire earth, drawing all people to Christ.

As recounted in this book, the story of Columban missionaries' engagement with the Church in North America mirrors that of the universal Church as it came to a greater understanding of God's mission throughout the twentieth century. At the outset, there was the clear distinction between countries that sent missionaries and those that received them. However, over the following decades, that distinction became blurred with the realization that regardless of where we live, all of us fall short of the demands of the Gospel and so are engaged in a lifelong conversion journey, as individual Christians and as members of a particular faith community.

Furthermore, throughout this past century, rather than being viewed as a one-way street, cross-cultural mission came to resemble a highway with traffic flowing in both directions. While family-faith life and seminary formation prepared Columban missionaries to embark on cross-cultural missions, their experience of sharing the Good News with peoples of others lands gave them a deeper appreciation of the mystery of God's action in the world and provided them with new insights into the Gospel message. Moreover, they witnessed the impact of international commerce and foreign policy decisions by their own government on the lives of the local people to whom they ministered in other countries. Upon returning home, these Columban missionaries eagerly shared their experiences and new perspectives with the communities that had initially sent them on mission, thereby completing the circle.

Another major change in our understanding of mission during this past century has been the growing realization that all the baptized are called to be missionaries. The Second Vatican Council affirmed that all Christians have both the privilege and responsibility of being messengers of God's love and mercy to the world around them. Of course, how and where one lives out that baptismal vocation depends on many factors. However, with this broader understanding of their Christian vocation, Columban supporters came to see themselves no longer as simply assisting missionaries but rather as expressing and sharing their own faith as partners with us in mission.

Every missionary has a twofold task: to come to know Christ so as to introduce him to an audience and to come to know a particular audience so as to introduce it to Christ. Since all of us encounter Christ through the lens of our own culture and within the mind-set of our own particular era, upon arriving in another country, Columban missionaries have to learn a new way of understanding Christ and of presenting his message in a manner that resonates with their new audience. Frequently, this task causes uncertainty as they slowly separate the heart of the Gospel, the actual gift, from particular practices, customs, and traditions—the wrapping paper. At the same time, they also have to search for new wrapping paper with which to present such a special gift to their new audience.

However, in the world today, it is not only Columban missionaries who are faced with this task. In every multicultural society, all baptized persons are called to move out of our own cultural comfort zone in order to share the Good News with people around us who have different backgrounds and traditions. Furthermore, as our modern world becomes increasingly shaped by advances in media, presenting the gift of the Gospel to younger generations using such new forms of wrapping paper will remain a major missionary challenge. Moreover, with further developments in technology and travel, more and more people will become part of the global village, resulting in as yet unimagined changes to our understanding of, and approach to, cross-cultural mission.

Within such a complex and fast-changing world, the celebration of the centennial of Columban mission provides us with an opportunity to reflect on our past and become more deeply grateful for the blessings we have received, so that we can continue to treasure and share them as we move forward. This book on the history of Columban missionaries' engagement with the Church in North America and the wider world is, therefore, a bridge between our past and our future. Its genesis dates back to a meeting of the U.S. Columban leadership team—the Regional Council—in 2010. As it looked ahead to the celebration of the centennial of Columban mission in 2018, it decided that the story of Columban mission, viewed through the lens of our presence in North America, ought to be researched and recorded, not only for ourselves, but also for our supporters and members of the wider Church, with whom we remain inextricably linked.

As the then U.S. Regional Director, Fr. Arturo Aguilar, looked around for someone who had the competence to undertake such a major task, fortune smiled on him. Sr. Angelyn Dries, OSF, professor emerita of American Christianity at Saint Louis University, not only was eminently qualified but also agreed to undertake this assignment as a labor of love. Columban missionaries in the U.S. region are deeply grateful for her painstaking research of our story during these past several years, and for bringing it to fruition in this book in time for the celebration of our centennial year.

Just as there are many hands at work behind the scenes to facilitate those on the frontline of Columban mission, so also did several people in the background contribute in various ways to this book project. Columban missionaries in the U.S. region wish to express our gratitude to Sr. Jeanne Janssen, CSJ, for her assistance in getting the project off the ground. We are also grateful to Michael Arbagi for bringing order out of chaos by structuring our archival resources. Both his and Rhonda Firnhaber's prompt responses to numerous requests by the author for specific archival materials greatly smoothed the process of her research. Finally, we deeply appreciate the commitment of Kate Kenny, the director of communications for the U.S. region, to keeping this project moving forward and, together with Marci Anderson, doing the final copyediting of this book.

To support Sr. Angelyn Dries, OSF, throughout the lengthy process of researching and writing, a group of Columban priests made themselves available to interview their confreres, as well as to provide feedback on various drafts of this book. The contribution of Frs. John Brannigan, John Burger, John Comiskey, Sean Dwan, Joseph McSweeny, and Tom Reynolds helped deepen various insights into Columban identity as well as broaden some perspectives on our mission during this past century.

Throughout 2018, as Columban missionaries celebrate a century of mission, we are pleased to be able to share with you this story about the engagement of the people of North America in our global mission. We are grateful to so many, both here and in other countries around the world, who have contributed by their missionary endeavors to particular paragraphs and chapters of this story. While certain individuals are referenced in the text, the contribution of so many others—whose names are written in invisible ink!—is an equally treasured part of our Columban story.

As Columban missionaries celebrate our centennial, the story of our past provides us with reassurance that God will continue to guide us and provide for us as we prepare to encounter a new century of mission. We look forward to you accompanying us also so that the next volume of our story can provide even greater testimony to God's unfathomable love and concern for all the people of our world.

Fr. Tim Mulroy
Director of the U.S. Region of the Columban Fathers

ACKNOWLEDGMENTS

Writing the History of the U.S. Region of the Columban Fathers

The author's first encounter with the Missionary Society of St. Columban happened in the 1969–1970 academic year. Two of us Sisters were hired to develop a religious education program for a parish that had closed its school the year before we arrived. Our main task was to train teachers for a first grade through high school religious education program in the greater Oconomowoc, Wisconsin, area. Some parents in the parish volunteered to be teachers, but we needed many more people. In mid-August we visited three seminaries/novitiates in the area. We hoped to draw the seminarians to our program and provide them with some teaching methods, materials, and guidance in teaching religious education. The Columbans were the only seminary to offer the opportunity to their college students. I did not know it then, but that encounter began a decades' long relationship (forty-nine years for me in 2018) with the Missionary Society of St. Columban. One Columban faculty member in 1969/70 was Father Thomas P. Reynolds, who has been assigned to the United States for about half of the Columban century and is on the Columban History Board.

The Columban Fathers U.S. Region History Project Board was formed during Regional Director Father Arturo Aguilar's administration. Sister Jeanne Janssen, CSJ, who was in charge of mission education, editor of *Columban Mission,* and held several other areas of office responsibilities gave sterling leadership to the direction of the history project at its beginnings. Many thanks also are due to Kate Kenny, who took on several of the tasks Jeanne held, including leadership of the History Project Board. Kate was copy editor of the manuscript and saw the project through to its publication. I am especially grateful to Father Thomas P. Reynolds and to Father John Burger. It was Father Burger who looked ahead to the centennial and suggested a history of the region. These two Columbans advised me on some of the fine points related to the region and provided insight, information, and other primary sources they had available. I am grateful for their avid interest in the history project. They both gave untold hours to reading and commenting on the stages of the book. Other History Board members include Fathers John Brannigan, John Comiskey, Sean Dwan, as well as Kate Kenny and Dan Eminger. My thanks to each of them for their reflections, corrections, and observations.

Archival Retrieval

You might have heard a variation of the Igbo and Yoruba (Nigeria) proverb, "It takes a whole village to raise a child." One could also say, "It takes a whole village of people and documents to raise a history." Archival holdings, oral histories, and interviews are central to writing a history. My first foray into the Columban archives located at the region's headquarters outside Omaha took place in August 1988. Father Paul Casey (1927–2005) was a gracious, helpful, well-organized archivist. My goal then was to gather documents on Columbans in China for a section of my dissertation. Some of that material ended up later in my *The Missionary Movement in American Catholic History* (Orbis Books, 1999). I later conferred with Casey as I wrote an article on Catholic Koreans in the United States, when I worked with the Korean community in Milwaukee throughout the 1990s. Columban Father Mort Kelly had served that community, traveling from Chicago for weekly Mass from February 1979 to July 1981, as did Father Gerald Wilmsen, SSC, from September 1983 through August 1984.

After I accepted the invitation to write the history of the U.S. region of the Missionary Society of St. Columban and was well launched into the project, I learned from Father John Burger that Casey had meticulously gone through correspondence, newsletters, and other key items to lay out the documentary evidence from the start of the U.S. region until 1982, as preparation for a Columban history of the U.S. region. Father Burger provided me a copy of the Casey material. I have referenced this document as the *Casey History* in the footnotes. The current archivist for the Columbans is Michael Arbagi, who graciously and swiftly provided a range of materials, including oral histories, biographical cards for Columbans, copies of *Columban Mission* and its predecessor, the *Far East*, as well as other Columban documents I needed. For the year Michael was deployed to Djibouti, Rhonda Firnhaber generously stepped in to keep the flow of information and items coming my way. I am grateful to them both.

Archivists from congregations of women religious who served where Columbans were located provided documents for the history. I especially want to thank Archivist Sister Rachel Shepherd, Sisters of Social Service, Encino, California. Through her I was able to contact Sister Angelia Ying in Taiwan through Sister Theresa Yih-Lan. Sister Rachel also provided wonderful primary sources and photos of the Sisters in the classroom. The pictures concretized some elements related to Columban mission among Chinese in Los Angeles. A big thank-you to Sister Anna Maria Pierto, IHM, archivist for the Immaculate Heart Community, Los Angeles, California. The treasure trove of materials she sent provides specifics of particular events and programs at the Chinese Catholic Center/Academy and the larger framework the Sisters and their students had in working among the Chinese, while at the same time illuminating Columban responsibility. Archivist Denise Gallo provided materials on the Daughters of Charity mission in Japan. Elizabeth Eisenhauer and Betsy Johnson, archivists for the Sisters of Mercy, Buffalo, New York, provided *Annals* of the Sisters' summer vacation week at St. Columban Seminary, Silver Creek, items related to the Mercy Sisters' mission in the Philippines, and the foundation of a Mercy Sisters Filipina community. In all these cases, women wrote with details about their daily work and thereby presented a clearer picture of Columban activity as well. Thank you.

Niamh Collins, archivist for the Missionary Society of St. Columban, Navan, Ireland, provided resources I was unable to find in the U.S. region archives and answered a number of questions relative to particular Columbans. She provided access to the interviews conducted earlier by Father James McCaslin for *The Spirituality of Our Founders* and other interviews conducted in the Columban region of Ireland. Her service was gracious and swift! In her absence, Father Neil Collins responded to my queries. Thanks to you both!

Thanks go to Laura Heimann, archivist at the Archdiocese of Omaha, who provided material on the Columbans from almost the start of their interaction with the Archdiocese, especially in relation to the Columban role in the beginnings of what became St. Mary's Parish, Bellevue. My gratitude goes to Robert Johnson–Lally, Director, Archives of the Archdiocese of Boston, for the material related to Richard Cardinal Cushing and the Society of St. Columban. Several visits to the Sarpy County (Nebraska) Museum and conversations with their staff provided historical background for the geographic area where the Society bought their first property in the United States.

Columban Fathers Thomas P. Reynolds, Joseph McSweeny,[1] John Brannigan, and Sean Dwan interviewed Columbans involved in aspects of mission related to the U.S. region. I am grateful to them for the many hours they gave conducting the interviews.

Houses of Hospitality

Not enough thanks can be expressed for the generous hospitality of the Columban Fathers who reside at St. Columbans, Nebraska, among whom I lived for several weeks over the years of the history project. Conversations around the table at meals often elicited stories about the Columban past. A special

---

[1]   Columban Father Joseph McSweeny (no "e" before the "y") was ordained in 1990.

mention of gratitude goes to Father Charlie Duster (1934–2017), the superior at the Columban Fathers' residence during the time I wrote the history. He was always gracious and solicitous that I was comfortable in my lodgings while I worked in the Columban archives. Thanks to Chef Jeff Lane, who provided delicious healthy meals, soups, and the occasional cherry pie!

I am grateful to Father Colm Stanley for his invitation to view the entire area that the Columbans originally purchased for their Nebraska seminary. His driving tour provided an excellent overview of the vast acreage that was so much a part of the conversation in the early days of the region. He also drove me to the graves of Chief Big Elk, the last full-blooded Omaha, and other Native Americans buried in the Bellevue cemetery. Special gratitude goes to Father Richard Steinhilber, former regional superior (1967–1970) and superior general (1970–1976) of the Missionary Society of St. Columban. He was the go-to person for many of my questions, given his unique leadership experience and many years in the Society. He is "one of a kind."

It was especially refreshing for me to meet the Columban Sisters since I had not known them prior to my visit. Their warm hospitality at their houses in Silver Creek, New York, and Brighton, Massachusetts, provided insight into their charism and on the work they did with the Columban Fathers both in the States and on mission. I am grateful especially to Sister Virgie Mozo, who made arrangements for my visit at Silver Creek and Brighton and to Sister Corona Colleary, who has been the administrator of the St. Columban's on the Lake Retirement Home since its beginning. She provided helpful background about the change of the building from a seminary to a retirement home.

Author Interviews and Contacts

Given that the Columban Sisters worked closely with the Columban Fathers, I am especially thankful to Columban Sisters Mary O'Dea (d. 2015) via Skype, Patricia Zandrews (via telephone), the Columban Sisters at Brighton, Massachusetts, and Silver Creek, especially Sisters Margaret Devine, Stephanie King, Evelyn Frieder, Margaret Holleran, Corona Colleary, Rose Dineen, Jean Fitzpatrick, Claire O'Rourke, Francesca Garvey (1924–2017), and Columban regional superior at the time, Sister Virgie Mozo. I appreciated the initiative Sister Corona Colleary took to contact some families who were involved in cooking and cleaning for the priests, seminarians, and retreatants at Silver Creek: Shirley Kanistanoux and Rosemary Krzyzanowski [nee McFarland].

I am grateful for interviews with Sister Marcella Regan, IHM, Sister Rita Connell, RSM, Sister Jeanne Janssen, CSJ, Sister Dorothy Mahon, RSM, Sylvia Thompson, and Connie Wacha. Special thanks to Janet Drey, former diocesan director of Youth Ministry, Des Moines, Iowa, for her story of the invitation to write the manual for the Columban films on *The Barrios* series and the effect the experience had on her life. These dedicated women significantly enhanced areas of mission education with a variety of competencies, skills, and personal appropriation of mission. Sister Catherine O'Brien, SND, sister of Father James O'Brien, SSC, generously provided some of her brother's personal papers that "fleshed out" material related to his mission education thoughts and involvement. Thanks to Sister Loretto Gettemeier, DC, who shared her experience and that of the Daughters of Charity in Japan and their interactions with the Columban Fathers in Wakayama.

Thank you to those with whom I held conversations about particular aspects of the region's history: Columban Fathers Thomas Glennon, Paul O'Malley, Charlie O'Rourke, Charlie Duster, Peter Cronin, Chuck Lintz, John Brannigan, and current regional director Father Tim Mulroy. Thanks to Father Richard Parle, Seattle, Washington; William Warborg, Johnson Creek, Wisconsin; and Reverend John Lam, SDB, St. Bridget Catholic Chinese Center, Los Angeles, who provided pertinent material for particular aspects of Columbans in the United States. Father Paul Tomasso offered some details about daily life at Silver Creek Seminary during his years there in the mid-1960s. Christine Cobourn Herman and Susan Thompson (the latter still has her calendars from seventeen years in the Columban Justice and Peace office!) were immensely helpful in providing specific information and insightful remarks about the development of the Columban Justice and Peace office, Washington DC, as did Columban Fathers Mark Mengel and Michael Dodd. Mark Saucier of the diocese of Jefferson City, Missouri, shared a history of the relationship between the Peru mission from that diocese and the Columban Justice and Peace office. Thanks to Scott Wright, director of the Columban Center for Advocacy and Outreach, who searched for materials for me and answered a number of questions for me. My last interview for the region history was with Mrs. Janette T. [Santa Cruz] Frye, who along with her sister were members of St. Columban Parish, Los Angeles, when the small community in the mid-1940s rented space on South Fedora Street. Mrs. Frye provided important information about those early days and the spirit that gave the sense that the Church is about the people. I am grateful for her embodiment of that generous, life-giving commitment to the Gospel.

Finally, a heartfelt thanks to some of the men I met at St. Columban Seminary, Oconomowoc, Wisconsin, all those years ago and who have made a difference in my life. Some of the residents were or became Columbans; others went on to serve their local communities in diverse ways: Father Bill Sweeney (Korea), Father Dick Pankratz (Philippines), Father Bob Lamby [1947–2002] (Philippines, USAF, Diocese of Cleveland), Father Sal Caputo (Korea), Father Paul Tomasso (Vicar General and Moderator of the Curia, Diocese of Rochester, New York, with service in the Diocese's mission in Mexico[2]), G. Benny Johnson

---

[2]   The Diocese of Rochester served a mission parish in Mexico from 1980 to 1990.

(President/CEO, New Orleans Chamber of Commerce, formerly Director, Archdiocese of New Orleans Office of Social Apostolate, then President, Greater New Orleans Community Foundation), John Brandon (active with his wife Janet in a range of ministries within their parish for decades, Owensboro, Kentucky), Father Victor Babin (Archdiocese of Miami), Father Horatio Yanez (Archdiocese of Seattle), Doctor Tom Yaeger (Family Practice, Guthrie Clinic, Sayre, Pennsylvania, with recent years as faculty member teaching other doctors), Steve Farenbaugh (General and Electrical Contractor, volunteer fireman, California), Tony Canzona (cattle rancher, northwestern Nebraska), Brother Kevin Dargan (Maryknoll Society, Shinyanga, Tanzania), Bill Warborg, who still remembers the fine English teacher he had at Silver Creek (MP Metal Products in Ixonia, Wisconsin), and Cy Svoboda (Professor of Psychology, Maryland University College). As noted earlier, faculty member Father Thomas P. Reynolds is on the Columban History Board. Christopher Farrelly (currently CEO/City Missioner of Auckland City Mission, New Zealand, whose mission is advocacy on behalf of those who are vulnerable or marginalized) and I met when I was doing my doctoral studies in Berkeley, California, and he was writing his thesis, *Missionary Spirituality in the World Today—From a Columban Experience* (Jesuit School of Theology, Berkeley, 1987).

The history of the U.S. region of the Missionary Society of St. Columban could not have been written without the interest, knowledge, resources, and assistance of all these persons. Thank you.

Footnote Abbreviations

When the reader sees the following abbreviations in the footnotes, the reference is as follows:

CFA-USA   Columban Fathers Archives, Region of the United States

CM   *Columban Mission*

FE   The *Far East*

INTRODUCTION

The story of the one hundred years (1918–2018) of the Missionary Society of St. Columban is filled with adventure, stress, and danger, with the humdrum of daily life, with martyrs (twenty-seven of them thus far, including Columban Sister Joan Sawyer), with innumerable personal and Society global connections and issues, with men who went from the familiarity of daily life and people they knew to lands and people unknown to bring the Good News. The story is charged with humor and courage, along with faith, hope, and love.

The people in this story lived within particular national histories and an evolving global Christianity. The history of the U.S. region of the Missionary Society of St. Columban interacts with movements of Catholic and American history. These *contexts* influenced the ability of the Columbans to grow in the United States, to provide desperately needed resources for the missions, and to further Catholic engagement in mission. Occasionally, however, the U.S. story needs to go abroad to see the relationships between the region and what is taking place in the Columban missions. The latter experiences will, in turn, affect the mission of the Columbans in the United States. The growth of the Catholic Church around the world will bring issues relative to "cross-cultural mission" closer to home, especially in relation to Columban candidates for priesthood or for lay missionaries from countries previously considered "mission countries."

A religious order or missionary society often forms itself around a particular focus of the Gospel and Catholic life. Franciscans and Jesuits, for example, have distinctive traits or characteristics they try to manifest in their day-to-day lives. The same is true of the Missionary Society of St. Columban. They were clearly influenced by Bishop Edward J. Galvin and Father John Blowick. However, the Society motto, "Be centered in Christ, not in self,"[3] and the image of Saint Columban as a "pilgrim" also offered spiritual and practical values that unfolded as the Society grew. Sister Mary Therese Bolan spoke of the origin of the Society's patron. She worked closely with Father E. J. McCarthy

---

[3]   The Latin text is, "*Christi simus non nostri.*"

as a laywoman in the Columban promotion office in Omaha almost from its inception and later joined the Columban Sisters.[4] She put it this way.

> One day, as [Fathers Edward] Galvin and McCarthy traveled to Belfast, they discussed possible names for the Society. They passed through a bleak area on their passage and discarded one name and then another. Galvin suddenly said, "St. Columban . . . that's our man." Galvin saw Columban as a missionary who had been a rugged man, had been through tremendous difficulty and all kinds of traditions and suffered terribly but had kept going on and had carried the faith with him.[5]

Bolan noted further, "It was only afterwards that Father Galvin adverted to the fact that [St. Columban's feast day] was his own birthday" (November 23).[6] While the feast day was celebrated in Ireland, Edward Galvin himself would campaign for the internationalization of the feast of St. Columban (559–615), whose feast appeared on the Roman Catholic Church universal calendar in the 1960s.

What Is History?

At its center, history is a story, a narrative, though it is more than a story. History is discovering significance in relationships between individuals and groups on multiple levels *over time*. Because of the time factor, larger meanings are often discovered in retrospect. In the case of the one hundred years of the U.S. region of the Missionary Society of St. Columban, this means we need to look at the larger framework or *context* in which the story emerges in this country, the patterns and anomalies we find, and the role that individuals and particular stories have within the bigger story. As Father Parig Digan, *Columban Intercom* editor at the time, noted, "Columban history should surely be more than a history of the Columbans."[7] How are individual Columbans part of the fuller story? Columban experience is a vibrant component in mission history. Columbans also contribute to migration and ethnic history, as well

---

[4]   Sister Mary Therese Bolan was the first American Columban Sister to complete her novitiate as a Missionary Sister of St. Columban in County Clare, Ireland, and first profession in 1931. She entered the Sisters when she was thirty-one years old.

[5]   Father Nick Kill interview of Sister Therese Bolan, August 1975, 8. Author received the document from Father Paul Casey, SSC, at CFA-USA in 1988.

[6]   Ibid., The feast of St. Columban was celebrated in the Catholic Church in Ireland as a local feast in Galvin's life.

[7]   Father Parig Digan, *Columban Intercom* (January 1972).

as to the history of the visual arts and prayer movements. In what ways did Columbans assimilate or revise mission thought and practice? In what ways did they contribute to new understandings of mission? As a Society not "born in America," how did the Missionary Society of St. Columban affect the life and thought of the Catholic Church in the United States? How did overseas mission experience influence the path Columbans took in the United States? What perennial motifs appear in the Columban experience? These questions will be explored over the next chapters.

History tells us about a past and a present and can provide insight into our future. To tell the story holds an important human and religious function. As Father Vincent Busch remarked about the tribal peoples with whom he has worked for decades in the Philippines, "People who can tell their story are in charge of their life."[8] Columbans have focused on telling the stories of thousands of people they served in many countries. It is now time to tell the Columban story.

Overall Framework

The history of the U.S. region of the Columban Fathers will unfold in two parts. **Part One, Development of a Corporate Columban Identity in the Region of the United States, 1919–2018,** explores the foundation and growth of the Society in the United States and the relationship between the U.S. region and the Society's headquarters in Ireland. After this introduction, which provides an overview of the group's beginnings in Ireland, six chapters identify the development and challenges the Society faced within various periods of American history and examine the unfolding of a "corporate" identity in the region. In brief, those chapters examine the Columban "initiation" into the United States and the conception of the Society as international rather national (chapter 1, 1918–1928), how Columbans faced the stressful times of the Great Depression (chapter 2, 1929–1940), the consequences of World War II for Columbans (chapter 3, 1941–1950), and a postwar "building boom," the growth of seminaries, and the threat of international Communism (chapter 4, 1950–1964). Chapter 5 (1965–1976) explores the impact of the social upheaval of the 1960s and 1970s and a renewed Catholicism at the Second Vatican Council as that affected the Society in its focus and seminary life. Chapter 6 (1977–2012) examines how the maturing theology of the Second Vatican Council related to mission location, emphasis, and the relationship between justice and preaching the Gospel. The Society's office for justice and peace in Washington DC addressed issues surrounding military dictatorships and global consequences of international development as seen in the Society's missions.

---

[8]   Interview of Father Vincent (Vinny) Busch, 1991. Unidentified interviewer. DVD.

Part Two, Attracting Catholics to the Support and Promotion of Mission, "retraces the historical terrain of the past one hundred years with cameo presentations"[9] that develop more fully the significant movements or particular contributions the U.S. region of the Columbans have made to the understanding and practice of mission. Chapter 7, "Mission Promotion and Mission Education," details the diversity, creativity, and consistency of Columban efforts to raise funds for and interest in their missions. Beginning with the *Far East*, later called *Columban Mission*, the use of film and latest audio/visual material and education processes to accompany the materials, the Society became a leader in mission education in the United States. Periodic mission promotion "events" to raise funds for missions were occasions to meet the Columbans informally in an atmosphere of enjoyment and relaxation while learning about mission life. Columbans developed strong relationships with their donors and never forgot the responsibility to be accountable for the gifts received.

Chapter 8, "Mission to Asian Communities in the United States," explores Columban ministry to three groups of Asian communities in the United States—Chinese, Filipino, and Korean. Columbans had an affinity for these groups in particular because of mission experience in those countries. At the same time, ministry with those communities provided Columbans a new way to envision mission within the United States. Through the work of several congregations of women religious who worked at the ethnic missions, the reader obtains a more detailed picture of daily life, especially among the Chinese.

Chapter 9, "The Whole Church Is in Mission," unfolds how the Columban Fathers engaged U.S. Catholics in the mission call. The coworkers include those specifically who follow the spirit of St. Columban as a Brother or a Sister or as lay missionaries or clergy volunteers (priest associates) to serve the missions. Chapter 10, "Development of the Local Church in 'Mission' Countries," illustrates how through Columban contacts in the United States opportunities were provided for the formation of congregations of women religious in China, Korea, Japan, and the Philippines and a Missionary Society in Korea. In addition to the formation of lay leaders through the Legion of Mary, these local women and men were effective in church leadership through providing schools, hospitals, and ministry among impoverished people. In turn, the growth of new congregations and missionary societies was another way of implanting mission values where Columbans served.

Chapter 11, "Retreats, Prayer, and Spirituality Movements," examines the Columban retreat ministry in the United States starting in 1929 with retreats given at the Columban region headquarters in Nebraska. Columbans engaged in more recent spirituality movements or spiritually oriented groups, such as Cursillo, Marriage Encounter, and Alcoholics Anonymous. Chapter 12,

---

9   Father Thomas P. Reynolds correspondence with author 27 March 2017.

"Columbans and the Earth—From Saving Souls to Saving the Environment," recalls that just as Columban pioneers in Nebraska had paid attention to issues of the land, so, in the present day, the concern for land, water, and the environment has many elements, ranging from Columban property at headquarters used for senior citizen housing to informing people of land/water degradation and its effects in mission countries. A brief "Conclusion" chapter recapitulates the history through the theme of Columbans as Pilgrims, "moving on," as had St. Columban in the sixth century, yet leaving a legacy with each step of their pilgrim journey.

Where Is St. Columbans, Nebraska?

A word about the location of the U.S. headquarters of the Missionary Society of St. Columban. "St. Columbans, Nebraska" exists only as a post office address in the United States. The Society's headquarters is about ten miles south of downtown Omaha and is located in Sarpy County, Nebraska. The Society is unincorporated land adjacent to the town of Bellevue, Nebraska, which touches on all sides of the property. A major thoroughfare close to the original western boundary of the Columban property was later named Galvin Boulevard in honor of Columban cofounder Bishop Edward Galvin. The road cuts through what had been a triangular piece of Columban land to the west of the street and a larger piece to the east of the boulevard. The other main road that goes through the old section of Bellevue and a block south of the Columban property is Mission Avenue. The latter street was named for Baptist missionaries Moses and Eliza Merrill, who arrived at the Indian Agency in Bellevue in 1833 to work with the Otoe in the area. In 1835, the Merrills moved eight miles west with the Native Americans and established the Moses Merrill Mission. In this book, sometimes "Bellevue" or "Omaha" is used in reference to the Columban headquarters, even though technically the Society is located in neither city. Considering that the nineteenth century Jesuit missionary Pierre de Smet had also formed a Catholic congregation straddling the Missouri River fairly near the hill where St. Columbans is located, it seems that this area of land was destined for mission, as well as being an important post for fur trading!

Foundation of Society in Ireland, 1916

First, however, we need a brief overview of the Irish origins of the Society to shed light on the development of the region of the United States. Father Neil Collins has extensively researched the beginning and growth of the Columbans with emphasis on the region of Ireland and then missions in Asia to 1954, so the reader can look to his book for more details about the early days and major figures.[10]

Several areas of Irish experience affected the origins of the Society. The **first factor** is the political world of Catholics in Ireland. Irishmen had died in the Battle of the Somme, France, one of World War I's largest and bloodiest military battles and Britain's first great offensive. Catholic Irish Nationalism was heightened (men languished in prison and died in the Spring Uprising of 1916). There was a strong movement to reclaim Irish Catholic culture, partially through a revival of Irish Gaelic.[11] As Columban Father Francis Hoare has written, "We cannot explain a historical movement simply in terms of conscious causality linking intention and consequence. While cultural representations that structure the motivation and behavior of the protagonists are not fully conscious to them, the representations can powerfully affect perceptions and intercultural interactions."[12] These profound Irish experiences and images at the Columban foundation (first informally called the Chinese Mission Society, then canonically the Maynooth Mission to China)[13] are seen in their literature and formation in Ireland. The bishops of Ireland gave the group permission in 1916 to raise funds to start a seminary, and in 1918 the group received ecclesiastical period. The early issues of the *Far East* published in the United States contained some pages printed in Gaelic. Other representations or symbols undergird the Columban world as will be seen later in the history.

Catholics are at home with symbols and images, of course. Their spiritual world is incarnational—i.e., physical representations of God, Mary, and the saints abound to connect the spiritual, physical, and sometimes political realms of life.

---

[10]   Neil Collins, *The Splendid Cause. The Missionary Society of St. Columban, 1916–1954* (Blackrock County Dublin: The Columba Press, 2009).

[11]   For background on the Irish context at the foundations of the Columbans, see Kevin Collins, *Catholic Churchmen and the Celtic Revival in Ireland, 1848–1916* (Portland OR: Four Courts Press, 2002), especially the introduction and chapter 2, Maynooth and the Irish Language. Bruce Nelson, *Irish Nationalists and the Making of the Irish Race* (Princeton, NY: Princeton University Press, 2012), especially the chapter on Eamon de Valera, who traveled through the United States and visited the Columbans in Omaha.

[12]   Frank Hoare, "The Influence of the Crusade Symbol and War Metaphor on the Motivation and Attitudes of the Maynooth Mission to China, 1918–1929," *U.S. Catholic Historian* 24 Number 3 (Summer 2006), 55–74, here 55.

[13]   In language of the Church's Canon Law, the Congregation for the Propagation of the Faith changed the language used by the Irish bishops "(a college for . . . the propagation of the Catholic Faith in China") to "a college for the Foreign Missions." Neil Collins, *The Splendid Cause. The Missionary Society of St. Columban, 1916–1954*, 50.

Edward Galvin (1882–1956) **and John Blowick** (1888–1972)

A few factual elements from the Society's beginnings are important to know before we concentrate on the U.S. region. The two Irishmen especially involved are Edward Galvin and John Blowick. Galvin returned to Ireland from China with the idea to initiate a missionary society for China missions. That meant the approval from the local bishop (in this case, it was Galvin's bishop of the diocese of Cork) and then of all the Irish bishops to raise funds and begin a seminary. Father John Blowick, by education a theologian, was the key person who had local contacts in Ireland and would guide the canon law process with authorities at the Vatican for the approval of the Society. In 1916, Galvin had permission to begin collecting for the Maynooth Mission to China.[14] As Edward J. McCarthy wrote, "When the Irish Bishops approved Father Galvin's plans at their meeting at Maynooth on October 10, 1916, there were in all only five of us available to begin the immediate task of raising funds for a new seminary to train missionaries for China. Father Blowick assumed leadership and the rest of us [Galvin, J. Heneghan, J. Conway, E. J. McCarthy] rallied round as best we could. . . . We were very young and some of us were very inexperienced."[15] In 1918 the Society was canonically approved, and the first students started at St. Columban's College, Dalgan Park, to become missionaries to China.

Galvin lead the first band of his missionaries to China in 1920. John Blowick became the superior after the Society's Congress, 1919, and vicar general from 1925 through 1946 and on the Council until 1952. He would "operate as the storm-trooper for Galvin in getting the project accepted by the Irish bishops"[16] and then took on organizing and developing the seminary. Sister Mary Therese Bolan (from whom we heard earlier) made the point later in her life, "Father McCarthy (one of the first five members of the Society) told me again and again that Bishop Galvin was the sole founder of the Society."[17] Not all Columbans have held to that position. Many Columbans have claimed both Galvin and Blowick as founders, each with different skills toward the foundation of a missionary society.

A **second factor** that affected the Society's development in the United States was that Ireland at the time had a surplus of clergy. Bishops "loaned" priests to growing dioceses in the United States for a certain period of time, especially beginning toward the end of the nineteenth century. Father Edward Galvin was "on loan" to the Diocese of Brooklyn. Father Michael Mee, born

---

14   For details on the history of the Irish origins of the Society, see Neil Collins, *The Splendid Cause. The Missionary Society of St. Columban, 1916–1954*, 14–85.

15   E. J. McCarthy, "A Few Personal Reminiscences, 1916–1920," CFA-USA.

16   Father T. P. Reynolds e-mail correspondence with author 27 March 2017.

17   Father Nick Kill interview of Sister Therese Bolan, August 1975. Typescript, 8. Author received the document from Father Paul Casey, SSC, at CFA-USA in 1988.

in County Monaghan, was ordained in 1910 for the diocese of Alton (now Springfield), Illinois, and taught there for a number of years before he entered the Society in 1918. Father Paul Waldron, born in County Mayo, was ordained in 1914 and taught moral theology at the seminary in the Archdiocese of St. Paul, Minnesota, before joining the Society in 1918. He became rector of the seminary in Bellevue, Nebraska, and the second U.S. regional superior. The surplus of other Irish priests who found their way to the United States proved a benefit to the Society as the missionaries sought opportunities for fund-raising and promotion across the country.

Why Come to the United States?

The First World War (July 28, 1914–November 11, 1918) had depleted foreign missionaries in China, especially the French missionaries, many of whom were elderly or who had been recalled to France as chaplains during the war. The dearth of missionaries from Europe opened the way for missionaries from elsewhere, especially from English-speaking countries.

In the United States, two situations made a difference on the Society's start on the western side of the Atlantic Ocean. The first development was the presence of great numbers of immigrants from Ireland (about 4.5 million between 1820 and 1930).[18] Many bishops in the United States in the late nineteenth century had Irish surnames, as was still the case until the last thirty-plus years. In addition to the large Irish immigrant population with potential for a sizeable donor base and seminarian pool, the country was a powerful neutral nation in 1916. However, the Society learned almost from the first day they arrived in America they needed to establish a seminary in the country. Otherwise, the Catholic Church would think them "foreign" and not give funds or their young men for mission.

The second situation was the formation of what became a national organization of Catholic bishops, starting with their summons to mission sending/funding society leaders in 1919, in the wake of the First World War. E. J. McCarthy received an invitation to attend. He also participated in the Catholic Students Mission Crusade, begun in 1918. The organization became the largest Catholic youth movement for high school and college students to learn about mission history and mission practice.[19]

---

[18] Gerald Shaughnessy, *Has the Immigrant Kept the Faith? A Study of Immigration and Catholic Growth in the United States* 1790–1920 (New York: The Macmillan Company, 1925).

[19] David Endres, *American Crusade: Catholic Youth in the World Mission Movement from World War I through Vatican II* (Eugene, OR: Pickwick Publications, 2010).

American Connections Prior to a Foundation in Ireland

Edward (Ned) J. Galvin (1882–1956), born in County Cork, was ordained from St. Patrick's College, Maynooth, in 1909 for his home diocese. He was one of the Irish priests "on loan" to the Diocese of Brooklyn, New York. At Holy Rosary Parish Rectory, where he would serve from July 1909 to 1912, he met Canadian Father John Mary Fraser, who was returning to China and eager to begin a mission society of priests for the China missions. Galvin left with Fraser right from Brooklyn on February 28, 1912. They visited Fraser's family in Canada before both set sail for China. Galvin served with Fraser from 1912–1916.[20] Not satisfied with Fraser's approach to the Chinese, Galvin left China for Ireland to get Irish priests to form a mission society. In 1916 Galvin stayed with Father Peter Yorke, a well-known labor priest in San Francisco, while on the way from China to Brooklyn. George Mundelein was auxiliary bishop in Brooklyn when Galvin had departed for China with Fraser. So Galvin stopped to see Mundelein, by then appointed archbishop, later cardinal, in Chicago. Eventually, as will be seen in chapter 1, Galvin started fund-raising for the mission in the Diocese of Omaha, returned to China in 1920, and remained there until 1953 when he was expelled.

With these cross-Atlantic connections, we now set sail with Edward Galvin and Edward J. McCarthy, who have their sights set to raise funds for the China missions and to start a U.S. region.

---

[20] Though Galvin left Fraser's mission to start a new Society, the history of Fraser's work in China is presented in Anne Tansey, "John Fraser," *FE* (January 1963), 16–17 as part of a monthly series on "Mission Leaders."

PART ONE

Development of a Corporate Columban Identity in the Region of the United States, 1919–2018

CHAPTER 1

Location, Land, and American Initiation (1918–1928): Edward J. McCarthy Shapes the Society of St. Columban in the United States

Columbans Arrive in Omaha

Father Edward Galvin returned to Ireland from China in 1916 by way of the United States, testing the waters for a potential location in America for a financial support base for the China Mission Society. In Omaha, he received his first encouraging word in the States from a "Maynooth man," Father Patrick J. Judge. Ned Galvin's final stop at his former parish in Brooklyn was a time of renewed acquaintances, great interest in his mission experience, and financial support for the mission from parishioners and friends. The "Galvinian" ladies in Holy Rosary Parish, who gathered regularly to meet, periodically sent the group's "dues" to him for his China mission, with one check for $2,500.[21]

Once the Irish bishops had approved the plan for a Society for Chinese Missions, the first five men who committed themselves to the venture spent a year collecting funds for the mission. They raised $150,000. With the successful launch of "The Mission" in Ireland, Galvin and Father Matthew Dolan sailed to the United States to find a site from which to promote the group's mission. The pair arrived in New York on December 3, 1917, the feast of the well-known

---

21   William E. Barrett, *The Red Lacquered Gate. The Early Days of the Columban Fathers and the Courage and Faith of Its Founder, Fr. Edward Galvin* (Lincoln, NE: Author's Choice Press, 1967, 2000), 89.

missionary St. Francis Xavier.[22] Galvin was received graciously by the archbishop of New York, who gave him letters of recommendation to visit parishes. No offer was given to settle there, however, especially because the Catholic Foreign Mission Society of America had begun a mission seminary in 1911 in Westchester County, north of New York City, thanks partially to the personal connection that James A. Walsh had with Monsignor, later, Bishop John J. Dunn. Walsh was wary of a mission society with Irish roots, a group whom he viewed as competition for mission funds, especially from Irish Americans. Galvin inquired in the archdioceses of Philadelphia and Saint Louis, with similar results. At a stop in Chicago, Galvin had hopes for a positive response when he visited Archbishop George Mundelein, whom Galvin knew as the former auxiliary bishop of Brooklyn. However, with the regional headquarters of the Society of the Divine Word Missionaries in his diocese, Mundelein thought that two mission seminaries could not be supported in the archdiocese.

After visits to other bishops, Galvin found an archbishop favorable to a Columban foundation when he called upon Jeremiah Harty, the bishop of Omaha. The ailing archbishop requested time to consider Galvin's request and to pray over the matter. On March 25, 1918, Galvin returned to the bishop's office for a response. Harty supported the idea but felt that perhaps Omaha wasn't "big enough for your work." When Galvin heard that, he remarked that "he was prepared to take the chance. God's Providence had brought him to Omaha and there he was going to stay."[23] Harty, born in Saint Louis, Missouri, was no stranger to missions. He knew of the historical Jesuit mission foundations in the Mississippi Valley and the Northwest. He had been archbishop of Manila from 1903 until 1916, when he was appointed to the Omaha diocese, comprising a much larger geographic space than Manila but with fewer Catholics.

In April 1918, Galvin set up a small office (#746) in the Brandeis Theater Building at Seventeenth and Douglas streets in "noisy"[24] Omaha. He lived for a time with Father Judge at Sacred Heart Parish on Binney Street. He then rented a house on the corner of Fowler and Templeton in North Omaha near Holy Angels Parish, where Father Patrick Flanagan was pastor.[25] Galvin received word that Irish-born Father Michael Mee (1886–1957), ordained for the Diocese of Alton (now Springfield), Illinois, had applied to enter the new mission Society.

---

[22] Matthew Dolan (1888–1957) incardinated in the Diocese of Kilmore, Ireland, after a brief time in China.

[23] E. J. McCarthy, "A Few Personal Reminiscences," (1916–1920), written in the 1950s. Typescript, 8.CFA-USA.

[24] E. J. McCarthy, *Historical Sketch*, 14. In 1919, a second office, #450, was rented in the Brandeis Building.

[25] Flanagan was brother to Father Edward Flanagan, who worked with young boys in trouble at home or with the law and eventually established the well-known Boys Town in Nebraska.

Mee helped with promotion work until he went to China in 1920 in the first mission band of Columbans. Galvin, anxious to travel the country to make known the China mission and raise funds, requested that Edward J. McCarthy (1890–1957) assume responsibility for the *Far East* office in Omaha.

McCarthy, tall, heavily built, and sporting glasses with round lenses, had studied for the Diocese of Cork, where he had been born in Ovens. He completed seminary work at St. Patrick's College, Maynooth, was ordained in 1915, and continued graduate work in philosophy. While on retreat in June 1916, he felt called to the China missions and sought his bishop's permission to do so. The bishop suggested he talk with Edward Galvin upon his return from China that year. McCarthy had read about Galvin, and his story "made a deep impression on me."[26] When the two met, they discussed how to acquire the permission of the Irish bishops to begin a China mission society. Upon approval, five men, including McCarthy, were committed to the mission and available to raise funds. McCarthy edited the *Far East*, did mission promotion, was business manager, and taught at the newly opened St. Columban's College, Dalgan Park.[27] He was now about to go to the United States to spread the word about the China mission.

After a rough sea passage from Ireland aboard the *Baltic*,[28] with ship lights extinguished so as to sail undetected by enemy ships, McCarthy arrived in New York on October 3, 1918. With him were fellow Society members, Fathers James Galvin (a distant relative of Edward Galvin), Alphonsus Kerr, Michael J. McHugh, and Richard Ranaghan. McCarthy reached Omaha, Nebraska, six days later. Twenty-seven-year-old McCarthy was appointed the first regional superior in the United States in 1919, and the other men were assigned to mission promotion work, as they awaited their assignments in China.[29] As regional superior, McCarthy became simultaneously a businessman, fund-raiser, builder, scholar, preacher, author, faculty member, sometime manager for the U.S. edition of the *Far East*, and pastor of St. Mary's Catholic Church

---

26   Edward J. McCarthy, *A Few Personal Reminiscences* (1916–1920), 1.

27   This Dalgan Park was located in Shrule, County Mayo. In 1941, the name, "Dalgan Park" transferred to a new location for the Columbans, Navan, County Meath.

28   Captain William Finch commanded the *Baltic*, a White Star Line steamship built at Belfast in 1904. During the First World War, he and this ship had brought General Pershing and the first armed American troops to England.

29   The latter three priests were part of the first group of Columbans to go to China in 1920. James Galvin was assigned shortly thereafter, along with Dr. Edward Maguire, to found the Society's Australia Region in 1919 at the invitation of Archbishop Daniel Mannix. The following year James Galvin went to China. Kerr managed the *Far East* from 1919–1920 and eventually incardinated in his home diocese, Down and Conner, Ireland.

in Bellevue (1927–33).[30] His administration would be the lengthiest of the regional superiors in the United States. His perspective and sensitivity toward what he saw taking place in the American Catholic Church would decisively, and at great personal expense, shape the Society's direction in that location.

A few days after their Omaha arrival, they sought more permanent headquarters for the canonical establishment of the Society in the United States. By the end of October 1918, they found a "fair-sized frame house" with about four acres of orchard and garden at 5035 Bedford Avenue, in the Benson area, newly annexed to Omaha.[31] Galvin and McCarthy moved there on November 11, 1918, Armistice Day, the end of the "Great War." A simple ceremony for the Society's canonical establishment in the United States took place on December 14, 1918, with Bishop Harty presiding in the presence of Galvin, McCarthy, and a few priests who were doing mission promotion.[32] While the Society looked to America for financial support of the missions and for recruits, McCarthy envisioned the Society with a more comprehensive role. "In whatever was to be done to develop the missionary potential of the Church in America, we were determined to lend a hand."[33]

In 1920, the *Far East* office moved across the street to a more spacious, five-room suite in the Courtney Building from which the Society promoted the mission to China through appeal letters, personal contacts, and the *Far East* magazine. When the Seminary was built in the Bellevue area, the offices were a half-hour streetcar ride from Bedford Avenue, though the priests eventually procured an automobile. The priests ate their Spartan lunch—bread, butter, and tea—in a corner of a small room in the offices.[34] Young women from the

---

30   Archbishop Joseph Francis Rummel to McCarthy 9 February 1929. *Casey History* (1929), 2. In March 1929, inviting Capuchin Father Theophilus to give a short mission to the parish, McCarthy described the physical setting of the parish: "We have no church but say Mass in a hall attached to the military post. There are a good many Catholics among the soldiers but I can do nothing with them. They never come to Mass or go to the Sacraments." McCarthy to Theophilus 28 March 1929. *Casey History* (1929), 8. The Capuchin did give the mission.

31   The property was formerly owned by Edward Creighton and then purchased by Erastus Benson, a land speculator. Creighton's wife, Mary Lucretia Creighton, and Edward's brother, John A. Creighton, carried forward Edward's and their idea to establish a college by providing land and buildings for what became Creighton College. After the Society moved from Bedford Avenue to Bellevue, the Servite Sisters of Mary rented the Bedford house in 1922 until they could build a novitiate in Omaha. A photo of the large wood frame building on Bedford Avenue is found in *FE* (March 1950), 17.

32   Katie Condon was the housekeeper and cook at the Bedford Avenue residence. She remained with the Society for twenty years before returning to Ireland. Interview with Sister Mary Therese Bolan, Tape 2, transcript, 9.

33   E. J. McCarthy, *A Few Personal Reminiscences* (1916–1920), 14.

34   Sister Mary Therese Bolan, "Early Days of St. Columbans in the States," 9.

Sodality in the area addressed envelopes and sent circulars to potential donors. One of the Sodalists, Margaret Bolan, urged Clare McKenna, daughter of a wealthy Omaha citizen, to assist with clerical work in the Columban office.[35] Bolan, who had office work experience, taught McKenna office fundamentals, and the latter became McCarthy's stenographer. After McCarthy met Margaret Bolan at a dinner at the home of Mr. and Mrs. McGawin, Margaret was soon hired as stenographer, bookkeeper, supervisor of the other women in the larger and "very busy" office, head of the post office, and in charge of the general desk in the main office. Margaret Bolan worked for the Columbans from 1919 until 1928, after which she sailed to Ireland to enter the Columban Sisters, newly founded in 1922.[36] With additional office space and more secretarial staff, the *Far East* subscriptions rose to 100,000 by the end of 1922.[37] The increased volume of work required more complex office equipment, some of which McCarthy "had never even imagined existed."[38] The Society used an envelope system for the first time, when they went to parishes for mission promotion and magazine appeals. People placed their donation into the envelope and wrote their name and address on the front of the envelope. The collected envelopes became the basis of the donor files. In addition to funds raised through these methods, McCarthy looked to potential areas of investment. He went through Galvin's vacated office desk and found a cluster of Liberty Bonds, sent by donors for eventual redemption. Unfamiliar with the Bonds, McCarthy learned of their value from the office staff.

Another area of investment he considered was the purchase of land. "Having come from the land myself I thought that land was just the kind of investment to give the Society some real security and income. How wrong I was."[39] Nevertheless, the property did give the Society some security and

---

[35] McKenna's father "ran a big saloon." Sister Mary Therese Bolan interviewed by Nick Kill, August 1975. Transcript in CFA-USA. Received by author from Father Paul Casey, CFA-USA, 1988. Nick Kill is a brother to Father Donald Kill, SSC.

[36] After Bolan joined the Columban Sisters, she returned to the States and cooked for the seminarians in Silver Creek, New York, served as a catechist, cook, bookkeeper and principal in the Catholic school in Westminster, California. She later served the Sisters at their house of studies in Chicago.

[37] The figure is given by Bolan, "Early Days at St. Columbans in the States," transcript, tape 2, 7. The high number might be due partially to targeting the Catholic Students Mission Crusade membership list.

[38] E. J. McCarthy, *A Few Personal Remembrances* (1916–1920), 17.

[39] Ibid., McCarthy noted, though, that by April 29, 1922, the Society in the States was worth over $300,000, while at the same time, Dalgan and Cahiracon were 25,000 pounds in debt. E. J. McCarthy, *Diary of Progress at St. Columbans, Nebraska*, 36, 44. Therefore, it would be the United States that would have to fund the China missions.

permanence and a place to call "home." Before the end of his service as regional superior in 1934, McCarthy would purchase a total of three large properties.

An important element that affected early Columban promotion in the States was the name of the mission group. Galvin held funds for the "Maynooth Mission to China." Informally, Galvin called it the "Irish Mission to China," the name printed on his office door in the Brandeis Theater Building. McCarthy pointed out, "That name could never stick. We had no idea of remaining a collecting organization for an Irish society. [The title] Maynooth Society, meant nothing to U.S. Catholics." But McCarthy glossed over the facts, as he continued, "From the beginning Father Galvin and I decided that the American region should eventually become native to the soil, an integral part of the missionary effort of the Church in the United States, and as far as I know that represented the responsible opinion in the Society as a whole."[40] Into the 1930s, Society publications from the United States held the legal title, the Chinese Mission Society of St. Columban.

McCarthy's responsibilities brought him a multitude of challenges during his lengthy tenure as regional superior until 1934. Sister Mary Therese Bolan, SSC, who worked closely with him in the office for years, described McCarthy as "one in two billion." She found him to be "considerate of others in every possible way," with a "knowledge beyond the average knowledge," possessing what she described as a "photographic mind." "He was a real genius and . . . a saint."[41] McCarthy's vision, talents, and keen observation of people and events forged the direction of the Society's future in America. In his almost sixteen years as regional superior, he raised substantial funds for the China missions, bought properties, built two seminaries, addressed local mail theft and the subsequent establishment of a post office on the Nebraska seminary grounds, handled investments and lawsuits, dealt with Presbyterian and Ku Klux Klan hostility, and kept open communication lines with Superior General Blowick in Ireland. In the midst of these challenging tasks, McCarthy found time to research and write about local church history, mission topics, and the life of Saint Columban. He emphasized the importance of nurturing various connections: within the Society (the relationship between the U.S. region, Ireland, and China) and with active engagement in key newly formed ecclesiastical and lay groups. The latter emphasis secured a broader Columban presence in the United States.

---

40   E. J. McCarthy, *A Few Personal Reminiscences* (1916–1920), 17. "The Chinese Missions Society" was the first of several legal aliases in the United States over the years. In 1925 the Office of Propaganda Fide changed the canonical name to the Society of St. Columban for Missions to the Chinese. Neil Collins, *The Splendid Cause* Columba Press: Dublin, 2009), 65. The name was again changed on July 3, 1935, to St. Columban Foreign Mission Society.

41   Sister Mary Therese Bolan interviewed by Nick Kill, August 1975, 8.

Lawsuits, Land, and Buildings

Within their first years, the Society encountered the American legal system. Two lawsuits occupied McCarthy's attention in 1921/1922. An Omaha attorney took the Society to court for breach of lease contract on the rented offices in the Courtney Building, where the *Far East* offices had been located. The Brandeis Investment Company Rental Property, which held the building McCarthy originally rented, was taken over by H. Wolf Company. It was the latter firm that brought the lawsuit. There was an informal agreement that tenants would rent for a minimal three-year period and, if leaving before that time, the tenant would give due notice and locate new renters for the space. McCarthy had spoken with Mr. Wolf about their situation, and there had been a verbal agreement that the Society need not worry about finding renters.[42] A rental contract, which tenants were forced to sign, came several months after McCarthy had rented the rooms. Prior to vacating, the Society had sought renters, though without success, at which point the Society received a letter from the H. Wolf Company attorneys. McCarthy noted, "Sufficient notice was given to both the Brandeis Investment Company and to the H. Wolf Company, that we intended to vacate these offices on May 1st [1922] and the notice was accepted and an effort was made to rerent the offices . . ." The regional superior suggested that "if these [offices] have not since been rented, the reason, very probably is that the rent being charged us was more than the value of the space represented or due to the depreciation in the value of the space owing to the condition in which the building was when we vacated."[43] On November 28, Attorney James H. Hanley, who had influence with the Brandeis Company, wrote to McCarthy that he had "taken the matter up with Brandeis and attached is the release protecting you and disposing of the matter. It would be well to put this release in a secure place."[44]

The second lawsuit related to architectural plans for a potential seminary on the Bedford Avenue property. The Omaha architectural firm of Ellert and Lahr brought their suit in November 1921. Mr. Ellert had visited McCarthy in the Brandeis Theater office in 1919 and 1920 and "solicited work, representing himself as a competent architect and guaranteeing service. At the time we had no definite building project before our minds, though in a vague way we contemplated building at some future time." The Society was "undecided whether our future buildings should be at Bedford Avenue property" or at the

---

[42]   The regional superior noted he spoke with the manager of H. A. Wolf Company, who said he would find new tenants for McCarthy. E. J. McCarthy, "A Diary of Progress at St. Columbans, Nebraska, 27.

[43]   E. J. McCarthy to Mr. T. Quinlan, Brandeis Stores, Omaha. 5 October 1922.

[44]   James H. Hanley to Rev. E. J. McCarthy 28 November 1922.

Bellevue, Nebraska, property that had belonged to the Bellevue Presbyterian College, land purchased by McCarthy in 1919. In any case, permission from the superior general (legally known as the president of the corporation and his councilors as the board of directors) was needed to proceed to the next step. A decision was made to build "a small building [at Bedford Avenue] which would serve temporarily as a residence and if we needed it afterwards as a seminary or college, it could be added to." The board of directors authorized McCarthy "to instruct Messrs. Ellert and Lahr' *to draw up tentative plans* [McCarthy's underlining] for a [possible Bedford Avenue seminary] building to cost about $30,000." At the time, purchase of the Bellevue College buildings remained an option the Society pursued. In the months of discussion, a proposed architectural style was raised for the Bedford location, and McCarthy requested that the company "draw me a water color picture of their idea." They did so, though they never suggested any charge for so doing. "Messrs. Ellert and Lahr knew very well, for I often told them that there was no question of going ahead with such a building as they were drawing," because the realization of the plan exceeded the amount of money allotted for the project and they could not go forward without permission from the superior general.[45]

In March 1921, the Society had opened negotiations to purchase the buildings of Bellevue Presbyterian College and made them an offer which, however, was not accepted.[46] McCarthy awaited a response to his letter to Blowick, as to whether the regional superior could then proceed with building, within the cost of $75,000. Plans submitted by Ellert and Lahr exceeded that figure considerably. The board of directors asked McCarthy for some contractor bids, and the bids were well over the allotted amount. McCarthy himself found the plans defective, but he asked two friends in the building trade to view them. "The evidence of these two independent and uninterested parties, together with the defects I myself discovered, and the fact that the architects had exceeded the instructions to draw plans for a $75,000 building decided me to place the matter formally before the board of directors [June 6, 1921] and it was decided at that meeting to dismiss Messrs. Ellert and Lahr and look for another architect." A key idea lying behind the decision of the board was "that seeing our Society was supported for charitable and missionary purposes, we had too much of a responsibility in dealing with public funds for all or any of

---

[45]   "Statement of Case Submitted for Lawyer's Brief," marked as 8-A-11-A.1 (last number unclear). See also C. F. Connolly to Rev. E. J. McCarthy, Courtney Bldg. 23 November 1921. The water color picture is probably the one pictured in late 1919 issues of the *Far East*.

[46]   Bellevue Presbyterian College opened in 1880 for the Christian education of local youth. Financial problems and a reduced student body during World War I forced the College to close in 1920. Bellevue College opened as a private four year liberal arts school in 1966.

them to be squandered on buildings that were defectively planned and which would cost an indefinite amount before they were completed and far more than what we were authorized to expend."[47]

Ellert and Lahr took the Society to court. On the afternoon of January 9, 1922, opening evidence was presented in Douglas County Courthouse before District Judge James M. Fitzgerald. Two days later, evidence for the defense was called. McCarthy wrote in his *Diary*, "Looks as if we may have to pay more than we expected. Suit claims $9,700." On January 13, the verdict was reached, with "$2,800 for plaintiff. It is more than we expected but we may be thankful to get out of it so well. The expert evidence on the plans and specifications showed them to be hopelessly defective and dangerous. It was the blessing of God that we got out in time."[48]

Scholar on the Nebraska Plains

Probably while dining at the home of an Omaha Catholic businessman, McCarthy heard about "the man who was selling [a farm] for the owners, a fine Catholic fellow, and one of the biggest real estate men in the city."[49] The 1919 purchase of the farm and 215 acres that belonged to the Presbyterian College in Bellevue, Nebraska, south of Omaha, would become the headquarters of the U.S. region of the Society of St. Columban and location of its first American seminary. "The situation and the possibilities of the place simply carried us off our feet." They sought the opinion of a "reliable valuer" about the land under cultivation, and the appraiser noted it was "tip-top land, worth far more than the owners were asking."[50] McCarthy appreciated "the scenic possibilities" the land offered for a future seminary. He also hoped that the "[Presbyterian] college

47   "Statement of Case Submitted for Lawyer's Brief," marked as 8-A-11-A.1 (last number unclear). See also C. F. Connolly to Rev. E. J. McCarthy, Courtney Bldg. 23 November 1921. In early 1922, another civil matter arose and McCarthy went to Papillion, Nebraska, to contest the Society's Bellevue taxes against Sarpy County. The County said the Society had to pay taxes on the entire property, including the farm, a different law than the Irish law McCarthy knew. After speaking with the Commissioners, a settlement was reached. The property was taxed for the last two years, when the Society was not living there. The Columbans paid the 1920 taxes for the year they rented the farm. At this point the property surrounding the new buildings was about 127 acres, to be used exclusively for the campus and pasture, while the remaining 87 acres of farmland ran into another tax lot. E. J. McCarthy, *Diary of Progress at St. Columban's, Omaha, Neb.* (1921–22), 13.

48   Ibid., *Progress*, 11.

49   E. J. McCarthy to My Dear John [Blowick] 19 June 1919.

50   Ibid., Seventy-five of the total acres purchased were located west of Fort Crook Road.

itself would fall into our hands," though that did not happen.[51] To purchase the property in the States, where the Society had little legal experience, McCarthy called upon "a very promising lawyer," James H. Hanley, a relative of a young Irish Columban, John P. O'Brien, assigned to China in 1920.[52] The attorney suggested that the "Presbyterians would be a difficult people for a priest or a Catholic institution to deal with. . . . It would be better to remain undercover and let [Hanley] conduct the transaction in [McCarthy's] name," with transfer of the property to the Society once the purchase was made.[53] The transaction was successful, "a safe investment for $50,000,"[54] even though McCarthy realized that some members in Ireland would oppose the action because they weren't interested in the "development" of the United States as a region.

McCarthy, ever the curious scholar, researched and wrote about the historical significance of the land the Society purchased in Bellevue. Pawnee, Oto-Missouria, and Omaha were among Native American tribes in the greater area. The Missouri River was the main transportation artery for the fur trade, other goods, and U.S. Army supplies to reach the troops across the Nebraska Plains after the U.S. Civil War.[55] Big Elk (1770–1846), the last full-blooded chief of the Omaha and baptized by the Jesuit missionary Pierre de Smet in 1846, was

---

51   *Mission Bulletin* (June 1921).

52   Bolan indicated this relationship. Hanley, of Hanley & Hopkins Law firm, remained the Society's legal advisor until his death. Sister Mary Therese Bolan, "Early Days at St. Columbans in the States," transcript tape 2, 14. Attorney James H. Hanley, "who has many friends in Washington," was able to get permission for the Columbans to have their own postal office on the seminary grounds, after the postal thief, who rifled through Columban mail, was caught. When this was taking place in 1922, Hanley was a candidate for Congress. E. J. McCarthy, *Diary of Progress*, 5 June 1922. Hanley also socialized periodically with the Columbans and acted as lawyer for some of the Chinese residents in the area. Hanley and Charles Porter, a Chicago businessman (see chapter 2) were lifelong friends of Father John Heneghan. As McCarthy described the relationship, Hanley and Porter "were the kind of men, sincere and generous hearted with strong, deep, simple, manly faith, who were always likely to find understanding in [Heneghan's] generous soul." E. J. McCarthy, *Life of Father Heneghan*. Typescript, CFA-USA. No date, but probably between 1950 and 1957. John P. O'Brien, uncle of Columban Andrew O'Brien, became bursar, rector, and vice rector at Silver Creek Seminary, after John's return from China. Later he was in charge of the retreats at Silver Creek and Derby, New York.

53   E. J. McCarthy, *A Few Personal Reminiscences* (1916–1920), 18.

54   E. J. McCarthy to My Dear John [Blowick] 19 June 1919. The Society would take possession after the tenants moved out in March 1920. McCarthy's letter to Blowick let him know the urgency of the action McCarthy took. "When I wrote to you last, I had no idea that anything like this was going to turn up so soon, and it was, I think, a case of being pushed into it by that Power that is pushing us into everything, one thing after the other." Ibid.

55   On the importance of the Missouri River for trade, communication and enjoyment, see K. Jack Bauer, *A Maritime History of the United States: The Role of America's Seas and Waterways* (Columbia: University of South Carolina Press, 1988).

buried at Elk Hill, north of Mission Avenue, the area the Society bought. This fact was apparently not well-known. When grading the Columban campus in 1922, his bones and those of other Omaha tribe were discovered.[56] Chief Big Elk's remains, along with those of fourteen other Omaha, were reburied for the third time in the Bellevue Cemetery in 1954. The town of Bellevue at the foot of the hill was home to Fort Crook, where soldiers were garrisoned to deal with Native Americans. When Omaha became the center of the Nebraska Territory, the population in Bellevue dwindled. Sister Mary Therese Bolan described Bellevue in the early 1920s as "all countryside." The town "consisted of—say six buildings for a Main Street and a few scattered houses." Cows grazed the land around the Bellevue City Hall. The town could be reached on the interurban line that ran from South Omaha to Papillion, the county seat, with a stop at Mission Station.[57]

The parish of St. Mary's, Bellevue, located since 1933 at the bottom of the hill below the Columban property, reflected historical connections with de Smet. The missionary was affiliated with Saint Mary's Church on the Iowa side of the Missouri River in the nineteenth century, but due to the river's undulating patterns that frequently submerged the land, the parish was reestablished on the Nebraska side.[58] Catholics in the area were few in the late nineteenth and early twentieth century. During "the Great War," services were held at nearby Fort Crook in a hall known during the War as the Military Service Club, built by the Knights of Columbus. The hall served as the gathering space for Catholic services until a new church was erected. E. J. McCarthy's *The Catholic History of Bellevue* (1933) was placed in the cornerstone.[59] McCarthy knew about the parish firsthand because on July 1928, Bishop Beckman asked the Columbans to assume temporary charge of the Catholics gathered at the military hall.[60]

---

[56]   E. J. McCarthy, *History of Catholic Bellevue* (1933), 5. The author does not know the burial location of the Native Americans after they were discovered on Columban property (the second burial of the Native American group).

[57]   Sister Mary Therese Bolan, "Early Days at St. Columban's in the States," transcript tape 2, 10.

[58]   The parish, named St. Mark's after the priest assigned to serve Catholics in a wide area around Bellevue, was renamed St. Mary's in 1933, when a new church was built, "to renew the tradition of Old St. Mary's and to honor the memory of Fathers De Smet and Hoecken, Nebraska's first Catholic missionaries." E. J. McCarthy, *History of Catholic Bellevue*, 5. The parish was put under the care of the Columbans in 1927, and Columbans still serve the parish for weekend liturgies.

[59]   Given that McCarthy was pastor when the new church was dedicated, it is not surprising that a map of Sarpy County and a wooden box from Bethlehem, containing various relics, including a stone from the Lourdes shrine and relic of St. Therese of Lisieux, were included in the foundation stone.

[60]   In May 1933, McCarthy wrote to Bishop Rummel about the group gathered at the military hall. It was no longer available for Mass because the military authorities

The Society property was also within eyesight and hearing of the airstrip added to Fort Crook in September 1918. Later named for Omaha native, First Lieutenant Jarvis Jennes Offutt, killed when his fighter plane crashed in France that year, Offutt Airfield became the base of the U.S. Strategic Command.[61] McCarthy was pleased with the airstrip location because it would "bring a good road near the Seminary"[62] and a possible closer mail route than Omaha.

A Fading Frontier and Accessible Omaha

By the time that Galvin and McCarthy arrived in Omaha, the Nebraska frontier was fading and Irish, Czech, and Polish immigrants had settled in Nebraska. The Kansas–Nebraska Act (1854) organized and opened the Nebraska Territory for white settlement. Railroads spurred the growth of towns along proposed rail routes, with town locations often determined by the railroad officials, who sought sites for families of the men who worked the railroad. Greeley County, Nebraska, was one of two locations proposed by the Irish Catholic Colonization Project, an effort to find work for newly arrived immigrants or for poor Irish in eastern cities, and championed by Bishop John Lancaster Spalding of Peoria, Illinois. Omaha had several Irish Catholic families who engaged in the public business of the area as lawyers, store owners, and land holders. Over the years, they would assist the Columbans in various capacities.

---

made other arrangements for the room. McCarthy wrote that "we have another hall though not quite so convenient for the people I am sure a church is necessary for the Parish spirit. I might add that the parish needs a church and a resident priest when possible, and much of the difficult I have had in building up the Parish even to where it is now is due to the fact that for some any years there was no priest here and many families fell away." E. J. McCarthy to Bishop Rummel 4 May 1933. Archives of the Archdiocese of Omaha. File Folder: Columban Fathers. Seven months later, McCarthy wrote the bishop saying he was willing to loan the parish in Bellevue $5,000 to build a church. E. M. McCarthy to Bishop Joseph Rummel 3 November 1933. A month later, McCarthy sent a Cashier check for $1,000 to Bishop Rummel from Omaha National Bank as an unsecured loan for the St. Mary's Church of Bellevue. 15 December 1933. File Folder: Columban Fathers. Archives of the Archdiocese of Omaha.

[61]   In 1941, the Martin Bomber Plant rented space at the base. The Plant produced the Enola Gay B-29 bomber, which delivered the atomic bomb over Japan in 1945. In 1955, June Allyson and James Stewart starred in the Cold War film, *Strategic Air Command*, which premiered in Omaha at the Storz Mansion, home of the descendants of Gottlieb Storz, founder of the successful Storz Beer Company in the midnineteenth century. In 1961 the Federal Aviation Agency built an aviation tower on land leased from the Columbans on the northern perimeter of their seminary property.

[62]   *Mission Bulletin* 1924 (August), 2.

Saint Columban Seminary, Nebraska:
"Heart of the Middle West"[63]

With the Bellevue Presbyterian College buildings no longer an option for use as a Columban seminary, Superior General Blowick sent a telegram to McCarthy on May 3, 1921, with permission to proceed with construction of a seminary on the earlier purchased farmland. In a letter to Blowick that same month, McCarthy expressed gratitude for permission and approval of a budget of $75,000. He indicated that "we have already been losing in prestige by not having some kind of seminary here."[64] The first seminarians were housed at the Bedford Avenue house in September 1921: the Americans, Thomas Powers (1902–1962) from the Bronx, Patrick Gately, and James Houlihan (1894–1954). In early 1922, a few others arrived and the students' retreat was preached under the direction of Father Arthur J. McGuinness (1893–1943), newly returned from China.[65]

Construction at the Bellevue site had begun and the cornerstone was laid on September 8, 1921.[66] Benefactors were invited to buy bricks for ten cents apiece. By the end of November, the smaller of the two buildings was almost completed and in mid-December the roof on the large building was finished, thanks to a record warm winter. By January 1, 1922, the small and large buildings were completely closed in, with a "good deal of inside construction done during the week." A fireproof altar was ordered from Daprato Altar Company, Chicago,[67] and on April 29, the men packed furniture at the Omaha office and Bedford

---

[63]   E. J. McCarthy, *St. Columbans. A Remarkable Missionary Movement of our own day!* [1931], hereafter called, *A Historical Sketch.*

[64]   E. J. McCarthy to My Dear John [Blowick] 26 May 1921.

[65]   Arthur J. McGuinness, born in County Cork, Ireland, was ordained in 1920 and in the first band of Columbans sent to China that year. After several bouts with malaria, he came to the United States in 1922 to recuperate. He was made bursar (1924–1929) when the Silver Creek seminary opened. As a member of the Society, he served in the Archdiocese of Detroit, where he died in Adrian, Michigan. He is buried in the Adrian Sisters Cemetery.

[66]   The cornerstone at St. Columban Seminary, Nebraska, included history notes of the Mission at its present stage; pictures of the priests now in China; various stations where they live; names of members of the whole Society; copies of different editions of *Far East* and other Society publications; autographed letter and photo of Bishop Harty; Sinn Féin flag; Victrola record of President De Valera's speech; and news items that might be of interest to future generations. *Mission Bulletin* (September 1921).

[67]   Daprato Company, founded in Italy near the Carrara Marble Quarry, had U.S. headquarters in Chicago in the nineteenth century. The company, recognized internationally for its high standards of religious statuary and decoration, continues to the present day.

Avenue.[68] On May 1 McCarthy was "very annoyed" that the final work was not finished, but they moved to Bellevue anyway. He remarked, "We realize that the only way to get the contractor out is to move in on him and run him out. Offices all fixed up and going in full swing."[69]

When it came time to grade the road up the hill from Mission Avenue to the Columban property, McCarthy went to Papillion, the county seat, to get approval and assistance from the County Commissioners. "There is the further understanding that the Road Commissioner makes the price and he will make it as low as he possibly can without losing face." Construction of the seminary had not escaped notice of Bellevue's citizens, who lived on the flat land near or just west of the River. When the County reneged on a promise of assistance, McCarthy hoped to obtain the services of the village board, "a Presbyterian outfit," to get a road, but the board "refused to help and we had to get their permission and grade it at our own expense. It is absolutely necessary to get a good approach to the building."[70] The work was accomplished and on the feast of Saints Peter and Paul, June 29, 1922, Saint Columban Seminary, "the Missionary College in the heart of America,"[71] was dedicated, with a procession around the two buildings, blessing them and the land with holy water, and a Solemn High Mass in the small chapel. In addition to ecclesiastical dignitaries, a large contingent of laity attended the celebration.

Bishop Harty congratulated Fathers Blowick and McCarthy by name and then addressed "you, the Catholic laity, the salt of the earth." He thanked the men and women for "your cooperation in this marvelous work of evangelizing not only in China but the whole world, for what you have done in gathering around this first group of buildings and in giving the aid of your own strength and wonderful assistance." Not only was this true for the laity present for the festivities, but, for "the hundreds of others scattered up and down through America, who have helped to build this house. Every brick in that college is an act of Faith and represents a sacrifice, perhaps of a child or of a mother toiling in her house, or of a poor laboring man."[72]

The 235 guests proceeded to a celebratory luncheon. The meal was catered by Albert Jones, "colored, at the rate of $2.00 a plate. He supplied everything:

---

[68] For a brief time after the Society moved to Bellevue, they maintained the *Far East* office in Omaha, to which the priests commuted daily. Given the condition of the roads at the time, this proved unfeasible and the office transferred to Bellevue.

[69] E. J. McCarthy, *Diary of Progress at St. Columban's, Omaha, Nebraska*, 29 April 1922.

[70] Ibid., 12 May 1922. McCarthy viewed the "Presbyterians of this Bellevue burg" as "a hundred years behind in their bigotry, . . . like a little nest of APAs that never got the sunlight of commonsense to shine on them." 1 April 1922. *Diary of Progress.*

[71] Editorial, "Our New Seminary at Omaha," the *Far East* (September 1922), 129.

[72] Ibid., 130–132, here, 131.

tables, cloths, chairs, eats."[73] The luncheon areas were decorated with colors of the Vatican and United States' flags. The photograph to mark the event featured bishops, clergy and a large representation of the laity standing in front of St. Columban's Seminary, with an American flag hanging from the outside balcony. The picture appeared in the September 1922 issue of the *Far East*. Twelve students were enrolled in the seminary, including Eugene Spencer (1898–1984), a second year theologian from St. Mary's Seminary, Cincinnati. He had enrolled in the Society seminary at Dalgan in fall 1921 and was the first American student ordained priest in the Society.[74] Father Paul Waldron, ordained at Maynooth in 1914 and a faculty member at the St. Paul, Minnesota, Archdiocesan Seminary before joining the Columbans in 1918, became the rector and faculty member of the new Columban Seminary.

While the Seminary was welcomed by the Catholics of the Omaha diocese, not everyone in the Bellevue area appreciated the Columban presence. One night the Ku Klux Klan mounted their hallmark fiery cross opposite the Society grounds.[75]

A Seminary at Silver Creek, New York

It soon became apparent that the Society needed a junior or preparatory seminary in the States along the lines of a "Classics" and Latin program. A five-year high school/Latin preparation preceded students' six years of ordination preparation (two years of philosophy, four years of theology) in Nebraska. The Columbans favored the preparatory seminary to be situated in the eastern part of the country. To find a suitable location, McCarthy took the train to western New York. He had "two fixed ideas about the [ideal] Site," that helped him identify a location in the Buffalo area, "the most desirable place in all America for a junior seminary." Using statistics from *The Catholic Directory*, he calculated that the Buffalo area would be at "the center of a thickly populated Catholic section along the Atlantic seaboard." His second requirement was that the site be situated near a railroad center and state highway, thus readily accessible for East Coast candidates, a point frequently illustrated in the *Bellevue Booster— Mission Bulletin* in the mid-1920s. Beyond these practical details, he hoped for

---

73   The events are described in E. J. McCarthy, *Diary of Progress*, 56–57.

74   Eugene Spencer, ordained in 1924, did promotion work for two years in the United States before he was assigned to China. He was repatriated to the United States from Hanyang after a year and then served in China again from 1946–1951, when he and the Columbans were expelled. He had assignments in Westminster, California, Glavetons, and San Diego, before retiring at Silver Creek five years before he died.

75   *Mission Bulletin* (August 1924), 2.

"scenic attractions [as he had sought for the Omaha seminary], an important, though perhaps much neglected factor in the growth of a boy's mind."[76] The property he viewed was situated thirty miles south of Buffalo.

McCarthy described the site as having a large frame house, an orchard, twenty acres of grape vines in a verdant wine production area (the Concord Grape Belt) of New York, and "a few hundred acres of land more or less" with the [Eagle] Bay for beauty and recreation.[77] However, the New York Central railroad lines passed through the southern eighth of the property several times a day.

In fact, the site, in the village of Silver Creek, town of Hanover, Chautauqua County, had been the location of Eagle Bay Farm, a midnineteenth century agriculture experiment. A journal of the agricultural reform movement, *Country Gentleman*, founded in nearby Rochester, New York in the 1830s, noted that "decreasing soil fertility, growing demand for food for an increasing population . . . and bonanza farming are all bringing new [land] problems to the front."[78] Scientific study took place on the farms to determine which breed of cow gave the best milk for babies (the Holstein did) or which provisions for chickens provided the most nutritious eggs (grains and high quality mashes did). By the time McCarthy viewed the farm, a different generation concentrated on the more lucrative vine production, with "bootleggers who ply their trade between the Canadian and American coasts on Lake Erie, under the protection of New York state troopers."[79]

After McCarthy left the owner at the time, a Mr. Pappas, and visited a few more places, he prayed the Litany of Our Lady of Good Counsel, a common practice for him. "'Silver Creek' kept ringing through my brain with an insistence that I could not deny." When they returned to close on the option, the owner raised the price. Disappointed, McCarthy returned a few months later, and because of circumstances related to the owner, the Society bought the buildings and land for $70,000, which was $55,000 less than the family had asked. While McCarthy termed the acquisition of the Bellevue property as a business transaction, that of Silver Creek "showed a definite Providence in the background."[80]

---

[76]   E. J. McCarthy, *Historical Sketch [1931]*, 22–23.

[77]   Ibid, 23, 25.

[78]   *The Country Gentleman. A Journal for the Farm, the Garden, and the Fireside. Devoted to Improvement in Agriculture, Horticulture, and Rural Taste: To Elevation in Mental, Moral, and Social Character.* July 6, 1911.

[79]   "The Bellevue Booster and Mission News Letter," 4 No. 1 (January 1924), St. Columbans, NE.

[80]   E. J. McCarthy, *Historical Sketch*, 22, 25.

McCarthy described the land and dwellings for the Society. They had purchased 260 acres of "first, touching second class, land right on the shore of Lake Erie" in an area called Eagle Bay, with a sandy beach. As he indicated, tongue in cheek, "The ownership of Eagle Bay is amicably divided between Uncle Sam and the Chinese Mission Society. The former owns the water and all the rights thereon, including the Canadian bootlegging trade, and the Chinese Mission Society owns the sand on the beach, the skating in winter, the swimming in summer and the fishing at other times of the year."[81] Twenty acres of the Society land contained vineyards.

The Chinese Mission Society, the legal name of the Society at the time, opened St. Columban's Preparatory College[82] in September 1924. The bishop of Buffalo invited Father Arthur McGuinness to give the sermon on St. Patrick's Day the following year as a formal introduction of the Society to the Diocese. The curriculum had five years of "Classics and Science" followed by "the innovation of a Spiritual Year, which began with a thirty day retreat and spiritual studies, character building and the study and practice of those virtues necessary for the work of a missionary."[83] The next branch of study was Philosophy, which, McCarthy wrote, gives the young man a grasp of the great fundamental problems of the universe."[84]

Students and priests lived in an eighteen-room frame house, formerly owned by a lawyer, "fitted with electric light, hot water heat, gas, bathrooms and running water supplied from the New York Central filling station a short distance away."[85] McCarthy alluded to the missionary tradition in Western New York of the Jesuit missionaries, some of whom were martyred in the area. A "Chinese Room," featured furniture, objects, and paintings with a China motif, as a visual reminder of the people to whom the seminarians would someday be sent. The Society used the farmland to provide food for the residents. Bursar Arthur McGuinness's White Leghorns and Rhode Island Reds, the breeds that the Eagle Bay Farm had favored, won two first prizes for two roosters at the Chautauqua County Fair. The barn and large chicken coop on the property

---

[81]   "The Bellevue Booster and Mission News Letter," 4 No. 1 (January 1924), St. Columbans, NE.

[82]   This is the title of the seminary as given in the lengthy booklet E. J. McCarthy wrote to describe the Silver Creek education program and history of the Society in his *Historical Sketch* [1931]. He also identified this location as the St. Columban's Preparatory Seminary.

[83]   "The innovation of the Spiritual Year was received with the greatest satisfaction" in the American region. "We realize now what we missed. It should strike the golden mean between a top heavy spirituality and none." *Mission Bulletin* (1924 September and October), 2. E. J. McCarthy, *Historical Sketch* [1931], 33.

[84]   E. J. McCarthy, *Historical Sketch* [1931], 34.

[85]   E. J. McCarthy to "My dear Doc O'Dwyer," 25 August 1924.

were later remodeled to accommodate more students, until a new building was later completed. A gas well on the property provided heat and cooking fuel for a number of years and has been reactivated.[86] The site fit well McCarthy's ideal location of a seminary for health reasons: young men had immediate access to a variety of nutritious farm products: vegetables, eggs, butter, milk, chicken, fruits, as well as fresh air and plenty of acreage for physical exercise. Eventually a gymnasium was built for exercise during the winter months.[87]

The first twenty-four students, including the six men who came from St. Columbans in Omaha and four of whom would be on their Spiritual Year, arrived on September 30, 1924. McCarthy thought that the Society could "house all the students . . . up to winter time. They will have to rough it a good deal, both priests and students, but if there is a prospect of having some decent living accommodations when winter comes, they won't mind a little pioneering."[88] The following year enrollment went to thirty. When the new seminary building was completed in September 1929, Silver Creek had forty-five students. McCarthy's 1931 history of the Society noted the importance of the Columban Sisters in making the place a home for students and faculty.

Columban Land and a Spiritual Topography

While the *Far East* described the new Seminary in Omaha as a "watchtower set upon a hill, a training camp for the future soldiers of the Cross,"[89] the U.S. regional superior imagined the property with different imagery: trees, flowers, and bushes. He soon set about to develop the terrain. The Columban Bellevue area seminary and later the Columban Silver Creek property bore "McCarthy's stamp."[90] His attention to the landscaping details in both locations indicates his sensitivity toward *place* and a corresponding, though perhaps not conscious, intersection with spirituality. When the men in Ireland found a location for the China Mission seminary, Ned remarked about the beauty of Dalgan: "We had all fallen in love with Dalgan, with the quiet, peaceful woods and its lovely

---

[86]   After the Society moved in, some of the farm implements and dairy stock were auctioned off.

[87]   E. J. McCarthy to "My dear Jim," 16 October 1924.

[88]   E. J. McCarthy to "My dear Doc O'Dwyer," 25 August 1924. That year McCarthy expected ten students to arrive at St. Columban in Nebraska: four would be novices and six, "too advanced for Silver Creek," would do the ordinary classical courses. Ibid.

[89]   Editorial, "Our New Seminary at Omaha," *FE* (September 1922):130. Cardinal Van Rossum of Propaganda Fide called the new seminary "a memorial and a light-tower." E. J. McCarthy, *Historical Sketch*, 1.

[90]   Bolan, *Early Days at St. Columbans in the States*, transcript tape 2, 6. CFA-USA.

gardens bright with flowers, its sluggish black river winding its way through the grounds and reflection in its deep dark pools, under dripping willows and tall ferns, the wealth of foliage and color along its banks."[91]

On the other hand, the Bellevue land was quite a contrasting site. A local farmer was employed to manage the farmland and existing fruit trees, with students helping in their free time and vacations.[92] The arable land was then rented to a farmer and, later, most of the farm land was sold.[93] At one point, McCarthy had inquired about buying additional land to the south of their property, so as to maintain a good view. McCarthy's letter to John Blowick described their location to be in a "fine rolling country, and the college is built on one of two hills looking right over the river along as fine a view as there is in the middle west."[94] However, McCarthy admitted that initially the site of the two buildings (the Seminary and the *Far East* office) looked quite bleak, with just a few trees and tall electrical poles, with wires strung from one to the other.

Perhaps remembering the lush greens of Ireland and of Dalgan Park specifically, McCarthy quickly began to cultivate what probably must have seemed to him a bare Nebraska flatland. Actually, the 1895 Nebraska legislature named the state, Tree Planters' State and demanded of settlers that they forest the region.[95] McCarthy "accepted landscape plans from Harold E. George [in Omaha]. Plans should enable us in time to make Bellevue a pretty place. It will take twenty years."[96] Mr. George had several specific ideas about grading the property to enhance the view and "feel" of the place. One thought was a projected quadrangle behind the two buildings, with "an even grade in order to give a certain refined and dignified formality to this portion of the grounds."[97] The first things planted in spring 1921, were many trees, both deciduous and evergreens. The seminary's hired worker, "that man Kelly," was told that new trees needed careful attention with proper watering, which apparently did not take place. Between lack of proper care and gopher activity, a large number

---

[91]   McCarthy quoted in William E. Barrett, *The Red Lacquered Gate*, 132.

[92]   A Father McCormick from Melrose, Iowa, intended to leave several thousand dollars in his will for the Society. He sent good references for Mr. M. F. Knowles as foreman for the Bellevue farm. E. J. McCarthy, *History of the Early Days of the Society*, 12 December 1922.

[93]   Bolan, *Early Days at St. Columbans in the States*, transcript tape 2, 13. Harold E. George, landscape architect, to Rev. E. J. McCarthy 2 September 1921.

[94]   E. J. McCarthy to "My Dear John" [Blowick] 19 June 1919.

[95]   After World War II, Nebraska was officially called the "Cornhusker State."

[96]   E. J. McCarthy, *Diary of Progress at St. Columban's*, 10 December 1921. McCarthy obtained the nursery stock from P. J. Flynn's Benson–Omaha Nursery.

[97]   Harold E. George to Rev. E. J. McCarthy 2 September 1921.

of trees needed to be replanted.[98] A few years later, when Superior General Blowick indicated that certain items were "disallowed" in the U.S. region budget, McCarthy spoke for attention to the landscape:

> Nebraska is a hard country to grow trees and shrubs. They need a great deal of care for the first four or five years. Last year owing to the desire to economize, we did not give them this care and the result was that we lost over $400 worth of trees during the summer. Similarly due to lack of care and the desire to economize in labor, parts of the lawn burned up and the grass failed. . . . On the allowance of this year's budget, we cannot possibly give the grounds the attention they need and consequently we may look for another tree and lawn failure. It looks like false economy. . . . If the amount were raised to $750.00 we could probably save the trees that are now growing and by next year they will have taken root sufficiently to take care of themselves afterwards.[99]

By January 1923, the Columbans had "secured control of the road leading south from the building and [we] will also have to figure in some planting there."[100] McCarthy had a partiality toward trees, linking them with Joyce Kilmer's, "Trees."[101] The poem was conceptualized especially in McCarthy's construction of a "Calvary Path" on the eastern side of the property, "a bare, bleak place" toward the top of the hill before McCarthy planted Norway maples, elms, mountain ash, cedars, and other trees ("where the birds can build their nests"[102]) that lined the walk.

At the end of the Calvary Path, one came face to face with an almost life-size "Limpias" Crucifix, a replica of which was also found in the Silver Creek and Bellevue seminaries. The crucifix had gained international prominence just after World War I. While the original hung in the sixteenth century Saint Peter's Church in Cantabria, Spain, a monk cleaning the cross witnessed the

---

98   P. J. Flynn to "Dear Father McCarthy" 17 April 1922.

99   E. J. McCarthy to "My dear John" [Blowick] 19 March 1926. The previous year, the Region had already economized.

100 E. J. McCarthy to P. J. Flynn 16 January 1923. The other entrance to the grounds was considered to come from Bellevue Boulevard on the other side of the property.

101 Bolan, *Early Days at St. Columbans in the States*, transcript tape 2, 6. Joyce Kilmer, *Trees and Other Poems* (NY: George H. Doran, 1914). Kilmer, an American from New Jersey, was killed in 1918 in France in the First World War.

102 E. J. McCarthy, *Historical Sketch*, 18, 19. His quotation reflects the Kilmer lines, "A tree that may in Summer wear A nest of robins in her hair."

eyes open and close on the figure, as did others, who reported more physical characteristics taking place. In 1919, one of two prominent Spanish citizens, who arrived in the church to denounce the phenomena as mass illusion, assented to the miracle. In a post "Great War" world, where uncertainties prevailed and the effects of war were deeply felt, especially in Europe, the message of the cross was a call to repentance and religious belief. A replica of the shrine of Our Lady of Lourdes in France was placed to the left of the crucifix, up against the hillside along the path. McCarthy, a devotee of Mary, under various titles, had many photos of the Lourdes grotto and its measurements taken, "so that this tribute to Our Lady at St. Columbans would be as near the original as possible."[103] On a more mundane plane and probably taking advantage of the gopher holes already on the land in Bellevue, the students managed to create a three-hole golf course for recreation.

McCarthy saw that the grounds at Silver Creek seminary were also landscaped with numerous trees, many of them obtained from the government. Father Daniel F. Houlihan oversaw the construction of the junior seminary, as well as the care of the trees and plantings in the picturesque location on Eagle Bay.[104]

The two Columban seminaries were visual, natural reminders to students and faculty of the relationship between nature and grace, people and land/water, and the need for a contemplative perspective—i.e., listening, attentive presence to the sufferings of people with the same attentive devotion as one paid to the sufferings of Christ in prayer.

The Catholic Midwest and the Columbans

The major Catholic population and potential sources for funding were situated on the East Coast, particularly in Boston, New York, Philadelphia and Baltimore, and for this reason, many mission groups desired to have a "foothold" in those locations. As noted earlier, Galvin did have a connection with George Mundelein, appointed archbishop of Chicago in 1915 and noted by a local newspaper in 1924 as the "first Cardinal of the West." Mundelein set about to move the U.S. ecclesiastical "center" to the Midwest, where jobs were plentiful and the ethnic Catholic population was growing.

The centerpiece of what Mundelein hoped would be a new geographic ecclesiastical capitol was the massive seminary he built outside of Chicago,

---

[103]   Bolan, *Early Days at St. Columbans in the States*, transcript tape 2, 16.

[104]   Daniel Houlihan (1896–1955) eventually was incardinated into the Diocese of Trenton, New Jersey.

in an area later called "Mundelein."[105] He showcased that location at the International Eucharistic Congress held at the seminary in 1926, an event which Ned McCarthy and other Columbans attended. Describing the "magnificent and inspiring Congress," McCarthy wrote to Bishop Galvin, "Your friend George [Mundelein] did himself proud. He put over a big thing and I am sure he knows it. In fact one paper was ambitious enough to remark that there was nothing now to prevent him from being pope (except, I presume, the fact that he's a Yank)." The railroad laid new tracks to connect Chicago's Union Station with the Seminary. "The Chicago priests and business men had strenuously objected [to the plan] but the Cardinal put his foot down" to have the event at the seminary. Nevertheless, McCarthy related to Galvin, "I never saw or could imagine anything like the faith and devotion that was displayed all through, beginning with the children's and ending with the men 250,000 strong. It was an inspiration from start to finish," as a witness to non-Catholics and in bringing back "hundreds—perhaps thousands—of men and women to the Sacraments in Chicago," this, according to local clergy. There were some logistical problems, however. "The trains and automobiles were jammed in the tremendous effort of bringing more than half a million people forty miles out of Chicago. . . . The trains that brought us to Mundelein had used up so much juice in the morning that they could not move in the afternoon until the distributors along the line were all recharged." It would be six o'clock in the morning when the last of the pilgrims returned to Chicago. McCarthy, along with Fathers James Galvin, John O'Donovan and John P. O' Brien, "walked across the countryside to another little place called Libertyville and took another train home."[106]

Mundelein's desire to shift ecclesiastical power to the Midwest aligned with the visual depiction of the Columban's geographic location, though for a different reason. Omaha, indeed, was the lynch pin of the Transcontinental Railroad and by the time the Columbans arrived, railroads had replaced river transportation for the movement of goods and people. McCarthy visualized

---

[105]   For an overview of Mundelein's leadership style, see Edward R. Kantowicz, *Corporation Sole. Cardinal Mundelein and Chicago Catholicism* (Notre Dame, IN: University of Notre Dame Press, 1983).

[106]   McCarthy to "Dear Ned" [Galvin] 6 July 1926. See, also, E. J. McCarthy, "The Triumph of the Eucharist," *Far East* (June 1926), 128–130, which further provides a history of some significant International Eucharistic Congresses. The opening Mass took place, however, at Grant Park Stadium and included a chorus of 50,000 children from Catholic schools in Chicago. James Galvin (1895–1965) was doing pastoral work in the US, after recuperating from his work in China. O'Donovan (1895–1959), well known for his fine singing voice, would be appointed rector at Silver Creek in 1927, teaching or directing students for twenty-three years, and John O'Brien (1894–1968), in the first group of the Society's missionaries to China, was appointed in 1924 to teach at Silver Creek.

an accessible Omaha with a U.S. map he constructed. The map appeared in the *Mission Bulletins* in the 1920s, in advertising of the Society, and even in the Columban booth at the Missionary Exposition at the Vatican in 1925. He pictured Omaha at the center of the country, with lines (presumably railroad lines) reaching north, south, east and west. He described St. Columban's Seminary as located "at the heart of the Middle West."[107] The map reminded the men at Dalgan of Omaha's location in relation to the rest of the United States. If Irish-born mission promoters found that potential Society candidates were reluctant to move from the cities along the eastern seaboard, the Columbans could show the young men that they would be only a train ride, albeit a long one, from their homes. After property in Silver Creek was later purchased, the same visual point was made.[108]

Nevertheless, Omaha, and certainly Bellevue, seemed remote to many American Catholics. Many young men had written to the Columbans about entering, but "for some reason [they] did not come. Perhaps it is that Omaha is too far, or at least they think so."[109] McCarthy was keenly aware that Columban presence and contact was needed along the eastern seaboard for influence, money and vocations. In May 1922, McCarthy had remarked, "All here are in favor of a house in the East as a feeder for St. Columban's, but the big question now is whether the time is opportune. Unquestionably, Philadelphia would be the greatest center in the East for Vocations." It was questionable whether Cardinal Dougherty would let the Society into the diocese.[110] The junior seminary at Silver Creek, New York, was a beginning. Eleven years later, McCarthy wrote to Superior General O'Dwyer that they found an ideal property in the Diocese of Providence, Rhode Island. "My Council and myself are urged to ask for permission for this new Providence foundation now because we feel that it is the last opportunity the society will have of establishing a foundation anywhere in the New England States." McCarthy had visited several bishops "in desirable dioceses along the eastern seaboard and invariably met with the same refusal, the excuse being that their dioceses were already crowded with religious enterprises of one kind or another." Citing statistics for Catholic population in Providence, Boston, Hartford, Springfield, and Fall River, which McCarthy noted "are very Catholic and I may add very Irish," he urged that

---

[107]   E. J. McCarthy, *Historical Sketch* (1931), 7.

[108]   Gas well at Silver Creek, Bolan, transcript tape 2, 13; E. J. McCarthy to Very Rev. Michael O'Dwyer 3 May 1933.

[109]   E. J. McCarthy, *Diary of Progress at St. Columbans*, 15 July 1922, 60.

[110]   Ibid., May 24, 1922. Harty, who knew Cardinal Dougherty when they were in the Philippines, did not intervene with Dougherty, because the prelate noted that "The [Philadelphia] Cardinal hates to be approached by intermediaries. Wants to feel that he can make up his own mind and that no one can tell him anything." Ibid.

the superior general give permission to purchase property in Bristol, Rhode Island. [111]

Shaping an *American* Region: Meaning of "Americanization"

The Society in Ireland clearly viewed the United States as a major source to fund "the big needs in China."[112] While the first Columbans who came to the United States traveled the country to raise money and gain interest in missions to China, they saw themselves as "being in the wings" until they could get to China. But as McCarthy moved into his role as regional superior, he expressed the view that the Society in the States needed to "Americanize." In addition to dealing with a republic that expressed nonestablishment of religion and, therefore, no financial support of the churches, he had several intersecting lines of thought about what being an American region meant:

-   the perspective that now is "America's Hour" to send missionaries abroad
-   Society participation in key ecclesial groups in the country
-   the adoption of certain "American" ways, which included the ability to make decisions that required local knowledge, rather than the Central administration making every decision about the region.
-   Columban presence in the United States heralded the development of the Society as an *international* organization.

America's "Hour" for Missions

The precedent for America's "hour" to send missionaries overseas after World War I echoed the voice of Bishop Herbert Vaughan, founder of the Mill Hill missionaries, who highlighted the theme at the centennial of the foundation of the U.S. bishops in 1889. Vaughan declared that U.S. Catholics had the same "national character" as did American Protestant missionaries in China. Further, American Catholics "possessed the tradition of the missionary spirit of St.

---

[111]   E. J. McCarthy to Very Rev. Michael O'Dwyer 3 May 1933. The Minutes of the Regional Council Meeting for 2 May 1933 indicated that the bishop of Indianapolis would give permission for a Terre Haute, Indiana foundation, where there is an orphanage with a debt of one hundred thousand dollars, which the bishop would give for that sum. McCarthy and his Council were asking the superior general for $50,000 to purchase the Bristol property. Extracts from Minutes of a Meeting of the Regional Council 2 May 1933.

[112]   E. J. McCarthy, *Diary of Progress at St. Columban's, Omaha, Neb.*, 45. This was also Galvin's idea. See, Neil Collins, *The Splendid Cause. The Missionary Society of St. Columban, 1916–1954* (Dublin: Columba Press, 2009), 43.

Patrick." With the "enterprise, courage, skill and adaptability of the American, conjoined with the Catholic and Apostolic spirit of the Missioner," the bishop predicted that American Catholics would lead the missionary world in the twentieth century.[113] The refrain further reflected the view of some of the Paulist Fathers, notably Paulist founder, Isaac Hecker, and Walter Elliott. In the United States for only a few months, McCarthy expressed the sentiments in a circular letter to potential donors. He observed, "Old nations that have been the mainstay of mission around the world, have been grievously affected by the Great World War" and "can no longer champion the Great Cause [of missions]; while *our* nation [italics mine], as if through the special designs of Providence, has emerged victorious from that same war." Therefore, "America must come quickly to their assistance." Referring to the reorganization of "her missionary forces" with the Catholic Student Mission Crusade and the group that later became the American Board of Catholic Missions, he continued, "A new missionary spirit is breathing through the land but her Catholics must throw themselves wholeheartedly into the great struggle for Christ."[114] The regional superior intended to engage the Society in what he saw to be a vibrant Catholic Church in the United States.

Columban Participation in Key U.S. Ecclesial Groups

McCarthy sensed the growing *national* character of the United States with structures of transportation connecting east and west but also with Catholics perceiving themselves after 1918 as American, not just as regional entities. This was a different emphasis of national than the Irish nationalism of the period. Just before and after World War I, many U.S. Catholic organizations formed *national* membership and gatherings. Among them were the German–American Catholic Central *Verein*, with its social justice oriented emphasis and strong regional roots. The group now held national conferences for members, as did the American Catholic Historical Association, the National Catholic Philosophical Association, and the U.S. Catholic Bishops, whose efforts to promote War Bonds made them realize the strength of their collective action and the potential of an organized, centralized vehicle for public and internal church purposes.

Beginning in 1918–1919, three groups formed nationally that affected missions were the Catholic War Council, out of which emerged the National Catholic Welfare Council[115] (today called the United States Conference of

---

[113] Herbert Vaughan, reprinted in *Catholic Historical Review* XXX (October 1944), 290–298, here 291.

[114] E. J. McCarthy to "My Dear Friend" (circular letter to potential donors in United States) 1 Dec 1919.

[115] For the history of the NCWC, see Douglas J. Slawson, *Foundation and First Decade of the National Catholic Welfare Conference* (Washington DC: Catholic University Press of America, 1992).

Catholic Bishops), the American Board of Catholic Missions,[116] and the Catholic Students Mission Crusade, the latter founded at the Divine Word Missionary headquarters outside Chicago and later moving to Cincinnati. McCarthy's active engagement at the start of two of the groups put the Society into the mainstream of a developing and organizing national ecclesial entity.

As regional superior of a mission society, McCarthy received an invitation from James Cardinal Gibbons, president of the Catholic War Council, to a meeting at the University of Notre Dame in July 1919, "to formulate a plan to unify, coordinate, encourage and promote various forms of Catholic activity under the direction of the hierarchy."[117] Father Michael McHugh, who would be on his way to Hanyang the following year, accompanied the U.S. regional superior to Indiana. The bishops had written a key pastoral in February 1919, that addressed several areas of Catholic life, including home and foreign missions. The Notre Dame meeting concretized the points addressed by the bishops. Bishops and clergy involved with education, social welfare, the press, missions, and other areas of Catholic life met in the University auditorium for an explanation of what they were to accomplish and then were placed in their respective groups to devise a plan to coordinate their area nationally. This was McCarthy's first *en masse* encounter with U.S. Catholic ecclesiastical leadership and he took a keen interest in the dynamics of the meeting.

McCarthy knew a few men in the missions group: Peter Janser and Bruno Hagspiel of the Society of the Divine Word, Dr. Francis Beckman[118] (Catholic Students Mission Crusade), who became a lifelong friend, Paulist Peter O'Callaghan (Catholic Missionary Union), and Joseph McGlinchey (director, Archdiocese of Boston Society of the Propagation of the Faith), "who took me under his wing immediately and introduced me all around."[119] Other

---

[116]   For an overview of the ABCM history, see Angelyn Dries, OSF, *The Missionary Movement in American Catholic History* (Maryknoll, NY: Orbis Books, 1998), 92–95. See also, James Gaffey, *Francis Clement Kelley and the American Dream* (Bensenville, Illinois: The Heritage Foundation, 1980). The present day successor to the ABCM is the U.S. Catholic Mission Association, though with a different configuration.

[117]   Certificate of Incorporation, Archives of the U.S. Catholic Conference, quoted in Douglas J. Slawson, "National Catholic Welfare Conference," Michael Glazier and Thomas J. Shelley, eds., *The Encyclopedia of American Catholic History* (Collegeville, Minnesota: Liturgical Press, 1997), 1005.

[118]   Beckman became bishop of Lincoln, Nebraska, in 1924, and during Harty's last illness, administrator of Omaha. In that capacity, St. Mary's Parish, Bellevue, was committed to Columban pastoral care in 1927.

[119]   E. J. McCarthy, *A Few Personal Reminiscences* (1916–1920), written in early 1950s. typescript, 23. McGlinchey was well acquainted with Edward Galvin and "remained one of the best friends of the Society." McGlinchey periodically sent burses to the Columbans, such as the $3,000 burse sent in May 1921. McCarthy devoted seven

mission organizations were represented, but two major players, Francis C. Kelley, founder of the Catholic Church Extension Society, and James A. Walsh, cofounder of the Catholic Foreign Mission Society of America, held opposing views for a coordinated plan for U.S. Catholic missions. Kelley and Walsh were on a missions subcommittee of seven who did the major planning for a national mission board. After the meeting and the whole group had affirmed a plan for what became the American Board of Catholic Missions, Joseph McGlinchey related to McCarthy that, at the subcommittee meeting, McGlinchey "had heard Kelley promise Father Walsh that in return for the latter's support of the mission board plan [that Kelley proposed], Kelley "would use his influence to have Maryknoll accepted by the hierarchy as the sole official American foreign mission society and have the 'Irish Mission' [Columbans] excluded from any participation in the proposed scheme. It seems incredible, but that was what my friend [McGlinchey] across the table was telling me and he was there."[120] The American Board of Catholic Missions, with a plan somewhat different from what was proposed at the 1919 meeting and subsequently refined did not begin officially until early 1926.

In retrospect, McCarthy observed that the "meeting turned out to be without doubt the most important and historic ecclesiastical gathering held in America in the first half of this [the Twentieth] century." At Notre Dame, McCarthy "saw a hope, which has never since been dimmed, no matter how slow its fruition might seem, hope in the vast missionary potential of the Church in the United States." He further opined, "Surely, I thought, all this restless, purposeful vitality I saw around me, must someday overflow to spread faith and culture over the far-flung heathen mission fields of the world. Any other conclusion seemed inconceivable."[121]

The Catholic Students' Mission Crusade (CSMC), founded in 1918, was a young organization at the time of the Notre Dame gathering of bishops and others.[122] But E. J. McCarthy recognized the value of the CSMC in motivating high

---

out of thirty pages of his single-spaced, "Reminiscences," to the meeting. McCarthy noted the continuing difficulties between the mission funding and mission sending perspectives in E. J. McCarthy to "My dear John" [Blowick] 26 May 1921 9.A.83.8.

[120]   E. J. McCarthy, *A Few Personal Reminiscences*, 30.

[121]   E. J. McCarthy, *A Few Personal Reminiscences* 23, 27. The American Board of Catholic Missions officially began in 1925, but one bishop on the standing committee to the advisory group to the board was Columban friend, Jeremiah J. Harty of Omaha. After a brief suppression of the National Catholic Welfare Council by the Vatican, mainly because of the intervention of two U.S. archbishops, the group incorporated again as the National Catholic Welfare Conference.

[122]   David J. Endres, *American Crusade: Catholic Youth in the World Mission Movement from World War I through Vatican II* (Eugene, OR: Pickwick Publications, 2010) provides an important overview and development of the Catholic Students Mission Crusade and the evolving spirit of the group, as well as reasons for the group's demise.

school and college students to consider mission. He was on the organization's board of directors in the 1920s, wrote *An Introduction to Mission Studies* for the group, participated in the national and local conferences, promoted the group in the *Far East*,[123] and provided personnel and exhibits of Columban mission work for the latter.[124] The Society used some items, sent from China for the 1925 Missionary Exposition in Rome,[125] at local CSMC gatherings, especially in the eastern part of the United States. The 1925 Missionary Exposition in Rome was highlighted in three issues of the *Far East* that year.

Language, Customs and American "Ways"

McCarthy suggested to John Blowick that when an Irish-born Columban came to the United States, the superior general should "have a talk with him" before embarking. While the new missionary would undoubtedly want to be sent to China and would consider an assignment to the United States as decidedly not mission work, the one sent should grasp "the fact that he is coming to this country to make good. The only way to make good is to become as sympathetic as possible with the work here and with the country." McCarthy realized that new members would want to "see the big things in the [China] mission" and that "the work here seems very secondary." But McCarthy counseled,

> "a man must have a certain amount of humility to fit in with it. . . . We don't exactly want men to forget Ireland, God forbid, [but] the men that come here should learn above all to be all things to all men. A man must change here even to his accent. Some are inclined to think that it is weakness

123   The Editor (E. J. McCarthy), "The Castle School of Crusade Leadership," *Far East* (June 1925), 136–138.

124   Edward J. McCarthy, *An Introduction to Mission Studies* (Catholic Students' Mission Crusade: Cincinnati, OH, 1925); "The Soundest Argument" [for missionary interest], Convention Secretary, ed., *To Defend the Cross. The Story of the Fourth General Convention of the Catholic Student's Mission Crusade* (Cincinnati, OH: Catholic Students' Mission Crusade, 1923), 56–57. Edward J. McCarthy, *An Introduction to Mission Studies* (Catholic Students Mission Crusade, 1925). Editor [E. J. McCarthy], "The Castle School of Crusade Leadership. A great new Factor in the development of the Missionary Spirit in America," *FE* (June 1925), 16–18. Edward J. McCarthy, "The Catholic Organization for the Missions," taken from the *Leader Book of the Catholic Students Mission Crusade*, and published in *The Mission Apostolate* (NY: National Office of the Society for Propagation of the Faith, 1941), 75–85. Several times in his correspondence, McCarthy referenced the significance of CSMC and the importance of Columban involvement in the group.

125   On the anthropological underpinnings of the 1925 Missionary Ethnology Exposition, see Angelyn Dries, "The 1925 Vatican Mission Exposition and the Interface between Catholic Mission Theory and World Religions," *International Bulletin of Mission Research* (April 2016), 119–132.

and *shoneenism*[126] that makes a man change his accent when he comes to America. On the contrary, I regard it as a man's duty to the Society. The same common sense principle that impels a man to learn the proper pronunciation of Chinese, should tell him to learn the pronunciation of English as it is adopted in any particular country. It is a false idea of national sentiment that keeps a man from doing it. . . . A man owes it to the whole society to adopt the outlook of the country in which he works, whether it be China, or Ireland or America and Australia, and that should be impressed on men before they leave Dalgan. It's easier than learning Theology and just as important."[127]

He reminded Superior General Blowick, "Over in Ireland conditions are more or less fixed, not so here. Mission activities are moving rapidly and if we have to keep sitting still waiting for decisions from Dalgan, the opportunities will slip by us and the Society as a whole will suffer."[128] McCarthy was sensitive to the energy and development he saw in the American church and he wanted the Society to be part of that experience. He wrote to Blowick, "One could not live three years in a country like America without realizing its importance, far more, I think, than any man who has never been outside Ireland could realize."[129]

Another area that the Columbans in Ireland were chastising the U.S. region related to the eventual addition of the letters "SSC" [Society of St. Columban] after their name, a procedure familiar to Catholic Americans. That made it seem to the Irish Columbans that the Society was a religious order. McCarthy explained that in the United States Catholics would not contribute to a Society with the title "China Mission Society," or even "Irish Mission Society," thinking that the group is foreign. This was especially true with respect to the American Board of Catholic Missions. The initials behind a priest's name followed "American" usage.[130]

The Columbans from Ireland did not forget their own historical and cultural roots. Most Irish-born priests did not perforce lose their accent after

---

[126] A derogatory word that signified preference for English customs, language, and perspective, over that of Irish. Given Irish nationalist sensitivity at the time, McCarthy's explanation makes sense.

[127] E. J. McCarthy to "My dear John" [Blowick] 1 Nov 1922.

[128] E. J. McCarthy to "My dear John" [Blowick] 18 June 1923.

[129] E. J. McCarthy to "My dear John" [Blowick] 29 December 1921.

[130] Edward Galvin had initially favored a regular novitiate for the men and, if possible, the development of a religious order. E. J. McCarthy, "Diary of Early Days of St. Columban, Nebraska," 28 April 1922, 36.

being in the States, nor did they necessarily lose interest in Irish politics. In 1920, Eamon de Valera, an Irish patriot, revolutionary, and politician, who had escaped from Lincoln jail, Lincolnshire, England, traveled across the United States to plead the cause of Irish freedom. He made a visit to Omaha. At the Bedford Avenue house the Society hosted a luncheon for him, Archbishop Daniel Mannix from Melbourne, Australia, Bishop Harty, and a few Omaha priests.[131] De Valera and Mannix wanted to be alone to talk Irish politics, so for this to happen, McCarthy drove them along the Bellevue "Boulevard," just a dirt road at the time, to the site purchased by the Society for its headquarters. McCarthy occasionally mentioned or commented upon contemporary Irish political issues in his letters to Blowick and elsewhere.

But McCarthy's perception of the Catholic Church in Ireland as "settled" and even staid could probably only be seen because of the foundation of the American branch of the Society on the "frontier" in Nebraska and the dynamic Church in the United States he saw before him.

The U.S. Region and Internationalization

Edward Galvin initially had thought the "Irish mission," as he termed it, would "BIND Ireland, America and Australia together in this work. Australia and the US have the funds and some vocations, too. We must not confine it within the four seas of Ireland but try to make it the work of the Irish race . . . both now and in the future most of the assistance will come from the Irish abroad and they must be BOUND CLOSELY to us."[132] The Society would be a kind of Irish mission diaspora. But McCarthy related to Blowick, "The Society has become international whether we like to admit that or not. It became international on that morning towards the end of Nov. 1917, when you and I stood at Kingstown pier and said goodbye to Caw [Edward Galvin] and Matt Dolan. We have committed ourselves to all that or rather God has committed us to it without us knowing it. It is now our duty to do what we can to develop the Society so that it will remain an international organization working as one unit."[133] He suggested that the close unity the men felt in various regions could

---

131   E. J. McCarthy, "A Few Personal Reminiscences," (1916–1920), 20. "Young Father Ed Flanagan, afterwards famous in his own right as Father Flanagan of Boys' Town" was present for the occasion. Ibid., The controversial Daniel Mannix, past president of St. Patrick's College, Maynooth, and well known to McCarthy, would have a fifty-year tenure as archbishop of Melbourne.

132   Edward Galvin to Joseph O'Leary, 16 August 1916 (CFCA, G-1:33), quoted in Neil Collins, 43.

133   E. J. McCarthy to "My dear John" [Blowick], 18 June 1923. Earlier, McCarthy had stressed the international dimension of the Society. In a letter to a Sister of Loretto,

not last for more than twenty or twenty-five years. McCarthy wrote that "The day that Father [Edward] Galvin published the first copy of the *Far East* at Omaha in 1918, he took the first step, rightly or wrongly toward making the Society international. . . . The events following . . . were the logical outcome of that step and we were pushed into them, one by one, by forces and circumstances over which I candidly think we have little or no control."[134]

The Columban administration at Dalgan needed to trust those "in the field," who knew the context, facts, and extenuating circumstances. Perhaps in the future there might be a "danger of a cleavage in the Society owing to different nationalities." McCarthy wrote to Blowick, "Now is the time to prevent that cleavage, but John, you can't do it by cropping off the branches. You have got to prevent it by strengthening the trunk of the organization." Americanization would mean that the country "would not remain simply as a collecting agency" for Ireland.[135] It would include eventual appointment of regional superiors born in the United States. McCarthy opined that a cleavage might occur at least "as long as Irish-born priests are in charge of the work [in the United States]." It would be possibly in the next thirty or so years, "that the Society must endeavor to formulate a policy and a constitution which will prevent this cleavage when American priests get into control, as they must."[136] Furthermore, McCarthy wrote to O'Dwyer, "I cannot emphasize too strongly my own conviction of the necessity of having as many American born priests as possible attached to this region and if possible connected with the Administration."[137]

Writing to Sister Antonella, a Sister of Loretto, whose community worked with the Columbans in Hanyang, McCarthy remarked that other communities should come to the United States, without dependence on the country for a start, either in men or money," to promote the mission spirit in the United States and "make America a big factor in the foreign missions. That is something that is above nationalism and it is Catholic in the widest sense. I think the idea of

---

Kentucky, whose community worked with the Columbans early on, McCarthy noted, "We have never accepted the protection or help of any government, and, please God, we never will. We go to China under no flag but the Cross and we feel that under that banner of Redemption we will be safe. From the outset, we set ourselves to establishing an international organization because we feel that we must be prepared to draw our resources from every field if we were to cope with such things as international wars." E. J. McCarthy to Sister Antonella, Sisters of Loretto 16 September 1921. CFA-USA.

[134]   E. J. McCarthy to "Dear Doc," 15 November 1924.

[135]   E. J. McCarthy, *Reminiscences*, 17.

[136]   E. J. McCarthy to "My dear John" [Blowick] 18 June 1923.

[137]   E. J. McCarthy to "Dear Dr. O'Dwyer," 5 March 1928.

nationalities is carried much too far in mission work. Everywhere in the foreign field, we have the saddest experiences of love of country before love of God."[138]

After years of seeing the deleterious effects of German or French nationalism on local Catholic communities, Edward Galvin recognized that if foreign missionaries were dismissed, the Catholic Church in China would suffer. When the Society was negotiating with the American Sisters of Loretto to come to Hanyang, China, McCarthy remarked, "We go to China under no flag but the Cross and we feel that under the banner of Redemption we will be safe. From the outset, we set ourselves to establishing an international organization because we feel that we must be prepared to draw our resources from every field if we are to cope with such things as international wars."[139] Galvin also reiterated the point in a letter to McCarthy from Hanyang in 1949, "We visualized the mission, not as a National entity, but as an International organization."[140] This was a change of the perspective Galvin and Blowick had held earlier. McCarthy further elaborated the point: the Society reflected earlier Columban monks, who embodied people of many ethnic groups and nations.[141]

Edward J. McCarthy as Regional Superior

The Public Face of the Society

At twenty-eight years of age and ordained for four years by 1919, Edward J. McCarthy was appointed the first regional superior of the Chinese Mission Society in the United States. He would bear many burdens and be tested in multiple ways over his next fifteen years in leadership. Fortunately, he possessed

---

[138] E. J. McCarthy to Sr. Antonella, Sisters of Loretto 16 September 1921, Hanyang folder, Loretto Sisters, 1920–23, negotiations re: going to Han Yang. 1.c.6. CFA-USA. Pope Benedict XV and Pope Pius XI, even more so, strongly chided the nationalist spirit of some European mission societies.

[139] E. J. McCarthy to Sister Antonella, Sisters of Loretto, 16 September 1921.

[140] Letter quoted in James McCaslin, *The Spirituality of Our Founders: A Study of the Early Columban Fathers* (Society of St. Columban, 1986), 52.

[141] E. J. McCarthy, *Historical Sketch*, 31, makes the point specifically. McCarthy further noted that Father James Conway (1892–1977) "was preparing to go to the Irish College at Salamanca to learn Spanish with a view to opening a new field for the Society in South America." In 1919, Conway went to Buenos Aires, Argentina, "to set up his office" and prepare a Spanish edition of the *Far East* to promote the mission in that country. E. J. McCarthy, *A Few Personal Remembrances* (1916–1920), 16, 18. However, with no support for the Argentine project, Conway left for a short stint in China and returned to Ireland shortly thereafter, traveling through the United States. He incardinated in the Diocese of Kildare and Leighlin in 1929. The idea of a promotion house in Argentina arose again in the 1930s. "Do you think it a suitable time to send a few priests to B. A. [Buenos Aires] to establish a branch of our organization there?" Dick Ranaghan to E. J. McCarthy 10 Jan 1934.

diverse talents and learned new skills to face significant challenges. As has been seen in the chapter, McCarthy handled many tasks and diverse tests each day. In so doing, he shaped the role of regional superior in relationship to the public, both in legal matters, public relations, finances and investments. Within the Society, the regional superior had to work out the pattern of association and structures of governance between the United States and the superior general in Ireland, as well as make decisions about the overall seminary experience of future missionaries. McCarthy also exerted pastoral leadership. This involved a personal concern for the men, along with practical judgments to be made that affected their health and well-being, and the development of patterns of life together in support of the mission. McCarthy's temperament, personal attributes, spirituality, physical health, intellectual and fine arts pursuits would each have a place, as well, in his exercise of leadership. A brief look at representative tasks and situations McCarthy met in the first ten years in the United States illustrate these multidimensional connections.

The first order of business for the Columbans once they arrived in Omaha and settled into their rented house was to raise funds for the mission in China. They did so by getting to know local Catholics and by engaging as many Catholics as possible to subscribe to the *Far East*. Sister Mary Therese Bolan characterized him as a "businessman to the nth degree." He made sure that those in the *Field Afar* and Society offices had the "most convenient and latest" implements to speed along the process of written communication. He handled investments, the purchase of real estate in two states (with parties unfavorable to Catholics) and a third state in 1933, raised and managed funds for the budget, allocated physical resources, and tended to the spiritual and ministry needs of the men. The requisite to raise funds was a constant pressure for him.[142] There were postal strikes, periodic theft of donor's money at the local post office[143] and a financial depression in 1922, all of which resulted in a downturn in donations those years.

Managerial tasks were both pragmatic and substantive, ranging from overseeing and providing for the *Field Afar* offices, booking trains and ships for the men from Ireland traveling across the United States on their way to China, sending *Ordos* (daily liturgical almanacs) and Mass Stipends to missionaries, and administration of the overall building construction and grounds for the Nebraska and Silver Creek seminaries.

Fund raising depended upon making the Society known in the United States. His presence at the foundation meeting of what became the American

---

[142]   Nick Kill interviews of Sister Therese Bolan, 1975.

[143]   One of these times was in late 1921. The Columbans alerted the postmaster, a trap was set, and the postal thief was arrested in January 1922. However, periodic thefts continued over the decades.

Board of Catholic Missions put him in contact with the "major players" of missions, both home and foreign. With that group not getting started until 1926, the Society had to rely upon funds from the National Society of the Propagation of the Faith office and personal contact with bishops. Bishops in the 1920s were often reluctant to have missionary societies into their dioceses. One of the exceptions was Bishop Michael Gallagher of the then Diocese of Detroit, which in the 1920s was experiencing a growth of Catholic population due to the automobile industry. McCarthy's active engagement with the Catholic Students Mission Crusade put the Society in touch with high school and college students, who were eager to "do something" for the missions.

While he noted that a good income was due to mail propaganda, he noticed a small recession in 1922, indicating job loss of some of their donors. Later that year, he mentioned strikes and financial depression as reasons for lower funds arriving for the Society.[144] Nevertheless, on December 11, 1922, he responded to 292 letters and on December 19, 362 letters sent by donors.[145] Then there was the problem of the mail containing donors' money being stolen at the post office. One of these times was in late 1921. The Columbans alerted the postmaster, a trap was set, and the postal thief was arrested in January 1922. Early on, the Society established a post office at their headquarters, which eliminated some of the problem of stealing, though not all theft, due to the route the mail followed to get to arrive at the Columbans.

McCarthy, who saw the United States as his "adopted country," (he became a U.S. citizen in April 1925) cultivated clerical and lay friends, found attorneys for legal work, and traveled across the country to negotiate with property owners and bishops. Fond of concerts and good shows, McCarthy also oversaw the establishment of trees and shrubs for two seminary properties.[146] He had established the seminary first at the Bedford Avenue location with a few students in September 1921, then in the new building outside of Bellevue and a preparatory seminary in Silver Creek. McCarthy spent several months in Silver Creek when that seminary opened in fall 1924. He dealt with questions about the structure of the courses, whether American students should go to Ireland for some of their education, at which seminary to take their philosophy courses, what type of program seminarians should have outside of the structure of the classroom setting.

---

[144]   E. J. McCarthy to "My dear John" [Blowick]. 1 November 1922.

[145]   These numbers point to the fact that McCarthy dictated letters to the secretary, who would use the same basic message to a number of people. The secretarial staff grew quickly.

[146]   Sr. Therese Bolan, "Reminiscences." CFA-USA.

Structures and Philosophy of Governance—What Is a Region?

Then McCarthy faced the pressures of governance. A new trail was made as the practicalities of a "region" were developed. Because "Ireland" did not have a feel for things in the States and seemed to want "to interfere with such [small] details," McCarthy felt further frustration because decision making that required more immediate action was weighed down by the slowness of communication across the Atlantic Ocean. McCarthy's vexation was poignantly expressed in a seven-page letter to Blowick. Topics ranged from choosing a site for a seminary, which location should be used for which purpose, and "promoting our classes in Senior classics." McCarthy noted of the latter point, "That is merely a small detail that I do not want to talk about if you decide that it is a good thing for the superior general to interfere in such details. Personally I would advise you not. It is starting a precedent which may, in future years, lead to trouble."[147]

With respect to the preparatory seminary location, McCarthy responded to Blowick's statement that "the Niagara area [one area McCarthy had looked at] cannot be a healthy center for growing boys and consequently cannot be thought of as a center for a school. What on earth put that into your head? Niagara and the hills around it are the health resorts of northern New York and Pennsylvania. . . . [McCarthy mentioned the Vincentian college and convents located along the gorge.] However, I shall do nothing about getting property in the vicinity of Niagara until you withdraw your opposition to that location." A little later in the letter, McCarthy remarked, "You must remember, John, that there are conditions which we can see here and which we cannot explain in all our letters. Even if we did, it would be difficult for anybody in Ireland to understand so far away from the actual field."[148] While Blowick certainly meant well, especially because he had visited the United States on his way to China, McCarthy observed that conditions had changed in the meantime and that it was imperative to find a location for the Society in the eastern part of the country. McCarthy ended his seven-page letter in a spirit of frustration.

> Now look here, John, I have simply exhausted all my powers of explanation in this letter. . . . I am tired of writing letters and explaining our position here. For goodness sake let us all try and feel that we are working in the interests of the Society as a whole and that we are not trying to put anything over on anybody else, and if we cannot understand the other man's point of view, or if we cannot see his consistency, let us

---

[147]   E. J. McCarthy to "My dear John" [Blowick], 18 June 1923.

[148]   Ibid.

try to account for it by the fact that we do not always have the background against which he is working.[149]

McCarthy's perspective would much later undergird the principle of subsidiarity, an organizing principle that matters ought to be handled and decisions made by the smallest, lowest or least centralized competent authority with attention directed to those most affected by the decision.[150]

Pastoral Elements of Regional Leadership

The first group of Columbans left Ireland for China in 1920 by way of the United States so that the missionaries would have a sense of the vast country and make personal contact with Americans, especially Irish Americans. Some of these contacts would be relatives, who would hopefully be generous toward the China mission. However, very soon after the first two groups began their mission in China, McCarthy welcomed back some missionaries who arrived to recuperate. First, however, the priests buried the first Society member to die, Father James O'Connell (1892–1921).

Ordained at Maynooth in 1917, O'Connell joined the Columbans the following year. While in the United States in 1919, he suffered a severe attack of influenza. He went to Phoenix, Arizona, where the Irish Sisters of Mercy tended to him at their St. Joseph Hospital.[151] After McCarthy received a telegram from the Sisters about O'Connell's weakening condition, he set out for Arizona by train, but because of flooding along the rail lines, he arrived too late. O'Connell died of an abscess of the lung. That Christmas McCarthy wrote: "We visited Father O'Connell's grave this afternoon [at Holy Sepulchre Cemetery, Omaha]. It is covered with snow. Wonder what big Christmas gifts he is planning to send us."[152]

---

[149]   Ibid.

[150]   Subsidiarity, a key principle of Catholic social thought, holds that nothing should be done by a larger and more complex organization which can be done as well by a smaller simpler organization. . . . This principle is a bulwark of limited government and personal freedom. It conflicts with the passion for centralization and bureaucracy characteristic of the Welfare State." David A. Bosnich, "The Principle of Solidarity," retrieved March 15, 2015 from http://www.acton.org/pub/religion-liberty/volume-6-number-4/principle-subsidiarity.

[151]   St. Joseph Hospital, Phoenix, was founded by the Sisters of Mercy in 1895 as a twelve bed sanitarium for indigent patients suffering from tuberculosis. *The Mission Bulletin* (U.S.A. Edition) noted that the Sisters of Mercy also tended O'Connell in California earlier. "The Society owes [the Sisters of Mercy] a great deal." *Mission Bulletin* (July 1921) 1. O'Connell's poem, "The Sanctuary Lamp," written a few weeks before his death, was printed in the same *Mission Bulletin*.

[152]   E. J. McCarthy, "Diary of Early Days of Progress at St. Columban, Neb.," Christmas, 1921, 7. McCarthy visited O'Connell the week before he died.

Another person whose health was of concern was McCarthy's classmate, Father Joseph O'Leary (1891–1974), ordained at Maynooth in 1915. He had joined Galvin in China for a few years and returned by way of the United States to join the Society in 1918. He was on the Council and teaching at Dalgan Park in the 1920s. McCarthy wrote "that [O'Leary's] health is almost broken down and that he fears the recurrence of the trouble he had while in America, and for which he was operated on in Philadelphia in 1918. May God grant that his fears are not correct. There is only one place in the world where he can get a proper diagnosis and proper attention and that is Rochester [Minnesota]. I have written to both him and Father Blowick to come at once to America and consult the Mayos [Doctors in Rochester, Minnesota]. [O'Leary] is resigning from *Far East* and Council."[153] In the U.S. O'Leary managed the *Far East* for some time, but ill health returned. He incardinated in the Diocese of San Diego, California, in 1938.

Analysis of the Problem of Poor Physical Health and Some Solutions

By the later 1920s, the health of missionaries and seminarians was of general concern in the Society. "Our priests are breaking down in health from work and worry [in China] . . . I am worried sick about it all."[154] In a letter to Superior General O'Dwyer, McCarthy provided a lengthy analysis of various aspects of illness and he suggested some solutions. "The health condition of our priests is a thing largely due to certain racial defects resulting from malnutrition and impoverished living conditions that our people as a race have been subjected to for generations. Our present generation of Irish boys and girls, including Irish American, are not of the same sturdy race as our forefathers. They are particularly liable to TB [tuberculosis] in this country as well as Ireland, more so I am advised by medical men than any other race except the American Indians, where similar causes have been at work."[155]

McCarthy made specific suggestions, particularly for the house in Ireland where some American and all the Irish seminarians lived. He indicated that there was "not enough attention to the dietary in our houses." The seminarians or missionaries are entrusted to men in excellent health, but, though solicitous, "do not appreciate what men suffer through monotonous and ill-cooked menus." This was "especially the case at headquarters in China and the priests on the

---

[153]   E. J. McCarthy, "Diary of Early Days of Progress at St. Columban, Neb.," 6 March 1922, 24. In 1889, Dr. William Worrall Mayo was invited by the Sisters of St. Francis, Rochester, Minnesota to be director of a hospital the sisters would build. St. Mary's Hospital was established in 1889 with the Mayo Clinic connected with the hospital. His sons, William James Mayo and Charles Horace Mayo joined him in the practice of innovative health care.

[154]   E. J. McCarthy to Ned Galvin in Hanyang, 27 April 1929.

[155]   McCarthy to O'Dwyer 8-C-17.39. 5 December 1928. *Casey History* (1928), 14.

missions know nothing about food values." Americans who never suffered indigestion in the United States "have suffered severely from the diet at Dalgan. Proper dietary is a scientific thing and should be studied like everything else."

McCarthy had inquired of American born Father Ambrose Gallagher what he thought was the cause of students' poor health. Gallagher, who had studied at Dalgan from 1924–1928, attributed illness to "lack of variety in food and especially to the sameness of breakfasts of bread and strong tea and hard boiled eggs. Why not try such things as fruit, cereals and coffee for a change and in addition give the students a good course in food values." [156] McCarthy was of the opinion that the physical problems of the missionaries in China began in the seminary. Among the recommendations McCarthy made to those at Dalgan was to "review thoroughly the dietary system of our houses and colleges and take expert advice on the matter, have proper menus drawn up and insist that these be carried out rigidly." And, as he had noted to the Society's superior general about other matters, McCarthy said, "There is all too frequently a tendency to false economy in this respect."[157]

The regional superior made an astute observation which suggested the relationship between physical and the spiritual, given the intensity of seminary life.

> It is quite possible that spiritual repressions lead to nervous repressions and they in turn lead to functional organic repressions which necessitate the constant use of medicine, also, I understand, a common feature of Dalgan life. Perhaps the Spiritual Director could find some remedy for this difficulty, but if it cannot be remedied, why not try to get students to resort to physical exercises like Müller's rather than pills? . . . The less students think about their health the better. Their spiritual life tends to make them introspective and it is very easy to divert that introspection from spiritual to physical ills."[158]

The Müller to whom McCarthy referred was the celebrated exercise gymnast of the era, the Dane, Jørgen Peter Müller (1866–1938). His popular book, *My System*, published in 1904 and translated into many languages, advocated a shedding of some of the Victorian "restraints" of the era in favor of sunshine, fresh air, and fifteen minutes of free body movement and exercise every day for men and for women. As noted earlier, McCarthy's "ideal location"

---

[156]   McCarthy to O'Dwyer 8-C-17.39. 5 December 1928. *Casey History* (1928), 14.

[157]   Ibid.

[158]   Ibid.

for a seminary embodied these elements: fresh air, sun, and exercise, whether "artificially" through something like Müller's exercise, through a bit of farm work and gardening, an improvised three-hole golf course, or basketball in a gymnasium. Later, in spite of the country's economic Depression, an expenditure was authorized for $818 for the construction of a handball court at St. Columbans, whereas half that amount had been authorized for building a cow and horse barn on the farm at Silver Creek.[159]

The importance of good health he linked to the "virile spirit" of the Midwest. "It is better for [the Society] to grow up with young and virile Catholic spirit that is developing here [in the Midwest.]"[160]

Then there was the situation with the seminarians at Silver Creek. With increasing enrollment (forty in 1929 and possibly sixty to seventy the following year), the Columbans had hoped for a few Columban Sisters to help with nursing care, cooking and other tasks related to making a "home" for the high school and college students. But, in the meantime,

> "Young boys are continually getting sick with different kinds
> of boys' complaints, diphtheria, scarlet fever and the like.
> Then, of course, there is always the flu and colds. At present
> when these boys are sick the priests have to carry their trays
> to them and nurse them. If a serious epidemic breaks out
> we have to get a nurse, but even that is unsatisfactory, for we
> find it impossible to get the proper kind of help so far from
> the city."[161]

In addition to a more nutritious and varied diet, exercise, and breathing fresh air to sustain good health, a long-term solution was sought for the needs of seriously ill missionaries—a house for recuperation especially for men with lung problems. Superior General John Blowick wrote to Paul Waldron the rector, faculty member, and retreat master in Nebraska, to inquire about finding a place for the men to rest. Blowick wrote, "At least three of our priests will, I am afraid, have to leave China soon on account of ill health and I would be glad if you would arrange with the bishop of Los Angeles to rent a house (or cottage) for them in some good healthy place. They are, I am afraid, not in a position to undertake anything like heavy parochial work."[162] Paul Waldron, having been appointed vice director of the U.S. region, was asked to look

---

[159]   O'Dwyer to McCarthy, 4 July 1932. *Casey History* (1932), 20.

[160]   McCarthy to O'Dwyer 8-C-17, 28. 5 March 1928. *Casey History* (1928), 3.

[161]   E. J. McCarthy to Ned Galvin in Hanyang, 27 April 1929.

[162]   Blowick to Waldron, 14 May 1924.

into the situation. He consulted with Father James Galvin, who was himself recuperating in California at the time. Waldron responded to Superior General Michael O'Dwyer that the men do not simply need "rest,"

> but first class care. Not a cottage—person needs to be cared for; good attention, food, etc. Climate is only half the cure. . . . That a place where the Sisters are in the place where they will be cared for. He (James Galvin) knows from experience. . . . In view of the above, I set about getting a healthy or the most healthy place I knew of or could learn combined with a Sisters Hospital where they handle such cases. The Sisters Hospital in San Diego[163] was the best I could learn of. I saw the Mother Superior. She is willing to take the priests. I told her that the complaints were mostly lung trouble and nerve trouble— general break up." [164]

For those with lung problems, the system at the Hospital was a series of special tents where patients lived and even slept. Waldron remarked that "it would be criminal to put them in [hospital] rooms if there is lung trouble. . . . The advantage of the tent was, according to the Mother Superior, the patient has open air always, and the patient is removed from the noise around a room in the hospital," yet has immediate doctor and nurse care.[165]

In fact, the Society did not acquire a "home for invalid priests" until March 1936, when a house was rented for about a year in Redlands, San Bernardino, California. The climate and location did not meet the needs of the men, but in 1937, the Diocese of San Diego offered the Society the guardianship of the historic, small Adobe Chapel of La Purissima in Old Town, San Diego, rebuilt that year by the Federal government. Father John McFadden procured a house nearby, where ailing priests could reside and from whence the Society could solicit donations for the missions. Father John Cowhig, who had served in China and would in two years start the Columban ministry among the Chinese in Los Angeles, was the first Columban to say Mass in the Chapel on November 2, 1938. The house served as a location from which Columbans could live and say Mass occasionally in nearby parishes, as well as at the Adobe Chapel. Columbans were affiliated with the Chapel until 1969.

---

[163]   Most likely this was the St. Joseph/Mercy Hospital in San Diego, established by the Sisters of Mercy in 1890. By 1904, the Sisters had opened a nursing school there, as well.

[164]   Paul Waldron to Michael O'Dwyer, 24 July 1924. This letter referenced the 14 May 1924 letter of Blowick to Waldron.

[165]   Paul Waldron to Michael O'Dwyer, 24 July 1924.

A Regional Superior's Personal Life

Physical Health

McCarthy reported to Blowick that, "During the last few years I have been nothing but a business man saying Mass. There was little of the priest or the student in my life, and since I have started again [after his operation in August 1922] I feel a 100% better in every way. It takes my mind off the greenbacks, and you know, John, it is easy for a man to lose his ideals, and with them will go a lot of other things that a man cannot do without. Being mixed up in the seminary to some extent gives me a greater sense of responsibility and I can live a more regular life."

However, on his visit to Ireland in 1924, McCarthy became a patient at Mater Hospital Nursing Home, Dublin, in mid-May. The state of his health caused Blowick "great anxiety and sorrow and everybody here is very much upset by it." While no information was given about the cause of his illness or whether he had surgery to relieve the situation, it took McCarthy until July to feel in better health.[166] He further suffered eye afflictions and while in Ireland, sinus troubles. No doubt his physical condition was affected by the immense pressures he felt: those coming from headquarters in Ireland, from concerns related to his responsibility toward the men in the United States, the responsibility for large funding of the Society mission in China, and for defraying the debt that Ireland had. Added to this, he had to deal with frequent bouts of loneliness, something he did not often share. But in a letter to Bishop Galvin, he noted, "It has been terribly lonely here for the past few years and that loneliness has been a big trial, bigger perhaps for me than most people imagine."[167]

Intellectual and Fine Arts Interests

McCarthy was a prolific writer. His smaller, but important history items included "Diary of the Early Days of St. Columban in Nebraska" (1919–1923), his "Reminiscences" (1950s) of those early days, and a "Catholic History of Bellevue" (1933) .[168] He wrote a monograph, "The Society of St. Columban. A Historical Sketch" (1931), which provides a brief history of the Society and important details about the seminary in Nebraska and the new minor seminary in Silver Creek, New York, to interest young men to join the Society. The latter booklet walked young men through the stages of seminary life and included photos of the newly built seminary and grounds.

---

[166] Blowick to McCarthy. 14 May 1924. 8-C-15.17. *Casey History* (1924), 4. However, in early 1925, McCarthy was ill once again.

[167] E. J. McCarthy to Ned Galvin 5 March 1926. 8-C-16.47. *Casey History* (1926), 3.

[168] E. J. McCarthy, July 1933, "The Catholic History of Bellevue." CFA-USA.

He had voluminous and lengthy correspondence with Society leadership at Dalgan, with Bishop Galvin in China, and with Society members in the United States. He wrote an abundance of letters on behalf of Bishop Galvin sent to Catholics in the United States for support of the China mission. McCarthy scripted two successful radio plays, one on St. Columban, one on St. Patrick, both of which aired on local and national radio. As indicated earlier, he penned materials for the Catholic Students Mission Crusade, including a chapter in *The Mission Apostolate* and *An Introduction to Mission Studies*.[169] Under his direction reproductions of fine art paintings from Europe and Asia graced the covers of the *Far East*. After the materials from China displayed at the 1925 Vatican Mission Exposition, he had some of the items sent to Silver Creek, where a lovely "Chinese Room" at the front entrance of the building was created, using the wall hangings, carved wooden sconces and ceramic tile painted in a Chinese style. A more scholarly work was his study of Montalembert, *Life of St. Columban, Notes and Critical Studies on the Life of St. Columban*.[170]

Spirituality

McCarthy's spirituality shaped the visual religious atmosphere at the seminary in Nebraska and to some extent at Silver Creek. The Lourdes Grotto was just one example of McCarthy's devotion to Mary. He had made an act of consecration to Mary.[171] He frequently prayed litanies and other prayers to the Blessed Mother. The looming presence of the Limpias crucifix in the Nebraska and Silver Creek seminaries reminded missionaries that the suffering they most likely would endure would be done in union with that Jesus. McCarthy faithfully observed a holy hour of prayer sometime during the night. Jesuit spirituality, particularly the Thirty-Day Retreat, undergird not only McCarthy's religious experience, but that of the region in general. He and Father James Wilson[172] made a Thirty-Day Retreat at the Jesuit novitiate, St. Andrew on

---

169   Edward J. McCarthy, "The Soundest Argument [for Missionary Interest]," Catholic Students Mission Crusade, 1923), 56–57; E. J. McCarthy, "The Castle School of Crusade Leadership," FE (June 1925), 136–138; Edward J. McCarthy, *An Introduction to Mission Studies* (Catholic Students Mission Crusade, 1925). Edward J. McCarthy, "The Catholic Organization for the Missions," *The Mission Apostolate* (Paulist Press: NY, 1942), 75–85.

170   The Count of Montalembert, *Saint Columban, with Introduction, Notes and Critical Studies* by E. J. McCarthy, SSC (St. Columbans: Nebraska, 1927).

171   This was the devotion advocated by Louis de Montfort (1673–1716), a French priest whose books, *The Secret of Mary* and *True Devotion to Mary* were known to McCarthy. Sister Mary Therese Bolan, 8.C.3., p. 10.

172   Father James Wilson (1890–1970) taught at St. Columban Seminary, Nebraska, from 1922–1924 and was elected to the superior general's Council (1924–1931), after which he served as director of probationers at St. Columban (1931–1933), rector, and then vice rector at St. Columbans, Nebraska (1933–1939; 1939–1947).

Hudson, New York, beginning on June 30, 1923. Later Paul Waldron would go to the Jesuit Novitiate in the Saint Louis, Missouri, area to observe the kind of formation taking place there, when the Society was instituting the Spiritual Year. The Jesuit retreats also prepared Waldron, and to some extent, McCarthy, for beginning retreats in Omaha, Buffalo, Derby, and Silver Creek and later at Bristol, Rhode Island.

But McCarthy also experienced what spiritual authors have called, the Dark Night of the Soul, an experience that took different forms in different people. Personal stresses, in terms of the overall well-being of individuals, decisions about projects that had lasting implications, and overseeing a brand new experience for the Society, put enormous pressures on McCarthy at a relatively young age. Early on he wrote to Blowick, "I am dying to get a talk with you about this whole American proposition. I am getting terribly out of my depth. This job is far too big for me, and it is only the Goodness of Providence that has kept us going so far."[173] At one point, McCarthy wrote explicitly about a "Dark Night" experience. In relating his thoughts about Father James Conway (1892–1982) who left China and had a "mental attitude towards China," McCarthy wrote to Jack [O'Brien?] that Conway had never gone through "any of the spiritual experiences that other fellows went through, temptations against faith and kind of thing which I understand was perfectly the normal experience for most men. I know it was my own and pretty severe at that." In that same letter, McCarthy referred to another Columban who traveled through Omaha on his way to China. The visitor was going through "the same kind of a spiritual crisis that comes in every fellow's life. It was well for me that I had experience of it in my own case and heard other men talk about it, and was able to treat the poor fellow as well as I knew how. He got out of it all at once, and I believe will make one of the best men on the mission."[174]

Some of his confreres viewed him as a "go-getter with unbounded energy and ideas galore." Today we might describe McCarthy as a Type-A personality. He did things "with flair and a touch of sentimentality."[175] While McCarthy

---

[173] E. J. McCarthy to John [Blowick?] 29 December 1921.

[174] E .J. McCarthy to "My dear Jack" [probably O'Brien] 22 June 1921. In the mid-1920s, McCarthy considered being a Trappist in China. McCarthy kept the letter in his desk for many months before he sent it to the Abbot in China. The Abbott responded "No, [McCarthy's] work was not to be a contemplative life, his work was where he was at the moment, with the Society." Sister Mary Therese Bolan, "Early Days at St. Columbans in the United States," p. 8. 8.C.3. McCarthy composed a prayer to St. Columban, which later was included in the *Raccolta*, a book published by the Vatican containing a list of approved prayers, novenas and the accompanying indulgences. The *Raccolta*, the Italian word for "collection," was published from 1807–1950.

[175] Edward Fischer, *Light in the Far East. Archbishop Harold Henry's Forty-Two Years in Korea* (NY: Seabury Press, 1976), 11.

might have seemed overbearing to some Society members or mercurial in temperament,[176] the versatility of his abilities to handle a multitude of tasks secured a place for the Columbans in the United States.

Conclusion

It is safe to say that the Chinese Mission Society would not have rooted in the United States without Edward J. McCarthy's acumen and energy in multiple areas. As regional superior in the country from 1919 to 1934, he established the Society in the United States and shaped it as "American" and at the same time "international" and promoted "inculturation" into America. His overall administrative style shaped what it meant to be a "region." Within a little over a decade in the United States, the Columbans had a building for headquarters and a major and minor seminary. He made sure that those in the *Field Afar* and Society offices in Omaha had the most convenient and latest implements to speed along the process of written communication. He oversaw investments, raised and managed funds for the budget for the U.S. and for Galvin in China. The need to raise funds was a constant pressure for him. On behalf of the Society, McCarthy interacted with significant Catholic groups forming on the national level: the National Catholic Welfare Conference, the American Board of Catholic Missions and the Catholic Students Mission Crusade. His tireless work took in buying and shaping land to embody beauty, fresh air for health, and nature appreciation as a step toward prayer for seminarians and priests. He was a parish pastor, attentive to the spiritual, physical and mental well-being of those in the region and a great and constant connector and communicator with Ireland, China and within the United States. The second regional superior for the U.S. region, Father Paul Waldron, would be appointed in 1934, but first the Society and McCarthy had to face the multiple challenges of the economic Depression following the 1929 Wall Street Crash.

---

[176]   Neil Collins, *The Splendid Cause. The Missionary Society of St. Columban 1916–1954*, 63.

June 1926 Far East _Page_02

CHAPTER 2

Mission in Stressful Times:
The Great Depression (1929–1940)

The decade from 1929 to 1939 was a trying and stressful time in the United States because of the great financial crisis that touched everyone. At the same time farmers from some of Nebraska's neighboring states, especially Kansas and Colorado, suffered the effects of the "Dust Bowl" years. In the depth of the Depression, between thirteen to fifteen million people were unemployed with no job openings available because many plants closed or decreased production. With a prevalence of impoverished families, children's education was often neglected, as they, too, sought small jobs to support their family. The psychological pressures of impoverishment formed a generation of Americans. The financial conditions of the nation would affect not only the ability of donors to support the Columbans, but also the Society which had to deal with its own financial issues.

Financial Storm Clouds Gather

The Society had come through their first decade with a home base, complete with substantial buildings to house themselves and the *Far East* offices. They were gradually becoming known to friends in America and had attracted young men who entered the mission seminary for the "Chinese Mission Society." The next decade of Columban life in the young region of the United States (1929–1939) presented several interconnecting critical issues: the small number of priests available for promotion work, the development of a preparatory seminary in Silver Creek, New York, and entrance into an "east coast" diocese in

48

Rhode Island, all of these things taking place in the shadow of the Wall Street Crash of 1929. In the middle of the decade, the U.S. regional superior would be asked to resign largely because of issues related to disagreement about his approach to investments.

The Financial Health of the U.S. Region— Sources of Income and Expenditures

Donors (family members, diocesan priests who had contact with Columbans, mission circles, and individuals), subscriptions to the *Far East*, Mass stipends, and circulars for a particular fund were important sources for mission income. The Columbans in the United States assigned to promotion work traveled the country preaching at parish churches on behalf of the Columban missions. "Supply work," that is, Columbans offering Masses when parish clergy were gone for a day or two, provided a small, though irregular source of funds but was another vehicle for making known the China missions. Some income came through rental of the farm acreage at the Nebraska location. Other funds came through endowments,[177] annuities,[178] and investments. Bishop Galvin set up a Bureau in Hanyang and later in Shanghai to collect funds in the United States for the China mission. Most of the logistics for Galvin's appeals were funneled through the U.S. region.

Regional Superior Edward J. McCarthy had observed a slight financial downturn in donations and fewer *Far East* subscriptions in January 1922, due to job loss of some benefactors. "Their little earnings are rapidly being used up in their efforts to keep soul and body together."[179] Periodic theft of the Society's mail at the post office not only resulted in lost donations, but McCarthy said that another effect of mail robbery was that it was "hurting business, as so many people who do not get answers [to their letters and donations] put it down to our bad business and carelessness."[180] Nevertheless, by February, he wrote that

---

[177]   Some examples of endowments for the Columbans are wills, Masses in trust, burses, and other monies or stock/bonds given for restricted use. Burses, from the French word for "purse," were often funds applied to the education of seminarians.

[178]   In March 1929, McCarthy was working on an annuity plan as a means of "fund-raising." E. J. McCarthy to O'Dwyer, 7 March 1929. Columbans use charitable gift annuities. This is a contract, under which a charity, "in return for a transfer of cash, marketable securities or other assets, agrees to pay a fixed amount of money to one or two individuals, for their lifetime." American Council on Gift Annuities. Retrieved from www.acga-web.org on 27 March 2015. A later chapter narrates the interaction between donors and the Society of St. Columban.

[179]   E. J. McCarthy, *Diary of Progress at St. Columban's, Omaha*, 7 February 1922.

[180]   Ibid., 13 January 1922.

"after three years in Omaha, the Society has made itself felt in a financial way and is regarded as a good security."[181]

Another category of income was money received from the investments the region made in stocks, bonds, or mutual funds. Between 1924 and 1930, the Chicago firm of Porter, Skitt and Company became financial advisers to the Society. Charles C. Porter, who became a good friend of the Society, handled the Columban account.[182] Porter retired from the firm in 1930 but he remained as an informal financial adviser to the Columbans, at least until 1934.

The Society made three large expenditures for property since their arrival in the States through 1933: the properties outside of Bellevue, Nebraska, Silver Creek, New York, and Bristol, Rhode Island. Monies were needed for offices and seminaries in those locations. There were the daily living expenses of the priests and seminarians, upkeep on buildings and grounds, utilities, supplies for houses and offices, modest salaries for farmer assistance, stenographers, cooks, grounds keepers, maintenance men, and house keepers. Priests assigned to promotion work required railroad passes or other transportation and living expenses, when they traveled. The region paid for room and board and made arrangements for Society missionaries from China, while they were in the United States.

The U. S. region, seen by the Society in Ireland as a major source for raising money, regularly sent monies to support the China mission. In August 1924, for example, Superior General O'Dwyer requested the U. S. regional superior to send 2500 pounds ($12,000) for that purpose. Sometimes Bishop Galvin wrote directly to the U. S. region for financial support. In April 1929, O'Dwyer requested the U. S. region to send 3000 pounds to a Shanghai bank "to pay off something [unidentified] in China," but "Fr. Coady [sic] will know the object of the money."[183] That same month, the U.S. region was asked to send Mass stipends to Galvin, and on the back of that missive, O'Dwyer wrote,

---

[181]   Ibid., 3 February 1922.

[182]   Charles C. Porter, a former manager of the bond department of the Trust Company, and James Skitt, a former manager of the bond department of the National Bank of the Republic, formed the Porter, Skitt & Company in 1922, along with Walter H. Damon, Chauncey G. Powell, and Maurice L. Stedman. The company was formed to conduct a general business investment bonds. Their office was at 29 La Salle Street, Chicago. Information obtained from "Form New Company," *Financial World: America's Investments and Business Weekly*, 38 (October 28, 1922), 581. Accessed through Google Digital Books, 13 April 2015. Porter was a friend of Charles O'Brien, who, before he entered the Society of St. Columban, had been a stock broker in Chicago and Kansas City and closely associated with Porter, who later was known as "The Saint of LaSalle Street." "Archbishop Harold Henry Anecdotes," no date, p. 7. CFA-USA Archives.

[183]   E. J. McCarthy to Bishop Galvin, 27 April 1929. This was most likely Father Nicholas Cody, bursar in Shanghai at the time.

"(by the way, you are big work in this department, here)."[184] But other requests for monies came in as well. In November 1929, O'Dwyer assessed the U.S. and Australian Regions 5000 pounds each, which was two-thirds of what was needed to conclude the purchase of the property at in Navan, for a new seminary and headquarters.[185] "The Irish region was asked to contribute 8000 [doesn't indicate whether dollars or pounds] toward the property because it is not purchased for the Irish region but for the Society."[186]

Problems began to surface relative to the collection of income. By 1926, fewer priests were available for promotion work because those in the United States had either been sent to China or were ill. McCarthy lamented, "The *Far East* had a circulation of 40,000 (1926) but that was small, "especially when you consider that in '21 when the priests were out campaigning it ran up to practically 80,000.[187] Because the American Board of Catholic Missions did not begin to function until after 1926, many U.S. bishops were preventing any mission appeals other than the Society for the Propagation of the Faith collection for several years. Fewer monies from that group were available as the Depression wore on and diocesan incomes fell. Missionaries could not preach on behalf of the missions in many dioceses, unless they had headquarters there. One advantage of Columban Richard Ranaghan's film on China (see chapter 8) was that he could announce at a parish Mass that the film would be shown that night in the parish hall and collections for the missions could then be made.

In 1929 Galvin planned to open a Hanyang vicariate private fund in the States for the sale of vestments that the Sisters of Loretto school girls had sewn and embroidered. The bishop suggested that Father Michael McHugh (1876–1959) run the operation and he would be responsible to Galvin.[188] This effort, which also intended to create a "circle of friends" for Hanyang vicariate, would provide funds in addition to money sent to the Bureaus in Hanyang, Shanghai, and from Society locations in the States. The latter were already sending out information, the *Far East*, and circular letters of appeal for the missions. Not only would the Hanyang collector in the States be associated with regional headquarters in the minds of

---

[184]   Michael O'Dwyer to E. J. McCarthy, 16 April 1929.

[185]   E. J. McCarthy to Hugh Donnelly in Australia, 30 November 1926.

[186]   O'Dwyer to McCarthy 14 December 1926. *Casey History* (1926), 11. O'Dwyer indicated "the terms on which the regional departments will find a home at Dowdstown is a matter of future arrangement between the Society and the Region." Ibid.

[187]   E. J. McCarthy to Romuald Hayes, 11 March 1926. 8-C-16.48.

[188]   An additional argument McCarthy gave against the plan related to jurisdiction. "I cannot fail to see possibilities and probabilities that may in future cause serious conflicts between the vicars apostolic or other mission superiors and the Society as represented by its Directors. I therefore hesitate to commit this Region to any policy that may give rise later on to such difficulties." E. J. McCarthy to Galvin 6 April 1929. *Casey History* (1929), 4.

bishops, priests, and people, but in some cases, donors received multiple requests from these locations. They were confused as to why the Columbans had so many of their places requesting money. McCarthy forcefully wrote against Galvin's plan for various reasons. For one thing, "With the best of intentions private collectors [such as Galvin's plan] will encroach on the friends of the Society, and in this region we are entirely dependent on the friends already made for our very existence."[189] Nevertheless, the superior general, who was in China at that point, approved the idea and Father Michael McHugh spent a brief time in the States in 1930–1931 to carry out the dual focus of Galvin's plan.

Financial Skies Darken

By 1926, the General Council in Ireland was becoming nervous about the financial picture in the U.S. region. McCarthy wrote a lengthy letter to Edward J. O'Doherty, a member of the General Council. "I note that [the Superior General] considers the American region as financially precarious. That view would be considered, to say the least, interesting by most of the men here if they knew of it." McCarthy indicated the percentage of the reduction on the U.S. region's debt and stated, "Our property and buildings at Silver Creek are entirely free of debt, as of January 1, 1926."[190] He then painted a more detailed financial picture to indicate the region's priorities:

> The property and buildings at St. Columbans [Nebraska] have only a 5 % mortgage of $20,000 outstanding and at the present time we owe only $20,000 to the bank at 5%. The interest rate is low and I am leaving this debt stand and investing in 6% investments to refund our obligations to annuities. So that the only debts that we are paying interest on at present amount to $40,000. Most of the other indebtedness is towards our annuity funds which we used, as you know, for building. All our burses are invested to date. Our actual funded investments in the shape of interest producing bonds and mortgages amount to $330,103.88. These average exactly 5.03% interest rate which as you can see amounts to approximately $16,500.00 a year.[191]

---

[189]   E. J. McCarthy to Galvin 6 April 1929. *Casey History* (1929), 5.

[190]   The final payment made on the purchase money for Silver Creek property changed hands on January 30, 1924.

[191]   E. J. McCarthy to Edward J. Doherty, 2 November 1926. 8-C-16.43. *Casey History* (1926), 3.

McCarthy put their experience into perspective and indicated to the General Council that the U.S. Catholic Bishops were having financial difficulty as well. Some diocesan priests were beginning to live without salaries, in order to provide parish services.

On another point, McCarthy indicated, that "Silver Creek has not asked us to send them any money since last September for their daily expenses. They have been supporting themselves on the farm and on money received as remuneration for Sunday supplies, etc. . . . We haven't even sent them interest on burses to which they are entitled and which we will credit to them at the end of the year, nor have we sent them the interest on Father Dillon's endowment fund which is designated for Silver Creek." McCarthy thought that nothing precipitous should be done about selling their investments. "Personally, I can see no reason for throwing anything overboard to weather the storm. I think that if we were rather to go ahead with more confidence and greater trust and faith in the Providence of God, it would be better for us all round. I do think that we ought to go slowly. However, we should not take any backward steps."[192]

The average rate of inflation for 1926 was 0.94 percent. That year McCarthy even indicated to Bishop Galvin in China, "I believe at the present time we hold an unique position in the United States in as much as we are probably the only religious Society in the country that is out of debt." However, he found that a "terrible position to be in," and wished the Society could "pledge some of our property and fund Hanyang and pay back our debt here in the course of time. We could easily do that with our strong financial position and I would not have the slightest hesitation in adopting such a course."[193]

By July, McCarthy observed that income had increased steadily thanks to the U.S. region's own propagation efforts, the procurators' strict budgets, and the circle of friends they had made. In 1924, the Society had only $175,000 invested, but by mid-November 1926, they had over $630,000. In fall, McCarthy had thought "their financial worries were at an end, and they hoped to build a new seminary at Silver Creek,"[194] which by that time was "disgracefully overcrowded," with "thirty-six lads."[195] The region could perhaps make a specific appeal in the *Far East* and through circulars, if O'Dwyer would not permit the region to borrow $40,000 to build. However, the average rate of inflation for 1927 would actually be 1.92 percent deflation. The superior general requested that the region wait a year to start building new quarters at the Silver Creek

---

[192] E. J. McCarthy to Edward J. Doherty, 2 November 1926. 8-C-16.43. *Casey History* (1926), 3.

[193] E. J. McCarthy to E. Galvin 24 November 1926. 8-C-16.79. *Casey History* (1926), 10.

[194] E. J. McCarthy to Patrick Cleary, 4 September 1926. 8-C-16.70. *Casey History* (1926), 9.

[195] E. J. McCarthy to "Dear Jim" [Wilson?], 1927. CFA-USA.

preparatory seminary and the new, impressive building opened for students in September 1929.

The Financial Storm

On October 24, 1929, "Black Thursday," Wall Street began to reverberate with the crash of the stock market. The effects of the Great Depression which affected all Western industrialized countries would last for twelve years in the States. McCarthy assessed the Columban financial climate in a letter to Father Romuald Hayes (1892–1945), director of the Australia region and first Australian to join the Society.[196] The Society's American friends also felt the pinch of financial conditions. "Of course, great numbers of average people took a severe loss in the stock market. Now they are trying to recover that loss and buying and selling, and business generally is slow. People really think they are worse off than they are. They say, however, that things will be back to normal by June and that even the stock market may boom again." McCarthy's attention was more focused "on the general prosperity of what we might call 'middle class' people and the poor. They are always nearer to God and more generous with His work." Though the regional superior realized he might have made a little profit from the sale of stock, he had confidence that a "far greater profit can be reaped because the stock is in a Chicago monopoly, and the general impression is that it will go back to where it was, and even higher, and split. This morning I have had an offer, for instance, to buy part of it at $400, which would net me right now about $2500 profit. I am biting a little bit, and have written to our Chicago banker [Charles C. Porter], but I am not at all keen on disposing of it."[197]

McCarthy worried more about real estate mortgages in Nebraska and Iowa. In early 1930, he wrote to Romuald Hayes:

> Farm mortgages are almost completely frozen assets at the present time, but, of course, they are ultimately sound. The present deplorable depression throughout the country cannot last always in a country of America's wealth. . . . Economy is our watchword here, all along the line. I sliced about $7000 off the Silver Creek budget a few weeks ago." So far, it has

---

[196] Romuald Hayes, born at Malvern a suburb of Melbourne, was regional director in Australia, beginning in 1924. He had been a member of the Society's 1931 General Chapter and was appointed bishop of Rockhampton, Australia, in 1932. He kept close ties with the Columbans.

[197] McCarthy to Romuald Hayes, 4 February 1930. 8-C-18.4.

been our worst year and there is little hope in the near future that conditions will right themselves. However, we are not too badly off. We can keep going very well with what we have and God will always provide what is necessary."[198]

The Columban fiscal year for 1930 ended well, "despite the general slump all over the country."[199]

However, concerns about income and the volatile financial situation underscored a greater need for donor funds. The China missionaries were depleting the money obtained through Mass Intentions sent to them. There was "insufficient endowment" for the number of seminarians. By 1932, the year that 25 percent of the work force was unemployed, there were 107 seminarians, compared with ninety-nine students the previous year.[200] Nevertheless, that year a new cow and horse barn on the farm at Silver Creek were approved for construction, as was a handball court for students at St. Columban Seminary. Students had complained during McCarthy's official "visitation" of the group that "they did not have proper outdoor facilities for games, and I feel this court is necessary and has been approved by the Seminary and regional Councils."[201] In the midst of the stressed financial times, McCarthy was appointed on May 1932, for another five year term as superior.

By 1933, with the rate of inflation at an average of minus 5.09 percent (though this was better than the 1932 average of minus 10.30 percent), McCarthy expected every priest and student in the region to take an active part to assist the Society in a material way, whether through their private collecting or though their own personal economy. Between students and faculty at the two seminaries, fifteen hundred dollars came out of their pockets toward filling the financial hole. The regional superior again noted that "the *Far East* circulation is falling off, our active friends diminishing in number and we have no other sources of income except through our Regional Offices."[202] In mid-1933, the region was switching from bonds to stock "as the stock market was favorable. Purchases were made but the bonds could not be sold fast enough to meet payments on the stock." The loan from their brokers "had been considerably reduced and will be eliminated altogether, as soon as the sale of bonds is

---

[198]   McCarthy to Romuald Hayes, 18 March 1930. 8-C-18.6.

[199]   Romuald Hayes to McCarthy, 16 December 1930. 8-C-18.20. Hayes was quoting McCarthy's earlier letter to him.

[200]   Nine students were in theology in Omaha, seven in philosophy and six men were probationers. September 1931. *Casey History* (1931), 1. There was no mention of the number of Silver Creek seminarians.

[201]   E. J. McCarthy to O'Dwyer 8-C-18.63. 15 June 1932. *Casey History* (1932), 20.

[202]   E. J. McCarthy to Kelly 8-A-31.20. 21 November 1933.

completed in a more normal market." In the meantime, McCarthy wrote, their stock purchases were protected by "stop loss" orders."[203]

As another, more drastic measure of economy, the superior general requested that no new students were to be accepted for the coming academic year, beginning in fall 1933.[204] McCarthy advised against this order because of possible long range effects and "that the action would be a serious break in continuity of classes and to a certain extent a disorganization of the tradition we have been trying to build in our houses during the past ten years." Furthermore, not accepting students "might be interpreted as want of confidence in God." [205] Even so, McCarthy was willing to carry out the superior general's instruction. Austerity remained the order of the day, even as McCarthy believed "things are beginning to brighten up." Students took on more manual work in the kitchens, around the house and on the grounds at the seminaries. Priests were alerted that no vacations would be financed for them, beginning in the summer of 1934.

A bright light in the midst of financial woes of the decade happened in 1930 with the arrival of the Sisters of St. Columban at Silver Creek, New York. McCarthy had hoped the Columban Sisters, founded in Ireland in 1922, would be able to come to the United States in 1928. He requested a sick room nurse, a bookkeeper and typist, because Silver Creek was too far from Buffalo to find local people with those skills. He had been negotiating with Mother Superior Finbarr (Nora Collins) to send five Sisters that summer,[206] but Bishop Galvin had also requested six Sisters in China. Galvin had priority, so the first Columban Sisters were sent to China in 1929. McCarthy lamented to Galvin, "You have no idea, Ned, how much we need Sisters down at Silver Creek. We have forty boys this year and next year we will have between 60 and 70, please God, with a big building to take care of." Boys who had diphtheria, scarlet fever "and the like," and those with flu or colds had to be "nursed" by the priests. Being far from the city, nurses were hard to come by. While McCarthy empathized with Galvin's need, McCarthy noted that the New York situation was less urgent when there were fewer students and a small house. "But now things are different. Our priests are breaking down in health from work and worry over there. Two of them have been practically off work since last Christmas and we cannot get any additional priests. I am worried sick about it all." McCarthy asked if Galvin would write to Mother Finbarr to let her know that the China situation could wait another year and thus send Silver Creek Sisters in fall. McCarthy

---

203   E. J. McCarthy to O'Dwyer 8-A-30B-4. 20 November 1933.

204   This is noted in E. J. McCarthy to Michael O'Dwyer, 29 December 1933.

205   E. J. McCarthy to Michael O'Dwyer, 29 December 1933.

206   Author interview with Sister Clare O'Rourke 23 October 2013. See also, Claire O'Rourke, SSC, *USA: Stepping Stones to China and Beyond. A Columban Missionary Presence.* (Brighton, MA: Columban Sisters, 2008), 14.

concluded, Mother Finbarr "had already given us a definite promise and all arrangements were completed. . . . Mother Finbarr, without intending it, has gone back on a very serious promise in an effort to comply with your wishes. I will deeply appreciate anything you can do in the matter."[207]

The first Columban Sisters arrived at Silver Creek on Christmas Day, 1930, much to the joy of the priests and students.[208] They settled into a frame house on the property and took over the management of the house and medical needs of seminarians. E. J. McCarthy touted the Sisters' work in the promotional book for the Silver Creek Seminary. "Two very important departments—the kitchen and the infirmary—are under the excellent supervision of the Sisters of St. Columban. Good health is an essential condition of every boy who aspires to be a missionary priest, and the Sisters do their part to maintain that good health by providing our students with proper wholesome food."[209] The Sisters canned apples, peaches, tomatoes, and pears grown on the property, thanks to having 1,500 large canning jars donated by Father Alphonsus of Holy Cross Seminary. Grapes were gathered and "obtained a good price" in 1936. While Mother Finbarr had said that the Sisters would not cook for the seminarians, during the height of the Depression the Sisters did take on that work.

The Sisters sewed cassocks, did mending and were pleased when Sister Gemma, known as a "good needlewoman," arrived at Silver Creek. The Sisters went to the Regional Catholic Students Mission Crusade conferences where they took orders for the cassocks and "fancy work." The infirmarian took care of the students when they became ill and carried food trays to them from the dining room. As McCarthy again observed, "a little care from experienced hands (of the Sister), sanctified with prayer, just at the right time, may save a lot of suffering in later life. Here again the Sisters' work is supreme." In 1939, when there was an epidemic of small pox in the area, the Sister-nurse vaccinated the priests and students as a precaution against the disease. Not only did the Sisters' ministry lighten the priest's load, the Sisters added new life to the area. The Sisters reached out to the neighborhood by teaching catechism classes. Father Kelly provided a monthly conference for the Sisters and the women felt the prayerful support of the priests.[210] Being that the first Sisters were from Ireland and accustomed to fairly moderate weather, there were many remarks in their

---

[207]   McCarthy to Galvin 2 April 1929.

[208]   Seven Columban Sisters from Northern Ireland, Ireland, and Australia arrived in Silver Creek, but soon four of them moved on to the missions. The Sisters saw the assignment as a "stepping stone to one's assignment to China." Claire O'Rourke, SSC, *USA: Stepping Stones to China and Beyond*, 14.

[209]   E. J. McCarthy, *Historical Sketch: The Society of St. Columban* (St. Columban, NE, c. 1931), 37.

[210]   *Annals of the Missionary Sisters of St. Columban* at Silver Creek, 1930s. Silver Creek, NY.

Annals about the amount of snow and cold in the area, where frigid winds blew off Lake Erie, and where the trees the seminarians planted on the bluff were not large enough to act as a wind buffer for the inhabitants.

Different Approaches to Investments

McCarthy, more familiar with the American financial scene than was the Society General Council, presented them an optimistic financial picture in the early years of the Depression. In 1931, he reported the economic atmosphere as "very tense," but he noted that in the last year, the "economic conditions have not hit us in the least as far as I can see." He remarked, "Our liabilities at the moment are slightly less than the par value [i.e., the initial public offering price] of our investments, but when a valuation is made in the present economic conditions our balance will really show a deficit, yet on the whole our investments have weathered the storm well so far." He added that while the Society was "not by any means out of the woods here in America," at this point they "did not have serious losses. Of course, the market value of our investments is seriously depreciated, but our interest rates are keeping up fairly well."[211]

Discussion between the Society's headquarters in Ireland and the United States on financial issues was ongoing and often conflictive. McCarthy noted that any changes in investments in the months since the April 19, 1933, letter from O'Dwyer, who gave particular directions about investments, were "in an endeavor to interpret the letter and spirit of the law, conscientiously to the best of our ability in the unusual period through which we have been passing."[212] McCarthy would get "Moody's view"[213] on the superior general's Council's further recommendations to sell particular stocks and bonds.

However, in November 1933, McCarthy wrote to Father William Kelly at the Bristol Spiritual Year house, sending him a list of the operating and capital expenditure in the region over the last year. "You will see that our normal cash expenditures exceed our actual case receipts by $6,356.19. Besides this annual deficit, our balance sheet shows a Regional indebtedness of $245,793.05, largely to be accounted for through depreciation and loss of [the value of] investments."[214] The situation was beginning to look more bleak.

In addition to pressures induced by the financial climate in the United States, the situation in the China missions had worsened, a reality McCarthy felt

---

[211]   E. J. McCarthy to Romuald Hayes, 24 September 1931. 8-C-18.51. *Casey History* (1931), 10.

[212]   E. J. McCarthy to O'Dwyer, 29 December 1933.

[213]   Moody's Corporation was named for John Moody, who set the standard for modern bond credit rating.

[214]   McCarthy to Kelly 21 November 1933. *Casey History* (1933), 27.

keenly, as can be seen in his fairly frequent interchange of letters with Bishop Galvin. McCarthy was managing Bishop Galvin's investments, in addition to overseeing those of the U.S. region. The bishop, strapped for cash in China, recommended to McCarthy which investments to sell. McCarthy wrote that the "Society has taken a wallop of $344,000.00 in depreciation of investments at our last valuation. This does not mean, of course, that they are lost but it will take us a long time and a lot of hard work and prayer to build up back to where they were."[215] All in all, McCarthy felt that though the country was in "abnormal times," "the structure of the region's investment account was still basically sound."[216]

A Decisive Year, 1934

The usually optimistic McCarthy acknowledged in late 1933 that he and the region "had gone through four of the worst years."[217] The superior general's concerns about the financial situation of the region came to a head in 1934, after a series of letters back and forth between Ireland and the United States. At the end of December 1933, McCarthy, with reference to some of those letters, wrote a seven-page, single-spaced letter to O'Dwyer laying out the history of the financial crisis in the United States, the manner of operating investments in the country, and what had ensued with recommendations from their investment counselor, as well as what was recommended by Father Joseph P. O'Leary, the regional bursar in the United States. O'Leary had given almost his whole time to handling what was deemed a "thorough and conservative handling" of the Society investments and had made a "fine [and extensive] study of the subject [of investments] from every angle.[218]

At issue were matters of liquidation of certain "speculative stocks" (the term the Council used), purchase of Government bonds, clarification as to whether the Council meant for the region to sell individual stocks or to sell everything "when the market is favorable." McCarthy noted that "Losses are much more likely to occur through hasty liquidation now and this is something we must guard against at any cost."[219] After consultation with his Council, the regional bursar, and Mr. Porter, the region did sell some of its investments.

---

215 E. J. McCarthy to Bishop Galvin 11 November 1933.

216 E. J. McCarthy to O'Dwyer, 29 December 1933.

217 Ibid.

218 Father Joseph P. O'Leary (1891–1974) was appointed regional bursar in 1932. After a new regional bursar was appointed in 1934, O'Leary continued with management of *the Far East* until 1937. Under a doctor's care for some time, he incardinated into the Diocese of San Diego in 1938 and eventually retired in Ireland.

219 E. J. McCarthy to O'Dwyer, 29 December 1933.

The superior general and his Council had proposed other drastic measures to deal with the financial situation. "The Council thinks that something must be done quickly to increase income, decrease expenditure and pay off some of the debt. It has some schemes under consideration—the principal one being to close up the theology faculty in Omaha next June, send the students to Rome or Ireland, relieve priests for propaganda, sell the Bristol property [which was purchased in August 1933] and transfer the probationers to Silver Creek or Omaha." [220] The same day that McCarthy sent that letter, he wrote to Father Richard Ranaghan, who was in Seattle on promotion work with his film on the Society's China missions.

> We have been simply thrown into a regular vortex and we must be crushed, I suppose, if the work is to survive at all. At the moment my usual optimism has completely left me and I can see no hope ahead except to save our annuities and I am working at that just now and letting everything else go by the board. But we must get in donations and that can only be done through collecting and begging. I do not think, Dick, you have any idea how serious the situation is or how dark the future looks from my point of view. I have tremendous confidence in almighty God but I know too that the seed must perish before it can fructify and death is hard for all of us. [221]

A few months later, McCarthy wrote to Father William Kelly, rector at the new formation house in Bristol, Rhode Island, "Our difficulties are purely internal, and as a result of the Society's policy which few outside it could understand, and thank God, things are beginning to show a little brighter."[222]

However, in February 1934, Father Paul Waldron, who was rector of St. Columban Seminary and a faculty member, was appointed by the superior general as a full-time regional bursar for America.[223] His term as regional bursar was short lived—just a few months, and a good friend of McCarthy, Father Michael J. Treanor, rector at Silver Creek, was appointed U.S. regional bursar in fall of 1934.

---

[220]   E. J. McCarthy to William Kelly 23 February 1934. *Casey History* (1934), 4.

[221]   E. J. McCarthy to Ranaghan, Seattle, Washington. 23 February 1934. *Casey History* (1934), 4.

[222]   E. J. McCarthy to William Kelly 4 April 1934. *Casey History* (1934), 5.

[223]   Waldron did not remain in that position for long, because at some point in 1934, Father Michael J. Treanor, rector at the Columban seminary at Silver Creek was appointed regional bursar.

Sometime in June, McCarthy became deathly ill and had an operation for the removal of a kidney. He spent some time in recuperation in Arkansas, probably at Hot Springs.[224] Bishop Galvin commented in a letter to Paul Waldron that McCarthy had suffered a lot, both before and after the operation.[225] Certainly the intense pressures and sustained stress over the previous five years exacerbated McCarthy's physical condition.

In what must have been a shock to McCarthy, the superior general sent a letter dated July 4, 1934, and asked McCarthy to send a letter of resignation as U.S. regional superior. McCarthy replied on July 17, accepting the Council's decision and received confirmation of his resignation on August 15, while he continued his recuperation at Bristol. The newspaper account announced that Father Paul Waldron was appointed as regional superior because of McCarthy's health, but McCarthy admitted to Sister Mary Therese Bolan that he was asked to resign because of his financial abilities regarding investments.[226] McCarthy remarked that the experience of being removed from his office "seemed to take the very foundations from my life and all my dreams and hopes and plans came toppling around me, but again it was worth it all, because out of the ruins, as a great inspiration, came the loyal and vicarious sacrifice of one man [Michael Treanor], whose memory I will never forget." McCarthy received a letter from Treanor shortly before the latter's operation. Treanor wrote, "I want to tell you something I have never told you before. When I knew about the difficulties the Society was going through in 1934 and you were sick in Arkansas, I offered my life to God for the [U.S.] region and its Director. Now I am going to hospital and I have a presentiment that this offering is going to be accepted." [227]

---

[224]   Nick Kill interview with Sister Mary Therese Bolan, August 1975. Transcript of tape, p. 10 and 16. Bolan mentioned both Arizona and Arkansas. Hot Springs, Arkansas, was a well-known location for its natural thermal waters and health spas, the latter going back to the midnineteenth century. In 1886, the town became the location of spring training for the Chicago White Stockings, later known as the Colts and known today as the Chicago Cubs.

[225]   Galvin to Waldron 3 August 1934.

[226]   Nick Kill interview with Sister Mary Therese Bolan, August 1975. transcript of tape, p. 10. See also, Michael Healy, *Other Days* (Onstream Publications: Blarney, Ireland, 2010), 53–54. Apparently, Father Edmund Lane, who was bursar for both Ireland and for the whole Society, came to the United States to sell off the shares, which were sold at rock-bottom prices. As "gilt-edged" investments, however, they were sure to recover eventually. Ibid., 54.

[227]   Father Michael J. Treanor (1897–1936) was regional bursar for just under two years. He died at St. Joseph's Hospital, Omaha, following an operation for a duodenal ulcer. Information and letter quoted in Eamonn Byrne, *Columbans in Student Catholic Action. Philippines 1937–2007* (Malate, Manila: Ample Printing Press, 2007), 18. The Columban Sisters mentioned Treanor in their Annals for 1936: "He was well prepared to go and had several of the Fathers with him at the end. He will be

McCarthy's Journey to the Philippines

Apparently, McCarthy did not return to St. Columbans, Nebraska, after continuing his recuperation at Bristol, Rhode Island. Father Waldron packed up McCarthy's belongings and shipped them to McCarthy's assignment in Manila, Philippines. On September 12, after fifteen years as regional superior, Ned McCarthy sailed from New York on the *Manhattan*.[228] Leaving the States was a heart wrenching experience for him. He had become a naturalized citizen of the country, had made great efforts to make the Columbans known to U.S. Catholics, and had gained recognition of the Society among younger Catholics through the Catholic Students Mission Crusade. He had located and purchased properties in three states to found a "trinity" of formation/headquarter houses.

On his way to the Philippines, McCarthy spent a few months in Ireland, where he visited with family and friends. He spent some time in Rome, stopped in France to pray at the Lourdes grotto[229] and other shrines in the country, traveled in the Holy Land with time in the holy places and a retreat on Mt. Carmel. The last two stops took place from late December through January 6, 1935. The visits to the holy places proved healing in some ways for him. In letters sent to Sister Mary Therese Bolan during that trip, McCarthy wrote of the significance of the Holy Land experience. "I suppose I could never convey in words all these days here have meant to me. I could never be the same again. It will always mark a dividing line in my life."[230] While he had felt a strong presence of the Blessed Mother at Lourdes, he equally felt the presence of Christ in the Holy Land, not in the fact of the then neglected fields, and ruined cities, "but just the same, it is filled with some beauty, some peace, some Presence that can only come from Him Who lived here and made it His pulpit from which He preached His Gospel to the whole world." And while he would always have the memories of what he had seen in the Holy Land, "the Tabernacle is the Reality. That has come to me as a tremendous realization. You know the difference between faith and knowledge and what I may call '*realization*.' If you don't, someday, please God, you will, and your life can never the same again."[231]

On board ship, McCarthy had a complete physical examination with the ship's doctor and wrote, "Everything, O.K. Health is fine, thank God." In his last

---

greatly missed because he was greatly loved by those who knew him and he was a good friend of the Sisters." *Annals*, 1936. Sisters of St. Columban, Silver Creek, NY.

[228]   Constructed in 1931, the *Manhattan* was the first large liner built in the United States since 1905.

[229]   Bernadette Soubirous, to whom a "beautiful lady" appeared in a cave on the outskirts of Lourdes, France, in 1858, was canonized in 1933.

[230]   E. J. McCarthy to "Dear . . ."29 December 1934. 8-C.20, 24. Letters from Father Edward J. McCarthy on his way to the Philippines.

[231]   Ibid.

letter to Sister Therese before arriving at the Port of Manila, McCarthy noted, "It is just about this time or a little later last year that I began to go under. It is hard to imagine that only a year has passed and that so much has happened since then. Life is a great romance after all." He reflected further, "If we knew [the last chapter of our lives], it would take all the thrill out of life when the pleasant things are the little surprises God gives us whether through pain or joy."[232]

With a lengthy voyage to Manila and with many Spanish speakers on board, he studied Spanish, in which language he would recite his daily rosary. He arrived in Manila on February 11, 1935, to begin his new assignment. The universities in the Philippines had been "secularized," so he worked with students through the Student Catholic Action movement at public universities in the Archdiocese of Manila.[233] McCarthy effectively used the radio as another means of evangelization and his talks were published as *Radio Sermons* (1938). However, in 1939, he suffered from nervous exhaustion and spent the next two years recuperating in Australia.

A later director of the U.S. region, New York City native, Father Peter McPartland (1912–1987), assessed McCarthy's importance to the region and Columban influence on the Catholic Church in that period. "Ned [Edward J.] McCarthy would have had an indirect influence because his area of mission combat was at a higher level. He and the Columbans had to fight for existence in this country and the people he had to convince were the bishops." McCarthy's close work with the Catholic Student Mission Crusade and knowing key persons in the formation of what would become the American Board of Catholic Missions were just two of the Columban influences nationally to this point.

Father Paul Waldron, Second Director of the U.S. Region, 1934–1939

Father Paul Waldron (1888–1976) was appointed the second U.S. regional superior on August 1, 1934. Born in County Mayo, he was ordained for the Archdiocese of St. Paul, where he taught moral theology from 1914 until 1918. He returned to Ireland to enter the young Chinese Mission Society and was assigned to the United States in 1921. He was simultaneously for a time, editor of the *Far East*, rector of St. Columban Seminary at Omaha, faculty member,

---

[232]   E. J. McCarthy to "Dear . . ." 26 January 1935.

[233]   For this story, see Eamonn Byrne. By 1957, 166 Columbans served in the Philippines, with four of them specifically directing the work of 20,000 members of Student's Catholic Action in the Archdiocese of Manila. Among E. J. McCarthy's writings in this context is E. J. McCarthy, *Catholic Action in the University of the Philippines* (1936).

and vice director of the American region since the early 1920s. He would serve two terms as director: 1934–1939 and 1939–1947 and would become well-known throughout the United States for retreats given to laity and priests. Because of his sterling reputation as retreat master, the retreats could "back up" the appeals given by the Columban promotion men because priests and bishops knew Waldron and could trust the Columbans to speak and promote missions in their parish or diocese (see chapter 12).

The first and the second regional directors were contrasting in temperament, personality, and intellectual interests. McCarthy's correspondence was elaborative, frequent, and contextual and his spirituality was devotional and affective. His choice to publish Comte de Montalembert's, *Life of St. Columban*, along with McCarthy's own critical notes and comments, reflected the nineteenth century romantic writing and ecclesial tradition.[234] Waldron's letters were generally short. The subject matter he taught—Classics, Moral Theology, Canon Law and Ascetical Theology—approached life from a "classical ordered view of the world." His personal disposition appeared reserved, detached, and somewhat rigid, and his spirituality tended toward the ascetical or purgative way.[235] He was, however, an inspiring speaker, particularly in the hundreds of retreats he gave over the years to priests, religious, and laity. He provided instructions and hints for public speaking for the men going out on promotion work.

As regional bursar for a few months in 1934, Waldron sought advice from the Catholic University of America's Canon Law faculty to inquire about Church Law regarding the adjustment of some annuities, whether a seminary building would count for partial investment of burses, and whether three farms on the Society property in Omaha could be sold. The Society originally held the mortgages for the farms and when interest was in default, they took them over by foreclosure. Having conferred with Superior General O'Dwyer, who authorized the sale of the farms, Waldron was able to accrue some monies from the sale in 1938.[236] The Bedford House in Omaha, which had housed the first few seminarians, was sold the previous year for six thousand dollars.[237]

O'Dwyer continued advising Waldron about which stocks or bonds to buy and sell. In one communication, after explaining the latest financial

---

[234]   Charles Forbes René de Montalembert (1810–1870) was a friend of Lamenais and Lacordaire, who spoke against Ultramontanist (strong emphasis on the papal powers) writers. The Comte's writing was described as fiery, yet polished.

[235]   The author is grateful to Father Richard Steinhilber for providing some background related to Father Waldron. Author telephone interview with Father Richard Steinhilber, 20 March 2014.

[236]   O'Dwyer to Waldron 30 June 1938, per Waldron's letter of request, 4 June 1938.

[237]   *Casey History* (1937), 9.

situation, Waldron referenced the judgment of the Moody Corporation man, Mr. Clarke, as to what direction the Society should take.[238] Things were starting to assume a somewhat more positive turn by 1937 and O'Dwyer wrote, "I wish to congratulate the Region and all the Priests on the great efforts that have been made to put the Region in a sound financial position. I appreciate these efforts very much and I feel that God will bless the priests and their efforts with ultimate success."[239] At the same time, though, the U.S. region was asked to send one hundred British pounds' "donation" to the expenses of Student Catholic Action in Manila (even though those expenses should have devolved on the Archdiocese of Manila) and to donate five hundred pounds to meet the expenses of the Society priests who were going to the Diocese of Cagayan de Oro.[240]

Three issues were often in the balance in the 1930s: the number of students in each seminary, the felt need to have a strong presence in an eastern diocese, and financial limitations. At one point at St. Columbans, Nebraska, the seminary was so overcrowded, that the rector alerted the superior general that they could not guarantee the health of seminarians and priests.[241] In 1937, the superior general indicated that, "given the strenuous efforts of the region to straighten out the financial difficulty," he would allow the number of entrants to Silver Creek increased from ten to fifteen young men per year.[242]

In the long run, had the Society held to the financial position McCarthy advocated, they would probably have come out better off. McCarthy noted this later in his life, when he wrote a fellow Cork man, Donal O'Mahoney, that when he left the States in 1934, he gave Mr. Porter eighty dollars to trade with and to give the proceeds eventually to erect a statue of Mary at Bristol. Two years later that money had grown to 380 dollars and Archbishop Cushing, having heard the story, supplied the remaining cost of the statue. McCarthy was also to demonstrate that through investments he continued to manage for Bishop Galvin for Hanyang.[243] Silver Creek outgrew the student dormitories, originally created from the large chicken coop on the farm. As it was, the heat was turned off there during the night in winter to save money. This action was no small

---

[238]   Waldron to O'Dwyer 26 December 1934.

[239]   O'Dwyer to Waldron, 7 July 1937.

[240]   O'Dwyer to Waldron 8 September 1938 *Casey History* (1938), 17.

[241]   See, for example, James Wilson to Paul Waldron 28 May 1935. Wilson was the rector at St. Columban's, Nebraska from 1933–1939, having been on the superior general's Council (1924–1931), director of probationers at St. Columban's Nebraska (1931–1933). The issue of overcrowding in Omaha came up again in 1939 as the Society looked to the next class for the 1940–1941 academic year.

[242]   O'Dwyer to Waldron, 20 October 1937. *Casey History* (1937), 10.

[243]   E. J. McCarthy to Donal O'Mahoney 2 November 1949. Elden Avenue, Los Angeles.

thing, as the Columban Sisters wrote in their *Annals*. The winds blowing over Lake Erie from the North swept across the property, which was located in the legendary "snow belt" in the country. Discussions about housing were also laced with arguments for and against the move of the regional headquarters from Omaha to Silver Creek or even to build a major seminary in the newly purchased property at Bristol, Rhode Island.

Property and Presence in a Maritime
Diocese: Bristol, Rhode Island

In April 1933, McCarthy noted that the Columbans were the only foreign mission society in the United States not represented in New England. In May, his Regional Council recommended that permission be asked of the superior general to purchase real estate to the value of $50,000 as an investment with the intention to have a foundation in the Diocese of Providence, Rhode Island. The Council saw it as the Society's last chance to establish itself in the Northeast. McCarthy indicated the feasibility of purchasing property, even though the Society was feeling the effects of the Depression. Property prices were low. With a return to more normal times, land would be out of reach and the value of land along the water would escalate in a revived economy. He had located fifty acres on Narragansett Bay, Bristol, Rhode Island. In the 1930s, Bristol County had a combined population of about 12,000 people and five Catholic Churches.[244]

With the property came a large frame house in good condition. While the purpose of the property beyond that of investment value was not settled at the time, McCarthy thought it would be an excellent location for the men during their Spiritual Year. That would thereby relieve congestion at St. Columban, Nebraska. Father O'Leary, the region's bursar indicated, "Considering the present financial status of our American Region there does not appear to be any serious reason against our purchase of the RI property up to the sum of $50,000. A remarkable change in the Market for the past two months [of 1933] has greatly enhanced the value of our holdings. There is a consensus of opinion that the acute state of the depression is past."[245]

---

[244]   At the time of the Columban engagement in the Bristol area, St. Mary's Church, had been founded in 1851 as a joint community with Catholics in Warren, Rhode Island. In 1855 parishioners began construction of a church building in Bristol. Other churches founded initially with ethnic groups in Bristol County prior to 1933 were St. Jean Baptiste (1877), St. Casimir (1908), St. Alexander (Italian,1915), Our Lady of Mt. Carmel Parish (Italian,1917).

[245]   O'Leary to McCarthy, 3 June 1933. *Casey History* (1933), 13. There was a slight rise in the stock market about this time.

McCarthy contacted Bishop William A. Hickey of Providence, Rhode Island, in whose Diocese they hoped to begin a foundation. Hickey had taken bold moves in his diocese during the country's Depression to create construction jobs (schools and churches) and to provide funds and services through establishment of a Catholic Charities organization. McCarthy assured the bishop that the Society's "financial position is exceptionally sound, even at the present time, which is not due to any virtue in us but to the goodness of God. We are not rich and we are not, I think, what one might call intensive propagandists, but Almighty God takes care of our needs."[246] Perhaps with an appeal to the bishop's conscience, McCarthy wrote in the following month, "We are the only mission society not in New England. I'm afraid that unless you see your way to permit us to establish ourselves [in the Diocese of Providence], we cannot hope for any other opportunity."[247] The regional superior assured the bishop that they would not be a financial drain on the Diocese. The bishop gave permission for the Society to be established in the diocese and suggested they inspect several suitable sites, particularly land along the Bay. As McCarthy phrased Hickey's perspective, "If we are going to a maritime diocese, we should locate on the seaboard, if it is at all possible, even though it may cost a little more."[248]

The superior general and his Council thought that the U.S. region should use any available funds to pay off their debts. The region "had put enough money into unfruitful real estate."[249] However, the Council did give permission on June 1to purchase property in the Diocese. On July 3, 1933, preliminary agreements for purchase of property in Bristol were signed. The thirty-four acres with frontage of 850 feet on Narragansett Bay, the large guest house referred to as the Gardiner Mansion on the Van Wickle–McKee Estate, and the golf club house were located on what was locally known as Ferry Hill. The Hill was so named because from that view one could see the boat that took people from Aquidneck Island to and from the Bristol dock.[250] A smaller building, the former golf club house, would also be included in the sale. The Bristol Golf Club had constructed the building in 1897 on the knoll in the meadow south

---

[246] E. J. McCarthy to Bishop Hickey, 10 March 1933, *Casey History* (1933), 2. Reference to "propagandists" was to a particular American founded missionary Society. The Columbans heard that same term later from the archbishop of Los Angeles, when the Columbans began work with the Filipinos and Chinese in that city. The Columbans were invited to come to some dioceses in Indiana about the same time.

[247] E. J. McCarthy to Hickey 7 April 1933.

[248] E. J. McCarthy to O'Dwyer 3 May 1933. Five-page letter, with attachment of Regional Council minutes of 2 May 1933.

[249] 1 June 1933 O'Dwyer to E. J. McCarthy.

[250] The large Aquidneck Island was home to three towns: Portsmouth, Middletown, and Newport, Rhode Island.

of the estate. The purchase price for land and buildings Charles Porter was buying for the Columbans was $42,500. Deeds were filed on August 15, 1933. The Blithewold Mansion, adjoining property, and gardens remained in the Van Wickle–McKee family.[251]

Purchasing the Property

The purchase of the property took some hard work. Just as the Columbans experienced antipathy from groups in Nebraska who disliked Catholics, so, too, in Bristol, the property owners were averse to selling to Catholics. Transactions to secure the property and buildings were largely the work of McCarthy's good friend, Charles C. Porter, who had been the Society's investment banker in Chicago, and to a lesser extent, General Callan, the contact person from Bishop Hickey's office. McCarthy proposed that Porter and Callan should interact with William McKee and leave the Columbans out of the negotiations. He had confidence in Porter's ability to bargain.

The land belonged to the Augustine Van Wickle family, who had given land for the Bristol Golf Club in 1896. Bessie Pardee had married Augustine Van Wickle, who died at a young age in a hunting accident. In 1901, Bessie then married William McKee, a friend of Augustine. McKee was a millionaire who knew the Van Wickles through hunting and sailing with Mr. Van Wickle. While both Mr. and Mrs. Van Wickle's families had made their fortunes in Pennsylvania coal, McKee had a successful leather manufacturing business in Boston and a home on fashionable Commonwealth Avenue. Until the Depression, the McKees lived in Boston in the winter and at Blithewold, as the estate in Bristol was called, in the summer. However, by 1931, McKee had lost a great deal of his wealth. They sold their house in Boston and lived year round at Blithewold, Bessie's inheritance from Augustine Van Wickle. For a while, the mansion was rented for a thousand dollars a summer. By 1933, when the Columbans were interested in the property, McKee was in reduced financial circumstances.

Charles Porter came to look more carefully at the property and the house. McKee and Porter negotiated over several months. Part of the land (24 acres)

---

[251] Today the Blithewold Mansion, Gardens, and Arboretum are a property of Preserve Rhode Island, independently owned and managed by Blithewold, Inc. For background on the Van Wickle and McKee families and the history of the mansion and property, see Alice DeWolf Pardee, *Blithewold, Bristol, Rhode Island* (privately published, 1978) and Margaret Whitehead, *Blithewold. Legacy of an American Family* (Booklocker.com, 2011). The strip of land between the Mansion and the edge of the property, which McKee was adamant to hold for privacy and so that it not be subdivided, now has several homes. What had been the graveled path separating the McKee property from the Columbans is now paved and named Van Wickle Lane.

was owned by the Ferry Hill Improvement Company.[252] Porter employed a Protestant lawyer,[253] because of McKee's dislike of Catholics. At one point McKee asked Porter if he were a Catholic. Porter's response was, "I was raised in a Baptist family and our family goes back for many generations of Baptists." He did not mention, however, that he was a convert to Catholicism. McKee, by several accounts, was difficult to deal with. Even normally even-keeled Porter admitted, "I had become tired of the long drawn out negotiations, especially as I felt the favors were coming from me to McKee's and not vice versa, to all of which [McKee's] attorney agreed but he falls back on the old alibi that his clients are very difficult to handle."[254] In the end, Porter said, "I have this feeling about it [buying the property]—we will only get it through prayer. I do not believe it is a matter so much of negotiation as changing the inclination of their minds and hearts into one of willingness to sell it to me and God must give them that, not me. So I hope you and the others will not let up in your prayers for this and for a successful conclusion of the escrow."[255]

An additional asset of the property was its lovely landscaping. Trees were maturing and framed the view of Narragansett Bay. Prior to approval to purchase the land, Porter had written to McCarthy that he hoped the superior general's response would be in the affirmative, "but if not, then He must have something else in mind. When I stood on that ground, I felt like raising my hands to Heaven and saying, 'Good Lord, I thank you for such a spot as this.' What a place for meditation down by the sea front in the evening or just at dawn."[256]

In June, Porter followed through with further background checks on the Ferry Hill Improvement Company, as to whether there were any restrictions on the property, and to learn of any Rhode Island real estate "quirks," as he called them. At the last minute, a delicate situation arose. It appeared another party was considering purchase of the same land, so Porter urged that the deal be closed quickly. But additional discussions with McKee continued

---

[252] The Ferry Hill Improvement Company (known as the Golf Club) was the corporate name for the land which abutted the Van Wickle, Howe, Mills, and Low properties. Richard V. Simpson, *Bristol* (Portsmouth NH: Arcadia Publishing, 2005), 116.

[253] Bishop Hickey "said I had acted wisely in using a Protestant attorney, as his firm would be spotted instantly as acting for the Bishop." 6 July 1933, Porter to McCarthy. *Casey History* (1933), 18. Bishop Hickey died of a heart attack three months later on October 4, 1933 at the age of sixty-four.

[254] Porter to McCarthy 6 July 1933, Porter to McCarthy. *Casey History* (1933), 17. An additional reason for McKee's disposition might have been that, in spite of the fact he had lost the money he borrowed to run his business, he could now defend her interests in the sale of the building and property.

[255] Porter to McCarthy, 10 July 1933. *Casey History* (1933), 19.

[256] Porter to McCarthy, 24 May 1933. 8-A-38.35. *Casey History* (1933), 12.

about restrictions of the property. As Porter wrote, "So long as the use of this property is for residence, school, college, church or religious institution, I can see no harm at all in this restriction for the next ten years."[257] The deeds of the new property were transferred on August 15, 1933 to the "Blue Spruces Corporation," the name under which Porter bought the property. Until things were settled legally and a cesspool issue was taken care of, Bishop Hickey suggested that the two Columbans assigned to Bristol stay with the Sisters of the Holy Cross and Passion, a short distance away and on the same side of Bay.[258] In the first months the Columbans lived at the Bristol house, they were renting from the "Blue Spruces Corporation,[259] until the title for the house was transferred to the Society.

The Society was technically able to move into the house on August 15 with keys delivered to the new owner on that date, but McKee's furniture and belongings were still there two days later. Porter informed McCarthy, "I am serving notice tomorrow and demanding vacating by 4 P.M. Just another of his [McKee's] nasty ways. . . ." The Society "will take possession tomorrow, if I have to take a cop and set the darn furniture out."[260] Kelly, anxious to get organized for the Probationers who would arrive in fall, wrote, "At long last we saw our new home this afternoon, took possession, met McKee at the front door, left him speechless, registered the new address and created all kinds of sensation. As a parting snarl McKee disconnected the sewage system of our house from his own and left us in a mess. We are figuring how best to meet this emergency."[261] Porter, too, described the situation that afternoon:

> McKee had taken one of his contrary spells and would not move out his furniture. Then, a half hour before we got there he apparently became quite angry and cut our sewer connection, although he was supposed to leave it connected until we could get in our own septic tank. However, we had General Callan on the job Saturday morning with one of his steam shovels, and I think everything will be connected by

257   Porter to McCarthy 10 July 1933 *Casey History* (1933), 18.

258   Kelly to McCarthy 22 August 1933. The bishop asked if the Columbans could also be chaplains to the Sisters of the Cross and Passion (Passionist Sisters) novitiate in Bristol. In 1959 the Sisters' property was sold to the Sisters of St. Dorothy, who located their Provincial House there.

259   McCarthy asked William Kelly and Michael Treanor, the latter the rector at Silver Creek that year, to act as Porter's board of directors for Blue Spruces "for the purpose of transferring the stock certificate of this Corporation to the Society." McCarthy [?] to Kelly 11 August 1933, *Casey History* (1933), 20.

260   Porter to McCarthy 17 August 1933.

261   Letter from Fr. Kelly 18 August 1933, *Casey History* (1933), 21.

night [which should] do temporarily until next year. McKee told one of the storekeepers in Bristol Saturday morning, from whom Father Kelly was purchasing some furniture, that he was extremely sorry that he had disposed of the property to me.[262]

By the time the land and buildings were in the name of the Society, the U.S. Region Council had determined that the location was ideal for the Probationers' Spiritual Year. A Spiritual Year had been advocated at the Society's General Chapter of 1924 and "an innovation received with the greatest satisfaction" by the region. "We realize now what we missed. It should strike the golden mean between a top heavy spirituality and none."[263]

Father William Kelly (1893–1985), who was vice rector at Silver Creek, was appointed rector and master of novices in August 1933. Seven men were expected in the first class in Bristol. The purpose of a year of formation for the Probationers, as they were called, was to intensify their spiritual life in a setting that promoted prayer and reflection. The Spiritual Year took place between the first five years of high school/college at Silver Creek[264] and the last six years of philosophy/theology at St. Columban Seminary, Nebraska.

Father Waldron provided "some very helpful suggestions" regarding the Spiritual Year. "We took on the regulations and schedule, with very little change, that Father [James] Wilson[265] sent us. I find myself in full agreement with you in the opinion that the isolation and small number and the absence of that encouragement and comfort that comes from seeing how others adjusted themselves all demand that the Probation year at Bristol be governed by a less rigorous and more elastic set of rules."[266] After the first six months, there were additional adjustments to the program. Father Kelly wrote that he was "rearranging the schedule for the next term. It will be a whole lot easier than the pre-Christmas one, more humane and, I think, more calculated to produce a well-balanced type." [267]

---

[262]   Porter to McCarthy 22 August 1933 *Casey History* (1933), 23.

[263]   *Mission Bulletin* (September and October 1924), 2. Father Paul Waldron, who conducted the thirty-day retreat when it was held at Omaha, had stayed the summer of 1924 with the Jesuits at their Novitiate in Florissant, Missouri to learn the Jesuit method of retreats.

[264]   Initially, the seminary was a five year high school, with Classics, Science, and Latin. E. J. McCarthy, *The Society of St. Columban, A Historical Sketch* (St. Columban, NE, c. 1931), 33. The five year pattern remained at least through 1949.

[265]   James Wilson was director of probationers when that experience was held in Omaha from 1931–1933.

[266]   William Kelly to Paul Waldron 1 January 1935.

[267]   William Kelly to Paul Waldron 16 January 1935.

The former golf club building served a variety of purposes for the
Columbans, including sleeping quarters, chapel, and recreation room. Father
Richard Cushing (1895–1970), director of the Society for the Propagation of the
Faith in the Archdiocese of Boston, visited the Columbans in 1938. He gave the
group "five hundred thousand dollars to take care of his expenses" and urged
that Bristol become the location of their theological seminary.[268] Paul Waldron
wrote to Kelly, that Father Cushing "has been a regular Prince Charming to you
people in Bristol."[269] Cushing heard Father Ambrose Gallagher "put on a '*Nox
Ambrosiana*,' and was so impressed with the story of the land of the 'midnight
sun,'" that he slated Gallagher to preach at the Boston Cathedral on Mission
Sunday. Gallagher was the first person to give the talk in Boston without having
overseas mission experience. Four years earlier, when the Columbans were
given that assignment, "it meant over a thousand dollars for them,"[270] and that
was still in the depths of the Depression.

After permission to buy property in Bristol had been given, O'Dwyer
added, "the Council still thinks that it would be well to have a definite policy
of future development in the USA."[271] But in 1938, discussion again arose as to
the possibility of Bristol as a major seminary location and Cushing indicated
he would help financially to make that happen.[272]

Early on, the Columbans erected a large outdoor crucifix toward the top
of the hill overlooking the Bay. A Mr. Cornell, a "good Providence friend in
the construction business," [273] "saw the crucifix from the Bay many times as he

---

[268]   William Kelly to Paul Waldron 16 August 1938. In the same letter, Kelly noted the
        amount of money Cushing was willing to give the Society were they to erect a major
        seminary at Bristol and suggested ways to have benefactors pair with them for that
        purpose.

[269]   Waldron to Father Kelly, 26 August 1938.

[270]   William Kelly to Paul Waldron 16 August 1938. Ambrose Gallagher (1898–1966),
        born in Tacoma, Washington, would become great friends with Cushing. Gallagher
        saw Cushing more regularly when the Columban was assigned to St. Columban
        Major Seminary in Milton, Massachusetts and Cushing became the cardinal
        archbishop of Boston. Gallagher did promotion work from 1934–44 in the States,
        was assigned to St. Columban, Bristol, from 1944–1945 and to promotion work
        at Milton, Massachusetts until his death. A street close to the Columban house
        in Bristol is named for him: Ambrose Drive. Gallagher's vocation story, "A Star
        Athlete," is featured in Richard J. Cushing, *Answering the Call* (Boston: The Society
        for the Propagation of the Faith, 1942), 5–25.

[271]   O'Dwyer to E. J. McCarthy 14 June 1933.

[272]   See, for example, Ambrose Gallagher to Paul Waldron 11 September 1938. See
        also, 16 August 1938 William Kelly to Paul [Waldron]. The population of Bristol
        County in 1930 was smaller than larger diocese along the Atlantic coast: 25,089.
        The population of the county, which included the towns of Warren and Barrington
        in 2010, the latest census was 49,875, a slight drop from the 2000 census.

[273]   William Kelly to Father O'Donovan (rector at Silver Creek) 22 August 1938.

passed by in his yacht. On finding out from a Dr. McCaffery who lived here, he came down and being in the construction business and always doing good deeds, he said he would paint the place. He did and now he is painting and papering the interior."[274] Mr. Cornell also donated the carpentry work done on the house.[275]

With the continued weakened economy, there was still the possibility of the Bristol house closing in 1934. Rector William Kelly reported that the house expenses for April would be under $400, and "thus you can see that we are more than supporting ourselves since we started to seek our own livelihood. Father Collins and the Chancellor say we would disgrace the Diocese if we closed down and did not wait for the [new] Bishop who will truly be a Father to us. We would never be forgiven. Letters answering our appeal say, 'It will never be said that New England fails to support an Irish Mission House.' I feel we should trust in God, it is His Work. That is why I wished to have permission to try the scheme."[276]

The Blessed Mother, under her various titles, featured in Columban religious art at all three Columban houses. An outdoor statue of Mary, Queen of the Missions, carved from white Carrara marble was ordered for the Bristol property from the Daprato Company in 1937. A company representative came to visit Father Kelly to see firsthand the site where a statue would be placed. Considerable attention was given to the design and composition of the statue. "We agreed that the globe [she would hold in her hands] was to be of a different color marble—greenish; that the fingers would have to be stronger and less delicate than [those pictured] in order to support the ball; that the cross surmounting the orb be done in gold-leaf."[277] The outside trim of the base featured three ascending pagoda style roofs. To prepare for the blessing of the statue on April 27, 1938, the young men did "a superb job" landscaping and planting. "They have planted almost thirty tall cedar trees at the back and half

---

[274] A. Gallagher to Waldron 11 September 1938. *Casey History* (1938), 17. At some point in 1935 twenty-eight stone steps were laid ascending the hill to the Calvary cross area. Kelley to Waldron 2 September 1935.

[275] There were at least two renovations at Bristol before a new building was constructed in 1950. Patrick O'Connor, "An Old House in New England," *FE* (December 1939), 18–19 provides photos of the original house. Overlooking the conflict with the purchase of the property, O'Connor noted, "From its first days in August 1933, this house has enjoyed the thoughtful kindness of well-wishers in Rhode Island and neighboring states." Ibid, 18.

[276] Gallagher to Waldron 28 April 1934. The scheme while unnamed referred to the Sons and Daughters of Saint Columban.

[277] William Kelly to Father Waldron 13 December 1936. The statue was financed partially through McCarthy's personal finances, with the rest of the money being provided by Archbishop Cushing. E. J. McCarthy to Donal O'Mahoney. 2 November 1949. McCarthy was living in Los Angeles at the time.

way around the sides. Inside this fringe the lawn has been raised and laid out in a heart shape.[278]

Weather Effects on the Narragansett Bay

Winter weather proved especially harsh in some years. In a January 1935, blizzard, "where in Providence, the drifts were on a level with the second floors of the houses," Bristol lost electrical power for ten hours and the "crazy old roof began to leak. But the boys are having a grand time sledding down the hill."[279]

A major weather event affected Bristol on Wednesday afternoon, September 21, 1938. "With an unbelievable suddenness," an intense hurricane hurtled up the East Coast, carrying moisture and winds from the Caribbean. That pattern of winds usually lessened, as it traveled up the coast and eventually veered off into the Atlantic. This time winds gained in strength and around Long Island made a turn inland, affecting Long Island, New Jersey and much of New England. The hurricane arrived in Bristol around three-thirty carrying intense winds, sheets of water, and a fifteen feet surge of water that rushed up the bay.[280] The tidal wave was particularly devastating as the storm took place during the autumnal equinox and full moon. While many lives were lost in the State and elsewhere, no one was killed in Bristol. Much of the heavy damage in the town took place along the shore, with the exception of the iconic State Street Methodist Church, which sustained heavy damage. The church's steeple and thousand pound bell were toppled, making the building unsafe. The church was later demolished. Every street in Bristol was affected with downed trees and power lines. The Columbans reported the situation on their premises:

> House, garage, clubhouse, statue and crucifix stood the test. Some tall trees were felled on the highway blocking up one of our entrances, but that was all. Down at the beach, things don't look so hot. If fact, you'd hardly know where the beach and bathing boxes used to be. Everything is gone—all the docks, boathouses, rafts, boat—from the [Mount Hope]

---

[278] William Kelly to Father Waldron 27 April 1938.

[279] William Kelly to Father Waldron 29 January 1935.

[280] In today's reckoning, this was a Category 3 storm surge. For an analysis of the 1938 hurricane's development and impact not only on the built environment and infrastructures, but on coasts and forests (a thousand square mile of forestland was devastated), see Stephen Long, *Thirty-Eight. The Hurricane That Transformed New England* (New Haven: Yale University Press, 2016). For information about the hurricane as it affected Rhode Island, see, Richard V. Simpson, "The Great Hurricane and Tidal Wave of 1938: Scenes of the Disaster in Rhode Island's East Bay." Roger Williams University, 2012. Paper posted at DOCS@RWU.http://docs.rwy.edu/hurricane_1938/1. See also, Richard V. Simpson, *Bristol, Rhode Island. Images of America* Series (Arcadia Publishing Company, 1996).

Bridge up to the top of the harbor. Bristol's waterfront has taken a frightful licking. The storm roared up the bay in a south easterly direction. Herreshoff's boatyard[281] is gone and all the boats in the great shed were smashed or rammed through the sides of the building and piled upon on the highway or carried into fields. We have no electricity, water, radio, or newspapers, so you probably know a lot more of this affair than we do. Island Park, just across the bridge towards Tiverton, was washed away, bridge and all.[282]

The Columban seminarians were on their weekly hike away from the Columban property at the time and felt the hurricane for about two hours as they trudged back to the formation house. A great number of trees were felled on the Blithewold property, fifteen of which blocked all the entrance to Congdon's house, a neighbor.

The number of Probationers decreased in the late 1930s. The suggestion was made that possibly some of the seminarians could come to Bristol, along with the Probationers, thus relieving the overcrowding in Omaha and shoring up the numbers for Bristol.[283] Rector Kelly at Bristol wrote to Waldron:

We are all happy at the prospect of more students for Bristol next year. Things just couldn't go on as they are now. Our best friends are sorry for us and think we are on the down grade because of the noticeable decrease in student numbers. . . . There is a lot to recommend the rather sensational suggestion of a brick building to accommodate thirty or thirty-five theologians. We've got to break the present vicious circle—we can't build till we get the money and we won't get the money till we begin to build.[284]

---

[281]   Located at the foot of Burton Street, Herreshoff Manufacturing Company was the largest boat builder in Bristol. Begun by Captain Nathanial Herreshoff, the company constructed yachts and later other types of boats. The company built the America's Cup yachts that successfully defended the Cup eight times from 1893 to 1934. Surprisingly, most of the Cup winners were mainly intact in their warehouses after the hurricane.

[282]   William Kelly to O'Donovan [rector at Silver Creek] 23 September 1938. *Casey History* (1938), 18. The local paper, *Bristol Phoenix*, published a hand-cranked mimeograph "emergency edition" starting Friday, September 23, 1938.

[283]   The suggestion, which did not materialize, created another problem. The purposes of the probation year and that of the seminary curriculum were different and would require two different sets of Columban leaders and "rules, which would be an awkward situation."

[284]   William Kelly to Paul Waldron, 23 November 1939. *Casey History* (1939), 24–25.

The questions as whether or not to build at Bristol, renovate the clubhouse to take in a larger number of seminarians, add on to the present house, or build a frame or brick building were debated. It wasn't until after World War II that a new building of brick was built at Bristol in 1951 and the Gardiner frame house was torn down, though the club house building was kept. St. Columban, Bristol, remained a formation house for many decades. In 1977 the building became a House of Prayer for a few years and then a retirement home for Columbans, a purpose it still has today. A lovely addition to the building was made in 1999, with ten rooms, each with a view of Narragansett Bay, a library and an extended dining room.

Other Columban Conversations in the 1930s

In the midst of all the financial difficulties and pressures of the decade, the Columbans were in the forefront of initiating retreats for laity in the United States. The Society's first retreat began on a trial basis at Omaha in the summer of 1929. The lay retreat movement was growing rapidly in spite of the Depression, and "the new Bishop of Omaha is particularly keen on its development, as indeed, are all the bishops."[285] Beginning in 1933, retreats were given at Silver Creek for laity in the Buffalo area during the summer when students went home. Through the initiative of laymen in the Buffalo area a house was bought in the neighboring town of Derby, New York, to serve as the location for a retreat house in the Diocese of Buffalo (see chapter 12).

As has been seen, McCarthy and the superior general had a concern about missionaries' health and of "broken down" missionaries from China.[286] Where could they recover their physical and mental well-being? In 1930, the superior general had requested several times that the U.S. regional director find a location for ailing missionaries, particularly a location in California. He asked Paul Waldron to scout the area, though he was not able to do so until 1936. The thought was to be near a parish so that ailing missionary could offer Mass periodically without having parish responsibilities. The major focus would be on recuperation of the men for a month or more.

---

[285] McCarthy to O'Dwyer, 8 February 1929. *Casey History* (1929). See *National Catholic Welfare Conference Bulletin* (1929), 13 for article on lay retreat movement. Eamonn Byrne says McCarthy founded the Catholic Layman's League in 1929. I presume he means in Omaha, because the Catholic Laymen's League was founded in 1909 with retreats given at Fordham University by Father Terence J. Shealy, SJ, who saw the twentieth century as the century of the laity. Laity's contemplative prayer on a Jesuit patterned retreat should lead to effective social action. Hence, the name of the group quickly changed to Laymen's League for Retreat and Social Service.

[286] McCarthy to Cantwell, 22 November 1930 8-A-46.

While the Society was experiencing the stress of financial curtailment, sadness entered their lives. Father Timothy Leonard (1893–1929), a member of the first Columban group to Hanyang, was killed by Chinese Communist–bandits in Nancheng diocese. Father Cornelius Tierney (1872–1931), also in the first group to Hanyang, was captured by the Red Army, then turned over to Communist bandits, who demanded ransom. Tierney was brought to a barracks, stripped of his clothes, hands bound, and scourged. After mocking him and throwing a red cloak around his shoulders, he was kept for five days, with one hand tied continuously to his body. He was taken to another remote spot and winter hardened his sufferings."[287] He also suffered the effects of malaria and died after five months in captivity. The Society now had its first martyrs upon whom to call for assistance and inspiration when each man faced difficult times personally and spiritually.

In spite of the Great Depression, McCarthy and Father O'Leary organized and made arrangements for American Catholics to attend the 1932 International Eucharistic Congress held in Dublin, Ireland. The year marked the 1500th anniversary of St. Patrick's arrival in Ireland (432). They chartered a ship and contacted bishops who would be leading the contingent from the United States. McCarthy and O'Leary put together a pilgrimage of opportunities in Washington DC to learn about Catholics in America before embarking for Ireland. Archbishop Francis J. L. Beckman led the group. He was bishop of Dubuque at the time, then named bishop of Lincoln, Nebraska, in 1924, and apostolic administrator of Omaha from 1926–1928.[288]

As something of an "inculturation" into the country, on September 3, 1935, the region was given permission to be recognized legally as the Saint Columban Foreign Mission Society, a title that resonated more with Catholics in the United States. The region was given another administrative duty: to take responsibility for the Philippines as a "Pro-region," a consequence of a decision of the Society General Chapter in 1932. Just what that meant remained ambiguous, however, and given the financial turmoil of the 1930s, it was not a high priority for the two regional superiors in that decade. McCarthy was to have made a "visitation" there, but he could not find the time to do so, because "these last years have been dreadful." Waldron indicated to the superior general, that he was "not clear on our relations toward the Pro-Region of Manila."[289]

---

[287]   Patrick O'Connor, "Father Tierney, Missionary of the Society of St. Columban," *FE* (May 1931), 3–5, 22. See also, W. S. McGoldrick, "Memories of a Colleague," *FE* (June 1931), 7–9. A large photograph of Father Tierney with the poem, "Father Tierney," composed by Father James J. Gilsenan, was published in *FE* (February 1945), 15.

    Bernard T Smyth, ed., *Part of the Bargain* (Dublin: Helicon Limited, 1963) is a collection of letters sent to and from Tierney, including those sent when he was captured by the Red Army.

[288]   "Eucharistic Congress," *FE* (June 1931), 10–12 contains some of the background and anticipated steps of the journey.

[289]   Waldron to O'Dwyer, 9 January 1935.

Conclusion

While land did not prove an investment in itself, as McCarthy had hoped, the Society's purchase of three sites in Sarpy County, Nebraska, Silver Creek, New York, and Bristol, Rhode Island, served the Society into its centennial year, albeit in a manner somewhat modified from the original intentions for the properties.

During the decade the U.S. region experienced high "in house" expectations: the region was to supply a large percentage of funds for China, provide a hefty portion of the purchase of property for a new headquarters and seminary in Ireland, and maintain the American region fiscally. Pressures increased with the loss of income from investments, the depreciation of government bonds, and multiple demands within the region for building, promotion, and finding a place for missionaries who were ill in China. Many subscribers and friends, loyal to the Society, were not able to assist them financially as they had before. The region was understaffed, seminary priests were overworked with several roles, and additional strain arose from some hostility from the Ku Klux Klan and from some Protestants. The combination of pressures sometimes affected priests' mental and physical health. Father E. J. McCarthy had connected with national Catholic organizations to make the Columbans better known in the United States and had engineered three large land purchases and building constructions over his time as the first regional superior, all this alongside a multitude of other tasks. The crushing pressures of the financial realities in the early 1930s and disagreements with the superior general on financial priorities lead to McCarthy's "resignation," a situation that was not foreseen, but one which led to a different leadership style in the person of Father Paul Waldron.

Waldron's working relationship with the superior general was expressed in a different manner than that of McCarthy in terms of finances, but the country did not experience a full recovery from the Depression until World War II, when the country entered the War as one of the Allied countries. Waldron was reappointed regional superior in 1939 and under his watch the Columbans would become army chaplains and be affected by World War II. Ironically, it would be because of the fine work as chaplains that the Columbans would become better known in the United States. Yet, in spite of these strains and without alluding to the dire financial picture for the Society, the *Far East* stories of the time focused on the needs of the Chinese people and emphasized local efforts at evangelization by Chinese Catholics.

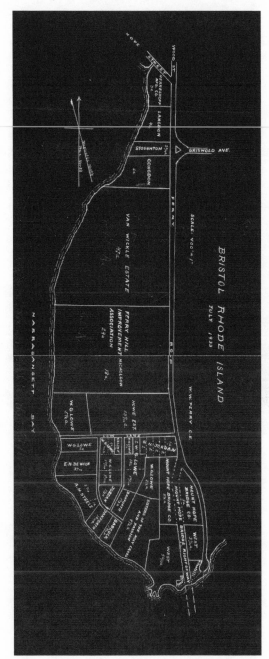

Bristol Blue Print July 1933

Bristol seminary, view from ferry road 1941

CHAPTER 3

World War II and Consequences for Columban Mission (1941–1950)

In many ways, the event which pulled the United States out of the financial doldrums of the Great Depression was World War II. Shaping a new generation of people, the global war impacted millions of people physically, economically, politically and spiritually. After America entered the war following the bombing of Pearl Harbor, the country ramped up defense plants and developed new technologies and materials for wartime use. Over ten million men were drafted into the army, women worked in the factories to take on jobs that men left behind when they were conscripted, and goods at home were rationed to have material available for wartime needs.

After the war, better economic conditions slowly developed for some groups. The Servicemen's Readjustment act of 1944 (PL 78–346, 59 stat. 284m), informally known as the GI Bill, enabled servicemen and women to obtain a college education or further work training, low-cost mortgages for a home and other benefits. One consequence was a housing boom in the United States. Japan was placed under occupation forces of the Allied Powers from 1945 to 1952, under the command of General Douglas MacArthur. This situation enabled Father Patrick O'Connor to have a base in Tokyo from which to provide news stories from Asia for National Catholic News Service. The war had made Russia a military superpower. By the end of the war a "cold war" developed between the western powers and Soviet bloc countries, lasting until 1989. The Columban promotion of the Legion of Mary gave a structure for local Catholic leadership, something which put Communists on the alert, a story which is told in chapter 4. In the United States a fear of Communism and its spread internationally gripped Americans.

The war created a complex situation for the Columbans with international connections. Ireland remained neutral, England would be bombed, Australia and New Zealand entered the war after Nazi Germany invaded Poland in 1939, and the United States was an Allied power against the Axis countries of Germany, Italy, and Japan. Columbans served as army or navy chaplains during World War II. Catholics in the United States followed Columban missions in war torn countries through the *Far East* and through weekly press releases. The Columban missions had grown since 1919 not only in China (Hanyang, Shanghai, Nancheng), but missions opened in Korea, in Burma (now Myanmar), especially among the Kachin people in the hills, and in the Philippines (Manila, Lingayen, West Misamis), though the country had been considered a "Pro-Region" of the United States since 1933.

Because World War II prevented mission travel from the United States, missionaries were available to open promotion houses in the 1940s and thus increase the geographic influence of the Society, even though the Society was still coping with the financial impact of the Depression. At the seminaries, the Society planted their "Victory Gardens" and dealt with rationing during the War, as did other Americans. Most poignantly, the Society felt the effects of their members killed in war zones. The *Far East* during this time reflected the reality of the war, as did their vocation literature. In the postwar years as the seminary population increased, the need to house those men reflected the building boom across the country.

But mission for the Columbans in the U.S. region grew in new ways at the same time. While having a presence in the eastern part of the country remained important to the Columbans for purposes of recruitment and fund-raising, several needs of the Society and of the Catholic Church in California coalesced to make that location an area of growth in mission for the Society during and after the war years. Fathers Paul Waldron (in his second term, which ended in 1947) and Timothy Connolly (1947–1952) would provide regional leadership in a time of growth but also of challenge.

Since the early 1920s, the Columbans had sought a location for missionaries who were ill and unable to continue work in the missions. They thought California would provide the best climate for physical recovery. The Archdiocese of Los Angeles needed help with a growing population of ethnic communities, particularly Mexicans, Chinese, and Filipinos.[290] Columban presence in these communities provided a favorable diocesan climate to open a promotion house in Los Angeles. The house could also be a base for missionaries in need of physical or mental recuperation. In the process, ethnic ministries also grew.

---

[290]   The story of the latter two groups is told in chapter 8.

Venturing West for Health, Promotion, and Mission

During the 1930s and 1940s, the Archdiocese of Los Angeles grew in population, especially among Mexicans and others who had come from various parts of the country looking for work during the Depression. A large number of Irish-born clergy served in the diocese, but there was still need for more clergy to serve in southern California.

In March of 1936, Regional Superior Paul Waldron visited the three bishops of California to thank them for their support of missions. Waldron also met with Monsignor Cawley, the vicar general of the Diocese of Los Angeles–San Diego,[291] "an unusually good friend and most interested in the Society." During their conversation, Waldron asked what chance the Society had of an opening for the Society there. Cawley indicated that the best chance would be now, because "after this [bishops'] administration, the door might be shut." Cawley remarked that Los Angeles was "a coming diocese," and with a view to the future, the Society should be established in the area. Waldron had in mind a place for "priests who might be coming homesick in years to come, as well as the chances to help [in parishes], especially since so many of the priests in L.A. are Irish. . . . The important thing was to be there to be available."[292]

At the time, Archbishop John J. Cantwell of Los Angeles, administrator for several months when the new Diocese of San Diego was carved from Los Angeles in 1936, gave permission for the Columbans to have a house "exclusively for the use of sick and convalescent priests." A place was secured in Redlands, California, in 1936 for that purpose.[293] The path had been paved for this situation through a connection with Father Laurence Forrestal (1894–1963), a former Columban and a former scripture professor at Dalgan. He had contracted tuberculosis and left Ireland on sick leave, serving in the Archdiocese of Los Angeles from 1925 to 1931, after which he incardinated in the Diocese of Los Angeles.[294] As pastor of a parish in Redlands, Forrestal

---

[291]   Between 1922 and 1936, John J. Cantwell was bishop of the Diocese of Los Angeles–San Diego. In 1936, Los Angeles as made an Archdiocese, with Cantwell as archbishop until 1947. In 1936 San Diego became a separate Diocese, with Bishop Charles F. Buddy as bishop.

[292]   Waldron to O'Dwyer, 17 March 1936. 8-A-24. 54.

[293]   Letter to Paul Waldron from Archbishop Cantwell. *Casey History* (1936), 3. The Society apparently had applied for such a house, though without success, in 1924 and 1929. "Local ecclesiastical policy at the time was to play down the notion that Southern California was a clerical sanitarium." No author, "Columbans in San Diego." February 1959. The four page item is a compilation of narrative and document excerpts. 8-B-19.

[294]   In 1925, Regional Director E. J. McCarthy contacted Forrestal and asked him to be his representative in relation to monitoring the situation in San Diego, as to when Father Patrick O'Connor might be able to be moved elsewhere for a different kind of

invited Father James Linehan to stay at his rectory. The missionary had been held prisoner by Chinese Communist guerillas for eight months and returned from China in ill health.[295] The Columbans rented a house in Redlands at 755 West Cedar Avenue, and Father Michael J. Treanor, the regional bursar from 1934–1936, was appointed to the house. However, Treanor became ill in mid-1936, so Cleveland, Ohio native, Father John McFadden (1894–1978) then came to Redlands in September 1936.

Soon it became clear that Redlands was not quite suitable for the Columban purposes. The area was remote from larger cities, did not have the climate that the Society saw as "rejuvenating," and priests probably could not get much "supply" work. Superior General Michael O'Dwyer, who "had been around both dioceses a good deal" [Los Angeles and San Diego], wrote to Waldron with "his impressions confirmed by the opinions of friends." Among the ten points O'Dwyer mentioned as favorable for the Columbans to establish themselves in the San Diego Diocese were the friendliness of the priests and the fact that Archbishop Cantwell did not at the moment have anything for them by way of a location. The Society "had better throw in their lot with the new Diocese of San Diego." [296]

John McFadden in Redlands recommended to Waldron that he attend the consecration of the new bishop of San Diego, Charles F. Buddy, at which time Waldron could consult friends who gathered for the occasion. Superior General O'Dwyer had also written, "Redlands is not the place for location—get out of it as soon as possible."[297] He added, the new Diocese of San Diego "is flourishing with a good lot of well-to-do navy and other people" and "is certainly a beautiful place."[298] McFadden and O'Dwyer met with Monsignor Cawley for an hour, though about "nothing very enlightening." McFadden wrote to Waldron, "The thing everyone is putting in my ears is that you [Waldron] should be at Bishop Buddy's consecration. They think you should come for his installation. Then

---

tuberculosis treatment. Apparently Forrestal was working with Mexican Americans. In 1926, McCarthy wrote to Superior General O'Dwyer that Forrestal, who at the time was still recovering from "nerves," has "pretty well mastered Spanish and is doing splendid work among the Mexicans in Orange, California. E. J. McCarthy to O'Dwyer 24 August 1926. *Casey History* (1926).

[295]   James A. Linehan (1901–1982) served in Hanyang, China from 1926–1932. He served at a Mexican parish, St. Anthony, Riverside, from 1938–1946 and then taught at Silver Creek Preparatory Seminary until 1964.

[296]   O'Dwyer to Waldron 14 December 1936. Re: Prospects in California 8-A-47.2. Handwritten letter.

[297]   Ibid.

[298]   McFadden to Waldron, 14 December 1936 8-A-47.11.

we will have done everything decent to prepare for asking him about moving to San Diego and asking about our charter in the diocese."[299]

Bishop Charles F. Buddy was installed as the first bishop of the new Diocese of San Diego in February 1937. He appointed Father Forrestal from Redlands to be his Chancellor and invited the Columbans to come to San Diego, "the sooner the better." Waldron, in a letter to McFadden indicated that the bishop "has a high opinion of your work there already, so congratulations to yourself and Jimmy [Linehan] on what you have done."[300]

The bishop offered the Society the guardianship of an historic Adobe Chapel of the Immaculate Conception in the Old Town section of San Diego, located near the corner of Congress and Conde streets. San Diego had been one of four military districts in California in the 1700s. The original Mission San Diego de Alcalá was founded by Junipero Serra in 1774. After movement of the mission by Serra himself to a slightly different location, an earthquake, war, and the secularization of the California missions in 1834, a new mission chapel was rebuilt from the crumbling original structure.

The Federal Government restored the small chapel in 1934, as a project for those who were unemployed during the Depression. Waldron described the chapel area to the superior general. "In the older section of San Diego the City has recently erected a small adobe chapel on the site of where the first Mass was said. The Bishop is going to have a priest or priests there to say Mass in that chapel, as the City is anxious that it should be used in some way and the Bishop wants the Blessed Sacrament there." Waldron shared his reasons with O'Dwyer as to the value of taking up the invitation. "It gives us some kind of a *titulus* for being in the City—rather than merely living in a rented house with no definite peg upon which to hang our existence. Secondly, the little chapel there will no doubt be opportunity for a voluntary apostolate of some kind open to the priests, which is better than doing nothing." Waldron opined that because of the chapel's historical value, visitors would stop by and contacts could be made with them, a small center for propaganda could be developed and spiritual exercises could be held, such as a triduum for a group of workers.[301] McFadden described for *Far East* readers, "many currents are blended in the Adobe Chapel of the Immaculate Conception, Spanish and Celtic, Mexican and Oriental, and the missionary ideals of St. Francis and of St. Columban."[302] The first Mass offered by a Columban in the Adobe Chapel was celebrated by Father John Cowhig on All Souls' Day, 1938.

---

[299]   McFadden to Waldron, 14 December 1936 8-A-47.11.

[300]   Waldron to McFadden 20 April 1937.

[301]   Waldron to O'Dwyer, 12 May 1938.

[302]   John McFadden, "In the Land of the Old Missions," *FE* (September 1938), 16–17.

In the meantime, John McFadden, now in San Diego, had overseen the building of a mission house, ready for the men by the end of September 1938, "and the Columban priests began to stream in."[303] Bishop Buddy blessed the new house on July 12, 1939. The Adobe Chapel and mission procure served several purposes. Guardianship of the Adobe Chapel provided a location for "battle scarred missionaries"[304] in the nearby house, the Diocese could have a weekly Mass at the Chapel, and those on promotion would have a home to which they could return after their journeys. The Columbans were also given permission to take up collections for the missions, which they did until 1942, when all such special collections were terminated in the Archdiocese. However, Waldron cautioned McFadden, "Keep in mind the purpose for which we are in San Diego. The primary end is not parish supplies. . . . Right now your main objective is to procure a place in [San Diego] where we may make a beginning and may try out this year with a view to deciding more definitely our procedure later on. . . . [The] great question is whether this place in Old Town would prove suitable as a center for propaganda work in California and I include under the term propaganda everything of a money-making nature."[305]

In addition to the Mission Chapel, Bishop Buddy invited the Society to work with Mexican Americans. McFadden wrote to Waldron that the bishop "has several Mexican districts that are not being looked after to his satisfaction. Either the priest is somewhat old, and hasn't the initiative to go after them, or some such reasons.[306] With little attention from the Catholic Church, some Mexicans "were drifting away from the Church and were being lured away to Protestant churches."[307] McFadden indicated that the bishop "asks the Society

---

[303] *Casey History* (1937) 6. For arrangements with the diocese on the building and financing of the house, see McFadden to Waldron 7 June 1938 and Waldron to Most Rev. Charles F. Buddy, 7 June 1938. Another source for the early days of St. Columban Society in southern California is, Father Gerard Marinan's nine-page history, "The Society in Los Angeles," written from Ireland, 3 November 1958. CFA-USA.

[304] Quoted phrase from John M. McFadden, "In the Land of the Old Missions," *FE* (September 1938): 16–17, quotation, 16.

[305] Unknown person, though probably Waldron to McFadden 11 August 1938, regarding San Diego. In addition to Father Richard Ranaghan being in the LA area in 1920, Father Thomas Quinlan, one of the first Columbans to China in 1920, stopped in various cities in Massachusetts, Rhode Island (and probably elsewhere) on the way to the West coast to give talks at parishes and get names of subscribers for the *Far East*. Letters from him to E. J. McCarthy indicate Quinlan traveled for this purpose from early April through the end of July 1920, until he arrived in San Francisco to await the others with whom he would sail to China. Folder 9-B-20. CFA-USA.

[306] McFadden to Waldron 12 May 1937.

[307] *Casey History* (February 1942), 21. No author cited, but probably taken from a parish booklet.

to let me work among the Mexicans in one of the districts here, organize a parish probably, be their padre, and give my whole time to it. . . . He thinks I know Spanish better than I do, and in brief, he wants me to take charge of some district and work it up." The town of Casa Blanca was one place mentioned because of the presence of a large number of Mexicans. Later in the letter, McFadden said that in terms of the length of the assignment, the bishop "would like me to hold [the area] at least till some of the Diocesan priests can be equipped for it. That makes me smile, considering my knowledge of Spanish and the people. It would be a full-time job, no doubt of it—with no time for St. Columban's."[308]

Waldron's Council favored the idea of accepting the work with Mexicans. The superior general gave approval for the venture. In the end, the Columbans were given two missions with Mexican–American populations: Casa Blanca (St. Anthony Mission, near Riverside,)[309] and Bryn Mawr, an unincorporated community near Loma Linda, where they served from 1941–1943.[310] The Columbans had departed Redlands in 1938 when they took up residence in San Diego and staffed the Adobe Chapel and served the Mexican community. Fathers James Linehan and John McFadden were considered to be "good Spanish speakers."[311] A formal Columban apostolate among Mexicans in the United States had begun.

Expansion of the Mexican Apostolate

Two years after the Columbans began work in San Diego, the Society accepted the invitation of Archbishop John Cantwell to serve the needs of the Mexican parish of St. Isidore, Los Alamitos, in the Archdiocese of Los Angeles.[312] The area was a distinct contrast to Columban experience on the east coast. The East tended toward crowded cities, large and small industries,

---

[308] McFadden to Waldron 12 May 1937.

[309] The Columbans served this community until at least 1951. Father Ernest Speckhart (1916–1980) from Newark New Jersey, served the Casa Blanca parish from 1944–1951, after he recovered his health in Colorado Springs the previous year.

[310] In 1945, the *Official Catholic Directory* for the United States listed a diocesan priest in charge of the Bryn Mawr parish.

[311] Waldron to O'Dwyer, 12 May 1937. Waldron pointed out to O'Dwyer the value of the two places (Casa Blanca and Adobe Chapel) in Southern California: "From time to time it will be nice for the priests to visit back and forth and avoid monotony for men who are resting or convalescing." Ibid.

[312] "You are hereby authorized to accept the archbishop's offer of a Mexican parish." O'Dwyer to Waldron 24 June 1941. St. Isidore Mission in Los Alamitos appears in the Columban *Green Book* for the first time in 1943.

and people with ethnic backgrounds from European, Eastern European, or Mediterranean countries. California had rich fertile land, which allowed for agriculture or cattle ranching and a wholesome climate year round. People lived in small towns, with the exception of Los Angeles, which had grown noticeably by 1940. There was a large Mexican presence including some land owners (ethnic Mexicans who descended from Spanish families going back to the eighteenth century) and some whose lineage included marriage with Native Americans going back the days of Spanish colonization. The number of Mexican Nationals—those who were seasonal workers—grew during World War II. With many men being drafted into wartime service, the work force was depleted at home. Not only was the famed "Rosie the Riveter" on the job, but the United States sought additional workers from Mexico for short term agricultural work through the *Bracero* program, beginning in 1942.

When Waldron had visited the archbishop of Los Angeles in 1941, he interviewed Father Michael G. Sheahan, a diocesan priest at a Santa Monica parish, to see whether Columban Father Robert Ross could be his temporary associate to gain experience serving the Mexican community and to learn Spanish.[313] Father Sheahan agreed and Ross came immediately to his assignment. In February 1942, John McFadden, joined by Ross in May, began the mission at Los Alamitos (St. Isidore) on Katella Avenue. The assignment took in a seventy-five square mile area, with Catholics numbering about 3000 people. A bicycle was the most maneuverable mode of conveyance across the fields. As McFadden described their mission, "we went into high gear, speaking Spanish, visiting homes, getting catechism classes under way, validating marriages, getting lapsed Catholic back to Mass and the Sacraments. There were happy times—the Twelve Nights before Christmas when we would pray at twelves homes in succession; the 'Posadas' it was called."[314] McFadden pictured for *Far East* readers their context in Los Alamitos:

> We have no mansions in our parish, but many hearths. Here, planned parenthood means getting ready for a houseful of children. Immaculate kitchens, neat lawns orderly gardens, endowments for college education, culture, quiet are rare. Our people are more impressed with the importance of living. . . . The catechism class is our chief contact with the children. The majority of them cannot read with much facility,

---

[313] This diocesan priest, whose name is spelled in some Columban correspondence as Sheehan, was at the Santa Monica parish at least from 1940 through 1944. The *Official Catholic Directory* lists the spelling of his name as Michael G. Sheahan.

[314] John McFadden, "The Story of My Priesthood," *The Maryfaithful* (March–April 1976), 4–6, here p. 5.

but we say the common prayers together. I read the questions with them several times and then call on some to repeat without the book. Timidity is a great obstacle to their learning anything. They fear to make a mistake, and without being absolutely certain, they do not care to venture an opinion.[315]

The people provided the priests with chickens, rabbits, milk, oranges and vegetables. The context afforded Columbans "a task with few material comforts, for the Mexicans are seldom well-to-do. [Therefore,] the priest to be accessible must forego some of the accessories of twentieth century living."[316]

As work increased with more Mexicans arriving in southern California, newly ordained Father Kevin McNally joined the other two Columbans and served at St. Isidore.[317] The Los Alamitos assignment also included Westminster (Blessed Sacrament), Garden Grove (St. Columban),[318] Independencia (Sacred Heart), Stanton (Our Lady of Guadalupe), and Manzanillo (Our Lady of Lourdes), *colonias* which initially had small numbers of Catholics associated with the mission.[319] Later, parishioners noted that all the missions "were served by these courageous, loveable, and persistent young priests."[320] Pastoring the scattered communities meant traveling many miles to meet the people in each small area. One Columban described the makeup of the communities. "Better

---

[315] Edward A. De Persio, "Where the Little Poplars Wave," *FE* (April 1943), 14. John McFadden, "Out California Way Among Mexican Americans," *FE* (June 1947).

[316] Edward A. De Persio, "Where the Little Poplars Wave," *FE* (April 1943), 16.

[317] Kevin McNally (1914–1984) then later served at Riverside and at the Columban parish, Westminster. He would later become pastor of a Mexican American parish in Navasota, Texas.

[318] Of particular note is the leadership of the Garden Grove Catholic Women, called together in 1934 by Grace Yeager. She and the other seven women at the time organized a Catholic Women's Club, for promoting the growth of Catholicism. Having lived in the area since 1923, she saw a need for "Catholic action," that is, evangelization and the need to gather together the few Catholic families spread over a large geographic area. Initially Grace taught English speaking children their catechism, while two Sisters taught catechism to children who spoke Spanish. Grace and the Garden Grove Catholic Women gave Bingo parties and card parties to raise money for a church building. When the Columbans came in 1942, there were fifteen families, and they raised five hundred dollars at their first bazaar, held in Garden Gove Park. In addition to the food which the women and men cooked, they sold the ladies' "fancy work." Eventually they raised enough money to build their church, thanks also to the carpentry skills of Father Ross. The first Mass was held in the chapel on Christmas morning, 1946. Folder: Westminster, Garden Grove, 4.23.1959. 8-A-50.

[319] Stanton and Independencia had a small mission chapel. Catholics in Westminster met at a hall. Some sources indicate that Los Alamitos at the start of Columban involvement included only Stanton, Independencia and Westminster.

[320] *Casey History* (1942), 22. "Blessed Sacrament Church [Westminster] in Review."

than ninety percent of these people were California-Mex. [I] would say that in '42 we had around thirty Anglo-Saxon families in the whole area to be found in Los Alamitos, Westminster and Garden Grove."[321] Later that year the priests and people remodeled an old church formerly used by a Japanese colony in Talbert. The building served as a parish church until completion of a new structure.[322]

Within a few years, the center of Columban ministry with the Mexican community shifted to Blessed Sacrament Parish at Westminster.[323] A new and welcome development took place in 1947 with the arrival of three Columban Sisters, who took up temporary residence at the priests' house in Los Alamitos.[324] Through McFadden's suggestion, Archbishop Cantwell had written to Mother Vianney Schackleton, superior general of the Columban Sisters in Ireland, to send a small group of Sisters for catechetical instruction of the children in each mission district. Sisters Margaret Mary McCarthy, Mary Vincent Lang, and Mary Therese Bolan were the first three to be sent to the mission. The day after their arrival on July 16, 1947, the Sisters began teaching about 800 children throughout the mission stations. The Sisters taught days and evenings after supper and Sister Bolan, who had been trained in bookkeeping and secretarial skills, wrote that she "began to develop her latent talent for teaching."[325] Father McFadden drove the Sisters to and from the locations. Mrs. Florentine Perez, "the lay person most responsible for the Westminster parish," sent two of her daughters as companions to assist the Sisters as they worked with the children.[326]

In the meantime, the priests and parishioners were building a convent in Westminster and the Sisters moved there in September, a few months after their arrival. Along with many parish volunteers McFadden who was handy with carpentry and related skills pitched in to build a school with eight grades. The building was ready for occupancy in autumn, 1948. The first year 150 pupils were enrolled. Bolan had a threefold role: superior, principal, and occasional catechist. She also managed the school office and kept track of

---

[321]   Father Kevin [probably McNally], *Casey History* (1942), 24. 8-A-50.5. The Columbans gave up Garden Grove, previously an outstation of Westminster, in 1953.

[322]   *Casey History* (1951), 4.

[323]   Father John McFadden was pastor of Los Alamitos and Blessed Sacrament parishes from 1942–1949, after which he resumed seminary work at St. Columban's, Bristol. The Columban commitment at Blessed Sacrament parish appears for the first time in the 1948 *Green Book*. St. Isidore and Bryn Mawr (also spelled, Maur) are listed for the last time in the in 1947 *Green Book*.

[324]   Father McFadden slept on a pew in the sacristy of St. Isidore Church, Los Alamitos. Father Ross went to live with a family in Garden Grove. Sister Therese Bolan, "Memories of the Columban Sisters Foundations in California." 1976.

[325]   Ibid.

[326]   Ibid.

fees and expenditures.[327] The Sisters served at Blessed Sacrament School until 1979, when they turned over the educational mission of the school to the Sisters of St. Louis.[328] Over the years, forty-eight Columban Sisters served at Blessed Sacrament School, including nine Sister Principals.

Ross and McFadden were known for getting around the vast area by bicycle, as noted earlier. This was an especially useful manner of travel, given the rationing of fuel during the War and the rugged terrain they crossed. McFadden served the Mexican community until fall, 1948, when he left for Milton, Massachusetts, to aid in building the Columban seminary the following summer.[329] Father Joseph Murrin was assigned to Los Alamitos in 1945.[330] The forty-four-year Columban mission at Blessed Sacrament parish ended in 1986, when diocesan priests were assigned to the parish. The area had grown considerably since the Society started ministry to Mexicans in that part of the Archdiocese of Los Angeles. Several parishes "spun off" from Blessed Sacrament or were subdivided from the original group.

The next geographic area the Columbans worked with Mexicans would be in Navasota, Texas, from 1959 to 1964. The Columbans took over the Diocese of Galveston mission from the Basilian Fathers, "who did the difficult spadework."[331] Father Kevin McNally, who had served the Mexican community at St. Isidore, was named pastor of the parish. In the meantime, other ethnic communities moved into southern California: Vietnamese around 1978 and that same year Koreans, who formed the Korean Martyrs Catholic Church in Westminster. The story of the Columban mission in the Korean community is told in chapter 9.

---

[327] Sister Ita Hannaway, SSC, *Tapestry in Mission* (Sisters of St. Columban: Ireland, 2008), 178.

[328] Hannaway states that in 1947 Archbishop John Cantwell requested Mother Mary Vianney to send the Columban Sisters to St. Isidore. The three Sisters began a school in 1947, which she refers to as being at Blessed Sacrament, Westminster. Three years after that, the Sisters began another mission, this time in East Los Angeles, Our Lady of Guadalupe. Ibid., 40–41.

[329] McFadden later accepted his first overseas assignment when he was fifty-eight years old: Buenos Aires, with the Argentine Apostleship of the Sea, then Lima, Peru. The Columban work with the Apostleship of the Sea ended in 1963.

[330] Not everyone who came to this mission was prepared to speak Spanish. Father Joseph Murrin (1916–2002), born in Parnell, Iowa, remarked about "being thrown out there without any preparation." James McCaslin interview of Joseph Murrin, 18 March 1987. Murrin was at Los Alamitos from 1945–1949, when the Columbans left that mission. Murrin returned to the area in 1967 as Pastor of Blessed Sacrament Parish, Westminster, until 1973. In January 1979, he was again at Westminster as Assistant Pastor for a few months.

[331] Rt. Rev. Msgr. Vincent M. Harris (Chancellor of the Diocese of Galveston) to Peter McPartland 9 September 1959.

World War II—The Columban Home Front in the United States

Before the involvement of the United States in World War II, Paul Waldron had sought Superior General O'Dwyer's advice about whether the U.S. region should invest in Australian securities. O'Dwyer was "not keen" on that but he suggested some investment in Canadian securities, "especially in Canadian foreign loans issued and payable in New York." O'Dwyer then informed Waldron, "It may be necessary for us to call on you [the U.S. Region] to pay pretty substantial sums to the mission by way of loan to the Irish and Australian regions in the course of this year, and if the war lasts, almost certainly next year." O'Dwyer wanted Waldron to know that and keep it in mind "when making your investments, so that you may be in a position to find the money quickly without having to seek out investments at an inopportune time."[332]

One effect of World War II at home was the government policy of rationing materials needed for the war effort. Items such as fuel, tires, cars, sugar, coffee, meat, cheese, canned milk, butter, and shortening were rationed. Ration books were needed to purchase these items and the Columbans were issued ration books as well. Bristol and Nebraska seminaries cultivated a "victory garden," as did the new Columban seminary in Milton, Massachusetts, where students grew corn and cabbage. The seminarians in Nebraska helped construct a "cave" or root cellar on the grounds in which to store over winter the vegetables grown there. An orchard was started on the grounds.[333] Silver Creek's farm continued to provide dairy products, eggs, fruit and vegetables, and meat products from hogs. Missionaries in Nancheng, Jiangxi Province, China, were also reported to have their "victory gardens" of vegetables because with repeated bombings, essentials were hard to obtain. One enterprising Columban mission grew tobacco, cured it, and "in the pipe it is not bad at all."[334]

Bishop John Francis O'Hara, head of the military vicariate of the United States of America from 1939–1945, requested the archdioceses and men's religious orders release some of their priests to serve as military chaplains. By 1944, the Archdiocese of Los Angeles would have twenty-two diocesan priests who were army or navy chaplains. The Columbans, too, received a letter from O'Hara and Waldron inquired of Superior General O'Dwyer whether any of the Columbans in the United States could respond to the request. O'Dwyer

---

[332]   O'Dwyer to Waldron 23 July 1940.

[333]   Seminarians working on the cave are featured in a photo in *FE* (January 1941), 4. While not specifically connected to war time, during the "Great Flood of 1943," wherein the Missouri River once again mightily wreaked havoc along its banks in some areas, Columban seminarians in Bellevue, Nebraska assisted with sandbagging to prevent the River from inundating the low-lying town's businesses and homes.

[334]   "War News from the Missions Bulletin" 3 February 1944.

would have no objection, but he had three stipulations. The man would have to do so "of his own free will, without any request or pressure from the Society authorities." The man should be over thirty years of age and under forty years old. Lastly, the superior should judge the person as to how "well-fitted he is to bring honor to his priesthood and to the Society."[335] The Columbans who became military chaplains in the United States Armed Forces in the first years of World War II were

Charles J. O'Brien (1941–1946, U.S. Navy hospital ship),

Thomas F. Powers (1941–1943, U.S. Army),

Patrick T. Brennan (1942–1945, U.S. Army), who had been evicted from Korea and was in the United States at the time,

Harold W. Henry (1942–1947, U.S. Army), who served in General George C. Patton's Third Army,

Peter McPartland (1942–1946, U.S. Army), who served in North Africa, Sicily and Normandy,

John Daly (late 1943–1945, U.S. Army, South Pacific), who was working with the Filipinos in Los Angeles before he applied for chaplaincy.[336]

Father Peter McPartland (1912–1987), who received seven military awards, spoke about some of his chaplain duties. On the base, much of his work was that of a pastor in a parish. He offered Mass, counseling, instruction for those interested in becoming Catholic. His ship embarked from Newport News, ...nia on November 1, 1940, for the North African invasion, just one of three ...n which he participated. He described one of his experiences:

in warfare, we were working like mad, working
...use there was pressure on and the injured
... so that you worked fast and you had no
... . You had the men in the medical

United States at the time of the bombing of Pearl
... his mission. He became a chaplain the Canadian
...ans were in active service as military chaplains during
... 1945), 18.

profession, those who were dying and you caught others as they were going out. It was a very, very stressful, not mentally stressful, but a demanding situation. . . . At one point in the night I saw a stretcher go by with a man who was dead and they were just stacking them all sadly outside the courtroom and I saw one go by that I hadn't seen. As soon as I finished my mission, it was dark, there was a blackout and it didn't bother me to climb over and get to the top of the pile to anoint him. It was mechanical in a sense, but it was something that had to be done. . . . that is an exaggerated example of what would occur.[337]

A few men from the United States later entered the Society after their service in the Armed Forces. After the war, Bishop O'Hara, the military delegate who had sent the request for chaplains, became bishop of Buffalo, New York, the diocese in which the Columban Silver Creek Seminary and the Columban-staffed retreat center in Derby were located.

The war prevented missionaries from leaving the United States for their missions and some Columbans assumed posts in America. Among these, Father Maurice Quinn was chaplain at a retreat house for women in Broadmoor, Colorado. Nearby, three Columbans were recovering their health at Glockner Sanatorium in Colorado Springs. Father Anthony O'Doherty, who had served in Nancheng, was chaplain at St. John's Hospital, Oxnard, California, and then served at Santa Ana as assistant pastor at St. Anne Parish. Other Columbans were assigned to promotion work.

The country's energy around the war was reflected to some extent in the vocation literature of the 1940s. In 1943, a monthly comic strip, "Commandos of the Cross," black and white drawings in the children's section of the *Far East*, pictured the history of the Society and of their work in the missions. Reflecting the values of devotion to one's country and willingness to sacrifice one's life, a section of the *Far East* aimed at young people, "Colum's Column," posed the question, "How can I become an officer in the Missionary army of our Lord?"

A Columban published booklet, *Cadets for Christ. An Invitation—A Challenge to the Youth of America*, answered the question. *Cadets* noted that "Alexander the Great wept when he saw no opportunity for further victories after he h[ad] conquered the then known world. Christ's Army, the Church, has still m[ore] victories to achieve. If He could weep, he would do so at the thought [of] many lands yet to be won with so few priestly officers to lead His Army." author provided a brief explanation of the training needed. The Co[lumbans] have "set up a clerical West Point at Silver Creek, New York, where[...]

---

[337]   Jim McCaslin interview of Father Peter McPartland, no date.

Christ are trained in the task of establishing beachheads of Christianity on far-flung pagan shores. This is a job for you. In your hands is placed the cross, that you may raise it high in lands that you will help to win for Christ." The Bristol seminary was a "spiritual flight school," after which you "start the advanced studies that will win you your wings as a full-fledged missionary."[338]

As the war came to an end, the Society wrote a *Far East* article on a Vocation Club for Servicemen. The idea was that upon return to the United States, veterans would take up their life anew and with overseas experience, they might consider becoming a missionary. Some former U.S. Armed Forces servicemen did enter the Columban seminary, though most would not have had a study of Latin in their background. They matriculated at the minor seminary at Silver Creek to study Latin for a year or so to get up to speed on their classics.[339]

Prior to World War II, missionaries had faced the Japanese invasion of China. The China mission experience was featured in a film that attracted large audiences around the United States. A. J. Cronin's novel, *Keys of the Kingdom*, was cast into a 1944 film, starring Gregory Peck, who portrayed a "Father Chisholm," a missionary priest and doctor in China. The model for the work of the missionary was, in fact, Columban Father Francis McDonald (1895–1971), a boyhood friend and medical school colleague of Cronin and to whom he dedicated the novel. Frank McDonald thought he was giving up a medical career for the priesthood. In fact, the sickness and suffering of people in Hanyang in the early 1930s was such that he resumed his medical skills, which were additionally needed after Japanese planes bombarded parts of China where the Columbans had their missions.[340] The July 1945 issue of *Far East* had a full page poster of the 20th Century Fox film on the inside cover, with a brief note to magazine readers: "The motion picture version of the *Keys of the Kingdom* has received Class A rating from Legion of Decency, with the warning that some of the film priest's statements could be understood in a sense as at variance with Catholic doctrine."[341] Three columns of "The Answer Box" that month were also devoted to *Keys of the Kingdom*.

Through the *Far East* and through press releases in the 1940s, the Columbans highlighted the fidelity of Catholics in Burma (now Myanmar), China, and Korea and the leadership laity took in spite of horrendous and

---

[338]   *Cadets for Christ. An Invitation* (Missionaries of St. Columban, 1944), 44.

[339]   Father John Burger indicated that the difference in background, maturity and experience between the somewhat older seminarians who had seen combat and the younger seminarians who were from fourteen to eighteen years old was, understandably, noticeable on a daily basis.

[340]   Columban Father McDonald's story is told in "A Key Man of the Kingdom," *FE* (February 1945): 5–7. Other stars included Vincent Price and Roddy McDowell, the latter playing the young Father Chisholm.

[341]   *FE* (February 1945): 1.

often life-threatening situations. Columbans reported over one thousand baptisms from June 1942 to June 1943 in the Nancheng (Nanching) vicariate. Father Robert Degnan wrote, "It would do your heart good to see the Church filled with Chinese Catholics, attending Mass and reciting aloud the special Mass prayers, or singing the hymns for Benediction."[342] After three years of missionary separation from their Catholics in Burma (now Myanmar), another Columban wrote "The priests here are overjoyed with the steadiness of the Catholics during our separation from them. With comparatively few defections, we find the main body with a more lively faith than when we last saw them. They organized themselves for prayers and took it very seriously."[343] Another example came from Korea. Kim Matthew, thirty-two years old at the time, volunteered to be a catechist when the Columbans were opening a new territory. The Columbans wanted to provide him with a salary for his ministry, but Kim "wished to work entirely for the sake of Our Lord and that he wanted only enough to support his wife and two children." Not only did he begin evening classes, he visited the parents of students, gave consolation to the sick and dying, prepared the body of the deceased for burial, and assisted the family in any way they needed. After Pearl Harbor and the possibility that funds might not be coming from the Columbans in Korea, the pastor suggested to Kim that he find another position. Kim refused. Though intimidated by the local police, who offered him a good job in the civil service on the condition he would give up the faith, Kim told the police "that the only way he could be made to quit was by death."[344]

At the same time, the Columbans emphasized that even through World War II and with physical destruction and intense danger in many areas, the missionaries continued their work, albeit with more emphasis on assisting the injured, tending to the dying, distributing food and other assistance to the displaced. A press release, also printed in the *Far East*, proclaimed that more than 92 percent of Columban missionaries (the pre–Pearl Harbor total) remained at their posts in China, Korea, the Philippines, and Burma (now Myanmar) at the end of 1943.[345]

---

[342]   "War News from the Missions," 3 February 1944.

[343]   "Mission News Service," 2 August 1945.

[344]   "War News from the Missions," 12 August 1943.

[345]   "Spot News From the Missions Bulletin," 9 December 1943.

Columbans Give Their Lives in Wartime

Given that most of the Columban missionaries were Irish and therefore considered neutral in the War, they were able to stay at their assignments in Asia. It is not surprising that Columbans experienced physical suffering and death during that time, as did their people. Six Columbans were killed in the Philippines[346] and Father Thomas Flynn was killed in Luzon in 1950 by Huk Communist guerrillas. Father Tom Murphy (1906–1945) was killed by an exploding shell in Burma (now Myanmar) while saying Mass in the chapel of the Leper Asylum, where the Columbans were interned.

Father John Heneghan (1881–1945), one of the Columbans killed in the Philippines, was well known to readers of the *Far East*. One of the first six members to join the Columbans in Ireland, he "frequently thought of Father Galvin away out in China all alone, praying before the tabernacle in a lonely, pagan village,"[347] Heneghan embodied abundant skills in both writing and speaking. He was appointed editor of the Irish edition of *Far East* in 1918 and remained so until he left for the Philippines in 1931 at the age of forty-nine. For fifteen years, his monthly articles appeared in the American edition of *Far East*. His book, *White Martyrdom*, the story of Bishop Damian of Molokai, who gave his life to the lepers by living among them in the nineteenth century, was serialized in the U.S. *Far East*. Heneghan's earlier book, *Pathways to God*, was considered a new way of writing about devotional or spiritual topics for readers. The Columban emphasized an "active, intimate friendship with the living Christ."[348] Father Paul Waldron, who would complete his second term as the

---

[346] Fathers Francis Douglas, Peter Fallon, John Heneghan, Patrick Kelly, Joseph Monaghan, and John Lalor were killed in the Philippines. Father Patrick McMahon was killed as a British Army chaplain in 1944. Parts of China were still occupied in the 1940s and foreigners were interned in China during World War II. Mention should be made of some Columbans who served as chaplains to internees in China or Burma (now Myanmar). Father James Stuart (1909–1955) saved lives of numerous refugees and American airmen during World War II in North Burma (now Myanmar). He received the British (OBE) Order of the British Empire, and the American Medal of Freedom. For the experience of several other mission societies incarcerated at the notorious Los Baños camp, Luzon, see James T. Carroll, "Sentenced to Death-Destined for Life: Catholic Religious and Japanese Occupation," *American Catholic Studies* 113 #3 (2002), 57–74.

[347] Father John Blowick's notes, quoted in Neil Collins, *The Splendid Cause. The Missionary Society of St. Columban, 1916–1954* (Dublin: The Columba Press, 2009), 32. Collins characterized Heneghan, at least at this early stage of editorship, with a "stirring mixture of Irish nationalism and Catholic crusade" and a "pessimistic view of the 'heathendom' of China." Ibid., 55.

[348] Heneghan's *White Martyrdom* was published by the Society of St. Columban, Milton, Massachusetts (1946).

U.S. regional director in 1947, continued the spiritual/devotional focus in *Far East* in his own monthly articles with reflections on the Sacred Heart.

Heneghan was in a Columban parish and center in Malate, a district located along the bay in Manila. By 1941, he was in poor health and was due for a vacation. Given the threat of war conditions, he decided to stay in Malate. With the strong possibility of an attack by the Japanese on Manila, the Columbans were given the option of internment at Santo Tomas prison for safety, but the men at Malate stayed with their people. By February 1945, as the Japanese evacuated Manila and destroyed everything in their path, Heneghan was one among five Columbans captured, along with some laymen of the parish. He was last seen in Japanese custody along with Filipino prisoners and most probably all were killed by their captors.[349]

The *Far East* editor, Father Patrick O'Connor, gave a personal tribute to the martyr and posted an excerpt of a radio address that Heneghan had given, "When the Fiery Trial Comes." O'Connor noted Heneghan's literary and vocal talents, along with an "active, intimate friendship with the living Christ . . . [which] kindled enthusiasm for the missions and for the cause of Christ everywhere."[350]

In the Philippines since 1930, Father John Lalor (1897–1945), was in Malate during the battle for Manila in 1945.[351] However, he was in Remedios Hospital, when the other Malate Columbans were captured. After the fall of Bataan, Lalor converted his school building into a hospital where he and a small staff took care of wounded Filipino soldiers, along with a section for American internees. The school-turned-hospital became a link to obtain medicine, medical supplies, clothing, food, and to send messages from the prisoners of war and internees. Lalor trained Filipino boys and girls to help with the nursing, as well as burying those killed. In July 1944, the hospital was cleared of all Americans. After a week of bombardment of the area, on February 13, 1945, he and the eighteen young people working with him had laid down to rest in a make shift shelter of tented mattresses and quilts. An American shell missed its mark and hit their building, which ignited their shelter, killing all of them. Five days later, Father P. Vincent McFadden was allowed into the rubble site. McFadden reflected upon the experience of seeing Lalor's dead body and of burying him where he died.[352]

---

[349]   E. J. McCarthy, *Life of Father Heneghan*, n.d. but between 1947 and 1957. Typescript. CFA-USA. McCarthy notes that Heneghan was "much more at home with divine than with human economies." n.p. Section II.

[350]   Patrick O'Connor, *FE* (May 1945), 2.

[351]   For the history of the Society of St. Columban in the Philippines up until 1953, see Neil Collins, *The Splendid Cause*, 186–225.

[352]   P. Vincent McFadden, "My Hardest Task," *FE* (May 1946), 9–10.

"As a priest, I often prepared men to die. As a hospital orderly in the internment camp, I had seen men die every day. Death is never nice yet somehow I got hardened to it. But seeing the lifeless body of Father Lalor at my feet was different. Here was a fellow priest, a man I had worked and prayed and played with. It was as if I was looking at my own brother. I had to summon every bit of my courage to bury him.

> I buried Father Lalor in the school yard he loved so well. Even as occasional sniper fire whistled and whined over our heads, I dug the shallow grave at the foot of the undamaged grotto of Our Lady of Lourdes. From a few pieces of rough wood, I fashioned a crude cross to mark his grave. And now Our Lady smiles down on a son who served her well, a son who feared no danger and ran every risk that souls might be saved.

> As I placed the cross above his grave, I prayed that the children of the children for whom he had done so much would occasionally halt in their play and say a prayer for their beloved Padre Lalor who truly died for his friends, than which there is no greater love." [353]

Fittingly, an appeal for mission funds linked the *Far East* readers with both the martyred Columbans and with the beleaguered Filipinos. "Wounds that show in shattered churches, as well as in bleeding bodies. . . . Wounds in stricken homes and broken hearts—these are the wounds of the Philippine people today. You bind some wound every time you help the work of the priests and Sisters." The appeal concluded, "The work of the six priests of St. Columban who have recently given their lives in the Philippines needs your help to continue. Wounds can't wait."[354] Once again, the Columbans placed their service in the perspective of what people in their missions were enduring.

Columban Portrayal of Armed Forces Personnel on the Missions

During World War II, the U.S. region issued weekly "War Bulletins," later called "Spot News from the Missions." The one page press releases, often with a map of the *Far East* countries attached, provided subscribers, donors, and the

---

[353]   Ibid., 10. A photo on that page shows him reading the burial prayers at the site.

[354]   Appeal for mission funds, *FE* (May 1945). Photos of the six Columbans killed in the Philippines, along with tributes from people who knew them are given in *FE* (January 1946), 13–14.

general public with a view of the effect of the war where Columbans served. The Columbans, particularly those who had Irish citizenship, stepped in to take on some of the work in Shanghai as chaplain to an internment camp, served in parishes wherein priests from Allied countries had been arrested, and, for a time, two Columbans taught at Gonzaga College and St. Michael's School for Russian Boys, because of the American Jesuits' internment. Two themes related to American servicemen emerged in the press releases in the 1940s, as well as in the pages of the *Far East*: American Catholic soldiers and their impact on other GIs and on Catholics in mission countries, and U.S. Armed Services' assistance to the Columbans.

The first theme displayed the stalwart faith of American servicemen. A telling large photo in the *Far East* represented the experience some in the Society had with "GIs" overseas. The cover photo featured two men wearing muddy boots, kneeling together after Mass, one a soldier in uniform and one a priest in his alb.[355] Father Lawrence D. McMahon, a Chicago native, returned to his mission in Bhamo, Burma (now Myanmar), after three years of internment by the Japanese in Mandalay, and reported that he had met GIs from every state in the Union. He observed, "Everyone is impressed by the militant faith shown by the Catholic soldiers in their regular attendance at Mass and fervent reception of the Sacraments." Not only was this example edifying, but he thought the GIs' witness "is bound to have a beneficial effect" for missionary work. "Prior to the war, many of the Kachin hill tribesmen were under the impression that all Americans were Baptists. Now when they see U.S. Catholic soldiers faithful to their religious obligations, the Kachins have to revise some of their mistaken opinions."[356]

The second theme related the interaction between Columbans on the missions and Armed Forces personnel, the latter providing assistance, both financially and in rebuilding schools and churches that had been bombed. The *Far East* had a tear off sheet directed toward service men and women during the War. The page was small enough to be clipped from the magazine and sent to a brother, son or daughter in the service, thereby alerting overseas personnel of Columban presence on the missions. Servicemen wrote to the Society and sent prayers and contributions for the missions. Periodically, letters from servicemen were printed in the magazine, including one from a Navy Lieutenant. "In almost every port we find the little churches which mission work has made available for ourselves as well as the natives." He mentioned that he and another

---

[355]   *FE* (June 1945).

[356]   "Mission News Service," 23 August 1945. Lawrence D. McMahon (1913–1989) was assigned to Burma (now Myanmar) in 1939 and remained there until 1972, when ill health forced his return to the United States. After McMahon's captivity, he was treated in India by Columban Father Richard Steinhilber's sister, Marion, who served there in the U.S. Army Nurse Corps.

man on the ship "are already members of St. Columbans, so before the evening rosary on board, he mentioned to the sailors he was sending a few dollars to you and would be glad to send other contributions your way. We collected this sum ($58.00) in five minutes. They are a wonderful lot, Father, and I am proud to be a member of them." The Lieutenant sent the letter and money, with the remark that the money was from the USS _____ Rosary Society and "we wish you to remember us as such."[357] Each month along with the recently deceased donors' names printed in the magazine, the names of those who had died in the armed forces were also listed.

After the war, some of the Columban missions benefitted from surplus materials from the American Armed Forces. Lieutenant Thomas M. Flatley of the U.S. Army wrote about his several days' stay with Father James McDevitt (1912–1981), the Columban Pastor of King of Kings Cathedral in Lingayen, Philippines after the Americans had landed. It was "in his GI wanderings" that he met McDevitt, "a man who loves Lingayen." After three years of Japanese occupation from 1942 to 1945, the bombings, shelling, and eventually, "the final stand of the Japanese with their scorched earth policy," the Philippines had suffered much destruction. The Lingayan Cathedral was in ruins. The rectory, convent and new chapel, which had been completed just before the war started, were also in shambles. Five of the Columban priests had been killed. No materials for rebuilding were coming into the country, but "thanks to the GIs in the vicinity, the priests acquired discarded wooden crates which formerly held airplane parts. These were creatively recycled to lay a floor and raise walls. The convent building walls read "this side up," "fragile," and "handle with care." Parishioners wove together palm leaves for a church roof, while a Filipino designed an altar made from bamboo.

Flatley shared McDevitt's rectory and its inconveniences and viewed up close the daily life of a missionary. As the Lieutenant put it, "I practically pulled duties with him." He served his daily Mass, saw the numerous people who came each day to seek help for the dying, a marriage, or for other assistance. The Pastor's diet was a bit enriched beyond rice and fish: "Thanks to the thoughtfulness of G.I.s, [Father] brags of dehydrated eggs and occasionally, potatoes." Pastor of an area with 40,000 people and the only priest available, McDevitt "sees grand possibilities of a postwar Jeep in his plans," as a way to get to people in the island's interior. Flatley concluded his article with an appeal. "If you can't give them (the missionaries) anything, offer your prayers or at least write to them."[358]

Another story in the *Far East* told of some U.S. Army Chaplains from Company 594 B and S Engineers in Luzon, who roamed the streets helping

---

[357]   *FE* (April 1943), 9.

[358]   Lt. Thomas Flatley, "At Home in the Philippines," *FE* (March 1946), 3–5.

the wounded and anointing the dying Filipinos. They were surprised to find the Columbans doing the same thing.[359] Some of the Company helped to reconstruct the bombed chapel in the city as well.

In 1941, a new method of constructing buildings quickly and cheaply for war time use was developed at Quonset Point, Rhode Island, near where a new Navy base (Davisville) was being constructed. In March 1941, as the military built up its readiness for war, two men from the George A. Fuller Company were asked by the military to design a hut based on U.S. specifications, but they needed to do so within two months. The Quonset Hut, from a Native American word for "boundary," was a versatile, mobile, and readily assembled multipurpose facility. After the War, the practical-minded Columbans were looking for a surplus army building to use for a chapel at the overcrowded Silver Creek. However, the town outbid the Diocese of Buffalo for the area's allotment, so the Society resorted to a Quonset hut for use as a chapel. The Bristol seminary also sought a Quonset hut for an office but none were available.[360] In the end, Bristol later built a new seminary.

Father Patrick O'Connor, *Far East* Editor, War Correspondent

The editorship of the *Far East* changed editorial hands since its early direction under E. J. McCarthy and Paul Waldron. As more missions opened in and beyond China, the magazine included articles about the Columban Fathers, Columban Sisters missions and the Sisters of Loretto, who worked with the Columbans in Hanyang. A new editor, Father Patrick O'Conner (1899–1987) would cut his editorial teeth as a newly ordained priest and he would go on in the next decades to become a respected foreign correspondent for the National Catholic Welfare Conference. He began with a shaky start, however, when, after ordination in 1923 at St. Columban Seminary, Dalgan, he became ill with tuberculosis shortly after his assignment to the United States. In July 1924, O'Connor apparently stayed at the rented cottage in Clear Lake, Iowa, "where the rising generations of the mission are refreshed during the summer holidays."[361] But by fall, he went for treatment of tuberculosis to St. Joseph/

---

[359] Dermot Feeny, "U.S. Chaplains Pitch In," *FE* (December 1946), 4–5, 20.

[360] Waldron to O'Hara, bishop of Buffalo, 7 June 1946; O'Hara to Waldron 12 June 1946. *Casey History* (1946), 11.

[361] By 1923, the Society rented a cottage in Clear Lake, Iowa, where seminarians from Omaha and the rector in July and spiritual director in August, as well as other Columbans spent vacation time. The summer retreat was given there for the seminarians. In the summer of 1923, the retreat was preached by Father Ignatius Hamill, SJ, of Creighton University, "a staunch personal friend of St. Columbans." The cottage was "understood as a real camping affair, where you cook your own

Mercy Hospital, San Diego, from at least September 1924, into the early months of 1926.[362] Father E. J. McCarthy, himself recovering from surgery, as well as having eye trouble, reassumed editorship for almost a year.[363] O'Connor had no experience in getting out a magazine (nor was he able to type). He did have literary talent and sensitivity.

From his hospital room, O'Connor wrote to McCarthy in Omaha with ideas and suggested a "tone" for some of the articles in the Columban the magazine. While McCarthy had suggested a serial feature, whose focus might be a "missionary new curate," O'Connor noted that any serial would need to be "snappy," a favorite word in his suggestions. O'Connor had written some short pieces with a "Chinese" flavor but with "Yank" vocabulary. He was running out of ideas along that line and felt he didn't have enough material to write further in that vein.

O'Connor, aware of the style and direction of a wide array of magazines, had his own ideas for the content of the *Far East*. He suggested a half or full page of jokes ("while people might skim through a magazine, they'll always read the jokes"); cookery recipes ("women read these avidly, I think"), and a "Question Box" ("Catholics—and, of course, Protestants—have difficulties over all kinds of ordinary things. They don' like talking with the pastor and they love that Question Box.")[364]

Writing from the hospital on Christmas, 1925, by now under treatment for about a year, O'Connor confided to McCarthy: "May I ask for special prayers for one of my intentions. I have lately been suffering pretty bad from what the spiritual writers call 'desolation.' It's a long time since I had so much of it. . . . Sometimes these blues—whatever they should be called—lift for a while. I think they have something to do with my barrenness in regard to short stories just

---

grub. The touch of the matronly hand will be absent from the pie-dish." *Bellevue Booster and Mission News Letter* (August 1923), 1. The pastor of Clear Lake, Father Bacci, placed his church at the disposal of the Society in the summers they were there and gave them a second hand Ford to use. "It is a sight for all Iowa to see two or three priests and about 12 students more or less travelling on this vehicle each morning [to church]. *Bellevue Booster and Mission News Letter* (August 1924), 1.

[362] St. Joseph Hospital was founded in San Diego in 1890 as a five bed dispensary, operated by the Sisters of Mercy. In 1924 the hospital moved to Fifth and Washington in San Diego and was renamed Mercy Hospital. O'Connor was a patient in 1924 and 1925. St. Joseph Hospital was a teaching hospital, and its medical practices were featured in "St. Joseph's Hospital, San Diego," The *California State Journal of Medicine* XIX, No. 5 (May 1921), 214.

[363] McCarthy had appealed to the superior general to send someone to work at the *Far East*, if even for a few months, because all personnel in Omaha, faculty and promotion staff were shorthanded. No one was available from Ireland.

[364] O'Connor to E. J. McCarthy 8 October 1925.

now. I simply feel like I couldn't ever make up a story again."[365] With the burden O'Connor felt to write some material for the magazine while recuperating, McCarthy thought they should get a Catholic short story writer for an occasional issue. This would take the form of a short story contest in the late 1930s and 1940s.

Back in good health again, O'Connor actively edited the magazine and wrote a children's section at the end of each issue. As "Nanky Poo," he presented mission news, wrote light poems ("Many Rhymes with some Reason"),[366] included a short story, sometimes obtained through a contest offered to the *Far East* readers,[367] and made young readers feel they were part of "Pudsy Kelly's Gang," all rallying around missions.[368] One could describe the tone of the children's section as "snappy," indeed. Letters from readers, photos of "*Far East* Fans" from around the country targeted high school students. A joke page appeared, as did the "Question Box." "Hints for the Home" (by MD) and "Stitches and Styles" appeared regularly to catch the attention of young and married women. The magazine featured articles about national and international Catholic events, such as the Eucharistic Congress and the Catholic Students Mission Crusade conventions, European Catholic cathedrals and shrines, and seminary life at Silver Creek. In addition to Columban Fathers and Sisters' missions and that of the Loretto Sisters, readers learned of the new community of Chinese Sisters founded by Bishop Galvin. Readers also read about the Columban mission among the Chinese in Los Angeles begun in 1940 and the outreach to the Filipino community there, starting in 1945.

O'Connor was well suited to writing and editorship and joined other editors of Catholic magazines and books, as a member of the Catholic Press Association (CPA). The Association had a few tentative starts going back to 1889 but solidified as an organization of editors of Catholic publications in 1911. In May 1944, O'Connor was elected president of the CPA but to comply with a government request, no conventions were held in 1945, so technically

---

[365]   O'Connor to E. J. McCarthy 25 December 1925.

[366]   O'Connor wrote the words for the early Columban hymn, "This Splendid Cause," the Society's "Rallying Song." The music was composed by Father George O'Neill, SJ. O'Connor thought, "the air is a nice one. . . . To my mind the air is a bit like the conventional college song or crusade hymn. It hasn't the spontaneous fire of a real war-song of a big Cause." O'Connor to E. J. McCarthy 25 December 1925.

[367]   Between 1943 and 1945, Mrs. Mary Lanigan Healy of Los Angeles won the contest at least five times.

[368]   O'Connor's poems were collected in *Pudsy Kelly's Gang*, by Nanky Poo (St. Columbans, NE, 1936), Third Edition. "A wandering minstrel I—A thing of shreds and patches, Of ballad songs and snatches, And dreamy lullaby!" Ibid., Frontispiece. The other "character" in the children's section was written by "Colum," who was Father Paul Waldron.

O'Connor was still in office in December 1945.[369] Given the Columban contacts overseas where war had touched millions of people, in 1945 O'Connor was appointed the official Foreign Correspondent for the National Catholic News Service for Japan, China, Korea, and Vietnam. In 1946 he was stationed in Tokyo, the heart of one of the defeated and nuclear bombed Axis powers and, for a while, a U.S. occupied country. From Japan O'Connor traveled to China, Hong Kong, Vietnam, and Indo-China to report on the situation of the Catholic Church and missions in the countries and to provide Americans and others with what he saw to be an objective view of the situations he encountered. A respected journalist, he was known to General Douglas MacArthur and interviewed Premier Zhou Enlai twice in 1947 in Nanjing and in Yenan, China. O'Connor's reports were published widely through the NCWC news releases, while some of his reports appeared in the *Far East.*

O' Connor established the Hua Ming News Agency at the Catholic Central Bureau in Shanghai in 1948, though that bureau was closed when Communists came to power in China. He then returned to Japan as his base. In 1950 he went to Korea as a war correspondent during most of the war. When possible, he "hitched rides" on military planes when regulations permitted.[370] He was later recognized for his journalism, winning the Catholic Press Association award in 1956 and the St. Francis de Sales Award in 1964 for "his long-term contributions to the Catholic Press."[371]

Another dimension of Columban involvement with military is the experience of Father John O'Donovan (1895–1959), who was assigned to the United States in 1924, after teaching at the seminary in Dalgan. He was rector of Silver Creek (1924–1930), professor of dogmatic theology at Omaha (1931–34), and vice director of the region (1934–1947). He then took on an unusual assignment while Japan was occupied by Allied Powers, as the Catholic Adviser under the direction of Douglas MacArthur, Supreme Commander of Allied Powers (SCAP).

Catholics also learned about Columban mission work after the war through two half-hour film programs that aired on television in 1948: one about

---

[369]   Patrick O'Connor to James A. Doyle, Executive Director, Catholic Press Association 1 March 1971. Folder: Patrick O'Connor.

[370]   Patrick O'Connor to James A. Doyle, Executive Director, Catholic Press Association 1 March 1971. Folder: Patrick O'Connor.

[371]   To: James A. Doyle, from Charles J. McNeill (Catholic Lists, Inc.). Later McNeill and Kane "persuaded several talented laymen to go to Nebraska to work with the Columban Fathers on their mission magazine: James T. Feely, Tom Galardi, and Vito Cioffero." Ibid., See also, "Father Patrick O'Connor, Bridging the Gap in Hong Kong: 1956–1970," China Reflections," published by the Columban Fathers in Hong Kong, Vol. 17 No.1 (January 2012), 7–8.

Columban work in Burma (now Myanmar) and one on Korea. A program on China was scheduled for 1949.[372]

Expansion of Promotion (Mission Procure) Houses

Sustaining the financial dimension of the missions remained a priority for the U.S. region. In addition to appeals in the *Far East*, the priests at the seminaries raised funds locally. Rector William Kelly at Bristol wrote that, "Bristol has many small circles to run weekly parties for us, and as we can, we work in an occasional large one." However, Bishop Galvin "says this is haphazard and without real stability or solidity. He holds that the man in Boston should go out merely to supply names to the bureau. The bishop's desire was that *every* Columban house should have a mission bureau, with a "man assigned full time for the job."[373]

Unable to go to travel to missions overseas during the war, Columbans assigned in that capacity were available for promotion in the States. By end of the 1940s, specific Mission Procure or Promotion houses had opened in San Diego (1941), Los Angeles (1941), Perryville, Maryland (1941), Milton, Massachusetts (1946), St. Paul (1948), Chicago (1948), and San Francisco (1949). [374]

Groundwork to open a Columban promotion house in Los Angeles had been laid in their mission among Mexicans, Chinese and Filipinos in the first half of the 1940s. Father Richard Ranaghan, one of men in the first band of the Society to head to China in 1920, had already made friends with people in the movie industry in Los Angeles, when he stopped there to get ideas about the development of what would become his classic film on Columbans in China. For a few months in 1941, the Society rented a bungalow on East Twentieth Street in Los Angeles. The physical arrangement of the house was not helpful for mission promotion, so they left that location in January 1942, for a house on Park Row, which was nearer to the Chinese population, something which Father John Cowhig, who had begun an apostolate among the Chinese in 1940, saw as advantageous.[375] As a promotion house, however, the house had disadvantages.

---

[372]   Society of St. Columban, Director, *News Bulletin* (1948/1949).

[373]   William Kelly to Waldron 2 September 1935.

[374]   A mission promotion house opened in Brooklyn in 1950, as a successor to the house formerly in Perryville, Maryland.

[375]   There was a difference of opinion between Father Gerard Marinen and Father Cowhig about the nature of Marinen's assignment to the Los Angeles house. Cowhig "was convinced that the house in Los Angeles and everything and everyone connected with it were there for the sole purpose of promoting the apostolate to the Chinese. . . . I was quite certain that Fr. Waldron's mind was that I should promote

The building was on a hill, remote from major areas of the city, and not easily accessible. Instead of spending money to rent another house, the Society then bought a house on Elden Avenue by 1942,[376] thanks to Mrs. Logan O'Brien, a good friend of the Society. She had searched the city for strategic locations for their house and had provided some of the furnishings in the house they had earlier rented.

The Perryville, Maryland, location came through the connection that Father Timothy Leahy (1894–1970) had with Edmond John Fitzmaurice, the bishop of Wilmington, Delaware. Born in Ireland, Leahy was ordained for the Diocese of Davenport, Iowa, in 1919. At some point he became a United States citizen. After he joined the Columbans in 1926, he did promotion work in Ireland and then was sent to Hanyang. Back in the United States in 1940, he was impeded from returning to China after the bombing of Pearl Harbor, so he was assigned to promotion. In the continued search to get openings in the Northeast, Leahy checked with Bishop Fitzmaurice, a relative by marriage, to see about opening a house in that diocese. The bishop gave permission and in 1941 the Society rented a house in the center of Perryville, close to the railroad tracks. There weren't any houses for sale. The "various government factories and projects were within a few miles: workers were pouring in; e.g., 20,000 naval cadets would be arriving in a week or so."[377] Leahy, who in the meantime joined the Canadian Forces as chaplain, had suggested strongly to the regional superior that there be several men in the house, especially for companionship. He observed, "Perryville is Protestant, bigoted, lonely, and the very reverse of stimulating for a man hoping to build up a propaganda machine in a completely new field."[378] After two years of rental, the Society did purchase a house in 1943, and in the summer of 1944, the *Far East* editorial staff was transferred from Omaha to Perryville, partially because of crowding in Omaha and partially because of the difficult situation in Perryville and the need Leahy stated for companionship for anyone sent to work from this location.[379]

In 1949, the *Far East* staff moved from Perryville to Milton seminary and a house in Brooklyn, New York, was purchased in 1950 to supersede the Perryville

---

Society interests in Los Angeles." Marinen indicated that the E. Twentieth Street house was rented at Cowhig's instigation." Gerard Marinen, "The Society in Los Angeles," (3 November 1958), 6. CFA-USA.

[376]   The SSC Archives *Green Book* is missing for 1942 but the 1943 book lists the Elden Avenue address, Los Angeles.

[377]   Timothy Leahy to John Loftus, 13 June 1943. Folder: Perryville, Maryland. Leahy's autobiography is Father Timothy Leahy, *Beyond Tomorrow* (Dublin: Massey Brothers Ltd., 1968).

[378]   Timothy Leahy to John Loftus, 13 June 1943. Folder: Perryville, Maryland.

[379]   The staff consisted of Fathers Patrick O'Connor, Edward De Persio, and Thomas Murphy.

house. Brooklyn was considered a prime location for the Columbans, especially after the war. New York was the port from which fifty missionaries came through from Ireland on their way to the missions, due to difficulty in obtaining a passage through the Suez Canal. They had large quantities of material for the missions to look after as they traveled from New York to San Francisco. While the Columbans had a Procure in San Francisco to arrange these matters, in New York the young men did not have that assistance. A second reason offered was the care of missionaries returning from China and elsewhere. Some of them needed hospitalization immediately when they came to New York, something the Society did not learn until New York relatives of the missionaries told them. A further "sentimental" reason was given: "Bishop Galvin is now an old man and many times has expressed the desire before he dies he may see the Society have a house in the Diocese in which it took root."[380]

Bishop Thomas E. Molloy gave permission to "establish a hospice [in Brooklyn] for the convenience of certain members of [our] Religious Community . . . before departure for other sections of our Country or of the world."[381] The "natural purchaser" of the house owned by Mrs. Mannix on President Street, was "our corporation at Silver Creek."[382] To obtain funds for the purchase in addition to what Dalgan had approved and the hefty "donation" Mrs. Mannix would give, Father Edward Maguire (1887–1957) noted that "the [Brooklyn] priests alone are certain to give us a substantial amount. I cannot tell you how happy they are that we are getting a Brooklyn home. In fact, they seem to be the friendliest priests I've met since I came to the country."[383] Maguire, Fathers Vincent McFadden and Michael Douglas were assigned to the house which opened in February 1950. Many in Brooklyn remembered Bishop Galvin, when he had been a Curate from 1909–1912 at Holy Rosary Parish. In 2014 the parish celebrated its 125th anniversary. They installed in the church a bronze plaque with an engraving of the bishop's face and a list of important dates in his life.[384]

The new promotion houses were in addition to Omaha, Bristol, and Silver Creek. With more locations, promotion teams were begun in those houses at the same time. In 1949, Father Timothy Connolly "called a meeting in Derby, New York, for all the [men] who were scattered round the country who were doing talks in churches and tried to set up some kind of organization—districts

---

[380] Director to Very Rev. Edward Maguire 31 October 1949.

[381] Bishop Molloy to [Edward] Maguire, 6 December 1949. *Casey History* (1949), 12. Maguire had opened the Columban house in San Francisco in 1947.

[382] Connolly [?] to [Edward] Maguire 24 January 1950.

[383] Maguire to Connolly 8-A-36.9 19 December 1949.

[384] John Marley, "Galvin Remembered," 25 November 2014. The material is from Marley's detailed account of Columban participation in the anniversary.

and promotion houses and that kind of thing."[385] The Chicago mission house, which also served as a vocation house to encourage men in the surrounding area to dedicate their lives to the missions, opened at 5714 North Sheridan Road in 1948. Father Thomas L. Convery was appointed the first superior of the group. A native of New Jersey and ordained in 1940, he would have known priests and people in the Chicago area because he had spent the previous five years as an assistant pastor in Oak Park, a Chicago suburb. Other Columban priests from the Chicago area were highlighted in the *Far East*: Patrick Brennan, superior of the Columban Asian Mission, Thomas P. Kane, Charles O'Brien, Lawrence McMahon, Robert Cullen, and the three priest brothers Robert Degnan (who was assigned to the Chicago house when it opened), Francis Degnan, and Charles Degnan. [386]

Other Developments Across the Region

A post–World War II surge in the number of seminarians across the country would necessitate construction at all three Columban seminaries. The Bristol seminary had the highest number of Probationers (24) in 1950, something which occasioned conversation about how to deal with what could be an overcrowded situation and perhaps too many Probationers for one director.[387] Father William Kelly in Bristol suggested that perhaps the incoming class of 1950 could possibly be divided, with one group under Kelly and the other group under the direction of Father Thomas Hanahoe (spiritual director at the St. Columban in Nebraska), or perhaps that students could take philosophy before they become Probationers. None of these suggestions was accepted, however, and the Probationers all came to Bristol.

Regional Director Timothy Connolly wrote to the priests during Easter Week, 1950, about the continued importance of frugality. He mentioned "the economy of the country going through a crisis" in 1949, the fact that "the Society has had to draw heavily on funds accumulated in better times because at present it is not balancing expenditure with income."[388] More seminarians meant a need for more space. The letter provides a window into one aspect of the spirit of the Society. After pointing out that the income of the region was

---

[385] Father James McCaslin interview of Father Peter McPartland (1912–1987), Columban Oral History Archive. Date of interview unknown.

[386] The Chicago Mission Procure was featured in *FE* (January 1949), 19. Readers learned some background on each of the Chicago Columbans named in the article.

[387] Kelly to Timothy Connolly, 8-A-32-49.

[388] Timothy Connolly to all the Priests of the [U.S.] Region 1 August 1949. *Casey History* (1949), 10.

expected to cover its domestic expenses with a small surplus, the problem was that the "surplus" still fell short of the amount of money expected to send to the missions by roughly $100,000. Urging "utmost care in incurring expenses," even though the men had not taken a vow of poverty, as did men religious, Connolly reminded the men about the region's obligation "not to fail in its duty to our brothers in the missions, the poverty of whose lives as compared with ours is—or ought to be—well known to every priest in the region. It is relevant here to draw attention to the magnificent spirit of generosity which inspires these missionaries of ours to give, without a thought, their personal funds and what should be their personal leisure to the service of their missions." With careful attention each month to the expenses of that period and with each one taking responsibility for his expenditures, "each priest can cooperate to achieve the goal of providing monies needed on the missions. Such cooperation has been generously given in the past. Thrift may not be a Columban charism but generosity and appreciation of the needs of the missions certainly are. So, too, are the spirit of self-sacrifice and hard work unaccompanied by the blare of trumpets, and, in most cases, unrewarded by any pat on the back."[389]

In spite of a tough financial picture in the region, the early 1950s would bring a "building boom" for the Society. The seminary in Nebraska in 1949 had added a building as a dormitory for major seminarians, Bristol would construct a new building starting in 1950, and Milton, Massachusetts, followed suit a few years later. The Columbans would again experience war time in their missions. This time it would be the Korean "Conflict."

---

[389]   Fr. Connolly to All Columban Priests in the Region of America. Easter Week, 1950. 9-A-11. CFA-USA.

CHAPTER 4

Postwar Building Boom and the Communist Threat (1950–1964)

After World War II, as Armed Forces men and women returned home to start families or return to the family life they left prior to the war, the veterans were assisted in a number of ways, including the provision of funds for professional training and higher education. Various housing finance plans became available and suburbs opened up a "building boom." With the number of seminarians gradually increasing in the 1950s, the Columbans had their own "building boom." Between 1949 and 1963, two new seminaries were built, and two other seminaries were remodeled and added buildings. The 1950s were a time of great patriotism and "revival" of religion in the United States, epitomized during President Eisenhower's administration with the inclusion of "under God" in the line of the pledge of allegiance: "one nation, under God." Evangelist Billy Graham frequented the Eisenhower White House. Church affiliation grew, especially among Protestants.[390] City dwellers moved to "suburbs" and southern Blacks and Puerto Ricans moved into the cities. For many people, it seemed that the 1950s were a time of stability and somewhat monolithic. In the 1960s, the eyes of the United States were being directed toward South America, through the Alliance for Progress, the Papal Volunteers for Latin America (PAVLA), and the Peace Corps.

A war in Korea and the growth of Communism in the "Cold War" era gave added depth to the measure of mission vocation and provided for the training of lay leaders, especially through Columban promotion of the Legion

---

[390]   Statistics for the declaration of church affiliation indicate a rise from 43 per cent in 1910 to 62.4 per cent in 1970. Sydney E. Ahlstrom, *A Religious History of the American People*, volume 2 (Garden City, NY: Doubleday, 1975), 448. See also, A. Roy Eckart, *The Surge of Religion in America: An Appraisal* (NY: Association Press, 1958).

of Mary. In the short time of the presidency of John F. Kennedy (January 20, 1961–November 22, 1963), the first Catholic to be elected to that office, the Cuban missile crisis, the failure of the "Bay of Pigs" invasion (Cuba), the "race to the moon," and threat of Russian invasion of the United States were part of the fabric of American life. For Catholics, and ultimately with an impact on Christianity around the world, Pope John XXIII on the feast of the Conversion of St. Paul, January 25, 1959, announced an Ecumenical Council of the whole church. This event, which opened on October 11, 1962, would have a major impact on every area of church life, including seminary formation, the relationship of the church to the world, and understandings of mission.

In the Columban world, Father Timothy Connolly, who had been U.S. regional superior from 1947–1952, was elected superior general at the 1952 General Chapter. The previous superior general, Father Jeremiah Dennehy, had died of cancer, four years after he was elected to that office (1947–1951). Father Peter McPartland became U.S. regional director (1952–1962), followed by Father Daniel Boland (1962–1967). Two Columban "giants" died a year apart: the founder of the Society, Edward Galvin, and Edward J. McCarthy, the first U.S. regional director. With the Columbans in Omaha, periodically having to fight to keep the post office they had in the regional headquarters, the establishment of a "Zip Code" system and two-letter state names on July 1, 1963, put the Columbans on the postal map as St. Columbans, NE, 68056.

Four Seminaries: A Building Boom

When Superior General Connolly returned from his visitation of the Society's missions and seminaries in 1954, he reported that his experience gave him "a new and clearer appreciation of the difficulties that confront us on the missions, and increased, if possible, the determination with which [the Columbans] are solving them." Missions in Asia, including the Philippines, and South America, had expanded greatly after World War II. Growth created a financial issue as well. Society income, which fluctuated depending on bequests, appeals, and donor's response to the magazine, was not keeping pace with the expansion, which meant that budget cuts would have to be made for everyone. A corollary, he wrote, was that "personnel in existing missions would need to be stabilized," the Society might have to be satisfied with "a much slower rate of progress," and "a ratio established between income and development." As had been the message of previous U.S. regional directors (including Connolly himself), "the more economically we can live and the fewer personal demands we make on the Society, the more money will there be for mission expansion."[391]

---

[391]   Superior General Timothy Connolly letter in [U.S. Region] *News Bulletin* (July 1954).

The letter came after the region had just finished two major building projects: a new house for Probationers at Bristol (1951) and a new major seminary in Milton, Massachusetts (1953–54). Building supplies were once again more available to the public and new materials for construction had been developed during wartime. Columban construction would also include reconfiguration of the vacated major seminary at Omaha (1953/54), an addition to the Silver Creek seminary (approval in 1961for expansion), a new college seminary in Oconomowoc, Wisconsin (cornerstone laid in 1962), and at the same time, a new office building (1961), chapel and the remodeling of the U.S. center of operations in Nebraska (1962–63). This could be called the Columban era of "bricks and mortar" to house and educate more seminarians in the post–World War II era and to organize Promotions with modern equipment and procedures.

A New Building for Columban Probationers in Bristol

At the start World War II, the Columbans in the United States had three seminaries, two of which followed the European model of education: at Silver Creek, a classical high school or minor seminary, which included an additional year of Latin[392] and a major seminary in Omaha, with two years of philosophy (Philosophers) and four years of theology (Divines). The Silver Creek seminary, however, did not have accreditation from the State of New York for certification.[393] The Society followed the pattern until the early 1950s, when a two-year program was added after high school to make a four year college course when combined with the two years of philosophy, though still without state certification. The yearlong program of prayer and study of the Columban Constitutions and material related to the spiritual life was held in Bristol before the young men began their studies at the Major Seminary. By 1954, 157 men attended their three seminaries.

The first major building program of the period took place at Bristol. The architect was Barry Byrne (1883–1967),[394] who would later be interviewed by Studs Terkel for his *Division Street: America* (1967). The original house and the clubhouse at Bristol had been renovated for various purposes, the latter facility pressed into service over the years for student recreation, a classroom, a

---

[392] Silver Creek remained a five year program at least until 1949, which included an additional year of Latin.

[393] The seminary curriculum at Silver Creek in the 1940s and 1950s included French, English, Arithmetic, Algebra, Geometry, History, Religion, Elocution, Sciences, Biology, Geography, Latin, Greek, and Ceremonies.

[394] Byrne's full name was Francis Xavier Ignatius Loyola Walter Barry Byrne. He was the oldest of six children, whose father died when Barry was thirteen years old. Barry became responsible for supporting the family.

dormitory, and a "getaway" place for seminarians.[395] In a letter to John Donovan, William Kelly, the director of probationers, laid out potential physical spaces to rearrange at Bristol with an upcoming class of fifteen or more for fall 1947, provided they could get a Quonset hut. The hut could be made into an office, the present office could become a classroom and the back part of the room, where the priests did their work, could become a dormitory. Taking out the side altars in chapel would accommodate more students, though "it would leave the Fathers with no place to sit at Benediction and Night Prayers. But we could get by."[396]

But in 1951, funds were made available for a new building with construction. Initially a three story dormitory with a school block building, the seminary was completed in 1952 and the old house torn down. Ambrose Gallagher, assigned to Promotion from the Bristol location, was called upon to oversee the Bristol construction, which was under contract with the Central Engineering Company. The diocese had a strong tradition of support of labor unions and when it was thought that the Columbans might employ nonunion painters for the interior in order to save costs, Mr. Pothier of Central Construction Company and some of the subcontractors "told us that we were getting adverse publicity in union circles, [some of whom] still felt sure that when they finished we would bring in the nonunion painters." Gallagher wrote, "Anyone of us who has been on propagation work knows that we cannot afford to antagonize the laboring class, the majority of whom are now unionized. We have been in trouble over such a small thing as tickets for benefits printed without the union labor. Our future support depends upon this class." He reminded the Society of the large amount of effort that had gone "into securing friends to assist us in our work. We would be finished if we lost their support."

The outcome of the painting situation was that the head of the union shop for painting was willing to use the paints the Columbans had purchased and apply two coats by brush for a cost that was $310 cheaper than a nonunion painter.[397] The cost of the Bristol building, which had asphalt tile floors and aluminum windows, was $1.00 per cubic foot. Byrne took quite a bit of time designing the drive from the street to the front of the building and around to the kitchen entrance. The land did not drain properly, a factor which would also impact the drain for the large refrigerator in the kitchen. The building

---

[395] "An idea that had been taking shape for some time about moving the classroom to the top floor was discussed with Barry. At first he didn't like it, but after a visit to the scene and much discussions and measurements he came around to our point of view enthusiastically." The dedication of the "Dormitory" at Bristol took place on June 4, 1951, with 1,000 people in attendance, according to a newspaper clipping. The building cost $250,000. *Casey History* (1951), 5.

[396] William M. Kelly to John (Donovan) 26 September 1946. *Casey History* (1946).

[397] Statement by Ambrose Gallagher 7 April 1951. *Casey History* (1951), 4.

sported a "modern feature" of glass blocks around the edges of the building. Problems soon arose with the heating system, a "bulge" in one of the outside walls, and a leaking roof, which had not been sealed properly.

The new building withstood Hurricane Carol, which struck on August 31, 1954. The storm direction followed the same pattern as did the more devastating 1938 hurricane, "though last Tuesday's version was mercifully shorter by several hours than the 1938 one." With winds of ninety miles per hour, the storm surge was up to 14.4 feet in Narragansett Bay, when it came on land just after high tide. There were seventeen deaths in Rhode Island blamed on the storm and its aftermath. In addition to destruction of hundreds of buildings, roofs torn off, thousands of downed trees, and ruined crops just at the height of harvest, all of Rhode Island lost electrical power. William Kelly at Bristol reported the consequences for them. "We probably will lose all the meat in our deep freeze. It will take at least a week to restore the power lines." Kelly further noted that "Everything built on the beach over the years has been swept away, of course, and we have lost about forty trees," while the shoreline was filled with debris."[398] A new Columban recruit, Robert I. O'Rourke, who had done some of his seminary training in the Archdiocese of Chicago, arrived by train and bus for his Spiritual Year at Bristol just two days after the hurricane went through. "Came into Bristol, trees all over the roads and no power and then I came to this building—it was a very impressive, very modern looking square. We would spend the whole year cleaning up the grounds after the hurricane. . . . The boss was Father William Kelly, of course. Barney Toal was the number two man."[399] Father Gerard Smith, engaged in promotion work at the time, was staying with his family at a nearby summer cottage. They "were very lucky to escape with their lives. Gerry lost everything except the clothes on his back. . . . No trace even of the foundations of the cottage remains."[400] In fall 1965, a Chapel Wing was built, with dedication of the square shaped chapel on September 25, 1966.

A New Seminary and a New Context in the Archdiocese of Boston

The physical location of the major seminary (the last six years of priesthood preparation) had been discussed in the 1930s and with fluctuating numbers of seminarians the topic rose again in the 1940s. The construction of a student dormitory in 1949 helped ease housing for a greater number of seminarians in

---

[398]   William Kelly to "Dear Pete" [Peter McPartland] 2 September 1954.

[399]   Joseph McSweeny interview of Father Robert I. O'Rourke, 2011. O'Rourke was missioned to Burma (now Myanmar).

[400]   William Kelly to "Dear Pete" [Peter McPartland] 2 September 1954. The hurricane was so devastating to the New England area, that the name "Carol" was retired from the list of names for hurricanes.

Nebraska.[401] As noted earlier, Richard Cushing had advocated a major seminary at Bristol on his frequent visits there. Now, as archbishop of Boston, he invited the Society to the archdiocese. The April 1945, *Far East* published the invitation and welcome that Cushing gave to the Columbans to open a "foreign mission seminary," one of two dreams he had for the Archdiocese when he became archbishop.

In December 1945, the region received permission to spend up to $70,000 for a seminary site in the Boston area and in 1946, the Columbans purchased a house in Milton, ten miles south of Boston. The historical and cultural heritage of the area put the Columbans in a setting that would be a challenge for their acceptance in the neighborhood. The Town of Milton, established in 1662, was formed from a section of Dorchester that the Native Americans called *Uncataquissett*. The "Blue Hills lands" were divided between Milton and Braintree in 1712. In the nineteenth century, the establishment of a new town (Hyde Park) and two other land divisions between Milton and Quincy, left the Town of Milton more or less with its current boundaries. One might get a sense of the mid to late 1880s social and cultural mind-set in Milton, suggested on the cover of Albert K. Teele's 1887, *A History of Milton*: "God sifted a whole nation that He might send choice grain over into the wilderness."[402] While the quotation was taken from Governor Stoughton's Election Sermon of 1668, Teele and the Organization of Town Historians who helped gather the documents, began the story with the Massachusetts Native Americans (the Neponset tribe, a remnant of the Massachusetts whose range was between the Blue Hills and Boston Bay), the removal of the Indians, land grants, farming, churches, civic institutions and a history of early businesses in the town of Milton,[403] ice block cutting and shipping, and the mill on the Neponset River crucial to creating and shipping products beyond the town and the state.

Forests had covered one of the three hills upon which Milton sat, but a fire had consumed the trees, with new growth only at the "brush stage" when settlers began their farms and identified the area as Brush Hill. Part of the area near where the Columbans would build was a swamp. Into the twentieth century, some farming continued, as did the mill businesses on the Neponset River. The forests had grown back in some areas. Some of the earliest homes in

---

[401]   When the Major Seminary program moved to Milton in 1953, the student dormitory building in Bellevue was used as an office building until 1961 when it became a retreat center, which purpose it still serves in 2017.

[402]   Albert K. Teele, *A History Of Milton from 1640 to 1877* (Boston: Press of Rockwell and Churchill, 1887).

[403]   One of the businesses on the Neponset River that flowed between Milton and Dorchester at that point, was the Baker Chocolate Company, founded in 1738 and still going strong, though the company is located elsewhere and went through a variety of ownerships.

Milton were located on Brush Hill Road, the street upon which the Columbans bought property: Milton's second oldest house, the Robert Tucker House, at 678 (c. 1670), the Deacon Nathan Tucker House, at 703 (1799), and the James Tucker House, at 823 (1804). The Philip Leverett Saltonstall family also resided on Brush Hill Road.

The Columbans purchased the estate located at 1372 Brush Hill Road, belonging to the Howard Johnson family, owner of the chain of Howard Johnson restaurants and, later, motor lodges.[404] He and his family had moved to Milton in 1932. The Johnsons, in turn, had purchased the land from the Hallowells, one of the "First Families" of Boston with long standing social and cultural prestige. These first families, most of them Protestant, included Adams, Cabot, Saltonstall, Lodge, Sears, Lawrence, and Lowell, who often married among other first families. The social and cultural dimensions of the neighborhood and its economic affluence, quite different from what the Columbans experienced in the Bellevue and Silver Creek areas, formed the backdrop for the resistance the Society felt when they decided to construct a new seminary building that would employ a different function and character than the architectural styles in the Brush Hill neighborhood.

The Society initially identified the Milton property as a minor seminary and residence for high school students who lived in the New England area."[405] In fall 1946, forty-nine students of high school age were enrolled at St. Columban Seminary, Milton.[406] The Johnson house held the dining hall, chapel, and residence hall for priests and staff. The stucco house that had belonged to the Hallowells was used for the student residence and classrooms. A smaller building contained the promotion office and administrative offices. Even with two large houses, the number of students proved a challenge to accommodate, so double decker beds were placed into their sleeping area. Classrooms and the Johnson House dining room were jammed.

---

[404] Johnson began his business near Quincy, Massachusetts, where he installed a soda fountain in a drugstore and developed a rich, creamy ice cream in twenty-eight flavors. His business grew quickly and soon he had restaurants in the northeast and along the east coast to Florida. After a downturn in business during World War II, by 1957 his business continued to grow again. Anthony M. Sammarco, *History of Howard Johnson's: How a Massachusetts Soda Fountain Became an American Icon* (Mount Pleasant, SC: The History Press, 2013).

[405] The fact is mentioned in Sister Ita Hannaway, *Missionaries Hand-in-Hand. A Celebration of the Laity's Participation in the Mission of the Missionary Sisters of St. Columban* (Wicklow, Ireland, 2010), 39.

[406] The Columban Directory, referred to as the "Greenbook," lists this high school population at Milton for just 1946.

A first thought about more space was to extend the existing Johnson house.[407] The stucco house proved sturdier and better insulated for the project. An architect, a Mister Wamsut, drew up plans for the addition to that house. But in the end, the Society decided that they would construct a new building for a major seminary.

Fund raising plans for a new building took shape. A brochure, the first page of which appeared on the cover of the March 1945, *Far East*, appealed particularly to Catholics of Irish descent to contribute toward the new foreign mission seminary in Boston. Unlike E. J. McCarthy's emphasis on the "American" face of the Society, the brochure drew upon the missionary heritage of Saint Patrick. A priest robed in Mass vestments held a shamrock placed in the center of a white cross. Light from the cross emanated onto a globe that showed "the Chinese Republic" and other Asian countries where Columbans had missions. On the bottom right of the picture was a quotation attributed to Saint Patrick: "We believe that the faithful shall come from all parts of the world." In the brochure, Archbishop Cushing provided abundant personal support to urge Catholics to take Memorials to build and equip the seminary.

Specifications were developed in October 1949, but approval was needed from the Town of Milton Board.[408] To appreciate the significance of a Catholic mission organization building an educational establishment in Milton, it is helpful to note the social environment surrounding a number of the Brush Hill Road families. Several "First Families" of Boston built country estates, large-scale suburban houses, and family "compounds." "Such men, in Boston's curious social oligarchy," wrote Cleveland Amory, "are not mere men; they are institutions."[409] In addition to the Hallowell family, the Lawrences, who had married into the Lowell family at one point, lived across the street from the Columbans. Bishop William Lawrence (1850–1941) graduated from Harvard University and succeeded Philips Brooks as Episcopal bishop of Massachusetts. The bishop had a winter home on Commonwealth Avenue, a summer home at Bar Harbor, Maine, and a fall-and-spring home in Milton.[410] His family

---

[407]   Interview of Father John Comiskey, 3 October 2013. Interviewer is not identified.

[408]   *Casey History* (1949) 27 October 1949.

[409]   Cleveland Amory, *The Proper Bostonians* (New York: E P Dutton & Co Inc, 1947), 312. Amory himself belonged to one of the Proper Bostonian families. Amory noted, however, that a "First Family institution" could not apply to those elected to the Senate. "They are too political; they cannot maintain the severe attitude toward personal publicity, which is perhaps the first requisite for a man's becoming an institution in Boston." Ibid., p.316.

[410]   Cleveland Amory, *The Proper Bostonians* (New York: E P Dutton & Co Inc, 1947), 314. McKee, who sold the Bristol property to "The Blue Spruces Corporation" (the Columbans), also had a home on Commonwealth Avenue before his finances

continued to live at the Brush Hill address, after his death. In 1998, the Brush Hill district was listed on the National Register of Historic Places.

In anticipation of building a new seminary on the property, the Society had attempted since 1951 to purchase the Morton Gould house next door and its four or five acres. The Gould land formed a small wedge shape between the two parts of the Columban property. An elderly Mrs. Gould lived there, where she raised some sheep and had several noisy, rambunctious dogs. The Society had many conversations with her about a possible purchase of the land over the next two years, but by the end of 1953, the Society gave up the idea. However, because of continued dialogue and the mutual kindness they had toward each other, Mrs. Gould "refused to sign a petition [that] a certain lady [in the Brush Hill neighborhood] tried hard to start, which would have endeavored to prevent our getting a building permit."[411] One of the reasons the Society was interested in Mrs. Gould's house and property was that it could have been used as a place for domestic help or for the Columban Sisters to live, should they work at Milton. Ambrose Gallagher mentioned to Regional Director McPartland, "We are out in the sticks and breakfast time comes early, snow storms come."[412] Having cooks and housekeepers on the premises would keep the academic year rhythm and daily *horarium* flowing more easily.

The Columbans again called upon Barry Byrne to draw up architectural plans for the major seminary. They probably had visited the Byrne designed Christ the King Church (1931) in Cork, Ireland, and would have been familiar with his style and philosophy of architecture. [413]

A contract with Walsh Brothers Construction Company of Cambridge was signed on December 26, 1951, for the new building for sixty students. Ground breaking took place on St. Patrick's Day, 1952, with Archbishop Cushing wielding the shovel. The path to completion of the seminary building was not flawless, however. Issues related to roofing and heating/ventilation systems needed to be corrected.[414] Father Joseph Murrin (1916–2002) was called to

---

plummeted). So, too, did the Currys, who, in 1952, moved their school for higher education (in 1952 called Curry College) to Milton.

[411]   Ambrose Gallagher to McPartland 14 January 1953. *Casey History* (1953), 8.

[412]   Ambrose Gallagher to McPartland 14 January 1953. *Casey History* (1953), 8.

[413]   For an analysis of Byrne's architectural style and emphases, see Sally Kitt Chappell and Ann Van Zanten, *Barry Byrne, John Lloyd Wright, Architecture and Design* (Chicago: Chicago Historical Society, 1982), which especially describes Byrne's forward thinking in relation to a renewed liturgy and the building in which it takes place, and Vincent L. Michael, *The Architecture of Barry Byrne. Taking the Prairie School to Europe* (Urbana: University of Illinois Press, 2013). The Columban projects are discussed in Ibid., 155–158. Michael interviewed Father Joseph Murrin, who oversaw the Milton Seminary construction.

[414]   See, for example, Barry Byrne to Potheir, contractor, 22 March 1952.

Milton to oversee the construction. Murrin was born and raised on a farm in Parnell, Iowa. Having heard Father Richard Ranaghan's presentation and film on the China missions, Murrin applied to the Columbans through his pastor and was accepted as a seminarian. Ordained in 1944, he worked for four years in the Columban Los Alamitos parish and was then appointed bursar and dean at the Columban Seminary, Nebraska, before moving to Milton. The versatility of skills required in successful farm life was good preparation for the task he took on at Milton. He "stayed there till all the kinks were out" of the building.[415] Murrin became well known for supervising the seminary construction and other buildings in Kwang Ju, Korea (where he also had a hand in the design of the buildings) and in Turramurra, Australia.

A separate contract was drawn up with Barry Byrne for the Milton chapel. Five hundred dollars was allotted for this, with the Columbans working with his ideas until they were satisfied. The construction cost seemed rather high to Superior General Connolly: "I know there is some reason but it is a real puzzle to me and would be to my Council, that a chapel designed to seat only about 150 should cost so much [$340,000]. It would be well when the time comes to have a detailed explanation of this."[416]

Byrne had been an apprentice in his youth with Frank Lloyd Wright in his Oak Park, Illinois, studio and had imbibed some of Wright's Prairie School of Architecture ideas. At one point, Byrne lived with two of the Wright sons in San Diego. He was a forerunner of liturgical renewal expressed through church architecture several decades before the Second Vatican Council. His articles in *Liturgical Arts, Commonweal, Catholic Art Quarterly, and American Benedictine Review* expressed his approach "to seek spatial solutions to problems of creating a new spiritual environment."[417] Among these problems was how to bring the congregation closer to the altar. His architectural drawings illustrated an integration of nave and sanctuary areas to link the priest and people.

The Milton Chapel, however, drew together congregation and celebrant "visually by modulating light and interior volume." The altar was elevated, not for separation from the people but for visibility. Byrne "exchanged physical interpenetration of the sanctuary and nave for their sensory unification . . . using long windows between structural piers to illuminate the altar rather than the nave . . . The walls and voids create the same enigmatic relationship between

---

[415]   Jim McCaslin interview of Father Joseph Murrin Columban Oral History Project 18 March 1987.

[416]   Connolly to McPartland 9 September 1952. The $340,000 was $40,000 above the cost approved a few years earlier for the entire seminary at Milton.

[417]   Byrne quoted in Chappell and Zanten, 10. Byrne's family was descended from the "famine émigrés forced to leave Ireland during the Great Famine, who came to Chicago from Prince Edward Island, the route of the poorest Irish." Michael, footnote 1, 184.

a feminine, light-filled interior and a masculine, lithic exterior of projected geometry."[418] An unusual and striking feature were the chapel windows, "massive squares set on end, their glass block grids marked by heavy zigzags of opaque blue blocks, a strident and youthful gesture." [419] The interior walls were constructed of cinder block and brick, which created an unadorned, uncluttered space, with a simple crucifix behind the altar and two candles on the extreme sides of the sanctuary. Not everyone appreciated Byrne's style. Reportedly, when Archbishop Cushing came for an ordination in the new chapel, he thought it too austere and offered to give money for a large carpet and other things to "soften" the atmosphere. In 1966 the chapel would be renovated with funds provided by Cardinal Cushing in remembrance of his Columban friend and card player, Ambrose Gallagher.

The faculty and students moved from their Bellevue location to the newly completed seminary at Milton in September 1953. The campus provided classrooms, living quarters for first and second philosophy students, the "divines," who were in the four years of theology, the faculty, the Columbans doing promotion, and guest rooms. The new chapel was ready in time for Easter services in 1954.

Another Columban building project in the 1950s, though to be constructed elsewhere but with influences from the United States, took place through the ingenuity of Harold Henry, bishop of Kwang Ju, Korea. He was visiting the States and looking for an inexpensive way to construct churches for the growing number of Catholics in his diocese. He purchased a geodesic dome at the cost of $2,500 to take back with him to Kwang Ju. The dome, the first of its kind for use as a church for his leper colony at Naju, was displayed on the Nebraska seminary grounds in time for the annual Columban festival on July 28, 1957.[420] The dome stood 19 ½ feet high, had a 39 feet diameter, 125 small stained glass windows in six different shapes, and 1200 square feet of floor space.[421] Bishop Henry had also requested the Byrne plans for his Korean churches. He had the basic floor plans but had to adapt them for his situation in Korea. Father Joseph Murrin, who oversaw the Milton construction, went to Korea to assist Henry for this and other building projects. [422]

---

[418]   Ibid., 156.

[419]   Ibid., 159.

[420]   *Newsletter* 19 July 1957. An artist's sketch of Harold Henry stands against a background which includes the geodesic dome, in *FE* (May 1960), 4–6. Henry blessed the dome church in Naju in November 1958.

[421]   *Newsletter* 19 July 1957.

[422]   In Korea, Murrin also designed and oversaw construction of schools, churches, and other buildings in the Diocese of Kwang Ju, when Bishop Harold Henry was head of the Diocese.

In the meantime, as the Columban Fathers were busy with their building project in Milton, the Columban Sisters in late October 1948 opened a house in Hyde Park, Massachusetts, a short distance from the seminary. The Sisters purchased the Peabody estate. Archbishop Cushing gave half the money to purchase the mansion and the Columban Fathers gave generously to help toward the other half of the purchase.[423] The Columban Fathers gathered some furnishings for them, including army surplus, such as "cutlery stamped with USN [United States Navy] on their dining room silverware."[424] The location was the Columban Sisters' novitiate and promotion house.

Possible Junior Seminary on the West Coast

Even though E. J. McCarthy had touted Omaha as the center of the United States and easily accessible by train from various parts of the country, the reality was that parents on the east or the west coasts would be reluctant to send their high school age boys to "the heartland." For that reason, the Society in 1952 considered opening a junior seminary on the west coast. With an impressive Columban presence in southern California among Mexican Americans and Filipinos, and with the Archdiocese of Los Angeles building many schools from which would come missionary vocations, a logical location for a seminary would be near the Westminster Parish, a hub for Columban work among people of Hispanic background.[425] The next conversation about a western junior seminary arose in 1957, with a visit to Rancho Buena Vista, Sonoma, for this purpose. The following year it was noted, "The matter of a west coast seminary keeps coming up for discussion." In January 1958, they had an "offer from a realtor in Sonoma" and were "still looking at sites around San Francisco."[426] In fall 1963, as the College seminary opened in Oconomowoc, Wisconsin, consideration was given to begin a two-year high school seminary in Camarillo, California, but by November 1964, the issue of a west coast junior seminary was dropped.[427]

---

[423]   The Columban Fathers "allowed the request of a loan when needed that was paid back interest-free over a period of time. . . . The Sisters therefore did not need a substantial bank savings account in the United States." Claire O'Rourke, SSC, *USA: Stepping Stones to China and Beyond. A Columban Missionary Presence* (Brighton, MA: Columban Sisters, 2008), 29–30. On these developments, see also, Sister Ita Hannaway, *Missionaries Hand-in-Hand. A Celebration of the Laity's Participation in the Mission of the Missionary Sisters of St. Columban* (Wicklow, Ireland, 2010), 39.

[424]   Claire O'Rourke, SSC, *Stepping Stones to China and Beyond*, 29–30.

[425]   *Casey History* (1953), 8.

[426]   *Casey History* (1958), 5. Letter from McPartland to [no receiver supplied], 13 February 1958, and same date McPartland to [Francis?] McDonald. Ibid.

[427]   Boland to Kielt, 20 November 1964. At this point, the Columbans were leaning toward a residence for students who would take classes in a local Catholic high

A College Seminary in the Midwest: Oconomowoc, Wisconsin

By 1958, the Society needed to renovate the Milton house used as the college, which was "bursting at the seams with twenty-six students." Thought was given to a possible addition to the stucco house or to construction of a new building. With "the unexpected developments on the drawing board," it became clear that the property was too small for an additional large structure.[428] There were just thirty-six acres of property and no possibility of gaining more adjacent land. In the meantime, discussion arose as to the feasibility of moving the first two years of college to the Midwest, so plans for a new building in Milton were dropped. One concern about moving from Milton was that the Seminary had recently been awarded a Massachusetts charter for their college.[429] Would leaving the state jeopardize the charter?

The Columbans at Milton were enthusiastic about a move to the Midwest. As Rector Daniel Boland put it, "I have never heard any proposal meet with such unanimous approval bordering on joyful glee."[430] Chicago was an active Promotion center for the Columbans, so setting up a college in the Midwest "would open up new contacts both with priests and people and with prospective vocations."[431] Statistics were compiled from eighteen dioceses in the Midwest as to the number of diocesan and religious priests, parishes, diocesan and religious seminaries, and the percentage of Catholics in each Diocese.[432] The names of

---

school. Ibid., This was looked back upon as an "experiment" and the Society thought they had enough going on with the new Oconomowoc seminary and with the changes that were happening in the Milton seminary program.

[428]   Richard Stokes to Peter McPartland 18 April 1959. 8-B-8. Stokes was the first rector of the seminary at Milton.

[429]   At some point in the mid-1950s, the college began an affiliation with Catholic University of America. Father Daniel Boland noted that the "Junior College had an inspection from CUA" in March 1959. Boland to McPartland, 16 April 1959. 8-B-8. Columban affiliation with CUA began earlier with the high school seminary in Silver Creek. Students took CUA faculty constructed tests in certain subjects, especially in Latin and in "classical" subjects. Schools complained about the high cost of exams, which were a money maker for CUA. Roy J. Deferrari, who became Chair of the Affiliation Committee in 1939, remarked about the unreliability of the exams themselves, "which were, all in all, put together hurriedly and carelessly and corrected in like manner." Roy J. Ferrari, *The Catholic University of America, 1918–1960* (Boston: Daughters of St. Paul, 1962), 192.

[430]   Daniel Boland to Peter McPartland 16 April 1959.

[431]   Richard Stokes to Peter McPartland 18 April 1959.

[432]   The dioceses surveyed included: Springfield (Illinois), Peoria (Illinois), Joliet (Illinois), Rockford (Illinois), Belleville (Illinois), Lafayette (Indiana), Ft. Wayne (Indiana), Indianapolis (Indiana), La Crosse (Wisconsin), Winona (Wisconsin), New Ulm (Minnesota), Dubuque (Iowa), St. Louis (Missouri), Cincinnati (Ohio), and Detroit (Michigan).

men's missionary orders were identified to see which societies had at least one formation house or seminary in the diocese. The compilation was done "to assess in advance the probable reaction of any of these dioceses to an additional seminary in their area."[433] The Archdiocese they chose was Milwaukee, which was written in pencil at the bottom of their typed information grid. After looking at several locations outside of the Milwaukee and Waukesha area, in 1961 the Society bought seventy-seven acres of farm property which included a small lake. Theodore F. Matt (1924–2009) owned the property, located in the Town of Oconomowoc, about thirty-five miles west of Milwaukee. An attorney, he was active in St. Catherine of Alexandria Parish, Mapleton, with civic involvement on the Oconomowoc Town Board and Waukesha County Board of Supervisors, among other engagements over the years. The Columbans purchased the southern part of his farm, while his family lived on the northern part of the farm, where he raised beef and poultry.

In July 1962, the Columbans had received bids to build, all of which were below the estimate. The bid from the Oliver Construction Company was chosen and a contract was signed on August 21, 1962. The Byrne plans for the Milton buildings were adapted for the Wisconsin project.[434] The plan was to include housing for 120 students. In the March 1963, *Far East,* readers viewed a drawing of the Oconomowoc seminary.

Ground breaking for the college seminary took place on September 7, 1962, and classes began on September 27, 1963, in spite of a bitter cold winter that set back construction. The first enrollment was eighteen new students, who joined the twenty-two "old-timers" who came from Milton. By fall 1965, a language laboratory was added, thanks to a grant from the Raskob Foundation for Catholic Activities. As had been true for the other Columban seminaries, students planted trees and bushes on the property. In winter, a makeshift ice

---

[433] Peter McPartland to Fathers Keegan, MacElroy, Whelan, O'Mahony, 8 May 1959. 8-B-8. Given that the Archdiocese of Chicago had many religious orders/societies, Columbans did not consider this area. However, according to Columban oral tradition, William Cousins, formerly auxiliary bishop in Chicago, had been appointed archbishop of Milwaukee and welcomed the Columbans to the Archdiocese. T. P. Reynolds correspondence with author 27 March 2017.

[434] The Oliver Construction Company began in 1945 with architect Oliver Wierdsma, who established the company to meet the needs of commercial customers. In looking at the bids from three companies for the chapel furniture, Barry Byrne recommended the Svoboda Industries (Svoboda Church Furniture) in Kewaunee, Wisconsin. The company was founded in 1883, by Joseph Svoboda, who was a woodworker and master carver in Vienna. Both companies continue to this day. The architectural companies under which Byrne designed Bristol (1950–1952) and Milton (1950–1964) seminaries were both under Barry Byrne Company, 1928–1952. St. Columban Seminary, Oconomowoc, Wisconsin (1962–1963) was under Barry Byrne & Parks, 1953–1959.

rink was created for hockey games.[435] A gymnasium provided opportunities for sports, especially basketball. The college team, "The Ramblers," played teams from other seminaries and other small colleges in southeastern Wisconsin. Through the years, seminarians went to local parishes to assist with religious education classes for the grade and high school students, assisted children with special education needs, and visited the elderly or the ill in convalescent homes.

Silver Creek Seminary and Regional Headquarters

The superior general wrote in January 1960, that the "Silver Creek's need [to expand] has moved to first place," and after estimates on the specific requirements to add on to the facility, the Columbans contacted a Buffalo architect, Mortimer Murphy, to draw up plans for the project.[436] A photo in the March 1960, *Far East* showed readers a sketch of the considerable addition. Father Charles Flaherty, the rector at Silver Creek, was in communication with the architect. Regional Superior Peter McPartland reassured Bishop Burke of Buffalo that the Society would not need a special fund drive in the diocese for the addition. A new chapel was added, the locker room section was extended, and ceilings were lowered in the main building to conserve energy. The former chapel became a recreation room. The close proximity to Lake Erie and the fluctuation of lake levels required a new approach to the sanitary bed which led to the Lake.[437]

At the regional headquarters in Nebraska, three projects expanded the physical space for work and living. In 1961 the two story office building, first used in 1949 as a residence for seminarians, became a retreat house "for the hundreds of area laymen who visit the grounds in the spring and fall for retreats."[438] A new, single-story edifice, situated to the west of the main house, was constructed for office space and a post office. A new IBM machine was installed in 1961, which allowed for a more efficient listing of donors and a "modern" feel to the office. By November that year, additional bedrooms and a lounge were attached to the main house, the offices and a small chapel were renovated to provide additional bedroom space, and a new chapel was built. The latter, attached to the west side of the main building, was dedicated in April 1962. Between 1962 and 1968, land in the northeast part of the

---

[435]   It seems that some land is just made for recreation. The spot where the seminarians' ice rink was located is now the playground for the Oconomowoc middle school that is housed in the former seminary.

[436]   *Casey History* (1960), 15. In September 1961, 109 seminarians lived and went to school at the Silver Creek location.

[437]   Flaherty to Keegan, 13 March 1961.

[438]   *Casey History* (1961), 4. Clipping 8-A-16, 29 St. Columbans Pushes Building Job.

Columban headquarters was leased for 99 years to the Federal Communications Commission for installation of a radar tower,[439] which controls air traffic in the region and for Offutt Air Force Base. The latter is located just southwest of the Columban property. The base is home to the Fifty-Fifth Wing, the largest wing in Air Combat Command and the second largest wing in the Air Force.

Education and Formation for Missionary Priesthood

How did one become a Columban missionary? What knowledge would students gain in these new buildings? What mission spirit would seminarians imbibe? There were formal and informal ways of education, undergirded by an understanding of what constituted a mission vocation. At Milton, formal education took place through a curriculum consisting mainly of philosophy and theology in the last six years of their formation. Philosophy and theology were taught mainly in Latin. There was not a mission curriculum, as such.

Seminary education took place within a structure of the day's activities, the "daily *horarium*." The year at the seminary in Bristol, the Probation Year (later called the Spiritual Year), focused more specifically on the spiritual life, but the Order of the Day for the men at Silver Creek and Milton in the 1950s and 1960, for example, looked similar to this day's organization:

Daily Schedule

Morning prayer, morning offering. Priests prayed the *Breviary* (or Book of psalms, scripture passages, and prayers) at various times during the day. Rosary was prayed daily.

Mass in morning (a second High Mass (sung) on Sundays)

Breakfast, classes and study periods, including some in the evening; lunch; afternoon classes; dinner

Time for sports[440] and recreation (singing, billiards, baseball, tennis, hockey, basketball), garden work on the seminary grounds, and hobbies, some of which included photography book binding, and making statues.

---

[439]   *Casey History* (1962), 5. Casey noted that in an interview, McPartland was not sure of the year.

[440]   A number of Columbans who went to the high school seminary at Silver Creek mentioned the availability of "lots of sports."

Rosary, benediction, spiritual reading, and evening prayer. Study in evenings.

Classes met from Monday through Saturday, with Wednesday and Saturday afternoons "free." Often seminarians assisted at various ministry situations on Wednesday afternoon.

Fourth year Divines were ordained on December 21, the former feast day of St. Thomas the Apostle, and finished their courses in the Spring semester.

At the Major seminary, where the students wore cassocks, additional prayer included Matins and Lauds of the Office of the Dead recited in the oratory on the First Monday of every month to remember Columbans who died in that past month. The sacrament of Penance was provided on Saturday mornings, the spiritual director delivered a talk regularly, and three-day retreat days were scheduled at the start and end of the semester.[441]

There was nothing specifically "missionary" about the *horarium*, except the discipline instilled and the assumption that the elements of daily Mass, prayer (including the breviary, when one was ordained), a choice of reading material at mealtime, some time for recreation—team sports or golf—and physical labor, would be part of a missionary's life along with pastoral work. Reflecting of his seminary days, Father Paul White, ordained in 1958, remarked, "I loved the seminary life and the big thing we got out of the Seminary was the discipline and living with other guys from different parts of the world [and country] and that was all good education because without that it would have been very difficult to make it on the missions." [442]

Informally, seminarians imbibed a sensitivity to mission through talks given by returned missionaries, as they shared their experience in China, Korea, or Burma (now Myanmar) and provided knowledge, inspiration, and embodiment of Columban ideals for the young men. One Silver Creek seminarian, William Schmitt, later ordained in 1968, commented,

> One of the things that was really good at Silver Creek, they always had the guys coming back from the missions and most of them would make an effort to stop by Silver Creek and tell

---

[441] See, for example, the *Normae* noted in Paul L. Keppner (1917–1999), to Regional Vice Director Hugh O'Rourke 12 October 1967. Keppner was rector at Milton seminary from 1962–63 and rector at the Oconomowoc seminary from 1963–1968. By the 1960s, the semester began and ended with just a one day retreat.

[442] Interview (interviewer not named) of Father Paul White (2013–).

us what they were doing. You could see the enthusiasm they had for going back. It wasn't like, I just finished three years of miserable life in some slum or something and, boy, I dread going back there. They were bubbling over with what they had done and the possibilities that were there and how they enjoyed it.[443]

The monthly Columban magazine was another way to learn about the Columban experience globally and, especially in the 1950s, stories of the Columbans who gave their lives in Korea shaped the students' perception of mission. Another formative element was the relationship of older Columbans to a younger generation. One example among many was the impact that Father Peter McPartland, ordained in 1936, had on a young Donald Kill. Kill's father and McPartland were grade school classmates and later their fathers worked together in the same office as clerks for the railroad. When McPartland came to Toledo, Ohio, to visit, he would stop in to see the Kill family. Father Kill remarked that "even though [Father McPartland] never went on mission to a country other than his own, his dedication to the missionary vocation was always obvious to me. He would often relate stories of other missionaries to us when he would visit. But most important for me was his joy in being what he was."[444]

Bishop Harold Henry came to Milton periodically, as one of the stops across the country to raise funds for his diocese. One time he invited Father Paul Park, a Korean priest from Henry's diocese of Kwang Ju studying English and Stephen Cardinal Kim's [Seoul] brother, Charlie, to stay at the seminary for six months. Father Charlie O'Rourke, ordained in 1957, later remarked that during his seminary years, "the combination of the two Koreans at Milton and the enthusiasm of Bishop Henry really promoted a great interest in Korea for us."[445]

The first few Americans who joined the Columbans took their last years of seminary in Ireland. Later, there would be an exchange of a few seminarians each year between Dalgan and Omaha/Milton. Because most of the Columbans on the missions were Irish, there was an opportunity for both groups to learn together and to become aware of the similarities and differences between Irish and American cultures. As Father Otto Imholte, ordained in 1963, one of the exchange seminarians expressed it, "I think it was to make the transition of

---

[443]   Interview (interviewer not named) of Father William Schmitt, Omaha, Nebraska, 1 October 2013.

[444]   "Father Donald Kill's Story," retrieved from Columban website, Region of the Philippines, 3 September 2012. Kill was ordained in 1972.

[445]   Father Sean Dwan interview of Father Charles O'Rourke. 3 October 2013.

meeting different nationalities in the missions a little less traumatic, so that you would be used to the Irish mentality and the Irish could be used to the American mentality, I suppose."[446] The exchange program was dropped in 1963, after a Society General Chapter recommendation.

The Irish-born faculty at Milton would have received their seminary education either at Dalgan or at an Irish university/diocesan seminary. Early on, an advanced degree for a Columban tended to be in Canon Law, such as that which Peter McPartland received in the late 1930s. But in 1948, Donal O'Mahony (1918–1993), nephew of Bishop Galvin, studied journalism at Denver, Colorado.[447] In 1955 Father Cathal (Charles) P. Coulter received a master's degree in Sociology and Anthropology at Fordham University, followed by attendance at St. Francis Xavier University, Nova Scotia, for study of the "Antigonish Movement."[448] Chicago born Father William Korenchan (1933–1966), ordained in 1957, studied there, as did Father Robert O'Rourke, who was sent after his ordination in 1958 to study the movement and to obtain a master's degree in economics.[449] The movement taught people how to work collaboratively to create credit unions and cooperatives. One place Columbans used the method was in Fiji, where, in 1953, the year after the Columbans accepted missions in the Fiji Islands, Illinois born Father Marion Ganey, SJ (1904–1984), arrived in Fiji to begin credit unions among the people. With Columbans engaged in that work as well, collectively over the Islands, one-fifth of Fijians were in credit unions by 1961. Father Seamus O'Connor unexpectedly found an outcome he had not anticipated when he began the credit union in his parish in Ba (Fiji). "Except that they went to the same Mass on Sunday, the mixed races (part European, Indian, Fijian) had little in common until I started a Credit Union. Now, when I want anything done, I have only to give the word to an enthusiastic interracial group who, for the most part, are officers of the Credit Union."[450] Working together for a

---

[446] Interview of Father Otto Imholte, 3 October 2013. Interviewer not named. The exchange also took place between Ireland and the Region of Australia.

[447] He was appointed Manager of the U.S. edition of the *Far East*.

[448] The Antigonish Movement, begun in Nova Scotia by Monsignor Moses Coady (1882–1959) and Reverend Jimmy Tompkins in 1920, was a program of adult education which used leadership training in credit union organization to promote democratic values and to build group trust and responsibility for their own lives. See Douglas Hyde, "A Cup of Kava," *FE* (December 1961), 16–17. Moses Coady, *Masters of Their Own Destiny: The Story of the Antigonish Movement through Economic Cooperation* (NY: Harper, 1939).

[449] Robert O'Rourke was missioned to Burma (now Myanmar), having obtained a visa in November 1962, but he had to leave the country by the end of 1966 due to unsettled conditions in the country.

[450] "Fiji," *Columban Newsletter* (October 1955).

positive financial outcome was an experiential factor that laid the groundwork for understanding scriptural foundations, such as, "We are all one body in Christ."

While there did not appear to be instruction in a particular "method" of mission for the Columbans, Superior General Connolly referenced Columban experience in an article he wrote about Pope Pius XII's concern for missions. Connolly named three papal mission themes: strategy, tactics, and general papal enactments with a missionary significance, and thereby affirmed underlying values Columbans espoused.[451] For the first theme, Connolly mentioned three areas, though not historically new to the Church: adaptation (the missionary seeks to implant Christianity, not the accidental trappings from his own country); the development of local clergy and leaders,[452] and the dissociation of missionaries from politics. Some of Pope Pius XII's mission "tactics" included translation of portions of the Roman Ritual into vernacular languages, and instruction to missionaries to "concern themselves closely with the social reforms demanded by justice and charity." [453] Connolly referenced Pius XII's concern for the persecuted Catholics in China and cited comments made by Columban Father John Casey (1920–1983): "The pope's letter of 18 January 1952 . . . was a short letter but it was a great help. It gave the Catholics confidence, they felt no longer isolated, they felt that the Church was proud of them and they became determined to live up to that good opinion."[454] Father Casey had himself been imprisoned by Chinese communists in 1952 and expelled from the country seventeen months later, in 1953.

Even though the seminary population grew in the mid-1950s into the 1960s, few photos of seminarians/seminaries were seen in the magazine during that time, except during their ordination, showing the men at the point during the ritual where they lie prostrate in the sanctuary. The men were not necessarily

---

[451]   Timothy Connolly, "Pope Pius XII and Foreign Missions," *The Furrow* (March 1957), 150–155.

[452]   The point was strongly emphasized early in the twentieth century by Pope Benedict XV's, *Maximum Illud* ("On the Propagation of the Faith throughout the World,"1919) and Pope XI's, *Rerum Ecclesiae* ("On the Propagation of the Faith throughout the World," 1926) and subsequent ordination of the first six Chinese bishops in modern times in October 1926. Columban promotion of the Legion of Mary is a prime example of the development of lay leaders to the time of Pius XII's papacy.

[453]   Connolly, "Pope Pius XII and Foreign Missions," 153. Pope Pius XII's two mission encyclicals issued in the 1950s were *Evangelii Praecones* 2 June 1951 ("On Promotion of Catholic Missions") and *Fidei Donum* 21 April 1957 (On Present Conditions of Catholic Missions, Especially in Africa).

[454]   John Casey, quoted in Connolly, "Pope Pius XII and Foreign Missions," 153. The Pope issued a second letter to Chinese Catholics on 7 October 1954.

identifiable.[455] Appeals were made in the *Far East*, though, to help the Society build the new Milton seminary. Cleverly put, one appeal said there would be 150 doorways in the new Milton seminary and each one to cost fifty dollars. The *Far East* reader was asked, "Would you buy, or help to buy 'A Doorway to the Kingdom of God?'"[456] In another issue, the appeal indicated that "there are 186 steps or risers for new seminary: $50–$150.00 each. Will you help supply these steps of charity for our seminarians?" However, in the 1950s and early 1960s, the *Far East* readers were not able to "follow" the seminarians in the magazine, as they had in earlier decades.

Men who enrolled in a Columban seminary felt they had a mission vocation, even if they themselves could not identify what that would mean. Father Paul Waldron in the late 1920s, framed "vocation" as a response to the call to have all people in the world be given the opportunity to know Christ and to be saved. "Priests! Priests! More priests! is the continual cry from the pagan world today." How "much good could even one zealous priest do in one of these countries— the glory he would give to God—the souls he would save—the consolation he would bring to the Sacred Heart of Jesus."[457]

Father John Blowick's, *Priestly Vocation* (1932), using a Thomist philosophical framework of rights, duties, and obligations, set vocation in the philosophical and theological category of ethics. His history of the theory of vocation noted that prior to the Council of Trent (i.e., before1545), seminaries, as thought of by twentieth century standards, were not known. Seminaries were a "product" of that Council, and there followed the language and underpinnings for "priestly vocation." He devoted only ten pages to mission in his 343 page book, five pages on "Recruiting—the Duties of the Supreme Pontiff, Bishops and Missionary Institutes," and five pages on "Impeding Missionary Vocations."[458] A mission vocation was also tied with "the fate of the unbaptized" and the imperative to seek them out.[459]

Father Paul Waldron later presented another perspective: the priest as a "personal sacrament." Apparently hearing the term from an unnamed priest caused him to reflect more deeply on the concept. "A mystery not unlike

---

[455]   From 1954 until 1958 there was a downturn (136 seminarians in all Columban U.S. seminaries in 1954 and down to 128 in 1958). Beginning in 1959, with 149 seminarians, the number grew to 232 by 1965.

[456]   *FE* (October 1951).

[457]   Paul Waldron, *Fishers of Men*, n.p. (c. 1925), 54. See also, the shorter version, Paul Waldron, "A Talk on the Priesthood," 1925. Columban publication, Nebraska.

[458]   John Blowick, *Priestly Vocation* (Dublin: M. H. Gill and Son, LTD, 1932).

[459]   Father Francis Mannion remembered a "Blowick article "on the fate of people who don't get baptized. He was very positive that people who are baptized go to heaven. Blowick said we will save as many Chinese as we can." Unnamed person interview of Francis Mannion 1 April 2011. Interview 1.

['the Incarnation, the Great Sacrament'] took place when Our Blessed
Saviour marked your soul with the character and made you His priest.
There was a taking over of your person by the Son of God." Of course, he
noted, there is the difference that exists between creature and Creator and a
priest's human nature was not absorbed by the divine. Nevertheless, "Christ
has taken you over. You too now can offer to God in the name of men the
homage by which they wish to be united to Christ. The homage and the
holiness of Christ pass through your hands."[460] While Waldron's letter is
undated, the image he used has moved away from a strictly philosophical
way to define one's vocation.

A "Director's Desk" page in a 1960 *Far East* provided a more mundane and
ecclesiastical jurisdictional perspective on the vocation. "One of the best ways of
describing the work of the missionary is to say that in the foreign missions the
priest does substantially what diocesan priests do at home. The work is under
the direction of a bishop—or in the case of 'mission designated' areas, under
a Prefect Apostolic."[461] This was a rather dry and unappealing way to express
what the Columbans lived on the missions, though his definition fit within the
categories that John Blowick had earlier designated.

How did young men find out about a mission vocation and specifically a
vocation expressed through the Missionary Society of St. Columban? Mission
magazines, such as the *Far East*, Columban talks and movies shown in Catholic
grade and high schools, and literature put out by the national Society for
the Propagation of the Faith office in New York were some of the places that
promoted mission vocations. Columban friend, Archbishop Cushing wrote
Answering the Call (1942), when he was director of the Archdiocese of Boston's
Society for the Propagation of the Faith. The book featured stories of some
Columbans, including Edward Galvin, Harold Henry, Ambrose Gallagher,
Cushing's good friend, and Cornelius Tierney.[462] The *Far East* advertised a
"Father Murphy Vocation Club" in the 1950s. Between 1958 and 1966,
Father Charles Roddy (1919–1987), born in Roxbury, Massachusetts, worked
in Promotion. Known for his enthusiasm, creativity and generous spirit, his
"famous 'Charlie Roddy Vocation Days,'" were held on the grounds of Milton

---

[460]   Paul Waldron, "Letters to a Priest," found in the Papers of Father Paul Waldron,
        undated. Printed in James McCaslin, *The Spirituality of our Founders. A Study of the
        Early Columban Fathers* (Maynooth: Society of St. Columban, 1986), 241–247, here
        241, 242. Waldron had a large influence with priests across the country because
        bishops invited him to give retreats to the clergy.

[461]   *FE* (March 1960).

[462]   Cushing's *Answering the Call* also noted the impact that Communism had upon
        missionaries and the missions. In 1956, when he as the archbishop of Boston,
        Cushing wrote *That They May Know Thee: Selected Writings on Vocation* (1956).

Seminary.[463] He gathered a large group of grade school children for the day, told them stories from the missions, showed them a mission movie and provided hot dogs and soda. He obtained some supplies for the occasion from army surplus. "He gave each child a small mustard cup saying it was a *saké* bowl or something."[464] In some dioceses, well-attended vocation conferences were held for grade and high school students in a central location in the 1950s.

In 1962, Regional Director Boland appointed Father Richard Steinhilber as director of vocations. At the time, this task was part of Promotion and every house was to take on that task, which was one of many, including "weekend supply work" in parishes. To have one person oversee, coordinate, and pioneer vocations work throughout the society was new to the region. To begin his work, Steinhilber, at the time on the faculty at the Milton seminary when he was appointed, went to Washington DC with Regional Superior Boland to attend a meeting of major superiors. At the time, "the men were dissatisfied with the operation for vocations. They had no literature, for example. Nobody was producing anything for them. There was some of the old stuff that maybe was lying around." One question that came up among the men related to accepting African American candidates. Steinhilber noted, "There was no rule against it but it was kind of, we didn't do it. So I got a statement to the fact that they [black students] were acceptable. It never really caused a problem because [we] only had a couple of applicants to begin with."[465] A more likely vocation "pool" would come from the ethnic communities where Columbans served parishes or ethnic centers and people knew them personally, especially in the Hispanic, Filipino, and Korean groups in California.

Then there was the question of the audience toward which vocation stories or advertisements for Columban life would be directed. Bishop Harold Henry complained to Superior General Connolly when the latter visited the country in 1958 that the *Far East* had too much emphasis on recruitment of high school and college students.[466] While a side effect of targeting people who had acquired a college education, profession, or established trade would be fewer expenses for the Columbans, the incoming men presumably would be more mature and have acquired skills or knowledge to build upon for mission as a Columban.

Sometimes "mission vocation" seemed more intuitive or "enfleshed," rather than reasoned out. Father Robert O'Rourke, ordained in 1958, had been a

---

[463]   Edward Naughton to Dear Father (obituary for Father Charles Roddy), 8 September 1987.

[464]   Joseph McSweeny interview of Richard Steinhilber 12 July 2012. Interview 2.

[465]   Ibid.

[466]   "Visitation of Korea, 1958" by Superior General Timothy Connolly. SSC Archives, Omaha, KOR Box 1/21.

student in the Archdiocese of Chicago seminary. At Mass one day at Mundelein Seminary, the priest said that a "man who sat in these same pews and walked these same corridors was killed in Korea. His name was Monsignor Patrick Brennan. So I kind of remember that."[467] Father Dennis O'Mara, ordained in 1961, recalled Columban Father Patrick Cashman, who gave a talk at his grade school. Father Cashman "had been working in the Philippines. I remember thinking for years he has a great sense of humor, he loves the Filipino people, he wants to get back there as soon as he can, and this impressed me greatly."[468]

The post–Vatican II period would bring many changes for the Milton seminary. A committee for Interseminary Cooperation in the Archdiocese of Boston was established in fall 1965, with Father Eamonn O'Doherty the chairman for the Undergraduate Theology Committee. The major seminary in Milton began to operate on a five-day week, with every Thursday off.[469] The academic year was divided into two semesters with first exams at the end of January. More substantially, though, by 1965 a national evaluation of seminary life and curricula had started under the U.S. Catholic Bishops, "to insert *aggiornamento* into seminary education."[470] Seminaries would move away from a Tridentine (with its "tracts," such as *de Deo uno et tres*) and European model of curriculum and mind-set that underlay priestly formation.

Communism and the Columbans, 1950s

An overarching specter of the growth of global communism weighed heavily on the United States in the 1950s. The post–World War II interaction of the two military superpowers—Communist Russia and the United States— and the subsequent "Cold War" led to a fear of the "Red Menace," a reference to Communist allegiance to the red flag of Soviet Russia. The *Far East* of the

---

[467] Father Joseph McSweeny interview of Father Robert O'Rourke, 2011.

[468] Father T. P. Reynolds interview of Father Dennis O'Mara, 20 February 2012. Patrick Cashman (1917–2002) was born at Bayonne, New Jersey, and ordained in Providence, Rhode Island, in December 1942. He served in the Philippines from 1950 to 1972.

[469] U.S. Regional *Newsletter*, 4 November 1965.

[470] Joseph Cardinal Ritter, "Foreword," in James Michael Lee and Louis J. Putz, CSC, *Seminary Education in a Time of Change* (Notre Dame, IN: Fides Publishers, Inc., 1965), v. The book provides an overview of the history of seminaries, educational problems in seminaries; selection of candidates, sociology, intellectual and psychological aspects of seminary life, and curriculum/teaching in seminary education. The Committee on Priestly Life and Ministry of the National Conference of Catholic Bishops was guided initially by Archbishop Paul J. Hallinan (1911–1968) of Atlanta. The Committee then was under the Chairmanship of John Cardinal Krol, archbishop of Philadelphia.

1950s and some of the Columban director's letters of the period referred to Communists as "the Reds." Missionaries and the people they served in Korea, China, Burma (now Myanmar), and the Philippines, experienced communist attacks, harassment, imprisonment, and even death. This section of the chapter will highlight three Columban "points of contact" with communism, each of which also had an impact on the seminaries: the Korean Conflict (1950–1953), the Legion of Mary and local development of churches, and the influence of Douglas Hyde, an English Communist who converted to Catholicism.

Korean Conflict (1950–1953)

Communist governance had moved well beyond Russia into China, the Philippines, and North Korea by 1950. Not only did the Columban missionaries suffer with their people the effects of World War II, but from 1950–1953 the "Korean Conflict" also created havoc and destruction of churches, schools, hospitals, and homes. One million Koreans in the South (600,000 in the North) would lose their lives with millions more displaced.[471] On June 25, 1950, soldiers from the Soviet-backed Democratic People's Republic of Korea crossed over the 38th parallel into the Republic of Korea south of that line. Within a few weeks, the United Nations troops, led by U. S. troops fighting on the side of the South, joined the war. Americans viewed the situation as a war against the growth of international Communism. An armistice was signed on July 27, 1953, and a demilitarized zone was created to separate the North from the South, a situation which remains to this day. No peace treaty has been signed.

At the outbreak of the war, thirty-six Columbans served in Korea, including in missions above the 38th parallel. Father Anthony Collier was the first Columban killed, shot on June 27, 1950, after a brief interrogation by Communist soldiers from the North. Shortly thereafter Montana born Father James Maginn was killed on July 7 and Father Patrick Reilly on August 29, 1950.[472] Between July 1950, and May 1953, Australian Columban Father Philip Crosbie (1915–2005), who had been a prisoner of the Chinese in 1941, became a prisoner of the People's Democratic Republic of North Korea, as did Columban Thomas Quinlan, who had been interned in World War II, and Father Francis Canavan, who died in captivity. They were part of a large group including Sisters, civilians, some of them Protestant missionaries or business people, and U.S. prisoners of war. Crosbie's compelling *March Till They Die*[473] recounts his imprisonment and the infamous Death March in Korea, as the prisoners were

---

[471]   Various statistics are given. The figures cited are from the online *The Encyclopedia Britannica*, "Korean War."

[472]   *FE* (July 1951).

[473]   Philip Crosbie, *March Till They Die* (Clonskeagh: Dublin, 1955).

compelled to march through Korea under horrendous conditions with the retreating Communist soldiers.

In the southern part of the peninsula, Monsignor Patrick Brennan (1901–1950), the prefect apostolic of Kwang Ju, Father Thomas Cusack (vice director of region), and Father John O'Brien[474] were taken into custody by the Communists in July 24, 1950. They were seen in prison and presumed among the slain on September 24 that year, the night of the general massacre at Taejon, as the Communist army was being routed from the area. These realities vividly brought home possible implications of a mission vocation.

Superior General Connolly visited the Columbans in Korea at the end of 1953 into 1954. The *Far East* readers learned about the plight of the Koreans in an article following his visitation there. He wrote a description of various physical aspects of the country—geographical features, the extent of the physical devastation of war, the presence of foreign soldiers and the characteristics of the Korean people. One admirable trait that Connolly singled out was Korean loyalty. "Missionaries have recently been killed in Korea, but never a missionary abandoned. If, in the red path of war, a missionary decided to stay with his people, then his people stayed with him. What he was willing to suffer, they too would endure. No missionary was left to endure alone."[475]

In an interview inquiring about the picture of Catholic life in the many war torn countries where the Columbans served, Connolly was asked, "What about the GIs [in Asia]? We hear a lot about their generosity." His response reiterated the same points Columbans noted about the GIs in World War II.

> I want to emphasize this strongly: The American GI has done more for the missions of Japan and Korea than 10 of his fellow Catholics at home. First in his generosity and second in the example he sets in going to the sacraments. Seventy-five per cent of the Columban plant in Chunchon, Korea, was destroyed in the fighting. Everything, including the Cathedral, was completely destroyed. Three years after the war had begun it was completely rebuilt. The Society had very little expense. It was rebuilt better than ever, not by the government or the army, but by the labor and donations of

---

[474] John O'Brien (1918–1950), born in Donamon, County Roscommon, Ireland, and ordained in 1942, was a chaplain in the British army until 1948, when he was sent to Korea.

[475] Father Timothy Connolly, "Looking at Korea," *FE* (February 1954), 6–8, here, 8.

the GIs themselves. I was amazed. That new plant came out
of the sweat and pocketbooks of the GIs.[476]

Certainly the presence of a convert to Catholicism and much decorated
former U. S. Army chaplain, Harold Henry (1909–1976), had a large influence
on the help that the GIs provided. Henry had arrived in the pioneer band of
ten Columbans to Korea in 1933, having finished his seminary training in
Dalgan, Ireland. A native of Northfield, Minnesota, Henry's first mission was
in Naju in 1935, when Korea was occupied by the Japanese.[477] Staying with
Prefect Apostolic Owen McPolin and other Columbans in Mokpo, Henry was
arrested by the Japanese there, then imprisoned in Naju for more questioning
after the Japanese bombed Pearl Harbor.[478] In May 1942, he was repatriated
to the United States as part of a prisoner exchange with Japanese prisoners.[479]
Through the intervention of Archbishop Cushing, who apparently overrode
the wishes of Regional Superior Waldron, Harold Henry became a U.S. Army
chaplain from 1942–47. He participated in the invasion of Normandy, later
receiving the Bronze Star for gallantry in action while serving with combat
engineering group in General George C. Patton's Third Army.[480] After the War,
Henry resided for a time at St. Columban Seminary, Milton, and then returned
to Korea in 1947.

After the death of Monsignor Patrick Brennan, Henry was appointed
apostolic administrator (later archbishop) of the Diocese of Kwangju in

---

[476]   Michael Heher, Denver, Colorado, interview of Father Timothy Connolly, March
1954. The interview is printed in Michael Heher, "The Undecided Giant." Connolly
Papers, CFA-USA. See also, *Columban Newsletter*, 5 July 1954. The rapport of
Columbans with U. S. troops also showed later in the Philippines, when a Columban
in Olongapo sought to get a sick child to this hospital in the midst of a typhoon.
A U. S. navy friend suggested the priest ask the Navy Admiral for the use of his
helicopter to transport the child and the priest. And that is what took place. "The
Admiral Won't Mind," *FE* (April 1966), 18–19.

[477]   Seven of the nine Columbans in Korea had been arrested by the Japanese and
held in prison or house arrest at some point during World War II. Edward Fischer,
Light in the Far East. Archbishop Harold Henry's Forty-two Years in Korea (NY: The
Seabury Press, 1976), 65. David Sheehan, "Old Reliable," *FE* (September 1965),
12–13 narrates the story of mission catechist, Thomas Choi, who was able to tend
to Father Harold Henry and Chicago born Father Thomas P. Kane (1914–1984)
while they were imprisoned by the Japanese at the start of World War II.

[478]   Harold Henry was arrested in Mokpo, then sent to Naju, and then under house
arrest in Kwangju prior to the prisoner exchange in 1942.

[479]   For this part of Harold Henry's life, see, Edward Fischer, *Light in the Far East.*
Archbishop Harold Henry's Forty-Two Years in Korea (New York: The Seabury
Press, 1976), 62–71.

[480]   "Columban Archbishop Henry Succumbs in Korea at 66, "Columban Fathers, News
Release, 3/5/1976. CFA-USA.

southwest Korea, Henry built a seminary in Kwang Ju ("the most important project of my life").[481] Seminarians from nine of the fifteen dioceses in Korea were taught in that location. By 1954, many building projects commenced, thanks to the Armed Forces Assistance to Korea Project (AFAK). Certain projects of a community nature, such as schools, churches, hospitals, and county government buildings were some of the specific projects that qualified. The Armed Forces provided surplus materials and their technicians' knowledge to the project, while local organizations supplied the labor and paid for it. Columban parishes benefitted from this assistance, as did the Father Kapaun Memorial Technical School in Kwang Ju, one of the largest projects for which the Columbans received help from AFAK.[482] Catholics in the United States heard many of Bishop Henry's stories on his several trips back home.

The Columbans had a strong presence in Korea after the Korean War. In November 1955, ten young Columbans joined the forty-seven other Columbans, who were half of all foreign missionaries in Korea. In 1958, the actor, Gregory Peck, would narrate a Columban-made film, *Path to Glory*, which used Columban archival films and photos explaining the history of Catholic life in Korea, starting in 1777 with its introduction through lay scholars and more recent material to that time, of the Korean War and the experience of the death march. Father John Vaughan had a large hand in its production onsite, with later assistance from Desilu Productions in California.[483] In fall 1958, the first U. S. lay missioners to Korea arrived in Kwang Ju to assist Bishop Henry. Mr. and Mrs. Edward Kreiss were from Oakland, California. He was a veteran of twenty-two years in the Navy with skills in accounting, architecture and teaching. His wife was an office manager and secretary. Unfortunately, due to Mrs. Kreiss's failing health, the couple needed to return to the United States in spring 1959.

The Legion of Mary

A key approach to evangelization Columbans used in China, Korea, and the Philippines was the Legion of Mary. The Dublin born founder, Frank Duff (1889–1980), held a civil service position, which he gave up to devote himself to an evangelization approach based upon devotion to "Our Lady," specifically under her apparitions to children in the town of Fatima, Portugal, in 1917 in combination with another Marian devotion, Louis Mary Grignon de Montfort's

[481] Columban Fathers. *Mission News Bureau*, press release March 5, 1976. 9.A.19. CFA-USA.

[482] "AFAK," *FE* (October 1955), 10–13.

[483] U.S. Regional Superior, Visitation of Korea, 1958. Desilu Productions was founded in 1950 in California by Desi Arnaz and Lucille Ball.

True Devotion.[484] Duff's devotional life combined with the practicality of his work in his parish Society of St. Vincent de Paul. The first meeting of the Legion of Mary was held in Dublin on September 7, 1927. Legionaries visited their neighbors, going door to door, to take a census so that the members and the parish priests could follow through to work with people who had "fallen away" from Catholic practice.

Frank Duff wrote a *Handbook* that laid out the prayers, structure of the meetings, and visitation methods. The words he used for organizational units were based on those of the Roman army. There was a marked similarity of methods and titles of the Legion and of International Communism. "Each adopted the nomenclature of the *legio* or legion of ancient Rome. The Legion of Mary uses *praesidium* as the name for the unit of organization, the branch. The Communists use the same term—who has not read reports of the meetings of the 'Supreme *Praesidium* of the Soviets'?" [485] Both groups used the word, "*Tessera* for the membership card, both of them red in color—the red flag of Soviet Russia and "the color of the Holy Spirit." [486] The Legionaries in Communist countries would be among the people most persecuted and would demonstrate that to be a Legionary was to "be in a school of supernatural heroism." [487]

The Catholic Church in Korea experienced substantial growth after 1953. Bishop Harold Henry thought the country had enough relief organizations and devotional societies after the Korean War. The church needed action groups of committed lay apostles. He heard a Legionary talk at a U.S. Army base in Japan, studied the *Handbook* of the Legion of Mary, and appreciated that the movement connected action and devotion, but "kept the itch for results in its proper place."[488] He began in 1953 with three *praesidia*: one for women, one for men, and one mixed group in Mokpo, the main Catholic center in the vicariate of Kwang Ju. He estimated that by 1960, the Legion was doing 50 percent of

---

[484]   Anne Tansey, "Instrument of Mary [Frank Duff]," *FE* (February 1962), 114–116. See also, Frank Duff, *The Spirit of the Legion of Mary* (Glasgow: J. S. Burns, 1956).

[485]   Anne Tansey, "Instrument of Mary [Frank Duff]," 115. Tansey quoted from the *Capuchin Annual*, 1956–1957. Filipino Communists were instructed to join or infiltrate the Legion of Mary and other Catholic Action groups in the 1950s. *Columban Newsletter* (October 1955).

[486]   Anne Tansey, "Instrument of Mary [Frank Duff]," *FE*, 115. It would be this very structure that Communists would use against Legionaries, terming them as subversives.

[487]   Leon Joseph Cardinal Suenens, *Theology of the Apostolate* (Divine Word Publications: Techny, IL, 1953), 54. For a description of a Legion meeting in Negros, Philippines, see, Bernard Smyth, "Legion in Action," *FE* (1956), 3–4.

[488]   Harold W. Henry, DD, "I Choose the Legion," *The Priest*, 16 (September 1960), 766–772, here 67.

the total convert work there and an even higher percentage of the instruction of Catholic children. Henry observed that confraternities/sodalities in a parish "ensure public order in the practice of devotional exercises of a more or less private nature. They serve many worthwhile purposes, and no place should be without them. But one must not depend on them to carry the fight, to act as 'combat teams' in the expansion of the Church. [Confraternities] are 'bread' rather than 'leaven,'" whereas the Legion was the leaven.[489]

Henry also attributed the growth of Catholic life in Korea to the "martyrdom of Monsignor Brennan, Fathers Cusack and O'Brien, along with 400 Catholics, and to the fact that during this Marian Year [1954] so many people are praying for the conversion of the pagan world."[490] He referenced the "Double Program" (*Pai Ga Oun Dong*) begun by Cusack, whereby a Catholic wrote down the name of a person he or she intended to lead to the Church during the year, said a daily Our Father, Hail Mary and Glory be to the Father for the conversion of the person. The Catholic "is obliged to admonish the person and to introduce him to the priest." The other half of the form upon which the Catholic wrote the name of a prospective convert was given to the pastor. Catechists or well instructed lay people took care of instructing those interested in becoming Catholics. Both approaches emphasized lay apostleship and lay responsibility for the growth in Catholic life.

Leon Cardinal Suenens, who championed the role of laity and the role of the Church in the world, and who would be a prominent voice at the Second Vatican Council, promoted the Legion of Mary as well. One major difference between Frank Duff and Suenens was that the cardinal's first emphasis was on the Holy Spirit and the work of the Spirit in the Trinity and in the Church before elaborating Mary's role in the apostolate.[491]

The Columban probably best known for the promotion of the Legion was Father Aedan McGrath (1906–2000), whose work in China was so instrumental in training lay Catholics for evangelization, that under the Communist government he and many Chinese Catholics were arrested and jailed, in his case for three years.[492] The Communists, knowing the structure of the Legion,

---

[489]   Ibid., See also, Harold W. Henry, "Korea's Amazing Convert Movement," *Mission Bulletin* (January 1959), 12–16.

[490]   Father Harold Henry, "Another 'First in Korea," *FE* (September 1954), 4.

[491]   Léon Joseph Suenens, *Theology of the Apostolate of the Legion of Mary* (Cork: Mercier Press, 1960).

[492]   Bishop Fulton. J. Sheen drew attention to Aedan McGrath's work with the Legion of Mary, when Sheen spoke at the National Catholic Students Mission Crusade held at the University of Notre Dame, August 23–25, 1954.
        Aedan McGrath, *Perseverance Through Faith. A Priest's Prison Story.* Theresa Marie Moreau, ed. and researcher (Xlibris, 2008). Eamonn McCarthy, compiler and editor, *From Navan to China: the Story of a "Chinese Irishman." Aedan W. McGrath*

viewed the group as a hostile, competing, and subversive organization.[493] After Father McGrath was expelled from the country, he shared his experience with the seminarians and was on the speaker circuit throughout Ireland, the United States and other countries. He was in the United States several times to speak with many groups across the country.

Influence of Douglas Hyde

Douglas Hyde (1911–1992), a former news editor of the *London Daily Worker* until 1948 (he had joined the paper in 1940), had publically renounced his Communism and became a Roman Catholic. He had studied for the Methodist ministry before embracing the ideals of the Communist party and wrote his intellectual/spiritual odyssey in *I Believed*, a book that became a best seller in 1950.[494] In 1954 he visited Columban headquarters in Ireland, where he gave a weeklong series of lectures on "Marxism in Theory and Practice." The Irish Press bought serial rights to Hyde's, *One Front Across the World*, which featured the Australian Columban Father Philip Crosbie in Korea and other Columbans in Korea and Japan.[495] The book was read at meals in Columban seminary dining rooms.

Based on his experience visiting Columbans in Korea and Japan, Hyde termed them the first line of defense against Communism. "The men who are holding the fort —and extending the territory in our hands—until reinforcements arrive, do not dramatise themselves or their life in any way. That, I have found, is typical of these Columbans anywhere. Perhaps it is that they are too close to the scene to see its drama, too unaware of their own sacrifices to see their significance. But to a man from outside, given the opportunity to see the thing as a whole, it is apparent enough."[496] Hyde wrote articles for the *Far East* on Student Catholic Action in the Philippines and on the eviction of Chinese from Indonesia. In the latter case, the Chinese, though born in Indonesia, were being sent to Communist China.[497]

(1906–2000) (Dublin: RAW Publishing, 2008*).* "China: Expulsion," *Columban Mission* (March 1972), 21–23 related McGrath's experience in the 1950s.

[493]   At the same time, Filipino communists were instructed to join or infiltrate the Legion of Mary and other Catholic Action Groups in the 1950s. *Columban Newsletter* (October 1955).

[494]   Douglas A. Hyde, *I Believed* (Putnam: NY, 1950).

[495]   Douglas Hyde, *One Front Across the World* was published in Ireland in 1955 with publication in 1956 by Newman Press, Maryland.

[496]   Douglas Hyde, quoted in *Hibernia* magazine, Dublin (Autumn, 1954) and published in U.S. Region *Columban Newsletter* December 1954. Hyde's visits to Columbans are referenced in U.S. Region *Newsletter* (August 1954 and December 1954).

[497]   *FE* (February 1960); *FE* (June 1960).

The overzealousness of Republican Senator Joseph McCarthy, who led a "hunt" in the United States for suspected Communists, with no person or group beyond his target, gradually was challenged. Army-Senate hearings were held and televised from April to June 1954. In December 1954 the U.S. Senate voted to censure McCarthy for his conduct. Nevertheless, Catholics still appealed to Our Lady of Fatima to overcome Communism and to convert "Godless Russia,"[498] while an additional "Mary" emphasis in the decade was a "Marian Year," a 1954 proclamation by Pope Pius XII in 1954. One of the last Columban references to the Communists as "Reds" in the *Far East* is in October 1960, where a few sentences from Dimitri Z. Manuilsky's 1931 lecture to students of Political Warfare in Moscow are printed in huge letters across the page: "War to the hilt between communism and capitalism is inevitable."

Death of Bishop Edward Galvin and Father Edward J. McCarthy

Two Columban "giants" died within a year of each other: cofounder of the Society of Saint Columban, Edward Galvin, and the first U.S. regional superior, Edward J. McCarthy. Bishop Galvin retired to Dalgan, where he died on February 23, 1956.[499] A group of Chinese students from University College, Dublin, headed by Father Lu were among those who came to his funeral Mass. The students bore two large mourning scrolls in Chinese characters.[500] Galvin's life and mission were remembered at a Solemn Requiem Mass offered at St. Mary's Church, Bellevue, with Archbishop Gerald Bergan of Omaha as celebrant. Galvin was commemorated similarly in the Brooklyn Pro-Cathedral and the Archdioceses of San Francisco and Los Angeles.

Edward J. McCarthy, who had shaped the Society in the United States from the beginning as the first regional superior in the United States and had impacted the development of Student Action in the Philippines had also been interned by the Japanese in Burma (now Myanmar) from1942 to 1945. Never one to be idle, he wrote a history of Catholicism in Burma (now Myanmar)

---

[498] Well-known Bishop Fulton J. Sheen gave "Chalk Talks" on television in the 1950s for the program, "Life is Worth Living." In a talk on Reparation (in the context of Communist Russia), Sheen noted, "The Communists are not the only ones who are guilty before God. We, too, as a nation are guilty. We have failed in some way. As Lincoln said: 'It behooves us then, to humble ourselves before the Offended Power, to confess our national sins, and to pray for clemency and forgiveness." "Chalk Talk," in Joseph P. Chinnici and Angelyn Dries, eds., *Prayer and Practice in the American Catholic Community* (Orbis Books: Maryknoll, 2000), 222–225, along with a reproduction of a prayer for the conversion of individual Communists.

[499] "Edward Galvin," *Those Who Journeyed With Us*, Missionary Society of St. Columban.

[500] *Columban Newsletter* (March 1956).

while he was there. After recuperation in England, he was again appointed to the United States in 1947 and lived at the Elden Avenue Columban house in Los Angeles. In early September 1957, he went out to mail a letter at a nearby mailbox and was knocked down in a freak accident when two cars collided and jumped the curb, knocking him down along with the mailbox and pole. He remained unconscious for two weeks with a fractured skull and extensive brain injuries before he died in Queen of Angels Hospital. He was sixty-six years old. [501]

Death of President John F. Kennedy

The United States, and probably much of the world, was shocked when the Catholic president, John F. Kennedy was assassinated in Dallas, Texas, on November 22, 1963. The Missionary Sisters of St. Columban at Silver Creek recorded their impressions of that day. Their house *Annals* mention that during September 1963, "Homesickness sweeps the study halls each year at this time. A stream of young students ebbs slowly away. Better now than later."[502] But the longest entry of that year summarized the high points of a lecture given on November 22 to the Sisters by Father Seamus Leddy (1918–2002), a faculty member at Silver Creek seminary. He had come prepared to speak about Saint Columban, given that the following day was the feast day of their patron. Leddy changed his topic to give "his impression of the day's tragedy [which lay] deep in our souls."[503] Leddy "likened [Kennedy] to Christ who laid down His life for us at noon on the First Friday."[504] Just as the foes of Jesus were left with "their sense of empty gain," so at the death of President Kennedy "a keen sense of insecurity has seeped over the people that looked up to the leader."[505] After commenting on the fact that Irish soldiers came at the request of Mrs. Kennedy, Leddy said, "Life must go on and the Vice President, L. B. Johnson, has stepped up to take the reins as President. God is with him."[506] The nation watched almost constant television coverage of every step of events from just

---

[501]   *Columban Newsletter* (September 1957).

[502]   *Annals of the Missionary Sisters of St. Columban*, Silver Creek, 22 November 1963. The *Annals* are hand written. Courtesy of Sisters of St. Columban, Silver Creek, New York.

[503]   Ibid.

[504]   Ibid.

[505]   Ibid.

[506]   *Annals of the Missionary Sisters of St. Columban*, Silver Creek, 22 November 1963. The *Annals* are hand written. Courtesy of Sisters of St. Columban, Silver Creek, New York.

after the shooting, right through Kennedy's funeral and burial. There would be more shocks and social upheavals that would follow in the United States by the mid-1960s.

Conclusion

Reflecting the post–World War II trend of increased home construction, the Columbans built, remodeled, or added to each of the four seminary locations between 1950 and 1965. While the number of Columban seminarians decreased from 156 in 1954 to 128 in 1958, the following year the numbers rose to 149 seminarians and continued climbing to 232 in 1965. Growth occurred in Columban mission areas, particularly in Korea, the Philippines, and the opening of Columban missions in Chile, Peru and Fiji in 1952.[507] New areas of Columban visibility in the United States came with a seminary in Wisconsin, a promotion house in Brooklyn, and new promotion locations in West Chester, Pennsylvania (1956), Houston (1963), and Denver (1963).

The specter of international Communism dominated American life in the 1950s, but the introduction of the Legion of Mary, especially the work of Aedan McGrath and use of the approach by other Columbans, was an evangelization perspective that provided formation for lay mission and embodied the importance of laity in the church, a strong emphasis in the Second Vatican Council. Douglas Hyde's books and lectures, "exposing" Communism but also showing the role missionaries played in countries affected by Communism, would reach a variety of audiences, from seminarians to the general public. The Columban relationship with American soldiers worked to the benefit of both groups in the Philippines and Korea. The army men had access to supplies and individual soldiers were willing to help with rebuilding, while the army men would have a sense of "home" away from home because of communication in English and a welcome atmosphere from the Columbans. On August 15, 1962, Bishop Harold Henry received Korea's highest civilian award: the Order of Cultural Merit Medal "for meritorious acts of friendship for helping to improve the welfare and happiness of the Korean people." The Columbans and the Catholic Church had still more martyrs in these years.

While the major seminary followed a standard seminary curriculum in the 1950s and early1960s, other formation factors, including the *horarium*, informal interaction with returned missionaries, reading about Columbans worldwide, and getting to know classmates, who might not have a chance to see each other after ordination due to mission assignments around the world, gave seminarians a connection to a larger mission. Later, they could support

---

[507] A mission in Japan opened in 1948 during the Allied occupation of the country.

each other in prayer and letters when they went to various mission fields. The Columbans had a tradition of martyrs in Korea and in Burma (now Myanmar), the latter country where Father John Walsh (1921–1964) was killed in 1964, possibly in retaliation for the earlier killing of two Buddhist monks by Kachin rebels. By this time in Burma (now Myanmar), reentry permits would be valid for only three months, a fact which would affect Columban decisions about mission there.

An individual's call to mission would mature through the years, would be tested sometimes, and understood in new ways when the young priest began his first mission. The framework for "mission vocation" philosophically moved from "ethics" to personalism and stronger scriptural foundations after the Second Vatican Council. In 1965, the American bishops laid a foundation for evaluation of seminary curriculum and life, a process that would become more structured by 1972. The Columbans in Milton were already engaged in 1965 in working with other seminaries to take advantage of fine theological and scriptural programs in the greater Boston region, especially those offered by the Boston Theological Institute.

Given the relative feeling of stability, especially in the 1950s in the United States, in spite of the threat of Communism, the next period in U.S. history would prove tumultuous—the events of racial conflict especially with the death of Dr. Martin Luther King Jr. in 1968, the Vietnam War, which deeply divided the American people. In the midst of these realities, serious consideration would be given to rethink perspectives on mission, scripture, attitudes toward "the world" and other dimensions of the Second Vatican Council and to incorporate those ideas into the lives of seminarians and priests. This would be accomplished through study, hope, faith, pain, trial, and error.

Bishop Henry

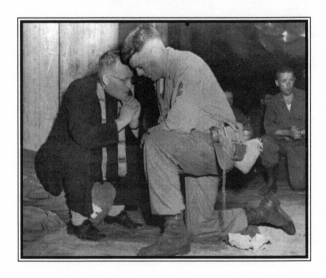

Father Geraghty with GI in Korea

Bristol, new seminary, 1952

x marks the site of new seminary, Bristol

CHAPTER 5

"The Times They Are a-Changin'" (1964–1976)

The motif of the next years in the United States (1964–1976) could be expressed in one sense by the folk singer Bob Dylan, whose 1964 song "The Times They Are a-Changin'" (an anthem for change, as Dylan considered it to be) captured some of the ferment of the period:

> Come gather 'round people
> Wherever you roam
> And admit that the waters
> Around you have grown
> And accept it that soon
> You'll be drenched to the bone
> If your time to you
> Is worth savin'[508]

In the United States, the assassinations of Dr. Martin Luther King Jr. on April 4, 1968, in Memphis, and Robert Kennedy on June 5, 1968, in Los Angeles, racism and civil rights issues were part of the ferment of the social, political, and cultural changes that had been brewing over the decades in some cases, and which came to the fore more spectacularly in the mid-1960s into the mid-1970s. Americans were deeply divided about changing class distinctions,

---

[508] Bob Dylan, born in 1941 in Duluth, Minnesota, performed the song for the first time on October 26, 1963, in Carnegie Hall. The song was first released as a single (Columbia Records) and then in an album with the same title in January 1964. His music was influenced by Irish and Scottish ballads.

growth of the women's movement, and the entrance of the United States into the war in Vietnam. At the same time, the church started to implement the perspectives of the Second Vatican Council documents. A 1970 document on priestly formation described the "signs of the times" that youth were facing. Youth possessed

> an ardent longing for sincerity and truth; they are noticeably very prone to take up everything new and out-of-the ordinary; they admire the world with its scientific and technical progress; we see them wanting to work their way more deeply into the world to serve it, with a sense of "solidarity" particularly with the poorer classes and the oppressed, and a spirit of community. But besides all this they have clearly a distrust for everything old and traditionally accepted; they cannot make up their minds, and are inconsistent in putting plans into effect; they show a lack of docility—very necessary for spiritual progress—with a disposition difficult and critical towards authority and the various institutions of civil and ecclesiastical society, etc.[509]

Even before the Vatican Council began, many commissions and committees had been at work, debating a wide spectrum of issues and writing the documents pertaining to multiple areas of Catholic life discussed and approved by the bishops. Columban bishops had participated in the Council, including the American, Harold Henry.[510] The ramifications of *aggiornamento* (renewal) would affect all Catholics and by extension, people of other faiths. Parishes, congregations of women and men religious, societies of mission, bishops, and other groups began to unpack the documents issued from the Council, in order to put into effect the direction the Council had developed.

The fourth and final session of the Second Vatican Council took place from September 13, 1965, to December 8, 1965. During that session, the formation of priests and the Church's missionary activity were among topics deliberated. Three Council documents came from the session that particularly affected the Columbans: the "Decree on the Church's Missionary Activity," "Decree on the

---

[509]   *The Basic Plan for Priestly Formation* (Washington DC: The National Council of Catholic Bishops, 1970), p. 17. The Latin name of the document is, *Ratio Fundamentalis Institutions Sacerdotalis.*

[510]   The other Columban bishops present at the Council at various times were John J. Howe (Myitkyina, Myanmar), Thomas Quinlan (Ch'unch'ŏn, Korea—South), John J. Dooley (Official of the Secretary of State, Indochina), Patrick Cleary (Nancheng, China), Patrick H. Cronin (Cagayan de Oro, Philippines), and Henry C. Byrne (Iba, Philippines). Superior General James Kielt attended the Council.

Ministry and Life of Priests," and "Pastoral Constitution on the Church in the Modern World."[511]

The Society held two General Chapters (1970 and 1976) with representatives from the Society coming from the Columban regions. Regional gatherings in the United States made concrete the directions and changes of the *modus operandi* for the Columbans in light of the Council documents. A note here should be made that during the Society's 1970 General Chapter, Father Richard Steinhilber (b. 1926) was elected the first American born superior general of the Missionary Society of St. Columban. He had been appointed the superior of the U.S. region in 1967. Steinhilber was born in Buffalo, New York, an area known well by the Columbans. After his ordination in 1951 at the Gregorian University, Rome, he received his Doctorate in Canon Law and was sent to the Columban major seminary in Milton, Massachusetts. He was Dean from 1957 to1959 and then a professor until 1962. He was then appointed vocation director for the U.S. region from 1963–1967. In 1967 Father Steinhilber was appointed director of the U.S. region. At the General Chapter held in Ireland in 1970, he as well as many other Columbans were surprised at his election. Prior to this, only men of Irish heritage had been elected superior general.[512]

Vatican II and Seminary Renewal

First, a little background on some reference points the Columbans used to alter the practices and education structure of seminary life between 1964 and 1976. The model for seminaries had been established after the Council of Trent. This Council held twenty-five sessions between 1534 and 1565, in a time when divisions of the church happened with Martin Luther, John Calvin, and others, and when politically influenced intrigues with consequences for local church life took place among prominent Catholic families in Europe. Diocesan clergy prior to the Council of Trent did not necessarily have a good education or spiritual formation for their work. The seminary system set up after 1565 (though not everyone was enthusiastic about this) was meant "to train men for devotion and loyalty to the church in a 'disturbed and undisciplined age' [here meant the various reformers, such as Luther and Calvin]."[513] Some of that

---

[511]   The Latin names for these documents are, in order, *Ad gentes divinitus; Presbyterorum ordinis; Gaudium et Spes.* They were issued on 7 December 1965.

[512]   When the Columbans were forced to leave Burma (now Myanmar) in 1977, Steinhilber helped the men move from the country. Information on Richard Steinhilber, biography summary sheet. CFA-USA.

[513]   James Michael Lee and Louis J. Putz, eds., *Seminary Education in a Time of Change.* (Notre Dame: Fides Publications, 1965), Introduction, p. x.

disturbance took place in the church itself, whose leaders were not necessarily paragons of virtue or of pastoral leadership, but were more concerned about the benefices that might come with the position. Particular values were inculcated in the Tridentine style seminary. "Seriousness of purpose, a great spirit of sacrifice, and above all ultradocility and uncritical obedience were demanded of candidates for the priesthood, who, the Council [of Trent] had decreed, were to be set apart from the world 'from their tender years.'"[514] In the United States, the latter took the shape of a minor seminary, or high school with residency, such as the Silver Creek location for the Columbans.

The "Decree on the Ministry and Life of Priests" was aimed at "giving more effective support to the ministry of priests and making better provision for their life in the often vastly changed circumstances of the pastoral and human scene."[515] The U.S. Catholic Bishops studied the seminary situation in light of all the other Vatican II documents and in view of the particular context of the midtwentieth century. In 1965, James Michael Lee and Louis J. Putz edited a volume which provided background for various elements of seminary life: education, both in curriculum and teaching styles, social dimensions, spiritual formation, and psychological development of students. Recognized experts in seminary related topics wrote the other chapters. Among the suggestions was that seminaries "should be located near universities, which benefits both groups."[516] The educational plan was to be four years of high school, four years of college and four years of theology. Philosophy was to be taught as philosophy not as an ideology. Theology should have a more "kerygmatic flavor" (i.e., reflective of scripture and the "Good News of Jesus").[517] Academic settings needed updated libraries, addition of lay faculty, inclusion of the arts and sciences with more emphasis on behavioral sciences, and participation in cultural events outside of the seminary. An internship in a parish setting prior to ordination was recommended.[518] A reform in relation to spirituality was to move toward "an ecclesial spirituality and away from sectarian piety." "Ecclesial" included a strong biblical and liturgical immersion and attention to the relationship of the church to the realities of the present time. There was some talk in the United States that perhaps a change in Catholic Church laws would allow for a married clergy.

---

[514] Ibid.

[515] "Decree on the Ministry and Life of Priests," in Austin Flannery, OP, General Editor, Vatican Council II. *The Conciliar and Post Conciliar Documents. New Revised Edition.* (Northport, NY: Costello Publishing Company, 1992), 863.

[516] Robert M. Brooks, O. Praem, "Social Dimensions of the Seminary," in Lee and Putz, *Seminary Education in a Time of Change (1965)*, 231.

[517] Ibid.

[518] Ibid., 232.

The application process to become a seminarian also received a more thorough approach. The process was that the young man would contact his pastor and ask him for a recommendation letter to be sent to the Society. Other items sent were the man's baptismal certificate, academic report, and a medical report from the family doctor. They might visit the seminary, if that wasn't too far from home. While those items were still included in the application process, additional forms needed to be completed, interviews conducted with the candidate, and a psychological test taken with results sent to the admissions person at the seminary. The latter test came up for discussion among the Columbans in December 1967.

On March 16, 1970, the Sacred Congregation for Catholic Education issued, *The Basic Plan for Priestly Formation*.[519] The following year, the Priestly Life and Ministry Committee of the National Catholic Conference of Bishops, a committee which had been active for some time, published helpful historical background for issues facing the seminary in a post–Vatican II church.[520] With the insights and all the documents from the Council, and specifically with the *Plan*, seminaries assessed their academic structures, curriculum, and formation processes over the next years, as they implemented renewal.

Renewal in Columban Seminaries: Milton and Oconomowoc

How did the Columbans address the issues and new perspectives? As noted at the end of chapter 5, interseminary cooperation was already building between the Columban Major Seminary and the Boston Archdiocesan seminary, St. John, Brighton, by fall 1965.[521] Father Eamonn O'Doherty was the chairman for the Boston Theological Institute's joint Undergraduate Theology Committee. In fall 1966, Columban students lived at Milton but attended classes at St. John's Seminary. *The Plan* (*Ratio*, 1970) recommended that the deacons participate in a semester or yearlong diaconate experience in a parish. In 1971, the Columbans had a large group of fourth year deacons that went for a few

---

[519]   *The Basic Plan for Priestly Formation* (Washington DC: The National Council of Catholic Bishops, 1970).

[520]   John Tracy Ellis, ed., *The Catholic Priest in the United States. Historical Investigations.* National Conference of Catholic Bishops. Committee on Priestly Life and Ministry (Collegeville, MN: Saint John's University Press, 1971).

[521]   Nationally, there was talk of Interseminary Cooperation, with a preliminary meeting in Washington DC sometime after August 30, 1967. Hugh O'Rourke and newly appointed director of vocations, Richard Steinhilber, attended. Rectors at the Milton Major Seminary during the period of this chapter include Fathers Eamonn O'Doherty (1962–1966), John J. Moriarity (1967–1972), Donald M. Wodarz (1973–1974), Charles Flaherty (1975–76; June 1977; vice rector of Major Seminary, director of Spiritual Year students 1978 through 1980.

months to the Columban parishes in St. Thomas and St. Croix,[522] but in the 1973/74 academic year, the Columban deacons were integrated into the St. John Seminary Diaconate program.[523] The 1976 Columban Society General Chapter would recommend an Overseas Training Program in locations of Columban missions before the seminarians were ordained.

Another recommendation was that a seminary be near a university. The Milton situation was relatively close to Boston College, among other places of higher learning. But the Oconomowoc College Seminary was not in that situation. They knew they did not have an updated library, resources, or faculty with adequate background for a full college curriculum. The Society was concerned that if any students left the seminary, the credits they accrued would not be accepted in other colleges and universities. Without proper accreditation veterans could not draw on federal monies to attend their college. On a national level, meetings were held by the hierarchy in Washington DC concerning interseminary cooperation, and Father Hugh O'Rourke was present for the meeting in fall 1967.[524]

The question still remained as to what to do with the college level of the seminary.[525] Rector Paul Keppner remarked, "Note the emphasis the Episcopal committee on Priestly Training puts on accreditation. If we cannot (or do not wish to) secure accreditation, will we seek amalgamation? . . . If amalgamation with other seminaries is not feasible, should we establish ourselves on the campus of a college or university in our own residence?"[526] On October 23, 1967, Keppner took the initiative to contact other Catholic college-level seminaries in Wisconsin as to whether seminary personnel would wish to confer about a possible amalgamation of college seminaries.[527] There did not seem to be

---

[522]   The two parishes in the Virgin Islands (St. Thomas and St. Croix) were begun as an opportunity for overseas mission for the men, a number of them American, who had been on promotion for many years in the States and were at an age where learning a new language became more difficult. The Virgin Islands was English speaking, but the Columbans found that some Spanish was needed, as well. Father Joseph McSweeny interview of Richard Steinhilber. Interview 2, 12 July 2012.

[523]   The purpose of the venture, a new idea at the time, was to provide some mission experience for the Fourth Year Divines. Columbans rented a house for them in the Columban parishes in St. Thomas and St. Croix. The program proved unfeasible, partly because there were too many seminarians for the small area and not enough thinking through what the program should encompass. Father Joseph McSweeny interview of Richard Steinhilber. Interview 2, 12 July 2012.

[524]   Keppner to Hugh O'Rourke, 30 August 1967. 8-B-11. CFA-USA.

[525]   In 1965, the two year College seminary at Milton ended. By fall 1967 Columban college students were at the four year college in Oconomowoc.

[526]   Report of Oconomowoc Seminary Rector Paul Keppner to Milton Rector Joseph McGlade 10 May 1968.

[527]   St. Columban's College and Seminary, Inc. was legally incorporated in the State of Wisconsin as a four year college. Keppner sent the "Questionnaire Sent to

enough support, or probably energy, for such a joint undertaking on the part of at least some of the seminaries. So, Keppner and the faculty continued to examine other options, including a move to an accredited four year college or university.

At a regional meeting held on March 25, 1971, "a unanimous decision was reached to close our seminary college at Oconomowoc, Wisconsin. It was also unanimously decided that beginning in September 1971, we will send our college students to the College of St. Thomas in St. Paul, Minnesota."[528] Father Hugh O'Rourke indicated some of the reasons for the change of venue. In addition to the continued rising cost of operations, the projected enrollment in the college for the 1971/72 academic year was just twenty students. While the college staff was "well qualified, at the present time no provision is being made anywhere in the society for personnel to teach at the college level. There is no possibility of our college receiving accreditation for granting degrees." The Society had to "face the question of whether we were justified in continuing to commit so much man power and money to an operation that promises such diminishing returns."[529]

After considering a number of seminaries in different Midwest cities with proximity to universities, they decided on the College of St. Thomas in St. Paul, Minnesota. Eleven students and a Columban formation team moved in time to start the 1971/72 academic year. They would live in Ireland Hall on the campus. Fathers Norbert Feld (rector), and John Comiskey (academic adviser), and Thomas Vaughan (spiritual director) were the initial formation team.[530]

---

the Rectors of College-level Seminaries in Wisconsin" on October 11, 1967. The questionnaire is attached to letters he sent to Hugh O'Rourke, the vice director of the U.S. region, the following day.

The College and Seminary "sought to retain an affiliation with Catholic University that it enjoyed as a junior college." On February 21, 1968, Rector Father Paul Keppner submitted a long report to the Catholic University of America (CUA) regarding the change from a two-year to a four-year college, and though he had not received word that the status would still apply, "we were told that the affiliation would hold good during the time required to process the change from a two-year to a four-year college." Paul Keppner to Joseph McGlade 10 May 1968. "History of Oconomowoc Accreditation." 8-B-12. Under Dr. Roy J. Ferrari's leadership the impetus of CUA Affiliation changed from exam taking to provision of materials for better teacher preparation, promotion of higher degrees for faculty, and a quarterly publication that provided course outlines, suggestions for newer textbooks, and articles on research on teaching. In the late 1950s state credentialing and standards were developed and by 1968 the Affiliation program of CUA ceased.

[528]   Hugh O'Rourke to "Dear Father" [a letter to all Columbans in the Regions] 5 April 1971. 8-B-12.

[529]   Ibid.

[530]   Father T. P. Reynolds was appointed to the St. Paul location but he remained in Milwaukee, Wisconsin to complete doctoral studies at Marquette University.

The Archdiocese of St. Paul seminary[531] was located across the main entrance from the College of St. Thomas on Summit Avenue. Jesuit and Franciscan formation houses were nearby. The Columbans would thus be mingling with other seminarians as well as lay students. The College was just two miles down Summit Avenue from the Society's pastoral house.[532]

In August 1974, the Society sold the Oconomowoc seminary buildings and land to the Oconomowoc Public School system for $500,000. Today the buildings and property are home to the Oconomowoc Public School Administrative Offices and Meadow View Elementary School. In keeping with the Columban tradition of planting trees and bushes, the Oconomowoc School system has been restoring the prairie land adjacent to the small lake on the property.

Changes at Silver Creek, New York and Bristol, Rhode Island Seminaries

Other changes were happening in Columban seminaries. Father Kevin O'Doherty, representing the superior general, came to Silver Creek sometime in 1964 to consult about whether to add on to the Silver Creek seminary. With 137 students at the time, possibly pushing to 140, he and Father Peter McPartland measured all the rooms of Silver Creek to decide whether any additions should be made to the buildings or whether to "wait it out for a year or two." Between that academic year and June 1968, the student numbers fell considerably. [533] As Father Steinhilber, who was vocation director from 1962–1966 remarked, "All of the sudden a tremendous effort of vocations and interest [in vocations] stopped. Just like throwing cold water on people. Not only with us but all over the country."[534]

On April 4, 1968, the Regional Council voted to close the seminary at Silver Creek, given that the projected student population was too low to have ten priests engaged in the work. That decision took place as the Columban Sisters were looking for a place to have a "mission" (and not only promotion) within the United States. The Columban Fathers gave a good portion of the property

---

[531] For a history of this important Archdiocesan seminary, founded in 1894 by Archbishop John Ireland, see Mary Christine Athans, *"To Work for the Whole People": John Ireland's Seminary in St. Paul* (NY: Paulist Press, 2003).

[532] A pastoral house for the Columbans was a location from which a priest did "supply work" in parishes or took on other pastoral responsibilities. It was not primarily a Promotion House. Cf. Father Joseph McSweeny interview of Father Richard Steinhilber. Interview 1, 11 July 2012.

[533] James McCaslin interview of Father Peter McPartland (1912–1987). Date of interview not known. Columban Oral History Archives, Dalgan/Navan.

[534] Father Joseph McSweeny interview of Father Richard Steinhilber. Interview 2. 12 July 2012.

and the seminary buildings to the Sisters. They would alter the internal areas to create a retirement home for women and men. Part of the agreement with the Sisters was that there would be up to ten accommodations available for Columban Fathers, if any of the men wished to retire there into the future. The buildings were remodeled with a view to the needs of the new residents.

From the home's opening on May 1, 1970, until 2016, one calculation is that a total of forty Columban priests have been in residence since the Sisters opened St. Columban's on the Lake Retirement Home. The home is a nonprofit, assistive-living facility administered by the Missionary Sisters of St. Columban.[535] In 2016, three Columban priests were in residence, one of whom is chaplain at the Residence. Some of the land at Silver Creek was rented to a farmer, even while the seminary was operating. The Society needed to pay taxes on that land because it was income producing. Eventually the farm land was sold, as well as the property "on the other side" of the railroad tracks.

Coordinating Seminary Formation

Given the alterations in the seminary programs and the direction needed with the new *normae,* the 1970 *Basic Plan,* and directives from the 1970 Society General Chapter, Father James McCaslin (1927–2003) was appointed the regional coordinator of the Columban Formation Program in 1971. He was a Creighton University graduate who served with the U.S. Army in Japan (1946– 48). He entered the Columbans two years later and was ordained in 1954. He served in the Philippines from about 1955 to the summer of 1966. He took a year's course in spirituality at the Catholic University of America, and in May 1968, he was appointed director of the Spiritual Year at Bristol.[536] Stepping into the position of Coordinator of the Formation Program, which encompassed all the seminaries, was no easy task. Not only were there multiple decisions to be made about education, spiritual practices, and daily routines in moving from one type of priestly and mission formation to that mandated by insights from Vatican II and new *normae,* but transitions were, perforce, uneven and difficult for all involved. St. John Seminary, Brighton, Massachusetts, where

---

[535]   The number is provided by Father Richard Steinhilber, who was regional director when the transfer was made. Father Joseph McSweeny interview of Father Richard Steinhilber. Interview 1. 11 July 2012.

[536]   Years later, McCaslin took time to absorb in a more formal fashion, the life, times, and spirituality of the early Columbans and that of St. Columban. The fruit of his reflection and study is, James McCaslin, *The Spirituality of Our Founders. A Study of the Early Columban Fathers* (St. Columban Society: Maynooth Mission to China, 1986).

the Columban seminarians took classes by 1966 had its own history of turmoil in that decade.[537]

Formation programs in religious congregations and apostolic societies across the country often bore the brunt of changes taking place in the 1960s and 1970s. The Columbans addressed the basic goals of formation at their 1970 General Chapter.[538] McCaslin's letter to the priests of the region a few months after he was appointed Coordinator captured well the various worldviews, experience, and perspectives that rubbed against each other and is worth quoting at length because it captured some of the conflicts of the time. Criticism about the formation program, McCaslin wrote, was based on "garbled information . . ., much on a failure to appreciate the problem the Seminary personnel have had to face in our recent past." [539] At the same time, "some criticism is undoubtedly justified." The program for the present seminarians "is different from that in which most of us were formed, and the end result will necessarily be a man somewhat different from ourselves. We must all learn to live with these differences and give one another credit for sincerity of purpose even where we cannot always understand or agree with each other."[540] Since Vatican II, the priest's role in the "modern world" has been reappraised, with seminaries the focal point of that search. Being "open to the world" took one form through field education, which, though a vital part of the program, "is a source of great confusion." [541] Mistakes have been made in that regard (deciding what types of work, how much work, what groups to engage seminarians with, for example), and the contact with various people "has not always been beneficial to immature men who didn't know how to handle it."[542] On the other hand, seminary staffs were not always sure what was the right thing to do. For example, seminarians were not asked to evaluate properly their use of freedom in their work. Apostolic activities were engaged in sometimes to the detriment of prayer and study. "We feel now we have enough experience

---

[537]   John C. Seitz, "'What better place?' Priesthood at St. John's Seminary, Boston 1965–1970." *U.S. Catholic Historian* 33 (Spring 2015), 49–82, details the nature of the conflicts at the seminary on the part of the faculty and the students.

[538]   The Basic Goals in missionary formation identified at the General Chapter were that formation "must ensure that in all its institutes of priestly formation the following goals are pursued: Missionary Motivation, Missionary Capacity, and Missionary Skills," each goal with an explanation of its intent. *Missionary Society of Saint Columban, General Chapter, 1970. Acts of the Chapter.* Printed and issued, 29 June 1971.

[539]   Father James McCaslin, To all the priests in the Region, 19 July 1971. CFA-USA.

[540]   Ibid.

[541]   Ibid.

[542]   Ibid.

to put everything in its proper perspective, and we intend to apply remedies where they are needed."[543]

Other factors McCaslin addressed included the fact that the seminarians began to see they could make a difference in their "own backyards and right now."[544] In other words, the challenge for formation was to keep the men's sights on mission beyond the United States. Toward this end, he wrote, "I myself consider it more and more necessary that we have a majority of our men with prior mission experience and who can be enthusiastic about that experience" and that the seminarians have mission experiences all along their formation time. Another area expressed by Columbans was the greater "freedom exercised by the student in coming and going and in their relationship with women."[545] While "concern was expressed that the men thought some seminarians were dating," McCaslin indicated that facts about individuals were needed in order to deal with individuals. The formation staff "seeks mature, responsible men who are better off learning how to handle things with direction, rather than simply obedient or fearful men who one day will have to face the realities of a very sin ridden world anyway."[546]

In his conclusion, McCaslin appealed to the men, "Please be patient with us. Change is very painful to everyone and never have we been confronted with so much so quickly. Mistakes have been made and will continue to be made. Pray for us, support us, inform us, ask us questions, and most of all give our students the example of a priesthood happily lived which will inspire them to go on."[547] In 1972/73, no students participated in the Spiritual Year, so James McCaslin was given a temporary assignment to the Milton seminary for that year. In 1976 the Columban students and several Columbans moved from Milton to a house in Cambridge, Massachusetts from whence they traveled to classes at the Boston Theological Institute. They received their degrees either through St. John's Seminary or Boston College. Beginning in 1978, a second house in the same location was begun for the Columban Spiritual Year.

McCaslin had some specific "backing" for his letter as far as the need for understanding of both groups. The 1970 General Chapter had addressed the relationship between older and younger priests in the Columban family. "Older

---

[543]   Ibid.

[544]   Ibid.

[545]   Ibid.

[546]   Ibid.

[547]   Ibid., To get a glimpse into the difficulties experienced by formation leadership during this time, the statistics that CARA (The Center for Applied Research in the Apostolate) compiled for the directors of novices in Women's Religious Congregations for this period indicate that about 50 percent of the directors of novices either left the community or had a nervous breakdown.

priests should likewise try to understand the mentality of younger priests, even though it might be different from their own and should follow their projects with good will."[548] Younger priests, in turn, should respect the age and experience of their seniors. They should "discuss plans with them, and willingly cooperate with them in matters which pertain to the care of souls."[549] The same principle would seem to apply between those who had made their Oath in the group and more experienced missionaries.

Repurposing Bristol Seminary

In 1974, Superior General Richard Steinhilber was on visitation to the United States and noted the particular interest in prayer he saw across the country by way of seminars on prayer, prayer groups, Thirty-Day Retreats (the Jesuit model of retreat), Directed Retreats, and Houses of Prayer. He saw the same attraction among the Columbans, "a good number of whom are involved with prayer groups." [550] The men inquired about new forms of retreat for themselves, including directed retreats, and had a "serious concern for suitable community prayer" in the houses. He wrote, "It struck me that possibly something could be done on a regional basis to provide for and encourage this worthy interest." Steinhilber raised the idea of the Bristol house as a year round Columban House of Prayer. A lengthy "Special Newsletter to the U.S. Region" included his remarks, Regional Superior Hugh O'Rourke's reflections, and James McCaslin's summation of a few types of retreats and prayer. Steinhilber wrote, "The atmosphere, the tradition and the facilities of Bristol make it ideal for this purpose," even if students were present. The Regional Council, after deliberation, gave unanimous approval for its immediate implementation."[551] Regional Superior Hugh O'Rourke commented further, "I believe that most of us would like occasionally to take some time away from the scene of our everyday activity."[552] The setting and quiet atmosphere at Bristol "can provide us with the setting we need for such reflection. I urge all men in the Region to

---

[548]   Father James McCaslin, To all the priests in the Region, 19 July 1971. CFA-USA.

[549]   *Missionary Society of Saint Columban, Acts of the General Chapter, 1970*, p. 87.

[550]   Regional Superior Hugh O'Rourke is quoted Superior General Steinhilber in, A Special Newsletter to Columbans in the U.S. region 11 June 1974. Superior General Richard Steinhilber noted that in his visitation of Columban houses in the United States, he observed that men were using local houses of prayer in their geographic areas.

[551]   Ibid.

[552]   Ibid.

seriously consider using the facilities at Bristol for this purpose."[553] With more
Columbans aging, as well, perhaps the Bristol location could also become a
home for retired Columbans. Father David Richers (1924–2002), a veteran
Korea missionary and vocation director (1971–1977), was appointed the
superior and bursar of the Bristol Retirement House and House of Prayer in
June 1977.[554] O'Rourke mailed a copy of the national directory of houses of
prayer (1979–80) to each Columban house in the region.[555]

Change of Regional Leadership

Between 1962 and 1967, Father Daniel Boland (1919–1967) served as the
regional superior. Under his direction many of the changes in the seminaries
were addressed. He would seem to be a fine choice for Columbans facing
education and formation issues. Born in Buffalo, New York, he had been on the
Silver Creek seminary staff beginning in 1944 and rector from 1950 to 1956.
From Silver Creek he was appointed rector at the Milton major seminary in
summer of 1957. His 1960 degree in education from Boston College provided
theoretical background for thinking through Columban education situations
in the United States.

Boland's appointment as regional superior included North and South
America (for five years) and pro-director of the Pro-Region of North America
(for three years). This meant visitation of the Columbans throughout North
America and which extended to Peru and Chile. His travels provided a sweeping
overview of the issues in the United States and the experience of Columban
mission in Spanish speaking countries of the Americas.

Guiding the region, along with his Council, would be a challenge, as was
be the case for anyone serving in major leadership of religious congregations
or mission societies during those years. However, Boland's situation was
compounded in January 1966, when he had an operation in Omaha for a
malignant growth. Over the next two years, a moderate degree of malignancy
appeared, though his lungs were clear of disease. In the middle of November
1966, and February 1967, he had further surgeries. By August 17 that year he
was suffering other afflictions. He died on September 2, 1967, in Buffalo, his

---

[553]   Ibid.

[554]   There were no men ready for the Spiritual Year in 1977. In 1978, the Spiritual Year
        would take place in Cambridge, Massachusetts in one of two formation houses the
        Columbans had. By this time, there was a National Directory of Houses of Prayer
        in the United States.

[555]   *Columban Newsletter* (November 1979). The regional superior noted that there were
        204 Houses of Prayer across the United States.

place of birth, and was buried at Silver Creek. In April 1967, Father Richard Steinhilber was appointed the new regional superior.

Exploring the Foundations of Mission after Vatican II

"Mission" was assumed in Columban seminary formation and lay at the heart of their lives and their magazine. Saving souls so they would not go to hell and converting people to the Catholic *religion* as main incentives for mission certainly had led Columbans and other missionaries to great heights of virtue. A mission theology course was not part of the seminary curriculum. However, the *Decree on the Church's Missionary Activity* (*Ad gentes divinitus*, 7 December 1965) and the "Norms" for Implementing that *Decree*[556] prompted explicit conversation and new underpinnings for mission. Father Donald Wodarz (1936–1994) was one of the first Columbans to engage in a formal study of the scriptural and theological foundations of mission and to do so in both Roman Catholic and ecumenical academic institutions.

Wodarz was born in Browerville, Todd County, Minnesota, in 1936, a very small town, whose population today is 290 people. He was a second generation American, with roots in Silesia. After attending a rural school for his first years of education, he went to St. Peter's School for the last four years of grade school. He somehow found the Columbans and went to Silver Creek and then to Milton in 1953, with a Spiritual Year at Bristol in 1954, and back to Milton to complete his seminary courses. Reflecting back on that seminary education, he "often complained of a lack of appreciation of American history and the American reality" among the largely Irish faculty members.[557] After his ordination on December 21, 1960, he went to Rome for a licentiate in Theology, where his thesis topic was on "Dialogue," which became "his fundamental approach to missiology. 'Dialogue' meant an openness to truth and particularly religious truth wherever it existed."[558] Wodarz was then appointed to missionary work in the Archdiocese of Cagayan, Philippines. In 1965 in Gingoog City he was on the faculty, a counselor, and chaplain at Christ the King College, which

---

[556] Pope Paul VI, *Ecclesiae sanctae, III*, 6 August 1966. Other documents related to mission followed over the next years, including encyclicals on the topic by subsequent popes and documents from the U.S. Catholic bishops.

[557] Cyril Hally, "Homily at the Funeral Mass for Don Wodarz," Australian Obituary for Father Wodarz. Hally said it was a "mild complaint, really." Hally worked closely with Wodarz in his years at the Columban Mission Institute, North Turramurra, Australia.

[558] Hally, "Homily at Funeral Mass for Don Wodarz." After Wodarz's death, Hally became the editor of the *Journal of South Pacific Mission Studies*, that Wodarz helped found.

had about 2,000 high school and college students. He learned firsthand the basics of Student Catholic Action and then worked with faculty to surface potential leaders from among the young women students. A training session of three days was set up and Student Catholic Action took off at the College. Shortly thereafter, the young men were trained and formed a SCA group. [559] The Columbans, starting with Edward J. McCarthy years before, were in the forefront of this movement in the Philippines and thus in the vanguard of training lay Catholic leaders.

He returned to the United States in March 1970, with an appointment to teach at the major Seminary in Milton. In March 1973, he was named rector, after Rector John Moriarty became ill. Wodarz engaged in the study of mission with a group of mission professors from various Protestant and Evangelical churches in the United States. In 1973, he, Dr. Gerald Anderson, with mission experience in the Philippines and soon to be named director of the Overseas Ministries Study Center,[560] and Dr. Ralph Winter, a mission strategist on the faculty at Fuller Theological Seminary, Pasadena,[561] formed the first executive committee of the American Society of Missiology (ASM), whose journal, *Missiology*, continues today.[562] The ASM sought to relate missiology to other scholarly disciplines and to promote cooperation and fellowship among those engaged in mission. Wodarz's ecumenical experience with this group and his study of the Church Growth movement while working on Professor Donald McGavran's papers at Fuller Seminary formed the background of his talk, "Foundations of Mission Theology," presented to the Columbans at their Nebraska headquarters on October 1, 1973.

Wodarz's years as rector of the Milton seminary were difficult for him, even traumatic, as Cyril Hally, a close friend and colleague in Australia noted. It was after Vatican II, "when seminarians were leaving, when two of his own

---

[559] Father Donald Wodarz, "Student Catholic Action," *Columban Fathers Missions* (April 1968), 4–6.

[560] Gerald Anderson was at Cornell University at the time and became director of the Overseas Ministries Study Center, Ventnor, New Jersey, in 1976. In 1987 the organization moved to its current location in New Haven, Connecticut, where it is a few blocks from Yale Divinity School with its huge collection (and tradition) of mission resources. Anderson remained director until 2000, almost a quarter of a century.

[561] Wodarz researched material for his dissertation on mission through Fuller Theological Seminary's School of World Mission, particularly the world growth theology of Donald McGavran (1897–1990), the founding Dean of the School. Wodarz's doctoral thesis was awarded a gold medal at the Gregorian University.

[562] For the history of the ASM, see Wilbert R. Shenk, George R. Hunsberger, *The American Society of Missiology: The First Quarter Century* (Decatur, GA: The American Society of Missiology, 1998). Wodarz continued the same ecumenical and mission association when he went to St. Columban's College in Turramurra.

staff left [the Society], and he felt to some extent that he was blamed, as rector of the college, for what was going on. Being a big person, with a big intellect, he understood perfectly well what was going on and that no one was really responsible. . . . But he did feel that to some extent he was held responsible. I don't think this hurt was ever healed, even though he could talk about it."[563] In June 1974, Wodarz was assigned to Rome to begin doctoral studies in mission.[564] He was then sent to teach at St. Columban's College in Turramurra, Australia. The next American Columban who completed doctoral studies in mission at the Gregorian University in Rome would be Father Robert Mosher in 1990. Ordained in 1980, Mosher was one of the first men who would have gone through a revised formation program with the emphases of the Second Vatican Council.

The *Normae* for implementing the Council's decree on missionary activity indicated that "the theology of mission is to become so much a part of theology, in the teaching of it as well as in the advancement by study, that the missionary nature of the church will be clearly understood."[565] One way the Columbans would do this in the United States was through a renewed Mission Education program, starting in 1979, with a suggested Mission Education program prepared by Richard Steinhilber, and a slide show organized by Father Colm Stanley and Vito Cioffero, former associate editor of *Sign* magazine. Cioffero was experienced in graphic arts and magazine production and assisted in various departments in Omaha at the time. The mission education program would grow in sophistication and influence over the years, as will be seen in chapter 7.

Diminishment for the Sake of Mission

By the end of the 1960s, it became clear that the Columbans were spread too thinly in the country. At an earlier time when missionaries were

---

[563]   Cyril Hally, "Homily at the Funeral Mass for Don Wodarz." Wodarz suffered a heart attack in fall 1976. In October 1977 he was at Omaha for additional recovery. Not only did he have the stresses of rectorship in what felt as uncertain times, he had just completed his doctoral studies.

[564]   Wodarz, Janet Carroll, MM, and Avery Dulles, SJ, prepared the "Memorandum on Evangelization," on behalf of the Major Superiors of Men Conference, in preparation for the 1974 Synod of Bishops, after which Pope Paul VI issued the apostolic exhortation, *Evangelii Nuntiandi* (*On Announcing the Gospel*), issued 8 December 1975. Memorandum Box 52 M. Miscellaneous. Major Superiors of Men Conference, CSP 1974–1976. Maryknoll Mission Archives, NY. In 1974, Wodarz also gave the principal talk at a Mission Theology Seminar, though the location and group to whom this was given are not clear.

[565]   Pope Paul VI, *Ecclesiae sanctae*, 6 August 1966, par. 1.

being evicted from China and later from Burma (now Myanmar), about fifty Columbans came to the United States to bide their time for their hoped for return to their mission. Given that the Society depended heavily upon the United States to provide mission funds, the returned missionaries were sent to existing promotion houses and opened new houses for that purpose. By 1970 it was clear to Father Steinhilber that there were "too many promotion houses, too many men engaged in promotion, who were needed in the missions and never got to the missions."[566] As he put it, "at the very beginning [of the Society] you had a handful of men in Ireland and the States, and Australia but most of the men were in the missions. Then all of a sudden we were starting to get this flip-flop mostly because of the targeting of Americans to do this work [promotion] at home."[567] In preparation for the 1970 General Chapter, the men at the 1969 Regional Convention recommended "that the Director continue to evaluate and review the existing promotion houses and operations in the U.S. region in light of expense and personnel."[568] After the houses were evaluated, the San Diego and Houston houses were put up for sale in 1970. The Columban house from which the San Diego Adobe Mission was served had been staffed by Columbans since 1938 (see chapter 4), but it had never been a profitable promotion house. The men mainly served the tourists on the history trail of the California missions. The St. Paul house went up for sale in February 1975 and the Denver house was sold in August 1976. The Society could no longer afford to have younger men sustain them. The priests were needed for the missions.

The 1972 *Newsletter* provided an overview of the Columban population in the United States: 139 priests (plus 6 seminarians with a permanent oath) worked in the United States in the following capacities:[569]

Regional Office	14
Vocation Work	6
Seminaries	10
Pastoral Houses	14
Pastoral Work, Supplies, Chaplains	36
Promotion Work and Retreats	30
Men 64 years of age and older	29

---

[566] Father Joseph McSweeny interview of Richard Steinhilber, Interview 2, 12 July 2012.

[567] Ibid.

[568] Seventh installment of information sent out by members of the Pre-Chapter Secretariat for distribution to all Society members, 8. Folder 1970. Papers to prepare for the 1970 Society General Chapter. CFA-USA.

[569] Source of Statistics: *Columban Newsletter* (January 1972).

That year more bedrooms were added to the main Columban building outside Omaha, because over twenty men were assigned to headquarters and the Society had a constant stream of visitors. An addition was put on to the office building and included a warehouse. On a more prosaic level, a Federal change particularly affected some members of the Society: the passage of Medicare, a national health program for people sixty-five years of age and older (one could apply when one was sixty-four), was signed into law by President Lyndon B. Johnson on July 30, 1965. This would impact individual Columbans able to apply for this in the next decades.

The Society General Chapter, 1970

A key word in Italian, *Aggiornamento* (Renewal) seemed to capture the intent and spirit of the Second Vatican Council, and the word was used ubiquitously. Congregations of men and women religious and Societies of Apostolic Life (the Columbans were in this ecclesiastical category) were mandated to assemble a General Chapter of their group after the Second Vatican Council to view their life and structures in light of the Council Documents. The Society's General Chapter held in Ireland in 1970 had that intent. At least a year of preparation took place in the Columban Regions. Surveys were taken. Issues were discussed at length and were recorded with divergences noted. Elected delegates from the Regions deliberated at the General Council held for almost four months prior to Christmas, 1970.[570]

As was true for previous chapters, the chapter deliberations were published in *The Acts of the General Chapter, 1970,* a 200 page document (including an index), that presented the context of various chapter deliberations, pertinent quotations from the Vatican II documents, material from the Society's Constitutions with recommendations for changes, Statutes, Mandates, and Recommendations from the chapter.[571] Topics ranged broadly and comprehensively to incorporate almost every aspect of Columban mission:

Rethinking our Aim and Nature with Vatican II

- Our apostolate and the relationships Columbans have with non-Christians, other mission institutes, episcopal conferences, local bishops

---

[570]   Archbishop Sergio Pignedoli addressed the Columban General Chapter. Archbishop Sergio Pignedoli, "Some Ideas on the Relevance of Missionary Institutes in the General Context and in the Local Churches," *Omnis Terra* XXXIII-2 (January 1971), 1–6.

[571]   One of the recommendations was that Father John Blowick be an ex-officio member of the chapter for life. *Acts of 1970 General Chapter,* 176. Blowick died in June 1972.

-    The apostolate in home regions
-    Personnel for the apostolate, including Volunteer Priests
-    Financing for mission
-    Formation for mission, including ongoing formation for Columban
     priests
-    Community structures
-    Communications
-    Missionary Spirituality, Priesthood, and Missions

Father Richard Steinhilber, elected superior general at the 1970 General
Chapter, wrote a preface to the *Acts*. The purpose of a Renewal Chapter,
he wrote, is "to make us a more effective missionary Society. We seek to do
together what we could not do as individuals." The chapter "attempted to set
out guidelines and establish structures for the achievement of our missionary
goals," with application of the principles left to the Regions. Father Steinhilber
continued,

> The Chapter stressed regional autonomy, coresponsibility,
> subsidiarity and team work on every level of the Society
> and in all aspects of our work. There will be differences of
> opinion in application of principles. These differences are
> not to be feared but welcomed. They are opportunities for
> living the Christian witness we preach. They help us to see
> problems as they really are, to form balanced policies and
> to discover solutions. Thus, our very differences can be a
> source of strength. Only, however, if we increasingly learn
> to communicate with one another, to respect each other's
> opinions, to listen with tolerance to views at variance with our
> own and try to see whatever is of truth in every opinion put
> forward. Only in this way will we arrive at that stage of 'one
> heart and soul' so essential for effective missionary work.[572]

Ideas such as subsidiarity and team work were in some respects new to some
Columbans and other Catholics. It would take time to work through just what
the ideas meant in practice.

---

[572]   Father Richard Steinhilber, *Acts of the General Chapter, 1970*, n.p. The *Acts* were
published in June 1971.

Other Dimensions of Columban Experience in These Years

In 1968, the Columbans celebrated their Golden Anniversary as a Society. In the United States, Father Charles Coulter, who was in charge of Promotion and on the Regional Council at the time, organized a wide variety of activities to celebrate those years in mission. Bishop Fulton J. Sheen, former director of the National Society for the Propagation of the Faith, and Douglas Hyde, former Communist turned Catholic, gave talks to celebrate the anniversary. Hyde was the keynote speaker at a banquet in the Americana Hotel following the concelebration Mass at St. Patrick's Cathedral in New York City. [573] Some celebrations featured talks given by a Franciscan, Cardinal Juan Landázuri Ricketts (1913–1997), the archbishop of Lima, Peru, where the Columbans had missions. That year the cardinal was the acting president of the Medellín Conference of Bishops.[574]

The Vatican II document, *Ad Gentes,* referred to the interaction of Catholics with "non-Christians," "separated Christians," and those "non-Christians." Father Daniel McGinn was appointed to the English-speaking section of the Vatican secretariat for non-Christians, in May 1971.[575] He had served in Japan from 1954 to 1961 and had acquired knowledge of Buddhism, both the underlying principles and what that looked like in practice in that country. As he described his work in the Secretariat's office, he had largely a "desk job" as a liaison with people from other religions, often dignitaries, who wished to have an audience with the Pope. In some cases, this would involve interaction with the Vatican's Secretary of State as well as Ambassadors in Rome. McGinn's understanding of Buddhist communities' dynamics would give special insight when people with Buddhist background might seek an audience with the Pope. His work later was called the "Welcoming Visitors" function of the Secretariat. He also engaged with others in the Secretariat to set up the annual conference related to dialogue with people of others faiths.

---

[573] Hyde stayed with the Columban Fathers at their promotion house in Bayside, Queens, New York. Information about Hyde's week in New York provided to the author by Father John Brannigan, 1 April 2017.

[574] The Latin American bishops, gathered in Medellín, Colombia, issued a document, "Poverty of the Church," on September 6, 1968.

[575] *Pope Paul VI* instituted a special department of the Roman Curia for relations with people from various religions. In 1988, the office was renamed as Pontifical Council for Interreligious Dialogue. Its purpose is to promote the spirit and principles underlying the Second Vatican Council document, *Nostra aetate*: to foster dialogue with people of various religions; to promote mutual understanding, respect and collaboration with people of different religious backgrounds. McGinn's one year appointment came from Superior General Richard Steinhilber, who, no doubt, would have been contacted by the Secretariat to provide a qualified person for the position.

The year prior to the Society's 1976 General Chapter, a regional meeting raised issues and concerns the men identified in several areas:

- Nature of the Society: "confusion about the meaning of the nature and purpose of the Society today"
- Persons: concerns for those retired, problem of isolation or alienation, but a desire to do something about these aspects of life
- Community life: what is the nature, need for, and implications of a Christian Primary Community for Columbans
- Spirituality: "not a communal acceptance of the meaning of spiritualty," diverse forms of spirituality
- Charity—"prevalent in desire and conviction"—but "how is that related to legitimate forms of plurality"
- Formation, and Government. The men noted particularly an "absence of a personnel counselor for the Region, a matter of concern to many."[576]

The Columbans demonstrated honesty in identifying their issues and a willingness to engage with the realities, in spite of their divergence of thought in some areas.

Conclusion

As was true for the Catholic Church in the United States, Columbans altered a Tridentine model of seminary structure, curriculum and formation, to one that reflected the immersion of the church in the world. As the oft quoted first lines of the *Pastoral Constitution on the Church in the Modern World* (1965) put it, "The joy and hope, the grief and anguish of the men [and women] of our time, especially of those who are poor or afflicted in any way, are the joy and hope, the grief and anguish of the followers of Christ as well." Field education with some kind of feedback from others about pastoral and personal strengths and challenges broadened a seminarian's experiential base by way of interaction with people from social, religious, cultural or economic background different than his own. Through the years the experience was called Pastoral Year, Clinical Pastoral Experience, Overseas Training Program, and Field Mission Assignment. Challenges abounded for seminarians and for those who supervised them. What did the development of a priestly spirituality that was "ecclesial," not simply devotional mean? How could one gain a deep

---

[576]   [United States] Regional Convention, 1975, "Diagnosis." Document #1 (P-I -1).
         CFA-USA.

knowledge and use of scripture for one's spiritual life and for preaching and teaching? What would identification of the particularities of one's own humanness require of each member? The questions were part of a larger shift that became fruitful over the years, but the process had begun. In addition to the resources offered at Boston Theological Institute and later at the Catholic Theological Union, Chicago, the Society could look for resources from among their members—from the men whose studies were in scripture, liturgy, theology or psychology. The Society had a sustained interaction with lay formation and retreat work which provided further insight for priestly mission formation.

The physical moves and alterations of the Columban seminary properties and buildings reflected the changes. Reuse or sale of Columban buildings to groups who served the interests of children and the elderly carried Columban mission more broadly. The time of change as the Society sought to "rethink our Aim and Nature with Vatican II" brought eagerness, hope, stress, resistance, and uncertainty. Rare is the Columban, or any Catholic living in the United States in this period who did not experience some, if not all, of those feelings. People in leadership on any level sometimes felt they sailed in uncharted waters.

"Changin' times," indeed. In 1976, Americans celebrated the bicentennial of the United States of America with parades, tableau, speeches, fireworks, historical reenactments, and conferences. From August 1 to August 8 that year, Catholics from around the world came to Philadelphia for an International Eucharistic Congress, whose theme was "The Eucharist and the Hungers of the World." That same year, the Columban General Chapter also met and similarly linked an emphasis on the Justice and Peace elements of mission. The fruits of that chapter would be taken up over subsequent years, including the establishment of a Columban Justice and Peace Office, a story told in the following chapter.

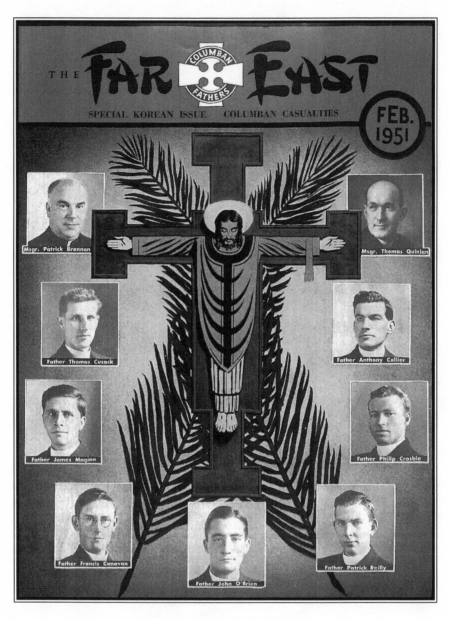

February 1951 Far East _Page_01

170

CHAPTER 6

"Action on behalf of justice . . . a constitutive dimension of the preaching of the Gospel." Implications and Challenges 1977–2012

The significant experience of the Second Vatican Council overflowed into new ways to think about and revitalize Catholic life and mission globally. Columbans examined a full range of Catholic perspectives on scripture, liturgy, relationships with other religions and approaches to the world, and lay formation. New mission emphases came to the fore to address the political, social and cultural realities of the people Columbans served. Mission involved helping people reflect on their experience in light of the Gospel, attain proper working conditions, and acquire appropriate skills and knowledge to create humane communities, often amid oppressive situations. Against the background of ecclesiastical investment in terms of social justice values, the chapter will focus on the inauguration and growth of a Columban Justice and Peace office, new Columban missions in Latin America, the relationship of inculturation and mission, the implications of an aging population, and "surplus funds" and property in the U.S. region. Another key justice theme related to land, ecology and the environment will be treated in chapter 12.

The U.S. Catholic Context: 1970s, 1980s

Building on the richness of the Second Vatican Council documents and Pope Paul VI's encyclical, *Populorum Progressio* (*On the Progress of Peoples*, 1967),[577] Pope Paul VI convened a synod of bishops in 1971 to develop further the social justice elements of Catholic life and thought. The synod document, *Justice in the World*, indicated the purpose of the bishops' deliberations: "Gathered from the whole world, in communion with all who believe in Christ and with the entire human family, and opening our hearts to the Spirit, who is the whole of creation new, we have questioned ourselves about the mission of the People of God to further justice in the world."[578] Probably the most remembered sentence in the document contained what seemed an explosive statement: "Action on behalf of justice is a constitutive dimension of preaching the Gospel."[579] Catholics wrestled with the meaning and implications of the sentence for years to come.

The U.S. bishops' 1971 *Pastoral on Mission Activity* affirmed the missionary vocation but raised the issue of the relationship of mission to development. "Salvation for some today means meeting people's needs in the temporal order. For others it cannot be found this side of eternity. The meeting of these two points of view constitutes the alleged conflict as to which is primary in the missionary effort, the development or the evangelization of people."[580] The problem of "development," especially related to the relationship between the United States and Latin America had its own difficulties.

The U.S. bishops published the key interventions they gave at the 1974 Synod, including that of John Cardinal Carberry (St. Louis, Missouri), "The Church: Essentially Missionary."[581] The bishops pointed out that shortly after the close of the 1974 Synod, the United Nations held a conference in Rome on the world food crisis. The two events were connected, "something which may not be immediately apparent. A major insight of this synod has been that work for justice and human development is intimately related to the proclamation

---

[577]   *Populorum Progressio* reiterated social justice emphases since Pope Leo XIII, *Rerum Novarum* (1891). Among the consistent values over the years are a just wage for employees, the right to organize and join a union, a right to fair and safe working conditions, and that the development of people and of the world's economy should serve the many and not just a few people. Later popes continued the themes: Pope John Paul II, *Sollicitudo rei Socialis* (1987), Pope Benedict XVI, *Caritatis in Veritate* (2009).

[578]   World Synod of Catholic Bishops, *Justice in the World* (1971), par. 1.

[579]   Ibid., par. 6.

[580]   Hugh J. Nolan, *Pastoral Letters of the U.S. Catholic Bishops*, Vol. 3 (Washington DC: U.S. Catholic Conference, 1987), 293–297, here 293.

[581]   United States Catholic Conference, *Synod of Bishops, 1974* (United States Catholic Conference: Washington DC, 1975).

of the Gospel. The food conference will turn the spotlight of international attention on an urgent and awesome issue of justice."[582]

The 1971 and 1974 Bishops Synods' emphasis on the social teachings of the Gospel coincided in the next decades with extensive support of social justice among a wide spectrum of groups, including the U.S. Catholic Bishops Conference, the Conference of Major Superiors of Religious Men, the Leadership Conference of Women Religious, and the burst of mission action through various North American political and religious groups, especially those with a stake in Latin America.

The bishops had formed an International Office of Justice and Peace in the early1960s. The associate secretary of the bishops' committee from 1973–1992, Father Bryan Hehir, was a major force in assisting Catholic groups to articulate justice and peace issues and how they would cooperate to approach various situations. Hehir, along with the U.S. Catholic Mission Council, men and women religious superiors, and Peter Henriot and Joseph Holland (Center of Concern, Washington DC), framed the content and processes for this purpose in national gatherings of major superiors of men and women (1977–1979). Major superiors were hearing from their missionary members about the impact of U.S. foreign policy or big business practices from North America on the people they served. Rather than responding as individual congregations, it would make more sense to combine efforts to address issues.

Between 1968–1987 the U.S. Catholic Bishops produced two key pastoral letters elaborating on the social justice dimensions of the Gospel: *The Challenge of Peace* (1983) and *Economic Justice for All: Catholic Social Teaching and the U.S. Economy* (1986).[583] The documents developed from the process of small groups for the bishops' listening sessions. Major superiors of missionary societies were one of these group. The process and subsequent bishops' document on the economy created a strong interest and sometimes alarm from the U.S. civic and business community, especially because the pastoral on economic justice touched a nerve in the body of capitalist economics.[584] So much so, the bishops' third document in this period, *To the Ends of the Earth: A Pastoral Statement on*

---

[582] Ibid., 83. Pope Paul VI issued an apostolic exhortation, *Evangelii Nuntiandi* (December 8, 1975), ten years after the Second Vatican Council. Much of the material in the pastoral reflected the 1974 Synod of Bishops' deliberations.

[583] For an overview of the U.S. Catholic Bishops' promotion of Catholic social teachings in this period, see Bishop William Murphy, "The Social Initiatives of the United States Conference of Catholic Bishops," *The Catholic Social Science Review* 18 (2013), 45–61.

[584] The Chair of the Bishops' Committee responsible to research and write the document, Archbishop Rembert G. Weakland, OSB (Milwaukee), wrote about the several years' formation of the document. Rembert G. Weakland, OSB, *A Pilgrim in a Pilgrim Church. Memoirs of a Catholic Archbishop* (Grand Rapids, MI: Eerdmans Publishing Company, 2009), 273–292.

World Mission (1987), received almost no attention from the public, even though it was intended as part of a triad of related issues.[585] Nevertheless, with this rich background and Columban mission experience, the Society created strategies to activate and unfold the relationship between mission and social justice.

Columbans in the U.S. region had supported boycotts of Nestlé Corporation for their marketing of infant formula in Third World communities, boycotts against the J. P. Stevens Company, the largest textile manufacturer in the United States, for failing to allow workers to unionize,[586] and the longstanding boycott of grapes and lettuce because of the working conditions of mainly Hispanic farm workers in California. The Columbans would know the latter experience from their mission among Mexican people in the Westminster, California area and in the next decade in Alamogordo, New Mexico.

In the context of this larger background we will examine the growth of a Columban *office* of Justice and Peace, the Columban experience in Latin America, from whence came so many of the "hot" sociopolitical issues addressed by the office, and inculturation, a term new to many but reflective of the relationship between the Incarnation and how that "looks" in cultures.

Formation of a Justice and Peace Office

Columban General Chapter Mandate

The 1976 Columban General Chapter connected social, cultural, political and economic situations to scriptural and theological understandings of mission. "Our special role as an exclusively missionary Society is in crossing boundaries of language, culture and faith to establish the Church and to assist local churches in bringing the knowledge and love of Jesus Christ to the unevangelized."[587] The call to mission is threefold: "to incarnate the Gospel in cultures which are not our own; to bring about full Christian liberation to the poor and the oppressed of the countries in which we work; to facilitate

---

[585] While the bishops published *To the Ends of the Earth* through their office, it is notable that the Overseas Ministries Study Center (OMSC), an organization sponsored by a large and diverse group of Christian mission researchers and missionaries, also printed the document. National Conference of Catholic Bishops, "To the Ends of the Earth: A Pastoral Statement on World Mission," *International Bulletin of Missionary Research* (April 1987), 50–57.

[586] J. P. Stevens had been founded in the midnineteenth century in Massachusetts but moved their headquarters to the Carolinas where labor was cheaper and there were few unions. On the boycott against J. P. Stevens, see Timothy J. Minchin, "'Don't Sleep with Stevens': The J. P. Stevens Boycott and Social Activism in the 1970s," *Journal of American Studies* 39 #3 (2005), 511–543.

[587] Missionary Society of Saint Columban, *Acts of the General Chapter, 1976*, #1, 1–4, p. 10.

dialogue between Christians and non-Christians."[588] In other words, mission addressed the Gospel in relation to culture, the poor and oppressed, and offered particular values to share with people of other religious traditions. How did this work out in practice in relation to the U.S. region?

The chapter resolution, "immediately to set up a Justice and Peace Office and that each Region establish a similar office or be affiliated with already existing offices of this nature,"[589] found fertile ground in U.S. Catholic life, given the wealth of statements from the U.S. bishops and Catholic practice. Regional Director Coulter appointed Father James McCaslin as Justice and Peace officer in the U.S. region in 1977. [590] Theologically the office embodied Vatican II documents and more explicitly the Bishops' Synod document, *Justice in the World*, from which the *Columban Newsletter* quoted a key sentence. "Action on behalf of justice and participation in the transformation of the world fully appear to us as a constitutive dimension of the preaching of the Gospel, or, in other words, of the church's mission for the redemption of the human race and its liberation from oppressive situations."[591] Columbans referenced the sentence often into the next decade.[592]

Given the number of national Catholic organizations already devoted to justice issues, Father McCaslin's first job was to find out what groups were in place nationally. He was appointed as Columban liaison with the Office of International Justice and Peace of the U.S. Catholic Conference partially for that purpose.[593] He was "to research and make recommendations how the Region can best fulfill its responsibilities in this important area,"[594] a kind of "consultation phase."[595]

---

[588]   Missionary Society of Saint Columban, *Acts of the General Chapter, 1976*, #1, 1–4, p. 10.

[589]   Ibid., #13, p. 14.

[590]   Father Eamon O'Brien was named to begin a Justice and Peace Office at the Columban Central Administration (Ireland) in 1977.

[591]   *Columban Intercom* (June 1977), 2. This issue of *Intercom* also laid out the Central Administration's initiatives for the establishment of a Justice and Peace Office.

[592]   See, for example. *Columban Mission Today*, Missionary Society of St. Columban General Chapter, 1982, p. 38.

[593]   For an overview of the role of the U.S. Catholic Bishops Conference in relation to promotion of teachings on social justice, see Bishop William Francis Murphy, *Catholic Social Science Review* (2013), 45–61

[594]   *Columban Newsletter* (September 1977).

[595]   *Columban Intercom* (June 1977).

From a Committee to an Office

With McCaslin assigned back to the Philippines in 1979, three Columbans were appointed to a Justice and Peace Committee: Fathers Mark Mengel (Chair, Chile/Cambridge, Massachusetts), Michael O'Loughlin (South Korea/Derby, NY), and Vincent McCarthy (Fiji/Omaha).[596] The group was appointed through 1982 with two more Columbans joining them.[597] The Columban intention was to "affirm, support and cooperate with what is being done by the U.S. Bishops Conference."[598] The *Report to Chapter, 1982* indicated they "tried to avoid duplicating the work of other established agencies in the same or related fields" and continued Columban cooperation with other national groups working on justice issues.[599]

The first objective of the Justice and Peace Committee had two parts: "to acquire a better appreciation of how the promotion of human rights is a constitutive element of the Gospel; to acquire a more critical awareness and understanding of socioeconomic realities, particularly as they relate to global justice and development."[600] The second objective was to educate home churches to help them acquire a similar awareness.[601] It would take some time for the Society to have an overview of the multiple organizations nationally and internationally and to decide what the Columban experience offered other groups.

In April 1983, Father Michael O'Loughlin was appointed Justice and Peace Coordinator. Regional Director Charles Coulter asked him to take some

---

[596] To get an idea of the large areas focused upon initially, O'Loughlin, in addition to issues related to Korea and China was to be informed on human rights, right to life, death penalty, women, labor, political prisoners. McCaslin in addition to social justice concerns of the Philippines, Southeast Asia, and the South Pacific, was to focus on peace, nuclear power, disarmament, chemical waste, and ecology. Mengel, who focused on Latin America, was also to concentrate on issues surrounding agribusiness, hunger, housing, Transnationals, and corporate responsibility.

[597] An experienced missionary in the Philippines, Father Brendan O'Sullivan, was on the Staff of St. Columban's Theologate, Cambridge, Massachusetts, in July 1980. The following June he was appointed to the U.S. Regional Commission for Justice and Peace. At the November 1982, Society General Chapter, O'Sullivan was elected a member of the superior general's Council until 1988. For an overview of O'Sullivan's life to that point, see "Father O'Sullivan's Parish: The World," *CM* (March/April 2001), 22–26.

[598] *Columban Newsletter* (November 1979), 73.

[599] "Report to Chapter, 1982. Region of the United States," 14. At the 1982 General Chapter, the Justice and Peace officers were to be referred to as Coordinators. Each of the three Columbans was responsible for particular areas geographically and issue related.

[600] *Acts of the Chapter, October 4–December 8, 1976,* #13, p. 14–15.

[601] Ibid., p. 15.

courses in sociology, political science, and justice and peace,[602] as well as to "find out more about the China issue."[603] In the meantime, the Regional Council decided to select contact people representing various areas of responsibility. The men would in fact replace the Justice and Peace Regional Commission. "Their duty would be to assist and collaborate with the J&P Office in fulfilling regional duties in J&P."[604]

In July 1984, Regional Director Peter Cronin asked O'Loughlin to open a Justice and Peace Office in Washington DC given that the Federal government, the U.S. Catholic Bishops' organization, and many justice groups were located there. O'Loughlin wondered, "Would I be capable of doing what they were asking me to do? Because [as a citizen of Ireland] I was a total outsider. The issues at the time were basically focused on the Philippines and then in Chile, the Pinochet thing. So reluctantly I decided I would go [to DC] and Peter Cronin was very supportive."[605] The Columban Justice and Peace Office opened in late fall 1984, or early 1985,[606] in a building where the CARA offices were located in Washington.[607] O'Loughlin introduced himself to the coalition groups, especially Korean and Filipino organizations and the Washington Office for Latin America, an NGO (nongovernment organization).[608]

O'Loughlin felt expectations from Washington groups that the Columbans could effect change for the better. Given that he attended many meetings and was away from the office, he hired what he initially thought of as a secretary to take care of the office,[609] "because I was going helter-skelter, running between the Korean coalition and the Philippine coalition and all the Latin American coalitions." [610] He hired Susan Thompson on November 1, 1985, as a full-time staff member. She would take leadership in Columban-focused areas until 2002.

---

[602]   O'Loughlin took courses at Queens College, Queens, New York. He moved to the Columban Bayside promotion house, closer to the college. Father Sean Dwan interview of Father Michael O'Loughlin, 2013.

[603]   At the 1976 Columban General Chapter, the incoming Central administration was charged "to establish a special Commission for the Chinese Apostolate and mission among Chinese." *Acts of the Chapter, 1976*, #4, p. 10.

[604]   *Columban Newsletter* (June 1983).

[605]   Father Sean Dwan interview of Father Michael O'Loughlin, 2013.

[606]   It is unclear whether the office officially opened in late fall 1984, or very early 1985.

[607]   The CARA offices were located in the former Viatorian Seminary at 3700 Oakwood Terrace, NE Washington DC.

[608]   The Columbans also made a financial contribution to the three groups mentioned. At some point, O'Loughlin became a naturalized U.S. citizen.

[609]   The only two categories on the application form for lay people to work with Columbans were "secretary" or "housekeeping." Thompson was neither. Author telephone interview with Susan Thompson, 20 December 2016.

[610]   Father Sean Dwan interview of Father Michael O'Loughlin, 2013

Her previous experience included years of shelter work for homeless people at first in her parish's church basement in Alexandria, Virginia. The project soon involved many other churches (eventually thirty-five) and became a large, effective presence in the city. Thompson was moving toward advocacy work for low-income housing to address the causes of homelessness. Her perspective was that "while some people might think of 'mission' as what was happening 'over there,'" her conviction was that "mission is wherever you are."[611] At the Justice and Peace office, she continued her interest in housing for homeless and low-income people but expanded to additional key areas the Columban chapter documents and the U.S. region expressed.

The workings of the office were fluid, in that she and McLaughlin were daily learning their way. At first, Susan tagged along with Mike to meetings, getting to know individuals and groups. During her seventeen years with the Columbans at the Justice and Peace office, Thompson worked with and provided leadership in many groups, especially in advocating for Third World concerns in Latin America, as participant and leader in groups focused on women's issues (on behalf of the Columbans she attended the 1995 International Women's Conference in Beijing)[612], and as cochair of a housing advocacy group in the District of Columbia. Thompson found that in her interaction with various constituencies, "you're a known entity being part of the Columbans. You are able to accomplish so much more with other groups." Father O'Loughlin later noted, "I [and this included the staff of other Columbans and Susan Thompson] was continually making contacts and I was beginning to feel a little bit more helpful, a little bit better than I did in the beginning. I was feeling more optimistic we could do something."[613]

The 1982 Society General Chapter connected mission education, justice and peace. The purpose of mission education and animation "is to develop awareness among Society members and the people of our churches of origin that justice is a constitutive element of the Gospel and an essential part of the apostolate of the missionary church."[614] O'Loughlin carried the message to Catholics in other settings. He gave four workshops on Justice and Spirituality,

---

[611]   Author telephone interview with Susan Thompson, 20 December 2016.

[612]   Father Richard Steinhilber invited Thompson to organize articles for an issue of *Columban Mission*, "Women—Where Hope Lies," (*CM* (September/October 1996) in view of the Conference. The issue was translated into Spanish and later, the magazine had its own Spanish edition. Susan also gave a talk at Columban U.S. headquarters about the Beijing conference.

[613]   Father Sean Dwan interview of Father Michael O'Loughlin, 2013.

[614]   Society of St. Columban General Chapter (1982), *Columban Mission Today*, 38. The 1988 Society General Chapter included Integrity of Creation as a new dimension of Justice and Peace work. At some point the Columban Washington DC office was titled, Justice, Peace, and Integrity of Creation.

"with a good turnout of those who were looking for ways to integrate a social analysis into their social programs."[615] He and Sister Dorothy Mahon, RSM, who provided leadership in mission education and was on staff at the Columban parish in Norwich, Connecticut, gave Justice and Peace workshops in the Northeast in June 1985. The Columbans collaborated with several mission sending groups in the United States to produce a filmstrip based on Gerald and Patricia Mische's, book, *Toward a Human World Order.*[616] The Columban Mission Education programs the region developed reinforced justice and peace values.[617] Columbans participated in periodic workshops or retreats centering on the topic of spirituality and justice held at one of the Columban houses in the United States to deepen personal understanding of this aspect of Columban life.

As the staff grew in experience and knowledge and the office's constituencies multiplied through the years, three intertwined approaches centered their hub of activity: **advocacy, education** for themselves and their constituents about particular issues, and **public witness**.[618] Columban programs over the decades are too numerous to describe adequately, but a few examples of each approach will illustrate the many facets of their work. Some examples overlap in their focus.

Advocacy

An advocate is one who pleads for another's cause, often because that person is unable to do so for any number of reasons. The United States gave monies or support to a government elsewhere, often as part of an arrangement that redounded to the benefit of the United States. Advocates in this context interceded on behalf of Columban constituencies who felt the negative impacts of international politics and business practices. Columbans brought their considerable experience and truth to the advocacy table. Some of their stories appeared in *Columban Mission* and other Columban media. When the Justice and Peace office in Washington became an active channel for justice issues related to the Philippines, the Society had abundant and firsthand knowledge of issues. Columbans had already taken initiative by the 1970s.

---

[615]   *Columban Newsletter* (September 1984).

[616]   The Franciscans, Jesuits, Pallotines, and Sacred Heart Fathers were among the collaborators. The full title of the book from which the filmstrip was developed is *Toward a Human World Order. Beyond the Security Straightjacket* (New York: Paulist Press, 1977).

[617]   For the history of the Columban Mission Education program, see chapter 7.

[618]   The categories were identified in author telephone interview with Susan Thompson, 20 December 2016.

Chicago born Columban Father W. Robert Burke (1923–2011) focused on the sugar workers shortly after he went to the Philippines in 1955. Except for four years when he resided at the Columban seminary in Milton in the 1970s, he served in Negros until 1993, after which he served the Filipino community in the Chicago area.[619] Father Burke was the "first Columban in Negros to see the need for a priest to be involved in social activism in response to repressive poverty."[620] In La Castellan (Negros Occidental), Columban Father Patrick Hynes (1925–2004),[621] diocesan priest Edgardo Saguinsin, and Jesuit Hector Mauri set up the first nongovernment controlled labor union for sugar workers (National Federation of Sugar Workers) in 1970. After Martial Law was declared in 1972, many members of the union were jailed and some killed. The Major Superiors of Religious Congregations in the Philippines published a study of the sugar workers' situation in 1975.[622] Columban Father John Brannigan was contacted in 1974 by the president of the Association of Major Religious Superiors of Men to conduct some of the research for the study, while he taught at San Vicente Ferrer Major Seminary, Jaro, Iloilo.[623]

One early case of the Columban Justice and Peace office advocacy in the 1980s vis-à-vis the Philippines' situation took place after Father Michael O'Loughlin met Rosemary O'Neill, a daughter of Congressman Thomas P. O'Neill of Massachusetts. She introduced O'Loughlin to her father, who was Speaker of the House of Representatives (1977–1986). O'Neill, an advocate for social causes, especially those affecting poor, unemployed or underprivileged people, took an interest in the Philippines situation and was aware of the arrests of clergy, women religious and others.[624] He advised O'Loughlin to get

---

[619]   Burke, ordained in the Archdiocese of Chicago in 1949, had several years as a parish priest before he entered the Society of St. Columban (September 1955) and left for the Philippines in November of that year.

[620]   Father John Brannigan correspondence with author, 1 April 2017. "Other Columbans at the time saw the poverty but they understood their priesthood in terms of sacramental ministry and building parish schools, which they did with enormous success." Ibid.

[621]   Father John Brannigan provided helpful background on Columban involvement in social justice in the Philippines, prior to the opening of the Columban Justice and Peace office in Washington. He suggested that "not enough credit has been given to Patrick Hynes' role in social activism." John Brannigan e-mail correspondence with author 1 April 2017. Assigned to Negros in 1950, Patrick Hynes (1925–2004) worked the next forty-six years in Negros parishes before he retired to Dalgan.

[622]   Association of Major Superiors in the Philippines, *The Sugar Workers of Negros: A Study Commissioned by the Major Superior of the Philippines* (1975).

[623]   Father John Brannigan e-mail correspondence with author 23 April 2017.

[624]   Tip O'Neill also worked with Senators Ted Kennedy, Daniel Patrick Moynihan and others between 1977 and 1985 toward a peaceful accord between warring groups in Northern Ireland. For O'Neill's memoir, see Tip O'Neill with William Novak, *Man*

a petition with at least fifty signatures of congressional members to begin a process toward a bill or other document to address the situation of arrests and factors related to the arrests.[625]

McLoughlin ended up with fifty-six signatures, an accomplishment which was just one of many achieved through the work and knowledge of the "highly qualified" and "very talented" Christina Cobourn, whom O'Loughlin was "fortunate to meet" at a conference.[626] Working in the Philippines with the Mennonite Central Committee, Cobourn knew several Columbans. Among the many areas she handled were communications and advocacy for human rights and development issues in the Philippines. O'Loughlin offered her a job at the Columban office. She was hired in 1987 as Asia director and remained on the Justice and Peace staff until 1992. Christina had tremendous knowledge and skills for congressional advocacy especially in human rights in Asia and sustainable development. She "had the ability and the personality as a lobbyist,"[627] as well as having numerous contacts in a wide variety of circles.

With O'Loughlin appointed vice regional director of the Columbans in 1987,[628] Father Mark Mengel was named to head the Justice and Peace Office where he remained until 1994. Mengel, a native of Holyoke, Massachusetts, had been Chair of the Justice and Peace Committee at its inception. He came with mission experience in Santiago, Chile, where Augusto Pinochet's military junta had overthrown the socialist President Salvador Allende. Pinochet, as head of a military government, began the oppression, killing and "disappearance" of thousands of Chileans from 1974–1990. Father Charles (Chuck) Lintz, a native

---

of the House. The Life and Political Memoirs of Speaker Tip O'Neill (New York: Random House, 1987).

[625]   Father Sean Dwan interview of Father Michael O'Loughlin, 2013. Congressman Tip O'Neal, along with three other prominent U.S. political figures of Irish extraction, led the movement toward issuing the St. Patrick's Day Declaration (1977) that denounced the violence in Northern Ireland, on through the Irish aid package upon signing of the Anglo-Irish Agreement (1985).
In 1984, Father James McCaslin wrote to President Ronald Reagan prior to Reagan's visit to the Philippines. McCaslin described the oppressive situations people experienced daily. "As an American I am further saddened by the apparent blessing my government has given to a regime that, at the present time, in no way represents the aspirations of the Filipino people." James McCaslin to "Dear Mr. President" [Ronald Reagan], 1984. CFA-USA.

[626]   Father Sean Dwan interview of Father Michael O'Loughlin, 2013.

[627]   Ibid., As of this writing (2017), Christina Cobourn Herman is program director at the Interfaith Center on Corporate Responsibility, New York

[628]   O'Loughlin remained in the DC area for another year or so before he went to Omaha. From 1988–1994, O'Loughlin was on the Board of the United States Catholic Mission Association. He was appointed U.S. regional director from 1991–1994 and was on the superior general's Council from 1994–2000.

of Rochester, New York, and veteran missionary in Korea, also joined the staff with Mengel.[629]

To "learn the ropes," Father Mengel attended every meeting possible relating to the Columban focus. Initially he would "stand in a corner to listen," but being a good listener as well as contributor, he soon became known to many people and groups. He was asked to be on a committee, "then, before I knew it, I'm chair of the committee, then I find myself on a Board."[630] That way, "I got to know people personally and could invite them to our events." Working with diverse individuals and groups, he learned that "a lot of times [the justice issue] is personal."[631] That is, pursuit of justice values was central to the identity of the person.

Education

Education for the staff came through reading, attendance at workshops, courses, talking with people in pertinent organizations, and meetings between Columban missionaries and agencies/government officials for whom the information or perspectives could be helpful. One of these many occasions took place when Mengel arranged to have Columban Father Shay Cullen meet with a Brazil delegation representing the National Street Children's Movement. The delegation was sponsored by the Washington-based Brazil Network, of which the Justice and Peace Office was an active member.[632] Father Cullen was known internationally for his work through the Preda Foundation, a group he founded in 1974 in Olongapo City, Philippines, to rescue sexually abused children from traffickers, brothels, and prisons.[633] The organization expanded services in several directions over the years, including therapeutic homes for the rescued children, handicraft projects, and a Preda Developmental Fair Trade program.[634]

---

[629] Mengel and Lintz lived for a while in DC with the Josephite Fathers and eventually moved to an apartment.

[630] Author telephone interview with Father Mark Mengel, Springfield, Massachusetts. 3 November 2016.

[631] Ibid.

[632] *Columban Newsletter* (March 1993). Father Thomas Glennon, then in Chicago, volunteered at the Eighth Day Center for Justice.

[633] *Preda* stands for "People's Recovery, Empowerment and Development Assistance." Father Cullen received many national and international awards for his work. Fr. Shay Cullen, "Preda Developmental Fair Trade," *Columban Mission* (2014 Vol. 96, Number 9), 8–10. The organization also provides therapeutic homes for rescued children.

[634] On the latter, see, Fr. Shay Cullen, "Preda Developmental Fair Trade," *Columban Mission* (June/July 2010), 8–10.

Mengel hosted representatives from the National Human Rights Coordinating team from Peru. They were attorneys and economists familiar with the Columban missions. As had O'Loughlin before him, Mengel set up meetings with congressional members or their aides to provide information relevant to the shaping of American foreign policies. The meetings were educational, laying the groundwork for advocacy on issues. Columbans participated in related boards and steering committees with the United States Catholic Mission Association, the Conference of Major Superiors of Men, other church groups, and organizations focused on a specific issue or country. The meetings were a two way education experience: the group learned about Columban areas of concern, while Columbans had a venue wherein U.S. Catholics and others joined expertise and skills to work for justice.

Thompson and Father Lintz provided mission education with justice/peace dimensions in the Washington area schools and in the Diocese of Arlington, Virginia. The East Coast Columban mission educators formed a group and they contributed material on justice related issues for *Columban Mission*.[635] The staff gave presentations to the annual conference of the Religious Education Convention. Connections with people of other religious backgrounds included Thompson's participation in the Interfaith Working Group on Trade and Investment Issues.

Mengel shared pertinent material with the Peru Peace Network in Jefferson City, Missouri. The Missouri diocese had sent missionary Sisters and priests to Peru since the early 1960s. By 1990, there were two parts to the diocesan interaction with social justice concerns in Peru. Missionaries from the diocese, still concerned about poverty issues, highlighted the increase in drug traffic and the government's reaction to *Sendero Luminoso* (Shining Path), the Communist terrorist group that killed thousands of people in Peru in the name of a "pure" communism. The missionaries formed a Peru Solidarity Forum to inform the people back home of their concerns. The Jefferson City diocesan advocacy group, the Peru Peace Network, was formed to monitor and advocate for appropriate legislation in the United States.[636] The cross continents' engagement was critical to obtain and disseminate knowledge of specific realities people faced daily, especially those with few resources. The Peru Peace Network continued into the early 2000s.[637]

---

[635]   *CM* (February 2010).

[636]   The Peru Peace Network was part of a national network. Author telephone interview with Mark Saucier, Mission Director, Chancery Office, Jefferson City, Missouri, 8 November 2016. Father Peter Woodruff, SSC, was on an Executive Committee of the Peru Solidarity Forum.

[637]   The group "fell off the radar" after the terrorist attack on the World Trade Center, New York City, on September 11, 2011. Information about the Jefferson City group from author telephone interview with Mark Saucier, Mission Director, Chancery Office, Jefferson City, Missouri, 8 November 2016.

In 1990, staff member Christina Cobourn spent five weeks in the Philippines to gather information on issues of Columban concern. "Since her return she has been working practically round the clock sharing some of her observations with various Washington groups."[638] On behalf of the office, Cobourn presented a statement on development, militarization and environmental concerns to the Foreign Operations Subcommittee of the Senate Appropriations Committee. Her positive reception "was a tribute to her expertise and awareness of recent developments in that country."[639] The approach also reflected an earlier Society General Chapter proposal that Columbans "associate where possible with the personnel of aid and development agencies to help situate their promotional activities within the context of the full mission of a local church."[640]

Father Michael Dodd was named the Coordinator of the Columban Washington office in September 1994.[641] Dodd found that with a history of O'Loughlin and Mengel at the helm and with the excellent work of staff members Thompson, Cobourn and John McAndrews, everywhere Dodd went, "the Columbans were known and known as a friend."[642] Dodd thought that given the political importance of the United States globally and the Washington area in particular, the presence of many offices representing the poor and disenfranchised around the world would be a fitting location to have Justice and Peace directors from other countries intern there under auspices of the Columbans. One hoped for result would be a cross-fertilization of ideas between local churches.[643] An internship program at the office, though not necessarily with Justice and Peace directors from elsewhere, would formally begin in 2005.

Father Dodd and Susan Thompson worked on advocacy issues, each of which required education for the staff and for the constituencies Columbans engaged. Topics ranged from toxic waste cleanup after the withdrawal of U.S. military forces from Subic Bay, Philippines, to a Border Working Group (United States/Mexico) on human rights and future policy implications affecting that geographic area. Susan Thompson met with the Welfare Reform Working

---

[638]   "Justice and Peace Office," *Columban Newsletter* (October 1990), 3.

[639]   Ibid., When Christine Cobourn was hired in 1992 for the project from the Columban Central Office of Justice and Peace, John McAndrew, a former Maryknoll lay missionary in the Philippines with experience in development work was hired as staff. Information provided by Mark Mengel, 10 October 2016 and Susan Thompson, 20 December 2016. McAndrew left the office prior to Father Dodd's appointment to the Columban Office of Justice and Peace.

[640]   *Acts of the Chapter, October 4–December 8, 1976*, Section 4, #14, p. 15.

[641]   Susan Thompson took on the areas Mark Mengel worked with, including Latin America and border issues between Mexico and the United States.

[642]   Author telephone interview with Father Mark Mengel 3 November 2016.

[643]   Author interview of Father Michael Dodd, SSC, Columban Office of Justice and Peace, 16 October 1994.

Group to advocate for ways to integrate housing issues into the welfare reform debate in Congress.[644] In Tucson, Arizona, Thompson and the others gathered with several groups actively involved in "border work," including the Diocese of Tucson, Catholic Relief Services, and Humane Borders and Border Links.[645] Thompson, on behalf of the Columbans, attended the Fourth International Women's Conference (1995) in Beijing. Afterward, she organized an issue of *Columban Mission* related to women's lives, bringing to light the effect of policies and practices particularly where Columbans had missions.[646] The issue was translated into Spanish and a few years later, a Spanish issue of *Columban Mission* was begun.

Public Witness

The **third strategic area** for the Columban Justice and Peace office was **public witness**, an action often related to large group participation. An advantage of these events was that they could be replicated elsewhere. One example of this is an "Economic Way of the Cross,"[647] that Susan Thompson helped develop. The idea was based on the Catholic devotional practice of the "Stations of the Cross." The tradition was that a priest and two servers walked down the church aisle, stopped at crosses marked on the walls, recalled fourteen interactions Jesus had with various people he met as he carried his cross to Calvary. The congregation prayed with the priest after reflection on each station. The idea was to join with Jesus in his suffering. In the "Economic Way of the Cross," the "stations" were designated at various locations in the District of Columbia. The group started at the Capitol building for "the first station: Jesus is condemned to death. The spoken reflection focused on the suppression of God's image/lack of authentic democracy. At each stop, the leader gave an explanation as to why that place was chosen as a "station." The group then prayed antiphonally in relation to prayer for change around the highlighted reality. From there, the group processed to the next "station." People prayed at the end of each station, "We pray for the coming of the New Creation. We believe that Another world is Possible." The stations marked "various institutions that cause people and communities throughout the world

---

[644]   *Columban Newsletter* (December 1993).

[645]   *Columban Newsletter* (Fall 2001), 4.

[646]   *Columban Mission* (September/October 1996). The title of the issue is, "Women—Where Hope Lies." (*Mujeres—Dónde Habita La Esperanza*). Brendan O'Sullivan, in his "From the Director" page, recounted the contributions of the Ladies Ancient Order of Hibernians to the Society. Ibid, 31.

[647]   The "Economic Way of the Cross" was sponsored by the Religious Working Group on the World Bank and the IMF.

to remain in poverty or, in the case of the station where Veronica wiped the face of Jesus, to acknowledge institutions which help people out of poverty."[648]

Susan Thompson was an organizer/participant in an interfaith pilgrimage along the U.S./Mexican border. The event took tremendous effort and time to organize. The Columbans wanted to call attention to the large number of people dying in border crossings from Mexico. The hope was that people on both sides of the border could make the pilgrimage from city to city at the same time and meet in Tijuana/San Diego, though only the U.S. pilgrimage was able to be made.

Another public witness was held in April 2000, in conjunction with the meetings of the World Bank and International Monetary Fund (IMF). The World Bank had been created for the purpose of development of countries, especially those in dire poverty circumstances. However, as the World Bank grew, the focus on poor people declined and debt grew out of bounds for poor countries while profit soared for the World Bank.[649] Columbans were already part of an Interfaith Working Group that came together on Trade and Investment issues and planned workshops to strengthen a faith-based understanding of the issues and problems.

Some public witness could have potentially serious implications. Columbans participated in several peaceful demonstrations that drew attention to harmful issues in Korea, the negative effects of the World Bank and IMF, and other matters dear to Columbans. Columbans from the office took part in some of the demonstrations: Mark Mengel, Chuck Lintz, and Mike Dodd, for example.

---

[648] Susan Thompson e-mail correspondence with author 11 January 2017. Among the other stations were, 2: Jesus bears the cross (Department of Labor/Exploitation of Labor/Sweatshops). 3: Jesus falls the first time (Department of Commerce/Local Chamber of Commerce/Idolatry of Money, Consumerism). 4: Jesus meets His mother (Department of Health and Human Services/Degradation of Family Life). 8: Jesus speaks to the women of Jerusalem (Homelessness in Lafayette Park/Double Burden of Economic Injustice on Women), and a fifteenth station: Resurrection of Jesus Signs and Seeds of Hope/Another World is Possible. *Economic Way of the Cross*, Religious Working Group on the World Bank and the IMF (n.d. but probably 2004). Copy provided author by Susan Thompson. The material was able to be reproduced readily and inexpensively. A similar experience of the Stations took place in the Columban parish in Brazil. While the stations were about Jesus and his way to the cross, these stations were also about peoples' homes, that became the "station." The family placed candles, pictures and a crucifix on the small altar they made for outside their front door. People processed from house to house and listened to the readings, prayers, and songs sung into a microphone system secured to the top of a car. "They sang along mightily." Transcript of interview of Father John Wanaurny, 1991. No interviewer identified. CFA-USA.

[649] For background on the development of the World Bank and its effects on specific countries and the feminization of poverty, see, Kevin Danaher, ed., *50 Years Is Enough: The Case Against the World Bank and the International Monetary Fund* (Boston: South End Press, 1994).

Susan Thompson was arrested at peaceful demonstrations several times. While she was not able to obtain any "official approval" from the office or U.S. region (there was the potential of arrest at the demonstration), there was never denial. The decision on her part was personal. She "did get the clear impression [from Columbans] that it would be an all right thing to do!" [650] The *National Catholic Reporter* listed the names and organizations of individuals arrested at various demonstrations, and she did not receive any Columban letters against her so doing.

2004 and Developments through 2018

In 2003 Amy Woolam Echeverria, the JPIC (Justice, Peace and Integrity of Creation) Coordinator in Chile, was transferred to the U.S. region as the Latin America Associate for the Columbans. The following year she was appointed JPIC coordinator/director of the Columban Office in Washington DC, replacing Mike Dodd. [651] During her directorship, a new international JPIC role evolved after an international meeting of the Columbans placed an emphasis on migration and its global effects.

The Columbans had a vast experience observing what happened to migrants in their mission areas. One example was Taiwan, where workers, often undocumented immigrants, came from the Philippines and Asian countries. Women and men sought jobs in the hope they could send money home to their struggling families. The conditions migrants often experienced were demeaning, unsafe and unhealthy. While these workers contributed to Taiwan's prosperity, they lived in fear of deportation or death as a result of their treatment at work or conditions in which they lived. The Columban video, *Walking from the Shadows*, provided an insightful look into the life of migrants who came to the Hope Workers Center, a gathering space for migrant workers begun by Columban Father George Herrgott in Chungli in 1987. At first the endeavor was small but the Center grew as an important locus for protection of immigrants working in Taiwan.[652] The Center promoted a spirit of cooperation among diverse ethnic groups and thus a more united stance when working for justice. Columbans also participated in protests in the country to draw attention to the injustices toward immigrant workers.

Still another name change for the Justice and Peace Office took place in April 2008, when the focus enlarged as part of the Columban U.S. Regional

---

[650]   Susan Thompson e-mail correspondence with author 11 January 2017.

[651]   The author is grateful to Amy Woolam Echeverria for the timeline she sent especially for the mid-1980s to 2013 and to Father Michael Dodd for filling in some of the timeline and information for that period.

[652]   The Columbans began a mission in Taiwan in 1978.

Plan of Action.[653] The Columban Center for Advocacy and Outreach's (CCAO) mandate included coordinating the region's invitation to mission programs such as internship, volunteering, and mission exposure trips. These things had been taking place through individuals in the region but now the Office could manage and develop this larger focus. The mandate allowed for an expansion of the program to include calling others to join the Columbans in mission in various ways. In 2008, the CCAO sent its first Mission Exposure group to Peru and the following year the Center launched Columban Volunteers USA, which placed full-time volunteers to work in the office. In 2010 the U.S. region/CCAO launched Columban Volunteers International, which had a pilot placement of people in the Columban migrant ministry in Taiwan.

In 2013, Amy W. Echeverria was appointed as the Society Central JPIC Coordinator, with the job description of Society Migrant Link Person rolled into that of Coordinator. To replace her, Scott Wright was hired in 2013 as director of the Columban Center for Advocacy and Outreach/U.S. JPIC coordinator. He had strong roots in the social dimensions of Christianity as it played out in the United States and in Latin America and had experience as a lay missionary in Central America. The CCAO 2016 mission statement indicated the direction of the office:

> The Columban Center for Advocacy and Outreach is the national advocacy office for the Missionary Society of St. Columban. Columban Missionaries are called to heal, reconcile, build bridges and create mutual understanding through dialogue which is expressed through our solidarity with marginalized people and the exploited Earth.
>
> Internationally recognized for their work on raising awareness of the ongoing threat of climate change, accompanying and defending the rights of migrants, and promoting sustainable economic justice, Columbans are committed to addressing the structural and root causes of oppression and inequality. As a result of decades of experience living, working, and standing in solidarity with impacted communities, Columbans have identified four advocacy priority areas: Migration, Environmental Justice, Economic Justice, and Peace and Conflict Transformation.[654]

---

[653]   In 1994, the Columban General Assembly referenced the office as the Justice, Peace, Inculturation and Dialogue Office.

[654]   Retrieved 7 July 2016 from http://columban.org/category/columban-center-for-advocacy-and-outreach.

The Columban Center focused information and the broad experience from Columban missions around the world. Columbans educated diverse groups toward an understanding of the injustices people experienced, connected people who felt denied of their human rights and right to a just livelihood, and challenged the assumptions around "development" and the role of the World Bank. Education, advocacy and public witness were some ways Columbans unpacked and lived the meaning of "Action on behalf of justice is a constitutive dimension of preaching the Gospel."[655]

The Issues

Justice for People Living under Military and Repressive Governments

The Philippines and Latin America were geographic areas with Catholic roots over centuries. However, people experienced situations where the government oppressed the people, tortured or killed citizens who objected to unjust policies, and where any organizing for workers' rights was quashed with force. A lengthy presentation opened the 1976 Columban General Chapter held in the Philippines: "Security in a Rapidly Changing Church and World." The speaker raised the question, "What does it mean for us Columbans that in Korea, Burma (now Myanmar), the Philippines, Peru, and Chile we live and work under military governments?"[656] Termed later as "low intensity conflict," the practice was a way to control populations and to assure compliance with military governance through death threats, disappearances and torture, a situation Columbans faced in several countries where they worked.[657] Among other key items, the Society General Chapter passed the proposal, "That a 'contingency plan' to cope with the expulsions of Columbans from a particular country be drawn up and the plan be communicated to the membership."[658]

In the case of the Philippines, martial law had technically ended in 1981 but the presidential and military powers remained the same. In fact, the military had tripled in numbers from 1972 to 1981. In 1982, President

---

[655]   World Synod of Catholic Bishops, *Justice in the World* (1971), par. 6.

[656]   *Columban Intercom* (June 1977), 2–6. Authorship not given. In the countries mentioned, there were military governments or dictators, each of whom had his own method of repression. Four years after the 1976 Chapter, the bloody "Kwangju Uprising," also called by UNESCO, "Democratic Uprising," took place from May 18–27, 1980, in the city of Kwangju, the provincial capital of South Chŏlla, Korea.

[657]   This insight was suggested to the author by Father John Burger.

[658]   *Acts of the Chapter*, October 4–December 8, 1976. #6, p. 13.

Ferdinand Marcos's government arrested many priests, Sisters, and other church leaders, who were described as "subversives" or "communists." In *Columban Intercom*, the Society printed sections of the February 1983, Philippine bishops' courageous pastoral letter. The document was written after the bishops "came to the conclusion together that we should speak our minds on our present problems, firstly, on the arrest and detention of priests, religious and Church workers in our social action programs, and secondly, on the deeper issues that undergird the action of the military against the Church."[659] Because of the fear that President Ferdinand Marcos would prohibit publication of the letter, the document was hand delivered to 3,000 parishes. A friend of the Columbans, Antonio Yapsutco Fortich, bishop of Bacolod, Philippines (1967–1989), was staunchly anti-Marcos.[660] Fortich had set up cooperatives with sugar workers and small land owners as a way to empower the poor. His house was attacked with a grenade, thrown by a congressman.

The Columban "contingency plan" was active when Columban priests were imprisoned and later deported from the Philippines: Brian Gore (1983) and Niall O'Brien (1983),[661] and Chicago native, Dennis O'Mara, deported from Chile[662] (1984). Gore had been "charged with taking advantage of his position and engaging in activities undermining social order and advocating principles contrary to national security."[663] O'Brien had been charged with the murder of the mayor of Kabankalan, Pablo Sola. Sola, in fact, had been killed by guerillas. The three

---

[659]   Philippine bishops' pastoral letter, cited in *Columban Newsletter, USA* (March 1983), 2.

[660]   On 26 June 1987, Bienvendo Tudtud (1931–1987), bishop of Iligan, Mindanao, was killed along with forty-nine others in a Philippines Airline crash as their flight headed toward Baguio City. Tudtud was ordained in Boston in 1959. He was well known for his work with Muslims, especially in southern Mindanao, where in the early 1970s there began an upsurge in violence between Christians and Muslims. He had a popular radio program. Edwin C. Mercurio, "Bishop Bienvenido Tudtud: 'The Lamplighter,'" *Inter-Religio* 12 (Fall 1987), 92–94.

[661]   For perspectives O'Brien held, his work and that of Brian Gore, and the stories of the people they shared life with in Negros, see Niall O'Brien, *Revolution from the Heart* (Maryknoll, NY: Orbis Books, 1991). See also, Alfred W. McCoy, *Priests on Trial* (Penguin Books: New York, 1985). Many copies were purchased by the Columbans in the United States. The book was noted in the *Columban Newsletter* (February 1985). Brian Gore returned to the Philippines and is working there in 2016.

[662]   Dennis O'Mara wrote a six page, single space article, "The Participation of Foreign Missionaries in the Movement Against Torture—'Sebastian Acevedo'—A Personal Reflection. He sent the material to the U.S. Regional Director Peter Cronin, with a handwritten note that perhaps a shortened version of his reflection could be used in *Columban Mission*. The shorter version is Dennis O'Mara, "Protests Against Torture, Wednesday, 14th of September 1983." Dennis O'Mara personal file for *Columban Mission*. CFA-USA.

[663]   *Columban Newsletter* (March 1983), 3.

cases involved Columbans who worked with the poor aiding them to establish their lives with dignity. The men enabled people to work together for a life that was not beholden to powerful leaders, who controlled every phase of life, threatened and carried out torture of workers and citizens. As it turned out, when President Ronald Reagan was on a State visit to Ireland in 1984, among the protesters he encountered was Niall O'Brien's mother, Olivia. She placed herself behind the mock bars in a "cell" outside the U.S. embassy in Dublin. "The image embarrassed Reagan and pressure was put on Marcos to release the [Columban] priests."[664]

Violence continued in the 1990s in the Philippines. In Negros, four Columban priests and a Sister of the Presentation were given "death warnings," a "not unusual act." One of the priests was eighty-four-year-old Father Edward Allen, who condemned violence in a homily.[665] The other three priests were Brian Gore, Neill O' Brien and Dennis O'Mara. Columbans were kept abreast of the priests' situations through regional newsletters, *Columban Intercom* and personal contact. Through Christina Cobourn in the Columban Justice and Peace Office, Niall O'Brien after expulsion from the Philippines had speaking engagements in several U.S. cities to inform people about the political, social and economic realities in the Philippines. One of these occasions was O'Brien's book launch, *Revolution of the Heart*. The U.S. Columban video, *Social Volcano*,[666] focused on the lives of sugar cane workers in the Philippines, one of the large groups Gore and O'Brien served.

Father Dennis O'Mara, in Chile since 1978 after teaching at Turramurra Seminary in Australia for seven years, was sent to a parish of about twenty thousand people in the port city of San Antonio. He lived for several months among Chilean clergy, from whom he learned about Chilean life and customs. He also benefitted from the quarter century of Father Hugh McGonagle's mission experience at that point. McGonagle had "discovered the family spirit in Chile, where we are working with the Church of the country to save a great Church established by Spanish missionaries four centuries ago."[667] The Archdiocese of Santiago had "great leadership from Raul Cardinal Silva Henriquez, SDB."[668] Four Columban parishes and communities formed part

---

[664]   No author, "Turbulent Priest with a Social Mission," *The Irish Times* 1 May 2004, retrieved online 11 December 2016. Niall O'Brien founded *Pax Christi* in the Philippines.

[665]   *Columban Newsletter* (October 1990), 7.

[666]   *Social Volcano* was produced in November 1985.

[667]   Hugh McGonagle, "*Bienvenida a Chile, Padre*." The *Far East* file, Ireland, n.d., but written just prior to McGonagle's return to Valparaiso, Chile in the Andes in 1962. 4 typed pages.

[668]   Father Thomas P. Reynolds interview of Father Dennis O'Mara, 20 February 2012. Cardinal Silva is pictured at a Columban parish in *FE* (1963 November), 13. O'Mara had conducted a seminar at the Columban seminary in Australia about ideas coming out of the bishops' conference at Medellín.

of the Vicariate of Solidarity. Among the many activities Columbans aided during the seventeen year military dictatorship of General Pinochet, were soup kitchens, shared meals and cooperative buying. In the process, people imbibed principles of human dignity and basic human rights. Most of the bishops in Chile at the time were committed to justice, accompanying the people,[669] and to a basic pastoral stance of what came to be called liberation theology. Father O'Mara himself, who had received his doctorate at the Gregorian University in Rome during the Second Vatican Council, was well aware of the social dimensions of Christianity through seminars and workshops and through interaction with people familiar with a theology that reflected the life of the people. With others, he gave "dynamic workshops and retreats" for parishioners, "very much in a context of liberation theology."[670]

In San Antonio parish O'Mara worked with unions and was chaplain of the jail. At one point, he was stopped from visiting the men. "The warden told me, 'we would like you to keep coming here, we appreciate your ministry. But you must have said something in your sermons because from what they told us, that priest, don't let him back in the jail again.'"[671]

O'Mara volunteered to be assigned to a Franciscan parish, San Luis Beltran, in Pudahuel, a section of the Santiago metropolitan region. The political atmosphere was violent in the country. In the 1970s, Columban Associate priests Bryan McMahan, Des McGillicuddy and Brendan Ford,[672] who worked in the city center parish, had been expelled by the government. On November 1, 1975, the Columban Center house in Santiago was stormed by military police. Henriquetta Reyes, the Columbans' housekeeper there was killed. A guest in the house, English medical Doctor Sheila Cassidy, was held in detention and subsequently tortured.[673]

In San Luis Beltran parish, Father O'Mara had been involved with a group who prepared to take up peaceful protests against the use of torture by police and soldiers. Recognizing his "foreigner" status, he did not suggest any particular action because the consequences for him would not be as heavy as those of Chileans. As O'Mara described the training in nonviolent gatherings, he said, "I took part in the planning meetings, the workshops we had, to teach

---

[669]   Father Thomas P. Reynolds interview of Father Dennis O'Mara, 20 February 2012.

[670]   Ibid.

[671]   Ibid.

[672]   O'Mara mentioned this group as "Bryan McMahan, a Franciscan priest, also a Columban associate." Father Thomas P. Reynolds interview of Father Dennis O'Mara, 20 February 2012. Father Desmond McGillicuddy is the vicar general of the Mill Hill Fathers (2016).

[673]   Cassidy wrote about her experience in Sheila Cassidy, *The Audacity to Believe* (London: Collins, 1977).

us about fear, about how to even stand when being pushed and about how to act towards the people who were not acting so nicely toward us. It was a very rich experience and at times a little frightening."[674]

He took part in several peaceful demonstrations against the use of torture by the Chilean security police and other security forces. On one day, he was arrested four times. In December 1984, the action the group took was to pass out Christmas cards at church in the city of Santiago. The message was that people have a Christmas without "Herod" and a New Year without torture. That day, five of the group were arrested and jailed for five days. On December 23, O'Mara was then deported from Chile by way of Lima and arrived in Miami on December 27, 1984.[675] In the Miami airport, Father Victor Babin, a Columban stationed at St. Benedict Parish, Hialeah, Florida, met him at the airport, amid shouts of protesters who heckled Father O'Mara, calling him "Communist, Marxist." The following day the Columban left for Chicago where his family, friends, and national and local press and television networks gathered to hear his story. Regional Superior Peter Cronin came to visit Father O'Mara and the family in Chicago in early January.

A Columban Justice and Peace office "alert" was sent to national justice coalitions, including the U.S. Catholic Conference of Bishops, conferences of major superiors, and justice and peace offices around the United States and Canada. The groups were in solidarity with the Columbans to protest the "continued oppression of the Chilean government and their use of deportation of church people who stand for victims of injustice." Father O'Mara wrote a letter to his people, stating, "My commitment to life demands of me a commitment to the Movement Against Torture, up to the ultimate consequence, in order to participate with others in the struggle against torture."[676] In San Luis Beltran parish, seventy religious and clergy fasted for forty-eight hours, ending the fast with a large public procession. The group was accompanied by people from the communities where Father Dennis served. The procession ended at the large basilica of Our Lady of Lourdes, where the vicar general presided at Eucharist.

Back in the States, O'Mara gave many interviews and talks to inform the public about the Chilean situation and the violation of human rights. After a short vacation and time with relatives, he took a course at the Mexican–American Cultural Center in San Antonio, Texas.[677] His next mission would be

---

[674] Father Thomas P. Reynolds interview of Father Dennis O'Mara, 20 February 2012.

[675] Information about the specifics of his deportation and the return to the United States are given in *Columban Newsletter* (February 1985), 3–4.

[676] *Columban Newsletter* (February 1985), 2–3.

[677] The Mexican American Catholic Center (now College) was established in 1972 in San Antonio, Texas by Father Virgilio Elizondo, a priest of the Archdiocese of San Antonio, Texas. Its purpose was to prepare Catholic leaders to explore Hispanic

among Hispanic people in a new Columban commitment, Alamogordo, New Mexico, in June 1985.[678]

Father Dodd reported another example of light in the darkness, due to successful efforts of Columban Father Robert Sweeney,[679] activist and adviser to social action groups in South Korea. He, along with the Columban Justice and Peace Office and organizations in the DC area focused on the strafing and bombing practice range at Koon-Ni, located south of Seoul.

> The U.S. action created havoc and instability in the lives of the local farmers and fisherfolk for almost 50 years. Despite the denials from the U.S. Forces Korea (USFK) and the South Korean Defense Ministry, it is a commonly held belief that in more recent times the range was managed and used by Lockheed Martin for tests of its new weapons. Packing it in after a hard day of demonstrating outside the facility in June 2000, the late Bob told Los Angeles reporter, Valerie Reitman, "The enemy isn't North Korea or Russia or anybody else, it is us." [680]

Justice in Relation to Third World Debt

The 1988 Society General Chapter mandated that the Central Administration Justice and Peace officer in consultation with Region Mission Units be charged to draw up a program of action regarding Third World Debt.[681] In 1991, the Columban Washington office hosted an international

---

culture and reach out to the large Hispanic Catholic population in the United States. Elizondo eventually developed a *mestizo/mestiza* theology. Virgilio Elizondo, *Mestizaje: Dialectic of Cultural Birth and the Gospel. A Study in the Intercultural Dimension of Evangelization* (Paris: [s.n.], 1978).

[678] Father Thomas P. Reynolds interview of Father Dennis O'Mara 20 February 2012, El Paso, Texas. The interview indicated that O'Mara went to Alamogordo, New Mexico. *Columban Newsletter* (May 1985), 1, noted he was assigned to Las Cruces, New Mexico. Las Cruces is the name of the diocese.

[679] Father Robert Sweeney (1935–2000), a native of Niagara Falls, New York, died unexpectedly in Seoul on July 29, 2000. Ordained in 1959, he earned a degree in canon law in Rome and was missioned to Korea for most of the years from 1964 until his death. Sean Dwan's interview of Father Robert Sweeney in the *Columban Newsletter, Korea* (April 1991), 4–6, provides insight into his personal, spiritual, social justice, and mission perspectives over the years.

[680] *Columban Newsletter* (September 2000), 3. Sister Teresa O'Connell, SSC in Korea provided the information for this newsletter and continued to be the point person on the issue.

[681] The 1988 Society General Chapter also included "Integrity of Creation" as a new dimension of Justice and Peace. *Acts of Missionary Society of St. Columban General*

Columban JPIC coordinators' gathering. "The group focused on three areas: the international debt, the environment, and women's issues. It was decided at the meeting to have a worldwide campaign focusing on the International Debt, [which] would be the focus of all the Columban offices."[682] One of the speakers was Marie Dennis from the Center of Concern, Washington DC. The significance of Columbans addressing this key issue might be placed alongside other actions in place at the time.

Advocacy groups in Washington DC had addressed the debt crisis of the 1980s but by the early 1990's, "debt had been replaced by campaigns focused on NAFTA (bilateral trade agreement)."[683] Christina Cobourn Herman, as Coordinator of the Columban Campaign on Debt and Development Alternatives, noted, "To keep the focus of advocacy groups on the international debt, the Columbans had a two-year campaign. I carried the debt issue into the *50 Years is Enough*[684] campaign on the World Bank, which was deeply involved in 'managing' the debt crisis, primarily through the imposition of structural adjustment policies imposed on indebted country governments."[685] The third

---

Chapter, 1988, chapter 3, 37–46. Along these lines a mandate was given to develop a program of education and plan of action about the "Ecology question," a topic that will be developed in chapter 12.

[682]   Father Mark Mengel e-mail communication with author, 10 October 2016. Father Mengel received the Hibernian Christian Charity Award in March 2016, in the Springfield, Massachusetts area. On the women's issues (later termed gender issues), Susan Thompson remembered there were Columban "representatives from Korea and Japan, who did a joint workshop on the issue." Thompson was also on the Alt-WID [Alternative, Women in Development] working group at the Center of Concern. Susan Thompson e-mail correspondence with author, 12 February 2017.

[683]   Christina Cobourn Herman e-mail communication with author, 13 October 2016. Mark Mengel noted that when he started in the office, democracy issues and promotion of human rights were in the foreground. When he left the office, the movement was toward trade and economic issues, a military environment in many countries and the international debt. Author e-mail correspondence with Mark Mengel, 10 October 2016.

[684]   Kevin Danaher, ed., *50 Years Is Enough: The Case Against the World Bank and the International Monetary Fund* (Boston: South End Press, 1994) provides background for issues related to policies of both institutions.

[685]   Christina Cobourn Herman e-mail communication with author, 13 October 2016. Christina was hired by the Central Justice and Peace Office in Ireland in 1992 specifically to work on the issue of international debt. Susan Thompson then took over the "Fifty Years is Enough" campaign. Cobourn wrote an article on the Third World Debt for *CM* (November 1992). JPIC office director, John McAndrew edited the *CM* (September/October 1994) that featured topics surrounding "Third World Debt. Why the Poor are getting Poorer." Articles provided brief observations of the effects of debt on the countries where Columbans serve. *CM* (February 2010) was devoted to "The Economy and the Economics of Poverty."

year of the Columban campaign (1995) brought to the fore "an examination of development alternatives."[686]

In 1993 a joint conference was cosponsored by the Columbans and the Maryknoll Society on the theme, "Witnessing to Justice in a Global Economy." The "Columban Campaign on Debt and Development" was a feature of the conference.[687] Topics presented ranged from children and violence in the DC area, to global situations in the areas of culture, factories, shopping and finances. A representative of the International Monetary Fund and one from the World Bank gave presentations, with a "lively exchange" with Christina Cobourn Herman of the Columban Campaign on Debt and Development,' along with a representative from Bread for the World, and James Hug, SJ (Center of Concern), who led the group in a process of theological reflection over the five-day conference.

Archbishop Desmond Tutu sometime in 1993 had suggested to Marie Dennis that "we consider a year of Jubilee in 2000."[688] About the same time, Martin Dent, a retired lecturer in politics at Keele University (England) stopped in to the Columban Justice and Peace Office to suggest the same idea.[689] Given that the staff was heavily involved in many areas, the staff's first response was "no way." [690] The issue continued to grow, and the Columbans significantly addressed the issue with others.

The U.S. Catholic Bishops document, *A Jubilee Call for Debt Forgiveness* (1999), challenged powerful "creditor institutions," such as the United States, to "provide some debt relief for some countries."[691] People who contract loans have an obligation to pay, "but this presumption may be overridden in certain circumstances. One such instance is when a country cannot repay its debt without critical reductions in spending for health, education, food, housing,

---

[686]   Christina Herman Cobourn e-mail communication with author, 13 October 2016.

[687]   *CM* (December 1993), 3. *CM* (November 1992).

[688]   Marie Dennis was on the Jubilee 2000 Campaign for cancellation of debt for poor countries and connected with several other organizations that Columbans focused. She has been active in a range of Justice and Peace groups, including the White House Task Force on Global Poverty and Development, the Washington Office on Latin America and *Pax Christi*. In 2017 Marie Denis was awarded the Public Peace Prize, a global recognition of her peacemaking efforts internationally.

[689]   Martin Dent and friend William Peters, a retired diplomat, linked the biblical understand of Jubilee with the modern debt relief program. They found Jubilee 2000 campaign in the early 1990s. Information on this point obtained from Susan Thompson.

[690]   Susan Thompson e-mail correspondence with author, 20 December 2016.

[691]   Administrative Board of the United States Catholic Conference, "A Jubilee Call for Debt Forgiveness," April 1999, Summary. Retrieved online at www.usccb.org/ issues-and-action, 15 September 2016.

and other basic needs, and when debt has become a serious obstacle to development."[692] Jubilee 2000 called "for a one-time cancellation of the backlog of unpayable debts to mark the millennium."[693] Debate over the international debt "cannot hide the human dimensions: children without health care and education, communities without roads and water, women without equality, people without hope."[694]

The statement, "which took a lot of work to get written,"[695] was issued in preparation for Jubilee 2000 to welcome the second millennium of Christianity and to proclaim a year of mercy.[696] All areas of Catholic life were involved, from the sacraments to scripture reflection to practical implementation of mercy and forgiveness in areas of society, international law, and daily life. As U.S. region Director Brendan O'Sullivan wrote, "Jubilee is a particularly appropriate time to reassess our way of living with the compassion of Jesus as a guide."[697] *Columban Mission* featured various facets of "Jubilee 2000" as evidenced in Columban missions globally.[698] Susan Thompson, who had been on a committee to decide whether Jubilee 2000 would continue after that year, was elected to the transition team of the Jubilee 2000/USA campaign. The organization continues today as Jubilee USA Network.[699]

---

[692]   Ibid.

[693]   Susan Thompson, "A New Moral Crusade," *CM* (November 1999), 28–30, here 29.

[694]   Administrative Board of the United States Catholic Conference, "A Jubilee Call for Debt Forgiveness," April 1999, Summary. Retrieved online at www.usccb.org/issues-and-action, 15 September 2016.

[695]   Author telephone interview of Susan Thompson, 20 December 2016.

[696]   "Archbishop Desmond Tutu Pleads for 'Jubilee'—Debt Release," National Council of Churches, news release, NCC 11/19/1996; Administrative Board of the United States Catholic Conference, "A Jubilee Call for Debt Forgiveness," April 1999. Retrieved online at www.usccb.org/issues-and-action, 15 September 2016.

[697]   Brendan O'Sullivan, "From the Director," *CM* (November 1999), 31.

[698]   *CM* (November 1999).

[699]   The team was responsible for determining if/how the thrust of Jubilee 2000 would continue as a grass roots organization with support from Washington based groups or whether it should die a natural death. The Columban Justice and Peace office over the years was involved on issues with *many* organizations with similar goals. In addition to the groups mentioned in this chapter, a partial list includes Jubilee, Medical Mission Sisters (and many other communities of women and men religious), Network, *Pax Christi*, Religious Task Force on Central America and Mexico, Africa Faith and Justice Network, Center of Concern, Interfaith Working Group on trade and Investment, Korean and Philippine Coalitions, and Peru Peace Network. List provided by Susan Thompson, e-mail correspondence with author, 17 January 2017.

North American Focus on Mission to Latin America

Another focus area of the Justice and Peace office was Latin America. Congregations of mission institutes and men and women religious in the United States had specifically been encouraged to send their members to Latin America to stem the tide of communism. In 1959, the Bishops' National Catholic Welfare Conference voted to reinstitute a Latin America Bureau. Archbishop Agostino Casaroli met with the major superiors of women and men religious at the University of Notre Dame (1961) to reinforce the Vatican request to send missionaries to Latin America. He laid out nine focus areas for missionaries, including rebuilding of the Church by the people themselves, promotion of local vocations, and missionary participation in cultural and language orientation strong enough to guarantee a respect for local customs and cultures.[700]

Close friend of the Columbans, Cardinal Cushing, sponsored a group of diocesan priests who formed the Saint James Society in 1959.[701] Their first members went to Lima, Peru. Cushing visited Latin America several times and was struck by the prevailing poverty and illiteracy he saw. A Cushing biographer noted that in the people he met and circumstances he witnessed there, he "saw qualities that made the Church so vital to the Irish immigrants of South Boston in their bitter conflict with Protestant Yankees."[702]

In 1961, a Vatican representative called together the U.S. major superiors of men and women religious/mission societies to address the religious situation in Latin America and to appeal to them to send missionaries there.[703] Several groups of men and women religious did open missions in Central and South America, as did the newly founded lay Papal Volunteers for Latin

---

[700] Material from the 1961 meeting at Notre Dame is found in box 10/8, Missions, Major Superiors of Men Religious Annual Meetings, Latin America Bureau, Archives of the Catholic University of America.

[701] Cushing had in mind a kind of "lend-lease" program of the priests from the Boston Archdiocese, since his diocese had a surplus of priests at the time. This was reminiscent, somewhat, of what happened in Ireland at the time of the founding the Columbans. On the history of the St. James Society, see Angelyn Dries, *The Missionary Movement in American Catholic History* (Maryknoll, NY, 1998), 183–186.

[702] John Henry Cutler, *Cardinal Cushing of Boston* (New York: Hawthorne Books, 1970), 191.

[703] Two years earlier, the Vatican called a two week conference in Manila with some of the same purpose. Attendees were the bishops of the Philippines and Oceania. The Vatican was alarmed at the growth of communism in that region. Four Columban bishops attended the conference: Patrick Cronin, Harold Henry, Thomas Quinlan, and Henry Byrne. The gathering "rekindled Columban interest in China and set the stage for their return several decades later" though in a different manner than their early missions. Columban Fathers, U.S. Region website, "100 Points of Light, 1959."

America (PAVLA).[704] The U.S. relationship with the southern hemisphere was complicated but countries there engaged public attention, especially after John F. Kennedy became president of the United States. While the Vatican goal was to reinvigorate participation in sacraments, provide more viable catechetical programs, and keep Catholics away from communist influence, the working mission dynamic in the next years also moved toward addressing the consequences of the "development" of the countries. The topic reflected the "Decades of Development" (1960–1970; 1970–1980) emphasis of the United Nations.

Columban Mission in Latin America

While the next pages of this chapter are not a history of Columban missions in Chile, Peru and Brazil, a brief look at a few situations provides a hint at the larger dynamics of mission and is indicative of issues that the Columban Justice and Peace Office brought to the attention of the Catholic Church and government in the United States.

Chile[705]

How did Columbans find their way to a section of the world that was not initially on their mission radar? Given the difficulties of access to Burma (now Myanmar) and China by the early 1950s and with the urging of the Vatican toward Latin America missions at the time, the Columban General Council decided to open missions in Argentina, Chile, and Peru.

Columban Father James Conway had gone to Buenos Aires, Argentina, in 1919 and prepared a Spanish edition of the *Far East* to promote the mission there. The city had a large number of Irish immigrants, so he explored the feasibility of a possible region; that is, a place to raise funds for mission.[706] He

---

704   The Pontifical Commission for Latin America announced in 1960 a program for lay missionaries. For an overview of PAVLA, see Gerald M. Costello, *Mission to Latin America: The Successes and Failures of a Twentieth-Century Crusade* (Maryknoll, NY: Orbis Books, 1979). For a recent assessment of the effects of the interaction of North American Catholics and other Christian groups' interaction with Latin American Catholicism, see Todd Hartch, *The Rebirth of Latin American Christianity* (NY: Oxford University Press, 2014).

705   *CM* (March–April 2003) provides several articles on "50 Years in Chile. Mission to the Urban Poor and Mapuches." Another Columban mission area opened in the 1950s in Fiji. Twelve Columbans arrived there at the invitation of the bishop of Fiji, Victor Foley, SM.

706   Conway studied the Spanish language at the Irish College in Salamanca, Spain, in 1919. In Ireland, Father John O'Leary, manager of *FE* (Ireland), prepared a special

didn't receive support from the Irish immigrants or from the bishop, so he left Argentina in January 1921.[707] In the next decade, despite the Depression years in the U.S. region, Bishop Galvin queried, "Do you think it a suitable time to send a few priests to BA [Buenos Aires] to establish a branch of our organization there?" [708]

The first Columban in Buenos Aires for a length of time would be Cleveland born Father John McFadden. After his mission in California, he served as chaplain in the Apostolate of the Sea ministry in Buenos Aires, from 1952–1962.[709] McFadden met Father James Loughran in Lima, Peru, before they left for Argentina, with a stopover in Santiago, Chile.[710] As it turned out, Father Loughran met apostolic delegate Monsignor Mario Zanin in that city. They knew each other from China. As they conversed over lunch and Zanin learned the Society hoped to open a mission in South America, he recommended a visit to the archbishop of Santiago, José Maria Cardinal Caro Rodriguez (1866–1958). After the two men met, Loughran communicated the request for missionaries to the Columban superior general and then the two Columbans continued on to Buenos Aires.

Loughran spent about a year in the United States learning Spanish and returned to Chile in early 1952. He worked in Santiago for about a year to gain some pastoral experience in the capital city. In October 1952, the cardinal established a new parish, San Andres, entrusting the mission to the Columbans, with Loughran as the first pastor. In the first fifty years of Columban mission there, thirty-four parishes or Christian communities were established from the original parish.[711]

In a *Far East* article, Mark McGrath, CSC, the future archbishop of Panama, laid out the Chilean historical, social and economic systems in place by the 1960s.[712] Santiago, the heart of the central valley, grew from 700,000 to almost

---

issue for Argentina. E. J. McCarthy, "A Few Personal Reminiscences" [1916–1920] (1919), 16, 17, 18, 19. CFA-USA.

[707] Conway left for China in 1921, going through the United States on the way. He was in Hanyang for about a month and then returned to Ireland, where he incardinated in the Diocese of Kildare and Leighlin. He later was appointed vicar general.

[708] Galvin quoted in Richard Ranaghan to E. J. McCarthy 10 Jan 1934. CFA-USA.

[709] John McFadden, "Still Going Strong," *FE* (April 1966), 8–9.

[710] Father James Loughran was sent to Latin America with Father Fergus Murphy, who died from a serious illness shortly after arrival in Lima.

[711] John Jennings, "Pioneering in Chile," *FE* (April 1960), 12–13, 19. The history and various facets of Columban life in Chile are found in *CM* (March–April 2003).

[712] Mark McGrath, "Report from Chile," *FE* (April 1960), 5–9 and *FE* (May 1960), 1–3. Father Marcos McGrath, CSC (1924–2000) taught at the Catholic University of Chile for eleven years. He became auxiliary bishop of Panama in 1961, bishop of Santiago de Veraquas in 1964, and archbishop of Panama in 1969 with retirement

two million people from 1940–1960. An immediate and almost predictable consequence was the growth of large cities where people were huddled together in slums with inadequate sanitation, conditions that favored disease, and minimal education for those from the countryside to survive in a city.

Columbans were deeply involved in social justice issues in the country and relayed their knowledge and experience to Columbans elsewhere. Chileans suffered the effects of the military coup that overthrew the democratic government of President Salvador Allende on September 11, 1973.[713] At the end of the Latin American bishops' watershed meeting at Puebla, Mexico, Fathers Mark Mengel and Chicago born Thomas Connolly were interviewed for an article in the *Washington Post*.[714] Puebla was concerned with "community and participation," values the Columbans also supported. Mengel and Connolly were involved in a hunger strike and other demonstrations with Chileans, in support of the rights of the majority impoverished people of the country. A Dorchester, Massachusetts native, Father Michael Cody arrived in Chile six months after the *coup*. He and Mengel were active in the vicariate for workers, the first of its kind in Latin America, with a central church and four small community chapels. Growth of small Christian communities and of what came to be known as Liberation Theology drew the alarm of some church officials, who saw it as too political. But many engaged in the process and the communities found it liberating. Reflection together on their experience and the Gospel provided insight, courage, support and direction in their daily lives, as people dealt with difficult daily realities.[715]

In 1991, six priests from the Archdiocese of Dublin were sharing the mission of the Columbans in Chile. Three of them applied to join the Columbans. Of these, Father Thomas Hanley continues work in Chile as a Columban. In 2003 a tribute was given to the work of the Columbans when the Senate in Chile granted "Chilean citizenship by grace" to Father Hugh McGonagle (died 2013), a founder of the Columban missions there.

---

in 1994. McGrath advocated for the reintegration of the Canal Zone into Panama and condemned the violence of the Noriega regime.

[713]   Chile returned to democracy in 1990, at which time nearly 50 percent of Chileans lived below the poverty line. See, Fr. Dan Harding, "Despite Progress, Work Lies Ahead," *CM* (March–April 2003), 3. Harding was regional director in Chile at the time.

[714]   Charles A. Krause, "For U.S. Priest in Chile, 'Liberation Theology' Means Bringing Dignity to Poor," *The Washington Post*, 14 February 1979.

[715]   There is a vast literature related to liberation theology and the history of missions in Latin America in the twentieth century. For an overview, see, Paul Seuss, in Stephen B. Bevans, ed., *A Century of Catholic Mission* (Oxford: Regnum Books International, 2013), 44–57.

Peru

The Columban mission in Peru opened in 1951/52.[716] Father Martin Forde arrived in Lima six months before Father Michael Fitzgerald, who left Ireland in June 1952. Forde, who had spent World War II in Lingayen, Philippines, was appointed to the United States for three years before being sent to the new mission in Peru. Fitzgerald, unable to obtain a visa for mission in Burma (now Myanmar), was then sent to Lima. They both oversaw a new parish, Blessed Martin de Porres, in what was called the October 27 District at the time. With the exception of five years of promotion work later in Australia, Father Fitzgerald served in Peru until his death in 2006.[717] Without a place initially for the missionaries to stay in the district, the two priests lived at the College of Saint Mary's (Marianists) and then with the Jesuits at the Parish of the Immaculate for about a year. Fitzgerald remarked, "I soon felt the warm affection of the people and their great spirit of solidarity and initiative to accomplish many things. It was with them that we built the San Martin de Porres parish."[718]

Shortly after the Columbans arrived in Lima, Juan Cardinal Landázuri Ricketts, OFM (1913–1997), was appointed archbishop of Lima in 1955 until his retirement in 1989. For many of Ricketts' early years as a church leader, Peru was under a military dictatorship. Later, Peruvians would be terrorized for twenty years by the Communist terrorist group, *Sendero Luminoso* ("Shining Path"). Ricketts was acting president of the Latin American Bishops Conference in Medellín (1968). "Landázuri Rickets believed the Church should distance itself from established social structures and forces and that it should not only endorse social change but actively promote it by playing a guiding role in the country's development and encouraging a sense of social responsibility in political leaders and the population generally."[719] In 1968, Ricketts was a

---

[716] Father Fitzpatrick left Ireland in June 1952. Once he arrived in Lima, he met Father M. Forde, who had arrived six months earlier. *CM* (June–July 2002) features several articles devoted to the history of the Columbans in Peru.

[717] Fitzgerald was named Episcopal vicar of the Columban mission area in Lima (Diocese of Carabayllo, one of forty-three districts of the province of Lima) in the 1990s. The diocese was erected in 1996.

[718] Fr. Michael Fitzgerald, "Remembering the Early Days," *CM* (June–July 2002), 4–5.

[719] James Higgins, *Lima, A Cultural and Literary History* (Cambridge University Press/ Signal Books, 2004), 196. See also, Jeffrey Klaiber, SJ, *The Catholic Church in Peru, 1821–1985. A Social His*tory (Washington DC: The Catholic University of America Press, 1992) for an overview of the relationships between the church, the strata of society, and the social implications that intertwined in this period.

speaker at several Columban Golden Anniversary gatherings in the States[720] and was a guest of the Columbans in Bristol, Rhode Island.[721]

Father Stephen Kealy, who had previous experience with Student Catholic Action in the Philippines, formed a large youth group in St. Martin Parish, where he was missioned from 1960–1966. As he noted, there was little else provided for them in circumstances of great poverty. He received money from the United Nations to build a youth club with recreational space. His youth choir of sixty members became well-known.[722] The group had 2,000 members from the parish of 60,000 and "was the biggest thing in town [in their area of Lima]."[723]

Kealy's approach was one way to provide skills and a sense of community among the youth who, he observed, had little else to occupy their time.

Being a missionary in Latin America in the 1960s and 1970s was often difficult for many reasons. The *Far East* readers were provided an overview of some of the social and political problems in South America.[724] Not everyone in Latin America supported the declarations of the bishops' conferences at Puebla and Medellín, nor the implications thereof, especially in relationship to the priority of the poor. Father Smith himself indicated that the priest's domain should be "God and heaven" and not poverty. "The Church can only propose the principles of social justice and at best offer a token relief to immediate social miseries."[725] Columbans struggled with questions such as, what did identification with the poor mean? Should a missionary live in a hovel or take on a "mundane" work such as driving a bus to earn his "daily bread"? What did it mean in the context of Latin America "to be like the people?"[726] What did a "preferential option for the poor" look like in practice? Did the perspective of the two noted

---

[720] Father Joseph McSweeny interview of Father Richard Steinhilber, 12 July 2012, Interview 2.

[721] Father James McCaslin, *It's Not My Fault. It's Gift* (printed in Hong Kong, 2001), 105. Ricketts was the principal guest of Superior General James Kielt, former superior general and former U.S. Regional Director Father Timothy Connolly, who was then a missionary in Peru, and Richard Steinhilber, incumbent director. Ibid.

[722] Father Michael Harrison interview of Father Stephen Kealy, Los Angeles. 25 January 1992.

[723] Ibid.

[724] Gerard Smith, "The Cross or Chaos, Historical Background for Problems in Latin America," *FE* (April 1963) 2–5 and *FE* (May 1963) 1–3. Gerard Smith, "No Shortcuts," *FE* (April 1966), 4–7. Gerard Smith (1913–1997) studied film making and television techniques, then went to Peru, Chile, and Argentina to make mission movies. He was appointed to Peru from 1968 to 1975.

[725] Gerard Smith, "No Shortcuts," *FE* (April 1966), 6.

[726] Father Joseph McSweeny interview of Father Richard Steinhilber, 12 June 2012, Interview 2.

Latin American Bishops Conference (CELAM) documents change what it meant to be a missionary priest? Columban responses to the questions took different forms in practice, which sometimes caused tension among the men. In the 1970s, Father Michael Harrison, who had the opportunity to travel to many Columban missions, remarked that he felt in Peru "quite a bit of tension" or even a "division between [the men] who were going conservative and traditional and [the men] who were, what they call it, progressive and left-wing."[727]

Amid these questions and conflict was the fact that in this same period, priests, Sisters, and Brothers were leaving their Societies and religious congregations in North America. When asked if he had any "heartbreaks" in his time as a Columban missionary, Father Stephen Kealy remarked, "The greatest heartbreak was seeing the large number of priests in Peru who left the priesthood [post 1965]. I think that is the only thing that I really felt disheartened about because many of them were close friends of mine, not only Columbans but those from the St. James Society, too. [This was] a group I was very close to and used to go on vacation with them. . . . That was really the hardest thing I experienced."[728]

The Columban Sisters also had missions in Peru. Born in northern Ireland, Sister Joan Sawyer (1932–1983) had spent most of her religious life in mission promotion in Ireland, England and Massachusetts. Then in December 1976, she was given an assignment to Lima.[729] In the parish in Condevilla, she visited families daily to find out ways to alleviate their difficult situations and sought to be the love of Christ toward each person. The Sisters evaluated their ministry in the parish and concluded they would move to work in the mountains of Recuay. After a few months there, Joan returned to Lima early in 1983 and was a pastoral agent in Lurigancho prison on the outskirts of the city. The overcrowded prison was foul smelling and dangerous. She became an intermediary between the prisoners and their families. She advocated for them at the Department of Justice to verify reasons for prisoners' incarceration and decisions about the court sentencing. On December 14, 1983, as Sister Joan was about to leave the prison, she entered the jail office and unknowingly walked into a situation where several prisoners were staging an escape. They had taken hostage two social workers. Sister Joan was taken as the third hostage. The prisoners herded the social workers and Sister Joan outside into an ambulance and then climbed

---

[727]   "Joe" (Father Joseph McSweeny?) interview of Father Michael Harrison. 31 March 2011.

[728]   Father Michael Harrison interview of Father Stephen Kealy, Los Angeles. 25 January 1992.

[729]   Sister Mary Joan did promotion work from the Hyde Park, Massachusetts, house from 1969–1972. She then earned a degree in social work at Mundelein College, Chicago. She became a naturalized U.S. citizen. A brief account of her life is Fr. Maurice Foley, "God's Humble Servant," *CM* (December 2014), 6.

in. About a mile from the prison, police were waiting for them. Rounds of bullets from police were fired into the vehicle. Sister Joan was struck several times and died shortly after being hit.

A northern sector of the Columban parish of Huasahuasi had "virtually been under the control of the 'Shining Path' from 1988–1991."[730] As the terror of the Shining Path abated, the Columbans worked toward reconciliation of families and groups in their parishes. "Rebels carried out summary executions of 'government collaborators.' One of these was Australian Josephite Sister Irene McCormick. The army then replied with savage reprisals," where innocent people were killed as well.[731]

These situations and tense conditions were defining moments for Columbans and other missionaries. No Columban had visited Huasahuasi since 1986. Furthermore, to rebuild a Catholic community among those who suffered so much and who were on the "opposite" side in the time of violence called for courage and prudence. To the Columbans' surprise, people were willing to rebuild relationships, though it would take some time to foster true reconciliation. *Columban Mission* kept the various facets of the Peruvian story before U.S. Catholics. The Columbans in Lima continued to work with migrants from the Andes. The theme of migration pictured the stark realities and questions rural Peruvian had when they moved to the populous city of Lima.[732]

In Peru since 1977, Father Christopher Baker described Columban mission in 2009. Teams of priests, seminarians, Sisters, associate priests, lay missionaries from other countries and fifty local Columban missionary collaborators go from their parishes to form small communities who lack pastoral helpers. The twelve parishes Columbans shepherded engaged in 100 projects to "help educate and empower the local people to make their full contribution to the Church and the nations."[733]

Brazil

In spite of the questions and difficult experiences just noted, the 1976 Society General Chapter resolved, "That the Society increase its commitment to Latin America,"[734] though it took some time to make this happen. The next General Chapter held in Lima, Peru (1982), saw the Society to be in the

---

[730] "Healing the Wounds," *CM* (April 1966), 16–17.

[731] Ibid.

[732] Peter Woodruff, *Columban Mission* (February 2010), 21–22. Woodruff worked for many years in Peru.

[733] Fr. Chris Baker, "Mission in Today's Peru," *CM* (June/July 2009), 3.

[734] *Acts of the Chapter, October 4–December 8, 1976*, Section 4, #4, p. 12.

"second phase of renewal."[735] Lima was a key location for chapter delegates to experience the immense poverty of the area and gain insight into what impoverished people faced daily. Three years after the Lima Chapter, the Columbans opened a mission in a third South American country, Brazil. At the time, Dom Hélder Câmara, Recife, Brazil, known as the "bishop of the slums,"[736] was probably the most recognized South American bishop for North American Catholics. He gave several talks as part of conferences organized by the U.S. Catholic Bishops' Latin America Bureau. His small but powerful book, *Spiral of Violence,* was read and discussed by many in the United States and elsewhere.[737]

Eleven Columbans were sent to start their mission in Brazil in 1985 in the six-year-old diocese of Barreiras in the state of Bahia.[738] The group, who spent six months in Bristol, Rhode Island, for "inculturation," arrived in Brazil in August and attended language school in the capital city, Brasilia. Six men were sent to the city and five into the interior of the diocese of Barreiras. The state of Bahia had a 40 percent rate of illiteracy. Among the missionaries who began work in the interior, Father Clarence Beckley, a native of Springville, Iowa, remained in the Portuguese speaking country until 2000. He had twelve years mission experience in the Philippines before coming to Brazil. The bishop of Barreiras, Ricardo José Weberberger, OSB (1939–2010), was "appreciative of our presence because we came in as five young guys."[739] Weberberger, consecrated as bishop in 1979 at forty years of age, brought two monsignors with him into the new diocese. They were in their mid-'80s and had been working in the area for fifty to sixty years.

With a scarcity of priests in the diocese, the Catholics celebrated Eucharist perhaps every ten years. Beckley reflected upon the Columban early years. The three priests decided they would visit every one of the barrios. Every morning they got into their Jeep and headed to a new location. "We surprised the people because they had never seen three priests together. 'No, we didn't come here to say Mass.' 'What are you here for?' 'To speak to you, let you know we are here now in your presence and what is it that you need from the Church?'"

---

[735] Society General Chapter, 1982, *Columban Mission Today*, 8.

[736] Dom Hélder Câmara ((1909–1999) was a prime mover in the formation of CELAM and helped organize the Medellin Conference in 1968. In 2015, the inauguration of the process of his canonization to sainthood was started.

[737] Dom Hélder Câmara, *The Spiral of Violence* (Denville, NJ: Dimension Books, 1971).

[738] Unnamed interviewer, interview of Father Clarence Beckley 18 October 2011, Miramar Retreat Center, Duxbury, Massachusetts. The diocese of Barreiras was founded from the diocese of Barra in 1979. Pope John XXIII had created many new dioceses in Latin America. In a short period of time, 160 new bishops shepherded new dioceses.

[739] Unnamed interviewer, interview of Father Clarence Beckley 18 October 2011, Miramar Retreat Center, Duxbury, MA.

The priests took notes on what people said and after the missionaries made the rounds of the area, they came back to say Mass for the people. Eventually, they had Mass for each area once a year, then twice a year. The people came together either on Saturday or Sunday "as a community of faith" to pray. Eventually "the priests trained communion ministers who could take the Eucharist to these areas."[740]

The bishop "really listened to the Columbans because it was really a new way to be in mission."[741] One example Beckley gave related to the way the bishop and the clergy interacted with him at the first meeting between the bishop and the priests of the diocese. He would sit in the front at a desk and all the priests were "like students sitting in a row." After that meeting, the Columbans suggested a different way to hold a diocesan meeting with him. They said, "Don Ricardo, why don't we just put the chairs around so that we can see each other, you can see each one. You know, he did it! He was so surprised with the dynamic. . . . This was something new for them."[742] Don Ricardo "had a very good vision of forming and working with people."[743]

The sacramental life of Catholics was important, but with the close observation of people's lives, the areas that affected daily life also showed up on the Columbans' radar screen. As Beckley remarked, "We were looking, how can we be kind of like the yeast among the people."[744] Having grown up on a farm, he observed closely the plight of small farmers in the Wanderley area.[745] He saw that wealthy ranchers were encroaching illegally on the lands of the small farmers. He took up the matter with the bishop and brought it to the attention of national newspapers. "The publicity resulted in a court order in favor of the people, which angered the ranchers who retaliated by blocking roadways with fallen trees." However, the Wanderley police then presented them with a court order to clear the roads immediately.[746]

---

[740]   Ibid.

[741]   Ibid.

[742]   Ibid., Beckley had used the dynamic in Manila in the Student Catholic Action groups. Don Ricardo was bishop of Barrieras for thirty-two years. Some of the other dioceses had as many as five bishops in that many years.

[743]   Unnamed interviewer, interview of Father Clarence Beckley 18 October 2011, Miramar Retreat Center, Duxbury, MA.

[744]   Unnamed interviewer, interview of Father Clarence Beckley 18 October 2011, Miramar Retreat Center, Duxbury, MA.

[745]   Wanderley is a municipal district and a municipality in the state of Bahia.

[746]   Unnamed interviewer, oral history of Father Clarence Beckley 18 October 2011, Miramar Retreat Center, Duxbury, MA. See also, "Brazil," *Columban Newsletter, USA* (October 1990), 7, for a condensed version of the incident.

Beckley's wide ranging knowledge gained from farming also helped him develop a plan for a swift, less expensive way to build small houses for people, and a large community center that also functioned as a church. The latter was built by the people, who could look at its parts and recognize their own work. Beckley's experience with construction made the building sound and safe. Sisters came to the center to teach about nutrition, sewing projects were initiated and health personnel and doctors became available for the people.

Chicago born Father John Wanaurny was another of the first Columbans in Brazil. He, too, had many years in the Philippines before arriving in Brazil.[747] He would serve the Diocese of Barreiras in many ways over his ten years there, including promotion of vocations in the diocese, accompaniment of the labor movement among farm workers, and catechetical development for adolescents. In May 1990, he was appointed the first vicar general of the Diocese of Barreiras.

A key reality in Brazil was the relationship between the government and the church. Should the church cooperate with the government to get needed services or should the church continue with its own program? Wanaurny thought the Catholic Church "was the only 'credible institution' in Brazil. . . . If we enter into the government's plans, we're the government, we're going to lose credibility like the government loses it all the time. If we go out to the people and say, 'come on, let's get into this, let's cooperate,' we'll find out someone is putting the money in their pocket and the program isn't getting off the ground at all. We're always in this position."[748]

Wanaurny highlighted another type of education that fellow Columban Liam Carey provided the parish. Carey prepared well for each session. His approach was a contrast in goal and process to that provided by the Brazilian government.

> The church at the grassroots, popular education, the Church
> is there with all its support, with all its resources, everything
> it can do. We have a lot of this great material coming out. We
> got ourselves a projector. Liam Carey, the greatest guy in the
> world, Liam goes out, plugs in the projector, slides in some of
> the Gospels or slides of some aspect of health education, then
> [has] a discussion and conversation of an hour or hour and a
> half with the people. That's where education is occurring in

---

[747] A forty-six-page, single-line transcript of an interview of Father John Wanaurny in 1991 provides insightful and informative details about the Catholic Church in Brazil, his own experience and perspectives, as well as that other Columbans there up to 1991. CFA-USA. With short periods of time away from Brazil for vacation or to tend to an ill family member in the states, Wanaurny was in Brazil from 1985 to 1995.

[748] Unnamed interviewer of Father John Wanaurny, 1991. Transcript, lines 21–26.

Brazil. At most other levels you have education that fits into a system that keeps people locked into the social system as it exists. It doesn't challenge it. There is no one that comes out of a school in our area that says, "There are too few people owning too much land in this country." They don't get educated to see that, it's not conscious awakening type of education. The church does that with the labor unions.[749]

Able to cull from their mission experience in Latin America, as well as in Jamaica and Belize for some of those years, the Columbans, along with the Office of Mission Education and Animation in the Archdiocese of Chicago, prepared a study guide for the *Aparecida* document produced by the Fifth General Assembly of CELAM that met in Aparecida, São Paulo, Brazil, 2007.[750] Using consultation with groups in their countries to gather the experience and thoughts of their people to draft their deliberations, the bishops chose Father Jorge Bergoglio, SJ, the future Pope Francis, to chair the committee that wrote the final document of their Aparecida meeting.

China Back in Focus

The 1976 Society General Chapter had mandated that the "incoming central administration establish a special commission for a Chinese Apostolate and mission among Chinese."[751] This required updated knowledge about China and Taiwan. The Justice and Peace Office continued to gather and share information about China and Korea. Dodd and others met the new Assistant Secretary of State for East Asia to discuss human rights in China and reengagement of dialogue between the "two Koreas."[752] *Columban Mission* published an issue devoted to modern China.[753] The Justice and Peace office staff continued to be informed about China through their contacts, through attendance at seminars, such as the Brookings Institute seminar, "Church and

---

[749]   Ibid., Transcript, lines 36–52.

[750]   *Study Guide for Use with the Aparecida Document*, available through the USCCB, 2010. The guide was published in English and Spanish.

[751]   Missionary Society of St. Columban, *Acts of the 1976 General chapter* #4, p. 10.

[752]   *Columban Newsletter* (Fall 2001), 4.

[753]   *CM* (November 1996).

State in China,"[754] and through Father Thomas P. Reynolds' initial involvement at the start of the U.S. Catholic China Bureau.[755]

An example of the mandate's fruition was the formation of the Association for International Teaching, Educational and Curriculum Exchange (AITECE) established in Hong Kong in 1988. Father Edward (Ned) T. Kelly[756] along with Australian Audrey Donnythorne founded and registered AITECE. While "not a subterfuge for proselytizing," the organization is a "medium through which Christians from other countries could assist in the modernization of China especially in the sphere of education."[757] The stated purpose was "to recruit English-speaking teachers qualified to teach English as a second language in Chinese universities. That purpose broadened into teaching other university disciplines through English in Chinese universities. Science was particularly important during the Deng Xiaoping 'catch-up-with-the scientific-West' period of Chinese history."[758] AITECE kept in touch with the Columban Justice and Peace office in DC. Beginning in 1996, the Columban China Mission Unit published bimonthly *Newsletters*, which included information about AITECE. Father Thomas P. Reynolds, then teaching at Loyola University in Chicago, was the first recruiter for the early years of the program.[759] Following service on the Society General Council in Hong Kong, Father John Burger also recruited teachers.

Another Columban initiative was to have Chinese seminarians come to the States to take courses in English and theology. At the invitation of Father Ned

---

[754] The seminar featured China scholars and China watchers who gathered to "further common understanding of the role of the church and the state in the lives of the People's Republic today." *Columban Newsletter* (Easter, 2002), 4.

[755] Father Reynolds later served as Columban representative on the board of the U.S. Catholic China Bureau from 1992–2002.

[756] Father Edward T. Kelly (1936–1994), who engaged in Chinese studies at Seton Hall, New Jersey, and at Columbia University, received the Chen Juang prize for advanced studies in Chinese. In Hong Kong he was asked to "assess the feasibility of Columbans taking on work among the Chinese in Hong Kong." Missionary Society of St. Columban, *Those Who Journeyed with Us* (1918–2010), 132. "Donnythorne was also adept at Chinese languages and eager to have English speaking teachers come to China. The acronym originally stood for Association of International Teachers of English and Cultural Exchange." Father T. P. Reynolds correspondence with author, 11 December 2016.

[757] *Manual for AITECE National Offices*, December 2001, 3. AITECE is "legally incorporated as a limited company in Hong Kong and has been granted charitable status by the Inland Revenue Department, and registered with the State administration of foreign experts affairs in Beijing as an approved organization for the introduction of foreign experts to work in cultural and education fields in China." Brochure for AITECE, published in English and Chinese (2015). CFA-USA.

[758] Father T. P. Reynolds correspondence with author 11 December 2016.

[759] Ibid.

Kelly, seminarians Ni and Liang and a Father Joseph Wang arrived from China in the late 1980s. They lived with the Columbans in Chicago while attending courses in English at De Paul University and in theology and scripture at the Catholic Theological Union.[760] Father Burger later sought locations for Chinese Sisters to study. Other groups eventually took on the task of recruiting Chinese priests and Sisters to study at Catholic universities in the United States.

One Columban influenced by Father Ned Kelly and later involved with AITECE is Father Thomas Glennon, from Queens, New York. He had gained an interest in China from Kelly, "who was working on his Chinese," while Glennon was a seminarian at St. Columban Seminary in Milton, Massachusetts. After ordination, Glennon was sent to the newly opened Columban mission in Taiwan in 1979 and served there for twelve years. Upon his return to the States, he lived in Chicago at the Columban house on Magnolia Street. Through Grace Chen, a Taiwanese student he knew from celebrating Eucharist at the Catholic University of Taiwan, he learned that "she and her husband hosted a Chinese Bible study in their apartment and [they] invited me to join them. From that beginning, I met other Chinese Catholics in the Chicago area that met regularly for Chinese Bible study." They were a "great group of people."[761] Father Glennon hosted some of them for bible study and prayer at the Columban house on Magnolia Street. Sometimes during those gatherings "the struggles they had in terms of discrimination particularly in the work place or the implication of some employers taking credit for work being done by Chinese employees came up. That was a painful thing, as was the realization their children were growing up with different traditions than the parents who had grown up in Taiwan."[762] In addition to Glennon's own counseling and pastoral skills he could offer, he invited Father Howard Lui, SJ,[763] to the house to conduct a two-day seminar for the group on inner healing.

Inculturation

A further dimension of mission came to the fore in the mid-1980s under the term, *inculturation*.[764] Before the Columbans opened their new mission in Brazil, the group spent a month in Bristol, Rhode Island, for inculturation.

---

[760]   Unnamed interviewer, interview of Father Thomas Glennon, n.d.

[761]   Unnamed interviewer, interview of Father Thomas Glennon, n.d.

[762]   Ibid.

[763]   In 2010 Father Howard Lui Ching-hay was the Jesuit superior for Macau.

[764]   Fr. Peter Woodruff, compiler, Kate Kenny, Connie Wacha, eds., *The Missionary Society of St. Columban, Columbans on Mission* (Xlibris, 2013), 238–332, provides many recent examples of Columbans and inculturation around the world.

What did that mean? What difference would that make for mission? Behind the word was the question, "What is the relationship between the Gospel and culture?"[765] Does the expression of Catholic prayer and practice look the same around the globe?

The Jesuit missionary to China, Matteo Ricci (1552–1610) learned Chinese philosophy and art, valued Confucian ethics, and adapted to Chinese customs, to have access to the ruling elite who valued these areas. He appealed to Chinese interest in science, especially in the field of mathematics, trigonometry, geography and cosmography. His thought was to interest the intelligentsia in Christianity and if that group became Catholic, they would influence the other groups in China. European and American anthropologists in the nineteenth and early twentieth centuries focused on studying aboriginal tribal customs, art, and world views in Africa.[766] Missionaries in the early to midtwentieth century began to use the words, "adaptation," or "accommodation." The Gospel needed to be "adapted" or "accommodated" to the culture.

The Columbans did not think of themselves as scientists, but the notion of inculturation considered other nuances of "culture" in relation to the appropriation of Catholic life. The Columban Society's *Constitutions and Directory* (1986) thought it important enough to include the word in their revised constitutions. "The Church has come to a far greater appreciation of Kingdom values in the world's cultures and religions and of the need to listen with them and truly inculturate the Gospel message."[767] In other words, did people have values in their culture (or religion) upon which Catholic life could connect or perhaps challenge?

Fathers Donald Wodarz and Thomas P. Reynolds provided an introduction to "inculturation," the term gaining use in the post–Vatican II expression of a global church understanding of the interaction between Gospel, mission,

---

765   In 1982, a Pontifical Council for Culture was formed to study the rift between the Gospel and culture in Catholic countries and to examine issues underlying the inculturation of the Gospel.

766   Father Trevor Trotter, on the General Council at the time he wrote to Father Sean Dwan in 2007, had sent Dwan an article written by Frans Wijsen, whose anthropology work was among East African groups. Wijsen, along with Peter Nissen later edited, *"Mission is a must." Intercultural Theology and the Mission of the Church* (NY: Rodopi (Firm), 2002.

767   Missionary Society of Saint Columban, *Constitutions and Directory (1986)*, 7. Another issue that arose in the mid-1980s was the topic of "Missions" or "Mission in Six Continents," raised initially when the Commission on World Mission and Evangelism met in 1963 in Mexico under the title, "Mission in Six Continents." Where God is active is an invitation to have churches be in God's mission. The theme was noted in the superior general's "Report to the General Assembly," held in Korea, 1988, 5–8.

and culture.[768] The five-day workshop for the Columbans was rich but intense with presentations about the word "inculturation," small group discussion, personal reflection, and prayer together. Wodarz, an American teaching at the Columban seminary in Turramurra, Australia, at the time, unfolded insights as to how the church historically inculturated around the world and how the Second Vatican Council value of "dialogue" with other religions related to inculturation. He reflected upon his understanding and experience of North American culture, its historical and perspective present realities. He posed the question, "Are there uniquely American cultural values that affect me positively and negatively and do these values affect me as a missionary?"[769]

Father Reynolds, then a lecturer at the Catholic Theological Union, Chicago, developed the biblical basis for inculturation in two ways: inculturation *in* the bible and inculturation *of* the bible in both Testaments. He queried, "What is the essence of the Christian message? Can that be inculturated without doing violence to cultural values in the host culture? Can the message be inculturated without transformation in the whole host culture?" And finally, "Is the real problem one of translation *for the host people* or one of translation *by the host people*?"[770] The workshop "concluded with a session whereby people reflected on some significant symbols that spoke to us and signified being Columban. As we remembered some of the persons, places and events of the past that shaped our society and our lives, we became more aware of the process of inculturation itself."[771]

The year following the workshop, Columban Sean Dwan initiated a journal, *Inculturation*,[772] wherein he urged the Columbans to write articles about the history of inculturation in Korea or about ways the missionaries understood and incorporated inculturation. The workshop and the journal made explicit the theoretical elements of Gospel inculturation in Columban situations.

The 1986 Columban *Constitutions and Directory* identified mission from the perspective of "crossing boundaries of country, language, race and culture," in order to "establish the Church among peoples to whom the Gospel has not been preached; help Churches mature until able to evangelize their own peoples; and promote dialogue between Christianity and other religious traditions."[773]

---

[768]   *Columban Newsletter* (February 1985), 1–3. The Inculturation Workshop was held in Omaha from January 21 to 25, 1985.

[769]   *Columban Newsletter* (February 1985), 2.

[770]   *Columban Newsletter* (February 1985), 2–3.

[771]   *Columban Newsletter* (February 1985), 3. Most likely, Regional Superior Edward Naughton wrote the overview of the inculturation workshop.

[772]   Six volumes of *Inculturation* were published in Korea between 1986 and 1991, with Sean Dwan, editor.

[773]   Missionary Society of Saint Columban, *Constitutions and Directory, 1986*, C. 102, p. 11.

Of course, many Columbans had been doing that already in some form or other. Father Chuck Lintz, ordained in 1970 and missioned to Korea, commented that he wanted in his first assignment "to live with a Korean priest. I wanted to learn about their life, to learn the language, to get closer to Koreans, and I felt that living with a Korean priest would be the best way to do that."[774]

There were nuances to discover, however. The Columbans at the same time faced the challenges and potential of the fact that there were within the Society various "cultures." First of all, there were differences among Irish-born, Irish immigrants to the United States or elsewhere, U.S. Columbans from other ethnic backgrounds, and still later, those from countries considered "mission countries." Much conversation went on in the Society, especially with respect to the latter group, prior to the 1986 Columban *Constitutions and Directory*. As Father Tim Mulroy reflected, "the acceptance of members from our mission countries awakened us much more than previously to the diversity that already existed but had been cloaked by a common English language."[775]

In 2008, the Columbans opened a Central Administration position, that of Researcher on Mission and Culture, "a new development within our Society and an important one."[776] Father Sean Dwan was highly qualified for the appointment. He had mission experience in Korea, had earned an MA in theology from Yonsei University, Seoul, and a doctorate in history of religions from the University of Chicago. He taught courses in cultural anthropology. As he reflected upon what his appointment might mean, Dwan highlighted key cultural aspects of Columban priorities, such as structural poverty, environmental destruction, migration, and intercultural living, for example."[777] He thought the office could assist Columbans to reflect upon and share their cross-cultural experience and make available to other mission groups their insights and learnings. These reflections would also "link the issues of inculturation with the dynamics of intercultural living."[778]

---

[774] Father Sean Dwan interview of Father Charles (Chuck) Lintz. 12 June 2013, Bristol, Rhode Island.

[775] Notes to author in review of this chapter of the manuscript. 17 February 2017.

[776] Father Trevor Trotter to Father Sean Dwan 18 March 2008. The author is grateful to Father Sean Dwan for providing background for the new research position in the Columban Central Office. Author e-mail correspondence with Father Sean Dwan, 14 through 26 July 2016.

[777] "Statement of the New Position of Researcher in Culture and Mission, *Columban Intercom* (2008), as Sean Dwan began his assignment.

[778] Part of Sean Dwan's honing of the goals of the Researcher in Culture and Mission. Author e-mail correspondence with Father Sean Dwan, 14–26 July 2016. The point is noted in the Columban *Constitutions*: "The members come from different nations and cultures. This diversity enriches and contributes to the ongoing life and work of the Society." Missionary Society of Saint Columban, *Constitutions and Directory, 1986*. C.202, p. 15.

The Columbans further contributed to a fuller understanding of the relationship between the Gospel, church, and culture through imparting their experience in *Columban Mission* and in mission education.[779] The U.S. region produced two sets of mission material that specifically explored the subject of culture in relation to mission. In the *Journey with Jesus Program* eighth grade students learned about "Culture: Gift and Blessing." As the program noted, culture shapes every aspect of our lives. "Many times we cannot see our own culture until we see someone else's culture." Since there are "so many expressions of culture globally, God must love variety."[780] An adult formation program, *Culture: The Web of Life* (2011) explored cultural diversity and how those traditions support daily life. The program examined ways to cross boundaries of language and culture to appreciate the traditions of other groups and to celebrate expressions of faith in various cultural traditions as a gift from God.

Closer to Home

While vigorous activity and careful thought were given to convey the impact of mission through the Justice and Peace office, the growth of new mission locations, and a more conscious reflection underlying theological frameworks for mission after 1976, other issues came to the fore in the United States. Columbans expanded the idea of "formation" not only to seminarians but to include ongoing formation and renewal for priests. Inculturation had practical ramifications for Columbans in the United States. The region's increasing number of members over sixty years of age and efforts to have local mission become more self-sustaining had effects on funds, houses, and land.

Formation of Seminarians and Ongoing Formation for Priests

An aspect of seminarian formation after the 1976 Society Chapter called for mission experience prior to their permanent oath. "A period in his proposed overseas mission should be considered normal and desirable for the Columban student."[781] The experience was called the Overseas Training Program (OTP) and later, the First Mission Assignment (FMA). The 1986 Columban *Constitutions*

---

[779]   Some research on inculturation in the 1970s through the 1990s was coming from the French. However, of interest on the subject is S. Iniobong Udoidem, *Pope John Paul II on Inculturation: Theory and Practice* (Lanham, MD: University Press of America, 1996.)

[780]   *Culture, Gift and Blessing.* DVD, Mission Education Program, St. Columbans, Nebraska.

[781]   Missionary Society of St. Columban, Acts of the Chapter, 1976, #312, p. 23.

and Directory elaborated upon the point to say the seminarian's program of studies in his initial formation "is designed to prepare students for the priestly ministry, for cross-cultural evangelization and mission particularly among the poor and oppressed."[782]

Priests ordained for many years were also encouraged to take courses in theology, scripture and "pastoral updating with the opportunity for spiritual reflection within the context of the Columban community."[783] This ongoing formation was a more sustained time beyond the annual retreat for reading, reflection, prayer, short courses, interaction with peers from various congregations, with laymen and laywomen.

In January 1978, Columban priests lived with the seminarians in Cambridge, Massachusetts, for that purpose. Regional Director Ed Naughton wrote an overview of Columban experience there, a program chosen by many Columbans at the time.[784] Naughton's report summarized the experiment of having priests in continuing education reside with Columban seminarians at Cambridge. This "has been an experience that practically all have found most favorable."[785] Living with the students and formation staff proved fruitful and enjoyable. "The early fears of living in such close community and the near trauma at the thought of cooking dissipated very quickly and comfortableness and healthy friendships took over." Some of the men reported that the "Columban community experience of living, praying, studying together has been the best part of the program." [786]

In fall 1984, the Columban Theologate moved to the Catholic Theological Union, Chicago, where the curriculum was focused on mission and international experience. "Staff and students in theology found the first year

---

[782]   Missionary Society of St. Columban, *Constitutions and Directory, 1986* D.215.1, p. 37.

[783]   Ed Naughton, "Report on Continuing Education in U.S. Region, April 1979. *Casey History* (1979), 15.

[784]   "Continuing Education," *Columban Newsletter* (June 1978). *Columban Newsletter* (April 1979), 7–9 gave further information about the men's experience in Continuing Education. Two other programs at the time were at the University of Notre Dame and at the Maryknoll Institute. Among other renewal programs Columbans attended at some point were the Ministry for Ministers Program (San Antonio, Texas), Catholic Theological Union, Chicago, the Spiritual Integration for Ministry Program (Regis College, Toronto) and the Jesuit sponsored renewal program in Berkeley, California.

[785]   Ed Naughton, "Report on Continuing Education in U.S. Region, April 1979. *Casey History* (1979), 15.

[786]   Ibid., The move from a large seminary building to a residential house was quite a change for the men. The seminarians at the houses in Cambridge took turns cooking, shopping and cleaning. They took on simple maintenance tasks and lawn care, all of which kept them "in touch with the work-a-day world as well as building self-confidence, initiative and teamwork." September 1978, Move to Cambridge. 8-A-38. *Casey History* (1978), 7.

at CTU refreshing and challenging. They are impressed with the missiological emphasis in the theological studies and pastoral ministry program."[787] The student body was representative of the cultures into which future missionaries would find themselves. From 1998 through the end of the 2011–2012 academic year, the Chicago location served as the International Theologate for Columban seminarians from the Philippines, Korea, Fiji, and Latin America. Starting in 2012–2013 seminarians did their studies in their respective home countries.[788] Subsequently, a Columban International Seminary (with study of philosophy and theology) was established in the Philippines with attendance at Loyola University (Ateneo) in Manila or at Maryhill.

Several practical and theoretical issues around living and studying as an intercultural group came to the fore in Chicago. While on one level the Society provided workshops and readings on *inculturation*, the Theologate was a kind of "hands on" laboratory in the complexity of *intercultural living*. The seminarians had different academic backgrounds, abilities in language learning, rural or city experience, and socioeconomic contexts from which they came.

Columban seminarians from Latin America, the Philippines, Fiji and Korea lived together with the Columban priests. The seminarians attended DePaul University to study English to prepare them to take courses in theology and mission at Catholic Theological Union. Rector Father Tim Mulroy, whose mission life had been in Japan, later made some observations about seminarian interaction with DePaul students.

> Some [DePaul] students had a religious background (not necessarily Christian), some had no religious background. I could see after the months went by that a lot of times students at DePaul related on a very human level with their classmates of different religious backgrounds and different nationalities. I think [the seminarians] found confidence at being able to reach out to people from different cultures, backgrounds and religions and use their English language skills. That's all they had to communicate with somebody from Saudi Arabia or Taiwan. I often felt it gave them a sense of the missionary life.[789]

---

[787] "Around the Region, *Columban Newsletter* (May 1985), 5. The Columban initial formation directors met in 1994 to work out new developments for the initial formation of seminarians "to better serve our vision of the future of mission." *Intercom* (April 1994), 68–69.

[788] Latin American seminarians were sent to the Catholic University, Santiago, Chile. Fijian seminarians went to the Pacific Regional Seminary, at which some Columbans were teaching.

[789] Father T. P. Reynolds interview of Father Timothy Mulroy, El Paso. Texas. 2 February 2012.

Working together in projects or tasks proved a tangible way to learn communication across cultural differences, "rather than just sitting down and talking about culture or talking abstractly about their backgrounds. . . . When differences and misunderstandings come up and then they sit down to talk, they have food for reflection."[790]

Father Je Hoon Augustine Lee, who had been part of the Columban Chicago program at one stage of his formation, was ordained in 2015. He spoke of significant areas of his development toward Columban priesthood.[791] He noted that Father Michael Riordan, his spiritual director, "helped me to get to know myself and taught me many creative ways to approach God and interact with people. His advice about learning to live with other people and enter into their situation was a big influence on my vocation and desire to work with others." Being an only child, Lee needed to learn "how to live with different people," especially in a close community.[792] In addition to taking time daily for prayer and reflection, Lee found it also important "to be open to learning from other people who come from different places and cultures."[793] Part of that experience was forged in Chicago. Father Lee is now one of the Columbans "remissioned" to Burma (now Myanmar).

Given the experience noted here of the Columban formation years at the Catholic Theological Union, this is a good time to mention a lesser known Columban influence in the United States: teaching in universities. Columbans pursued higher degrees in Rome and elsewhere to teach at their seminary colleges and theologates. An admirable example of teaching in academic institutions is the work of Irish-born Father Thomas P. Reynolds. Ordained in 1961,[794] he taught at Columban seminaries in Silver Creek (1966–1968) and Oconomowoc (1968–1971). When the latter seminary closed, he moved to Milwaukee, where he earned a master of arts degree in theology and a doctorate in religious studies at Marquette University in 1979. After a three year mission assignment in Peru and a year of Mission Education through the office at Columban headquarters, he was appointed to a Columban house in Chicago, where the Columban Theologate had moved to take advantage of the academic and library facilities of Catholic Theological Union (CTU). Over his several decades in Chicago, Reynolds wore many hats. One important area

---

[790]   Ibid.

[791]   Father Lee's experience of formation is found in Father Timothy Mulroy interview with him, "Called to Serve. Thoughts from a Newly Ordained Columban," *CM* (May 2015), 16–17.

[792]   Ibid.

[793]   Ibid., 17.

[794]   For the five years after ordination, Reynolds pursued Language and Literature Studies in Spain, France, Germany and at the University of Wisconsin–Madison.

related to academics. He taught Christology at CTU from 1984–1986 and later served the CTU consortium in significant ways: Columban trustee (1992–2008), chairman of the Academic Affairs Committee (1993–96), and chairman of the board (1996–2008).

In 1986 Father Reynolds was offered a teaching position at Loyola University, Chicago, where he taught Christology. He observed that Loyola's Institute of Pastoral Studies (IPS) did not have a course in mission theology, so he strongly advocated with the IPS director for such a course, especially given that the program was a *pastoral* institute. Pope John Paul II's encyclical, *Redemptoris Missio (On the Permanent Validity of the Church's Missionary Mandate.* 1990), had challenged bishops "to see themselves as ordained not simply for their own diocese but for the universal church, . . . for the salvation of the entire world."[795] Furthermore, all Catholics were called to mission and people engaged at a pastoral institute should have a mission focus. After Reynolds held many discussions with IPS on the importance of mission theology, the director charged Reynolds to develop and teach such a course. Reynolds did so for ten years with classes well attended.[796]

An Aging Membership

Regional Director Michael O'Louglin wrote, leadership "is constantly being besieged by problem-driven change rather than by vision-driven change."[797] Of course, since the beginning of the Society in the region, problems galore presented themselves. Often they were problems of growth and expansion of the Society. By the late 1970s, internal realities came more to the fore. One factor was an aging membership. Obviously that is not a situation unique to the Columbans. It was more noticeable to them because after 1971 fewer men entered to "replace" those who died. During that year sixty-six students were in all phases of formation in the United States. A year later, there were thirty-eight seminarians. A population growing older impacted the structure of their work

---

[795]   Father T. P. Reynolds correspondence with author 27 March 2017. Reynolds quoted *Redemptoris Missio* par. 63 and 67. Before he came to the Columban College Seminary, he had taught at St. Columban Seminary, Silver Creek until that closed. He was ordained in 1961 and has spent a half century in mission in the United States.

[796]   While CTU in Chicago continues a vigorous curriculum related to mission, a focus on mission history, missiology, mission studies or even global Catholicism is fairly nonexistent in Catholic higher education in the United States. Undergraduate majors in Catholic Studies rarely treat the topic. De Paul University, Chicago, launched the Center for World Catholicism and Intercultural Theology. Their focus is conversation and study of the global South and the relationship between globalization and the Catholic Church's future as a truly worldwide church.

[797]   Michael O'Loughlin, *Columban Newsletter* (March 1993), 1.

in the region and on the missions. The reality called for creative, significant decisions that addressed their life within a strong Blowick/Galvin tradition but also within the spirit of the Society patron, Saint Columban.

O'Loughlin viewed an actuarial study that indicated for 1994, 300 of 650 Columbans worldwide would be over sixty years old. The projection was that by 2002, 400 of 540 Columbans would be over sixty.[798] Archivist Father Paul Casey noted the statistics for the U.S. Columbans in 1992:

30–40 years old   1 Columban
40–50 years old   12
50–60 years old   30
60–70 years old   36
70–80 years old   22
80–90 years old   7   Total Number of Columbans in U.S. Region: 108[799]

In 2016, there were 391 priests in the entire Society.

The Society had its first member turn 100 years of age in 2014, Father Bernard (Barney) Toal. Born in Philadelphia but growing up in Gloucester, New Jersey, Toal was ordained in 1943 at the Cathedral of St. Joseph in Buffalo, New York. He had been influenced by Father Richard Ranaghan who came to speak about missions when Toal was in grade school. While not specifically mentioning Ranaghan's famous film on China, Toal was impressed when the missionary prayed the Hail Mary in Chinese. Ranaghan later visited the Toal family home.[800] After ordination Toal worked with Mexicans in Arizona for about a year. He was missioned to the Philippines in 1947. Father Toal might be known best in the United States as a spiritual director and director of the men in their Spiritual Year (1951–1968) in Bristol, Rhode Island.[801] He was then missioned to Peru for ten years. He died at St. Elizabeth Nursing Home in Bristol, Rhode Island, in 2015 at 101 years of age.

One area impacted by an older Columban group was future planning for Columban ministry. To obtain some data on their situation, the U.S. region contacted the Center for Applied Research in the Apostolate (CARA) to survey Columbans about issues and perspectives they had in the areas of mission, formation, and charism. Columbans knew the organization because CARA and the Columban Justice and Peace office were in the same building. Furthermore, CARA had been started with a $5,000 contribution from the major superiors of

---

[798]   *Columban Newsletter* (March 1993).

[799]   Paul Casey, *Columban Newsletter* (April 1992).

[800]   Father Michael Harrison interview of Father Barney [Bernard] Toal, 12 May 1992. Interviewed at a retreat house outside Los Angeles.

[801]   For the last ten of those years Father Toal was director of probationers.

mission sending congregations, after they read an article by Cardinal Cushing on "The Modern Challenge of the Missions" (1961). The idea was to assist future planning not just on hunches but on scientific data. In this case, a survey of the appropriation of Columban charism, apostolates, personal and communal life, resources for apostolates and planning for the future provided data as to which issues were key considerations for the men, as they thought about the Society as a whole and their individual place in their region. People who worked closely with the Society were also tapped for their perceptions of Columbans and their ministry.

What is notable in the selected results from the surveys conducted in 1979/80 and 1989/90 is that there was unanimity between Columbans and those working with them as to the importance of the first three areas of ministry: mission awareness, vocation recruitment, ethnic minorities. The fifth area noted as important is the same for both groups: retreat work. Columbans placed the Columban Justice and Peace office as fourth in order of importance, whereas the non-Columbans had the homeless as their fourth choice. The non-Columban group was even slightly higher in their emphases than the Columbans. (See CARA summary at end of chapter.)

Statistically, the percentage of men either retired or unavailable for ministry soared dramatically from 2.28 percent in 1979 to 29.8 percent ten years later. The percentage of Columbans involved in mission centers and the number of promotion houses decreased from 34.28 percent to 17.5 percent.[802] While the percentage of men in Administration and the General Mission House in Omaha doubled, the actual number of men remained the same: fourteen Columbans.

One reason for a larger number of older priests in the United States was that many Columbans in the U.S. region were in a "second career" in promotion work, for example, having served in Columban missions. Furthermore, the region is one of a few places where Columbans can retire or receive care and support when they are infirm or ill.[803] In spite of the number of older Columbans, new possibilities for mission opened, not only with lay missionaries but with the creative and significant work along the Mexican/U.S. border and the focus on China. Christopher Saenz from St. Mary's Parish, Bellevue, Nebraska, a parish with historic Columban influence, was ordained a Columban priest in June 2000, and was missioned to Chile, where he did his Overseas Training Program. At formal discussions in several parts of the country prior to the 2012 Assembly (Chapter), the Columbans wrote, "We feel that even as we get older we can still continue to make a contribution. However, given our lower numbers and decreasing energy we feel [the Society] needs to have fewer foci because

---

[802]   See reasons for the decline below.

[803]   Observations of Regional Director Father Tim Mulroy to author, 17 February 2017.

we cannot continue to operate as we have before. We suggest that a method be found to enable those who will engage in future mission to decide what it will be and how they will do it."[804]

Divestment of Funds, Land and Houses. A New
Expression of Columban Mission

In 1970, U.S. Regional Superior Father Richard Steinhilber was elected director of the Society of St. Columban. By that time, with an efficient staff and up-to-the date office machines "the U.S. office was really churning and bringing in money. Things were great and that's why we needed a goal at that time. How much money should we collect? How do we set our sights in terms of the appeals we run and the amount we try to raise? Do you refine the appeals themselves to particular groups?" He proposed that the men on the missions think through a three year budget. In a way, "that [idea] was a failure because they submitted a [proposed budget] for the next three years and we could meet all of their objectives [financially] in one year. You're back to trying to figure out what do we do with this money."[805]

The Columban Central Administration required funds from the region that were considerably less than previously requested from the United States. The missions had less physical expansion and therefore less need of capital expenditure. There was a new sense that local people on the missions should engage in the projects and invest some time and service to make the church, school or center happen. Father Clarence Beckley in Brazil was one example of the latter approach, as noted earlier in the chapter. An excess of monies presented a problem: no one wanted to collect funds unless there was a real need.[806] While keeping reserve funds for emergencies, for the health and retirement needs of the men,[807] for upkeep of buildings the Society still held, for employees' pensions, and the education of current seminarians, what should be done with the "excess" money and still be faithful to the intentions of donors? Between 1982–1988 the region did give money to a variety of groups who

---

[804]   U.S. Regional Pre-Assembly 2012 meetings, held in February at Columban locations in the United States. Summary.

[805]   Father Joseph McSweeny interview of Father Richard Steinhilber, 13 July 2012, Interview 3.

[806]   "Regional Report," *Columban Newsletter* (June 1979), 8–9. The issue is also mentioned in *Columban Newsletter* (May 1979). See also, *Columban Newsletter* (June 1979), 7–10.

[807]   In 1990, the residence in Bristol needed to have asbestos removed. In 1991, the issue was remedied. In April 1992, construction was coming to a close for a lovely extension on the Bristol house, with each of the bedrooms having a view of the bay. The dining room was expanded and new common rooms allowed for various leisure activities.

applied for the funds and whose aims were within the venue of the Columban stated mission goals.

In September 1978, another idea emerged: the use of land as a form of mission. The U.S. Catholic Bishops, aware of a housing crisis for the elderly and for people with a low income, wrote on that subject after their annual meeting in November 1975. *The Right to a Decent Home. A Pastoral Response to the Crisis in Housing* indicated an "increasing awareness of the limitations of land and resources and the implications of these limitations on efforts to house our citizens. Since only a fixed amount of land is available and housing needs are growing, legitimate questions may be raised regarding the amount of land a person owns, the manner in which it is used and the regulation of land ownership by society."[808] The bishops then quoted from Pope Paul VI's, *On the Progress of Peoples*: "Private property does not constitute for anyone an absolute and unconditional right. No one is justified in keeping for his exclusive use what he does not need, when others lack necessities."[809]

With those ideas in mind, Columban leadership in 1978 considered the "possibility of donation of about 19 acres of [Columban] Bellevue property for subsidized low-cost housing for the elderly."[810] Regional Director Coulter and his Council wrote a *Proposal on Housing for the Elderly* and sent it to the region. Coulter noted, "For well over a year we have been looking at ways in which we can use our surplus property here in Bellevue in line with the call from the U.S. bishops and our Columban accent on stewardship and accountability. We plan to donate whatever acreage is necessary of our total Bellevue, Nebraska, property for subsidized low-cost housing for the elderly. The rationale behind this plan is found mainly in the U.S. Bishops' pastoral, *The Right to a Decent Home*."[811] Quoting the thoughts and intent of the document, Coulter wrote, "This attempt to answer the call of our Bishops and use our Columban property for the elderly should keep us mindful of the need to be good stewards and trustees of God's creation, exercising that trust for the common good and benefit of our sisters and brothers."[812]

The Society had done its homework to find out how many houses were available for subsidized low-cost housing for the elderly in the Bellevue area.

---

[808]   U.S. Catholic Conference, *The Right to a Decent Home. A Pastoral Response to the Crisis in Housing*, 20 November 1975. Par. 52.

[809]   Ibid., Par. 53.

[810]   *Columban Newsletter* (September 1978).

[811]   The Columban *Proposal on Housing for Elderly* is found in *Columban Newsletter* (March 1979), 1–2 and *Casey History* (March 1979), 11–13.

[812]   Ibid.

There was clearly a need for more, given the demographics of the region.[813] A plan was set up for a nonprofit separate corporation of local citizens and Columbans called, "The Bobbio Corporation,"[814] to which the Columbans would deed the property. The U.S. Federal Government Housing and Urban Development Program (Title 202) would fund the design and construction. A native of Buffalo, New York, Father Donald Devine, who had been Bishop Harold Henry's secretary in Korea for many years, was appointed to act as the director's "liaison on the Omaha Senior citizens' Housing Project."[815] In May 1982, a project application was completed to create Bellewood Apartments on ten acres of Society land on the northwest side of the Columban property. Groundbreaking took place on October 5, 1983, for Bellewood Courts to be managed by Mission Park Housing, Inc. The forty-eight apartments filled quickly. The Columbans decided a few years later to provide more assistance using the Federal Government Housing and Urban Development money (HUD). Thirty-six additional apartment units were begun in September 1990, with occupancy available in mid-June 1991.[816]

At the same time, the Society also took care of the needs of its senior priests who wished to retire at the Bristol house. The location had served as the U.S. region's formation house for probationers since opening in 1933, as well as a promotion house. In 1977, the Society designated the location as a house of prayer, a retirement home for Columbans, and promotion house, the latter continuing the summer festival and bazaar. In 1991/1992 asbestos was removed and rooms were rebuilt with accommodations better suited for older persons. A major building project began in July 2000, with a lovely extension on the Bristol house. Each of the twelve new bedrooms had a view of Narragansett Bay with provision for those who might need assisted living. The dining room was expanded toward the Bay. New common rooms allowed for various activities. Father James Dwyer wrote about the house. "It is a great place for anyone to visit but especially Columbans. The spirit here is great, the staff is wonderful.

---

[813] The philosophy, background of research of the need for housing, and steps taken in the project to that point are given in C. Coulter Report, *Columban Newsletter* (September 1978), 4–7.

[814] Bobbio, located in northern Italy, is the town where St. Columban (542–615) died and is buried.

[815] *Columban Newsletter* (November 1978), 4. The original members of the nonprofit corporation (Mission Park Housing, Inc.) were Charles Coulter, president; Dr. Charles Longo, vice president; Eugene Ryan, treasurer, Don Devine, secretary; Mr. Bernard Kouba; Mr. and Mrs. Kenneth Wessling; Richard Steinhilber; Peter McPartland. McPartland, Devine and Ryan "assumed responsibility for the couple of hundred pages of documentation that will be involved." C. Coulter, 11 May 1982. *Casey History* (1983), 18.

[816] *Columban Newsletter* (January 1991), 5.

The physical beauty of the area, especially at this time of year [summer] is breathtaking."[817]

Back office at Columban headquarters, Nebraska, an additional "shared space" between the Columbans and the public opened in spring 1985, when the post became a local post office for the public under contract with the U.S. Postal Service. At the time, two employees from the mission office were in charge of running the office.

Other mission dimensions were vigorous during this time period. Chapter 7 will convey the expansion of the Mission Education program. Chapter 8 will present the array of ethnic groups to which the Society committed itself within the United States. Chapter 12 will explore issues related to land and environment, a topic that literally brings the region history full circle.

Conclusion

In the heat of the battle, so to speak, leadership, and perhaps the men themselves, might have felt as did Michael O'Loughlin quoted earlier: leadership was "constantly being besieged by problem-driven change rather than by vision-driven change." But the range of efforts of the U.S. Columban region proved to be diverse, far-reaching, and effective both in the country and in the missions. In the evolution of their Justice and Peace office, Columbans were both initiators and supporters of groups aligned for similar mission purposes. Columbans addressed key justice issues in countries where the Columbans served and raised up the plight of people affected by the growth of the World Bank and the International Monetary Fund. Columbans did not highlight themselves but worked with others to be a conduit that made inclusion and collaboration possible to address local and global issues faced in the missions and in the United States. As outsiders in mission countries, Columbans could see more clearly how systems dehumanized or took advantage of the people they served.

New commitments in Chile, Peru and Brazil had different social, political and ecclesiastical contexts. By the 1960s strong Latin America ecclesiastical leadership provided direction for social justice areas and a call for government accountability. The Columban area of most tension probably revolved around interpretation of the bishops' synod statement, accepted by the Society, "Action on behalf of justice is . . . a constitutive dimension of the preaching of the Gospel." The ways in which Columbans interpreted the intent of the statement were problematic in some cases. How does one live among the people? What

---

[817] Dwyer was the new superior at the Bristol house. *Columban Newsletter* (Summer 2002), 2.

focus should predominate in a mission response to poverty and oppression? In a way, the question was raised, "Did one need to be a *priest* missionary to do that? [818]

Inculturation, a word that might sound the most esoteric of the mission vocabulary of the past forty-plus years, gave the men an appreciation for their own internal "cultures," as well as new sensitivity to the cultures where they worked and ways people could deepen their understanding of Catholic life, prayer, and "being church." Social services (medical needs, food distribution, etc.) were not secondary means of mission but part of the fabric of mission engagement as they were part of life. Less separation between spiritual and physical realms made the Incarnation more "real."

Internally, Columban divestment of land, buildings, and funds underlined a value important to the Society from the beginning. They were stewards for the sake of mission, not owners. Divestment demonstrated a deep sensitivity to donors and to the justice dimensions of investment. An aging Society had practical ramifications. The men were provided simple but adequate accommodations and enrichment opportunities in their retirement home, if they wished to retire in Bristol. Mission commitments needed to be rethought across the regions. On the other hand, the initial commitment to the "Far East" was reengaged in new ways. Echoing the 1971 Synod of Bishops, the U.S. region had "questioned ourselves about the mission of the People of God to further justice in the world." The region probed, sometimes hesitatingly, yet boldly, the "times," their charism, and their mission situations. They conveyed innovation, leadership and accomplishment nationally and internationally in relation to justice/peace issues and made a difference in the lives of the people served. Columbans felt a reciprocal spiritual, personal and communal support of many thousands of people in the United States and elsewhere.

---

[818]   On this point, see Joseph McSweeny interview of Father Richard Steinhilber. Interview 2. 12 July 2012.

Region of Missionary Society of St. Columban
CARA Studies of 1979 and 1989 Comparison[819]

Year	1979	1989
Members	175	114
Regional Average Age	not given	61.2 years
Percent of men retired or unavailable	2.28%	29.8%
Mission Houses/Centers	34.28%	17.5% (more mission houses closed by this year)
Pastoral and Chaplaincy	21.14%	23.7%
Regional Admin & General Msn Office	6.85%	12.3% (while percentages are different, 14 men were assigned in both years)

Apostolates Considered Appropriate
by Columbans and Non-Columbans
Top 5 choices (1989/90)

Apostolate	Columbans		Non-Columbans' Response	
	%	Rank	%	Rank
Mission Awareness	96%	1	99%	1
Vocation Recruitment	93%	2	96%	2
Ethnic minorities	88%	3	89%	3
Columban J&P Office	64%	4	68%	6 (# 4 was Homeless 83%)
Retreat work	61%	5	78%	5

---

[819]   *Final Report of the Surveys for the Assessment of Society Commitments for Columban Fathers,* Eleace King, IHM (April 1990), Georgetown University. A copy of the CARA survey, 1980 (marked as 1979 here, the year it was administered) has not yet been located in the CFA-USA but is available through the Catholic Theological Union Library, Chicago. "The Identification of Issues Related to Planning for the Future: Missionary Society of St. Columban." Columban responses edited by Paul Besanceney and J. Christopher O'Brien (Center for Applied Research in the Apostolate, 1980).

Father Bernard Toal Baptism

Father Bernard Toal

PART TWO

Focus Areas in Columban History

CHAPTER 7

Mission Promotion and Mission Education

Vocation appeals, promotion, and mission education were intertwined with different emphases over the years. In many respects, that remains true today. As Father Richard Steinhilber explained the situation, "Promotion was doing appeals, running parties and raffles, showing movies, having a big event once or twice a year. Every house would have a festival and the Fathers went out on appeals. The [men went] into the Irish clubs, showed movies, went to the Knights of Columbus, anyplace where you could promote the missions." [820] The men in the promotion houses did mission appeals on weekends or were asked to substitute for parish masses if the pastor was away (this was called "supply work"), made contact with potential donors and arranged for large and small events to raise funds. The promotion house also did vocation work which meant priests visited schools and spoke about the missions. The vocation director was under the authority of the local superior and subject to activities that the superior might want to plan. The vocation man had no authority to do what he saw important for vocation promotion, because he needed to follow the direction of the local superior. This situation might not leave time for vocation contacts. [821]

Father Richard Steinhilber was the first vocation director for the entire United States region, when he was appointed by Regional Superior Daniel Boland in 1962. Thereafter, the vocation director had more freedom to concentrate on vocations, as he saw fit, and not be impelled to do some of the

---

[820] Father Joseph McSweeny interview of Father Richard Steinhilber 11 July 2012. St. Columbans, Nebraska, Interview 1.

[821] Ibid.

other tasks for which the promotion house was responsible. Chapter 5 explored various understandings of "vocation" the Columbans held over the years until the Second Vatican Council. This chapter will pursue the ideas of promotion and mission education in that same time period.

What Is Mission Propaganda/Promotion?

Soon after E. J. McCarthy arrived in the United States, he wrote to John Blowick that it was a "regular thing for the *kirk* (church) in the United States to be looking for money."[822] The implication was that the American government system of nonsupport financially of *any* church meant that Catholics were used to financial appeals for their church services and activities. Among the ways the U.S. Columbans raised funds for their missions were "circular letters," personal letters to donors, subscriptions to the *Far East*, burses,[823] annuity plans[824] and mission appeals by individual Columbans who spoke in parishes, schools, in homes, and at regional or national conventions. Toward this end, missionaries engaged in "propaganda." This was a process that involved a relationship with promotion, fund-raising, vocation, and education. Recognition of the connection among these activities was not always self-evident and needed to be brought to the fore from time to time.

When Columbans were assigned to mission "propaganda," as they termed it in the early days, they had in mind a word that harkened back to the Roman Catholic Church's College of Propaganda, a seminary in Rome that educated priests for missions around the world.[825] But the Columbans also "included under the term, propaganda, everything of a money-making nature."[826] The word, propaganda, eventually assumed a pejorative meaning of persuasion from a biased perspective. Mission "promotion" seemed more what the Columbans had in mind: fund-raising to support the China missions, while acquainting U.S. Catholics with the Chinese Mission Society.

---

[822] E. J. McCarthy to John [Blowick] 29 Dec 1921.

[823] Burses are permanent income designated for a particular purpose by the sender, such as education of seminarians or a particular mission, in the early days, specifically for Hanyang.

[824] For example of early advertisement for annuity, see *FE* (August 1933), last page of issue.

[825] The Sacred Congregation for the Propagation of the Faith (*Sacra Congregatione de Propaganda Fide*), founded in 1622, was the official papal office that held responsibility for areas considered as "mission territories" globally. Since 1982, that Office is called the Congregation for the Evangelization of Peoples.

[826] [unknown] to John McFadden, August 1938.

In 1933, Regional Superior McCarthy had definite ideas about personal qualifications for "propaganda work in this country." The priest should have a "well-balanced outlook and a more than ordinary spiritual life, for the work is hard, discouraging and spiritually dissipating." Further, he needed "a tough skin, to be unselfish, and humble, for he is going to meet with hard knocks . . . and frequent disagreeable experiences from pastors who are struggling with their own problems," especially in the time of the Great Depression. McCarthy concluded that the promoter should be a "good preacher, have some experience of the missions and of America and a sympathy with both, . . . be sociable, and know the value of money."[827] Newly ordained missioners in Ireland came to the United States for promotion work, until they left for China.[828] That way, American Catholics would be able to follow the work of the men they met at the parish talk by reading about them later in the *Far East*.

Paul Waldron, the second regional superior, sent hints for public speaking to the men doing promotion, but each priest was on his own in how to proceed with the content. The promoter contacted influential Catholics in the area and local bishops, who were central to obtaining speaking engagements in parishes. Waldron himself wrote a "Propaganda Sermon," that he gave at the end of his popular retreats to laymen, wherein he made an appeal "on behalf of the work of the Maynooth Missionaries," to urge retreatants to become members of the "Irish Mission League."[829]

By 1950, fifty-five Columbans, a number of them formerly in China and waiting for China to reopen to foreigners, were situated in fourteen promotion houses across the United States. Four of these houses opened at the time: St. Paul, Minnesota, and Chicago, Illinois (1948), San Francisco, California (1949), and Brooklyn, New York (1950). The houses were to raise enough funds to meet the mission assessment determined by the superior general for the region. Secondly, a small portion of the money would be used to support the expenses of the house. Because of the large number of new promoters, Regional Superior Timothy Connolly in 1949 called a meeting in Derby, New York, for all Columbans around the country assigned to promotion. The gathering was intended to give support and confidence to the newly assigned promotion men. A number of them were young and untrained in the skills or knowledge required for promotion. They needed to "learn the ropes." Promotion Teams were begun at the designated houses as a support to each other.

---

[827] E. J. McCarthy to O'Dwyer 29 Dec 1933, pp. 6, 7.

[828] After the foundation of the Missionary Sisters of Saint Columban in 1922 and the first mission of the Sisters to China, the Sisters sailed to China without coming to the United States, a venture which would have been expensive for them.

[829] Reverend P. Waldron, "Outlines for Retreat Conferences," Twenty-Ninth Conference. n.d., 60–61. Paul Waldron personnel file.

A General Mission Office was established by Father Charles Coulter at Columban headquarters as a centralized, direct fund-raising operation of the region in 1967. Donors could send their gift directly to that Office. However, a promotion house remained a primary personal contact between Columbans and donors.

In an effort to learn from professionals what the Columbans might do to increase their skills in promotion, in 1967 they invited Lee Dreves, from Holland Dreves Poff & Reilly, Inc.,[830] a public relations, fund-raising, and advertising consultation firm, to help the Society assess their approaches in promotion and to suggest "more efficient ways of supporting the Columban Fathers."[831] One of the ideas Dreves proposed was a Columban Missions-Aide Program. The idea was based on the axiom that "the closer involved one becomes with an organization, the higher is the likelihood to support the activities," a principle he saw applicable to the Columbans and their benefactors.[832] Vatican II emphasized that "every Catholic must be missionary, but very few people have any idea whatsoever how they can fulfill this obligation. We intend to enlighten them." The basic idea Dreves suggested was closer contact with donors, who would be willing to register as a Columban Missions-Aide. He proposed a target group of the 6,500 people who had responded in Columban mailings that they would appreciate a monthly reminder to support Columban mission activities. He outlined a wide variety of actions that would take individuals "into our confidence." The Columbans would keep "Missions-Aides "as close to actual mission activity as possible," through monthly suggestions of specific situations, and prayer or sacrifices toward that mission.[833] The idea was not picked up at the time, but it took a somewhat different turn later with the Companions in Mission.

In preparation for the 1970 Society General Chapter, the men raised the issue of too many promotion houses. Local promotion houses, especially those established in the early decades of the region, had annual events that had grown to be large, which sometimes involved the assistance of an outside coordinator

---

[830]   Robert Holland took over his father's advertising agency in Omaha and expanded the services offered when he created the Holland Dreves Poff & Reilly Inc. firm. Holland was one of the first people in early 1960 to invest with another Omaha resident, Warren Buffett.

[831]   "Columban Missions-Aide Program," Presentation by Mr. Lee Dreves. Appendix 4. Regional Promotion, Results, Etc. (1967). Four pages. 9-B-26.

[832]   Ibid.

[833]   Ibid., 1. The Society's 1970 General Chapter stated, after quoting the *Ad Gentes* Decree on the point, that all Catholics are called to mission, "We, as a missionary institute, are a voice reminding the People of God of this responsibility and channel through which they can discharge it." *Acts of the 1970 Society of St. Columban General Chapter*, p. 67.

and the need to pay for the hall in which the event took place. The result was that the amount of funds raised for mission was proportionately not worth all the effort and expense to run the event. Sometimes the popularity of some fund-raising activities diminished over the years. The U.S. region also raised for consideration at the 1970 General Chapter the need to make local mission churches self-supporting. The region put forth the position: "So that priests on the mission are made aware of the importance of making the local church self-supporting and recognizing the sacrifices made by Columban benefactors at home, we recommend a Chapter reconsideration of the possibility of instigating promotion work in mission areas where feasible. (vote unanimous)."[834]

Columban leadership in Promotion/Development came through a willingness to assess what was happening with the men in the region, to consider the changing circumstances of mission life itself, and to learn what modern public relations firms could offer as practical assistance. By the late 1960s, the Promotion Office "was really churning and bringing in money and things were great." So, Father Steinhilber put forth the idea of goal setting for what the missions needed. "How much money should we collect? How do we set our sights in terms of the appeals we run and the amount that [we need]. Do [we] refine the appeals themselves to particular groups?"[835]

While raising money for the needs of the missions remained important, the relationship between funding (eventually called Development), promotion and education were evidenced when the Columbans were recognized in 2008 as founding members of the National Catholic Development Conference in 1968. Charles Coulter, director of development and promotion, was instrumental in founding the largest, single organization dedicated to Catholic philanthropy. The organization sees Catholic development as a ministry of ethical fund-raising through education, resources, networking and advocacy.[836] The Society also was a consultant and a drafter of the document, "Principles and Guidelines for Fundraising in the United States by Arch/Diocesan Agencies and Religious Institutes," issued in June 1977.[837]

---

[834]   Papers presented by the U.S. region in preparation for the Society's General Chapter. Promotion, 7.

[835]   Father Joseph McSweeny interview of Father Richard Steinhilber 13 July 2012. Interview 3.

[836]   The NCDC was composed of people who were originally members of the Catholic Press Association. Another national development that affected the intake of funds for missions was the Mission Cooperation Plan administered through the U.S. Catholic Mission Association in the early 1970s. Mission societies in the United States were each allotted a particular number of mission appeals per year. In 1975, the Columbans gave 354 church appeals and 29 appeals at military installations.

[837]   C. Coulter to Dear Father [letter to all Columbans in the United States] 11, July 1977, with principles and guidelines attached. CFA-USA.

The *Far East/Columban Mission* Magazine

One promotion outcome was that many people would subscribe to the Society magazine, the *Far East*. For the first few issues of the Chinese Mission Society of St. Columban, the Irish edition of the magazine was used or modified for an American audience.[838] Decidedly "Irish" in orientation, the magazine displayed Gaelic symbols on the cover and in the magazine, with articles written in Irish Gaelic and English. In the United States, editorship of the *Far East* went back and forth among the Columbans in their Nebraska seminary, sometimes one of many jobs the editor held. The regional superior was, in effect, responsible overall for the magazine, but the seminary staff was "doing too many things, so the *Far East* suffers."[839] In 1924, Father Patrick O'Connor, known as "Paddy," became editor of a U.S. region edition of the magazine for twenty years. The tone of the American version of the *Far East* was humorous, informative, and filled with stories of the missions and some of O'Connor's poetry.[840] A man of literary talent, O'Connor became president of the U.S. Catholic Press Association from 1944 to 1946. At the end of World War II, the National Catholic News Service appointed him to represent them in China, Japan, Korea, and Vietnam. He was well-known in East Asia as a roving correspondent in the 1950s and 1960s, winning the Catholic Press Association award in 1956 and 1964.[841] Father Donal O'Mahoney (1918–1993), who had been missioned in Nancheng for about three years, then studied journalism in Denver and held an apprenticeship at the *Denver Register*. He became manager of the *Far East* and editor from 1955–1965. After the decade, he was assigned to the Philippines.

As seen in earlier chapters, the *Far East* played a significant role in conveying to people in the United States—and men and women in the Armed Forces during World War II—what life in the missions in Asia was like for the people who lived there, how they embraced Catholic life, what their challenges were, and who the Columbans were who pastored them. E. J. McCarthy's appreciation for widely recognized European religious art resulted in prints of the art in the magazine. Soon, though, striking paintings, especially from China and

---

[838] *FE* (April 1945) stated Edward Galvin was the magazine's founder, first editor and manager.

[839] E. J. McCarthy to [O'Dwyer], 18 February 1923.

[840] Pseudonyms for the authors of columns that appeared in the children's section of the *Far East* in the 1920s included Checkers (Paul Waldron), Benen, Nanky Poo (Patrick O'Connor), and, Colum (James Gilsenan). O'Connor's poetry for young people was published as Nanky Poo, *Pudsy Kelly's Gang*, with the third edition in 1936.

[841] Patrick J. Burke, SSC (1917–1990) was a National Catholic Welfare Correspondent in Korea (1959) and Saigon (1966).

Japan, also appeared on the magazine's cover. The May 1925, issue featured a painting of Mary and a young Jesus, both with Chinese features and garments, painted by a Chinese artist, following the important 1924 Shanghai meeting of the bishops, during which they dedicated China to Mary. The editorial, "The Soul of a Chinaman," challenged stereotypes that readers might have about Chinese people:

> The soul of a Chinaman. In spite of ourselves the word strikes unmusically upon our western ears. To most men the Chinaman is just the yellow man, instinctively associated with the Chinatown of our big cities and with the things of Chinatown, gambling dens and opium—in short, to most men he is just the "heathen Chinese." But the picture is far from true and we are beginning to see him, not as prejudice has painted him but as God has created him, a man with an immortal soul whose eternal destiny is like ours, heaven.[842]

To produce a magazine required access to good stories. Beginning with Bishop Galvin, a prolific and conscientious letter writer, the missionaries in China wrote letters to the U.S. regional director, describing their mission situations. Parts of the letters were used to create articles for the magazine, so subscribers and donors would get an inside view of daily mission life. As the decades wore on, *Far East* editors had a difficult time getting material, especially when situations of war, poverty, and disasters overwhelmed everyone on the mission. One such time was when Bishop Galvin wrote, "An air raid compelled me to leave this letter. 18 Jap planes just here; they bombed Hankow. Hanyang escaped this time."[843] Even though by the 1950s the missionaries were given a small stipend to write an article about their mission, the editor had to remind the men to write. Each issue provided information about the Columban missions and the people with whom they worked and brought in much needed finances for the missions. Occasional appeals were placed for something in particular, such as funds for a new seminary building at Milton or a roof on a Columban chapel in Korea, or a pony to traverse the mountain trails in the Philippines.

The number of pages in the magazine fluctuated over the years. The June 1954, issue had grown to thirty-two pages with a "self-cover" and color inside, in contrast to twenty-four pages during scarce resources of World War II. By 1960, however, the *Far East* had twenty pages. In 1963, the Columbans requested the assistance of a publisher consultant, James F. Kane, on the board of directors

---

842   "The Soul of a Chinaman," *FE* (May 1925), 97.

843   Galvin to My dear Paul [Waldron] 16 July 1935.

for Sheed and Ward, to evaluate the *Far East*. Having read the previous twenty-six issues, Kane judged the magazine to be second in the field of a multitude of U.S. Catholic mission magazines. With some "extra effort and thought," the publication could be "outstanding and excellent." Kane "deduced" that the editorial purpose of the magazine "to make readers more mission-minded, aware of foreign customs, outlook and habits; to inform them of the Society's work; to ask for their financial and spiritual support, and to entertain and inspire them." He indicated it was "editorially imperative that the purpose be *defined*" for the reader and not "deduced."[844]

Kane further observed that "Certain themes crying aloud for popular presentation in a mission magazine were not being treated in the *Far East*," particularly themes in Pope John XXIII's pivotal encyclical on Christianity and social progress, *Mater et Magistra* (1961), and "the great questions of the day [that] greatly affect the Columban Fathers, such as poverty abroad, international justice, foreign aid, the emerging peoples, Peace Corps, lay volunteers on the missions, foreign students in the U.S., and the American 'image' abroad."[845]

His evaluation came at a time when the General Mission Office (fund-raising), the Vocation Office, and the Central Clearance Bureau,[846] each with office staff, did not necessarily see their relationship to each other or realize their interconnected purpose in relation to the magazine. Clear delineation of responsibilities, coordination of all departments with that of the *Far East* and with each other, would strengthen each department.

In the 1960s, the two phrases, "Columban Fathers" and "the Far East," were in large print on the cover. The Promotion staff met in 1967 and one of the points for discussion was the content of the magazine. Father Eamonn O'Doherty provided his impression as to whether the magazine was doing an "efficient job of promotion. Was it being turned out mechanically, following methods of the 1930s and 1940s?" He thought that there was "plenty of room for improvement in the content (previous editors had been aware of this need and did something about it)." With improvements, there was no need for a radical change, nor should it be replaced by a monthly newsletter, and there should not be a teen-ager's page." The magazine had two purposes: "present the missions to the American people," particularly the work of the Columbans, and to be sure that the articles are "aimed at *our* readers. An article might be fine

---

[844]   To: Very Reverend Daniel Boland Re: The *Far East*. John F. Kane, publisher consultant. 27 March 1963.

[845]   Ibid., Boland was regional superior at the time. In 1965 the magazine still contained a humor section, "Miles of Smiles."

[846]   Father Donal O'Mahony, SSC, had established the Central Clearance Bureau in 1952.

for other magazines, not for *ours*."[847] Once again the issue was raised as to how to get material from the missionaries for the articles. The Central Clearance Bureau established earlier was intended to have all the Columban Regions submit their material or articles, which could then be published in any of the Regions. This would maximize the Columban input and not place pressure on one or other man to gather and write material for articles.

In January 1967, the *Far East* became *Columban Fathers Mission*,[848] and a few years later, *Columban Mission*. As the Society took on missions in Latin America, the name needed to reflect the change of geographic emphasis and the mission perspectives of the Second Vatican Council, some of the points Kane had noted. In 1969, Vito Cioffero, formerly associate editor of *Sign* magazine[849], was hired as art director at the Columban headquarters. He served as associate editor of the Columban magazine and assisted other departments with his skills in art, photography, layout, and design. As Cioffero moved into the magazine overall and into related dimensions at the office, Father Steinhilber, who at the time was responsible for the magazine, remarked about the "joy of the thing at the time," that Cioffero and his wife, Pauline, who knew well the magazine world, "had lots of ability, a lot of contacts, a lot of imagination."[850] Cioffero (died 2006) was associate editor of the magazine for many years and remained with the Columbans until retirement in 1999.[851]

In 1973, the magazine was again reviewed by James Kane, who at this point was a principal in Kane–McNeill Management Consultants, New York.[852] He spent a week with the staff to review everything about the magazine from

---

[847] Folder: 1967 Regional Promotion, Results, etc. Appendix 3, Content of the Magazine. 9-B-26.

[848] In 1966, Robert Reilly, who had been in charge of public relations for Creighton University, worked with the Society on all advertising and promotional material. Reilly, "a close friend of the Columbans," had written a small paperback on the life of Bishop Galvin. *Columban Newsletter* (August 1966).

[849] *The Sign*, was a national Catholic monthly magazine published by the Passionists from 1921–1982, initially to disseminate truth" and to offset "the pernicious influence of the lurid secular press." Between 1920 and 1950, subscribers followed the work of the Passionist missionaries in China, located close to the Columban Society's Hanyang mission. Robert E. Carbonneau, "The Sign," in *The Encyclopedia of American Catholic History*, Michael Glazier and Thomas Shelley, eds. (Collegeville, MN: The Liturgical Press, 1997), 1297.

[850] Father Joseph McSweeny interview of Father Richard Steinhilber 13 July 2012. Interview 3.

[851] Vito Cioffero was employed by the Columbans in Nebraska from 1969–1999, according to payroll records.

[852] This McNeill is most likely the same McNeill of the Holland, et al., firm that spoke to the Columbans in 1967. McNeill Kane had conducted a study of office operations at the Catholic Near East Welfare Association in New York City in fall 1967. See, *CNEWA WORLD* (September–October 2001), n.p.

aims, content, circulation, layout production, size/color, income, costs, to future plans. He provided an eight-page report. Having seen the development of the magazine since his analysis about six years earlier, Kane noted, "The layout, appearance, and presentation of material now bear all the marks of a professional product." He had a number of points related to the ratio of money spent to produce the magazine and the funds that came in as a result. In his last visit, he had commented that there was not an expressed editorial stance. This time he remarked, "We became ever more solidly convinced of the worth of the editorial investment, and noted the improving response visible in the direct dollar returns. In recent years there has been much closer coordination of the editorial product with the overall regional promotion effort." Again, along monetary lines, he calculated, "At our current cost of 4.5 cents per copy for each issue of *CM* mailed we conclude that the immediate return to the Columban Fathers on the magazine investment is now an irreplaceable adjunct of the total promotion effort of the Society."[853] Kane remained an informal adviser to the Columbans on these issues until his retirement.[854]

Columban Mission continued in its development. In 1982/1983, the Catholic Press Association awarded First Place for General Excellence to the magazine.[855] During the 1980s and early 1990s individual magazine issues featured Columban missions in a particular country. In 1987 and 1988, for example, the February issues featured Korea in many of the articles. Some issues had short reviews of books related to mission. But issues in the next decades were also becoming thematic, especially with social justice themes: "Why the Poor are Getting Poorer" (October 1994), "Catholic Social Teaching" (October 2011); "Mission in Difficult Places" (August/September 2011 and October 2014). The vocation of all to mission continued in importance for vocation to the priesthood, lay vocations and the vocation of families (December 2004, October 2007 November 2010, March 2011).

In April 2008, Kate Kenny was hired as managing editor of *Columban Mission*. In June 2011, she was appointed director of communications, which included editorship of the magazine. Sister Jeanne Janssen, CSJ, mission education and communication director, had that position and left to teach at Avila University. Before applying for the position, Kate was unaware of her Columban connection. When the opening was posted on the Columban website, she mentioned to her in-laws that she had applied for the job with the

---

[853]   *Columban Newsletter* (March 1973), 3. The four-page Newsletter provided excerpts from Kane's eight-page report.

[854]   Father Joseph McSweeny interview of Father Richard Steinhilber 13 July 2012. Interview 3.

[855]   Father Steinhilber was *CM* editor, Pauline and Vito Cioferro, Colm Stanley and Billie Pesek were on the CM staff.

Columban Fathers. She found out that her father-in-law had subscribed to the Columban magazine for many years. Kate had worked in the publishing field, and possessed many skills in written, visual, and oral communication. She also brought energy, insight and a love for mission. As Kate remarked years later, "We go where God leads us at the time. It becomes clearer later, what the path has been."[856] Under Kate's editorship of *Columban Mission*, geographic areas, such as Fiji, are still highlighted, but thematic issues carry larger themes: "Earth/Wind/Sand/Sea" (June/July 2010); "Radical Discipleship: Mission in the Post-Modern World" (July 2010). More recently, themes have highlighted, "The Power of Forgiveness" (March/April 2015); "Practical Spirituality (June/July 2015); "Faith in Daily Life (March/April 2016). The issues continued to focus on the interaction of Columban missionaries (priests, sisters, laity) with the people they serve. Through all the issues of the magazine, one gets a sense of the joys and sufferings of the people, something of their culture, the deep connections the Columbans have with the people, and the diverse ways the mission of Jesus is rooted and grows.

Columban Mission had ridden the course of a century of twentieth century printing history! They started with "copy" sent out for typeset, then pasted on boards for markup and resent for printing. Then the printing process happened through large, noisy IBM machines. Most recently the entire issue of the magazine is done on an office computer.[857]

Promotion and Mission Engage
the Visual and Film Arts, 1921–1970s

The objects that Bishop Galvin and the missionaries sent from China became Columban "spokesmen" in the United States through a 1926 Missions Exposition at Chicago's Municipal Pier on Lake Michigan. The Columbans set up a major exhibit, thanks to the "efforts of one of our Fathers, who studied Chinese art and whose work at the 1925 Vatican Mission Exhibition awarded him a diploma from the Holy Father."[858] Chinese vestments and embroidery

---

[856] Author telephone interview with Kate Kenny, 29 March 2016.

[857] Father Steinhilber recounted these developments. Father Joseph McSweeny interview of Father Richard Steinhilber 13 July 2012. Interview 3. The IBM tapes contained donors' names and addresses. One of the priests took the tapes home each night. In case of a break-in at the office, no one could steal them.

[858] "St. Columbans at the Congress Exhibition," *FE* (1926),136, 138. Photo is from *FE* (1925), 52. Richard Ranaghan was the organizer of the Exhibit in Rome. Father Joseph P. O'Leary, "who has made a special study of Chinese Art of the late Ming Period,' designed this stall at the Vatican Exposition. On the importance of the yearlong event, see, John J. Considine, *The Vatican Mission Exposition. A Window on*

pieces from the Sisters of Loretto embroidery school in Hanyang were displayed. Intricate ivory pieces by noted Nanking artist, Sun Tah Sing were on display. Visitors viewed paintings on silk by Ching Yeun Kao and other exquisite Chinese silk and embroidery pieces. One part of the exhibit featured the reconstruction of a typical Chinese fashionable room of the Ming Dynasty.

The stars of the Columban exhibit in Chicago were two large pictures of the lakes of Hangchow, etched in silver and plated on copper, with myriad colors appearing, depending on the angle of the reflected light. The cultural objects were "calculated to completely change one's ideas of Chinese people."[859] If Americans had contact with Chinese at the time, it was most likely at a Chinese laundry in their city. Americans could have surmised that the Chinese, who spoke little English and performed a mundane task, had no "culture." The elegant art exhibited through a variety of media proved otherwise.

The Ranaghan Tradition

Some Society promoters with no mission experience could not convey a sense of immediacy of the missions, much as they desired to do so. A step in the direction of providing Americans with a vicarious experience of mission life

---

the World (New York: Macmillan, 1925). The Congress Exhibition in Chicago in 1926 followed up that Mission Exposition.

[859]   *FE* (1926), 136.

came through an idea of Father Richard Ranaghan.[860] A man of enthusiasm, imagination, boundless energy, and creative ideas, Ranaghan developed the Society's experiment in film as a mode of mission promotion. One of the first members to take the Society oath in 1920, he did promotion work in the United States until he and the first Columban mission band sailed from San Francisco on the SS *Nile* in July 1920. Ranaghan took advantage of being in California to learn the rudiments of film making in Los Angeles. He convinced E. J. McCarthy to purchase a movie camera, a "heavy, clumsy looking thing like a miniature Bren gun,[861] which had to be set on a large tripod and took quite a little time to get into action."[862]

After some time in Hanyang, Ranaghan returned to the United States having made a movie to capture life in the Chinese missions. The film, to which he had "devoted a terrible amount of planning and work and worry to the production of his masterpiece,"[863] arrived in the United States in the summer of 1921. With curiosity and anticipation, the Columbans and their friends viewed the silent film in downtown Omaha. The theater manager was reportedly impressed with the artistic value and quality of the film, better than some produced in Hollywood, he remarked. Subsequently, "retouched and new copies of the film were made for Ireland and Australia, titles and subtitles with suitable readings attached according to the headings sent from China."[864]

The movie became a "Talkie," thanks to the efforts of a New York producer Ranaghan knew,[865] and the "Talkie" became *The Cross and Dragon* by the 1930s. To add sound to the film, Ranaghan traveled to Los Angeles for promotion work and made the acquaintance of two of the Crosby brothers, Bing and Larry, Bing's publicist. Bing had moved there in 1929, at a time when four major film companies had shifted the film capital from New York to Hollywood. Ranaghan got Bing Crosby to sing "*Adeste Fidelis*" and "Silent Night" as background for *The Cross and Dragon*.[866] The two songs were recorded "with the understanding that Crosby's share of the royalties would go to the missionary's fund."[867] In

---

[860]   Richard Ranaghan (1889–1937) was ordained in Ireland for the Diocese of Down and Connor, Ireland, in 1914 before he joined the Society in 1917.

[861]   A lightweight rapid-firing machine gun used in World War II by Allied Forces.

[862]   E. J. McCarthy, "A Few Personal Reminiscences," (1916–1920) [written in the 1950s].

[863]   Owen McPolin to E. J. McCarthy 25 August 1921.

[864]   *Newsletter* (August 1921).

[865]   E. J. McCarthy to O'Dwyer 31 Dec 1931.

[866]   The recording took place before 1935, when Crosby's Decca Records version of "Silent Night" became the largest selling record in the world.

[867]   See Richard Ranaghan to My dear Paul [Waldron] 2 July 1937, a seven-page handwritten, "Ideas re: propaganda," 29 June 1937. Bing Crosby also recorded, "Stabat Mater" and "St. Columban's Marching Song" for the Society. "Notes on

November 1936, the Society received about $650 from the Crosbys. After Ranaghan's death in 1937 contact was lost with the brothers. The money from the record by that time "went to a trustee account to be spread among Church groups of all denominations everywhere."[868]

Ranaghan regarded film as a money maker, even though the cost of production seemed exorbitant initially. While Regional Director McCarthy did not provide funds for the next phase of the film, "he put it up to the community at Silver Creek and they kicked in enough personal funds to get it started. He got in touch with some producer in New York and between them they have turned out 6,400 feet of sound (music, poetry and drama) with Dick's best efforts in the movie line. . . . The movie has become a talkie."[869] For Columbans who might raise the objection that a film project would "neglect the real work of propaganda [i.e., mission appeals and subscriptions to the *Far East*], he noted that priests' promotion work took place mainly on weekends at parishes. The man "hasn't much more to do during the week," so he could feature the film in schools or other parish gatherings, thereby educating Catholics about the missions, while raising funds to support the missions.[870] In the 1930s, some pastors, inundated with many requests, tended not to sanction mission appeals at the Sunday Masses, perhaps also fearing adverse effects on parochial financial support during difficult financial times. The China missionary pointed out the popularity of film for the public, who were willing to pay to see New York or Hollywood films. The American penchant for new media would entice people curious to see something about China, especially portrayal of real life scenes. *The Cross and Dragon* easily paid for itself over the years.

Ranaghan urged the Society to send personnel specifically to learn film production as a means to mission promotion. "If Doc Dwyer [Superior General] has a man with plenty of 'gray matter' and a taste for mechanics, the U.S. Director should ask for him and put him to learn all the secrets of the art of motion picture making here in the United States."[871] One person would be a writer, a second specialist would learn photography, and a third Columban would become proficient in the mechanics of a sound camera and studio. Ranaghan had many more ideas for mission promotion but, unfortunately, he

---

Father Dick Ranaghan." CFA-USA. No author given but probably the archivist in the undated year of the notes. The document cites several pieces of correspondence that reference Ranaghan's work in film.

[868]   "Notes on Father Dick Ranaghan." CFA-USA.

[869]   E. J. McCarthy to Michael O'Dwyer, 31 December 1931.

[870]   Parts of the film were also shown at the Catholic Students Mission Crusade national and local conventions, with a good amount of money obtained in that manner.

[871]   Richard Ranaghan to My dear Paul [Waldron] 2 July 1937.

was killed in an automobile accident near Council Bluffs, Iowa, coming back from a mission promotion trip in 1937.

His suggestions were effected after World War II. Father Gerard Smith (1913–1997) was sent to the United States from Ireland to learn film making and techniques of the emerging television media. He then went to Peru, Argentina, and Chile to make mission movies. In 1958, Fathers Sean Dunne and John Vaughan were in South Korea to create a film about the experience of Columbans and other missionaries during the Korean "death march" of 1950. The compelling black and white film began with the history of the Catholic Church in that country and the important role and witness of laity, something which continued through Columban promotion of the Legion of Mary. In 1960, Dunne brought the film, *Path to Glory*, to the United States for processing. As had Ranaghan before him, Dunne went to Hollywood, where the film was produced by Desilu Productions, a company formed by Lucille Ball and Desi Arnaz. The 1964 version of the film was edited for use with the United States Air Force with narration by the actor, Gregory Peck.[872] In a three-minute "afterward," actor Pat O'Brien encouraged the audience to support both the Columbans and the Catholic Church in Korea. While the original film was shot against the background of Catholic rhetoric against Communism of the late 1950s, a later version of the film no longer had that emphasis in the forefront. The film remains popular and is now in DVD format.

Father Cathal (Charlie) Coulter

The Ranaghan legacy was again taken up in the United States by Father Cathal (Charlie) Coulter (1931–2014), who was enthusiastic about Ranaghan's audiovisual approach to mission promotion. Coulter's interest in film making began at the seminary at Navan, where he had access to a 16mm camera and experimented with the media. After ordination in 1954, Coulter was sent to the United States for promotion work and vocation recruitment.[873] From September 1959 to April 1960, he traveled the entire country with Bishop Harold Henry,

---

[872] Gregory Peck (1916–2003) is buried in a mausoleum underneath the Cathedral of Our Lady of the Angeles in Los Angeles.

[873] Coulter received a master's degree in anthropology/sociology from Fordham University in 1955. During this time, Jesuit anthropologist, J. Franklin Ewing organized mission conferences at Fordham and taught classes to introduce missionaries to the use of anthropology in mission. Renowned sociologist, Joseph Fitzpatrick, SJ, taught courses and was a specialist on pastoral care of Puerto Ricans in New York. After Fordham, Coulter spent some weeks in Nova Scotia to learn about cooperatives and credit unions through the Antigonish Movement, as did many Catholic missionaries and others for decades. The Antigonish Movement, under the direction of Father Moses Coady, was an extension department of St. Francis Xavier University, emphasizing training for social and economic development.

who raised over a million dollars for a diocesan major seminary in Kwang Ju, South Korea. The two usually stayed at the house of the bishop, which, for the Irish-born Coulter, proved to be an "interesting introduction to the American Church; to see it from the inside and also to learn how they thought, operated, and worked."[874] While on the road, Coulter gleaned insights on public relations and the use of public media for raising mission funds. Between 1960 and 1967, Coulter was based in West Chester, Pennsylvania, doing vocation and promotion work over an enormous territory from New Jersey to Florida, but he also worked with Father Gerard Smith in film productions, "usually driving and carrying equipment!!"[875]

Coulter, a man of vision and creativity, became regional promotion director at St. Columbans, Nebraska, in 1967. By that time, office staff had increased, many of them lay people, and the department had purchased new technology for mission promotion. Direct mail was keeping the Society financially afloat, and Coulter learned from a management consultant how to understand computers and their potential for the mission cause.

Because the promotion office was well run,[876] Coulter's interest turned to the possibility of film for mission education. He knew the early popularity of Ranaghan's, *The Cross and Dragon*. People rented the film from the Nebraska headquarters and then returned the film after it was viewed. Coulter reasoned that "because it was our mission message we were trying to sell, we would give the film for free and they paid only for return postage."[877] More substantially, Coulter's film work developed in a reinvigorated Vatican II perspective on mission and the Church's relationship with people of other faiths, both of which had consequences for mission education and the Society's renewal General Chapter of 1970.[878]

---

[874] Interview with Father Cathal Coulter. No date, but c. 2011. Coulter became a naturalized U.S. citizen around 1974.

[875] Cathal P. Coulter, *Memoirs*, 95. Unpublished. CFA-Ireland.

[876] Peter McPartland was assigned to the General Mission Office with responsibility for the monthly donor, wills and annuity programs, designated gifts and scholarship, and represented the Society at the Foundations Organization in New York. Director's *Newsletter* (15 September 1969).

[877] Cathal P. Coulter, *Memoirs*.

[878] After the Second Vatican Council (1961–1965), the Vatican Office for Societies of Apostolic Life (the canonical designation of the Columbans) and Institutes of Consecrated Life (men and women in religious life, whether Sisters, brothers, or clergy) asked these men and women to review their constitutions and other documents to have them reflect the perspectives affirmed in the Council documents. The 1970 Columban General Chapter filled that purpose with the process continuing until 1986, when the Society's revised constitutions were formally promulgated.

An Expanded Mission Education Program

Among the many topics the men deliberated during the 1970 Chapter was the apostolate in Home Regions—i.e., how is one a missionary in one's home country. The Columbans placed their mission call in the larger fundamental reality: "The Church on earth is by its very nature missionary, since according to the plan of the Father, it has its origin in the mission of the Son and the Holy Spirit."[879] In this light, the Society assisted the People of God to evangelize through at least three objectives:

1. "The forming and strengthening of missionary concerns by an educational program which provides information, inspiration and motivation;
2. The recruiting, training and sending of missionaries to the nations;
3. The seeking of spiritual and material support for the missions."[880]

What converged was the realization that vocation promotion, seeking funds for the missions (promotion), mission education, and missionary life were all interrelated and, therefore, all parties involved needed to be in *communication* with each other and to be knowledgeable about the endeavors of all departments at St. Columbans, Nebraska. This was exactly the point that John Kane, the publishing consultant for the *Far East*, had made in 1963.

In 1971, the vocation directors in the U.S. region, in light of the difficulties they experienced in vocation work and in support of the 1970 General Chapter, made several proposals to the director:

"That Promotion houses be known as Mission Education centers.

That Promotion and Vocation men be considered mission educators.

That the Superiors of houses be considered as mission education coordinators."[881]

---

[879] *Ad Gentes Divinitus (On the Church's Missionary Activity)*, par. 2. 7 December 1965.

[880] *Missionary Society of Saint Columban General Chapter, 1970. Acts of the Chapter*, 68.

[881] *Casey History* (December 1971).

Under Regional Director Hugh O'Rourke, the Society immediately moved on the Promotion recommendation from the General Chapter.[882] O'Rourke, a former missionary in Burma (now Myanmar), appointed a committee of four men involved in vocation recruitment, promotion, and mission education to "formulate a program of mission education, to test the program for a specific period, and to present the experience of the pilot program to the individual houses."[883] The Mission Task Force Committee, chaired by Father William J. Carney, wrote material on sixteen topics to provide the region with "suitable presentations on mission education for all age groups" and "as basic material for vocation talks" on missionary priesthood.[884] The themes in their thirty-nine page document included the history of Catholic missions within and from the United States, theological foundations of the missionary nature of the Church, missions and development, the laity, the parish, the family and missions, the missionary vocation, and a mission liturgy. The Committee, however, did not feel competent to prepare presentations that involved audiovisual media.

The Committee also made some practical observations. Columbans were less willing to return to the States from their missions to do promotion or vocation work. New audiovisual materials were needed for parish and group presentations. A "talk on the missions" no longer sufficed. Charlie Coulter realized that young people had grown up in a visual, rather than a print world. The Committee recommended that the Columbans produce and/or distribute new films on mission in view of the mission perspective of the Second Vatican Council and the Society's General Chapter.[885] He produced, "Columban—Man with a Mission," a monthly program sent *gratis* to classrooms across the country in 1971. Along with the film, a colorful brochure was sent for classroom use and for displays on bulletin boards.

A Focused, Developmental Mission Education Program

The Columban Promotion Committee meetings in the 1970s coincided with the plan of the United States Catholic Bishops Conference to sponsor a two-month course on communications/media, held at Loyola University, New

---

[882]   A Regional Promotion Committee was to be set up to "devise means of collecting and producing material for our magazines and appeals; to draw up if possible a plan of promotion in its own area; that the Promotion councilor "coordinate the production of mission films to fill the needs of the home regions." Missionary Society of St. Columban, *General Chapter, 1970, Acts of the Chapter*, # 103, 104, p. 188.

[883]   William J. Carney to Hugh O'Rourke. 26 March 29 1972. The other committee members were Fathers James Kielt, Fintan Keegan, and Charles Duster.

[884]   Hugh O'Rourke to Dear Father, 25 August 1972.

[885]   Cathal P. Coulter, *Memoirs*, 94.

Orleans, Louisiana, in 1974. Charlie Coulter's participation in the classes and his work at Xavier University[886] in that city provided the practical elements of production: writing a script, producing radio and television programs, and creating a short film.

Coulter took two photographers with him to South Korea that year to work on new mission films. But they had great difficulty because of the subject matter: Father Noel S. Ryan's work with the Young Christian Workers, who were being exploited in factories. Given the pressure of the Korean Central Intelligence Agency with respect to that mission, Coulter took his cameramen instead to Father David Sheehan's parish in Kangjin and to Cheju Island, producing two films: "To Celebrate a Harvest" and "The Shepherds of Halim."[887]

In 1975, Coulter teamed up with Chvala Productions, Omaha, Nebraska, and the two principals, Ronald Chvala and his brother, William Chvala. That year they made three films in the Philippines and four films in Fiji the following year. They later filmed material in Columban missions in Latin America. Some of that footage would be used later for *The Barrios* mission education materials. The Chvala brothers started to work with the Columbans in the 1970s and have continued in various ways with the Society into the twenty-first century. Their first class filming in Columban locations, collections of music from Columban mission areas, and great skill in producing films is a story needing to be told.

In 1976, Coulter summarized the work of the region in a paper for Columbans around the globe. He put the creation and use of films and other media in the context of Columban film production, almost from the first day in the U.S. region. He reminded the Society that the "typical American high school graduate" is of an "audiovisual generation." The Columban films had discussion guides with helpful questions to draw out students' thoughts and to present information that could supplement what students saw. Coulter recalled that Pope Paul VI's *Evangelii Nuntiandi*, as well as the Society General Chapter, had suggested "that the Church would feel guilty before the Lord if she did not use these powerful means . . ., a modern and effective version of the pulpit."[888] After Father Coulter's term as regional director (1977–1983), he continued film/video work, writing and producing twenty-two mission films,

---

[886]   In his "Columban Oral History Archive," [n.d.], Coulter referred to work at Saint Francis Xavier University in New Orleans. It is unclear whether he attended Xavier College (now a University), founded by Mother Katharine Drexel in 1915, or Loyola University, the latter a Jesuit university.

[887]   Ibid., 97. Coulter provided some background on the Columban pioneering use of audio visuals in, Father Charles Coulter, "Audiovisuals in Mission Education—U.S. Region," *Columban Intercom* (September 1976). By 1972, several Columban filmstrips were also in use.

[888]   Charles Coulter, "Audiovisuals in Mission Education—U.S. Region." *Intercom* (September 1976).

most of them with the Chvalas. Over the years the films won several national and international awards.

The title regional promotion director "was changed [to Mission Education Director] to reflect the focus of the work in the U.S. region: to educate the 'home church.'"[889] As the materials of the time noted, "We are called to be educators and a voice that motivates, gives direction and provides a channel that people may use to discharge their missionary duties."[890] Columbans newly appointed to Mission Education/Vocation work, while rich in mission experience abroad, might not necessarily be aware of educational directions or the tenor of the United States. The Columbans sought assistance from mission educators. A Mission Education Task Force had begun in 1978 and Coulter, as regional superior (1977–1983), appointed Father Peter Cronin as director of the Task Force in 1980. The Task Force was mainly Father Cronin and Sister Mary O'Dea, SSC (d. 2015), the latter who developed the nucleus of the program, *Come and See.*

Sister Mary O'Dea, an experienced grade school and religious education teacher, had some "colorful years" at the Hispanic school, Our Lady of Guadalupe, in Los Angeles. She then taught for eight years at Blessed Sacrament School, Westminster, California, where she served also as Principal (1972–1975). The Columban Sisters left the Westminster school in 1979, at which time Father Coulter invited Mary to come to Omaha to write a mission education program.

Starting in fall 1980, she lived at the Columban residence and during the academic year used her considerable knowledge and experience to develop a program for elementary schools and eventually for high schools. In preparing the materials, Sister O'Dea was aware of the needs of teachers, who might not have the background for the material, but who could benefit from the experience of missionaries. Her timeline for the *Come and See* program was a five-day session in the grade school. If a missionary used the program in the grade school, an important element was to tell the story of their mission. While she worked at the Columban headquarters, she often conferred with Vito Cioffero in the *Columban* magazine office and found him creative in his approach and supportive of her work.

Sister O'Dea and Father Cronin "field tested" the program in Sioux Falls, South Dakota, for about ten days and in June 1980, Mary made a presentation to the Columbans when they gathered for their annual meeting.[891] She was transferred to Silver Creek, New York, and visited parishes in that area to

---

889 *Casey History* (February 1980), 1

890 Ibid.

891 Information about Sister Mary O'Dea's development of the program obtained through a Skype interview with her in Lima, Peru. Author interview of Mary O'Dea, 19 February 2014.

promote the *Come and See* program. She presented a workshop at a National Catholic Education Association conference, which gave a still wider exposure to the Columban mission education materials.

The program Mary developed took another step forward, when she suggested that Father James O'Brien, one of the Columbans who had formed a Team Ministry in St. Peter and Paul Parish, Norwich, Connecticut, along with Sister Margaret Devine, SSC, should meet with the Superintendent of Schools in the Diocese of Norwich to discuss the possibility of presenting the program to the Principals.[892] Sister Dorothy Mahon, RSM, involved in religious education and liturgy as part of the Team Ministry at St. Peter and St. Paul, worked with the *Come and See* materials for use as a *parish* program. After five years working with the Columban materials, Dorothy offered her services *gratis* to the Columbans in 1983 to develop and adapt materials for the three Connecticut dioceses and the Diocese of Providence, Rhode Island. In 1985 she put together resource materials for a Program for Adults, with a focus on the church in the Philippines. "Dorothy has worked long and hard to develop these materials, well described in a handsome brochure. The materials go a long way towards enhancing a global faith context." [893] The program was modeled on the national RENEW program for parishes and was designed for small groups.

While in Norwich, Father James O'Brien, who "took to religious education, like a duck to water,"[894] was appointed in 1983 as director of mission education, a "big title but no one, including myself, knew what it meant. There was a common understanding that I was Promotion Director" (fund-raiser).[895] However, as was seen above, there was a steady development wedding promotion and mission education, continuing after the 1976 General Chapter.[896]

O'Brien had served in South Korea since 1957, was assigned to the U.S. region in 1976 and appointed a member of the formation team for the seminarians at the Columban seminary, Milton. While at Milton, he assisted

---

[892]   Author telephone interview of Sister Margaret Devine, SSC, 10 April 2014. See, also, information on mission education in Jim O'Brien, "Columban Journey, 1956–2006," a paper O'Brien prepared to be read when his classmates assembled in Ireland to celebrate their Golden Jubilee of priesthood. He was not able to join them because of ill health. Papers provided to author by O'Brien's sister, Sister Catherine O'Brien, SND.

[893]   *Columban Newsletter* (12 November 1985).

[894]   Author interview of Sister Margaret Devine, SSC, 10 April 2014.

[895]   James O'Brien, *Vitae*, extended version. Paper courtesy of Sister Catherine O'Brien, sent to author 2 June 1913.

[896]   The press release from the Quincy, Massachusetts Promotion House reiterated that the role the Columbans had at the house was "not another method of collecting funds, but [the Columbans were] contributors of their mission experience to the home church." *New Columbans at Quincy*, Press Release, AA87-2. [1987].

part time at St. Patrick Parish, Stoneham, where he was involved in the religious education program and particularly enjoyed youth ministry. A further experience that shaped O'Brien's approach to mission education was his six years on the Columban pastoral team at SS. Peter and Paul Parish, Norwich, Connecticut, from 1977 to 1983. While in Norwich, he drove to Hartford once a month to celebrate a liturgy for Korean Catholics and to preside at their weddings. An insight he carried into mission education was, as he put it, "in Korea he put a lot of effort into building churches, but now he put effort into building Church." His reflections upon Korean culture "proved most valuable" for his work in mission education.[897]

When O'Brien moved to St. Columban's, Nebraska, in February 1983, the promotional side of office operations was going smoothly, so he ventured more deeply into mission education. At a Columban gathering, he argued for a shift in emphasis from mission *appeals* (a priest traveling from parish to parish, asking for financial assistance at Sunday Masses) to mission *awareness* through *education*. In a memo to the director of the U.S. region, O'Brien inquired whether "there is a gradual and more definite shift toward "awareness" in the magazine (*Columban Mission*) and in appeal letters?"[898] In other words, did mission appeals in whatever form engage the audience in an *awareness* of mission and urge them to respond to their call to mission wherever they lived? His assessment of the magazine and appeal letters was that they often were "touching" in their approach—i.e., stories appealed to sentiment, rather than demonstrate an "awareness approach."[899] One outcome of a changed attitude would be that an informed and evangelized Catholic population would be more likely to support the missions and live their baptismal mission vocation. The masthead on the material sent from his office included in red ink: Mission *Awareness*.[900]

Far more than semantics, mission *awareness* aimed for adult formation. Education about mission would need to involve all Columbans who were asked to do mission appeals in the States. Regional Superior Michael O'Loughlin later wrote to the superior general: "Personally I don't like the word promotion, it is misleading because what really is at issue is mission Education/Animation." The mission education programs begun under the direction of James O'Brien

---

[897]   James A. O'Brien. Notes affixed to his biographical information. Paper courtesy of Sister Catherine O'Brien.

[898]   J. O'Brien Memo to Director U.S. Region re: Preliminary Mission Education Report 11 October 1983. CFA-USA.

[899]   J. O'Brien memo to Director and Council 5 May 1984.

[900]   Author telephone interview with Sister Rita Connell, RSM, 1 July 2013.

"have been the major contribution of the Region," even though the Columban houses could do much more in the follow-up to the programs.[901]

Mission education/awareness was more involved than producing and showing a film, VHS, CD-ROM, DVD, or use of the latest technological tool. Program development required the combined skills and knowledge of many people. O'Brien suggested that the Columbans "look into the possibility of moving Sister Mary O'Dea's well-developed program into professional hands for publication and promotion. If the current trend further develops, it may be more than we can handle in house."[902] After consultation he recommended to the regional director that a new position, associate Mission Education director, be added to the office. "This position calls for a person qualified with an educational background with a creative touch and a comprehensive vision of the mission of the Church."[903] O'Brien hired women with expertise in curriculum development, religious education, and experience in the teaching/ learning process to create what would become the most recognized Catholic mission education program in the country.

He contacted the Provincial of the Mercy Sisters in Omaha to inquire whether they had someone with the background and interest to work with him. Sister Rita Connell, RSM, an experienced parish religious education director in Iowa, was hired as associate director of Mission Education from 1984 until May 1990. In the early 1980s, Rita had participated in a workshop given by Father Thomas Sweetser, SJ, "Profiles of a Healthy Parish," and one of the healthy marks was that a parish had a sense of mission beyond its own boundaries.[904] She saw the Columban work as a way to influence parishes and schools in that direction. She oversaw the development of the mission education materials, introduced the Columban mission promoters to the materials so they would feel confident to use them in parishes and schools, presented the Columban programs to attendees at national mission conventions, and developed many other elements for mission education.

To create and develop the curriculum itself,[905] O'Brien, through his acquaintance with Sister Mary Jo Maher, IHM, at annual U.S. Catholic Mission

---

[901]   Michael O'Loughlin to Father Nicholas Murray 19 April 1991.

[902]   J. O'Brien memo to Director U.S. Region re: Preliminary Mission Education Report 11 October 1983. CFA-USA.

[903]   J. O'Brien memo to Director U.S. Region re: Preliminary Mission Education Report 11 October 1983. CFA-USA.

[904]   Sweetser is founder and director of the Chicago based Parish Evaluation Project. His team gave leadership development workshops around the country, beginning in the early 1980s to bring out the best in the parishioners and the staff. A book related to the point Rita Connell made is Thomas P. Sweetser, SJ, *Successful Parishes: How They Meet the Challenges of Change* (San Francisco: Harper & Row, 1983).

[905]   In May 1983, O'Brien had met with Sisters Mary O'Dea, Margaret Devine, Dorothy Mahon, Joan Rigney (National Office of the Society for the Propagation of the

Association gatherings, learned about Sister Marcella Regan, IHM, then working in Juarez, Mexico. She had the ideal background to design and test a new mission education program. Marcella was an educator and catechist for many years, was her Congregation's Religious Education Consultant, a Catechist Trainer for the Archdiocese of Detroit, and a missionary herself. O'Brien invited her in 1984 to update Mary O'Dea's "Come and See Program," a school program with five lessons per grade, which had already proved itself a success.[906] Sister Marcella Regan then developed a parish religious education edition, with one lesson per grade, teacher manuals, art from the featured countries, handouts, videos, and elements that engaged all the senses in learning. This comprehensive approach led people in charge of programs to learn effective ways to present the content.[907]

O'Brien spoke with Sister Marcella at length about a perspective to be conveyed to young people.[908] In his reflection on the Gospel passage where Jesus said to those who became his apostles, "Come, and see," it struck O'Brien that a mission education program should do just that. The videos, activities, readings, and other elements of the program should help students put words to their experience of God. The program should share with students how Jesus acted and worked in other countries. As a later director of Mission Education said of O'Brien, "Instilled within him was the teaching that a missionary goes to find God in the people and to learn with them and to share the Gospel."[909] The perspective was a definite shift in the focus of some mission societies whose literature and visual products idealized the hard work the missionary did in foreign lands.

Sister Marcela then created a program from scratch and recast the material with a "scope and sequence" for grades kindergarten–grade 6, a process that created continuity and development of ideas throughout the curriculum. For each grade a different country where Columbans were missioned was featured. She developed lesson plans, added songs, prayers, maps, art from the featured country, and handouts to enhance the video, engaging all the senses in

---

Faith), and Columban Fathers Michael Harrison and Michael O'Loughlin for an initial review of the program and materials. *Columban Newsletter* (November 1984).

[906] "In consultation with Sr. Mary O'Dea, I recommend a second printing of 25 sets of the Mission Ed program." The original sixty sets were needed where they were. J. O'Brien memo to Director, U.S. Region re: Preliminary Mission Education Report 11 October 1983.

[907] Marcella Regan's work is noted *in Columban Newsletter* (January 1991), 4.

[908] Regan found O'Brien to "have a deep spiritual sense" and "working with him to be a spiritual experience." Author interview with Sister Marcella Regan, IHM, 20 June 2013.

[909] Sylvia Thompson, "On the death of Father James O'Brien," 2009. Paper courtesy of Sister Catherine O'Brien.

learning. Classroom teachers, responsible for preparing many subjects and for myriad classroom responsibilities, and volunteer religious education teachers would not have time or resources to plan sessions as full and rich as what the Columban program offered.

A plan for junior and senior high students, *Challenged and Empowered*, was developed along with materials for the teacher. Janet Drey was invited by Father Peter Cronin to work with particular materials related to the film Father Charlie Coulter had shot earlier in Peru (*The Barrio Series*, 1987). Drey was a skilled and well-known educator in Des Moines, Iowa. As director of Youth Ministry for the Diocese of Des Moines with many years of success during the time of Bishop Dingman's leadership. With a change of ecclesiastical leadership there, a number of diocesan staff resigned, including Janet. The Columban invitation following that experience proved a "graced time for her. I was open to what might come and feel blessed because of the experience with the Columbans."[910] She viewed the Barrio films, which "were very well done."[911] The perspective Father Coulter took in the film was "hopeful healing in for the women's experience in the barrios of Lima."[912] Janet became "immersed in the lives of the people and listened to them to understand their lives in order to connect with them." [913] She was "moved by what she saw and heard and the experience stretched her." In writing the manual to go with the series, I sought to make available in the First World what people in the Third World experienced."[914]

Throughout all the programs, students came to greater mission awareness. Teachers themselves were evangelized. O'Brien invited Charlie Coulter to produce a "Teaching Come and See" film to introduce teachers to the program and perspective, so as to have mission permeate classrooms and parishes.[915] This was also the theme of the 1986 video, "Teaching Global Awareness." By that time, O'Brien observed,

> We sense in the region a more positive consciousness and acceptance of mission awareness. The general attitude is

---

[910]   Author telephone interview with Janet Drey, Des Moines, Iowa, 21 March 2017.

[911]   Ibid.

[912]   Ibid.

[913]   Ibid.

[914]   Ibid.

[915]   "Teaching *Come and See*," script by Charlie Coulter. Mary Kay Mueller, narrator. Produced by Bill and Ron Chvala (1986). The film was shot at the local parish, St. Mary's, Bellevue, Nebraska. When the United States Conference of Catholic Bishops published the *Catechism of the Catholic Church* (1994), the Columban Mission Education Office provided corresponding paragraph numbers of the Catechism with the material from the Columban programs.

that we have passed beyond the promotion thrust (heavy on
financial assistance) to a realization that mission awareness
in a wider perspective is the role of the home region. This
means education through various resources such as *Columban
Mission* and the materials offered by the mission education
office. This greater realization has gradually surfaced as
the members struggled with Society documents. . . . Not all
actively pursue this approach in their ministry, but there is
general acceptance of our new thrust. [916]

The *Come and See Program* continued until fall 2007, when a new program
for Grades 1–8, *Journey with Jesus,* began that semester. The latter program
was thematic for each year, whereas *Come and See* had focused on a particular
country for each grade.

By 1984, a revised mission program included a focus on young adults
("People with a Mission") and Lenten programs with a mission emphasis.[917]
In addition to adult formation of those who taught the school and parish
programs, adults were the targeted audience in other videos. Father Thomas
P. Reynolds wrote the script for the Coulter and Chvalas' video production,
"Send, Receive, Set Free," to introduce Catholics to the U.S. Catholic Bishops'
document, "To the Ends of the Earth: Send, Receive, Set Free" (1984). A later
video, "From the Ends of the Earth," produced with a Spanish and English
edition for the Adult Rite of Christian Initiation programs, carried the twofold
theme: "Call to Mission" and "Living the Mission."

During the time Sister Marcella developed the kindergarten–grade 6
curriculum in the evenings and eventual weekly "day off" from her regular
classroom (1987–1994),[918] she lived in Mexico and Michigan. She experimented
in classrooms and religious education programs to assess the effectiveness
of the material and flew to Omaha for occasional meetings to develop the
next stage of the program. To handle the art work, layout, and format of the
program, Patti Samson, Sister Rita Connell's sister, was hired. Patti happened
to have been finishing courses in graphic arts at the time and her skills were
immediately engaged at St. Columbans to create material based on the ideas
the staff discussed for each unit. O'Loughlin commented to the superior

---

[916]   James O'Brien to Director, U.S. Region Annual Report for 1985. 17 January 1986.

[917]   *Columban Newsletter* (November 1984). After the annual meeting of USCMA, where
        Columbans heard that the ideas of the mission education program for grade and
        high schools needed to have a similar program for adults, a work group of people
        from the Northeast gathered at Bristol, Rhode Island in June 1984 to provide
        direction for such a program.

[918]   The Columbans made financial provisions to hire a substitute teacher for these
        days.

general, "There is no way that I could see ten hardworking, full-time committed Columbans making this kind of impact for twice the cost."[919] The programs were, indeed, a success.

Given the demographics of the Catholic Church in the United States by the early 1990s, O'Loughlin noted, "We are presently considering engaging in Mission Education among Hispanic communities. This is a project we have contemplated for a long time. We see a real need for cross-cultural mission groups such as ours to have educational materials available for the increasing number of Hispanics in the U.S."[920] The program would begin in a modest way, given the energy and scope for Columban mission educators who worked in Hispanic communities.

In 1989, a parishioner from St. Mary's Parish, Bellevue, just down the hill from the Columban headquarters, had learned that Sister Rita Connell would be moving from her position in the Mission Education office. Sylvia Thompson already had several experiences working with the Columbans. After graduation from high school, she first met the Columbans when she moved from South Dakota to the Bellevue area and for two weeks stuffed mission appeal envelopes at the Columbans before she embarked on her college years. After marriage to George, who was in the U.S. Navy, the two of them went to the Philippines, where Sylvia worked with the Columbans as a religious education teacher. Returning eventually to the Omaha area, she became the director of the religious education program at St. Mary's Parish in Bellevue. Having worked in the parish for many years, Sylvia recognized that the "mission story" was not evident there. Jim O'Brien hired Sylvia as his assistant on July 1, 1990, to replace Rita Connell. After his heart attack in 1993, he put her in charge as director of Mission Education. Father O'Brien remarked that Sylvia "has grown into the job and taken it to new heights. Without lay people of her caliber the program would be dead. It was a big move on the part of the Columbans and helps us see our way into the future."[921] Sylvia, in turn, hired Connie Wacha, her former secretary at St. Mary's, to assist her as Connie did do so ably, first as the contact person from whom to obtain the growing number of excellent Columban materials.

In addition to updating existing programs and materials, Sylvia also worked with others to create videos on new themes. For many years, Columbans had seen the effects of climate change, deforestation, and industrial processes that adversely affected the people with whom they worked, especially in the Philippines. From Quincy, Massachusetts, O'Brien suggested that a Mission

---

[919]   Michael O'Loughlin to Father Nicholas Murray 19 April 1991.

[920]   Michael O'Loughlin to Rev. John Grace, SPF Office, Chicago, 1 July 1993.

[921]   James O'Brien's listing of his assignments over the years, along with his annotations. Paper courtesy of Sister Catherine O'Brien.

Awareness program be developed based on Columban Father Sean McDonagh's work on climate change.[922] Taking a holistic approach, Father Vincent Busch, born in Western New York, was missioned to the Philippines in 1975, working on the island of Mindanao. Beginning in 1984, he produced numerous award-winning videos that focused on Columban mission in Asia. The 1985 Mission education program featured the video, *Social Volcano,* which centered on the sugarcane workers in the Philippines. Several of his books raised the relationship between the life of the earth and the life of humans who use that earth, including *The Human Soil* (1980) and *Hope for the Seeds* (2000). His book, *Creation Mandala* (2004), highlighted the Subanen women, who particularly suffered from malnutrition and lack of education. Some of their condition was due to the effects of deforestation in their mountainous area. The sale of the women's mandalas, which resemble Native American "Dream catchers," provided the women with money to meet their needs. The enterprise also raised their feelings of self-worth.

O'Brien had noted that because few Columbans were available to promote the mission education program, a "network of associates" could enhance the Columban effort. He stressed the concept because "we see our main thrust as adult education with educators.... Simply put, they are in key positions and have much impact on youth, whom we now see as our secondary target audience."[923] O'Brien hoped for a core group of ten Columbans (there were six highly active Columbans in the work) who would network with our associates. "We see the associates—full and part time—as Partners in Ministry and essential to advancing our M/Ed presence. They are qualified, competent and interested educators who are looking for support that only a Columban can give." O'Brien continued, "The bottom line is that we do not have the Columban personnel to do the job and so must turn to the associates." This was not a one way street, however. "The associates through their expertise and enthusiasm facilitate the Columbans assigned to the work and give them support as well as open new avenues."[924]

With O'Brien's encouragement to "get the educators together," Sylvia began the Companions in Mission program in 1992. In addition to some Columbans, the group comprised men and women, most with overseas mission experience, who worked effectively in mission offices or in mission education situations.[925] The Companions in Mission met once a year for an extended weekend and

---

[922]   The topic returned: "Mission Awareness Committee to discuss this at their next meeting, 2007." Regional Council Report (May 2007).

[923]   James O'Brien to Director, U. S. Region, Annual Report for 1985.

[924]   Ibid.

[925]   For O'Brien's overall Mission Education Office Vision for 2000, see Jim O'Brien to Brendan O'Sullivan [Regional Director] 13 July 1993.

were in regular communication with Sylvia. At the first invitational gathering twenty-five people assembled. Over the years the number grew sometimes to sixty participants. The weekend, supported financially by the Society, was rich in community building. The group learned about the new Columban mission materials and received input from Columban priests, lay missionaries and participants about global mission realities (human trafficking, migrants and labor conditions, the Catholic Church in a Taiwan mountainous area), or about issues such as mission education and the college campus. The group prayed together, drew on the rich cultural traditions from Columban missions, and held a festive final evening, often richly laced with music and dance from people where Columbans served.

Sylvia Thompson's gregarious disposition, creativity, and exuberance enriched the Companions' weekend and the connections she made with educators around the country. This was seen in the addition of Columban Mission Associates, people hired to represent the Columban mission education program at national conferences, local diocesan gatherings, and other venues. Among these, Sister Rosemary O'Malley, CSJ (1932–2006), a former missionary in Peru and Chile and a former staff person at the Chicago Hispanic Missions Office, was invited to promote Columban programs and to animate local church diocesan educators. She did this with great verve between 1992 and 2001.[926] Sister Rosalie Callen, CSJ, with a rich background in teaching and religious education, worked in the same capacity for thirteen years, mainly in southern California. She and Sister Colleen Nolan, OP, took the *Journey with Jesus* themes and scaled those for Adult Education. Sylvia Thompson left her position as director of Mission Education in February 2003, to tend to her elderly parents. Connie Wacha remained working with the mission education program and Companion weekends.

Sister Jeanne Janssen, CSJ, was hired that same month as the new director of Mission Education. As was true for Sylvia, Jeanne had Columban friends and was knowledgeable of Columban missions. In 1972 she was missioned to Japan and met many Columbans at language school, a "forging experience."[927] Her next mission was in the Philippines, where she served in an urban slum on the fringes of the Columban parish, Malate. After her return to the States in 1994, she worked with Katie Pierce at the Center for Mission Studies in New York, where Jeanne learned about the Columban initiated AITECE program (Association for International Teaching, Educational and Curriculum

---

[926]   Sister Rosemary O'Malley, was a director and teacher for the Archdiocese of Chicago Spanish Language Program from 1988–1992. As a Columban Mission Associate, she promoted the Columban Mission Education Programs in San Francisco, Los Angeles, and Chicago. Sister Colleen Nolan, OP, and Father Charlie Duster teamed up to promote the SSC Mission Education programs in the Chicago area.

[927]   Author interview with Sister Jeanne Janssen, CSJ, 15 April 2014.

Exchange), the first structured Catholic agency for working in mainland China. Through this program, Jeanne taught English in China between 1997 and 2000. Old friends met when Father John Burger, a Japanese language classmate of hers and by that time the U.S. regional director, met her at the Omaha airport in 2003 to interview for the position of mission education director.

Jeanne brought to the office over twenty years of cross-cultural and teaching experience. She "felt at home right away. I walked into a home, a life, and a job, which used her best experiences."[928] Under her leadership, several new programs were written and produced. Sister Carol Jean Willie, SC, the NGO representative of the Sisters of Charity Federation at the United Nations (2007–2015), authored the material for the *Journey with Jesus* Program, beginning in 2007. Her background included a doctoral degree in multicultural education with experience teaching African Americans, Native Americans, Haitians, and people from other Caribbean countries. She also engaged with a number of Interfaith committees. The *Journey* program carried forward the directives of the U.S. Catholic Bishops: "We call for a renewed commitment to integrate Catholic social teaching into the mainstream of all Catholic education institutions and programs."[929] The program deftly and beautifully combined insights of Columban missionaries, scriptural perspectives, and social justice teachings for students to understand our world. Mission was not "going out to those poor people out there," but included the ability to go out of oneself to others different from us and learning of the richness of God's expression in the world.[930]

The *Journey with Jesus* Program was addressed to children from kindergarten through eighth grade. The preschool used the DVD, *Vinny's New Day* and the kindergarten focus was *Children of the World*. Themes were carried through for each grade: *Families of the World, Building Communities of Peace, Respect for All God's People, Care for Creation, Respect for Different Faith Traditions, Standing on the Side of the Poor, Beyond Borders: Migrants, Immigrants and Refugees, Culture: Gift and Blessing.*[931] Helpful teacher materials, prayer cards, original songs, and suggestions for "at-home connections" came with the audiovisual.

---

[928]   Ibid.

[929]   U.S. Catholic Bishops, "Sharing Catholic Social Teaching: Challenges and Directions," 1998. When the U.S. Catholic Conference of Bishops published the *Catholic Catechism* in 1997, the Mission Education Office prepared a guide to use the Columban programs and material, as it aligned with specific sections of the *Catechism*.

[930]   Carol Jean Willie, SND, "Program Orientation" for *Journey with Jesus*. DVD. CFA-USA.

[931]   In 2011, an Adult Formation DVD and accompanying materials was developed: *Culture, The Web of Life*. The three goals of the program were to explore cultural diversity and traditions in the world and how they support daily life; to discover

The Companions in Mission gatherings continued under Jeanne Janssen's direction. After her first two years in the ministry, a more complex administrative structure was put in place at Columban headquarters after Father Arturo Aguilar became regional director. Her work expanded beyond the mission education office in January 2009, with additional responsibilities as communications director. So, in addition to Mission Education, she edited the magazine, and oversaw all publications that went out from the Mission Office, including appeal letters, and pamphlets. Additionally, all department heads comprised the Mission Office Management Team. They were also members of a regionwide management group.[932]

Well over 200,000 people annually participated in the popular, innovative Columban Mission Education Programs around the country.[933] The Columbans were generous with funds for this promotion area and their programs became the leading mission education materials on all levels of grade and high school and were used by other mission organizations.[934] The United States Catholic Mission Association presented the Society of St. Columban with a Mission Award in 2010 "in recognition for excellence and creativity in Mission Education and Promotion" for over twenty-five years. Sister Jeanne Janssen and Regional Director Arturo Aguilar accepted the award on behalf of the Society. As Sylvia Thompson remarked, "The Columbans have the sense that it is God's Mission. They and their programs are a generous gift to the American Church."[935] Jeanne's "take away" from her years in leadership at the Columban headquarters reflected that the job was a "perfect fit for her" and "I used my best experiences: cross cultural." She observed, "The true missionary knows the cue as to when they should leave. It was a gift in saying, 'yes' and in saying, 'good-bye.'"[936] Jeanne left her leadership position in May 2011, and went to Avila University, Kansas City, Missouri. She uses her considerable skills in the International Student Office and teaches in the Department of English as a Second Language.

---

ways of crossing boundaries of language and culture in order to experience the rich cultural traditions of one another; to celebrate our faith and the cultural diversity of Catholic worship as a gift from God.

[932] Author e-mail communication with Sister Jeanne Janssen, 21 January 2016.

[933] Regional Director Father Arturo Aguilar noted in 2010 that in the twenty-five years of the mission education program, over 2,250,000 children and young people were introduced to mission through over 150,000 teachers and catechists using the Columban mission education curriculum. *Columban Mission* (November 2010), 23.

[934] "Columban Journey—Jim O'Brien, 1956–2006." Paper courtesy of Sister Catherine O'Brien.

[935] Author interview of Sylvia Thompson 21 August 2013.

[936] Author telephone interview of Sister Jeanne Janssen, 15 April 2014.

After Jeanne moved to her next ministry, Connie Wacha, hired for a part-time position by Sylvia Thompson in 1991, took on more responsibilities, a pattern since beginning her work at Columban headquarters. She entered orders for video materials that schools and parishes requested and completed the paperwork connected with the communication. She set up media and took care of myriad details in the logistics for the annual Companions in Mission gathering. Slowly she became involved in planning the weekend. While Connie came with some computer skills, she also taught herself additional skills, as the need arose, and worked on some design elements for the Columban materials. For a number of years, she was an editorial assistant for *Columban Mission*. Her earlier international experience was in Okinawa, where she worked with Franciscans in the 1970s. She was baptized and confirmed a Catholic in 1976 with the sacraments administered by the bishop of Okinawa. She reflected, "Mission has always been in my heart. When mission really gets into your heart and soul, it doesn't let you go." Her work with the Columbans "helped her grow." She felt among the Columbans "an international feeling." Missionary stories "keep the mission experience alive, listening to their stories."[937] Connie retired in 2015.

The many decades of this form of Mission Education are winding down, but the mission message is directed in other ways.[938] Most recently, for example, the United States Catholic Mission Association has made available the Columban coauthored study guide for the Latin American bishops' Aparecida document and study guide for Pope Francis's, *Laudato Sí* (2015). The latter guide was developed by the Columban Office of Justice, Peace, and Integrity of Creation in Washington DC.

Conclusion

The public venue of Columban life had several strands: vocation, promotion, and education. Over the years new understandings of those connections and the development of each area with professional assistance kept the promotion of mission more generally in the foreground for the Society. From the beginning of the U.S. region, the Columbans had a keen appreciation for and sensitivity toward their donors, a relationship which will be treated in chapter 9.

The Society of St. Columban looked to the United States as a major source of funds, especially after World War II. The economic structures of mission promotion evolved from the assessment the superior general gave to the region

---

[937]   Author interview of Connie Wacha, St. Columbans, Nebraska, 25 August 2015.

[938]   The Mission Education Office announced that effective on 31 December 2016, the Columbans would end the mission education program. .

to contribute a certain amount of funds annually, based on mission needs. More promotion houses opened at the end of the 1940s, when missionaries awaited assignment elsewhere. Promotion work placed different kinds of expectations on the men than if they were in a mission station. The region provided tools for alleviating some of the burden of promotion, such as "Hints for the Promoter," Promotion Teams, and classes in public speaking, including Dale Carnegie courses. Men who were successful at a certain type of fund-raising in larger cities, such as having a major well-recognized singer appear for a benefit, set the bar higher for everyone else. Columbans were successful in raising funds, especially by the early 1970s. At one point, Father Steinhilber indicated, "Too much money could create false expectations that the 'cash cow' would always be there." [939] He wanted mission areas to rely on their own countries with mission mechanisms to make missions more self-supporting and mission minded toward other groups." Donors were generous and by the 1970s, Father Steinhilber expressed the irony: "With money, you always seem to have the problem—Either you have too much money and no vocations or we have too many vocations and not enough money. That's just the way it was."[940]

In the promotion activities, the magazine, and mission education programs, Columbans included laity and women religious and created a relationship that raised mission consciousness globally. Even the effort to have local communities in poorer countries become self-sustaining, is a tribute to the belief that Columbans want to have resources shared, no matter how small the resource. The magazine early on, especially under Patrick O'Connor, sought specifically to attract women and child readers, though, most likely, the woman was the one who held the subscription or at least read the magazine.

The Columban Mission Education program came to be viewed not so much as a "money maker" for the missions, but as having a mission in its own right: to educate people in the United States to understand, embrace, and live mission. The combined efforts of a mission education staff produced successful programs for schools, parishes and Adult Education groups. A mission "full circle" can be seen in the Columban video, "As Water in the Desert," set in the towns of El Paso, Texas, and Juarez, Mexico, where the Columbans work. The film highlighted the baptismal waters that unite Christians into a family and contrasted that with the disconnection among people who live where the waters of the Rio Grande River flow. Young Korean American adults from Southern California came with Father Tony Mortell and saw for themselves the effects of this water divide for the daily life in the Mexican communities. The young adults even in just a week of interaction with people along the border

---

[939]   Father Joseph McSweeny interview of Father Richard Steinhilber 13 July 2012. Interview 3.

[940]   Ibid.

came to new personal understandings of Catholic life and mission. Mission had come full circle in the group that Columbans had served since the early 1970s in Southern California. As was true for Columban mission education and promotion, people were invited into mission not only with the Columbans but into a community with others in mission.

The Society continued the Ranaghan pioneering work in film and consequent use of new audiovisual developments to convey the mission message. In anticipation of the Columban Centennial, each week the "One Hundred Points of Light," a three-minute website video, provides significant "points of light" in Columban history. Through the activities of promotion and mission education, Catholics and others are drawn into the circle of Columban mission to experience, if only vicariously, the variety and diversity of God's expression in human life through distinct people's lives around the globe.

February 1940 Far East

February 1964 Far East _Page_01

THE FAR EAST

OUR LADY OF THE ORIENT—By a Chinese Painter

May, 1925

May 1925 Far East_Page_01

Mission Exhibit Postcard, Providence, RI

CHAPTER 8

Mission to Asian Communities
in the United States

"Wherever (the Columbans) are,
we should be going into ethnic communities."[941]

Except for aboriginal groups who lived in what became the United States, everyone else was an immigrant from West Africa, Europe, Eastern Europe, Asia, and in more recent times from Central America, Russia, sub-Saharan Africa, or from countries with Islamic heritage. The expanding borders of the United States west of the original thirteen colonies eventually included people whose origins were in Mexico or who were "Native."

In 1884, the bishops of the United States at the Third Plenary Council of Baltimore identified the variety of peoples and Catholic groups already in the country in need of pastoral or mission presence: immigrants newly arrived from Europe, "Indians and Colored," adults and children who needed education in the Catholic faith, and "Home and Foreign Missions."

Of the numerous ethnic communities who settled in the United States by the twentieth century, Columbans worked with Chinese, Mexicans, Filipinos, Koreans, Japanese, and Vietnamese. The chapter will highlight Columban mission among three of the groups: Chinese, Filipinos, and Koreans, with a high concentration of this cross-cultural mission taking place on the West Coast, a natural point for groups arriving from Asian countries. In all cases, the long-term fruitfulness of these endeavors reflected enterprising Columban pioneers, intrepid women religious, and ardent lay leaders who made a commitment in some form to "grow" the mission.

---

[941] Response from Superior General to Director's Annual Report, *Columban Newsletter* (April 1984).

Mission to the Chinese in the United States

Chinese Immigrants to America

With Columban sites focused on China from the Society's origin in 1918, immense energy, effort and finances were sent in that direction. However, the Chinese in the United States had been in the United States well before that year. Chinese arrived in the nineteenth century to work mainly on the transcontinental railroad, as miners, and in the eastern part of the country, as laborers in the clothing industry. The American writer, Jack London (1876–1916), had a Chinese cook and helper at his ranch in Glen Ellen, California. Looked upon as "cheap labor," Chinese were often harassed by other workers, who saw Chinese as lowering wages for everyone else. The well-known cartoonist, Thomas Nast, captured the stereotype of the Chinese in his *Harper's Magazine* drawings. The Chinese Exclusion Act of 1882 and its extension in 1892 intended to close the door to new immigrants from that country. The Paulist Fathers had a mission to Chinese in San Francisco, starting in 1903.[942] By the time the Second Catholic Missionary Congress was held in Boston in 1913, attendees met Chinese Catholics from that area and were served a Chinese meal.

In 1919 Regional Superior McCarthy's letter to donors drew attention to two needs: the education of American missionaries and the "religious and moral education of those Chinese students [1500 at the time] who are flocking to American universities."[943] McCarthy met two Chinese young men who visited the Columbans in Omaha. They attended Columbia College in Dubuque, Iowa, and hoped to matriculate at Creighton University. "They may later become the nucleus of our Chinese Students Hostel at Omaha."[944] While that project did not materialize, when McCarthy received a letter from Bishop Galvin, alerting

---

[942] For an overview of the mission to the Chinese in California in the first two decades of the twentieth century, see, Charles A. Donovan, CSP, "The Paulist Mission to the Chinese in San Francisco since 1903," *U.S. Catholic Historian* 18 (Winter 2000), 126–141. For missions to the Chinese in the early twentieth century throughout the United States, see, Angelyn Dries, OSF, *The Missionary Movement in American Catholic History* (Maryknoll, NY: Orbis Books, 1998), 108–111.

[943] E. J. McCarthy to "Dear Friends," 1 December 1919.

[944] E. J. McCarthy, "Diary of Progress at St. Columbans, Omaha, Neb." [October 21, 1922]. When the Society hoped to buy the Presbyterian College on what would be the eastern part of the land the Society bought, McCarthy thought that one of the buildings on that campus could be "devoted to a Chinese hostel for our Hanyang Chinese who may be sent to Creighton University. The tram car runs to the door and it will be most convenient for these Chinese students." E. J. McCarthy to [unidentified], 19 September 1920. The Society wrote about the Chinese students in *FE* (November 1923), 171–172 and *FE* (January 1924), 5–6.

him to the presence of Chinese students in the United States and a suggestion that the Columbans work with them, McCarthy responded:

> I have been in touch with this situation for quite a while through Father Keogh, who is the Secretary of the Catholic Alumni Association, but my problem is to get a suitable man. I believe he should be an American and should have some Chinese experience. I do not expect the Superior would give us a man for that work, in any case. There is no question about the need for such a work, but what can be done. . . .

> There is only one practical way of meeting this situation and that is to let a priest free and let him go around to the Universities and meet these Chinese students and put them in in touch with the Chaplains of the Newman Clubs. . . . I understand Father [John] Cowhig is a likely man for such a work."[945]

The *Far East* in 1923 and 1924 included articles about the presence of Chinese students in the United States.

St. Bridget's Catholic Chinese Center, Los Angeles

Several years later, Father John Cowhig (1897–1986) opened a mission among the Chinese in the United States but not in a university setting. Cowhig, who had served with Bishop Edward Galvin in Hanyang, China from 1924–1934, began a ministry among the Chinese in Los Angeles.[946] Cowhig had met Paul Yü-Pin (1901–1978),[947] vicar apostolic of Nanjing (Nanking), along with

---

[945]   E. J. McCarthy to Bishop Galvin, 18 May 1933.

[946]   Cowhig had returned from China in ill health, and in 1935 he was assigned to promotion work and did so in Brooklyn and Boston. "He is very keen on this undercover contact work. As he is a good mixer, he will find it a whole lot easier than appealing in churches." Kelly to Waldron, 24 November 1935. Cowhig then spent a short time with the Cistercian community in Valley Falls, Rhode Island. In 1936, he went to Mayo Clinic for an assessment of a condition which was probably a reoccurrence of amoebic dysentery, as well as physical and nervous exhaustion. When Regional Superior Paul Waldron made a visit to several bishops in California that year, he noted that Monsignor Cawley, vicar general for the Los Angeles Diocese, had suggested in addition to a house for missionaries in need of recuperation, the Columbans might "later get interested in the Chinese in the city." Paul Waldron to Dr. O'Dwyer, 17 March 1936.

[947]   Born in northern Manchuria, Yü-Pin studied at the *Propaganda Fide* seminary in Rome and stayed in the city for four more years as a lecturer and librarian. Upon his return to China, he was appointed spiritual director for Catholic Action among

his secretary, Father Ferdinand Lee, when they were in San Diego. As special envoy of the Chinese National Government Relief Commission, Yü-Pin was touring the United States to gather funds for refugees from Japanese-invaded Manchuria. When Cowhig asked him for advice about a Chinese mission, Yü-Pin suggested going to Los Angeles, which had a larger Chinese population. Archbishop John Cantwell[948] of Los Angeles and director of the Confraternity of Christian Doctrine, Father John K. Clarke, were eager to begin an outreach to the Chinese.

Having secured the permission of Archbishop Cantwell, Cowhig then canvassed the area to assess the possibilities to locate the mission, while finding financial support for himself as chaplain for the De LaSalle Christian Brothers[949] and their students at Cathedral High School, located at 1253 Bishops Road in Los Angeles.[950] He had two rooms on the top floor of the school.[951]

---

young Catholic teachers and gave active support to Chiang Kai-shek's government. He spent the years of World War II in the United States. The Imperial Japanese army had offered a substantial reward for his capture. Some of his speeches and writings were printed in the United States at the end of the World War II. See *Eyes East: Selected Pronouncements of the Most Reverend Paul Yü-Pin* (Patterson, JN: St. Anthony Guild Press, 1945). Raymond J. De Jaegher, *Life of Archbishop Paul Yü Pin* (Saigon, Free Pacific Editions, 1959).

[948]   Permission for a missionary society to enter the diocese was a delicate matter at the time. On the one hand, "the Passionists from China and Maryknoll refused to do this work [mission to Chinese in Los Angeles] with the excuse that there was no prospect to such an undertaking." On the other hand, the archbishop's sister, Ursuline Mother Regis, remarked that "the reason he [the Archbishop] did not want [the Columbans] in the archdiocese previously was (quote): 'I did not want two robbers in the diocese—one Maryknoll was bad enough.'" John Cowhig, "Report, Chinese Language School," Catholic Chinese Social Center, c. 1948. Columbans in Los Angeles: Chinese Center, 8.A.48. In other words, the archbishop thought that missionary societies would be more interested in seeking funds for their seminaries than in assisting in the ministry. Regional Superior Waldron suggested ways for Cowhig to address the fact that Columbans desired to serve the Chinese people and had extensive background to do so. See Waldron to Cowhig, 6 August 1940, *Casey History* (1940), 5.

[949]   This congregation of Brothers is known by several names: Brothers of the Christian Schools, the Christian Brothers, and the De La Salle Brothers. Cathedral School was located on the site of the Old Calvary Cemetery. The Brothers started teaching first with a seventh and eighth grade group of boys in Lincoln Heights, added a ninth grade the next year and for the 1925/26 academic year moved to the Bishops Road site.

[950]   A popular narration of the history of the Chinese Catholic Center is found in Editor, "Chinese Blossoms," *FE* (July 1942), 12–14, and Ann James, "Chinese Yanks at Queen Mary's Court," *St. Joseph Magazine* (December 1944), 2–3, 13. See also, Patrick O'Connor, "Christ in Chinatown," *FE* (April 1945), 12–14.

[951]   Father Joseph Crossan (1891–1974) who served in China from 1920–1939, was working with the Chinese in Los Angeles [not clear what dates]. He lived at the Brothers' school and assisted Cowhig periodically, but as soon as the Columban

Cowhig described three Chinatown sections in Los Angeles. District 1 was "New Chinatown, situated on North Broadway. District 2 was China City, situated on New High Street, North Spring Street, Main and Los Angeles Street. District 3 was located on San Pedro Street, between Ninth and Thirty-Fifth Streets." He indicated that the "better class Chinese" and merchants lived in New Chinatown, where the Center would be started. Cowhig observed of the Chinese in that area, "In many respects, they are more difficult to influence, but once their confidence is gained, they are the most loyal and sincere." The Chinese who lived on San Pedro Street, he noted, "mix and intermarry with Mexicans, colored people, and white, and thus are not as influential among the Chinese as are those of New Chinatown."[952] Cowhig also described the areas in terms of Protestant influence: Presbyterian and Nazarene Churches were on the East side; the Congregationalists were in the vicinity of Ninth Place and San Pedro Street; and the Old and New Chinatown were under Methodist influence.[953]

As Cowhig walked through the streets, he found it challenging to gain people's trust. He observed discrimination against Catholics from Protestants, who were successfully making conversions among Chinese, the spirit of what he called "the materialistic education of the public schools,"[954] and hindrance from a Catholic group, he considered "political." He appreciated the "Old China" spirit that he observed among elderly Chinese: "religious minded, sincere Buddhists, who have a great love for family life." Cowhig remembered Francis Xavier's axiom regarding the Chinese: "You must first go in their door before they will come in yours. You must first prove yourself to the Chinese before they will respond. Once their confidence has been gained, they are most responsive and loyal."[955]

Cowhig found an invaluable ally and friend in Dr. Stanley H. Chan (Chan Shau Hong), at the time a lecturer in Oriental Studies at the Protestant Claremont and Pomona Colleges in California.[956] Cowhig contacted Chan

---

rented a house in Los Angeles on E. Twentieth Street, he moved there. Crossan had to leave the United States toward the end of 1942 for about a year because he was in the United States on a Visitor's visa. He went to Canada. Gerard Marinan, "The [Columban] Society in Los Angeles," 3. CFA-USA. Marinan wrote a monthly "Colum's Corner" and "Pudsy Ryan's Diary" in the *Far East* for twenty years.

[952]   John Cowhig, "Report, Chinese Language School," Catholic Chinese Social Center, c. 1948. Columbans in Los Angeles: Chinese Center, 8.A.48.

[953]   John Cowhig to Archbishop McIntyre, c. 1948. 8.A.48

[954]   John Cowhig, "Report, Chinese Language School," c. 1948.

[955]   Ibid., Cowhig also noted that the Protestant churches were financed by American missions and supervised by a Chinese minister.

[956]   Chan received a master's degree from Stanford University, was working on his doctorate in political science, and had previously taught at Peking University. Chan

and asked his cooperation to "get into the Chinese doors," and offered him a meager hundred dollars a month. Chan remarked that he needed to keep his position at the colleges in order to support his family. As these negotiations were under way, Chan and his family decided to learn more about Catholic life, took instructions, and were baptized. When that took place, the two colleges would not allow him to teach for them.

At great sacrifice for himself and his family, Dr. Chan continued the mission with Cowhig in Los Angeles. With the small salary from the mission and just twenty dollars from the archbishop, but with permission secured for the Columbans to appeal in churches for financial support,[957] Chan and Cowhig began a Chinese Language School, or "The Mission," as Cowhig called it, in New Chinatown in 1940 on North Figueroa Street. While people were wary of a Catholic priest, the Chinese respected the educational leadership that Professor Chan provided in the city. Chan directed the school at "Our Lady's Chinese Center," his wife was a teacher, and Cowhig was appointed chaplain. Cowhig obtained some local aid through the Coordinating Council of the City of Los Angeles and "persuaded" the Ladies Auxiliary of the Ancient Order of Hibernians, to sponsor the endeavor."[958] The Catholic Church Extension Society, through a donation of a Mr. Mulcahy, provided a good portion of the monies toward building expenses. The building was renamed St. Bridget's Center, in honor of Mulcahy's mother (Bridget). In addition to serving as a language school, the Center was used as a recreational hall and small church. To attract new members, classes in English were taught, "so necessary for the Chinese housewives who must deal with the various storekeepers in a foreign tongue."[959]

Cowhig noted, "The Church in Los Angeles was accused by the Chinese of being Pro-Japanese. Many and not a few of the influential people believed this. By associating with the children and with the influential Chinese, plus the great prestige of Dr. Chan as an educator, we were soon able to win their confidence and respect."[960] The first Mass was celebrated at the Center on Christmas,

---

had a brother who taught at Stanford University and another brother who took Stanley's place at the two colleges.

[957] Once the school opened, Cowhig gave Chan all the tuition money. During Chan's work with the Chinese Academy, he taught Oriental Studies and Political Science at Loyola University in Los Angeles, thanks to the influence of Father Cowhig. Chan later became Chair of the Political Science Department at the University.

[958] *St. Bridget's Catholic Chinese Center, Golden Jubilee, 1940–1990* (Privately Printed), 14. Cowhig listed an overview of the four language schools of the Protestants and the Chinese Six Company (three schools) in the districts. See, John Cowhig, "Report, Chinese Language School," Catholic Chinese Social Center, c. 1948.

[959] [John Cowhig, no date, but written in 1948]. CFA-USA, 8-A-48, 117.

[960] Cowhig's account in *Casey History*, "Events in 1941," 9.

1940, classes started in March 1941. The Center was officially dedicated June 7, 1942, in an elaborate celebration attended by over 700 people, 300 of them Chinese.[961] The Center was given an exquisite banner of the Good Shepherd, painted by an eminent Catholic Chinese painter, Chang Shan-tse, a convert to the Catholic faith.

Father John Cowhig pointing out features of Chang Shan-tse's painting to students at the Chinese Catholic Center. (CFA-USA)

Chang and his wife were baptized in 1938, having been converted through the work of Bishop Paul Yü Pin. In 1939 the couple came to the United States where Shan-tse's paintings were exhibited at the World's Fair in New York, and at some point he joined the bishop for some of his journey through the United States. Chang became known as the "Tiger Artist," due to the use of the tiger, rather than the traditional dragon, to depict the new Chinese spirit. He used his artistic gift for evangelization, in his portrayal of Catholic themes in a Chinese style with Jesus depicted with Chinese features.[962]

---

[961]   Dr. Chan was one of nine people who was confirmed at the dedication.

[962]   Chang gave two water colors to Fordham University, each valued at $5,000 at the time. One of them was a "Christ the Good Shepherd." For background on the artist, see Paul Yü-Pin, "Chang Shan-Tse Rests in Peace," *America*, 64 (1940), 286–287. Chang died in 1940.

Sisters Assist with the Mission among the Chinese

Cowhig invited the Immaculate Heart Sisters, who had conducted a summer school for Chinese children at Queen of Angels Grammar and High School, to teach English to the students at the Chinese Center, and the Sisters did so for eight years.[963] The Catholic China Academy, a name suggested by Dr. Chan, began with five children and grew to one hundred, with students attracted from the patriotic and Protestant schools because of Dr. Chan's scholarship and reputation. Cowhig noted that initially, "they were very much opposed to me as a priest."[964]

Cowhig was concerned about prejudice on either side between Chinese and other groups in the area. His remarks, spoken in Mandarin at the dedication ceremony, reflected the theme. "The spirit of the world always has been selfishness and hatred. The spirit of China always has been fraternal friendship and this friendship has been universal in spirit and beautifully expressed by Confucius when he says, 'within the seven seas, all are brethren.'"[965]

Later, Cowhig remarked that at the Center, where there was a "complete Chinese atmosphere and they feel perfectly at home," the same Chinese children in public schools "feel an inferiority complex, and as a result, they do not associate or play with other pupils. They positively do not mix with Mexicans and for that reason I have absolutely failed to get them to attend the neighboring Catholic Plaza School."[966]

He attempted to diffuse the prejudice. One way came through their singing, dancing, and dramatic groups to provide entertainment for a wide spectrum of the city. Audiences ranged from public school teachers, people at War Bond rallies, audiences at Immaculate Heart College, and citizens listening to them perform on the steps of City Hall. Classes in Dramatics and Dancing were conducted by Sister Mary Noemi Crews and a student from Immaculate

---

[963]   Interest grew in the Center and among those who became benefactors were volunteers from Immaculate Heart College and Immaculate Heart High School, Bing Crosby, Charles Skouras, who was the president of Fox-West Coast Theaters, and Mr. and Mrs. Chadwick Woo. Volunteers from Immaculate Heart College assisted with children in weekend or summer programs. For photos of the Catholic Chinese Center, see Jenny Cho and Chinese Historical Society of Southern California, *Chinatown and China City in Los Angeles* (Mt. Pleasant, SC: Arcadia Publishing, 2011), 97–99.

[964]   John Cowhig, "Report, Chinese Language School," Catholic Chinese Social Center, c. 1948. Columbans in Los Angeles: Chinese Center, 8.A.48.

[965]   John Cowhig to "My dear Paddy" [Columban Father Patrick O'Connor], 8 June 1942. 8.A.48.

[966]   John Cowhig, "Report, Chinese Language School," Catholic Chinese Social Center, c. 1948. See also, John Cowhig to Very Reverend Timothy Connolly (Columban regional superior) 9 February 1948.

Heart College.[967] Sister Mary Noemi had been a professional actress prior to her entrance to the convent and taught English and Public Speaking at the college. The student, "a Miss Eugenia Puchinelli, a girl of great talents and wonderful apostolic zeal," had prepared the young people for these public performances through her dancing classes. Cowhig attributed the success of the American–Chinese War Bond Drive to her able talents in directing the children.[968] In the summer, a man was hired to coach basketball teams, which ended up being Chinese, American, and Mexican.

Sister Candida Wei, the first Chinese Sister to enter the Sisters of Social Service, worked at the Center from 1942–1946 and from 1958–1961. She taught catechism classes, was in charge of the choir, and organized a Girls' Club and a Mothers Club in the 1940s. The latter group sewed for the refugees in China, as well as for the needs of the Center and chapel. Young married women, American born Chinese, formed a Mandarin club, where the women discussed Chinese culture and that of other nations and studied Mandarin, under Sister Candida's instruction.[969]

For some years, the Center also had a grade school, conducted by a Sister of the Immaculate Heart of Mary community and two lay teachers, one of them Chinese. With the school gaining more students, Cowhig sought permission from the new archbishop, James McIntyre, to build a four-room school. The prelate, who had come from the Archdiocese of New York, was not familiar with the local Chinese situation and he denied the permission. With the great demand for Sisters in an archdiocese expanding quickly with new immigrants,

---

[967] An informative overview of the Catholic Chinese Center is found in Sister Noemi Crews and Timothy Chan, "A Pictorial History of the Catholic Chinese Center in Los Angeles Chinatown, 1940–1990, *Gum Saan Journal* 13 (June 1990). Copy provided to the author, courtesy of Sister Anna Maria Pierto, IHM, Archivist, Encino, California. Cowhig instructed Sister Noemi in 1942 simply to sit on the porch, as the children walked to language school. Her partner for the summer was Sister Francella. "A few courageous youngsters came in after language school to make our acquaintance." Sister Francella taught piano and Sister Noemi started a dramatics class. Ibid., 5. Through Sister Noemi and her sister, Sister Joseph, also a former actress, several other former actors helped out the Chinese Catholic Center in various ways.

[968] See, also, Thomas W. Kilsaw, Director, National Origin Groups to Archbishop J. J. Cantwell (n.d., but in June 1945). By 1946, the Language School, located on the East side of town on East Twenty-Second Street, was under the supervision of a Mr. T. M. Ching, whose father was Minister to Mexico and at the time of Cowhig's letter, the Minister to Chile. John F. Cowhig to Fr. De Persio, 10 January 1946.

[969] Information from a report of the work of the Sisters of Social Service among the Chinese in Los Angeles. Original in Archives of the Sisters of Social Service. Copy in Archives of the Columban Fathers, "LA Chinese Center, 1948." 8-A-48.

the Immaculate Heart Sister was needed elsewhere. The Academy closed in 1951 and Cowhig retired in 1954.[970]

The Center expanded in other directions when Columban Father Anthony O'Doherty (1904–1979) was appointed to the Center. O'Doherty had served in Kienchang and Nancheng (Nanjing) from 1934 until 1947. He was tapped by 20th Century Fox for their film, *The Left Hand of God*, starring Humphrey Bogart, who impersonated a fictitious Father O'Shea, killed in war time China. O'Doherty was on the Hollywood set for about six weeks in 1954 providing technical and other advice. The movie was based on a book of the same name, written by William E. Barrett (1900–1986), who later wrote, *The Red Lacquered Gate*, the history of Bishop Galvin and the early days of the Columbans. [971]

O'Doherty made visits to homes and work places of the community, directed them toward services they needed, and encouraged them in Catholic practice. The work was furthered after his request to the Sisters of Social Service to serve the mission. Sister Candida Wei returned to the Center from 1958–1961. Sister Angelia Ying, born into a Catholic family in Beijing, had heard of the mission the Sisters had opened in Shanghai. After a visit there, she began her Novitiate with the Sisters of Social Service in Los Angeles in 1947, with the hope of returning to work in China. But her superior asked her to serve at St. Bridget's Chinese Center in 1954.[972]

A look at one of the annual reports Sisters Candida and Angelia sent to their religious superior provides an overview of their work and their context. Father O'Doherty had requested Sister Angelia to "assist the Mission" in order to "bring the Chinese people into the Church," as well as to have them appreciate their culture. She indicated that "little is known about Father's views and attitudes. Father has but little time to give to the Center for he seems to be always in a hurry to get away." Therefore, she was "left to her own initiative to see what is to be done." She characterized him as "not aggressive and not very vocal." The only conferences the Sisters had with him were for new programs or modifications of existing programs, though even after the conference, "he doesn't help with what is to be done."[973] Perhaps his advisement to the film people was a partial reason for his disposition, at least in 1954. When he was away, other Columbans came to say Mass and for almost a year, Columban

---

[970] Cowhig moved to Colorado Springs, Colorado and became a well-known amateur astronomer. He had a large sophisticated telescope near the property where he retired.

[971] William E. Barrett, *The Left Hand of God* (New York: Doubleday, 1951); William E. Barrett, *The Red Lacquered Gate* (Sheed and Ward: NY, 1967).

[972]

[973] Sister Angelia (Ying), SSS, annual report, 1958. The use of a car was included in the Sisters' annual contract, in order to visit the Chinese in their homes and places of work.

Father Leo Lyons (1917–1988), "well-liked by young and old," worked with the Chinese.[974] Lyons had returned from the Philippines in 1949 in ill health and was recuperating in Los Angeles at the time.

Father O'Doherty wanted to begin the Legion of Mary among the Chinese and asked the Sisters to organize the ministry. As Sister Candida began to realize, they could not do so unless they began with leaders who were "communion rail" Catholics—i.e., practicing Catholics. The Sisters knew it was not yet the moment to begin the Legion, and "Father was appeased of the thought for the moment." Other things needed to happen first. Some of the women and older men did not speak English and "found life hard to go about." Father O'Doherty did not "have any specific work outlined" for her, so she organized English classes, where the lessons to "young and old and in between" were explained first in the Chinese dialect and then taught in English. She "began to know her people, and the people began to know her, her religion and so forth." Sister Candida wrote to her superior, "To teach English is not the basic work of a Sister of Social Service but working among these people, one has to get them interested in something they have an interest in. It is always at the back of one's mind of what is the principle a Sister would really wish to teach; however, one has to use means to reach the end. The means is English, the end is Catechism."[975]

Sister Angelia did most of the family visits. The Legion of Mary eventually did begin at the Mission. The two Sisters taught catechism in Chinese in people's homes and at the Center, taught crafts classes, organized young adult choirs, began annual parish festivals, Altar Societies, provided Chinese culture classes for children and offered other ways for Chinese Catholics to socialize, while at the same time having the people assume more responsibility for the church. An annual bazaar in the summer brought together many Chinese from around Los Angeles and was attended by the Columbans in the Los Angeles area. A Chinese luncheon, Chinese games, and many gifts donated by Chinese merchants, not only became an important social event for all the Chinese in Los Angeles, but it also "brought a pretty good income to cover the church expenses."[976]

---

[974] Sister Angelia Chieh-Liang Ying, "Memoir of My Work at the Catholic Chinese Center, Los Angeles," May 2014. Document provided to author through auspices of Sister Theresa Yih-Lan, SSS, Taipei, Taiwan, May 2014.

[975] Sister Candida (Wei), SSS, annual report, 23 July 1958. During this time, Sister Candida spent a year as a Parish Social Worker in Oakland, California, across the Bay from San Francisco.

[976] Sister Angelia Chieh-Liang Ying, SSS, "Memoirs," provided to author through auspices of Sister Theresa Yih-Lan, SSS, Taipei, Taiwan, May 2014.

Growth of St. Bridget Catholic Center and
Final Years of Columban Presence

Father Matthew Quinn (1918–2007) was the third and last Columban who served the people at St. Bridget's Chinese Center from 1963–1980. He had been missioned to China in 1946 by way of Shanghai and Hanyang, where, in July 1947, Bishop Galvin assigned him to Yo Pa, a village with several mission stations in other villages, and a church without a priest since the Japanese invasion in the late 1930s. After a few months, the area became unsettled with frequent rumors of bandits in the area. With the situation becoming more restless in early 1948, he and the less experienced missionaries were sent to Columban headquarters in Hanyang. Within a month, the Nationalist armies collapsed around Peking (Beijing) and Galvin sent the newer missionaries to Shanghai, with hope that the situation would change for the better. Three of the newer missionaries, including Quinn, were seriously ill and were sent to the United States. Quinn made his way to the Columban house on Elden Avenue in Los Angeles, where John Cowhig visited from time to time.

After a few short term commitments in Brooklyn, Silver Creek, and Chicago, and recuperation from an operation and the return of tuberculosis, Quinn was assigned to the Chinese Center in Los Angeles in 1963. He found that he was performing marriages of the children that John Cowhig had baptized. Columban Sisters Teresita Yu, a Chinese from mainland China, and Rita Geraghty, served the Chinese community in the 1960s, with visitation of people in their homes and with music lessons and music groups, respectively. Quinn also observed that the Center physically was "run down"[977] and the Chinese were becoming indifferent about its condition, yet they still desired a "place." So Quinn said to them, "If you want a place, you have to help me build it." The people built a kitchen, extended the building, put in a new altar," and that "made them feel good about it. . . . They thought that I was great, but they did it all themselves with very little help from the diocese." Periodically, the Columban regional superior inquired whether Quinn wanted any monetary assistance for the work in the Chinese Catholic Center. Quinn thought the offer generous but he considered it ironic that the Columbans would help out a Chinese parish for his sake "in one of the richest dioceses in the country" and the "powers that be in the city weren't too interested."[978]

---

[977]   Father James McCaslin interview of Father Matthew Quinn, 22 May 1987. Columban Oral History Archive, Dalgan Park. Quinn was chaplain to the students and to the Brothers, in addition his pastoral duties at the Chinese Center.

[978]   Ibid., The archbishop at the time would have been James Cardinal McIntyre, who was archbishop of Los Angeles from 1948–1970.

The Center grew from about forty families when he arrived to 250 families when he left. With a population increase through immigrants from Hong Kong with few resources, Quinn found they came to him with their needs. In a typical day, after saying Mass for the Brothers, Quinn would visit the Chinese in their homes, perhaps take care of a task related to the Brothers' school, contact the St. Vincent de Paul Society for items for the new immigrants, and then after supper, visit people in their homes. A Sister of Social Service came on Saturday for religious education classes. After she left, the Columban Sisters helped with classes. There were about fourteen students in class, and at one point lessons ceased. But then, a Sister of Social Service, not knowing that Quinn needed help, knocked on the Center's door. "Father, we would like to help you." And the Sisters of Social Service continued to work at the Center at least until 1987.

The Center also expanded through the efforts of American/Chinese "oldtimer, Mrs. Fong," and some of the older ladies. "The women particularly were a great force, because they brought a lot of their goodness with them and they brought their families with them." Many of the women were widows. "But their children, some of them, the newer breed of Chinese, were beginning to assert themselves because they were highly educated and they belonged to the Church. Now they know what the Church is all about and they can do it a lot easier than the old folks."[979]

Quinn "enjoyed nineteen happy years" at the Center, and, as he reflected back on life with the Chinese, he remarked that "he would have put more pressure on the diocese [Archdiocese of Los Angeles] to do more for the community." While he never became proficient in Chinese, he "would take their worries, their anxieties, and their cares, and worry about them and [I] would pray about them." He thought, "Maybe I was better off not to know Chinese [too well], then I wasn't going to brush them off. I was extending myself, in other words." He was "very grateful that the Columbans sent me to Los Angeles."[980] In his last year at the Center, the Human Relations Council of Los Angeles gave public recognition to "the perfectly empathetic Irish pastor" for his service to the entire Chinese community.[981] After almost twenty years, the task became

---

[979]   Ibid.

[980]   Ibid., From the start of the Catholic Chinese Center, the Columbans' intention was to "hand back" the administration and direction of the Center. The contract between the Columbans and the Archdiocese was formally terminated on 1 March 1980. In 1977, Quinn had requested that the Columbans find a replacement for him, "not because I'm tired or bored with the place. God has blessed my life here in many ways, but I feel that the mission is ready to take off in a new direction with younger and bolder visions." Quinn to "Dear Charlie [probably Coulter, Regional Director] 16 August 1977.

[981]   Sister Noemi Crews and Timothy Chan, "A Pictorial History of the Catholic Chinese Center in Los Angeles Chinatown, 1940–1990, *Gum Saan Journal* 13 (June 1990), 20.

too much for Quinn. At age sixty-two he served in a Hispanic parish for three years and then in other parishes in the Archdiocese of Los Angeles for thirteen more years.

Through the combined efforts of the Columban priests, the Sisters of Social Service, the Immaculate Heart of Mary Sisters and their students, the Sisters of St. Columban, Chinese Catholic laity, and donors, the Catholic Chinese community had become known in Los Angeles. Converts with Chinese cultural roots found their spiritual home in Catholic life at St. Bridget's Catholic Center. After Quinn moved from the Center,[982] the work was carried forward under the direction of Father Peter Tsang (1980–1991), an ex-Salesian priest and native of Shanghai, who spoke Cantonese, Mandarin, and English. The Columbans, whose first mission was China, had served the Chinese in Los Angeles for forty years.

Columbans and the Filipino Apostolate

Origins of the mission

The mission of the Columbans among Filipinos in Los Angeles began with a visit to a lonely, sick Filipino, Francisco Velasco, who had a lengthy stay in Ward 6000 of the General Hospital of Los Angeles. He came to the city from Chicago looking for work, was injured in a work related accident and suffered a badly twisted spine. He had few, if any, visitors. When Columbans learned about his plight, they visited him weekly in the hospital, until his death in 1945. Few people were at his funeral because Catholic Filipinos had no place to gather and no way to contact the growing number of Catholic Filipinos in Los Angeles. However, Francisco's desire to help Filipinos was expressed as a self-offering for them. As he said to Columban Father John Daly, "I am offering my suffering for my beloved country and my people and for your success among my people here in Los Angeles."[983]

Boston born James O'Kane (1913–1992), ordained a Columban priest in 1940, had been held back from going to the missions in the Pacific because of World War II.[984] He directed his mission informally among Filipinos in Los

---

982 "The Archdiocese [of Los Angeles] notified us that it was formally terminating our contract with St. Bridget's Chinese Center, Los Angeles. Father Matt Quinn . . . will remain at the Center until it is handed over March 1, 1980. The Archdiocese wants to appoint as administrator a priest who speaks Mandarin and Cantonese." *Columban Newsletter* (November 1979).

983 Francisco Velasco quoted in Edward A. De Persio, "Philippine Island in California," *FE* (July 1945), 8.

984 James O'Kane (1912–1992) was appointed to the Philippines in 1945, where he worked in Luzon and Malate.

Angeles for about a year. The Filipino population at the time was estimated to be between ten and fifteen thousand and most of the organizations directed toward them were run by Protestants. The apostolic delegate, Amleto Cicognani,[985] expressed his concern that someone attend to the spiritual needs of Filipino Catholics, "many of whom were being weaned away from their traditional Catholic faith," with little done to remedy the situation.[986] Archbishop John J. Cantwell and Bishop Joseph T. McGucken[987] expressed a similar concern and encouraged the ministry. The archbishop gave the Columbans permission to start a church for the Filipinos and Father John Daly became the first pastor.[988]

Some background on the situation of Filipinos in California and in Los Angeles might be helpful to understand Filipino circumstances socially, religiously, and legally. By the mid-1940s, Filipino men held mainly agricultural jobs in the Bunker Hill area, were gardeners, or house boys, and lived in the "historic" Filipino town. Filipina women were maids, care givers and nurses. With more men than women living in the area at the time, women sometimes married Anglos, Chinese, Japanese, or "Negroes." A woman so doing was ostracized by the whites and she was forced to mix only with Filipinos. Children born from these marriages also felt discrimination. California state law at the time forbade marriage between Filipinos and people of other ethnic groups. Other discrimination included Filipino men who had served in the U.S. Army and lived in the States could not obtain citizenship in the 1940s. Because of widespread discrimination, Filipinos "developed a complex which they carry even in regard to their Church."[989]

Direction for Mission

This was the local context when Father John Daly (1903–1988) arrived among the Filipinos. He had been teaching mathematics at the Silver Creek seminary since 1924 until his appointment toward the end of 1942. Daly came to Los Angeles for a brief time serving the Filipinos, when he volunteered for

---

[985] Amleto Giovanni Cicognani (1883–1973) was the apostolic delegate to the United States from 1933 to 1959.

[986] Jim O'Kane to "Dear Father," 17 June 1942. CFA-USA.

[987] Bishop McGucken was appointed bishop of Sacramento in 1957 and then as archbishop of San Francisco in 1962.

[988] These facts were reported by Francis Hoza, "St. Columban's Catholic Church for Filipinos, Los Angeles," 30 May 1948.

[989] Francis Hoza, "St. Columban's Catholic Church for Filipinos, Los Angeles," 30 May 1948. For details on California's laws regarding marriage between "whites" and other races, especially from Asia in the 1920s and 1930s, see Leti Volpp, "American Mestizo: Filipinos and Antimiscegenation," *Law Review, UC Davis* 33:795 (1999–2000), 795–834.

the Army Chaplains Corps in 1943. Father Francis Hoza (1916–1987) was then released from parish work in Pasadena to shape the ministry at what would be named St. Columban Parish, Los Angeles. After Hoza's arrival in early September 1943, he went with Daly to meet "Filipinos in key positions and other families who were interested in our work." They also attended gatherings to meet as many Filipinos as possible, "but what was more important, the people who met me would remember me when I called at their homes."[990]

Daly wrote to Regional Superior Waldron that it would take Hoza "a long time to get the knowledge of the problems and the conditions as well as to get established to the extent that I have." He further observed, "The work is difficult and it is like nothing else that I can think of. Only a person who has been working with the people can realize how much is to be done and how little can be done for a long time." While Daly had made "a host of friends" among Americans and Filipinos, he could not say "that there are any great results from a religious standpoint."[991]

Daly had opened a Center, "an expensive proposition without much visible results," and Hoza requested that Daly close the Center. Initially, when Hoza visited families and urged them to go to the parish church in their area, he heard about their experience of discrimination. "Many felt they were not wanted in their own church because of their race, and I could not convince them otherwise." Not knowing exactly how to proceed, he did a study of social work among Filipinos, one result of which was that he realized that the Filipinos did not want another social club or organization. Various kinds of social service work set up to assist the group often met with failure.

Hoza had been thinking of a church as a place of identification and formation for Filipinos, a church in "which they would not be strangers, but [a church] that belonged to them."[992] He noted two views about the proposition. Some people thought this would bring together the Filipinos. Others said it would segregate them, "which is the last thing anyone wants to do." Hoza's view

---

[990]   Francis Hoza to Father O'Connor, 22 March 1945.

[991]   John Daly to Father Waldron 1 September 1943. A three-page paper, "The Filipino Question," (no author indicated, but probably John Daly), dated c. 1941, provides statistics and information on Protestant national and local organizations that engage Filipinos, including Filipino students enrolled in colleges in the United States and Filipino focused newspapers and magazines.

[992]   Edward A. De Persio, "Philippine Island in California," *FE* (July 1945), 8. Father John Burger has suggested that perhaps Hoza was influenced on the importance of gathering together people from the same language/culture because of Hoza's experience growing up in a Slovak parish (St. Mary's Church) in Uniontown, Pennsylvania.

was that a church would give them prestige and independence in the city," and in the end, few held the opinion that a church would segregate the people.[993]

Hoza later wrote to Regional Superior Waldron that Daly "made it clear to me" that the mission was "to be with Filipinos and their families, no matter what color or race the non-Filipino was—so long as either the husband or wife was Filipino." Hoza further mentioned to Waldron that the archbishop gave Daly "the faculties of a pastor in regard to all these people, without technically being a pastor. But none of these things were put into writing. All were handed down by word of mouth from the archbishop to Father Daly to myself."[994]

In addition to issues related to marriage situations and irregular church attendance among adults, there was the need to educate children in their faith. Without a physical place of some sort, Hoza could not begin classes for them. If they had a church, a place for them to gather, "there would be more chance of parents willingly cooperating in [the education of their children] and once I got the children interested in coming, I figured it would help to bring more of the parents also." He observed that "parents are very much attached to their children and will do what they think is best for them."[995]

Where should a church be located? Hoza surveyed the city and found that Filipinos lived mainly in two districts. While one district had more families than the other, the people were more transient. In the other district, the number of Filipino families was smaller, but families were settled and were large. It was in the latter district that Hoza found a space for the Filipino community to gather. For two years (1945–1946) a dozen families gathered in a leased building (1035 S. Fedora Street).[996] For many years the building was a Japanese school and center. When the U.S. government gathered the Japanese together and sent them to internment camps in the United States during World II, the building was used by a Protestant congregation for a short time. That population dwindled and the building stood vacant.

The rented space would be the start of St. Columban Parish with a ministry to Filipinos. The rented building, while not in the best condition but "respectable enough," had a large hall with a stage. The enterprising Hoza constructed a platform and steps in front of the stage and built a Communion rail, "which gives it the appearance of a Sanctuary." There was space in the hall for classrooms as well. The Sunday attendance ranged from seventy-five to one

---

993 Francis Hoza to Father O'Connor, 22 March 1945.

994 Francis Hoza, "St. Columban Catholic Church for Filipinos, Los Angeles," 20 May 1948.

995 Francis Hoza to Father O'Connor, 22 March 1945.

996 This general geographic location might also have been chosen to begin the ministry because it was within walking distance of the original Columban house. Information obtained from Father John Brannigan, 20 November 2014.

hundred people. Special services drew a larger crowd and the church was filled. He realized it would take time to draw the group because they were not used to regular Sunday Mass or were not married in the Catholic Church because of the discriminatory situation they faced in California. But by March of 1945, Hoza could report that the people "are encouraging one another to more frequent attendance at Mass. The non-Catholic wives in several instances have already started to take instructions."[997] Pastor Hoza was busy with baptisms, marriages and funerals. He conducted a choir, instructed converts, held catechism classes for children and prepared to organize some societies in the parish.

To get a glimpse of the "atmosphere" of the community at the time, the story shared by the oldest living member of early St. Columban's parish [2017] when it was located on S. Fedora Street captures the spirit of the community at its inception. Mrs. Janette T. [Santa Cruz] Frye[998] and her sister Mary Elizabeth lived next door to St. Columban Parish in its early years (mid-1940s) when the church was started in the rented building. Because of their proximity, the two young girls spent their days over there when they weren't in school. The sisters and their friends learned to sing all the songs for Sunday and weekday Masses (at that time in Latin), learned other church songs, and enjoyed being together. Father Hoza bought food items at the Safeway store and then made lunch for all of them. She and her sister were baptized in 1949 (technically her sister at St. Columban, she at St. Thomas), because of the "kindness of the [St. Columban] community, its spirit and Father Hoza. I love those people. The parish grounded me in my faith."[999] Janette remembers Father Hoza sawing wood, hammering nails, and working on other phases of shaping the rented building into their church. [Father Hoza] "was truly a priest—caring, a preacher, a teacher."[1000]

Growth of St. Columban Parish

With more Filipinos joining the parish, the Archdiocese then purchased the city's oldest but unused fire station, which was transformed into the Filipino's

---

[997]   Francis Hoza to Father O'Connor, 22 March 1945. The leased building is now home to Newton Academy. The latter information was obtained from Father John Brannigan, 20 November 2014.

[998]   Mrs. Janette Frye now lives in Denver, Colorado, and has been a lay Third Order Franciscan for thirty-eight years. She described the mixed ethnic area as the "working poor" at the time. Children from various ethnic backgrounds went to the same public school. "We were together. World War II helped that integration culturally." Of African American heritage herself, she became knowledgeable about Filipino culture, food, and language growing up in this context. Author telephone interview with Mrs. Janette T. [Santa Cruz] Frye, 21 April 2017.

[999]   Ibid.

[1000]   Ibid.

first church at 125 S. Loma Drive. The property was situated on Crown Hill, the former oil boom area of old Los Angeles.[1001] Again, thanks to Father Hoza's carpentry and construction skills, his "tireless energy and resourcefulness" and the efforts of parishioners "from all walks of life," who pitched in digging sewer lines, pouring concrete floors, painting and decorating the church,[1002] the community had a fitting space to gather for worship and fellowship. The enhancement of the interior and change in the exterior of the building came through various donors. The two small windows in the front of the church building were donated by the "Beachcomber boys," who also made other contributions through "the endless sweat they have uncomplainingly given whenever Father asked for their help, or any time an occasion arose." Mrs. Encarnacion de Leon ("of the prominent LVN Movie Studios"),[1003] Mrs. Vicente Lim, widow of General Lim,[1004] and the families of Vincent Bello, Ralph Peña, Augustine B. Cruz and Mariano R. Gorospe were among the donors of the stained glass windows set into the long sides of the church. The Stations of the Cross were donated by Lady Carrie Estelle Doheny, "wife of the late oil magnate," Edward, and the colonnades toward the back of the altar were from movie star Loretta Young's fireplace.[1005]

The tower, which formerly housed a fire bell, now contained a historically significant bell. Cast in seventeenth century Spain, the bell was recovered intact after World War II underneath the ruins of the destroyed church of Our Lady

---

[1001]   The parish area is part of the designated Historic Filipinotown, declared such in a resolution proposed by Eric Garcetti, former city council member and current Mayor (2014). Information provided by Father John Brannigan, SSC, pastor of St. Columban Church (2014).

[1002]   Teo Alemania, *Silver Jubilee Souvenir Book, 1968*. St. Columban Parish, Los Angeles.

[1003]   The LVN film studio was formed in the Philippines in 1938 by three families: De Leon (L), Villonco (V), and Navoa (N) families and became one of the largest film studies in the Islands. Long-lived and respected actor Leopold Salcedo married Encarnacion de Leon, which brought him to LVN studios.

[1004]   Vicente Lim was the first Filipino to graduate from the U.S. Military Academy at West Point (1914). He was a World War II hero, a brigadier general under General Douglas MacArthur, and survivor of the Bataan March. Unfortunately, he was captured by the Japanese and beheaded, while on the way to join MacArthur in Australia. Vicente's image appears on the Filipino 1,000 peso bill.

[1005]   St. Columban Parish, Los Angeles, *Parish Bulletin*, 11 September 1960. Carrie Estelle Doheny was the second wife of Edward Lawrence Doheny (1856–1935), who drilled the first successful oil well in the Los Angeles City Oil Field on Crown Hill in 1892. He sold his properties in 1902 and moved the oil business to Mexico with his holdings as the Pan American Petroleum and Transport Company. By the 1920s, this was the largest oil company globally. Doheny and Carrie Estelle Doheny were generous philanthropists to Catholic schools and other endeavors. The Doheny Mansion in Los Angeles is currently part of the Mount St. Mary's Doheny Campus south of downtown Los Angeles.

of Antipolo (Patroness of Peace and Safe Voyage) in Rizal Province, Philippines. A member of St. Columban congregation eventually transported the Antipolo bell to the "ex–fire station church."[1006] The first Mass was celebrated in the renovated building on January 1, 1947. St. Columban Church was the first Filipino Catholic Church and probably the last ethnic Catholic Church so designated in the United States. Columbans had contact with Filipinos who were struggling financially and with upper classes of Filipinos, some of whom probably went back and forth to the Philippines.

Father Gerald Byrne, SSC (1910–1972), who had served in the Philippines from 1939 through World War II, followed Hoza as Pastor of St. Columban Church in 1949. Byrne acquired the house next to the original small church to serve as a rectory and gathering space for parish organizations. Byrne observed that "that parish is the most successfully run organization of any kind among Filipinos in the U.S., whether religious, civic, or political."[1007] With the parish growing, property was purchased adjacent to the fire station. The next Pastor, Father Patrick Dermody (1898–1990), had been a missionary in China from 1924–1951 and after four years in Utah, the missionary was assigned in 1957 to serve St. Columban Church and remained with them until 1973.[1008] During his pastorate a new church was constructed on the property, which had more space after the demolition of the "firehouse church." Money for the building was raised through pledges, donations, Filipino feasts with food, dance and music, benefit teas and luncheons, bazaars and many other activities that brought in needed finances while at the same time were opportunities for the community to interact and work together for their church. The congregation celebrated the first Mass in the new church on September 10, 1967. Among the fine murals in the church is one of the beloved culturally and religiously significant Santo

---

[1006] Information about the bell given by Fr. Patrick Dermody, SSC, Pastor, to "Friends of St. Columban." 30 June 1968 and from Teo Alemania "Brief History" in the *Silver Anniversary Souvenir.* In both accounts, it is not clear whether Dermody or Byrne purchased the property for the Archdiocese, though it appears that Byrne did so. Comparison of the 1925 photos of Engine Company No. 58, 137 South Loma Drive with photos of the 1960 St. Columban Church reveal a considerable change to the exterior of the building, with possible addition of square feet to the building. The address for St. Columban Church on a 1960s parish bulletin indicates the address is 129 S. Loma Drive.

[1007] *NCWC News Service,* 19 March 1951. Not title.

[1008] For a brief time in 1957, Father Leo Lyons (1917–1988) of Providence, Rhode Island, served the parish, but had to withdraw due to illness. After his ordination in 1943, he was in the Philippines from 1945 until 1949. He left the country affected by tuberculosis for much of his life. He spent most of his active ministry in Los Angeles area parishes, particularly Blessed Sacrament, Westminster.

Niño de Cebú (Holy Child).[1009] During his pastorate, Father Dermody was able to clear the debt accrued in building the church.

Over the years, the parish had the challenge of living in a sometimes difficult neighborhood. The large Belmont High School was across the street.[1010] Students drifted over to the church and stole from the poor box a few times, the church building was defaced, and other acts of disrespect or vandalism took place.

In the mid-1980s, Father Paul O'Malley, who had just come from a six-year experience of Team Ministry in Norwich, Connecticut, brought to the Filipino community some of the emphases of continued renewal after the Second Vatican Council. During his pastorate from 1983–1985, he started a parish council, after he brought speakers from Loyola Marymount College to present ideas on Vatican II and parish life. The Council also provided emphases on a renewed Order of Permanent Diaconate. The parish had a "wonderful permanent deacon" who was in the first class of deacons during Father Dermody's time and who still served the community during Father O'Malley's pastorate. Previously the deacon had worked as chaplain at a Long Beach hospital. Lay leadership was also demonstrated through a large, inspirational youth choir, a thriving Legion of Mary,[1011] whose members were also active parish leaders. Laity provided religious education for public school children on Saturdays. When O'Malley came to the parish, there were just two Eucharistic ministers and a few readers. He opened a program to train more people in both ministries.[1012]

The Los Angeles riots in March 1992, affected the people in Koreatown more than the Filipinos in the city, but the turmoil happened while Father Stephen Kealy (1924–2007) was pastor from 1989–1994. Some of the

---

[1009] The vested statue was given in 1565 to Queen Juana of Cebú, when she was baptized by Magellan's chaplain.

[1010] The land on Crown Hill was the site of many oil wells after Edward Doheny's successful oil well drilling in that area. The site, now with abandoned oil wells, which had often been placed cheek by jowl, the decrepit Belmont Hotel, and a somewhat functioning pumping plant for the Los Angeles City Oil Field, was purchased by the Los Angeles Board of Education in 1921. "At one time the Belmont High School, built in 1923 on the site of the former Belmont Hotel, was considered to be the largest public school in the United States." Quotation from Father John Brannigan, SSC, the present pastor of St. Columban Church (2014). Among the famous graduates of the high school are actors Ricardo Montalbán, Anthony Quinn, and Catholic actor and producer, Jack Webb, famous for his portrayal as Sargent Joe Friday on the television show, *Dragnet*.

[1011] The Legion of Mary had a weekly well organized "Adorers" group, who maintained an all-night vigil before the Blessed Sacrament.

[1012] *Those Who Journeyed with Us, 1918–2010* notes that Boston native, Father Patrick Lavin was pastor of the Filipino parish in 1988, though he died suddenly on 18 April 1989. He had been a missionary in Mindanao from 1950–1969.

parishioners were not strangers to him. Kealy kept in touch with students he knew in the Philippines and, as it turned out, some of his former students in Manila were now in his Los Angeles parish. One former student became the wife of the parish council president (Mrs. Ned Pascua). Kealy, who "enjoyed everywhere [he] went, the people, and the different nationalities," was familiar with the social dimensions of Christianity. He had attended the key meeting in Rome on lay mission in 1951, engaged in leadership training of young adults through Student Catholic Action in the Philippines and was Chaplain of the University of the East in the 1950s.[1013]

Archbishop Roger Mahony who was particularly aware of the needs of the diverse Catholic population in his Archdiocese, made his first visit to St. Columban Parish and Filipino Center to administer the sacrament of Confirmation upon parishioners in May of 1990.[1014] On a practical level, the spot where the former fire station stood, Kealy built a rectory, which was begun in 1991 and completed in 1992.

A joyous event occurred during the pastorate of Father Robert Conley (1930–1999).[1015] A replica of the revered statue of Our Lady of Antipolo (Our Lady of Peace and Good Voyage) was visiting Filipino communities across the country headed to its final destination in the National Shrine of the Immaculate Conception in Washington DC.[1016] There it would be enshrined

---

[1013] Quotation from Fr. Michael Harrison interview of Father Stephen Kealy, Los Angeles. 25 January 1992.
For mention of Kealy and leadership of Catholic students in the Philippines, see, Eamonn Byrne, *Columbans in Student Catholic Action. Philippines, 1937–2007* (Manila: Ample Printing Press, 2007), 80–83 and 277. Columban E. J. McCarthy founded the organization in 1935 in Manila and remained its director until 1939. For his talks given in person and on the radio to the Student Catholic Action, see E. J. McCarthy, *Radio Sermons* (Manila: Student Catholic Action, 1938). In 1957, there were 166 Columban priests who were working in the Philippines. Four of them directed the work of more than 20,000 students in SCA in the Archdiocese of Manila. *Mission Bulletin* (1958), 748. The Columbans had a large commitment to the Philippines with over 220 Columbans serving various dioceses at one time.

[1014] Mahony had learned to speak Spanish from the Mexican workers he knew who were employed by his father in the latter's poultry processing business.

[1015] Born at Warren, Rhode Island, Conley was appointed to Japan after his ordination at St. Columban's Seminary, Milton, Massachusetts. After promotion work in the United States and mission in the Virgin Islands, he was part of the intentional Team Ministry in Norwich, Connecticut. Conley was the second of the Norwich Team members to pastor the Filipino community in Los Angeles. I have not been able to find the exact dates for Conley's pastorship, but by deduction from many sources, it seems he became pastor starting sometime in late 1993.

[1016] On the incorporation of a multitude of ethnic groups into the National Shrine in Washington DC as part of the heritage of U.S. Catholicism, see, Thomas A. Tweed, *America's Church: The National Shrine and Catholic Presence in the Nation's Capital* (NY: Oxford University, Press, 2011).

in a in a specially designed, Filipino themed small side chapel in the crypt of the Basilica. The visit of the statue to St. Columban parish was particularly festive, as the ceremonies, prayers and music were joined by the voice of the Antipolo Bell in the Church's tower.

After a little over a year as pastor, Father Conley became ill and Father Ronald Kelso, a friend of his, was appointed to the parish in 1995, an assignment that became effective in January 1996.[1017] Born in Philadelphia and ordained in 1973, Father Kelso's mission experience was in Japan, so he was not able to speak the Filipino dialects. However, some Filipino priests celebrated Sunday liturgies in various dialects for parishioners. The parish continued to thrive and their well-known St. Columban Choir performed several concerts in Rome. As Kelso noted, "Anything and everything Filipino was active in the parish." During his pastorate, he began a ministry to recent widows and widowers and produced a photo directory of parishioners. "I found [my time in the parish] to be a wonderful experience, and I was able to bring together many factions in my short term there."[1018]

Father Kelso was followed by Father Colm Rafferty as pastor, beginning in 1997. Born in County Derry, Ireland, he worked on the island of Luzon, Philippines, where, in 1990, he had introduced the *Retrouvaille* (Rediscovery), a weekend experience for couples with troubled marriages. As pastor of St. Columban in Los Angeles, his influence spread to other parishes of Filipinos in the greater Los Angeles area, where he often gave talks. As an observer remarked, Father Rafferty's "ministry to Filipinos and Filipino America breaks down barriers, shattering ethnic cultural stereotypes." Filipinos outside of his parish were surprised to hear an Irishman "speaking Tagalog [one of the Filipino languages] with ease."[1019] Father Sean McGrath also resided at the parish, assigned to Promotion for the Columbans. McGrath's imagination and Rafferty's support led to some intriguing fund-raising events to raise money for the education of Filipino seminarians.

The current (2017) Pastor of St. Columban Parish, Los Angeles, Father John Brannigan, had taught in San Vicente Ferrer Major Seminary, Jaro, Iloilo, and engaged in campus ministry in Manila. In the early 1970s when sugar cane workers were protesting for better wages and for respect for their human rights, Brannigan researched the conditions of the workers in terms of making

---

[1017] Father Ron Kelso was appointed to Japan in October 1996, but that became effective in 1997, so Father Kelso served St. Columban Parish for about thirteen months. Dates courtesy of Father John Burger.

[1018] The author is grateful for information on the period obtained by e-mail from Father Ron Kelso, 7 December 2014.

[1019] Father Colm Rafferty is noted in Dominic Pulera, *Sharing the Dream: White Males in Multicultural America* (NY: Continuum, 2004), as a "'white male' who crossed cultural boundaries to communicate well with ethnic groups." 150.

practical some of the social justice principles the students studied in class. When Columbans Brian Gore and Neil O'Brien were in a Negros prison in solidarity with Filipinos arrested in 1983 for trumped up charges that they had killed a municipal mayor and his cohorts, Brannigan became the liaison between the foreign press and those in prison during the time of the trial of the "Negros Nine" in 1983.[1020] Brannigan later was an adviser to the apostolic nuncio in the Philippines (2000–2007).[1021]

As had Father Stephen Kiely before him, Brannigan engaged with Student Catholic Action in the Philippines and provided an overview of that Columban work in a "Summary Report of Columban Involvement in Campus Ministry, from 1976–1983."[1022] He arrived at St. Columban Parish, Los Angeles, in November 2007, and, after a short vacation to see relatives and friends in Ireland, he was installed as Pastor on February 10, 2008. He brought with him decades of experience living in the Philippines in turbulent times and in settings where he was teaching and forming future leaders in the Philippine church.

The demographic situation in the parish had changed considerably over the years, with the movement of Filipinos toward the suburbs. Some longtime parishioners drove twenty or thirty miles for Sunday liturgy, with about 500 people attending weekend liturgies. Wednesday and Friday evening Masses, which are the evenings of a novena and the large Households of Faith (prayer groups) are well attended. Boys and girls up to the age of eighteen form the Knights of the Altar, those who serve Mass. With fewer people living in physical proximity to the church, the parish council became a Group Leaders' meeting.

[1020]   The story is told in chapter 6, "Action on behalf of justice . . . a constitutive dimension of the preaching of the Gospel." Implications and Challenges, 1977–2012.

[1021]   Father John Brannigan correspondence with author, 1 April 2017. In the Philippines, Father also taught in Maryhill School of Theology and the Institute for Formation and Religious Studies, the latter from 1990–2007.

[1022]   Eamonn Byrne, *Columbans in Student Catholic Action, Philippines 1937–2007* (Manila: Ample Printing Press, 2007), 227–239. Brannigan was Chaplain for the National College of Business Administration and the Philippine School of Business Administration from 1976–1983. For an early history, see Victor J. Sevilla, *Guide to Catholic Action in the Philippines* (Pasay City, PI: Pious Society of St. Paul, 1953). Sevilla viewed Catholic Action under the guidance of the hierarchy as a "defense against paganism." Ibid., 26–27. The first National Congress of Catholic Action was held in Manila, in 1925. The Congress showed a church in transition, both with a realization of the key role of laity within the church and society and the necessity to address social evils. However, many old attitudes remained, with a reaction to the potential of the new by stressing "conservatism, excessive preoccupation with trivial and old-fashioned points of 'morality' (dances, separation of boys and girls in schools), and authoritarian and clericalist attitudes and norms." John N. Schumacher, SJ, *Readings in Philippine Church History* (Quezon City: Loyola School of Theology, Ateneo de Manila University, 1979), 366.

Next Phase of Columban Mission among Filipinos

The Filipino Center at St. Columban Parish is the location of the Santo Niño de Cebú Brotherhood, a type of mutual support society, composed of men and women, who meet regularly and hold a huge annual religious event at the parish, centered on devotion to Santo Niño. Other Filipino groups gather at the Center, though they are not necessarily parish members. Many Filipino Catholics have made their way financially and have moved elsewhere. Other Catholic Churches host Filipinos. Perhaps there will be a new stage in Columban involvement with the Filipino community, given their ministry at St. Columban Parish, Los Angeles.

In the Omaha area in 2016, Father John Comiskey is the formal spiritual adviser to the Filipinos in the Archdiocese of Omaha. Columban Fathers Valentine Kyne and Thomas Shaughnessy assist the Filipino community at times. The Society has contact with them through the Omaha Chapter of the *Cofradia del Santo Niño de Cebu*, the Fil-Am Organization of Greater Omaha, and other groups.

Korean Apostolate in the United States[1023]

Korean Immigrants to the United States

The apostolate with Korean/Korean American communities represented a particular type of cross-cultural experience ecclesiastically, socially, and in structures of "authorization" with respect to Korean and U.S. regional direction. The ministry further raised the question: Should Columban engagement with immigrants in the United States from countries where Columbans were technically "in mission" be considered a valid apostolate in a "home country" of a mission sending group? The answer came from Columban experience beginning in the 1970s and from the 1976 General Chapter statement that

---

[1023] Since 1948, the Korean peninsula has been divided at the 38th parallel into the Democratic People's Republic (North Korea) and the Republic of South Korea. The term "Koreans" is used throughout the chapter to refer to immigrants from that peninsula. I have relied on the helpful background for the development of particular Korean Centers found in the histories of the apostolate as written by Columban Fathers Sean Brazil and Tony Mortell, and the Minutes of the January 11–12, 1982 meeting held in Omaha, Nebraska, with the regional director and the Columbans involved in the Korean apostolate. Information from the latter gathering is found in the *Columban Newsletter* (May 1982). For an insightful overview of the experience of different generations of Korean Americans, see, Simon C. Kim, *Memory and Honor, Cultural and Generational Ministry with Korean American Communities* (Liturgical Press: Collegeville, MN, 2013).

referred to "Reverse Mission." The largest number of Columbans working with ethnic communities in the United States worked with the Korean/Korean American communities.

The Society of St. Columban began their first mission to Korea in 1933. It would be the Columbans who served there so well who assisted Korean immigrants in the United States, especially as the number of Koreans grew by the mid to late 1970s. The presence of Koreans in the United States had been hastened through passage of the 1965 Immigration and Naturalization Act, which replaced a quota system of immigration.[1024] People with skills needed in this country—medicine, science, and technology—were a favored group. The government looked for doctors and nurses to staff city hospitals who served the poor. In 1970 there were 9,314 Koreans entering the United States and six years later, the number grew to 30,803. Considering the robust and lengthy involvement of Columban missionaries in Korea, the Columbans would be a logical group to address the needs of Koreans in the United States.

Columbans became involved in the apostolate in three ways: through Korean invitation, through a bishop seeking to address the needs of Korean immigrants, or through Columban initiative, the last often in conjunction with the first and second approach.

Korean Invitation to Columbans

Father Edward Quinn's story is an example of the first way—the persuasive efforts of Koreans themselves to seek pastoral care. The Korean Catholic Church had grown immensely after the Korean War, due in part to the assistance of the Catholic Church in war-torn Korea and to the work of the Korean Legion of Mary.[1025] Some of those fervent Catholics came to the United States. After twelve years of parish work in Korea, Father Quinn, who grew up in Omaha, Nebraska, was on vacation there. After his visit with his family and friends, he was eager to return to Korea. However, he was appointed vocation director for the U.S. region in 1969 and lived in Chicago. He was also to give mission appeals around the Midwest. By March 1972, he was assigned full time to ministry among the

---

[1024] The first Korean immigrants were sugar cane plantation workers in Hawaii, beginning in 1903, though Hawaii was not yet part of the United States. The second group was mainly "picture brides" or wives of American servicemen who served in the Korean War, 1950–1953. From the Armistice until the Vietnam War, there were roughly 100,000 U.S. servicemen (two army divisions) in Korea. After Vietnam War escalated, Korea still had one division, about 50,000 servicemen and women. In 2016, there are 24,900 U.S. troops in South Korea. *Air Force Times* 6 January 2016.

[1025] The Legion of Mary story is told elsewhere in this book. Aedan McGrath is the Columban most recognized for promotion of the Legion in China.

Koreans in Chicago, even though he tried to convince his superior that other Columbans would be interested.[1026] This is how it happened.

Four Korean Sisters invited Father Quinn to their convent in Chicago for Korean meals and to have him provide them with the sacrament of Penance. The Sisters were in touch with the Korean Catholics in the area and asked whether Father Quinn might celebrate a Mass for the group at the Columban house, located at the time on Hamilton Avenue on the far south side of Chicago.[1027] While the Columban house was large, about 200 Koreans came for Sunday liturgy and the house was packed. Catholic Koreans then "persuaded" Quinn to offer a monthly and then twice-monthly Mass for them at St. Sebastian Church in the northeastern part of Chicago. The group was then invited to have a Center at Queen of Angels Parish in North Central Chicago.[1028] When the parish convent became vacant, Quinn helped to fix up the building. He located beds and other items for the twenty-six bedrooms, in hopes of having boarders. The rent could offset the costs of maintaining the residence part of the building. With the availability of the bedrooms at the Center, Korean immigrants could have a temporary home before they were better situated to go out on their own. Quinn, who was assigned full time to the Korean ministry in March 1972, stayed at the Center and the Korean Sisters cooked and cleaned for him.[1029] English classes were provided and three month courses were given for Korean doctors, pharmacists, and nurses to prepare them for state board exams. In addition to Mass and sacraments, a catechumenate was started. What came to be called the Korean Martyrs Center at 4115 N. Kedvale Avenue, Chicago, was also used by the Korean Association and other Koreans for their functions.[1030]

[1026]   The fact that he was assigned full time to the Korean apostolate is stated on Quinn's personnel file card. Initially reluctant to work with the Korean Catholics, Quinn gave the superior general a list of seven Columbans he thought would be good in the ministry. The superior general's response was, "You do it." Interview of Edward Quinn, 5 April 2012. Quinn was assigned to the Columban Fiji mission in August 1973.

[1027]   Father Joseph McSweeny interview of Father Edward Quinn, 5 April 2012. First interview.

[1028]   The physical locations in Chicago where the Columbans served the Korean community was provided to the author by Father Thomas P. Reynolds.

[1029]   Father Joseph McSweeny interview of Father Edward Quinn, 5 April 2012. First interview.

[1030]   "Much of the success of the apostolate is due to the pastor of Queen of Angels Parish, Father Jim Voss. 'He has never refused us anything we asked and has done much to help integrate the Koreans into the total Christian community,' says Fr. Grady." 17 June 1976. *Casey History* (1976), 5. See also the Columban Press Release 6-17-1976. CFA-USA.

When Father Quinn was missioned to Fiji, Father Francis Grady was assigned to the Korean Martyrs Center.[1031] Grady, a native of Swampscott, Massachusetts, had taken a year of courses in Business Administration at Boston College prior to his entrance to St. Columban College in Milton. He was appointed to Kwang Ju, Korea, in 1968 before his ministry to the Koreans in Chicago began in 1973. Unfortunately, the gymnasium at Queen of Angels Parish, where the Koreans celebrated Sunday Mass, burned down. Cardinal John Cody, archbishop of Chicago, made sure that the Koreans were taken into consideration when he gave money to rebuild the gymnasium, even though some parishioners expressed a dislike of the Koreans. Grady's friend, Father Mort Kelly (1942–1989) was in charge of the Korean Center from 1977–1981.[1032] In 1984, Columbans Charles J. Carolan (1936–2003), Gerald Wilmsen and seven leaders from the Korean community offered a weekend seminar with a Basic Christian Community emphasis. The team repeated the experience for the Korean Catholics in Cleveland. In addition to liturgical services, the Center sponsored neighborhood gatherings for Bible study and prayer and held occasional Marriage Encounter weekends, which were led by a Korean priest and a husband/wife team from Chicago.

In 1990, while Father Charlie O'Rourke was pastor of the Korean Center, the Archdiocese of Chicago expressed interest to have the Koreans and other ethnic groups more integrated into mainstream diocesan wide events.[1033] The following year, O'Rourke celebrated his sixtieth birthday, *Hwangap*, a traditional Korean event to mark a man's "senior" status in the community.[1034] The event also marked the twentieth anniversary of the Korean Center and Auxiliary Bishop Timothy Lyne concelebrated the liturgy. The Korean Catholics

---

[1031] Grady was the first Columban to accompany Korean orphans to the United States in 1972 through the Holt International Children's Services (HICS). Columban Oral History interview with Father Francis J. Grady, 24 August 2011. HICS began in 1955 following the Korean War, after Harry and Bertha Holt petitioned the U.S. Congress to permit the adoption of seven children from Korea. By the early 1980s, Korean attitudes toward the "orphans" changed. Korean adoptions tapered off.

[1032] Father Mort Kelly also made periodic pastoral visits to Korean Catholics in Cleveland, St. Louis, Champaign-*Urbana*, Indianapolis, and eventually, Milwaukee (the latter, from February 1979 to July 1981). The members of the Korean community in Chicago remember Kelly's ability know each member by name. Eventually, Korean communities in Itasca and Rosemont were begun from the Chicago area.

[1033] *Columban Newsletter* (October 1990), 4.

[1034] O'Rourke wrote briefly about his experience in Korea, indicating that "Being available to give hope to the whole person is what Christ was all about when He tried to nourish and heal people's minds and hearts at the same time." Through the goodness of supporters "back home," he could "supply mothers in the parish with sewing machines and with their sewing skills they were able to put food on the table and send their children to school." Charles O'Rourke, "To Follow Him. A Message of Hope for the Future," *Columban Mission* (May 2009), 10–11.

generously provided airline tickets so former Columban pastors could attend the festivities as well.

Bishops' Invitation to the Columbans

The second way the Columbans began to work with Koreans in the United States was through the request of a bishop who knew about the Columban missions in Korea. In 1976, Raymond Hunthausen, archbishop of Seattle, Washington, wrote to Regional Director Charles Coulter: "It occurs to me that the Columbans may have available a priest who has served in Korea, who would be willing to come here to minister to the needs of the Koreans on a more permanent basis."[1035] Hunthausen also wanted Columbans to accept a parish so he could release his diocesan clergy to engage in programs for personal and spiritual renewal after the Second Vatican Council. In the process, the parish would provide an opportunity for the "Columban style of ministry" in a parish [to] be effected. That is, "people could gain a sense of a larger church and a mission spirit," [1036] something the Columban documents referred to as "Reverse Mission."

The Columbans signed a contract with the Archdiocese to work at St. Edward Parish, Seattle, which had a mixed demographic population. The first three Columbans sent to the parish were Richard Parle, who was named pastor, Horacio Yanez, and Thomas Dunne. Shortly after their arrival, Parle began to work with Koreans in the Seattle area. After five years, he resigned as pastor to serve the Korean community full time in the Northwest region of the country, starting in 1981. In the Archdiocese, Parle was also well-known because of his diocesan work on various levels, including the Board of Religious Education and the Diocesan Tribunal. As Korean American Father Simon C. Kim has observed, Parle, who helped rebuild the Catholic Church near the Korean demilitarized zone (DMZ) in his fifteen years in Korea, now worked with Korean immigrants to build their Catholic communities in the United States.[1037] In the process, Parle, who had incardinated into the Archdiocese in 1983, made other Seattle area Catholics more aware of a larger Catholic world.[1038]

[1035]   Raymond Hunthausen to Charles Coulter, 3 December 1980.

[1036]   Information obtained from author telephone conversation with Father Richard Parle, 11 July 2014.

[1037]   Parle's work with and love for the Koreans in the United States was featured in Simon C. Kim, *Memory and Honor, Cultural and Generational Ministry with Korean American Communities* (Liturgical Press: Collegeville, MN, 2013), 66–68.

[1038]   In the Eastern U.S. Father Francis Holecek was assigned to the Korean apostolate for the Archdiocese of New York from 1979 to 1983. After a year or so in Korea, he was then appointed to the USA Korean apostolate and served at St. Gregory Nazienzen, Koreatown, Los Angeles. Fathers Michael O'Loughlin and William

Columban Initiative in Conjunction with First and Second Invitations to Korean Apostolate

California

In November 1978, Father Francis (Frank) Mannion was appointed for a full-time apostolate among the Koreans in the United States. Over his fifty years with this community in Korea and the United States, he would become one of the most influential Columban leaders in the Korean apostolate. He brought over twenty-five years of experience in the Diocese of Chuncheon and the Archdiocese of Seoul, beginning in 1954.[1039] The consequences of many years of war and upheaval in Korea were the loss of five million people through death marches, malnutrition, minimal clothing and shelter, and the dislocation of families. After the "cease fire" in 1953, material assistance began to arrive from the United States through Catholic Relief Services, which, Mannion said, "gave more than all the other societies put together" to assist the people. His early ministry was sometimes related to sacraments and sometimes to food (mainly flour, cornmeal, grains, and powdered milk) and clothing distribution. However, Thomas Quinlan,[1040] who had been released from a North Korean Communist prison in 1953 and was made bishop in the Diocese of Chuncheon, made it clear that the Columbans were not to be thought of as a "relief Society." The primary reason for mission was evangelization and the sacraments, not social work. [1041]

Schmitt celebrated Sunday Mass for Korean Catholics in the Buffalo, New York area. For the pastoral work of Father James O'Brien among Koreans in Connecticut, while doing parish work in Norwich, Connecticut in the mid-1970s, see chapter 7. In 1980, Korean Catholics came for Sunday liturgy to the Derby, New York Retreat House, staffed by Columbans.

[1039] Mannion, from County Galway, was ordained December 21, 1952, and appointed to Korea in 1953. He served in the Diocese of Chuncheon (1954–1955), Seoul (1957–1961), and again in the Diocese of Chuncheon (1962–1967, 1969–1978, with most of the latter time as vice director of the Korea region, before he came to the United States for the Korean apostolate.

[1040] Bishop Thomas Quinlan, SSC (1896–1970), who had been imprisoned during the World War II, was the first superior of the Columbans in Chuncheon. He was named regent of the apostolic delegation in Korea in September 1953 and consecrated bishop in the Seoul cathedral in 1955. He was appointed vicar apostolic of Chuncheon and bishop in that Diocese until 1966. Mannion's impression of Quinlan was that, "like a lot of the priests at that time, they were authoritarian. But he was a great man." Later in the interview Mannion called Quinlan, along with Bishop Harold Henry, and Brian Geraghty, the latter regional superior in Korea, "100% missionaries." Interview #1 with Father Frank Mannion, 1 April 2011. For the history of the Diocese of Chuncheon, see Thomas Stewart, "History of the Diocese of Chun Cheon," typed manuscript, CFA-USA.

[1041] Interview #1 with Father Frank Mannion, 1 April 2011. When Mannion arrived in Korea in 1953, he said there were thirty-three Columbans in the country and when he left in 1978 there were 149 Columbans.

During Mannion's last years in Seoul (1969–1978), Koreans were moving to the capital in large numbers looking for work. The result was a burgeoning city with large areas of poverty and continued displacement of people. New factories grew up (a number of them backed by U.S. investment) in need of cheap labor. Over the years, Korea became more prosperous, though wages in the city remained low, especially for women. Because Mannion had a good eye for property, the archbishop, later cardinal, Stephen Kim Sou-hwan asked him to explore sites for future parishes to serve the large numbers of villagers moving to the city. Frank bought property for a good price for the Archdiocese to begin twenty parishes in Seoul. Though the government had begun with democratic values in the late 1940s, military regimes and dictatorships made life difficult for people after the 1950s. In 1979, President Park Chung-hee was assassinated. It would be during the 1970s that the United States received an influx of Korean immigrants.

In the Diocese of Orange, California, Bishop William Johnson asked the Columban regional director for a priest to serve the Koreans who were arriving in the diocese in large numbers. Frank Mannion was appointed full time to the Korean apostolate there in December 1978. Born in County Galway, Mannion had been a celebrated football player in Ireland. This gave him a certain *cachet*, especially among Irish-born priests, of which there were many in southern California. He began the Korean Martyrs Catholic Center, Westminster, California, and served that community for eleven years. Mannion saw his main work in Orange County as "evaluating new Catholics."[1042] From the Center in Westminster, Mannion traveled to some outstations,[1043] where Korean Catholics gathered for Sunday Mass once a month. One of these stations was in Los Angeles, where, in 1979, Mannion laid the foundation for a Center in Koreatown.[1044] He chose St. Gregory Nazienzen Parish as the location for the Koreans, because he knew the pastor, a former high school classmate from Ireland. The following year, when Father Tony Mortell was assigned to that community, it was designated as St. Gregory Nazianzen Catholic Center.[1045] The

---

[1042] Interview #3 of Father Francis Mannion, 1 April 2011.

[1043] The mission stations were in (San Chung?), San Diego, Las Vegas, and San Bernardino. The Korean community at Westminster split into three communities: Anaheim, Riverside (with a Korean priest, Father Kou), and Las Vegas, which was initially visited once a month by a Columban.

[1044] "Another group of Christians in Los Angeles at St. Gregory Parish, who didn't get along with the league [Legion?] and wanted to have their own place and came after me to get it. I started it for them a year later, with opposition from St. Gregory's, but it was OK. It worked out fine." Interview #2 of Father Francis Mannion 1 April 2011.

[1045] Mortell also initiated Korean Youth Bible Study Groups and Vocation Awareness programs. *Columban Newsletter* (October 1990), 4. While Mortell was pastor at St. Gregory, he divided it downtown and also started a mission in Torrance, California.

Center would have one of the largest Legion of Mary *praesidia* in the United States by the late 1980s. Mortell served that Center for almost eleven years.

By 1989 when Mannion took a short break from the apostolate because of health issues and was assigned to an American parish, twenty Korean Catholic Centers were active and growing in Southern California, some of them begun by the Columbans. Mannion's work with Koreans was legendary, so Koreans invited him to work with their group, which was about seventy strong. A year or so later, when a new center for the "Americans" in the parish was on the drawing board, the pastor suggested the Korean Catholics disband because their numbers were smaller than the "Americans." When Mannion mentioned the situation to the Koreans, they said, "No, we will find another location." They rented a school for Sunday Masses, one in English and one in Korean. After about five more years, thanks to gifts from the Koreans, Mannion purchased a new site and a church was built there."[1046] He noted that "Koreans wanted their own place and didn't want to be mixing up with Americans and be told they were messing up things. The Koreans were prepared to pay for [building new centers]."[1047]

Korean Catholics did not build schools but they came together for Sunday Mass and Religious Education, usually followed by a meal together, socializing, celebrating Korean holidays, and holding other events at the Center. Centers included catechetical programs, bible study, and Korean language classes for children. Shrewd, resourceful, and an entrepreneur, Mannion gave over fifty years of service to Koreans in that country and in the United States.[1048]

Lessons from Mission in Korea

Dublin born, Father Sean Brazil became a runner and golf enthusiast, both of which he continued along with his mission work.[1049] His first assignment, after

---

[1046] Oral History Interview #3 of Father Francis Mannion, 1 April 2011. Mannion said the Society bought the property, but he did.

[1047] Interview #2 of Father Francis Mannion 1 April 2011.

[1048] Two overviews of the history of the Columbans in the U.S. Korean apostolate and issues raised are, Tony Mortell, author of an eight-page document on the history of the Korean American Catholic Community, 1993. No title is given, but page numbers are 9–16. The paper was written for the U.S. Assembly 8–11, 1990. Angelyn Dries received the document from Father Sean Dwan, 26 March 2014. Sean Brazil, "Korean Apostolate, USA), a paper for the U.S. Assembly May 8–11, 1990, 1–7. The Mortell document might have been the document following Brazil's paper, with the hand written "1993" on the first page as incorrect.

[1049] Sean Brazil, "Personal Memoir," 30 November 1997, written on Korean Martyrs Catholic Center, Westminster, California stationery. In Korea, Brazil won the American Express Pro-Am of 1974 with a Taiwan professional golfer, Ku Tchi-Shen. As Brazil humorously noted, the professional "shot a 4-under par 68 and I improved

ordination in 1954 was to Mokpo, Korea, where he served at Holy Cross Parish. Father Thomas Moran had begun the Legion of Mary, which, as noted in an earlier chapter, the Columbans used with great effect.[1050] Brazil remarked that, "in whatever parish I worked in, the Legion of Mary has been my right-hand."

He was appointed to the Huksan Islands off the Mokpo coast in the China Sea. As would become fairly typical in Korean Catholic history, lay people gathered groups together for prayer on Sundays. In the case of Huksan, it was a father and daughter who had fled from North Korea who led the group. Superior General Timothy Connolly made a visitation to the missionaries in the rugged island environment. He asked Brazil and Cornelius Cleary, "What is the most important thing for you two young Irish Missionaries out here in the middle of the China Sea?" Brazil answered, "a solid prayer life to sustain you each day . . . with all its challenges." Cleary responded, "a good grasp of Chinese characters will be most useful to understand the Koreans and their language." Connolly responded, "Both answers are true but the most important thing is to show the people that you really love them, and they will love and respect you." Brazil remarked, "How true."[1051]

Brazil returned to Mokpo as Pastor of Holy Cross Parish (1964–1970), "the years of huge baptisms,"[1052] and then he was appointed to Seoul. With immigrants from villages arriving in great numbers and with demographics changing in Seoul, neighboring parishes gave him lists with names of about 1,200 Catholics who were somehow "lost," either because of moving or were not engaged in the church for various reasons. Within a year Brazil found a thousand of them, in addition to the new Catholics he baptized. After four years in the Archdiocese of Seoul where he began a new parish in the area of Sangbong Tong (St. John the Apostle), he took his vacation in Ireland, and returned to Seoul to start another new parish. His description of those years represents the continued growth of Korean Catholicism in that period. "I was again assigned to an empty field to start another new parish at Chang-Dong (St. Theresa). My first Mass was said in the basement of a vegetable market . . . less than 50 attended. At the end of 4 years we had our Church built and about 2,500 Catholics attending. Today there are two parishes with a total of 13,500 Catholics."[1053]

---

the card by 6 shots due to an eagle 2 on the par 4 hole. SO I HUMBLY SAY I DID NOT WASTE ALL MY TIME IN KOREA WORKING FOR SOULS." Ibid.

[1050] At the time of Brazil's arrival, the Legion of Mary handbook was being translated into the Korean language.

[1051] Sean Brazil, "Personal Memoir."

[1052] Ibid.

[1053] Ibid., While at this parish in Korea, Brazil was on the Director's Council and was elected to the Senate of Priests for the Archdiocese of Seoul, as spokesperson for

New Realities for Koreans in the United States

Father Brazil was assigned to the Korean apostolate in the United States and replaced Frank Mannion at Korean Martyrs Catholic Center, Westminster, in 1989. Brazil observed that Korean immigrants were "faced with the huge problem of their children becoming very Americanized . . . and not really interested in learning the Korean language," a not uncommon issue for the children of immigrants. Brazil saw the work of the Columbans as relating to the adults, given the Columbans' experience in Korea. At the same time Columbans related to the younger generation "and things American." The generation of young people born in the United States, or having coming to the United States as young children, would be a new focus for Columban pastoral care by the early 1980s.

In 1997, as Brazil reflected back on twenty years of growth of the Korean Martyrs Catholic Center, Westminster, he observed that the people's dream at the start was to have one Mass in Korean. "Today twelve Masses are offered in the diocese of Orange in Korean each Sunday. All this is due to the wonderful Korean Catholics, who like their Ancestor Martyrs continue to spread the Good News. It is and has been a joy to journey with them."[1054]

Growth of St. Gregory Nazienzen, Koreatown

Born in County Cork, Father Tony Mortell, who studied at St. Columban's College, Navan, was one of the exchange students to the United States at the Columban Major Seminary, Milton, Massachusetts. Missioned to Korea in 1961 and after a year of language study, Mortell worked in the Archdiocese of Kwangju, where, among other things, he produced a regional magazine, *The Columban Chosen*. The name was probably a play on the word *Chosun* (Korea), wherein he reported happenings of interest to Columbans in Korea. He occasionally wrote poetry, some of which was published in *Columban Mission*. Mortell was appointed to the Korean apostolate in the United States in September 1979, where he began his ministry at St. Gregory Nazianzen, in Koreatown, Los Angeles.[1055] When he arrived, there were sixty Catholics and

---

non-Korean priests. From 1978–1982, Brazil was in Sung-Nam (Diocese of SuWon), where he replaced Frank Mannion, who left for the United States to begin the Korean apostolate in Orange County. After Brazil left the United States, he spent eight years in Ireland in the *Far East* office and was a member of the Regional Council.

[1054] Sean Brazil, "Personal Memoir."

[1055] For a description of the demographic changes in the Los Angeles area where the Columbans began their ministry, see Tony Mortell, 1993, unnamed document on history of Korean America Catholic Community. CFA-USA.

when he left for some ongoing education in January 1991, the congregation had grown to about 2,400 people.

Mortell especially emphasized the development of young adults at St. Gregory and at other Korean apostolate locations. He held bible study groups for college students at various locations in the greater Los Angeles area, but he also promoted leadership among that age group in the parish. One example is that of John Chang, a college student coordinator and a confirmation teacher at Valley Catholic Korean Center. Chang wrote about his experience and that of groups of high school students from the parish over a three year period helping Hurricane Katrina (2005) victims recover. He and his group were assigned to work in people's homes heavily damaged by the flood. They interacted with the home owners, tiled floors, painted walls and cupboards, and did other physical work to restore the buildings. In the process, they "learned the human stories housed within the walls." He and the group also learned "humility towards work that may never be noticed by anyone, thankfulness for what each of us is blessed with, and the value of truly knowing the meaning of a hard day's labor." [1056] Mortell also brought Korean students to the Columban mission in Juarez, Mexico, exposing them to situations not only of poverty but to structures that keep poverty alive.[1057]

Dallas, Texas: A Korean Apostolate and "Reverse Mission"

The Columbans accepted another venue for a Korean apostolate, which simultaneously provided an emphasis on "reverse mission" in a diocese. The invitation is an example of the second way Columbans became involved in the Korean apostolate. The bishop of Dallas, Texas, Charles V. Grahmann, invited the Columbans to work in St. Andrew Kim Parish, established by a priest from the Diocese of Pusan, Korea in 1977. Founded with the help of a Korean congregation in Houston, Texas, the Dallas group was thriving by the early 1990s. There were 1,200 registered members, a variety of organized church activities, and an active Legion of Mary *Curia* with eleven *praesidia*. The group was using three buildings: a Sanctuary, Fellowship Hall, and Residential Hall, the latter having an office each for a pastor, a woman religious, an administrator, and several classrooms. By the early 1990s, however, the Korean community was in need of a new pastor. Bishop Grahmann and the majority of that Korean community, who had approached the Columban regional superior with their

---

1056 John Chang, "Operation Helping Hands. Aiding Our Brothers and Sisters in Christ," *Columban Mission* (May 2009): 12–14.

1057 Tony Mortell, "Memories of Juarez," *Columban Intercom* 27 No. 6 (November–December 2005), 301.

request, preferred to have a Columban with cross-cultural experience, be English speaking, and have served in a parish in Korea.

The offer from Bishop Grahmann also assisted the Columbans, because the invitation provided a different geographic region than the "overcentralized Ethnic Apostolates in the California area." The invitation would offer an opportunity to be "reverse missionaries into the local Church, that is, to engage in Mission Awareness in that area of the country," a theme raised in the 1976 Columban General Chapter and by Pope John Paul II's 1990 encyclical, *Redemptoris Missio.*[1058]

Fathers Mark Mengel and Brendan O'Sullivan visited the bishop in October 1991, to view potential sites for both ministries and a possible ministry among Hispanics. Their report to Regional Superior Michael O'Loughlin elaborated upon the Korean experience in the parish. They met with the Koreans, the bishop, and some clergy, and visited potential sites where the Columbans might live. The report indicated "typical issues" within the Korean community: the experience of the next generation, cultural, and language problems in the United States. The priests also highlighted the value the bishop placed on ministry with Hispanics, who "were coming mainly from Mexico, seemingly untouched by church, one way or another." The Columbans expressed to the bishop, who was himself spearheading many ways in which to meet the spiritual and other needs of Hispanic people, that Columban presence would be a "missionary venture," not for Columban fund-raising. "Working with Koreans was a point of insertion but we were there to help the Bishop to make the diocese more missionary."[1059]

A contract between the Society of St. Columban and the bishop of Dallas was signed by the regional director and the bishop and sent to the superior general. In fall 1992, Columbans began their several pronged mission, living at the mainly Hispanic Immaculate Conception Parish in Grand Prairie, Texas. Father Frank Mannion was appointed for the Korean ministry there in 1992 and in March 1993, Father John Hogan[1060] replaced Mannion. Columbans Robert O'Rourke, Denny O'Mara, and Barney Toal served the mainly Hispanic community. Father Bill Morton arrived in 1993 to work in mission education and vocation work using the parish as his home base. The parish became a hub in the next year or two for Columban lay ministry and Hispanic ministry, in

---

[1058]   Mike O'Loughlin to Most Rev. Charles V. Grahmann 26 March 1991. The regional director also noted that the Columbans "would not want to give the impression that our missionary presence demands fundraising or a Vocation Apostolate, as such."

[1059]   Brendan O'Sullivan Report on Dallas Visit, 14/17 October 1991, to Mike O'Loughlin, Director, USA.

[1060]   John Hogan worked with the Koreans in the Dallas area until June 1999 and then served in the Korean parish in the Diocese of Orange until June 2008.

addition to pastoral care of Korean Catholics. Regional Director O'Loughin had particularly indicated that Dallas could become central to many Columban Chapter directives and ideas that "we so generously talk about on the open floor." The people assigned there could "prepare the way for some Mission Ed Programs, Laity in Mission endeavors, and other forms of involvement that animates from our missionary charism."[1061]

Intersections and Issues in the Apostolate

Several factors intersected in the Korean apostolate, more noticeably than in the other ethnic communities the Columbans served due to the number, timing, and locations of this apostolate. Three main areas needed to coalesce for the ministry to happen: the levels of governance within the Society of St. Columban; the relationship between the local bishop, other diocesan realities and structures, and the apostolate; and the dynamics of the Korean/Korean American ecclesiastical communities.

Levels of Governance within the Columbans

Before a Columban in Korea was assigned to the Korean apostolate in the United States, several authority levels needed to work together. The people involved were the superior general, who assigned all Columbans, the director of the U.S. region, who would be responsible for the apostolate, just as he was for other aspects of the U.S. region, and the director of the Korea region, who needed to agree to "release" a man from that region for the U.S. apostolate for a designated period of time. In December 1977, at the onset of the formal appropriation of the ministry as a Columban venture, the U.S. region Director Charlie Coulter met with Korea region Director Charlie Carolan to discuss a "working arrangement," whereby that region would provide staffing on a rotating basis for the Korean Catholic Center in Chicago and possibly elsewhere.[1062] Carolan presented the idea to his Council and region. An understanding was approved by the Columban Central Administration, "whereby the Korea Region would provide staffing, on a rotating basis, for certain U.S. Korean Apostolates."[1063] A final issue of assignment to the apostolate, in addition

---

[1061]   Michael O'Loughlin to Reverend Robert O'Rourke, 24 April 1992.

[1062]   *Columban Newsletter* (December 1978), 2.

[1063]   *Columban Newsletter* (September 1979). By this time, seven Columbans were working part time with Korean Catholics around the country in addition to the priest's main duties. By November 1979, contracts were approved for Columbans to work in the Archdioceses of New York (Father Frank Holecek), Chicago (Father Mort Kelly),

to appropriate qualifications and willingness on the part of the missionary, was that an individual either had to be a U.S. citizen or acquire a residency permit.[1064]

The Korean Apostolate in Relation to Other Columban Apostolates in the United States

Of the ethnic ministries in the United States, the greatest number of Columbans served Korean/Korean American groups. The potential for the ministry surfaced after the 1976 Society General Chapter identified "Reverse Mission" as an important element in being a missionary in one's home country. The U.S. regional leadership gathered Columbans to discuss what that meant for the United States. One outcome was the formalization of the Korean apostolate.

In January 1982, Regional Director Charlie Coulter convoked a meeting in Omaha with five men in the Korean apostolate to discuss their experiences and "to help administration discern the value and need for our involvement . . . as a missionary group."[1065] The meeting helped to "dispel the feeling of emotional isolation, which necessarily is part of this work." Koreans tended to be cut off from the mainstream of life in the United States and from parish life in dioceses and experience the "emotional stress of ghettoized communities." So too, a Columban in the Korean apostolate could "easily fall victim to the same stresses and feel both a geographical and psychological isolation from not only his fellow Columbans but from the rest of the Church (in the United States)."[1066] After free-ranging discussion over two days and a meeting with the regional administration, two key objectives were identified and accepted. Columban work in the Korean apostolate in the United States was first, an "extension of the Society's overall commitment to the evangelization of the Korean people,"

---

and Los Angeles, in addition to the 1978 contract with the Diocese of Orange, California (Father Frank Mannion). In 1985, Father William Schaefer became moderator of St. Brigid's Korean community in Westburg, Long Island, New York, while he studied fulltime for a master's degree in social work.

[1064] Such was the case, for example, of Irish-born Father Miles Roban, who waited a year before his residency permit came through and then was assigned by the Los Angeles Archdiocese to the Korean apostolate. *Columban Newsletter* (September 1989).

[1065] In January 1978, thirty-two Columbans working in pastoral situations in the United States met with the regional director to exchange views on pastoral work in the region. This was part of the conversation around the question, what does it mean to be a missionary in one's home country?" A longer meeting was held from April 10–14, 1978, one section of which was "Apostolates to Overseas Peoples in the U.S. Region, Pastoral Contracts in U.S. Region."

[1066] *Columban Newsletter* (May 1982), 3.

and second, that the apostolate is a "contribution of the local Home Church to cater to the needs of a minority group."[1067]

Another meeting was held in California with the regional director in 1984 following a Columban workshop there. The group drew up a plan of action for Columban future presence and service to the Korean community.[1068] This time the group focused on the needs of the second and succeeding generations. "As a bridge to a people in transition we offer more than a service as caretakers to the first generation. We strive to assist the young into the total integration of the U.S.A. Catholic Church," a position that Charlie Carolan had actively promoted in Chicago.[1069] There were differences of opinion on this point, however, as ethnic diversity came to be seen as a strength in the expression of Catholic America. With Pope John Paul II's speech, "Work of Welcoming of the Stranger," and the U.S. Catholic Bishops' documents that addressed diversity of ethnic communities as a gift to the Catholic Church, a model of assimilation of ethnic groups into a supposed "mainstream" gave way to the realization that "culture is an integral part of a person and not just some accident like a coat that can easily be taken off and put on."[1070]

The Columbans in the Korean apostolate in California met informally to assess needs, share experience, and query, for example, whether or not a new Korean Catholic Center should open or another Columban might be needed at a certain Center. Regional Director O'Loughlin noted that the Korean apostolate "is not an easy apostolate, much more difficult than working in Korea"[1071] for several reasons: the intersection of many issues involving an Asian culture meeting an "American" culture; different generations of Koreans who lived in one house, experiencing several cultural, marital and economic problems in their adjustment to the United States; and because Columbans whose knowledge of Korean language and culture, while valuable, now had to adjust to a changing America as well.

[1067]   *Columban Newsletter* (May 1982), 3. Several pages of the *Newsletter* outlined the meeting, elaborated the needs in the apostolate, and indicated the personal qualifications and experience Columbans would need to work in the apostolate.

[1068]   *Columban Newsletter* (November 1984).

[1069]   *Columban Newsletter* (November 1984), 3–4. Several articles in the Korea Region *Newsletter* presented the work of the U.S. region among Koreans in the United States. See, for example, *Korea Region Newsletter* (April 1989) and (July 1989).

[1070]   Pope John Paul II, *Work of Welcoming the Stranger,* 17 October 1985. Examples from the U.S. Catholic Bishops in the 1980s are *The Hispanic Presence. Challenge and Commitment,* 1983; *What We Have Seen and Heard, A Pastoral Letter on Evangelization from the Black Bishops of the United States,* 1984; *Together a New People. Pastoral Statement on Migrants and Refugees,* 1986. Quotation from Tony Mortell, unnamed paper on the Korean American apostolate, c. 1993, p. 13, though the paper was probably prepared for the 1990 Society Assembly.

[1071]   Michael J. O'Loughlin to Bishop Grahmann, February 1991.

Issues raised by Columbans not in the Korean Apostolate

Generally, Columbans assigned to the United States worked in promotion, mission education, vocations, or development. Sometimes it appeared to U.S. regional administration or to individual Columbans that there was a degree of independence shown among some of the Columbans in the Korean apostolate, rather than the men seeing the apostolate as a *Columban* ministry. The concern of the regional directors was that this presumed attitude might lead to men getting used to working alone or to a lack of openness to taking on a different ministry, should that be deemed necessary by the regional director. As one director framed the issue, the men need "to keep the Korea Apostolate in a proper Regional perspective."[1072]

Some Columban confreres questioned those in the Korean apostolate on the feasibility of beginning a Center in a particular area, because there were few or no Catholic Koreans there. Father Mannion remarked, "The question is not that there are no Korean Catholics, but there are Koreans to become Catholic. The work we did in the States was more evangelical, like getting new people to come to the church, rather than serving the people that were Catholics already."[1073]

Mannion also pointed out the strong presence of Korean Protestant leaders in the United States eager to have Catholic Koreans join them. Protestant missionaries from the United States to Korea, beginning in the nineteenth century, were numerous and effective. While Korea held the distinction in modern times of having received the Catholic faith as a result of evangelization by laity, in the twentieth century there were fewer Catholics in Korea than there were Protestants. Some of the Korean Protestants came to the United States to start their own congregations among immigrants and among Korean students in U.S. universities. Mannion cited two examples of women the Columbans would have known in Korea. Because of "lack of a Catholic Center," one woman, a cook for fifteen years at a Columban parish in Korea and a daily communicant, became a member of a Protestant church in California. Another woman, a recognized leader of the Holy Mother Society at a Columban parish in Korea, became a leader in a Protestant church in San Jose.[1074]

[1072] Michael O'Loughlin to Derek Harris 3 September 1991.

[1073] Interview of Father Frank Mannion, no date, presumably 2012.

[1074] The stories are noted in Frank Mannion, "The Los Angeles Apostolate," *Korea Region Newsletter* (July 1989), 8–9.

Relationship of the Apostolate to the Local Diocese

The second intersection for Columbans in the Korean apostolate related to the jurisdiction of the bishops in the United States. Before a Columban worked in any diocese or in a particular apostolate, he needed to have authority to do so from the bishop where the missionary would be working and who would authorize his "priestly faculties" to administer the sacraments in the diocese. As seen earlier in this chapter, sometimes a bishop himself took the initiative to invite the Columbans for the ministry. By the 1970s, Korean communities were beginning to grow in the United States, and some dioceses in South Korea saw themselves responsible for the development of the "Korean Diaspora" around the world, naming a Korean priest as a national coordinator of the Korean apostolate.[1075] The Korean priest was responsible on one level to his "home" diocese that sent him. Pastoring a Korean/Korean American community was a kind of "mission" situation for him. Nevertheless he would have been under the jurisdiction of the local U.S. bishop.[1076] These ecclesiastical intersections sometimes proved difficult, even though it was against church law to have a bishop from another diocese have any jurisdiction in a local bishop's diocese. Stephen Cardinal Kim, who in 1978 had requested that the Columbans work with Koreans in more areas than Chicago, made periodic visits to the Korean communities in the United States to see how they were faring in their Catholic faith and in their interaction with the Catholic community in general.

[1075] For example, at the time that negotiations were taking place for Immaculate Conception Church in Dallas, Texas, Father Augustine Park was the coordinator of the Korean apostolate. In 1990, forty-four of the fifty-two priests who served the Korean communities in the United States and Canada were of Korean origin. Thirty-five of those priests were "on loan" from Korean dioceses. Sean Brazil, "Korean Apostolate, USA," a paper for the U.S. Assembly, May 8–11, 1990, p. 3.

[1076] The *National Catholic Directory*, Seoul, South Korea, publishes an annual listing of "Overseas Korean Missions." Father Tony Mortell in 1993 noted that the appointment of Korean priests had changed. At first Korean priests who were in the United States for a sabbatical term or academic year helped the Korean communities. The appointment became full time later. "This was a lonely situation and thanks to the efforts of the various Presidents of the Migration Pastoral Committee, and those of Fr. Augustine Park, President of the North American Korean Priests Association, priests are now appointed in consultation with the United States Catholic Conference, the Catholic Conference of Korea, the bishop of his diocese of origin, as well as the one he will work in." The Korean priest would be assigned for a definite period of time. Tony Mortell, Paper on the history of the Korean American Catholic Community," 10.

Dynamics of Mission among Korean/Korean Americans [1077]

The third area of intersection was the dynamic within Korean Catholic communities. Generally, these groups began informally, with a priest meeting with the people once a month, sometimes in a home, then bimonthly, and then once a week. When the group met regularly they sometimes did so in a rented facility, with eventual development into a multiservice center, at which point a building was either purchased or constructed for this purpose.[1078]

As had other immigrants before and after them, Koreans coming to the United States in the 1970s, often felt frustration, anger, and disillusionment. Some might have wished to return to Korea, but they could not do so because of their children, whose education was vitally important. While the men came for the betterment of the family, they often had a harder time to adjust than did the women. "Grandmothers" or "Grandfathers" who came with the family or after the family arrived in the States, often became isolated, especially if the Korean community was small. They did not have opportunities to learn English or to "fit in" to a social circle outside of Korean families. Even within clusters of families, there might be limited social contact. As a group with a strong status tradition rising from Confucianism, Korean immigrants faced an "American" culture which seemed "freer," with fewer social boundaries that appeared more fluid, at least for some people. While the men had "status" in Korea, even though they might have not had "wealth," they now had no "place" in the United States and would need to start at the bottom of the ladder, if they worked in American companies. Some of the men and sometimes the women began their own small businesses. Tae Kwon Do experts developed a clientele beyond people of Korean background and held popular regional and national competitions.

Immigrants looked for a "home" where they had a sense of belonging, recognition, and an opportunity to demonstrate their skills to other Koreans. Sometimes, a community became political, especially for the men, causing a group of Koreans to break from the original group and begin another center. Koreans sometimes came to the centers mainly for socialization, not because it

---

[1077] For elements of the larger picture of mission to the Korean community in the United States, see Angelyn Dries, OSF, "Korean Catholics in the United States," *U.S. Catholic Historian*, 18 (Winter 2000): 99–110. I am also grateful to Father Charles O'Rourke for his insights and for lengthy conversations about experiences he and other Columbans have had with the Korean communities in the United States. I profited as well from informal conversation with other Columbans in the Korean apostolate.

[1078] Perhaps the Korean parish that had the greatest physical risk was in Canoga Park, California. At one point, intense brush fires threatened the area where many Koreans lived. In 1994 the building in Northridge was affected by an earthquake.

was a Catholic center. But Catholic Koreans, some of whom knew the Columbans from Korea, also came with their energy, responsiveness and enthusiastic faith. Often it was Catholic laity who sought a priest for their community. Centers flourished with Sunday liturgies, a catechumenate, religious education classes for elementary school children, bible study, student groups, an informal school where children learned the Korean language, Korean holiday celebrations, and dinners together where families brought their food specialties to the meal. The Legion of Mary provided communal strength for their prayer and opportunities to learn how to evangelize their neighbors. Korean Catholics were financially generous and supportive of their Center or parish.

Columbans quickly recognized the difficulties families faced when their Korean or American born children attended local schools and interacted with people whose values differed from the values important in cultures with a Confucian background. This group of young people, sometimes referred to as a "1.5 generation" often struggled between the two worlds. Columban Father Sal Caputo provided an insight into family and society pressures men and women experienced in Korea, pressures they carried with them to the United States. Usually living in an extended family situation, Koreans went through the usual family stresses: birth of children, death of a family member, marriage, and illness, but the Confucian culture added other pressures.[1079] The structure of the language was based on a complicated hierarchy of relationships. Because the first born son carried on the family name and was responsible to support his parents in their old age, their family and siblings, there was a commensurate pressure upon the wife to bear a son. If that did not happen, there was a possibility that she and her daughters would be evicted and the husband could marry another woman. Education was of immense importance, and pressure mounted to educate the children, so as to be successful for competitive college entrance examinations with limited openings. Wives particularly felt the burden and spent extra time tutoring their children to be sure they could excel in the exams. Economic pressures sometimes resulted in the husband living in another city, sometimes for years, while the family remained at home.

These pressures were compounded living in the United States. Either success or failure in business could adversely affect a marriage. Young people dealt with loneliness and their identity between two cultural worlds. Finding

---

[1079] Father Sal Caputo, "Pressure Points in Korean Family Life," *Columban Mission* (February 1992), 4–8. Caputo served in South Korea from after his ordination in 1976 until 1999. During much of that time, he worked with family issues, abuse in the family, and Marriage Encounter. After his studies at Fordham University, he had a ministry at the intercity bus terminal in Seoul. A *Columban Mission* article drew upon Caputo's, "The Resilient Nurturing Survivor. A Study of Women as the Prime Family Provider," a thesis he wrote to complete an Advanced Professional Diploma in Religion and Religious Education at Fordham University (1988).

a marriage partner was another challenge. Sometimes a mother returned to Korea to seek a young lady for her American born son. Contacts with other Koreans in a given geographic areas also limited potential marriage partners, when it was assumed that Koreans/Korean Americans would marry within their group. A social service center at a parish provided guidance for new arrivals in the country but also served as a counseling center for those with family problems, mental health issues, addictions,[1080] or physical problems. To address conflictive family issues, some of the Columbans engaged in individual counseling and were team members for Marriage Encounter weekends and Gamblers Anonymous meetings.

Archbishop (later Cardinal) Roger Mahony of Los Angeles, also mentioned the "special challenge" of second and third generation Korean–American youth, who are "experiencing the confusion of adapting to two cultures, languages and ways of life."[1081] Father Sean Brazil summed up one issue of identity formation. "Is the Korean American Catholic Community just a colony of the Catholic Church in Korea, or, is it some sort of funnel to direct the people as quickly as possible into the 'American Church.' Or, does the Korean Faith as expressed in its culture here in the U.S. have a special witnessing value?"[1082] The latter was clearly his perspective and that of many local Korean Catholic Centers as well.

Columbans addressed the needs of second generation identity formation, especially that of young adult men and women. Korean American students in college felt psychological pressure from well-organized proselytizing evangelical groups on public campuses. Tony Mortell's effective Bible study group at the University of California, Los Angeles, with a second branch at California State, Long Beach, provided a venue where peers could express their Catholic beliefs, share the insecurities of identity formation, and find friends with whom to socialize outside of the study group. The study group was also an opportunity for Koreans with no religious affiliation to learn more about Catholic life and practice.

[1080] Father Paul White began Gamblers Anonymous groups in South Korea and did so for Koreans in the United States, when he returned here from Korea. See chapter 11.

[1081] Mahony quoted, *Columban Newsletter* (January 1991), 4.

[1082] Sean Brazil, "Korean Apostolate, USA," paper for U.S. Assembly, May 8–11, 1990, p. 4

Conclusion

In 2016, Father Gerard Dunne was the only Columban assigned full time to the Korean apostolate in the United States. He was pastor at St. Joseph Catholic Korean Center, in the Archdiocese of Los Angeles since 2013, but he had served the Korean Catholic Centers in Southern California since 1998. Dunne is part of a rich heritage of Columban engagement with the Korean community in the United States. The combination of energetic lay leaders, Columban expertise, "local knowledge" of civic, ecclesiastical and business practices, and love for people with a Korean American heritage enabled the Koreans and the Columbans to navigate American life.

Korean Catholic Centers with Columban pastors provided a supportive meeting place for Catholics and were expressions of ethnic experience, social engagement, and heartfelt Catholic life. The Centers further acted as a buffer between Koreans and groups who disliked them and the sometimes confusing entry into a multicultural world they now inhabited in the United States. Centers served as a way for lay leaders to exhibit initiative in the Catholic community through catechetical teaching, music ministry, or the Legion of Mary, and at the same time provided social standing for its leaders. The downside of the latter point is that Korean patterns of hierarchy and the importance of power for men sometimes carried over into a split in the Korean community.

Columban leadership in the development of viable Korean Catholic communities and the formation of Korean/Korean American Catholic leaders clearly stands out among missionary societies in the United States, both in terms of number of missionaries involved and the quality of pastoral care.

Columban missionaries had a significant presence in Southern California in relation to Asian communities, though their apostolate to Korean/Korean Americans took root in many cities across the United States. Viewed in "canonical" or ecclesiastical language, most of the centers for the ethnic groups noted in this chapter were designated as "Centers." For all practical purposes, however, the centers functioned as a parish. The practice of identifying them as centers was partially due to the experience of the Catholic Church in the United States, especially in the nineteenth century, when some French Canadian, German, Polish, or other European immigrants bought property, found a priest to serve them, and held control of the land and buildings, which led them to assume they could name their pastor, apart from any relationship with the bishop of a diocese.[1083]

[1083] The practice was called, "lay trusteeism." For a further explanation of the development of the nineteenth century experience, see Patrick Carey, *People Priests, and People: Ecclesiastical Democracy and the Tensions of Trusteeism* (Notre Dame: University of Notre Dame Press, 1987).

In some cases, the centers hosted gatherings of people not affiliated with the parish but with the ethnic community. While Columbans served ethnic groups who experienced discrimination, those ethnic communities were not necessarily favorably inclined toward other ethnic groups. Nevertheless, the Columbans boldly and creatively served the groups, and in the case of the Filipinos in the 1940s, firmly declared their willingness to meet the spiritual needs of that group, in spite of prejudice and legal discrimination. Public music and dance performances by members of the Chinese Catholic Center resulted in new understanding of Chinese culture among some citizens of Los Angeles.

As the situation warranted it, Columbans were able to connect with women religious who engaged in the apostolate to a particular ethnic group, thus strengthening the impact of the total Center. Lay people were active in various kinds of leadership, especially through catechetics, choirs, and the Legion of Mary. In the issues of the *Far East* in the 1930s through the 1960s, particular laity from the three countries were identified as key evangelizers in overseas Columban parishes. The implication was that people from those immigrant groups could be and were leaders in Catholic life in the United States.

The initial foundation of a center served a particular "generation" of immigrants, and over the years Columbans addressed new pastoral and human issues which arose with the birth of the next generation. Columban mission experience provided appreciation and knowledge of the cultural and social background of the three groups followed in this chapter, but Irish-born Columbans were also adjusting to the changing shape of the Catholic Church and society in the United States.

Invitations from bishops, Chinese, Filipinos, and Koreans in the United States released the talents and initiative of Columbans and let them draw upon their overseas mission experience in a new context. As Superior General Bernard Cleary wrote to U.S. region Director Peter Cronin, "Wherever (the Columbans) are, we should be going into ethnic communities."[1084] The challenge was to use mission experience in a new context—the United States and its diversely ethnic Catholic Church. Columbans chose to serve in what were sometimes uncomfortable situations at the intersection of ethnic, social, and ecclesiastical cultures. Sometimes Columbans were companions, guides, advocates, and pastors. At other times, they were a challenge to the ethnic communities, Columban superiors and the rest of the Catholic Church. It was not always easy to see "the variety of ways in which God comes to people serves to bring out and develop different facets of the inexhaustible riches of the Gospel."[1085]

[1084] Response from Superior General to Director's Annual Report, *Columban Newsletter* (April 1984).

[1085] Pope Francis, *Joy of the Gospel* (*Evangelii Gaudium*), November 24, 2013. (Washington DC: United States Conference of Catholic Bishops, 2013), par. 40.

Catholic Chinese Center, L.A. 1941 front

Fr. Cowhig with children 2

315

CHAPTER 9

The Whole Church Is in Mission

Beginning with E. J. McCarthy, who was on the Board of Catholic Students Mission Crusade (CSMC) in the 1920s, the Columban Fathers encouraged the development of mission awareness and vocation among high school and college students through attendance at local and national CSMC conferences in the United States. Appeals were made through the *Far East/Columban Mission*, Columban vocation talks around the country, and through high quality mission education materials. Though not called to become a Columban priest, some Catholics sought a deeper commitment to mission through association with the Columbans in some form. This chapter will briefly highlight the Columban Sisters, particularly their work in the United States, the Columban Brothers, the Sisters of Loretto of Nerinckx, Kentucky, priest volunteers and lay apostles (called Columban lay missionaries today). Other people who felt connected to the Columbans and mission were numerous loyal donors. The Society of St. Columban continually in one way or other, promoted mission among all members of the Catholic Church, though "the manner of connecting" to the Society varied. The Columbans collectively embodied a message that the whole Church is called to mission.

Columban Sisters

Foundation in Ireland

Columban life also took shape in the foundation of the Missionary Sisters of St. Columban. In 1917, Father John Blowick hoped to begin a congregation of women religious who would work with the Columban Fathers in their missions.

He expressed this as a need for "auxiliaries" to serve as catechists, school teachers, and nurses, for example. He gave several talks about the need and informally mentioned the possibility to others. Frances Lewis Maloney, who later became Mother Mary Patrick, showed interest and was one of the first women to commit herself to the mission vocation as a Sister. In the first few years conversation among the interested women and with the Society clarified the nature of that commitment. By the time the first Columban priests were missioned to China in 1920, permission from Rome was given to establish a missionary religious congregation of Sisters who focused on engagement in apostolates that furthered preaching the Gospel in China. Specifically, Rome had authorized the bishop of Killaloe to establish in his diocese "a congregation of Sisters to labor with the missionaries of the Maynooth Mission to China."[1086] In 1922, the first postulants gathered in Cahiracon, County Clare. The first profession of the women was celebrated in 1924.[1087] Seven Missionary Sisters of St. Columban left for China in 1926, accompanied by Mother M. Finbarr (Nora Collins, 1885–1977)[1088]. Collins had received her nursing education and training in New Hampshire and was a nurse in Cork City for several years. Sister Mary Patrick was in the mission band and served in China for ten years before she later served as the superior general in Ireland.

To the States: Assistance to the Columban Fathers

Father E. J. McCarthy was eager to have the newly established Congregation of Missionary Sisters of St. Columban in the United States. In fall 1924, he wrote to Father James Wilson in Ireland,

> about a foundation of our Sisters in the States. We would be glad to have that as soon as possible. My idea was to have a novitiate at Silver Creek. In a few years our student body will be large enough to justify us in putting up a new building and the present seminary could be made a sisters' novitiate. Until that time, we might be able to use our house at Bedford Ave., Omaha. We would be glad to have some sisters as soon as possible in both Omaha and Silver Creek to oversee our kitchens and domestic economy. I would not favor them in

---

[1086]   Ita Hannaway, *Take Your Place . . .*, p.26.

[1087]   The women became a congregation of pontifical rite with approval of their Constitutions by the Holy See in 1947.

[1088]   Ita Hannaway, *Mission Unimagined: The Story of Mother Mary Finbarr Collins of the Missionary Society of St. Columban* (Wicklow, Ireland: Missionary Sisters of St. Columban, 2006).

the offices until such time as they are able to take them over altogether without any outside help and that will be many years hence, as far as I can see.[1089]

McCarthy had requested that Mother Finbarr send Sisters to the United States in 1928, but Father Galvin's need in China was more insistent. Given that he was the founder of the "Chinese Mission Society," or "Maynooth Mission to China," the Sisters also went to China, as did a second group of Sisters the following year.[1090] Finally, in 1930, after visa delays and the Sisters Assembly, seven Columban Sisters arrived by ship in New York. They took the train to the small town of Dunkirk, the station nearest Silver Creek. They arrived at their new mission on a cold, Christmas Eve Day. With help from local people, the Fathers had readied one of the wood framed Victorian style houses on the Silver Creek property for the Sisters. E. J. McCarthy ordered books for their library and sent paintings for their rooms.[1091]

The Sisters often did time consuming work that was essential to the running of the larger mission endeavor. The Sisters cooked, canned the farm's apples, pears, peaches and tomatoes and did many other tasks to ease the financial strain of feeding a growing population of mainly high school young men, as well as the priests and Sisters.[1092] The Sisters made the place a home, as noted in earlier chapters. But they did far more than "oversee the kitchens and domestic economy," as Father McCarthy suggested. They were also the infirmarians for the students. The Sisters sewed cassocks for a year or two and learned from a local craftsman to make clay figurines for Christmas cribs. These were income producing activities. Later on, one Sister printed out Christmas cards for Bishop Harold Henry in Korea, when there was not a quick and easy way to do so. Rita Garvey (Sister Francesca) from Parkersburg, West Virginia, and the first American to enter the U.S. novitiate in 1946, typed Father John Heneghan's hand written memoirs. After the Sisters moved to Hyde Park, Massachusetts, Sister Genevieve Hickey wrote letters for Columban Father John V. Dunne, who was going blind.

The Columban priests were chaplains to the Sisters and periodically gave them talks on a variety of subjects. In 1937, Father Ambrose Gallagher spoke

[1089] E. J. McCarthy to My dear Jim [Wilson] 16 October 1924.

[1090] The Columban Sisters story in China is told in Edward Fischer, *Maybe a Second Spring: The Story of the Missionary Sisters of St. Columban in China* (New York: Crossroad, 1983).

[1091] Claire O'Rourke, SSC, *USA: Stepping Stones to China and Beyond. A Columban Missionary Presence* (Brighton, MA: Columban Sisters, 2008), 17–21.

[1092] "Father Alphonsus of Holy Cross Seminary very kindly donated 1500 large canning jars." *Annals of the Missionary Sisters of St. Columban, Silver Creek, New York.* Diary entry from October 1936.

about the history of the part of New York where the Silver Creek seminary was located. He noted the early role of the Erie tribe, the migration of the Iroquoian speaking Seneca (the westernmost group of the Six Nations) into the area, with "a settlement on the river between here and Buffalo," and the early Catholic days in the diocese.[1093] During Holy Week that year, Father John O'Brien gave the Sisters two lectures a day on Christ's "Seven Last Words."[1094]

Financially, the Sisters were dependent upon the Columban Fathers until 1946.[1095] For example, E. J. McCarthy took care of the Sisters' travel needs. During the Depression, the Society had drawn up a new contract with the Sisters at Silver Creek, lowering stipends for the Sisters working at the seminary. The *Far East* contained occasional fund-raising and vocation appeals specifically for the Sisters. After World War II, the new superior general of the Columban Fathers, Jeremiah Dennehy, and Mother Mary Vianney Shackleton, the new congregational leader of the Sisters, conferred about the financial relationship. With their Councils the two leaders decided to separate their financial base from each other. As Mother Mary Vianney noted, "This separation probably should have taken place" in 1930.[1096]

Generally, the priests' main work was with the students, though Father Kaiser hired boys from the neighborhood to work in the fields.[1097] Sisters at Silver Creek also cared for people in the community. Sister Ignatius "began a weekly catechism class with M. Eskey's little daughter."[1098] Sister Mary James would meet Rosemary Krzyzanowski [nee McFarland] at school and take her to Sheridan for religious education class for First Communion and Confirmation. Rosemary's mother sometimes brought her along to help in the kitchen.[1099] Sister Pius was an organist. For the summer retreats neighbors volunteered to help with cooking, cleaning, and laundry. As Shirley Kanistanoux remarked

---

[1093] *Annals of the Missionary Sisters of St. Columban*, 1937.

[1094] Ibid.

[1095] John Blowick made sure that the new institute complied with canon law and that the Society would "guarantee the material support of the congregation." Sister Ita Hannaway, *Take Your Place . . .*, 43.

[1096] Mother Mary Vianney quoted in Claire O'Rourke, SSC, *USA: Stepping Stones to China and Beyond*, 63. Apparently, Mother Vianney's brother, Columban Father Abraham Shackleton (1908–1978), who was assigned to Silver Creek, had suggested the idea to her.

[1097] Author interview with Shirley Kanistanoux, who was eighty-four years old at the time of the interview and Rosemary Krzyzanowski, St. Columban on the Lake Home, 22 October 2013. Shirley also mentioned a Josephine F. [last name not remembered] who cooked at Silver Creek and lived in a small house on the property.

[1098] *Annals of the Missionary Sisters of St. Columban*, 1936.

[1099] Author interview with Shirley Kanistanoux, St. Columban on the Lake Home, 22 October 2013.

about the retreats, "Boys had to clear the tables and bring the dishes to the kitchen. The boys waited on the men on retreat, because women weren't supposed to have contact with the men."[1100] Once a year at Christmas, the Sisters held a large party for the volunteers and staff at Silver Creek complete with live band. Sometimes the party was catered. Sometimes others pitched in to prepare the food.

In 1936, the Sisters held a raffle to raise funds for the missions, even though people were still feeling the effects of the Depression. The winner of the raffle was the aunt of a seminary student. "She was simply delighted, choosing $25 instead of the hamper, as everyone in the family was out of work. The Fathers at the College were most generous in buying tickets and $46 came in, which far exceeded our expectations."[1101] In 1956, Sister Francis Borgia MacMahon was assigned to the Development Office for the Sisters, beginning a long period of service in raising funds. She felt her gifts were well used in that capacity. She began the first of what became her famous "lawn fêtes." The event took place in June before the seminarians went home. The fund-raiser involved people from the surrounding area[1102] and seminarians, who helped set up tables, chairs and tents on the seminary's expansive property.[1103] Attendees could obtain information about Columban missions and participate in games, music, raffles, food, a good time for all, and an opportunity to talk with the Columban Sisters. Sister Borgia also traveled to the greater Buffalo area to visit Columban supporters.

Sisters' Mission Expands Beyond Silver Creek Seminary

The Sisters moved their American novitiate to Hyde Park, Massachusetts, from Silver Creek, New York, in 1948. They were able to do so thanks to Archbishop Cushing who provided half of the money while the Sisters raised funds for the other half. In 1953, Mother Vianney came to Chicago to find a

---

[1100] Ibid.

[1101] *Annals of the Missionary Sisters of St. Columban,* 1936.

[1102] Claire O'Rourke, SSC, *U.S.A. Stepping Stones to China and Beyond, A Columban Missionary Presence* (Brighton, MA: Columban Sisters, 2008), 69–70. Shirley Kanistanoux and Rosemary Krzyzknowski were among the many neighbors who pitched in. Shirley also mentioned a Josephine F. who cooked at Silver Creek and lived in a small house on the property.

[1103] Father Paul Tomasso, a Columban seminarian through his college years in Oconomowoc and later ordained for the Diocese of Rochester, New York, remembered vividly in a positive manner, both setting up for the retreats and the work of the Columban Sisters while he was a Silver Creek seminarian. He experienced the Sisters as providing a "homey atmosphere to the place. They were 'sisters' to the seminarians. Theirs is an "unsung history." Author interview of Father Paul Tomasso, Rochester, New York. 22 September 2013.

house for Sisters pursuing a degree there. Bishop Galvin, who had inherited a house in the city, suggested that the Society give the Sisters the building. "Mother accepted [the house] with great delight."[1104] The home would also serve as a location for vocation and mission fund appeals. Galvin's gesture would typify a statement later made by Columban Sister Evelyn Frieder, as she reflected on her mission life: "When you're a missionary, you start something and then let it go."[1105]

The Columban Sisters were key persons in the parish school at the Columban parish, Blessed Sacrament, in Westminster, California. The Sisters felt a fine collaboration with the Columban Fathers. The Sisters had full run of the school, whose population was mainly of Mexican background, a story told in chapter 3.[1106] The Sisters also taught at St. Polycarp School in nearby Stanton, California. Later in East Los Angeles, they had responsibility for Our Lady of Guadalupe School on Hazard Street. After Vatican II, some of the Columban Fathers at Milton provided lectures to the Sisters about the topics and issues the Council raised.[1107] The beginning of a concerted effort in mission education in grade schools, high schools and parishes was effected through the work of Sister Mary O'Dea (see chapter 8).

About the time the possibility arose that the Silver Creek seminary would close, the Columban Sisters' General Chapter in 1968 urged the Sisters to begin a ministry in the United States and Ireland that would be a "reverse mission for returned missionaries and a way to give back services to long time benefactors.[1108] That same year, Father Richard Steinhilber approached Sister Francesca Garvey, regional superior at the time, inquiring whether the Columban Sisters might want the location for their needs. The Sisters, who had been thinking about a service to the elderly, conferred with the Carmelite Sisters in South Boston. They steered the Columban Sisters away from a medical model of service and toward a home for elderly women and men. The Sisters

---

[1104] E. J. Galvin to "Dear Mac" [most probably, E. J. McCarthy], 24 September 1953. The house was located at 6635 N. Ashland Avenue, Chicago. The Sisters moved there in 1954.

[1105] Author interview of Sister Evelyn Frieder, 22 October 2013, Brighton, Massachusetts.

[1106] Author interview of Sister Margaret Devine, 22 October 2013, Brighton. "On the missions overseas, the relationship between the Columbans priests and Columban Sisters depended on who was in charge, on both sides." Author telephone interview of Sister Patricia Zandrews 23 January 2014. The *Far East* used the Sisters' stories in their promotion.

[1107] Author interview of Sister Margaret Holleran, September 23–25, 2013, Brighton, Massachusetts.

[1108] Author interview of Sister Corona Colleary, 20 October 2013, Silver Creek.

repurposed the buildings and remodeled rooms and hallways for use by an older population, especially those with limited income.[1109]

Papers were drawn up between the two Columban groups on June 30, 1969. A fixed annual amount was stated to be paid quarterly by the Sisters. However, not long after the contract was signed, the Columban Fathers conveyed most of the property as a gift to the Sisters. Father Hugh O'Rourke initiated the legal transfer to the Sisters. Provision was also made for up to ten Columban Fathers to live at St. Columban's on the Lake Retirement Home, a policy which continues today. In 1970 the Sisters moved their quarters to the third floor of the building. The residence has become home to a variety of women and men, including parents, relatives of priests and Sisters with family on the east coast, as well as others in the vicinity who have heard of the enriching environment offered at the Home.

From the opening of St. Columban's on the Lake Home on May 1, 1970, Sister Corona Colleary has been the home's administrator. She took courses at Cornell University to become state certified for the task. Under her leadership they again surveyed for natural gas and found it anew on the property. Sister Corona was also certified as a water treatment operator and wastewater treatment manager because until recently, water was taken from Lake Erie and treated for use on the campus. Columban Sisters from the missions provided some of the pastoral care of residents. Sister Theresa Malloy, who served in Korea, supervised the nursing staff.

The Sisters moved their U.S. regional location from Hyde Park, Massachusetts, to Brighton, Massachusetts, in 1980.[1110] The house had been willed to the Sisters by Mr. and Mrs. Joseph McBrearty, along with the couple's savings. Joseph McBrearty was a Boston traffic patrolman and his wife, Anna, was a teacher at a business and finishing school. Joseph particularly noticed the Sisters driving a car, something unusual to see in 1948 Boston. The Sisters befriended the couple and after Mrs. McBrearty's death, the Sisters and he were in touch periodically by phone and visits. On the edge of Boston and readily accessible by car and public transportation, the house provided a good location for returned missionaries, whether they were visiting relatives and friends, or

---

[1109] While the building was remodeled, the Columban Fathers still used the third floor and the Sisters assisted the priests. The Limpias crucifix was taken down in the remodeling. With lowered ceilings the crucifix no longer fit the space and was placed in a stairwell for many years. Eventually the Sisters donated the cross to a Catholic parish in Buffalo for their church. Author interview with Sister Corona Colleary, 20 October 2013, Silver Creek.

[1110] Missionary Sisters of St. Columban, 73 Mapleton St. Brighton, Massachusetts. The novitiate returned to Silver Creek to a separate refurbished dwelling on the grounds. For further locations of the U.S. region's novitiate, see Claire O'Rourke, SSC, *U.S. Stepping Stones to China*, 79–80.

whether the Sisters participated in development, mission education, or were in retirement. Wherever the Sisters might have been in mission, Sister Margaret Devine's talk given at the funeral liturgy for Sister Anna Tseng (1921–2012) could be true for each of them, "We missionaries face transitions and we leave bits of our hearts in many places."[1111] As of 2017, Sisters remain at the Silver Creek location. In October 2016, the Sisters' Brighton house was sold and the deed handed over to new owners. The Sisters left the Archdiocese of Boston after sixty-eight years of service there.[1112]

Columban Brothers

In the early days of the Society, many areas of a new foundation needed to be addressed almost simultaneously: approval by the bishops of Ireland, approval by the appropriate Vatican office, funding, location of a suitable home for the Society, and the education of the missionaries. Other areas about the development of the Society were less clear, such as structures of leadership. Initially, Edward Galvin favored a regular novitiate and possibly the development of a religious order.[1113] The "novitiate" concept became known as the Spiritual Year at the General Chapter, 1924, and was referred to as such. The idea of Columban "Brothers" would fit into the model of religious life. In 1922, McCarthy had mentioned "many applicants for Brotherhood."[1114] On May 22 of that year, two "applicants as lay brothers called today: a farmer from Randolf, Nebraska [Mr. Taggart]; the other [unnamed] and "a convert of ten years"], an engineer on the Northwestern Railroad, living at Council Bluffs Iowa. As far as one could judge, they are two splendid men and just the kind to form the nucleus of a brotherhood. Looks as if God is pushing this development on us now."[1115]

Father John Blowick submitted a document to the Office of Propaganda Fide in Rome for permission to begin establishment of Columban Brothers. In 1924 a Brothers' Novitiate was established in Ireland.[1116] While McCarthy considered

---

[1111]   Sister Margaret Devine, Funeral Mass Reflection for Sister Anna Tseng, St. Columban's Chapel, Silver Creek, 3 December 2012.

[1112]   Information about the Brighton house provided to author by Sister Corona Colleary 12 March 2017.

[1113]   E. J. McCarthy, "Diary of Progress at St. Columban's, Omaha," 28 April 1922.

[1114]   Ibid., March 1922.

[1115]   Ibid.

[1116]   "A Call for Brothers," *FE* (Irish Edition) (April 1924), 54. The article noted that the Brothers were "part of the lay apostolate." Neil Collins has drawn up a list of the ten Brothers with their religious name, date of entrance into the Brotherhood, and death date.

Dalgan an "ideal place for the Spiritual Year and Brothers' novitiate, [1117] he was eager to begin a novitiate for Brothers in the United States. He wrote to Father James Wilson, "I have written to the Superior about brothers. We would like to start them here immediately if we may. Our numbers would be very small but we must make a beginning sometime." He suggested the American brothers could have their novitiate at St. Columbans in Omaha, because there "would be few students over the next four years, until this first year's class comes along."[1118] O'Dwyer and his Council decided, however, that an American novitiate for Brothers "is not at present to the best interest of the Society and therefore does not sanction it."[1119] While McCarthy indicated at the start of his *Historical Sketch* (1931) that the Society had 20 Brothers by that date, he later wrote on another page of the booklet that there were eleven lay Brothers.[1120]

Brothers generally were responsible for office work or helping in some physical capacity in Dalgan. By the mid-1930s, the Columban Brothers were in charge of an orphanage in Ying-Wu-Chow, China. One of the Brothers there was Brother Colman (Peter Ryan, 1903–1971). He had been a salesman prior to his entrance into the Columbans. After learning the basics of building construction, he went to China in 1933, where he was in charge of an industrial school. After being forced out of China, he became well known for major construction projects in the Philippines: the Cathedral, seminary, and Immaculate Conception College buildings, all in Ozamis. In 1954 he completed a high school in Clarin, Ozamis, in six weeks, at a cost of six thousand dollars. The building, which would accommodate 200 students, had six classrooms, a stage, office and clinic.[1121]

The number of Brothers did not grow beyond the ten brothers who remained in the Society. Discussion arose in the early 1960s about a concerted effort to recruit men to become brothers. Two probation Brothers were in formation at Dalgan in fall 1965.[1122] At the Society's U.S. Regional Convention in 1972, the delegates decided: "At this time, we recommend that the Society does not develop any program for the recruitment of Brothers in this Region."[1123] The vote was eighteen to zero (one abstention).[1124]

[1117] E. J. McCarthy to "My dear Jim" [probably Wilson] 16 October 1924.

[1118] Ibid.

[1119] Superior General to Rev. E. J. McCarthy 5 November 1924.

[1120] In the end, ten Columban Brothers, all from Ireland, remained in their lifelong commitment.

[1121] *Columban Newsletter* (March 1954).

[1122] *Columban Newsletter* (November 1965).

[1123] Preparatory meetings for U.S. Regional Convention, 1972. CFA-USA.

[1124] Folder: Regional Conventions, 1969, 1972. 8-A-7. CFA-USA.

Sisters of Loretto, Nerinckx, KY

Edward Galvin was eager to have women religious serve along with the Columban Fathers in China. While the Sisters of St. Columban were still in the process of developing as a missionary congregation, E. J. McCarthy inquired of Galvin whether he might want a seasoned women's congregation from the United States to come to China. He had in mind, the Sisters of Loretto, whose Motherhouse was in Nerinckx, Kentucky.[1125] Founded in the "wilderness" in 1812, the congregation had many experienced educators. In addition to their schools, the Sisters were engaged in missions among Native Americans and Mexicans in Texas and the Southwest. They had funded the Father Nerinckx Burse for the Columbans and gave a thousand dollars for the Columban church and school in China.[1126] McCarthy called them the "biggest mission boosters" in the country.[1127] He saw the Sisters preeminently suited for China."[1128] While the Sisters were not a Columban group, there is no doubt that interaction with each other at the initial stages of Columban mission, the Sisters were one of the keys to the success of the China mission, and hence, to the development of the Columbans.

With a view to a key practical element needed, McCarthy urged that the Society "consider American Sisters because they'll be able to finance their work, while the Irish sisters might not be able."[1129] After appropriate interaction between the Superior General Blowick, Mother Clarasine Walsh and the Vatican Congregation for Religious, the latter who would authorize the Sisters to engage in work beyond their approved Constitutions, a contract was signed on March 7, 1923, between the Sisters and the Society of St. Columban. Six Sisters of Loretto left their Motherhouse in Kentucky on September 12, 1923. They were accompanied by Father Patrick J. MacAuley, "a vigorous, genial

---

[1125]   For histories of the Sisters of Loretto in China, see Antonella Marie Gutterres, *Lorettine Education in China, 1923–1952: Educational Activities of the Sisters of Loretto in China, Hanyang and Shanghai (Taipei: United Publishing Center, 1961)*; Janet Manion, in Ann Patrick Ware, ed., *Naming Our Truth*: Stories of Loretto Women (Inverness, CA: Chardon Press, 1995). To see the work of the Sisters of Loretto in a larger context, see, Angelyn Dries, *The Missionary Movement in American Catholic History* (Maryknoll, NY: Orbis Books, 1998), 120–121, 129, 143–144, 146.

[1126]   E. J. McCarthy, *Diary of Progress at St. Columban's, Omaha, Neb. 29* December 1921, 8. In Hanyang, the Loretto Sisters met the first seminarian who benefitted from the Nerinckx burse, Father Michael Fallon. Ordained in Ireland in 1925, he died in China on June 7, 1928.

[1127]   E. J. McCarthy, *Diary of Progress at St. Columban's,* Omaha, Nebraska, 29 December 1921, 8.

[1128]   Ibid., 2 April 1922, 32.

[1129]   E. J. McCarthy to My dear John [Blowick] 29 December 1921.

personality" and Father Francis A. Murray.[1130] The group arrived in Hanyang on October 19, 1923.[1131] The Sisters of Loretto would become an integral link in the Columban mission in China.

Month by month during the 1920s and fairly regularly thereafter, the *Far East* readers followed the "Pen Pictures," written by "A Sister of Loretto." "Letters from Loretto," with variations on that theme, became the title of the article by the 1930s. While the Sisters had hoped for and intended to start a high school, Galvin asked if the Sisters "would be satisfied to have a home at the Embroidery [School] and to be given charge of same in place of school."[1132] Galvin would not able to afford a high school for the Sisters.

The Sisters' successful embroidery school, which supported the young girls' catechumenate, also increased the number and quality of the items and enlarged the market. The Sisters sent twenty large cases of embroidery for the exhibit sponsored by the Columbans at the 1925 Vatican Mission Exposition in Rome.[1133] The Sisters were active in other activities in the Hanyang area, sometimes informally. The Embroidery School became a center of trouble when a Communist organization was started among the girls, most of whom had not been baptized [c. 1926].[1134] The invasion of the Red Army into Hanyang uprooted the Sisters in 1926, and they went for a time to Shanghai but returned for the consecration of Bishop Galvin in November 1927. The embroidery school reopened with 200 young women. The Communists returned in 1931, and floods of the Yangtze and Han Rivers led to starvation. The Columban Sisters, priests, Sisters of Loretto and the Chinese Virgins of Mary fed and took care of the people who were coming down with cholera, malaria, smallpox, and diphtheria in the encampments on the hills. As a Sister of Loretto put it at the time: "Think of it—we are conducting a school, a catechumenate, looking after 250 girls, making all the mattresses, pillows and sheets for the Red Cross Emergency hospital, visiting the camps, giving inoculations, nursing the sick, baptizing the dying, burying the dead and a host of other things. And all

---

[1130] Francis A. Murray served the missions in China until 1948.

[1131] An article in *FE* looked back on the first ten years of the Sisters of Loretto in China and noted the two Columban names. *FE* (October 1933), 9. Patricia Jean Manion, SL, *Venture into the Unknown: Loretto in China* (Independent Publishing, 2006). For the debate about the value of Catholic schools in relation to the goal of the missions: converts, see Neil Collins, *The Splendid Cause* (Dublin: Columba Press, 2009), 112–113.

[1132] Neil Collins, *The Splendid Cause*, primary source quoted, 114.

[1133] See photos in *FE* (1925) that displays some of the embroidered items in the Exposition.

[1134] Shackleton, "History of Hanyang, China." Typed manuscript, n.d. CFA-USA. The author is most probably Father Abraham Shackleton (1908–1978), who served in Hanyang from 1936–1946.

this, during what Bishop Galvin has called 'the days of terror and confusion and black despair.'" [1135] To this was added the training of a new community of Chinese Sisters, established by Bishop Galvin (see chapter 11).

After the Communists left the area in 1933, one Sister noted that "the numbers of Chinese asking for baptism are far greater than the priests can provide for. . . . It is consoling to think that the fervor of the old Catholics increased remarkably during the trouble."[1136] Sister Justa was giving religious instructions to a rickshaw puller and learned that he was ill. "She was most anxious to baptize him before he died. She was called out to him one day. He was dying and had not been able to speak for several hours. Sister baptized him and he cried out, '*Yaso jo wo.*' [Jesus, save me.] He never spoke again, dying a few hours later."[1137] The Sisters of Loretto did eventually open a high school, though that was in Shanghai, 1933, after an invitation from the Jesuits.

As was true for most missionaries in war torn situations, the women's initial roles dissolved into diverse responses in the crisis, as the effects of bombing appeared all around. After the "all clear" sign, the Sisters baptized some who were dying, the wounded were taken to the Columban hospital, while many bled to death on the streets. Hundreds of people sat at the convent door asking to be taken in. Stores were closed, windows bricked, warnings were given that buildings might be dynamited. The Sisters of Loretto described one of those days, November 1, 1938.

> The hardest day yet evacuating the Refugees. We left home at 7:30 a.m. Gave them some food and tried to get them up. They would not go unless we went with them. Men and women fell on their knees begging us to care for them. What misery. Sisters Justa and Nicholas were to go with them. A woman with Sister tried to commit suicide. Sister Clementia . . . looked after the left-overs—babies left behind as the people said they could not take them; so they just left them and went. Many [refugees] were sick and could not go. Sisters of Loretto are acting as traffic cops, directing the refugees. The [refugees] are breaking into houses that have been locked and are occupying them. All are asking us to live in the Zone with them, they are that afraid.[1138]

[1135] Michael J. O'Neill, "Silver Jubilee. The Loretto Sisters Show Twenty-Five Years of Progress," *FE* (October 1948), 14–15.

[1136] "Letters from Loretto," *FE* (February 1933), 11.

[1137] Ibid.

[1138] 1 November 1938. Folder: Han Yang Diary, by the Loretto Sisters, 1927–1947. 1.c.5 CFA-USA.

Poignantly, in December 1941, as the United States joined in World War II, the Lorettine diarist wrote, "Dismissed the Han Yang girls [at the embroidery school]. They cried; we did, too."[1139]

Lay Auxiliaries/Lay Apostles/Lay Missionaries

When Galvin wrote to McCarthy that he needed a carpenter in China, McCarthy wrote back, "Everyone knows we are doing a little in the lay apostle line." [1140] The idea of a lay apostle was that he/she had a "secular" skill such as carpentry, bookkeeping, or medical/nursing needed on the missions. Lay people doing this work meant that priests could catechize, baptize, say Mass for their congregations, and engage in various types of pastoral work. Lay mission work was thought to be a few years of one's life overseas, not necessarily a lifelong experience. The Columbans had a few lay auxiliaries in Hanyang early on in the mission.

On January 28, 1921, Doctor Robert F. Francis arrived in the Prefecture of Hanyang, where he was in charge of the Columban Medical Mission for four years. He was the first American Catholic doctor to enter the medical mission service in China. Born in South Bend, Indiana, he was a graduate of Notre Dame, earned a medical degree from American University of Chicago with a further degree from the Boston College of Physicians and Surgeons. He had traveled through parts of Africa and China, "which convinced him of the importance of the Medical Unit in connection with missionary work, and he offered his services to the Hanyang Mission."[1141] Initially he was to tend to the medical care of the Fathers themselves, but the more pressing need was the Chinese. Galvin remarked, "He has labored unceasingly among the poor of this Prefecture, healing the sick and caring for the abandoned ones of the Master. He was always at the post, ever ready to respond to the call of suffering."[1142]

In early February 1921, Mr. Otto Scheuerman, a native of Rochester, New York, inquired of Regional Superior McCarthy, whether he knew of "an address

---

[1139] 26 December 1941. Folder: Ibid.

[1140] E. J. McCarthy to My dear Ned [Galvin], 6 September 1921. McCarthy noted in his *Diary of the Early Days*, "The first lay auxiliary arrived—Jerry Sheehy, May 18, 1922."

[1141] Abraham Shackleton, *History of Hanyang, China*, typed manuscript, n.d., 37.

[1142] Galvin quoted, "Our Medical Mission Loses Zealous Worker," *FE* (March 1925), 66. When Otto Scheuerman arrived in China, a Dr. P. J. Donoghue arrived at the same time. The latter was born of Irish parents in British India. O'Donoghue became a Paris Foreign Mission priest and served in Rangoon. Notes written in file: Folder: Han Yang—Lay helper. Otto Scheuerman, 1921. 1.C.1 (1891–1973). CFA-USA. For a brief overview of the medical mission of the Columbans in China, with doctors who were laymen, see, Neil Collins, *The Splendid Cause*, 102–3.

for work with lepers under Catholic auspices. I assure you this is not an idle inquiry but it is a worthy object I have in view."[1143] He was thirty years old and a bookkeeper and cashier in the office of H.B. Graves Company, a well-known downtown furniture store in Rochester. During World War I he had gained medical experience over fifteen months in the U.S. Army. McCarthy sent him a letter of agreement to work with the Society. McCarthy listed him as a lay auxiliary, so he could receive a clerical rate for his ticket to China. McCarthy's letter to the State Department to secure a passport for Otto stated that he "is a member of the Chinese Mission Society of Omaha, Nebraska . . . and will engage in missionary work."[1144] He left for China on December 5, 1921.[1145] Scheuerman worked as a medical administrator under the supervision of the medical doctor in the central part of the Hanyang area, in conjunction with the medical activity of the priests of the Chinese Mission Society. He remained in China for twenty-two years, and in addition to his medical work, he was a construction supervisor and bookkeeper.[1146] After Otto's death in 1973, his nephew, Charles, wrote to Father John J. Loftus, who knew Otto when the priest served in China (1926–1935), to mention that "Otto did not talk much to the family about his China experience, because he thought his affairs were inconsequential or uninteresting."[1147] However, Otto was interned by the Japanese at the "start of hostilities, and after being held in prison camps in China, Uncle Otto was repatriated via the MS *Gripsholm* in December, 1943."

On November 26, 1921, the second Columban mission band left Seattle for China. The group included Mr. Thomas J. Sullivan of Buffalo, who volunteered his service as a lay missionary. He was a brother of Daniel P. Sullivan, already working at Hanyang (1920–1922).[1148] Thomas Sullivan was Chief Clerk in the Toronto Hamilton & Buffalo Railway Company. He had been in service during World War I with a cavalry unit. By November 1924, Doctor Robert Francis unfortunately suffered a nervous breakdown. The extent of the suffering he saw must have felt overwhelming. The Sisters of Loretto noted, "Dr. Francis

---

[1143] Folder: Han Yang—Lay helper. Otto Scheuerman, 1921. 1.C.1 (1891–1973). CFA-USA.

[1144] E. J. McCarthy to State Department, 30 November 1921. Hanyang—Lay Helper. Otto Scheuerman, 1921. 1.C.1 (1891–1973).

[1145] E. J. McCarthy, "Diary of Progress." 1921–1923.

[1146] Neil Collins, *The Splendid Cause*, indicated the latter works for Scheuerman, 102.

[1147] Charles Scheuerman to Father John Loftus, 22 January 1974. Folder: Hanyang—Lay Helper. Otto Scheuerman, 1921. 1.C.1.

[1148] Folder: Hanyang—Lay Helper. Thomas Sullivan, 1921–1922. 1.C.3. CFA-USA. During the year or so that both brothers were in China, the Columbans sent fifty dollars a month to their mother, when another brother, Frank, cautioned against Thomas going to China One of the reasons was that his railway job income would not be available to his mother, who needed financial support.

leaves for the United States going directly home (New Orleans). He is quite well again, but needs a rest."[1149] The *Far East* readers learned about his work and in a photo he wore a white pith helmet, white long sleeved shirt and trousers and held a cane.[1150]

In the early 1920s, exploration of the theme of "the Mystical Body," with all parts of the body important for the mission of the church, led to active lay groups such as the Young Christian Workers and Young Christian Students. Their purpose was to study, pray, and work together to influence the social and work world in which they lived. By the 1950s the lay mission movement grew through the Grail (arrived in the United States in 1940), Women Volunteers for Africa, the Lay Mission Helpers of Los Angeles, Catholic Social Action, and the Papal Volunteers for Latin America (PAVLA). The first laity from the United States to work with the Columbans in Korea arrived to donate their services to Bishop Harold Henry in late November 1958. Mr. and Mrs. Edward Kreiss from Oakland California brought skills that would be helpful to Henry's diocese. Mr. Kreiss had served in the U.S. Navy for twenty-two years and had training in accounting, architecture, and teaching. His wife, Rita, had experience as office manager and secretary. Unfortunately, the couple needed to return to the United States in spring 1959, due to Mrs. Kreiss's failing health.[1151] Rita wrote about their experience as "lay apostles" and the couple's impressions of mission life in the *Far East*.[1152] As a young girl, she had attended the Cathedral of the Holy Cross School in Boston, where Father Richard Cushing visited them periodically with stories about missionaries. The orange penny box ("five dollars meant being able to adopt a pagan baby") was on the corner of the teacher's desk, a visual reminder to students to sacrifice something for the missions. Her husband Richard became a naval officer. After he retired from the navy, the couple "agreed we would like to give to God a year or so of our lives in thanksgiving for all He has given us." Their pastor at St. Jarlath Parish, Oakland, California, was a helpful guide to them for the year, as they prepared for Korea. Another Oakland priest, Monsignor Thomas F. Scahill introduced the couple to the Columban missionaries and to Bishop Harold W. Henry.

[1149] *FE* (May 1925), 112. There is mention of a Father Murphy, "in charge of recruiting young men for Chinese Service." This might have been either Father William Murphy or Father Fergus Murphy, both of whom were in China at the time. For lay missionary groups or individuals who went overseas in the early twentieth century, see Angelyn Dries, *The Missionary Movement in American Catholic History*, 119. Elsa Chaney provided a brief description of the lay mission organizations sending members overseas. Elsa Chaney, "The Sleeping Giant," *FE* (April 1960), 1–4.

[1150] "Our Medical Mission Loses zealous Worker," *FE* (March 1925), 66.

[1151] *Columban Newsletter* (November 1958). Forty-nine Columban lay missionaries are listed in the Columban *Greenbook*, 2016.

[1152] Mrs. Edward (Rita) Kreiss, "Lay Apostles in Korea," *FE* (September 1959), 10–13.

Eventually the couple arrived in Seoul and Bishop Henry himself with an entourage of twenty priests (Columban, Korean diocesan and Salesian), several Sisters and their students, and what seemed like the whole population of Kwangju and neighboring towns greeted them with flowers and speeches. They arrived in the post Korean War period when large numbers of Koreans were converting to the Catholic faith. Rita Kreiss was Bishop Henry's personal secretary and "kept so busy I haven't had a chance to get homesick." She worked with Susanna Hong, a fourth-generation Catholic from Jeju Do, an efficient typist. Rita did visit other areas beyond the bishop's headquarters. One visit made a deep impression on her: the leper colony, where she went with the bishop when he dedicated a new chapel he recently built for them.[1153] She wrote, "I can't begin to explain how pathetic these poor souls are, nor how well they are taken care of, nor how kind the Bishop is to them and how much he loves them and how much they love him in return." At this location, Bishop Henry started Perpetual Adoration of the Blessed Sacrament in the chapel, with "the lepers taking turn in pairs, praying for their benefactors and the benefactors of the Vicariate."[1154]

A movement had been growing in the twentieth century to involve lay people in mission or "the apostolate," as it was sometime called. Some groups employed elements of the Canon Josef Cardijn model of lay involvement in their world (Young Catholic Workers, Young Catholic Students) arising in the 1920s. Cardijn's approach used a "see, judge, and act method," which later was the same dynamic in early Liberation theology. Beginning in 1950, other apostolate/lay mission groups were modeled on "Catholic Action," those also with an evangelization approach of "like to like." That meant farmers evangelized among farmers, industry workers with their peers, etc., an approach advocated in the Vatican II Decree on the Lay Apostolate.[1155]

In a 1960 *Field Afar* article, Elsa Chaney provided readers with an overview of lay mission groups in the United States, picking up on Pope Pius XII's idea that the laity are a "sleeping giant" in terms of mission.[1156] A chart showed the names of lay mission groups, their headquarters, training program, length of mission service, and focus of their mission. Chaney wrote that the work of lay people in missions and at home is

---

[1153] This is probably the geodesic dome Henry had on display in Nebraska during the annual Columban festival.

[1154] Kreiss, "Lay Apostles in Korea," *FE* (September 1959), 12.

[1155] *Decree on the Apostolate of the Laity (Apostolicam Actuositatem.* 18 November 1965), par. 13.

[1156] The "Sleeping Giant" idea was also used in Columban retreats given in the 1950s. Columban leadership in retreats is related in chapter 11.

primarily one of transforming and animating the temporal order; lay people therefore do not in any way replace the priests and religious in missions but go to perform their distinct lay task in the mission environment: to bring the principles of religion into all spheres of ordinary daily life, into the developing industries and business life, into education, medicine and the arts, into the professions and emerging political structures.[1157]

The author expressed a common perspective of the time, that the laity had their "sphere" of action, as did the clergy. The laity thus worked in the "temporal" order and the missionary priest attended to the "spiritual" order. A 1963 *Far East* issue brought home the latter point, but with the premise that all are called to mission.[1158] In fact, however, as has been seen in the Columban history, the priests were engaged in construction or reconstruction of churches, schools, seminaries and other dimensions of the "temporal" order.

Lay Mission after Vatican II

Two years after Chaney's article, the Second Vatican Council's, "Decree on the Apostolate of the Laity,"[1159] gave expression to a new awareness of church in relationship with the world, with society, and with culture. The "spheres" of church and world, of clergy and laity were not separate and distinct, but they were part of a cohesive whole. The document drew on the earlier Mystical Body imagery, reminding people that in the living body of the church, "no member plays a purely passive part."[1160] Laywomen and laymen "were called by God to make of their apostolate, through the vigor of their Christian spirit, a leaven in the world."[1161]

The Society's 1976 General Chapter held in Manila specifically addressed the topic of lay missionaries.[1162] The chapter proposed "that the Society initiate an experiment which would encourage qualified laity to participate in our

---

[1157]   Elsa Chaney, "The Sleeping Giant," *FE* (April 1960), 1–4, here, 1–2.

[1158]   *FE* (October 1963).

[1159]   *Decree on the Apostolate of the Laity.* See also, the Vatican II document, *Light to the Gentiles* (*Lumen Gentium*, 21 November 1964), par. 31.

[1160]   Ibid., par. 2.

[1161]   Ibid.

[1162]   The author is grateful for Father Thomas P. Reynolds' compilation of statements about lay missionaries in the Society of St. Columban documents from 1976–2006.

missionary work."[1163] Perhaps the Society did not collectively recall that the U.S. region did have laymen associated with the Columbans in China (and in the late 1950s the Kreiss couple for a short period in Korea). Nevertheless, the strength of several decades of promotion of mission for laity in the twentieth century and the presence of U.S. lay mission groups overseas was an opportunity for the Columbans to rethink the relationship lay missionaries could have with the Society and how the relationship could be of mutual benefit.[1164]

Columban Mission Today, the document produced by the Society's General Chapter, 1982, devoted three pages to "Lay Missionaries." Regions were urged to take more initiative to implement the policy on lay missionary vocations. The chapter directed that a Lay Missionary coordinator be appointed for three years to assist Regions in the development of procedures for screening and orientation of lay missioners, the dissemination of existing lay mission organization programs, and the provision of workshops on the laity's role in transcultural ministry.[1165] No one was specifically appointed, and the responsibility was assumed by a member of the General Council. Between 1982 and 1988, twenty-seven lay missionaries were recruited and sent on mission under Columban auspices.

A concrete direction toward coordination was taken after the 1988 General Chapter, held in Pusan, South Korea. The chapter document, *Becoming More Missionary*, stated, "We have facilitated lay people in the past and will continue to do so."[1166] In April 1989, a Columban from Australia, Father Warren Kinne, studying in England in preparation for returning to the Philippines, was invited by Superior General Nicholas Murray to be the Society's Central Lay Missionary Coordinator and "to get a lay missionary program onto a secure footing."[1167] While lay people were engaged in cross-cultural mission at the

---

[1163]   *Acts of the Society of St. Columban*, General Chapter, 1976, #5, p. 11.

[1164]   Pope Paul VI, *Evangelii Nuntiandi* (December 1975) also encouraged the Society to address the possibility of lay people being connected with the Society. Father T. P. Reynolds e-mail to author 18 May 2016. For the Columban Sisters and their relationship with laity participation in relation to the Sisters, see, Sister Ita Hannaway, *Missionaries Hand-in-Hand. A celebration of the laity's participation in the mission of the Missionary Sisters of St. Columban* (Wicklow, Ireland: Dermot O'Connor and Associates, Ltd., 2010).

[1165]   *Columban Mission Today*, General Chapter of the Missionary Society of St. Columban (1982), 65–67.

[1166]   Missionary Society of St. Columban General Chapter (1988), *Becoming More Missionary*, par. 26.

[1167]   Author e-mail correspondence with Father Warren Kinne, 7, 8 August 2016. The 1988 General Chapter delegates read a draft of a *Handbook for Lay Missionaries*. A number of them were concerned about the potential financial consequences of some of the statements for the Society.

time, the endeavor did not have a unified program.[1168] Kinne formally began as Coordinator in the first half of 1990 with an office in Dalgan Park. He had many challenges before him: obtain knowledge of the people/programs in the regions, be able to communicate with lay missionaries and the Columban priests (not all of whom were sold on the idea of lay mission), and develop along with Lay Missionary representatives a handbook that clarified responsibilities and provided sources for a spiritual foundation for missionaries in the Columban tradition.

Kinne, who would later spend many years in China,[1169] set up three area gatherings to reflect on and assess the lay mission program in the regions and to develop a more cohesive lay mission formation program across the Society. The gatherings took place in Hong Kong (1991), Jamaica (1992), and a plenary meeting in Tagaytay, Philippines (1994). In 1993 Kinne had visited the orientation programs in the Philippines, Korea, Fiji, the United States, and Ireland.[1170] This organized, consistent focus provided him with a clear view of the strengths and weaknesses of existing formation program. He also worked to see how the link between laity and clergy could be a true "partnership." In early 1994, he reported that about fifty lay people were engaged in mission with the Columbans that year or were in orientation for mission. Father Kinne regularly placed articles in *Columban Intercom* to inform the Society of developments in the lay mission program. He provided some challenges to the Society in terms of involvement with the laity and included stories about lay missioners.

At the three gatherings, the groups had drafted and refined a document on lay mission within the Columban context. The Columban founders' intention was "to bring the Good News of the Gospel to people who had not yet heard it," with efforts aimed especially to the people of China.[1171] "From the beginning, [the founders] envisaged that Sisters, Brothers, Lay People and Priests would participate in this missionary enterprise. Hence, within the early Columban family, there were various and distinct charisms. Appropriate formal and

---

[1168] Warren Kinne noted that in 1990, the Philippines received six Korean lay missionaries. Later that year, the Philippines sent three Filipinos to Lahore, Pakistan. Earlier lay mission groups served in Chile, Pakistan, and Taiwan. Author e-mail correspondence with Warren Kinne, 7, 8 August 2016.

[1169] Kinne had some Chinese heritage. See *Columban Mission* (January 1992), 28–30 and Peter Woodruff, compiler, *Columbans on Mission* (Xlibris, 2013), 203–208.

[1170] *Columban Intercom* (January/February 1994), 14–18. While in the United States, Kinne met in Chicago (Drexel Avenue house) with Fathers Bill Morton, George DaRoza, and Thomas Browning. Michelle Harrison and Monica Messa were completing their preparation for a Taiwan assignment. Columban seminarians took their courses at the Catholic Theological Union at the time.

[1171] From the draft of the Hong Kong Document, quoted in Kinne e-mail correspondence with author, 8 August 2016.

informal structures were established to ensure that these charisms would not only be mutually complementary but would also retain their true identity . . ." Quoting the scripture passage, "By this shall all know that you are my disciples if you love one another," the document indicated that "all members of the Columban family," whether they be men, women, lay or clerical, those with permanent or temporary commitment "should strive to create a partnership which enables us to work together in a supportive and complementary way, celebrating each other's unique gifts and personal ministry."[1172]

Columbans in the United States had mixed feelings about a lay mission program in the country. In 1992, Vice Regional Director Brendan O'Sullivan challenged the men in his report on the Jamaica Lay Missionary Conference. "The past few General Chapters and Interregional Meetings have promoted the idea of partnership with laity in Mission. However, the Columban Lay Missionary Program has progressed slowly in most countries. . . . The question for us in the U.S. Region is whether we are willing to put our energies into promoting the Lay Missionary Program. I think it is worth the effort."[1173] Another factor in hesitancy might have been that some missionaries serving in the United States were from countries where Columbans had been serving for decades. Their presence raised the focus of "mission on Six Continents"[1174] and brought to the fore the idea of cross-cultural and intercultural mission.

At the Columban 1994 General Chapter in Chile, the theme of "partnership" again came to the fore. While the assembly affirmed the need for partnership ("the preferred way of being on mission today")[1175] the chapter members were of different minds about the program or its future direction.[1176] In the meantime, a "Lay Missioner Policy Handbook," the ongoing work at the three

---

[1172]   Ibid., See also, Warren Kinne, "A Developing Partnership," *Columban Intercom* (April 1994), 63–65 for the fruit of the Lay Missionary Conference, Philippines, 1993.

[1173]   *Columban Newsletter* (April 1992), 2.

[1174]   The term, "mission on six continents" was the theme of the 1961 meeting of the World Council of Church and its Commission of World Mission and Evangelism. The implication was that Europe and North America were also in need of mission. A map of the world found in John Considine, *The Vatican Mission Exposition, A Window on the World* (Macmillan, NY, 1925), which recounted the 1925 Vatican Mission Exposition, indicated all the countries of the world, including the United States as mission countries. Europe was not included. The United States was included primarily for its missions among Native Americans and African Americans. Catholic thought on "mission on six continents" remained controversial, but *Evangelii Nuntiandi* (1975), the inauguration of the Vatican Pontifical Council for Culture (1982), which merged with the Pontifical Council for Dialogue with Nonbelievers in 1992, the perspective of Pope John Paul II and the Pontifical Council for New Evangelization (2010), established by Pope Benedict XVI all acknowledged the need for evangelization of historically Catholic countries.

[1175]   *Choose Life*, the document from the Columban General Chapter (1994), par. 51.

[1176]   Ibid., par. 53.

Lay Mission Conferences Kinne had convened, was approved by the Columban General Council in June 1994. By the end of that year, the Columbans had 59 lay missionaries. Forty-one of them were in their first term, with four in their second term and 14 preparing to go to mission overseas.[1177]

The idea of "partnership" might seem a slippery term to some, maybe equally as ambiguous as other terms that were used to talk about the relationship between Columban priests and others who wished to affiliate with the Society. The experience of the Mission Unit in Pakistan provided a practical experience of what the term meant.[1178] Living mission together provided multiple examples of developments with lay/ordained, female/male working in partnership. Added to the mix was the fact the group represented many cultures themselves working in an Islamic country that itself had a variety of cultures. The key to having the experience move from "talking about partnership" to "lived-experience of partnership" was aided by the fact the Columbans were a "small enough sized group with a good openness and acceptance of the possibilities."[1179] Important, too, was that partnership developed in the process of addressing the inevitable difficulties that occur when something new is emerging. Yet when talked out and shared in true love and honesty they can become very life-giving." They found that, "Sometimes issues need to be talked out and processed over and over again."[1180] Of course, a great deal of patience, a vibrant spiritual life, and a sense of humor helped immensely.

Many practical questions needed to be worked out, some of them related to finances: could someone with a family to support become a lay missionary? What if the whole family came with the person? If lay missionaries took on two or three terms (a total of nine years, for example), would there be some type of remuneration toward eventual "retirement," etc.

Father Warren Kinne was the first of two Columban priests in charge of the Lay Mission Office, which is now headed by a lay person. In 2016, the Coordinator of the Lay Missionary Central Leadership Team is Gracia Kibad. Father Kevin O'Neill, superior general, is the liaison with the lay mission leadership. As of mid-2016, 272 women and men have served as Columban lay missionaries since the start of the formal program.[1181] While a history of the

---

[1177] "Partners in Mission," *Columban Intercom* (July/August 1994), 156.

[1178] Dan O'Connor, "No Other Way. Partnership Here to Stay," *Columban Intercom* (September/October 1995), 199–200.

[1179] Dan O'Connor, "No Other Way. Partnership Here to Stay," *Columban Intercom* (September/October 1995), 199.

[1180] Ibid.

[1181] The lay missionary number is cited in Columban Lay Mission Team, "Participating in God's Mission," *Columban Mission* (August/September 2016), 6.

Columban lay missionaries is yet to be written, the story of two of them provides a hint about the diversity of experience and contexts they brought to mission.

Columban lay missionary, Leanne Hester, was sent to Taiwan. The Columban Fathers had opened missions in the industrialized diocese of Taipei and Hsinchu, Taiwan, in 1978. One of the Columban missions was among the Atayal, a large ethnic group, the original inhabitants of Taiwan. The group lived in the mountains of Miaoli County, a government established reservation. "The aboriginal people in Taiwan suffer from poverty in sharp contrast to the majority of the population. They are in danger of losing their culture and natural resources."[1182] Because of Leanne's linguistic skills she was asked to edit the third edition of the Atayal missal. She remarked in the *Journey with Jesus* series, "What good is this God, I questioned, who hears but does not respond to a person in distress? Gradually an answer came to me: not only does God hear those cries, but God uses our ears to listen—the ears of people like me."[1183] In 2016, ten Columban Lay Missionaries served in Taiwan.

Elizabeth Yean Sin Lim, a twenty-four-year-old South Korean, was assigned to Fiji, where, along with the Columban priests and Sisters, she would visit the homes of people, while still learning the language and customs of Fijians of the area. Father Hugh MacMahon had told the lay missionaries, "Make friends with the local people. Mission is not a one way street, it is the give and take of friends."[1184] She wrote, "It is a strange and happy experience to find ourselves speaking their language, making and eating their food. They don't have much but they share the food they have and always appear at peace. It occurs to me how different our increasingly destructive way of life is from theirs."[1185] Unfortunately, a few weeks after she wrote the letter to a fellow lay missionary, Elizabeth contracted hepatitis and died in the hospital on November 11, 1994. Father Hugh McMahon flew from Korea with her parents. They arrived three days before she died. Elizabeth was the only Catholic in her family. Her father asked the Columbans to bury her in Fiji "in the Catholic way," when he learned

---

[1182] "Columban History in Taiwan," 16 February 2010, www.columban.org, retrieved 8 August 2016.

[1183] *Journey With Jesus*, Grade 8 *Culture: Gift and Blessing*. Columban Mission Education Office. Leanne Hester also served as a volunteer in Casa Vides in the frontier community of El Paso, Texas, and Ciudad Juarez, Mexico, through accompaniment and service of undocumented immigrants and refugees. Her poem, *Lejos del Hogar*, is in *Misión Columbana*, n.d., but during the time that Father Brendan O'Sullivan was U.S. regional director (1995–2000).

[1184] "Final Letter from Lim Yean Sin (Elizabeth) to Lee Kyong Suk (Justina), 9 October 1994, *Columban Intercom* (January/February 1995), 31. See also, "Death Comes for a Lay Missionary," *CM* May/June 1995), 20–22.

[1185] "Final Letter from Lim Yean Sin (Elizabeth) to Lee Kyong Suk (Justina), 9 October 1994, *Columban Intercom* (January/February 1995), 31.

that cremation services were not available. The Suva Korean community, including the ambassador to Fiji, visited Elizabeth's parents and Columbans at the lay missionary house.[1186] The Columbans commented at the time, "In the perspective of faith we expect that the grain of wheat which has fallen to the ground will produce much fruit."

A surprising "fruit" was the baptism of Elizabeth's parents "in her church" in Korea, December 3, 1995. A touching letter from Elizabeth's father to her written a year after her death was printed in *Columban Intercom*. After musing whether Elizabeth knew her parents were at her bedside that last three days of her life, her father wrote, "Your Dad had to go there at that time to realize that you were in the front line of a Catholic movement for reconciliation between the original Fijian people and the immigrant Indian people. . . . While there, the photo we took at the Mass became your portrait and this year on the November page of the Fijian Catholic calendar your picture appeared with the caption, "Let us remember you as our daughter." He then explained that he and his wife had gathered with the youth Elizabeth had worked with in Korea prior to Fiji and offered a Mass together. A Mass was also celebrated in the child care center in Song Nam (South Korea) where she had worked. Her father visited the latter place several times. "There I saw many people who sacrifice themselves in helping those who live under a cloud, to live a better life. As your Mom and Dad looked into your life's work we became convinced of how good your life was and we embraced your Catholic faith and this, too, will fulfill a great desire you had." He concluded the letter, "Praying for your eternal rest and in gratitude for the baptism you brought us. Your Dad."[1187]

The canonical (church law) structures were clear for religious life and for priesthood. However, the structures appeared less clear for lay people who felt called to mission, whether for a designated number of years or for life. As did several U.S. congregations of women religious, who explored the relationship of the "Associates" (or variations on that theme), so, too, the Columbans at their General Assembly in Sydney, Australia (2000), examined the development of the lay missionary vocation in the Columban context around "structures whereby the Columban Lay Mission Program moves forward toward greater autonomy."[1188] Laity could not be "members," a term with church law implications. As Father Kinne expressed the situation, "The old conundrum seems to remain—the direction of integration or separation.

[1186]   The funeral is described in, "Funeral of Elizabeth Yean Sin Lim," *Columban Intercom* (January/February 1995), 32.

[1187]   *Columban Newsletter* (April 1996), 75.

[1188]   Columban General Assembly document, *Columban Mission in the Third Millennium* (2000), #87. Two structures were to be a Central Coordinating Team, elected for three-year terms and local coordinating teams. Ibid, #92.

However, the concertina experience of 'partnership,' that word with so many nuances, continues to be the unifying image that the Program has had from the beginning."[1189]

In 2004, a Lay Mission Coordinator served in the Columban Central Administration Office, and lay missionaries were appointed as region or Unit coordinators. In 2006, Lay Missionaries were represented at the Columban General Assembly held in Ireland. They had transitioned from being a "program" within the Society to being Columban Lay Missionaries (CLM).[1190]

In 2012 Columban lay associates gave presentations at the Columban General Assembly (formerly called General Chapter) in Los Angeles. In 2016, the Columban Lay Mission Team expressed their mission and identity.

We are an intercultural group of women and men, single, married couples and families with children, who feel called to respond to God's mission by crossing boundaries of culture, gender, creed and race. With joy, we witness to a new way of being Church by finding and celebrating God's loving presence as we seek to live a simple way of life and journey in communion with the poor, the marginalized and the exploited earth. In partnership with one another, with the Columban priests, and with local communities, we participate in building bridges of dialogue between peoples of diverse cultures and faiths as we strive to be catalysts of transformation in building God's kingdom."[1191]

In 2016, there were fifty-one Columban lay missionaries, with one of those in the United States. While the situations and contexts that lay missionaries came from and entered into changed over the years, reflection on the experience probably left many with the same sentiment that Dan Sullivan, the lay missionary in early 1920s China expressed. "We are all so very, very small at times, and this fact has been brought to me many, many times while here. Rest assured that I am leaving China and St. Columban's mission, a bigger and broader Catholic than when I entered it, thanks to the kindness and forbearance of the Priests here."[1192]

[1189] Warren Kinne, "A Silver 25th, not yet quite Gold." Material sent to author from Father Warren Kinne, 8 August 2016. The text is his reflection on the Silver Anniversary of the Lay Missionaries, 2015. After work with the Lay Missionaries, Kinne has spent many years in China. See, Fr. Peter Woodruff, "Getting a Start in Life. Friendship is at the Heart of Being a Columban Missionary." *Columban Mission* (June/July 2016), 4–5.

[1190] Father T. P. Reynolds' e-mail correspondence with author, 18 May 2016.

[1191] Columban Lay Mission Team, "Participating in God's Mission," *Columban Mission* (August/September 2016), 6. The issue includes stories from Columban lay missionaries in several countries.

[1192] Daniel Sullivan to E. J. McCarthy 1 June 1922. Folder: Hanyang—Lay Helper, Dan Sullivan, 1920–1922. 1.c.2. CFA-USA.

Priest Associates

From Columban beginnings in the United States, diocesan clergy from Ireland who served parishes in the United States were interested in the Society of St. Columban, not only as benefactors, but as priests with an interest in joining the Society. In the United States, Father Michael Mee was one such case. But diocesan priests were also interested in working alongside missionaries outside of the United States, at least for a few years. By the 1950s, as more lay people became interested in overseas mission, so, too, diocesan priests became "clergy volunteers" (more recently called Priest Associates) with the Society of St. Columban. Between 1956 and 1979 over seventy priests had served with the Society, mainly in Chile and Peru, even though a more formal program for volunteer clergy launched first in July 1979.[1193] The Priest Associates told their stories in the pages of the *Far East*. Father William Keane, an Irish priest volunteer, served in Lima.[1194] Father Robert Watson wrote of his experience in the slums of Peru.[1195] Priests from the United States applied to Columban headquarters in Nebraska. A Priest Associate was instrumental in founding the Manuel Duato School for Special Needs located next door to the Columban Central House in Lima, Peru.

Another step was taken at the 1976 Society General Chapter. A proposal was passed that the Society "accept volunteer priests from the countries in which we work," provided they were "willing to work with us in cross-cultural situations."[1196] In other words, priests from Korea and the Philippines, for example, would be accepted for a designated period of time as volunteer priests with the Columbans. The program for volunteer clergy was launched with a brochure in July 1979. That month's *Columban Newsletter* indicated that "from the beginning our Society, diocesan priests from the various home countries in which we are based have worked with us in our missions."[1197] Given all that experience, a six page document which followed the *Newsletter* included various elements of suitability needed in the priest volunteer. He should be "old enough to have found himself in the priesthood, young enough to learn a new language and adaptable." The suggested age of the candidate was between thirty and forty years old. Normal good health, emotional balance, "the ability

---

[1193]   *Columban Newsletter* (July 1979).

[1194]   William Keane, "Looking at Lima," *FE* (January 1963), 8–19.

[1195]   Robert Watson, "Trinity of Misery," *FE* (November 1963), 6–8.

[1196]   Missionary Society of Saint Columban, *Acts of the Chapter (October 4–December 8, 1976)*, 11 # 6.

[1197]   *Columban Newsletter* (July 1979). Following the *Newsletter*, a six-page document provided information about the program for diocesan priests, including a suggested contract between the priest's bishop, the priest, and Columbans.

to see and live with other viewpoints, a basic contentment and happiness in the priesthood, a full commitment to personal celibacy, and a mature acceptance of the limitations of any form of apostolate rounded out the picture. The *Newsletter* also contained a suggested contract between the priest's bishop and the priest."[1198] There was less hesitancy on the part of the Society about the priest volunteers. The fact they were brother priests and shared Holy Orders seemed a strong bond. The financial questions raised about lay missionaries were not in the fore, because after mission service the priest returned to his home diocese to be assigned duties there and receive remuneration and lodgings, as he did before leaving for the missions.

The plan, however, was aimed at diocesan priests in the United States seeking to work in Columban missions elsewhere. As had been true for thinking about "cross-cultural mission" with lay missionaries, so, too, some Columbans wondered about accepting priests from "mission countries" to work alongside Columbans. Given that a Society decision was made to do so, in 2016, the makeup of the priest associates reflected a century of Columban locations for mission.[1199] No diocesan priests from the United States were on the roster.

Priest Associates	Home Country/Priest Volunteer	Mission Assignment
12	Korea	Peru or Chile
1	Ireland	Chile
1	Peru	Fiji[1200]

Donors and Benefactors

The Columbans had many ways over the years to seek funds for their missions. Priests were appointed specifically for promotion, whether at the seminaries or in other Columban houses around the country. At promotion houses, special dinners, annual bazaars or "fêtes," concerts, and fashion shows were just a few of the ways Columbans and their helpers brought together people from the area for celebration, raffles, music, food, and a good time. The event made the Columbans better known and people gladly contributed to the missions. Golf outings held the same purpose. Sometimes the planned event became quite large, with well-known singers or performers entertaining the guests in a public auditorium rented for the occasion. Funds also came from subscriptions to the Columban magazine, through direct mailings, wills,

---

[1198] "Volunteer Priests Working with St. Columban's Foreign Mission Society," *Columban Newsletter* Enclosure (July 1979), 2.

[1199] Statistics taken from *Missionary Society of St. Columban Greenbook, 2016.*

[1200] Father Nilton Iman tells his story in *Columban Mission* (May 2016), 4–5.

bequests and annuities. As seen in earlier chapters, Columbans developed strong relationships with the soldiers in the U.S. branches of military service. The latter assisted in reconstruction of mission buildings after war time. Knowledge of Columban work sometimes led to further donations from individuals. The Columbans specifically had permission to give mission appeals at various U.S. Air Force, Army, and Navy bases in the country.

The U.S. region developed a strong and faithful donor and benefactor base over the years, partially due to the spiritual and attitudinal perspective the Columbans held toward their benefactors. Regional superiors reminded the men about the relationship between donor's generosity and the lifestyle of the Columbans, the latter to be one of sparing use, a concept that was later specified in a Society General Chapter. "We are a Society of beggars, in the sense that we must beg from our mission-minded laity for our own support and that of our missionary work. We must have a sense of responsibility and stewardship when Society funds are in question, and of deep gratitude to our benefactors."[1201] A few years later, Regional Superior Coulter and his Council wrote to the men about preparation of their local house budgets, which should "be a group effort, stressing the individual responsibilities of the members." One outcome of the budget process was "to make us more aware of the sacrifices our benefactors make and the grave responsibility to use funds wisely and not to waste." Budgeting had practical consequences in daily life. One example was that, "the size and style of the Society cars should be modest, as befits missionaries."[1202]

Given the size of the United States and large number of Catholics, the Society leadership in Ireland expected the U.S. region to supply a hefty portion of monies for missions. Or, as Father Steinhilber termed it, "the American region was the bread and butter source. [The Columban administration] kept putting most of these [priests] on promotion, Americans, which made sense. But at the same time it was making the U.S. personnel servants of the rest."[1203]

The relationship with benefactors was again identified in the 1982 Society General Chapter, which noted some reciprocal obligations to donors: "gratitude

---

[1201] *Acts of the 1970 Society General Chapter*, 69. The perspective reflects the experience Galvin had when he went to China with John Fraser, prior to the foundation of the Columbans. They took the train from Brooklyn to Toronto and eventually to Vancouver, from which they sailed to China. In the dining car, Fraser would not spend more than a dollar for their dinner. "Five cents," Fraser said, "will buy a baby when we get to China and it strikes me that it is worth mortifying ourselves just a trifle in order to be able to send a few of the abandoned little waifs to heaven." *Father Galvin's Trumpet Call, Chekiang. A Record of a National Missionary Enterprise.* typescript. n.d. 4.B.21. CFA-USA.

[1202] Regional Council Letter to the U.S. Region, November 1978.

[1203] Father Joseph McSweeny interview of Father Richard Steinhilber, 12 July 2012.

to show the same care and concern for our benefactors that we owe to our relatives and friends; an obligation in justice that involves accountability to our supporters for the resources they have entrusted to us for our work."[1204]

The Columbans drew upon "the ties that bind" for financial support: their families, friends, and Irish and Irish/American relationships. Sometimes families offered "in kind" donations, as was the case of a farmer in Iowa who provided food to the Nebraska seminary from his farm in the 1920s. At the Columban Los Angeles house during the World War II years, Mrs. Logan O'Brien "did a lot for us in the way of carpeting and furniture. The main altar in our chapel was donated." "Mr. Hilton, the hotel man," donated some of the beds. Hilton's son attended Loyola High School. One of his teachers was Michael Heneghan, who was Father Tom Heneghan's brother. That connection led to a Columban interview with Mr. Hilton.[1205] Sometimes a relationship offered legal or financial counsel, as was the case with attorney James H. Hanley in Omaha and James F. Kane's advisement on the Society's magazine, even after he retired.

Columbans also had financial support from groups. The Irish Mission League, set up in Ireland by Edward Galvin and then in Great Britain, established a permanent organization of benefactors. They would share in the spiritual benefits of Columban mission and provide a permanent income through annual donations to support the seminary and the missions in China. A promoter was in charge of a unit or circle with twenty members, each of whom "subscribed" one shilling a year. The money was collected by the promoters and forwarded to the Society. The idea behind the League was to "reunite the scattered sons and daughters of St. Patrick into one great missionary army to fulfill again in our age the Divine destiny that God has entrusted to our race."[1206] While political independence of Ireland and Gaelic as the official language of Ireland had been goals there in the early 1900s, Irish Americans would have other goals, but they could unite around the "tie that seems to be in the very essence of the Irish Character, the tie of religion."[1207]

In the United States, Father Paul Waldron gave a talk on the Irish Mission League at the end of his retreats in the 1920s. William Kelly, rector at Bristol, thought it would "give flesh and blood and put life and soul into an idea that we often discussed at Silver Creek; how to build up in this country, without treading on toes, something as reliable and unspectacular as the Mission

---

[1204] Society of St. Columban, *Columban Mission Today*. (1982) Society of St. Columban General Chapter, 80.3, p. 38.

[1205] Gerard Marinan, "The Society in Los Angeles," November 1958. Typescript. CFA-USA.

[1206] Galvin quoted in, "An Irish Mission League," *FE* (April 1918), 4.

[1207] "An Irish Mission League," *FE* (April 1918), 4.

League in Ireland." Kelly heard it said that "the Mission League is the one real solid and sure source of revenue that the Society has in Ireland."[1208] Father Richard Ranaghan tried to establish the League under the title, St. Columban Mission Circles, but without much long-term success. The U.S. plan was a fifty dollar Honorary Perpetual Membership for benefactors who made substantial contributions to the society in money or services."[1209]

The women of the Holy Rosary Circle, Brooklyn, the parish that Father Edward Galvin served before he went to China, remain active donors with interest in the Society. While the original members are deceased, their descendants continue to give to the Columban Fathers, even though the women have moved elsewhere.

The Ladies Ancient Order of Hibernians (LAOH) is the oldest and perhaps the largest financial supporter of the Columbans in the United States.[1210] In a visit to Chicago in March 1935, Bishop Galvin met Mary McWhorter, a member of the LAOH. Learning of her interest in missions, Galvin and she set up a support group, the Mission Helpers of St. Columban, with Mrs. McWhorter the president. The women grouped themselves into sections of twelve (twelve Columban Apostles), with a section leader. "That way," Galvin said, "I can fit any friends I meet harnessed to a definite work." Mary worked to get support from the AOH ladies and Hibernian men. "I am meeting the lady heads of 75 AOH units tomorrow night. My idea is to build up a list of friends who would stand by me from year to year. The Pastors whom I have met have taken kindly to the idea. It is something new."[1211] The women received a membership card, a holy card which pictured St. Columban on one side and a prayer for the missions on the back. Galvin, through Father Patrick O'Connor, sent 2000 copies of the card to McWhorter.

Later that same year, Mary McWhorter was appointed the national chairman of missions at the annual LAOH convention in Baltimore. After the convention, Bishop James Griffin of Springfield, Illinois, wrote to Mrs. McWhorter to congratulate her on her appointment. He had visited with Galvin while he was in the States and wrote to her that Galvin "would have broken under the strain were it not for the fine encouragement given by the AOH and the LA. As you know, some ten days before the Baltimore convention, his

---

[1208] William Kelly to Paul [Waldron] 7 May 1934. Folder: Bristol/Kelly, 1933–1935. CFA-USA.

[1209] E. J. McCarthy, "A Few Personal Reminiscences, 1916–1920," written in early 1950s.

[1210] Since 2006, the LAOH have also supported the Missionary Sisters of St. Columban.

[1211] Galvin to Paul [Waldron], 28 April. Galvin stayed at St. Attracta's Church in Chicago. The church, started by Polish immigrants in 1904, was rebuilt by Italians in 1960. When it closed in 1990 the congregation was mainly Hispanic.

diocese was flooded out in two different places and he certainly showed signs of discouragement."[1212]

In 1940 Galvin described to McWhorter the growth in Catholic life in the twenty years since his arrival in the Hanyang vicariate. He noted the presence of five churches, three convents, three catechumenates, an embroidery school, orphanage, dispensary and central headquarters for the priests of the mission. The Catholic population had grown from 18,512 to 55,338. The Hanyang vicariate moved from forty-fifth place in the number of Catholics to eighth highest in China. But, Galvin cautioned, "We do not speak of these successes in a spirit of boasting but rather that our friends may know what has been accomplished with their constant and generous help. It is their work, as well as ours, and to them we offer our heartiest thanks for their loyalty, their financial aid, and their earnest prayers."[1213] More recently, the a local chapter of AOH awarded Father Mark Mengel, pastor of Holy Name parish, Springfield, Massachusetts, the prestigious Christian Charity Award.[1214]

Some donors knew an individual Columban and donated toward a project the missionary hoped to initiate. Such was the case of Gerald Rauenhorst, Carl and Angela Kent, and Colonel and Mrs. Rowland, who were generous contributors to the Korean missions of Bishop Harold Henry.[1215] Joseph and Katherine Reilly had for decades contributed to the Columban missions. In 1972, Katherine had the opportunity to visit the Columban missions in Korea at the invitation of Father Sean Brazil.[1216] Mrs. Reilly told him, "the Lord has been good to me all my life and anything I have He gave to me. I plan to give it back to Him while I am alive." While she was "not brave enough to sacrifice [her] life" as a missionary, she noted that the "least we can do is to help you to realize your dream, which, in fact, is His command 'to go to all nations.'"[1217] She

---

[1212] Bishop James A. Griffin to Mrs. Mary F. McWhorter, Chicago, 3 August 1935.

[1213] Galvin to Mrs. McWhorter, 24 September 1940. CFA-USA.

[1214] The AOH and LAOH give the annual award to recognize someone in the community "who truly seeks to improve the quality of life for people of the Hampden and Hampshire counties." 19 February 2016 article retrieved from www.iObserve.com, Catholic Communication News.

[1215] Edward Fischer, *Light in the Far East* (NY: The Seabury Press), 172, 123–125. One Rowland donation, for example, made possible the building of a brick church to hold seven hundred congregants. The church was named St. Martin's Church, in memory of Mrs. Rowland's father. Ibid., 125.

[1216] *CM* (October 1972), 19–20. Sean Brazil's memoir notes, "We can never forget the generosity of a lady from Santa Barbara, Katherine O'Reilly (RIP), who gave almost $65,000.00 to build St. John the Apostle parish in the area of Sangbong Tong in the Archdiocese of Seoul. "Individual History of Sean Brazil, 30 November 1997," seven pages, typescript, single spaced. Typed on stationery from the Korean Martyrs Catholic Center, Westminster, California. CFA-USA.

[1217] *CM* (October 1972), 19.

spent a month in Korea to learn about the Columban missions. She commented on the friendliness of the Korean people, the love the people had for the priests and Sisters, and the "community spirit when the farmers get together to help with the rice planting." But she also saw firsthand the "long hours people work in factories—as much as 16 hours a day—the poor farmers, with no equipment, doing all the work by hand, the huge loads that the men carry on the A-frame and the women on their heads." [1218] Katherine went on a sick call with Columban Father Francis J. Royer from Chicago. They walked several miles into the countryside to anoint "old Mary Kim on her dying bed." As they walked back to the parish building, Father Royer remarked, "Even for that one sick call, it was worthwhile becoming a missionary."[1219] With all the memories of Korea, Katherine said to Father Brazil, "If you only knew the joy it gives me to send the Columbans a donation, you would not hesitate to ask, you would not deprive me of the opportunity and the joy of giving."[1220]

Other donors provided funds to the Society to use as the men saw fit. In most all cases, the giving was more than writing a check. It was a leap of faith that somehow the donor's prayers and money would enable the growth of Catholic life, especially in areas of the world where Christ was not known. Each donor has his or her own story of faith that prompts their generosity. Cyrilla Duprel (1924–2015), whose story begins in Berlin, Wisconsin, is one example. As Polish settlers arrived in Wisconsin, her mother's father, Albert Hopka, met Father Bronislaus Buczynski, who was assigned to pastor the Polish settlers in the Fox River Valley region. Mr. Hopka offered his home and family table as the location for the celebration of Sunday Masses in 1870.[1221] This marked the beginning of what became St. Stanislaus Parish, Berlin, Wisconsin. The "table leadership" continued into the next generation. Her parents, Margaret Hopka and John Ogurek were married in that parish on January 17, 1911 and came to the Omaha area. Cyrilla and her twin were born in Bellevue, Nebraska, in 1924. The family lived at the bottom of the hill, neighbors to the Columbans at the top. Cyrilla's father was a noncommissioned officer who worked at Fort Crook about two miles from their house. The family walked to Mass there on Sunday mornings.

[1218]   Ibid., 20.

[1219]   Ibid.

[1220]   Ibid.

[1221]   The Hopka kitchen table was later placed in the parish church. On the table a plaque indicates that around that table the first Mass was offered for the people who formed St. Stanislaus Parish. Author telephone interview of Cyrilla Duprel, and "History of St. Stanislaus Parish, Berlin, Wisconsin," retrieved through Archdiocese of Milwaukee website, December 2013.

On some Sunday afternoons, the priests and seminarians (the "men from the Chinese Mission Society, as her family thought of them") walked down the hill past the family house and toward the Missouri River. On their return trip, they stopped at the Ogurek family house, left their muddy rubber overshoes outside and sat around the kitchen table, while Cyrilla's mother fed them lemon meringue pie or the flavor of the day. She and her sister used the front steps of the seminary as their playground and would pray at the Marian grotto to the east of the seminary. She remembered Father E. J. McCarthy's booming voice and Father Patrick O'Connor ("he had wonderful eyes and was saintly"). She remembered Fathers Richard Ahern, who had returned in ill health from China, and John McFadden, a teacher and later rector at the seminary. McCarthy came back to visit the family on his way to California in the 1950s. Cyrilla left Bellevue after she and Duke Duprel, an army man, were married in the Ft. Crook Chapel on New Year's Eve, 1942. After Mr. Duprel's service in Okinawa, the Philippines, and Japan during World War II, the couple moved to Nashville, Tennessee. He was hired as a construction engineer at the Tennessee Gas and Power Company. The couple had four children.

Around 1980, when Cyrilla had some financial stability, she began to donate to the Columban missions, though she had not seen or spoken with a Columban since she left Bellevue. She had kept an illustrated diary of her Bellevue childhood that included hand drawn illustrations of the seminary campus.[1222] In 2013, she was delighted with a visit from Father John Comiskey when he attended a conference in Nashville. She showed her visitor some photos of the "early days of the Columbans" and her diary. Fr. Comiskey remarked, "The Columbans and their ministry around the world are part of Mrs. Duprel's fondest memories; moreover, they are part of her spirit. She has been with the Columbans every step of the journey in all parts of the world, not physically but in prayer and devotion."[1223]

Two characteristics stand out clearly in the Columban understanding of their relationship with donors, whether people gave a dime or a thousand dollars: inclusion into the Columban "family" and a sense of Columban accountability toward donors. In a 1960s letter in the *Far East*, Regional Superior Daniel Boland laid out the scenario of newly ordained missionaries going to their missions saying goodbye to their families, with tears on both sides because of physical separation. Nevertheless, each man "feels privileged to be called upon to assist in Christ's work for souls." Boland then brought donors

---

[1222] Information gleaned from "Mrs. Cyrilla Duprel's Story," Columban In-house Communication (March 2013) and author telephone interview with Cyrilla Duprel, 19 March 2013.

[1223] "Mrs. Cyrilla Duprel's Story," Columban In-house Communication (March 2013). Her obituary noted that Memorials were invited to be given to the Columban Fathers: see, www.MarshallDonnellyCombs.com.

into that intimate circle: "These are your missionaries—you have helped us to educate them through your prayers [and charity]."[1224] A few years later at the Easter season, when catechumens were baptized in the Columban missions, Boland wrote, "We like to think of you our Associate Missioners here at home as 'proxy' sponsors for these newborn children of God. The power of your prayer speeds across the seas to infuse the Spirit of God into the words and actions of your priests."[1225] Father David Richers, missioned to Korea, reiterated the connection. "We can't do anything without our benefactors back home. People prayed for me. My mother's weekly letters told me that. We have to remember the spiritual part of the donor process. That goes hand in hand."[1226]

Given the Society's tremendous sense of responsibility toward donors, it is not surprising the Society was a founding member of the National Catholic Development Conference (1968), the largest single organization dedicated to Catholic philanthropy. Regional Director Charles Coulter was also a leader in drafting the Conference document, "Principles and Guidelines for Fundraising in the United States by Arch/Diocesan Agencies and Religious Institutes (1977).

In the 1970s, one form of Society accountability was a report of the regional director "to our friends." The document was a Statement of Revenue, Receipts, Expenses, Transfers and Deficit for the fiscal year, along with the Opinion of the Certified Public Accountant. The Society indicated the sum total given to each region and the number of locations/type of mission work (parishes, mission stations, catechists, schools, development projects). A letter from the regional director accompanied the facts and descriptions. Father Hugh O'Rourke noted, that while the report is "mostly about money because that is something that can be easily counted and audited," in fact, the report is "mainly about people—the people we serve, mostly in the poorer nations of the world— and you, our friends." Recognizing that the donor's gift was part of their "ready cooperation in our common missionary vocation," the Society's work on the missions and through the mission education program in the United States, the magazine, vocation recruitment, seminary training and support of sick or aging missionaries, were all designed to stress the missionary nature of the Church and "your own role as a missionary spreading the Good News of Christ."[1227]

[1224] Daniel Boland, "From the Director's Desk," FE (September 1963), 14. In the same issue, Robert Brady, related the story of Clara Westropp, Cleveland, Ohio, originator of Mission Circles. Robert Brady, 'Going Around in Circles," FE (September 1963), 14–16. Brady wrote, "Although some missioners may feel that they are going it alone, in their hearts they know they can't. They need help, organized help like that which the Mission circle provides, to make their work effective." Ibid., 16.

[1225] Daniel Boland, "From the Director's Desk," FE (April 1966), inside front cover.

[1226] Unnamed interviewer of Father David Richers. videotape, 10 April1992. CFA-USA.

[1227] Father Hugh O'Rourke, "A Report to Our Friends . . . From the Columban Fathers, 1976." 9.B.24. CFA-USA.

The Columbans, in turn, had a spiritual obligation toward their benefactors. "In order to carry out our missionary task we depend upon the spiritual and material generosity of our benefactors. Therefore, they have a special place in our celebrations of the Eucharist and prayers."[1228]

The story of St. Mary's Parish, Bellevue, provides a rich embodiment of various aspects of giving. The presence of the Columbans at the parish has been felt deeply. Father E. J. McCarthy was appointed to shepherd the small group of Catholics who formed the nucleus of the parish in the 1930s, and he gave money to start a physical space for the group to worship. Over the years and continuing to this day, the Columbans assist the parish for Sunday Masses and parishioners have given generously to the Society financially. As noted in chapter 7, Sylvia Thompson, former director of the parish Religious Education program, then directed the Columban Mission Education Office, along with assistance from another St. Mary parishioner, Connie Wacha. Christopher Saenz's family is from the parish, and he was ordained a Columban missionary in 2000. He has been serving in Chile for many years.[1229] The parish remains a firm supporter of the Columbans. Not surprisingly, St. Mary's Parish has a "sister parish" in Chile.

Conclusion

Columbans pointed beyond themselves to mission and to the people they served. Engaging a wide range of people in mission, the Society had an appeal to Catholics for many levels of involvement in mission. The Society knew they needed Sisters for the mission's success. Initially the Society provided financial resources and continued with spiritual resources for the Columban Sisters and the Sisters of St. Mary of Hanyang and promoted their life and stories in the magazine. In the United States groups of religious Brothers whose mission related to teaching or medicine (Christian Brothers or Alexian Brothers, for

---

[1228] Missionary Society of Saint Columban, *Constitutions and Directory* (1986), D.230.3, p. 38. Another factor related to donor money is the investment of funds. The Society's forward looking thought on this is discussed elsewhere, but in 1978, the Regional Council endorsed membership in the National Catholic Coalition for Responsible Investment, a national organization formed in 1973 and composed of several national Catholic groups including women and men religious congregations. The particulars and implications of this step are given in *Columban Newsletter* (November 1978). See, Pope Paul VI, *Populorum Progressio* (*On the Development of Peoples*, 26 March 1967), #26.

[1229] Father G. Chris Saenz, "The Homegrown Columban," retrieved from the *CM* Region of Britain website, 15 February 2016. The same material is found in, "I wasn't Always Like This," ZoomInfo cached page. Missionary Society of St. Columban, www.columban.org, retrieved 10 May 2016.

example) tended to have a good number of vocations to the brotherhood. Brothers' communities with a manual labor or clerical skills emphasis only and connected with a priest community generally did not acquire many Brothers. Such was the case with the Columban Brothers who were mainly from Ireland. While there was movement in the Society to reinstitute Brothers, the U.S. region (and the Society) decided not to do so. The development of lay missionaries identified with the Columban Fathers took a few decades to mature. The challenging part of the relationship tended toward financial issues. In what way was the partnership mutual? For how long would the service be given? Lay missionaries provided cross-cultural experience for U.S. parishes that broadened an understanding of "Catholic." The Society's respect for and appreciation of donors is almost palpable throughout the region's history. They had a deep sense of responsibility toward donors and felt accountable to them. Columbans made donors feel a part of the Columban "family." In turn, donors felt connected with the Society and with that larger world. For a century, Columbans have engaged the whole church in mission.

CHAPTER 10

Development of the Local Church in "Mission" Countries

The chapters thus far have shown several examples of the development of local church leadership, especially that of laity where Columbans served overseas. This chapter provides a brief sketch of five communities of women religious and a missionary society of priests influenced by Columbans who were either from the United States or who had U.S. connections. Columbans had some shaping of the groups' development and thereby promoted local church leadership.

China: Sisters of St. Mary of Hanyang

The year 1924 was significant for the Catholic Church in China. The first national Council of Catholic Bishops was held in Shanghai, the first such meeting in the modern China. The *Far East* featured an article and large photograph of the Council of China, which had been called by Cardinal Celso Constantini.[1230] The Council addressed what today we might call "inculturation" issues, which stressed the importance of respect for Chinese clergy, a call for church architecture and art that reflected Chinese culture, rather than a transplantation of European models of beauty, and the need for the development of local seminaries and religious communities for indigenous vocations. Six Chinese priests were appointed bishops, and Constantini accompanied them to

---

[1230] For Constantini's background overview of the 1924 Plenary Council of Chinese Bishops, see Francis Chong, CDD, translated by Barry, M. M., "Cardinal Celso Constantini and the Chinese Catholic Church," *Tripod* (Spring 2008).

Rome for their consecration.[1231] The Council dedicated China to Mary, under
the title of Mother of God. The year after the council in Shanghai, the May
cover of *Far East* displayed a two color reproduction of a painting, "Our Lady
of the Orient, by a Chinese artist." The explanation provided drew attention
to the Chinese features of mother and child. Chinese art now had new subject
matter with Catholic themes. "While some people might find it scandalous to
see Mary depicted in this manner (Jesus, too, for all that)," the editor reminded
the readers that "some of the great paintings of Mary from Europe have her
with physical characteristics of the period or country [Europeans] considered
beautiful."[1232] On the same page as the painting explanation, readers saw a
photo of a recently ordained Chinese priest. A few pages later, readers viewed
the photo of a catechist in Edward Galvin's parish. The theme of indigenization
or emphasis on promotion of local men and women to serve their churches was
key to the 1924 Council in Shanghai.

Having worked in Hanyang for almost a decade, in 1931 Galvin began
St. Mary Parish with sixty Catholics. In addition to Mass, the sacraments and
pastoral opportunities, the Columbans opened a night school for men to
study catechism after their workday. The number of converts increased. Who
would work with the women in a similar fashion? Certain parts of China had
a tradition of a women's group Virgins (Latin: *virgines*).[1233] By the mid-1930s,
China had 6,211 *virgines*. They served mainly as catechists and teachers, though
some conducted embroidery schools, printing presses and carpet factories.[1234]
Some Virgins had arrived in Hanyang after the floods of 1931 and remained in
the area.[1235] They, the Sisters of Loretto, and Columban priests worked together
to feed and care for the starving, stricken refugees who flocked to the city to
escape flood and communists. The Sisters of Loretto described the emergency
situation. "We are feeling fine but too busy for words. Think of it—we are
conducting a school, a catechumenate, looking after 250 girls, making all the

---

[1231] Paul Wang Jiyou, *Le Premier Concile Premier Chinois (1924): Droit Canonique Missionaire
       Forgé en Chine* (Paris: Éditions du Cerf, 2010).

[1232] *FE* (May 1925), 98.

[1233] For an overview of the Chinese virgins (in Latin, named by the Congregation of
       the Propagation of the Faith as *Virgines*) with reference to the Columbans in China,
       see, Sister Sue Bradsaw, OSF, "Religious Women in China: An Understanding of
       Indigenization," *The Catholic Historical Review* 62 (January 1982), 28–45. Bradshaw
       highlights the Sisters of Loretto and their work with the Virgins in Galvin's
       diocese, 41–43. See also, Jessie G. Lutz, ed., *Pioneer Chinese Christian Women: Gender,
       Christianity and Social Mobility* (Bethlehem: Lehigh University, 2010).

[1234] Sister Sue Bradshaw, OSF, "Religious Women in China: An Understanding of
       Indigenization," *The Catholic Historical Review* 62 (January 1982), 38.

[1235] For a brief history of the Sisters of St. Mary, see Neil Collins, *The Splendid Cause*,
       127–129.

mattresses, pillows and sheets for the Red Cross emergency hospital, visiting the camps, giving inoculations, nursing the sick, baptizing the dying, burying the dead and a host or other things." Yet, despite the tremendous difficulties of the war, the "vicariate work goes on in a movement of unprecedented dimensions."[1236]

Women were instructed about Catholic life through St. Mary's catechumenate. Bishop Galvin, who had given the Virgins a simple rule in 1931, indicated that "great progress in the parish is largely due to the efforts" of the Virgins. Among their works, they visited the Catholics in the city and in the countryside, had charge of a dispensary, and taught in the parish catechumenate. In 1936 they instructed 200 women converts.[1237] Galvin wrote to Father Paul Waldron in Omaha, summing up some of the women's ministry. "The Virgins of Mary teach and take charge of women's catechumenate and try to do the work of the curates in the central station, while the three priests devote almost all their time to visiting and examining outside schools and sending in women to the central station for final instructions. What they have done in those two parishes is remarkable."[1238]

In March 1939, Galvin received permission from the Congregation for the Propagation of the Faith[1239] to begin a religious community of Chinese women. The nucleus of the new community, the Sisters of St. Mary of Hanyang, were the Virgins who had been doing such effective work in the area. [1240] Through various stages of the development of the group, readers in the United States followed their lives through the *Far East*.[1241] Bishop Galvin opened the novitiate for the Chinese Sisters on March 25, 1939. Two Sisters of Loretto, Sisters Justa

---

[1236] Galvin to Waldron 24 February 1938. 8-A-[26?]. CFA-USA.

[1237] Galvin to "Dear Friend" [the Ladies Auxiliary of the Order of Hibernians] 10 October 1936. The dispensary was under the direction of Columban Father Eugene Spencer (1889–1984), who served in China from 1926–1943 and 1946–1951. Spencer, born near Detroit, Michigan, was the first American student ordained in the Society. The catechumenate was under the general direction of Father Joseph Hogan (1900–1946), who died in Shanghai. He worked closely with Galvin to develop the Sisters of St. Mary.

[1238] Galvin to Waldron 14 February 1938.

[1239] Sometimes this office was referred to as *Propaganda Fide*. After the Second Vatican Council it was renamed the Congregation of Evangelization of Peoples.

[1240] For an overview of the Chinese virgins (in Latin, named by the Congregation of the Faith as *virgines*) with reference to the Columbans in China, see, Sister Sue Bradsaw, OSF, "Religious Women in China: An Understanding of Indigenization," *The Catholic Historical Review* 62 (January 1982), 28–45. See also, Jessie G. Lutz, ed., *Pioneer Chinese Christian Women: Gender, Christianity and Social Mobility* (Bethlehem: Lehigh University, 2010).

[1241] See, for example, the issues of *Far East* for (May 1939), 4–6; (Midsummer 1939), 4–5; (February 1940), 6–8

Justyn (director of novices) and Clementia Rogner (superior), who had some command of the Chinese language, were appointed to prepare and direct the Chinese women in the basics of religious life.[1242] One of the criteria for admittance was that they were from a family of third generation Catholics, "to ensure freedom from superstition and solidarity in the faith,"[1243] and that the women have a basic education. Galvin said the Sisters "should be trained using their own language, in a fashion that would not frighten or discourage them."[1244]

Galvin observed, "The little Chinese Sisters are doing really well. Imagine—they will make their vows next October. They are 20 in all, 13 novices and 7 postulants. For good will and trying to be saints, I doubt if you could beat them yourself. But it has taken a lot of work."[1245] Galvin saw the need for the Sisters to obtain continued formal education once they made their profession of vows in the community.

An unfinished newly built church was converted into a women's catechumenate. They taught in the building during the day and at night the women slept there. "Most of the instruction is given in village schools throughout the parish but we bring the women into the catechumenate for three weeks, where the Sisters influence is invaluable, where they get to know each woman personally. They give the women special instruction and prepare her for baptism, confession and communion. It gives those pagan women an atmosphere of Christianity which they could get in no other way."[1246]

By 1948, the Sisters of St. Mary were in charge of elementary schools (collectively 800 students), including a school turned over to them by the Sisters of Loretto, and two medical dispensaries. They were hoping to open a maternity ward in Hangyang city.[1247] In 1949, the Sisters of St. Mary had twenty-six professed Sisters with thirty women in the novitiate and postulate. When the Communists marched into Hanyang, "the professed Sisters could remain but had to wear "secular" clothing, live in Christian families and support themselves through work in a hospital or prison. Galvin asked the one Chinese Sister of Loretto and the professed Sisters of St. Mary "to seek dispensation as a precautionary measure."[1248] In 1952 when the Sisters of Loretto were expelled communists took over their Hanyang convent.

[1242]   FE (March 1939), 16.

[1243]   Bradshaw, "Religious Women in China," 42.

[1244]   Bradshaw, "Religious Women in China," 41.

[1245]   Galvin to Mrs. McWhorter, 24 July 1940.

[1246]   Galvin to Waldron 14 February 1938.

[1247]   Michael J. O'Neill, "Silver Jubilee," FE (October 1948), pp. 14–15.

[1248]   Bradshaw, "Religious Women in China," 42.

Under communism, foreign missionaries were imprisoned and expelled from China. Galvin summarized the reasons the Chinese Communist government gave for his expulsion in 1952: "opposing the establishment of the Independent Church there, for bringing into being the Legion of Mary, for antipatriotic propaganda against the government, for disobeying the orders of the government, and for destroying the property of the people."[1249] From the Columban seminary in Silver Creek, New York, he wrote to the Presentation Sisters in San Antonio, Texas. "My Chinese Sisters are outstanding in their loyalty . . . Pray for them."[1250] The year after Galvin's letter, "evidence indicated that Sister Isabel Huang, the Sister of Loretto, had been martyred,"[1251] probably because she had joined a "foreign" community.

The Columbans returned to China with the AITECE program (1988) and moved their headquarters to Hong Kong in 2008. In fall 2011, two Columbans visited ninety-one-year-old Sister Li Fen Fang, a Sister of St. Mary of Hanyang in Hanyang province. Galvin had arrived in her town, Chang Dang Kou, when she was a young girl. His work "generated a great renewal of faith and practice in the community, along with rapid growth through conversions of individuals and families."[1252] She eventually joined the Sisters of St. Mary of Hanyang. When asked what thoughts she wanted to share from her story, she remarked,

> During my lifetime, there has been much hardship for us Christians. This was a real burden in my heart, as I sought to always be faithful. Today, there is much more freedom and less danger for Christians. I would like people in the future to be aware of the sacrifice and suffering of those who went before them. Cherish your freedom in faith and continue to love and spread it. What I have done, I did for the Church. As Christian people, whether Sisters or lay Catholics, we are all responsible to share our faith. By our testimony, we can touch people. Even if we fall short, even if we don't achieve all we

---

[1249] E. J. Galvin to Sister Magdalen [letter written from Honkong] 4 October 1952. Galvin was on his way to Ireland via the United States.

[1250] E. J. Galvin to Mother Magdalen and Sisters [Presentation Sisters, San Antonio, Texas] 12 March 1954. CFA-Ireland. The Texas group had been formed from Ireland. Galvin noted that Mother Magdalen could send a letter to "our mutual friend," E. J. McCarthy, who was living in the Columban house in Los Angeles at the time. Sister Peter Corcoran (1919–2013), born in Cork, was a cousin of E. J. McCarthy and was a member of the San Antonio Province.

[1251] Bradshaw, "Religious Women in China," 43.

[1252] No author cited, "Almost a Century of Faith," *Columban Mission* (June/ July 2013). Retrieved from http://Columban.org/14853/magazine-archive/ almost-a-century-of-faith/.

really want to do, we should do as I did. I always tried to do
the best I could at this, even if it was imperfect.[1253]

In 2016, Sister Li, born in 1920, lives with the much younger Sisters of St.
Mary. She is the last of the original vocations Bishop Galvin received into the
community.

Korea: Sisters of Charity, Seton Hill Sisters

The mother of a Columban missionary turned out to be a key link to the
arrival of the Seton Charity Sisters in Korea. David Richers (1924–2002) had
served in the U.S. military during World War II. He entered the Columban
seminary after the war and was ordained in 1952. The following year he was
appointed to Kwangju Prefecture, Korea, where he was assistant pastor in
Mokpo and then pastor at Noan. On a visit home to his family in Altoona,
Pennsylvania, in October 1959, his mother insisted that they make a visit to
the Sisters of Charity (the Seton Sisters) in Greensburg, Pennsylvania, to solicit
their prayers for his mission. Mrs. Richers had graduated from Seton Hill
Academy and felt she had received an excellent education from the Sisters.

So, on October 6, 1959, the two of them drove to the Sisters' motherhouse
to speak with the Sisters about Richers' mission in Korea. "The Council and
the other Sisters began to feel his zeal for his apostolic vocation and for the
missionary work of his Congregation in Korea. We felt first his great dedication,
his desire even in the present moment to be back in his mission parish."[1254]
The Richers' visit came just at the time the Sisters were celebrating because
their foundress in the United States, Elizabeth Ann Seton, had just been
declared "Venerable." This was the first step of the process toward official
church declaration of sainthood. The Sisters were looking for a way to express
gratitude to God for the inauguration of Seton's step toward sainthood. As
Richers and his mother visited informally with the Sisters during the afternoon,

---

[1253] No author cited, "Almost a Century of Faith," *Columban Mission* (June/July 2013).

[1254] *Community Bulletin* (December 1, 1959) of the Sisters of Charity, Greensburg,
Pennsylvania, is found in the Columban Archives, U.S.A., as well as in the Archives
of the Seton Hill Sisters, Greensburg, Pennsylvania, from which the document
emanated. The author is grateful to Sister Sara Louise Reilly, SC, archivist in 1994
when I first contacted the congregation about the mission to Korea, and to Sister
Louise Grundish, archivist for the congregation in 2014, who provided "A Brief
Chronology of the Apostolic Mission of the Sisters of Charity of Seton Hill in Korea."
Community Bulletin (December 1, 1959) Sisters of Charity, Greensburg,
Pennsylvania.

the Sisters in the convent talked with each other. Enthusiasm grew for a possible mission in Korea.

Archbishop Harold Henry from Korea was in Minneapolis at the time and able to visit the Seton Sisters. He arrived a few days after the Richers' visit. After conversation with Mother Claudia Glenn and her Council about the possibilities and challenges in Korea,[1255] Henry invited the Sisters to begin a two-pronged mission in his prefecture: to start a school for girls, ages six to sixteen and to begin a community of Korean Sisters. "It seemed to the Council that Mother Seton was calling us to this effort."[1256] Acceptance would be an "act of thanksgiving for this great blessing."[1257]

The Sisters were so enthusiastic about accepting the mission that 100 of them volunteered to become the first Seton Sisters in Korea. After Council deliberations, four Sisters were chosen: Sisters Thomas Aquinas Carey (superior), Mary Noreen Lacey, Marie Timothy Ruane, and Martin de Porres Knock.[1258] The choice of Sister Thomas Aquinas as superior appeared apt, according to Father David Sheehan, who knew well the Seton Sisters and worked with them many years. Sheehan wrote in his memoirs, "Sister Mary Agnes Carey [Thomas Aquinas] was such an outstanding human being that the success of the Seton Sisters in Korea is due in large part to her marvelous faith and humanness." He then went on to describe the stellar qualities of the other three founders of the Korean region of Seton Sisters and expressed gratitude to them for their help in his missionary life.[1259]

The Sisters arrived in Mokpo, Korea, in November 1969 and lived with native Korean Sisters of the Caritas Congregation. The Sisters studied the Korean language and culture and at the same time made plans for a school for girls they hoped to build in Mokpo. In 1961 Father Richers, newly appointed pastor in the rural village of Kang Jin (Province of Cholla Nam Do), had an offer from the local founders of Kum Neung Middle School for Girls. The school board was no longer able to finance the school. Bishop Henry accepted the group's offer, provided that a four year high school could be added to the Middle School. Henry asked the Seton Sisters if they would be willing to accept

---

[1255]   Shortly before his visit to the Seton Sisters, Henry wore a background article on Korea and the post–Korean War situation. *Mission Bulletin* (January 1959).

[1256]   *Community Bulletin* (December 1959), Sisters of Charity, Greensburg, Pennsylvania.

[1257]   "History of the Korean Mission of the Sisters of Charity." 6-A-72. CFA-USA.

[1258]   "Brief Chronology of the Apostolic Mission of the Sisters of Charity of Seton Hill in Korea, 1992."

[1259]   David M. Sheehan, *A Columban Missioner Forty Years in Korea* (Chonnam National University, 1996), 92. While he expressed a wish to be buried in the Seton Sisters' cemetery in Kang Jin, he is buried in the Sheehan family plot at All Saints Cemetery, Des Plaines, Illinois.

the rural school, which came with property and buildings. A year after the Sisters arrived in Korea, they began to staff and administer the school renamed St. Joseph School for Girls and undertook mission work with the poor.

In 1965 two Korean young women entered the Sisters' congregation, after completing a six month postulate in Kang Jin. They arrived in the United States in September that year and completed their initial formation as Sisters of Charity. Both women were graduates of the Jesuit Sogang University, founded by the Wisconsin Province of Jesuits in April 1960. In 1970, the two Korean Seton Sisters were on the faculty at St. Joseph School for Girls in Kang Jin.[1260] With more applicants to the Sisters, a new novitiate building was erected in Kwangju in 1979. The Sisters branched out in 1983 to open Eun Hae School for the Handicapped. That same year, Sister Shin-Ja Lee was awarded a master's degree in theology from Duquesne. She would later succeed Sister Marlene Mondalek as director of formation in Korea.

With more Korean women professed as Sisters of Charity, the community branched out still further, working at several parishes, two ministries with the blind, and a Seton Retreat House. The latter ministry, where Sisters of Charity direct retreats each month, opened in 1989 in Seoul. In 1992, Seton Day Care Center for Children was started at the Sisters' Regional House in Kwangju. The same year, Sisters took on three additional parishes, including Sorak Catholic Church located near the North Korean border. By 1993, the Korean region of the Sisters of Charity had 155 Korean women: forty-six with perpetual profession, thirty-four in temporary profession, thirty-seven novices, nineteen postulants, and twenty-three live-in affiliates. Four American Sisters were also working in the country. The Sisters of Charity served in the Archdioceses of Kwangju, Seoul, and the Diocese of Chon-Ju.

The growth of the community reflected the growth of Catholicism in the area. Columbans were quick to note the positive influence of the Seton Sisters of Charity. Father David M. Sheehan, who would serve the Koreans as pastor, teacher, chaplain, and spiritual adviser for almost fifty years, shared his regard for the Sisters in his memoirs. Prior to his arrival, no students from non-Catholic families had been baptized. In the fourteen years of his pastorate in Kang Jin, he baptized several thousand people, among them 700 students from St. Joseph's School. He wrote, "I have often spoken about the influence the Seton Sisters' School had on the families of the girls enrolled [at St. Joseph School] and attribute the growth of the Church in Kang Jin primarily to the tremendous example of the Sisters and their teachers on everyone in the town

---

[1260]   Sister Sung-Hae Kim returned to the United States in the mid-1970s to study theology at Harvard University, where she received her Ph.D. (1981). She returned to Korea to teach at Sogang University.

of Kang Jin and indeed on the entire District."[1261] There certainly was mutual respect and regard by the Seton Sisters for Father David Sheehan, who was described as "an easy, outgoing person" and "truly a very fine gentleman," the latter an admired Korean trait.[1262]

Korea: Poor Clare Nuns

A point worth noting in Sheehan's friendship with Archbishop Henry related to the invitation Henry gave to another American women's community to come to Korea. When Sheehan was a young priest in Mokpo, he saw Harold Henry as a big brother. Sheehan "challenged" Henry, "generally in a nondocile manner, but [Henry] was patient and understanding" over the seventeen year that Henry was bishop of the diocese. "Our friendship was always a reality bu only in the later years did Henry open his heart and talk about his inner life."[126] Sheehan's comment about Henry might reflect the value on the "inner life" tha the archbishop felt, though seldom expressed.

Harold Henry, who had invited the Seton Sisters to the diocese of Kwangji also invited a group of cloistered nuns, the Poor Clares, to Jeju, an island i the southernmost part of his diocese.[1264] To help people on the island have steady income after the Korean War, several projects were initiated relate to the land. They were loosely grouped together as the Isidore Developme Association. The Association was an umbrella for many efforts, several them initiated or encouraged by Father Patrick J. McGlinchey, a man full ideas and able to make them happen. Young girls, whose families were in gre need, were taught how to weave. A spinning factory was expanded, using flee from sheep imported from Japan in 1958. Spinning wheels were made fro discarded bicycle wheels. A credit union was opened. An agriculture school w launched to teach young farmers the latest farming methods. Starting witl few pigs, McGlinchey expanded the Isidore farm when he brought 450 cat to the island, not an easy endeavor in the 1950s, as they had to be transport over water to the island and a wharf and corrals built to accommodate the

---

[1261] David M. Sheehan, *A Columban Missioner Forty Years in Korea* (Chonnam Natio University, 1996), 25. Sheehan in his fifty years in Korea was appointed Engl Professor in the Kwangju Seminary. He later returned to Kang Jin, his forr parish, where he served as chaplain to the Seton Sisters.

[1262] James Feely, "Language of Love," *FE* (April 1972), 7–8, here 7. The article beg with a simple rendering of the basic Korean "alphabet."

[1263] David M. Sheehan, *A Columban Missioner Forty Years in Korea*, 83.

[1264] Edward Fischer, *Light in the Far East. Archbishop Harold Henry's Forty-Two Years in K* (New York: Seabury Press, 1976), 165 on Poor Clares. Henry was made a monsig in December 1954, a bishop in May 1957 and archbishop in March 1960.

These were just a few of the many things happening on the island in addition to all the catechetical and pastoral commitments.

As McGlinchey had lots of ideas and was able to make them happen, the same could be said of Archbishop Harold Henry.[1265] He decided that his diocese needed a group of people whose sole mission was prayer for the whole church and the world. On a visit back home to family in the Minneapolis area, he asked the Poor Clare Nuns, who lived in Bloomington whether they would come to Jeju Do, not for an "active" purpose, such as catechetics. Rather, Henry said, "They must sacrifice themselves every day in their lives of sacrifice and prayer. Rather than tell people about God they are to tell God about the people. In this way truly they will be the leaven in the community, invisibly transforming it, molding it along the lines He wants."[1266]

The Poor Clare Nun Henry met first in the 1960s was Sister Anne Condon. Condon was the abbess—the elected leader of the monastery—from its inception in 1954 until 1967. Sister Anne was already a pioneer in having established the Minneapolis area convent after the Poor Clares received five acres of Bloomington, Minnesota, farmland from Marie St. Martin for a dollar. After Harold Henry's visit and invitation to begin a monastery in his diocese, the nuns discussed the possibility and prayed for guidance in their decision. As Sister Helen Weier, also a pioneer in the group for Korea, remarked, "God asks, and that's where you go." [1267] Sister Kate and Sister Donna were the first Poor Clares to go to Korea in 1969. Sister Kate studied at the "Columban language school" in Korea. Miss Frances Kwon and Miss Gabriella Choi came from Korea to the Minneapolis area for their studies and to learn about life in the Franciscan contemplative cloister. Archbishop Henry was at the Minneapolis monastery to invest the two women in the habit.[1268] The women returned to Korea in 1970 with four American Poor Clares to begin Poor Clare life on the island: Sisters Anne Condon, Helen Weier, Kate, and Donna.

[1265] Columban Father David Sheehan, himself a legend in Korea, was at Harold Henry's funeral on March 1, 1976. A "vast throng" of people gathered to pay their last respects "to that very wonderful person. I realized how many special relationships existed in his life of forty years as a missioner to Korea. Cardinal Kim paid him the ultimate compliment, 'He was a Korean!'" David Sheehan, SSC, *A Columban Missioner. Forty Years in Korea* (Gwangju: Chonnam National University, 1996), 96.

[1266] Edward Fischer, *Light in the Far East. Archbishop Harold Henry's Forty-Two Years in Korea* (New York: Seabury Press, 1976), 165.

[1267] www.poorclaresminneapolis.org. Retrieved 3 May 2016.

[1268] A newspaper clipping, undated and not identified except as 6.A.62.20 CFA-USA gives information about the two Korean women and Harold Henry's remarks about the importance of a cloistered community whose mission is prayer. The Korean Poor Clares are featured in *CM* (February 1982).

For several years, the Sisters worked to get the monastery up and running on Jeju. The property was adjacent to the farm development project Father McGlinchey ran. They made Mass wine that was used throughout the entire archdiocese. They had a small dairy, which they learned was not helpful to their schedule for prayer in the monastery, given the exigencies of cattle and calving.[1269] They turned instead to farming aloe vera, a subtropical crop used for medicinal and health products. Eventually the four pioneer Poor Clares returned to the United States when the Korean women were established as a thriving Poor Clare foundation. Pioneering must have been energizing for Sister Anne. She lived to be 102 years of age (1913–2016). As of 2016 there are six Poor Clare monasteries in Korea. [1270]

Japan: Daughters of Charity

Columban Father Arthur Friel (1916–2002) was chaplain in the Royal Air Force in Europe from 1942–1946. In 1948, having studied Japanese for two years in Shanghai, he was appointed regional bursar for Japan and Korea and then superior of the Wakayama, Japan region. Columbans gathered from the mountain and coastal parishes at the "head Columban house" in Wakayama, Island of Honshu, once a month or on feast days. As the priests informally talked with each other, they realized a large number of children they saw were "special education children," with muscular dystrophy or some form of crippling. [1271] Though the Japanese loved their children, these physically handicapped children were kept at home and did not receive physical treatment or educational opportunities. Given what Friel saw of the work of the French Daughters of Charity, he contacted the French Province of the Daughters of Charity who had opened a mission in Japan in 1933 with a house and hospital in Osaka. They directed him to contact the superioress general at their Motherhouse in Paris.

However, there was a U.S. connection to the French Sisters in Osaka. The "Wolfhound Soldiers" (the Twenty-Seventh Infantry Regiment Wolfhounds),

---

[1269]   Sr. Roberta Ryan, "A Chapel for Cheju, *CM* (February 1982). For an overview of the Isidore farming operation and the influence of the Poor Clares in the area, see Francis Herlihy, *Swords and Ploughshares. Fifty Years of Mission in Korea* (Melbourne, Australia: Dove Communications, 1983), 212–220. Father Sheehan mentioned the Poor Clares briefly in David. M Sheehan, SSC, *A Columban Missioner. Forty Years in Korea* (Korea: Chonnam National University, 1996), 106.

[1270]   Information about the Poor Clare monastery found at http://www. poorclaresminneapolis.org.

[1271]   Author telephone interview of Sister Loretto Gettemeier, DC, St. Louis Province, 17 January 2017.

who met the Daughters of Charity in war torn Osaka after World War II, began what became a decades' long connection with the Sisters. The Wolfhound soldiers pitched in with food, clothing, medical care and financial assistance for 200 orphaned children. The soldiers even built two wings on to the home. The Wolfhounds work with Sister Genevieve and the orphans at Holy Family Home became so well-known that Hollywood produced a movie about them, "Three Stripes in the Sun."[1272]

The collaboration continued, and in 1964, Daughter of Charity Sister Maurice Naquin, a pediatric nurse, was sent to Osaka for thirty-six of her fifty year mission in Japan to work at Holy Family Home. She recalled the value of the continued tradition of the Wolfhound soldiers and veterans.[1273] The "Wolfhound" tradition of "passing the helmet" and throwing in money to support the Japanese orphans continues today.[1274]

Following up on Father Friel's request, the DC superioress general in Paris contacted Sr. Catherine Sullivan, Provincial of the West Central Province in the United States and asked her to send American sisters to Wakayama to open a hospital for physically handicapped children. At that point, Friel, being the region's procurator, was busy buying land and designing buildings for present and future parishes in the area. That included property at Nishihama, Wakayama Prefecture for the soon to arrive Sisters.[1275] The first four U.S. Daughters of Charity, Sisters Mary Moran, Angela Sheehan, Baptista Casper, and Mary Patrick Collins left for Kyoto on September 24 and arrived in Japan on October 10, 1954.

These first Daughters of Charity went to language school in Kyoto for two years, then brought a teacher from Kyoto to Wakayama for the next group of Daughters who studied Japanese for two years before they began their ministry.

In a few years the Sisters, with funds from the U.S. province, built the hospital for physically handicapped children. Sister Baptista Casper was the administrator and secured the services of a Japanese physician and surgeon.

[1272]   Columbia Pictures, 1955.

[1273]   Information on the first two decades of the Daughters of Charity mission in Japan from author conversation with Father John Burger, SSC, and from "Sister Maurice Naquin Shares Memories," www.themesageonline.org/local_news/article/id/11224.com retrieved 8 July 2015. See also, Sister Daniel Hennefin DC, "The Daughters of Charity at Carville: 1891–1981," *Vincentian Heritage Journal* Vol. 2 Issue 1 (1981), Article 4, pp. 55–80. The article, which gives background on the Daughters of Charity work and leadership in medicine, is available at http://via.library.depaul.edu/vhj/vol2/iss1/4.

[1274]   An example is provided with that Unit of soldiers in Kunar Province, Afghanistan, in 2011. Defense Video Imagery System, "Wolfhound Soldiers Continue World War II Tradition Started in Osaka," 1 May 2011. Courtesy story. Retrieved online.

[1275]   The biographical card for Arthur Friel noted the purchase. CFA-Ireland.

She worked with government officials in Wakayama to ensure the hospital was well established and accepted. The Columban Fathers saw to it that children came and soon the hospital was at capacity. A school was also established in the hospital. Through the years, the Columbans served as chaplains and supporters of the Daughters of Charity and their works.

Sister Loretto Gettemeier arrived in 1956 and remained in Japan until 1968, a key time in Catholic life with the changes theologically and liturgically in the time of the Second Vatican Council. Over the years, she taught in the Japanese public high school, Wakayama University and with the public school teachers who taught at the school in the hospital. She instructed those already who were Catholic and those who desired to become Catholic. On one occasion, a group of twelve Buddhist men asked her to teach a course on the Bible in English. As she said, "I prepared more for this class than I did for anything else in my life! I had to look at my life in a new way." [1276]

As Sister Loretto reflected upon her life in Japan, she noted, that because she had to teach the Japanese the essentials of the faith, she had to reexamine them herself. For the Japanese devotions and acts of piety were not of the essence. The questions the Japanese asked her made her think about essentials. "The Columbans had to do that, too."[1277]

Sister Loretto remarked upon the work of the Columbans in Japan. "The Columbans loved the people." One of the many examples where she found them sensitive to the situation of the poor people took place at the parish Christmas Mass at midnight. People came to and from Mass using public transportation—bus or streetcar. The transportation would have stopped by the time Midnight Mass was finished, so the Columbans had a party for the parish. People played the games they enjoyed together, sang ("Japanese people love to sing") and had breakfast at the parish center until the buses ran again at five in the morning.[1278]

The Columban priests directed to the Daughters of Charity young Japanese women who expressed an interest in becoming Sisters. Sister Loretto was asked to work in formation and direct these aspirants. From the start, the Sisters had decided that Japanese women in formation would receive education, as did the American Sisters. Some Sisters' congregations had a tradition of "native" Sisters not receiving an education. The number of Japanese Daughters of Charity grew over the years to the point where there is now an autonomous Japan Province of the Daughters of Charity with their provincial house located in Kobe-Shi. As of 2017, one American Daughter of Charity remains in Japan.

[1276]   Author telephone interview with Sister Loretto Gettemeier, DC, 17 January 2017.

[1277]   Author telephone interview with Sister Loretto Gettemeier, DC, 17 January 2017.

[1278]   Ibid., The author is grateful to Sister Loretto Gettemeier, DC, for her clarification of the Daughters of Charity history in Japan.

Philippines: Sisters of Mercy

Columban Father Edmond G. Bahl (1918–2001) born in Buffalo, New York, was ordained in 1943 and sent to the Lanao Prelature of Ozamis in the Philippines in 1946, the year the country became an independent republic.[1279] Bahl saw the value of schools as "the only way to reach the kids."[1280] He set up a high school in Mindanao. Later he became president of St. Columban's College, one of the schools he had founded. Father Bahl knew the valuable ministry the Mercy Sisters brought to the Diocese of Buffalo, as well as the Mercy medical ministry to Columbans elsewhere in the United States. The Mercy Sisters had been summer guests for the day in the 1920s and vacationed in some summers in the 1930s at the Columban Silver Creek seminary. Bahl's niece became a Buffalo Sister of Mercy (Sister Mary Elizabeth Walter). With these connections to the community, Father Bahl contacted the Mercy Sisters to ask them to send their Sisters to Lanao Province.

The community accepted the invitation and sent four Mercy Sisters to start their mission in a corner of Mindanao, Philippines, in 1957. The Sisters spoke at a student assembly at their Mount Mercy Academy, Buffalo, where three former Mercy Academy students, now Mercy Sisters, spoke to the young women in the auditorium about their "plans for spreading the mantle of mercy" in Tubod, Lanao Province, Mindanao, Philippines.[1281] This would be the first foreign mission of the Buffalo Mercy Sisters. Sisters Miriam John Nash (superior), Mary Mark Long, and Mary Harriet O'Connor mentioned some elements of the future mission. The Sisters reminded the students that their work expressed the Mercy vows of service to the poor, sick, and ignorant. A fourth Sister, Christina Dineen, a graduate of Mercy High School, Niagara Falls, was visiting her parents in that city on the day of the Assembly.

Many preparations were made for the Sisters' journey including collection of supplies contributed by family and friends and objects for their chapel. A new white habit was sewn for the Sisters and modified for the heat and humidity they would experience in the tropics. "Modeling" the habit was done a few times before their departure and proved to be quite a novelty for those who saw it.

Several Masses were offered for and with the missionaries and their various constituents. On January 20, 1957 Father John J. O'Connor sang a High Mass for the Sisters and their families. Two Columbans (Peter Boland, vice rector at Silver Creek, and Hugh O'Rourke) were present for the Mass and breakfast at the Chapel at Mount Mercy on January 27, 1957. Boland recalled to all the

---

[1279] Columban Patrick Cronin was appointed Prelate Ordinary of Ozamis in 1955.

[1280] Edmond Bahl, *Those Who Journeyed with Us* (1918–2012).

[1281] Buffalo Box 99, V A-3 Philippine Mission—General Materials, "Early History of the Philippine Mission, 1957, 1. Mercy Heritage Center, Belmont, North Carolina.

priests many of his experiences as "steady altar boy for Mt. Mercy."[1282] Father Edmond Bahl's sister and family visited the Sisters because they would be living in the same neighborhood.

After saying their final "good-byes," the Sisters took the train from Buffalo to New York City and across the country to San Francisco, from whence they sailed on the Glenville, a Norwegian ship. They made a stop in Chicago, where the Columban Sisters met them. When the porters at Chicago's Union Station saw the luggage tags listed for the Philippines, the men pooled their pennies and gave the Sisters nineteen dollars for the mission. After a few days with the Columban Sisters, the Mercy Sisters returned to their train with a final stop in San Francisco. Father John des Rosiers, the Columban bursar, met the Sisters at the station and transported them to the Mercy Sisters in Burlingame, just south of San Francisco. When it was time to leave for the ship on February 19, "D day—Departure Day," Mother Callista from Burlingame accompanied the Sisters to the ship. Father de Rossiers met them there to be sure they were safely settled and luggage stowed for the three week trip to the Philippines. He returned after their supper on the ship to check that all was well. After many hours of loading, the ship finally left the dock on February 20 at 5:30 a.m.

Once the ship docked in the Philippines, the Sisters were not sure who would meet them. A man on shore "asked if we were 'for the Columban Fathers.' He told the Sisters to give their baggage to the man who represented the Catholic Welfare Association."[1283] Then the Mercy Sisters saw two priests in white cassocks. "We had wished so hard that they would show up before the passengers left the ship so that it would not look as if we had not been met. The priests were Fathers Nowak and [William] Godsil," the latter representing Bishop Patrick Cronin.[1284] "The Bishop is in good form, he said, the Sisters are coming. He was very pleasant and courteous. The priests said we were most fortunate in the record passing of our luggage."[1285] The Sisters wrote that when they arrived at the Columban house "we were met by the noise of a new building going up. The present house is very old. The priests at the house took care of getting the Sisters trunks from the ship and got them through Customs inspection." Father Kelly [probably Mark] took them to the immigration office to pick up forms to complete the immigration process, which saved them time the next morning when Father Kelly again saw the Sisters through the remainder of the entry process.

[1282] Buffalo Box 99, V A-3 Philippine Mission—General Materials, "Early History of the Philippine Mission, 1957, 1, p. 5. Mercy Heritage Center, Belmont, North Carolina.

[1283] Buffalo Box 99, V A-3 Philippine Mission—General Materials, "Early History of the Philippine Mission, 1957, 3, p. 3. Mercy Heritage Center, Belmont, North Carolina.

[1284] Ibid.

[1285] Ibid.

The Columban Fathers took them to the Church of the Malate, the only Columban church in Manila and recounted the death of five Columban priests there during the World War II. They no doubt heard the story of one of those Columbans, Father John Lalor, who converted his school building into a hospital during the War. He and the eighteen Filipino young men and women he trained nursed the wounded for many weeks. After a week of strong bombardment, the group, who had a makeshift tented shelter of mattresses to rest from the labors of the day, were killed by an American shell that missed its mark and exploded. Father Lalor was buried where that happened.

The Sisters first worked in the schools Father Bahl and the Columbans had founded in the area. Between 1958 and 1966, the Sisters taught at three school/academies. In 1965 they opened a Family Life ministry and would soon have a hospital of mercy. They found in Father Bahl "a generous and steadfast friend," who "guided and assisted them in countless ways and heartily supported opportunities for expansion of their work."[1286] In 1971, a Mobile Clinic arrived in Iligan City, which let the Sisters provide professional medical care and follow-up with poor people of the area. The Clinic was possible after Sister Rosemary Petrie, RN, had collected twenty thousand dollars through the school children of the Diocese of Buffalo through "an intensive effort"[1287] on her visit home in 1969. The specially designed clinic "on wheels" was shipped through the Dr. Jose P. Rizal Memorial Foundation in the Philippines. Father Bahl's niece, Sister Mary Elizabeth Walter, served in the Philippines between 1979 and 1986. Between 1957 and 1971, twelve American Sisters were assigned to the Philippines for various periods of time.

Father Bahl was "instrumental in getting vocations for [the Mercy Sisters] from among the Filipino young ladies."[1288] Bahl's sister and brother-in-law, Catherine and Joseph Walter opened their home to Filipina students who wished to complete their college courses to become nurses or teachers, "and often, to become Sisters of Mercy."[1289] Between 1958 and 1971, nine Filipina women were in their formation program with the Mercy Sisters in Buffalo. Sister M. Soccoro Largo, the first Filipina postulant, made her final profession in 1966 in Jagna, Bohol. By 1973, there were "3 Filipina Sisters to 1 American

---

[1286] "Father Bahl's Legacy of Support to the Philippines Continues," *Heart of Mercy* (Summer 2001), 1–2. Sisters of Mercy, Buffalo, New York.

[1287] No author cited, but probably Edmond Bahl, typescript for possible article for *Columban Mission*.3-20-73. CFA-USA.

[1288] Ibid.

[1289] "Father Bahl's Legacy of Support to the Philippines Continues," *Heart of Mercy* (Summer 2001), 2.

Sister with responsibility evenly shared among them."[1290] In 1971 a postulancy was opened at Kolambugan, Lanao del Norte, and the following year a novitiate opened for Filipinas in Del Monte, Bukidnon.

Mercy ministry developed with additional health centers, hospitals (one with a Clinical Pastoral Education Chaplaincy Program), schools, family life ministry, various types of social action engagements, and a "Women Arise" Project (2000). Another example of the Mercy "charism" was the Indigenous People Apostolate the Sisters began in Sibugay Province, Mindanao. Started by Sister Corazon Dongallo in 2001, Sister Elva de Castro has directed the center since 2011. Ministry is multifaceted, ranging from reading classes for women, daycare centers where teachers are from their tribe, teaching Subanen and other indigenous groups to know and protect their legal rights, connecting people with government and nongovernment resources, instructing women in laws regarding violence against women and children, and learning ways of sustainable agriculture.[1291]

A more recent Mercy mission was begun by Sister Helen Bongolto, who, at the invitation of Sister Alegado, the local superior in the Philippines, was invited to study ecology (Luzon). In 2014, Sister Helen then used some of the Mercy Sisters' land to start the Mercy Center for Alternative Re-Creation of the Earth (MCare). The focus is on "creation-centered spirituality, sustainable agriculture, a learning center to teach ecology and advocate use of alternative medicines using herbs sold at our store."[1292] Poor indigenous women and children remain an important focus for the Sisters in the Philippines.

A Mercy Sisters General Chapter in 1972 designated the Philippines as a "Region/Area" connected to Buffalo. Structurally, the Mercy Sisters had formed the Institute of the Mercy Sisters of the Americas (1991). In 2004 the community had 36 vowed Filipina Sisters with four in formation. In 2017, there are forty Filipina Sisters of Mercy.[1293]

Through Columban interest and support and the connections Columbans had with the Buffalo Sisters of Mercy, new mission activity on the part of the Buffalo group intersected with the interest of Filipina women to enter

---

[1290] No author cited, but probably Edmond Bahl, typescript for possible article for *Columban Mission*.3-20-73. CFA-USA.

[1291] Information gathered from "Sisters carry Mercy mission to 'vanishing tribes' in Philippines," *In Harmony*, a publication of the New York Pennsylvania and Pacific West Mercy Sisters (Fall 2013), 12. "Indigenous people of Philippines focus of Mercy mission," *In Harmony* (Summer/Fall 2016), 7.

[1292] Retrieved 2 March 2017 from SistersofMercy.org/blob/2016/06/14/qa.

[1293] In January 2008, the Sisters of Mercy in Buffalo and Rochester, New York, Erie, Pennsylvania and the Philippines formed the Sisters of Mercy NYPPaW Community (New York, Pennsylvania and Pacific West).

religious life. American and Filipina Mercy Sisters worked together for the sake of effecting mission in the Philippines, "spreading the mantle of mercy."

Korean Missionary Society

Another area of local church development is mission societies that are similar to the Columbans. In other words, local Catholics who sense a call to work in "mission areas" come together for that purpose. With a vigorous growth of the Catholic Church in Korea especially after 1950, it is not surprising that in 1975 the Catholic Society of Korea for Foreign Missions (now called the Korean Missionary Society) was founded.[1294] John Choi Jae-seon, bishop emeritus of Busan, Korea, at the time, noted the action was "a way to show our gratitude to those who gave so much for the Korean Church."[1295] The goal of the Society is to send priests to evangelize long-term in countries underserved by clergy.

Shortly after the Korean Missionary's foundation, Father Chuck Lintz, a native of Rochester, New York, and parish priest in Korea after ordination in 1970, was asked if he had an interest in helping a newly founded foreign mission society in Korea. The invitation appealed to him, "Because when you form individual Catholics you have that person formed. If you train priests, their influence will multiply."[1296] He began work as director of formation for the Korean Missionary Society in September 1977. He lived and prayed with the men and devised apostolic programs focusing on cross-cultural experiences and on people who were impoverished so that the students could discover their true vocation. Many left, but those who stayed did so having a better realization of missionary life.

Challenges abounded on both sides. While he spoke the Korean language there was always a difficulty of communication at a deeper level. He learned to "live with frustration," and thus "I grew in my own faith."[1297] Through regular spiritual direction, he tried to help them share their lives and their experience of God, where God is in their lives, and help them see how God loves them."[1298]

[1294] For a short history of the Society, see "Korean Missionary Society, A Small Tool to Serve a Great Purpose," an interview with the Society's Superior General Father Andrew Kim Young-jae, *Asia News* (6 June 2014).

[1295] Korean Missionary Society, "A Small Tool to Serve a Great Purpose," an interview with the Society's Superior General Father Andrew Kim Young-jae, *Asia News* (6 June 2014).

[1296] Brendan O'Sullivan interview of Charles Lintz, 17 January 1996. See also, Father Sean Dwan interview of Father Chuck Lintz 12 June 2014, Bristol, Rhode Island.

[1297] Father Chuck Lintz e-mail correspondence with author.

[1298] Father Chuck Lintz e-mail correspondence with author, 18 January 2017.

The time with the Society was for Lintz "energizing, fulfilling, a high point [for me]."[1299] He remained with the Korean Mission Society until 1987, when he was assigned to the Columban Justice and Peace office in the United States.

In 2014, the Korean Missionary Society had ninety-five members.[1300] By 2016, Society members had served in China, Cambodia, the Philippines, Mexico and in several other countries. In Alaska, the Society's first U.S. mission, this means ministering to Native Americans and to people in rural areas.[1301]

The Columbans shaped church leaders not only in their parishes, including the effective Legion of Mary, the Society was instrumental in encouraging the development of indigenous women religious congregations and a mission society who sought mission overseas in gratitude for the gift of faith received from missionaries in Korea. This was a further dimension of ecclesial leadership.

Conclusion

In these several stories, albeit briefly told, it is clear that Columbans had a sense of building up the local churches through local leadership. [1302] The Columbans recognized what the Sisters had to offer the local church. The example had been set by Bishop Galvin himself in China and has continued in other countries where the Columbans serve.

[1299] Brendan O'Sullivan interview of Charles Lintz 17 January 1996, and Father Chuck Lintz e-mail correspondence with author, 18 January 2017.

[1300] Korean Missionary Society, "A Small Tool to Serve a Great Purpose," an interview with the Society's Superior General Father Andrew Kim Young-jae, *Asia News* (June 6, 2014).

[1301] The Columban Fathers also provided some funding for building the formation house in Tagaytay for the Mission Society of the Philippines.

[1302] A brief mention must also be made of a Sisters' community founded in the Philippines, though the contact of Columban Father Edmond G. Bahl (1918–2001) from Buffalo, New York. His niece was a Sister of Mercy in Buffalo, New York. Bahl was sent to the Philippines in 1946. He saw the value of schools as "the only way to reach the kids." (*Those Who Journeyed With Us, 1918–2010*). He set up a high school in Mindanao. Later he became president of St. Columban's College, one of the schools he had founded. Given that he knew the Mercy Sisters in Buffalo, he was instrumental in bringing the group to the Philippines. Beginning in 1960, many Filipino women joined the Mercy Sisters.

CHAPTER 11

Retreats, Prayer, and
Spirituality Movements

Over the century of the Columban Society's life, individuals have weighed in on whether there might be a specific Columban spirituality. If so, what would be the characteristics? The type of retreats and spiritual movements in which Columbans engaged reflect some of the values identified in Columban spirituality. Columbans at the start of the Society (Galvin, Blowick, McCarthy, Waldron, J. Heneghan, for example) noted some features: the life of St. Columban as a missionary monk, priesthood, and personal and communal prayer, for example. Father James McCaslin explored the matter at length. He took course work in spirituality at the Catholic University of America in the mid-1960s, after which he was assigned to the Probation House, Bristol. While there he was invited by laity to make a *Cursillo*. After several years as regional coordinator of the Seminary Formation Program in the early 1970s, he was appointed retreat master at Derby, then a year later at Omaha with the same role until 1980, when he was reassigned to the Philippines. Before leaving for his mission, McCaslin raised the question at a house meeting, "Is there a Columban spirituality?"[1303] The interest stayed with him and he wrote to the superior general and his Council about the value of a book on the spirituality of the Columban founding priests.[1304]

Given endorsement to do so, McCaslin spent some time in the Columban archives in Ireland poring over the primary sources. In 1986 the Society published McCaslin's manuscript, *The Spirituality of our Founders. A Study of the*

[1303] *Columban Newsletter* (May 1985).

[1304] Bernard Cleary to Rev. Fr. James McCaslin, Philippines 19 September 1983. CFA-USA.

Early Columban Fathers. Using writings, letters and sermons of Galvin, Blowick, McCarthy, Waldron and other early Columbans, McCaslin thoroughly identified and elaborated upon the elements of a Columban spirituality. The traits included emphasis upon the importance of priesthood for mission, devotion to Mary, personal prayer, humility, poverty, hospitality-gratitude, suffering and endurance, and obedience. He then reflected how those values and practices applied to the present world and church. McCaslin noted that the over the years the men "worked hard, were constant in prayer, and at the same time they knew how to relax and enjoy life" through golf, cards, and spinning tales.[1305]

Along a different line, McCaslin pointed out that ecumenism was "not a highly favoured practice of early Columbans."[1306] If a Protestant missionary visited a Columban mission, should one return the call? The early Columbans had a motivation to save the Chinese not only from hell but from heretics, which included Protestants of all stripes. As "men of the Church," the early Columbans were "loyal sons who thought with the Church in everything."[1307] For almost half of Columban history, that meant a hierarchical church, which highlighted the role of priests and bishops. A shift started with Pope Pius XII's affirmation of the role of the laity expressed in the World Congress of the Lay Apostolate held in 1951. Those meetings were held that year in many countries, including the Philippines. Many other lay movements in the church globally provided background for the Second Vatican Council, that brought to the fore the importance of all members of the church in an active manner. Historically, what are some of the spiritual experiences Columbans provided or shared with laity? In what way did Columbans assist in the spiritual development of laity?

Retreats for Laity, Columban headquarters, Nebraska

In the early 1920s, the Columbans had their hands full. They were settling in at their brand new St. Columban Major Seminary outside of Bellevue, Nebraska. They sought young men to become seminarians for the missions. With a small staff, they established seminary life academically and spiritually. They published a monthly *Far East* and raised funds for mission support. They made connections with various Catholic groups and with people from many walks of life in the country. They had farm property to cultivate. Nevertheless, the Society early on ventured another mission, that of retreat direction.

[1305] James McCaslin, *The Spirituality of Our Founders: A Study of the Early Columban Fathers* (Ireland: Maynooth Mission to China, 1986), 176.

[1306] Ibid., 173.

[1307] Ibid.

In 1909 a Layman's Retreat League formed in the New York area under the direction of Father Terence J. Shealy, SJ, of Fordham University. The inaugural retreat weekend was held July 9, 1909, with eighteen men. The focus of the group was the personal spiritual development of the men as well as the overflow of that spirituality into their work. The group's title was Laymen's League for Retreats and Social Studies, changed shortly thereafter to Laymen's League for Retreats and Social Service.[1308] The movement grew in other parts of the country. By the early 1920s, a Laymen's Retreat League was active in the Omaha diocese. Periodically the group's leadership met for a weekend conference with men from other regions to share information and experience, listen to speakers, and pray together.

Lay retreats, especially after the manner of the Jesuit Spiritual Exercises, were recommended in 1929 by Pope Pius XI. He promoted them not only for "that inward peace of the soul" but for another "choice fruit, which redounds to the great advantage of the social life: namely that desire of gaining souls to Christ which is known as the Apostolic Spirit."[1309] The lay impetus for retreats gathered national momentum in the 1930s and 1940s.[1310]

Father E. J. McCarthy was approached by the Knights of Columbus to make the seminary available for retreats. Several of the men were members of the local Laymen's Retreat League, for whom McCarthy had given a talk. In August 1929, he conducted the first lay retreat at St. Columban Seminary with eleven men in attendance.[1311] The retreatants used the rooms vacated by the seminarians who were home for the summer. The summer retreats became a regular feature at the seminary. In 1931, five retreats were given.[1312] Lay retreats in Omaha and Silver Creek were featured in a *Far East* issue in 1939.[1313] The program began on Friday evening and ended with breakfast early

---

[1308]   In 1912 the Laymen's League bought a large house in Malvern, Pennsylvania, and built the Manresa Retreat House there in 1921. This is the oldest and largest Catholic retreat house for lay retreats in the United States.
See also, Gerald C. Treacy, SJ, "The Beginning of the Retreat Movement in America," in *Proceedings of the First National Conference of the Laymen's Retreat Movement in the United States of America* (Philadelphia: Laymen's Weekend Retreat League, 1928), 13–20.

[1309]   Pope Pius XI, *Mens Nostra*, 29 December 1929.

[1310]   This type of retreat declined in the 1950s as Catholic Action came to the fore and revived in revised form in the 1960s and 1970s. In the late 1970s the National Catholic Laymen's/Catholic Laywomen's Retreat Conference became Retreats International.

[1311]   The family names of the men represented a variety of ethnic backgrounds: Bell, Greise, Kennedy, McDevitt (who was president of the Omaha Catholic Men's Retreat Association), Murphy, Tusa, Kaiser, Daly, Krajicek, Libentritt, and Peasinger.

[1312]   Retreat directors for summer, 1931 were Fathers James Hayes, Michael Treanor, Patrick O'Connor, John O'Donovan, Joseph P. O'Leary, and John McFadden.

[1313]   "Lay Retreats in St. Columban's," *FE* (October 1939), 10.

on Monday morning, as the men went off directly to their place of work. The weekend included several conference talks, morning and evening prayer, daily Mass, Stations of the Cross, visits to the Blessed Sacrament, examination of conscience (and presumably the sacrament of penance, as it was then called), and on Monday morning, a renewal of baptismal vows.[1314] The men were asked to keep silence during retreat, except for an hour or so after dinner. For the closing Benediction the men processed from the seminary building praying the Rosary along the Calvary Walk toward the illuminated grotto of Our Lady of Lourdes.

Father John O'Donovan was appointed director of the Omaha Catholic Laymen's Retreat Conference, between 1933 and 1947.[1315] Father Paul Waldron, who became known over the years for his retreats across the country, gave summer weekend men's retreats at St. Columbans in the early 1930s. Over the years he developed twenty-nine outlines for retreats, modeled on the Jesuit "Spiritual Exercises." Topics began with the Love of God, sin, hell, penance, prayer and ended with the resurrection, retreat resolutions, three conferences on the Sacred Heart,[1316] and a conference on the Mass. His twenty-ninth conference was a "Propaganda Sermon," in which he appealed for support the work of the "Maynooth Missionaries." He asked for prayer for the people where the Columbans served, encouraged the men to keep well informed about Columban missions (i.e., read the *Far East*), and become members of the Irish Mission League, by giving a dollar a year to support the missionaries.[1317]

After the Columban seminary opened at Silver Creek, Columbans gave summer retreats to laymen from the Buffalo area, beginning in June 1933. McCarthy suggested that "through such retreats we could get into the finest kind of contact with the best Catholic men of the neighboring communities."[1318] Father John P. O'Brien (1894–1968), in the first group of Columban missionaries to Hanyang, was then sent in 1924 to the Columban seminary at Silver Creek. He was a spiritual director, faculty member, seminary vice rector (1934–

[1314]   Program of Retreats for Catholic Men, conducted by the Columban Fathers, St. Columbans, Nebraska, Summer 1931. 8.A.19. CFA-USA.

[1315]   Information noted on Father John O'Donovan (1895–1959) biography card. CFA-USA. It is not clear if that is the name of the building at Omaha or if the idea was he was chaplain to the Laymen's Retreat League in Omaha.

[1316]   Waldron's reflections on the Sacred Heart continued through his late 1940s column in the *Far East*, "The Sacred Heart Lives."

[1317]   Paul Waldron, "Outlines for Retreat Conferences," no date. This is a sixty-one page document, with the Propaganda Sermon located on 60–61. Mention is made of the Columban missions in South America, so the document is probably after 1952.

[1318]   E. J. McCarthy to O'Dwyer. 8-C-17.31. "Lay Retreats in St. Columban's," highlighted the lay retreat experience in Nebraska and New York Columban seminaries. *FE* (October 1939), 10.

1940), and rector (1940–1947). This very busy man was also engaged in the summer retreat program. Of special note in July 1941, he and Father Martin H. Marnon conducted a retreat for men who were blind.[1319] Father Marnon was the Moderator of the Catholic Guild of the Blind, Inc. and was on the faculty of the Minor Seminary in the Diocese of Buffalo. Marnon wrote to the Chancellor of the Diocese, "There must be at least 500 Catholic Blind in the diocese, scattered over the eight counties. We have reached only about half that number with six counties practically untouched."[1320] The picture of the two priests and the retreatants appeared in October 1941 issue of the *Far East*. Columbans also reported on the laity in China who took time to attend retreats, in spite of difficult times in 1944.[1321]

Of course, meals had to be prepared, rooms cleaned, beds made and laundry washed and folded in preparation for the retreatants. In the summer at Silver Creek, a few local Columban seminarians came to wait on table and help out. Josephine Firmann, who lived in a small cottage on the seminary property for many years and cooked for the priests and seminarians, also was chef for the retreats and helped with cleanup. Rosemary Krzyzanowski [nee McFarland]'s mother, Rose, a cook at Silver Creek, also did so for the retreats. Shirley Kanistanoux and her friend, Nancy, rode their bikes to the seminary to help out for the summer retreats during the 1940s. They set tables and did the dishes. Shirley remarked that "many women in the neighborhood worked the retreats.[1322]

In the 1960s, another Columban became well-known for retreats. Father John V. Dunne, born in County Westmeath, was ordained in 1940 and later appointed to Hanyang. With the Communist takeover he was forced to leave China and worked in Student Catholic Action in the Philippines. With his eyesight beginning to fail he was sent to the United States in 1964. He eventually became blind though this condition did not stop his ministry. Dunne remained engaged in retreats and by the early 1970s became well known in the Boston area as a priest who did the Sunday televised Mass for many years.

St. Columban Retreat Center, Derby, New York

[1319] A photo of the men and their guides is found in the *Far East* (October 1941). n.p.

[1320] Information about Father Martin H. Marnon (1900–1965) and quotation are courtesy of Sister Jean Thompson, Archivist of the Diocese of Buffalo.

[1321] "Chinese Find Time for Lay Retreats," *News Release*, St Columban's Foreign Mission Society, 8 June 1944.

[1322] Author interview with Shirley Kanistanoux, who was eighty-four years old at the time of the interview and Rosemary Krzyzanowski. St. Columbans on the Lake Retirement Home, 22 October 2013, Silver Creek, NY.

A larger venue for Columban retreats became available to enhance the Silver Creek tradition of lay retreats at the minor seminary in 1945. The Laymen's Retreat League in the diocese of Buffalo promoted weekend retreats. Because the men had participated in the Silver Creek retreats, it is not surprising that the League invited the Columbans to be involved in a retreat center. In the discussion that ensued, the Columban Regional Council suggested that the League first approach the bishop. The Council reminded the Columbans that the Society "is not in a position to assume any financial responsibility for the project, owing to heavy demands for its own missionary work." The region, however, "would be prepared to accept the responsibility for running the retreat house and conducting the retreats."[1323] In November 1945, Superior General O'Dwyer cabled Regional Superior Waldron: "Authority for the acceptance of Buffalo offer retreat house approved."[1324] The following year Father Peter McPartland, who had come from chaplaincy in the U.S. Army during World War II, was "assigned behind my back" as retreat director.[1325]

After more clarification among the principals and in consultation with lawyers, the "St. Columban's Laymen's Retreat League" purchased the Hans Schmidt estate: a house and sixteen and a half acres of land overlooking Lake Erie in Derby, New York, about fifteen miles from Silver Creek.[1326] The group incorporated on December 30, 1947. That year Father John P. O'Brien was placed in charge of the retreat house, where he remained until his death in May 1968. With many years' experience at Silver Creek as vice-rector and rector (1934–1947), he knew well the people and situations of the Buffalo diocese.

The Laymen's League paid off the debt on the house and property in 1949. The intent of the League was that the Columbans hold the property for as long as Columbans gave retreats for laity there. After much discussion related to paying of a mortgage and other monetary and responsibility issues, the St. Columbans Lay Retreat League transferred title of the retreat house to the Columban Fathers in early 1950. In 1952 after Waldron returned from Ireland, where he had been vice director of that region, he was assigned to the retreat

---

[1323] John O'Donovan to Paul Waldron 22 October 1945. 8-A-43.1.

[1324] Cable to Paul Waldron from Michael O'Dwyer, 12 November 1945. Retreat numbers at Silver Creek were on the increase (1100) in the summer of 1945. Paul Casey compilation of sources for history of Derby Retreat House, p. 2. Typescript.

[1325] James McCaslin interview of Father Peter McPartland, n.d. Columban Oral History Archive, Ireland. The phrase seems to mean, "behind [McPartland's]back." McPartland had served with the North Africa, Sicily and Normandy invasions during World War II. He was decorated with seven battle awards. The assignment at the retreat house would certainly have been a contrast to his World War II experience.

[1326] The original name of the Schmidt house was the Suncliff Manor." Information provided to author by Father Thomas P. Reynolds, 27 March 2017.

house where he remained until 1967. From that base, he gave many retreats to clergy, religious, and laity around the country.

To make a long story short, over the years questions about responsibility and intent of the language in the retreat house deed continued to rise, when an extension was needed on the building, repairs were required, or other practical issues arose. There was also the question as to whether the house should be treated as a regular Society house.[1327] In the meantime, Columbans regularly gave retreats for laity, though the house ran a deficit from the early 1970s.

In 1978, a full assessment and review of the Derby Retreat House situation began in the region. Father Coulter outlined the facets of Columban responsibilities at Derby. The house and its property were the responsibility of the retreat master (Father Seamus O'Reilly) and bursar (Father Joseph Murrin). "Their primary work is the promotion and giving of retreats and the maintenance of the house and property for these purposes." Additionally, they were to be "responsible for the handling of new names, enrollments, donations and Mass stipends, as in the past, and local supplies [i.e., saying Mass at parishes in the surrounding area, when the pastor asked them to do so] insofar as these are compatible with their primary work, retreats."[1328] Fathers Michael O'Loughlin and William Schmitt were also assigned to the Derby Retreat House for Mission Education and Vocation work in the area. Thus, the retreat center served multiple purposes for the Columbans.

However, the Society continued to subsidize the retreat center. This raised the question of accountability to benefactors for the use of funds. Regional Director Charles Coulter broached the point. "Respect for the donors' intentions demands that we take a close hard look at the way benefactors' donations are used at the various levels in the region down to individual members."[1329] Given this perspective, in 1981 Coulter explained that the expansion of mission commitments "makes it increasingly difficult to provide specialized personnel and funding for retreat work here at home." The Society had taken on missions in Latin America, Fiji, Pakistan, Taiwan and Vanuatu in addition to the earlier Asian missions. "The Missions have first claim on our personnel and resources, since missionary work is the primary work of the Columban Fathers."[1330]

[1327] Among the Columban fund-raising activities conducted by the house in 1965 were retreat offerings; dollar-a-month donors; dime banks, a form of a miter box, advertisements, and patrons for the annual Communion breakfast; tickets for the annual Communion breakfast. R. Steinhilber, "Summary of the History of St. Columban's Retreat House, Derby, New York. 27 February 1969. 8.A.43.

[1328] Charles Coulter Review by U.S. Regional Council, 30 May 1979.

[1329] *Columban Newsletter* (September 1977), 2.

[1330] "Proposed Statement on Derby to go to the Diocese for their comments and publication," October 1981. 8.A.43.

The closing and transfer of the retreat house property to the Diocese of Buffalo took place in March 1982.[1331] The arrangement also kept with the intention of the Laymen's Retreat League. "At the invitation of Bishop Edward Head, the Columbans will continue their presence in the Diocese for mission education and vocation work."[1332] Columban Fathers James O'Reilly and Leonard Lavallee[1333] assisted the new diocesan director of the Retreat House until December 1982, after which time an evaluation would be made. Bishop Head generously gave a check for $10,000 to be used in the Latin America Missions "in recognition of all the Columban Fathers have done for the Diocese through the past years."[1334]

Columban involvement with lay retreats beginning in the 1920s was part of a new understanding in the Catholic Church of the importance of lay people not only for the church but for key roles in society. Lay spirituality and devotions had both personal and social dimensions. Paul Waldron presented an overview of the theological and spiritual foundations of lay retreats and their magnitude in the States.[1335] In 1930 there were 18 permanent retreat houses and 43 seasonal houses. By 1955 there were four times as many year-round retreat houses (72) and twice as many seasonal retreat centers (86) for laity. Waldron attributed the growth to the influence of Pope Pius XI's encyclical, *Mens Nostra* (1929). The Pope expressed a desire that clergy, religious and laity experience

[1331] The U.S. Columban Archives holds a large volume of material on the interaction of the Columbans with the Catholic Laymen's League with respect to the ownership of the retreat house in Derby and the relationship of the house to the Society. The questions continued to be raised as new Society directors were appointed, as the financial arrangements changed for Columbans at Derby, and as the Columban situation with respect to the missions changed. As SSC archivist Father Paul Casey noted, "Reading [the file on the Derby Retreat House] is like watching reruns of the same movie. The same two or three questions keep resurfacing over the years under successive Superiors General and [Regional] Directors." Among the many documents, one thirty-five page, single-space history of the St. Columban's Retreat House, Derby, was compiled from the primary sources and is probably the work of Father Paul Casey. Quotation, p. 31. A more concise history to the end of 1968 was compiled by Father Richard Steinhilber, 27 February 1969. 8-A-43.

[1332] Father Coulter made the request of the bishop. Coulter to Rev. Msgr. Donald W. Trautman, VG. 19 October 1981. 8-A-43.

[1333] Leonard Lavallee (1930–1995) was born in Providence, Rhode Island. The year after his ordination in 1955, he was in Japan between 1956 and 1967, after which he returned to the United States. Between 1981 and 1984 he was on the retreat team at Derby.

[1334] Most Rev. Edward D. Head to Reverend Charles Coulter, Director, Columban Fathers, 11 December 1981. 8-A-43.

[1335] Paul Waldron, "Lay Retreats in the United States," *The Furrow* Vol. 7 (July 1956), 387–395.

the "Spiritual Exercises," that is, the spiritual tradition as handed down by the Society of Jesus.[1336] A key paragraph in *Mens Nostra* indicated:

> Besides that inward peace of the soul, there springs forth spontaneously another most choice fruit [of the retreat] which redounds to the great advantage of the social life: the desire of gaining souls to Christ which is known as the Apostolic Spirit. For it is the genuine effect of charity that the just soul, in whom God dwells by grace, burns in a wondrous way to call others to share in the knowledge and love of that Infinite Good. . . . [especially] now, in this our age, when human society is in so much need of spiritual graces; when the foreign Mission fields, which "are white already to harvest" demand the care of apostles adequate to their need.[1337]

Waldron noted that retreatants form "a cross-section of the community: business, various professions, laborers, management, farmers. They pray side by side. If the men are from the same parish, they can see each other in a new light and influence their working environment." Whatever work one did to earn a livelihood, the men needed to "evaluate [their] relations with customers and clients, patients or employees in the light of Christian principles. Do we conform to what Christ has indicated He wants us to do?"[1338] He stressed the importance of a "balanced religion." Noting that one's neighbor is a neighbor *after* Mass as well as *during* Mass," Waldron cautioned against "an attitude of soul which, while being pious in the conventional sense of the word, could be embarrassingly individualistic; a man of prayer, but sublimely thoughtless of the fundamental rights and just claims of those who are associated with him."[1339] Following Pope Pius XII's emphasis on the important role laity had in the church and the world, Waldron concluded his article, "Out of the silence and thought and prayer and dedication of the retreat will come men and women of action."[1340] His retreats generally followed an Ignatian pattern, not only because of Papal support but Waldron had been formed in the Spiritual Exercises himself.[1341]

[1336] Pope Pius XI, *Mens Nostra* ("On the Promotion of the Spiritual Exercises for Laity") 20 December 1929. Par. 4.

[1337] Ibid., par. 4.

[1338] Paul Waldron, "Lay Retreats in the United States," 390.

[1339] Ibid., 392.

[1340] Ibid., 395.

[1341] For the Ignatian influence on the Columbans, see James McCaslin, *The Spirituality of Our Founders: A Study of the Early Columban Fathers* (Ireland: Society of St. Columban. Maynooth Mission to China, 1986), 56–66.

In 1968, Father Daniel McGinn was appointed director of the Columban Retreat Center, Derby. While there were challenges galore with his having come from promotion work for several years, "all of a sudden you were almost back like you were a missionary again."[1342] Usually between forty-five to eighty men would come, depending on the parish assigned for that weekend. In preparation for conversation with Regional Superior Steinhilber who would be coming to Derby for a conversation about the retreat center, McGinn drew up a seven-page set of notes outlining his thoughts for the formation of lay retreatants. He indicated the function of a retreat house: "to assist in the formation of lay leaders in prayer life, liturgical participation and theological understanding as they relate to the problems of today."[1343] Under each of those areas, he named specific practices. For example, under "Liturgical Mass," he noted communal prayer and singing, lectors, and dialogue homilies. Given the importance of communication in a retreat, a "talk on the Psychological Dimensions of Openness" would be important. His examples for this point included a talk by a layman who would "talk on how the Decree on the Laity has personally influenced his life." Or, someone "of the junior side of the 'generation gap' might speak of what they look for in their Christian fathers."[1344]

The latter reference reflected the fact that some people were frustrated and others were excited about changes in the church. "It was a very interesting time to be in a retreat house, because you had to accept the idea that the old paradigm of the Church is slowly dying." More than saying Mass in English rather than in Latin, "the people have to see that they are the ones who offer the sacrifice of the Mass, not [just] the priest. . . . What has to happen is the people have to have some kind of a feeling that they're not going to something this priest is going to do for them. They're going to offer the sacrifice of the Mass with the rest of these people who are called Church."[1345] McGinn noted that differences in attitude toward the effects of the Second Vatican Council were reflected in the Retreat Center's board of directors at the time. "The age and intellect of the Board reflects the general body of retreatants. We have polarized positions on almost every aspect and everything in between."[1346]

[1342] Daniel McGinn to Dick (Richard Steinhilber), 1969, 1. 8-A-43.23. CFA-USA.

[1343] Ibid.

[1344] Ibid., 3.

[1345] Father Joseph McSweeny interview of Father Daniel McGinn, Bristol, 29 March 2011.

[1346] Ibid., In 1979, McGinn took a renewal course at the University of Notre Dame at the same time as did Father David Sheehan, who commented specifically about the experience and renewing friendship with McGinn, a classmate. David M. Sheehan, SSC, *A Columban Missioner. Forty Years in Korea* (Gwanju: Chonnam National University, 1996), 28.

Retreats at St. Columbans, Nebraska, after 1965

After the Second Vatican Council, many parishes or dioceses offered workshops and classes to unpack the meaning of the documents from the Council. Active laity became renewed with deeper understandings of Catholic life for the "modern age." Attendance at retreat houses across the country generally was down, at least in places that had the format that worked well in the 1920s to the time of the Korean War. The Columbans in Nebraska reviewed their own situation of summer retreats. An interim committee of Columbans was set up to explore possibilities with the Laymen's Retreat group. The Columbans remembered that leadership of the retreat movement was primarily in the hands of the laity. A suggestion was made that the men and women's retreat groups could cooperate and possibly merge "into one Archdiocesan Lay Retreat Apostolate, something the Archbishop favored. Under the jurisdiction of the Archbishop the group would enjoy autonomy." Columbans would "provide facilities and would accept responsibility for spiritual guidance."[1347]

The idea was timely because the Archdiocese had created an Archdiocesan Pastoral Plan. The author of the talk to the retreat leaders, after suggesting the men and women's groups merge and cooperate for the greater good, said, "Whether we like it or not collegiality as stressed by Vatican II is an irresistible trend in the Church. . . . The day is gone when the Diocese or parish was an island."[1348] The diocese had started deaneries, around which a more cohesive local sense of church could happen. Perhaps a combined Retreat League would have a representative on the deanery and parish levels.

Conversation about retreats at St. Columbans continued. In 1977, James McCaslin gave the already scheduled Women's Retreat League Fall retreats.[1349] The retreat apostolate was listed that year as a form of pastoral work. Nine other Columbans at headquarters would join "the retreat givers team" in June 1978. "Giving retreats will be a team effort, using a team of two priests for each retreat. No one man will be overburdened. The team effort will also provide a variety of speakers and counsellors for the retreatants."[1350] Another group of

---

[1347] "Copy of words spoken to meeting of Retreatants at St. Columbans. 17 December 1973." No author indicated. The document is located in an unlabeled folder and box on retreats at St. Columban's, Nebraska.

[1348] Ibid., The meeting with the retreat leaders was apparently initiated by the Columbans.

[1349] In 1977, retreats were listed as one of the basic Columban apostolates in the category, pastoral work.

[1350] Lay Retreat Program, St. Columbans, 30 June 1977. Unlabeled folder and box on retreats at St. Columban's, Nebraska. CFA. In 1977 the retreat promoters were Fathers Denis Bartley, James O'Neill, Peter McPartland, Terry Crowe and Charlie

Columbans became a team to promote retreats. Many practical suggestions were made about the process. "No doubt," Charlie Coulter wrote, "it puts a burden on men who already carry a heavy workload. Its success will depend on the good will and spirit of cooperation of the men in the house. In this day of sharing responsibility and community action, I am grateful for that support and cooperation."[1351] The plan was to be evaluated after a year.

More recently, the St. Columban Center though no longer staffed by Columban priests is available for rental for weekends or evenings for retreats planned by groups from local parishes or organizations, such as *Cursillo*. A lovely outdoor pavilion added to the east of the Retreat Center in 2014 is also available for retreats. Many times the contact for reservations has been through a Columban known by someone in the retreat group. Additionally, prayer groups meet weekly or monthly in the large room at the Residence building on the grounds, sometimes with a Columban, who has nurtured a prayer group. One example of this has been the Centering Prayer evenings guided by Father Charlie O'Rourke and retreats given several times a year by a team of Columban priests and laity. During the late 1990s and into the 2000s, the Retreat Center was the location of the annual Columban Companions in Mission, for most of the time under the leadership of Sylvia Thompson. Companions were men and women from across the country in influential positions to share information about the Columban mission education programs and able to give workshops to teachers and other groups using the materials.

Columbans and Lay Spirituality Movements
after the Second Vatican Council

Columbans themselves were urged after the 1976 Society Chapter to engage in ongoing education and spiritual renewal for themselves. The 1979 Interregional Convention noted, that renewal of the Society's members was a "top priority if we are to make an effective contribution to the Church's mission in today's world." The Convention also *expressed concern* 'about the reluctance of some to avail themselves of the opportunities which are being provided.'"[1352] As noted in chapter 6, Columbans did take the opportunity for renewal in

---

Coulter. The priests who gave retreats were Fathers Steinhilber, Coulter, Crowe, Shaughnessy, O'Neil, Ryan Brennan, Dolan and Parker. Ibid.

[1351] Lay Retreat Program, St. Columbans, 30 June 1977. Unlabeled folder and box on retreats at St. Columban's, Nebraska. CFA. The retreat promoters were to meet with Father James Ryberg, who had been employed by the Better World Movement.

[1352] "Renewal and Continuing Education Policy—U.S. Region. *Columban Newsletter* (April 1979), 1.

Milton, Notre Dame, and a Maryknoll program. The programs developed new dimensions of spirituality and life for the men and reaffirmed commitments to mission.

As laity had initiated retreat movements, so, too, other types of spiritual and communal organizations for laity outside of a parish structure arose during the last half of the twentieth century. The Columbans were aware of these and were encouraged to engage with them. In an earlier chapter attention was given to the pioneering work of Aedan McGrath in promotion of the Legion of Mary as a way of lay leadership in the missions in Asia and elsewhere.[1353] A recommendation of the 1972 U.S. Regional Convention stated,

> Recognizing that the Spirit of God is moving through the church today and that among many of the laity in our Region, there is a search for true spirituality, and recognizing that we have a duty to the Church in this country, in the interest of spiritual renewal both for our members and the laity of this Region, this Convention encourages the Columban priests of the Region to involve themselves with laity in Movements of spirituality.[1354]

As noted in chapter 6 the Columbans had designated their house in Bristol as a House of Prayer, a movement that grew throughout the 1970s for priests, religious and laity.

The connection between one's relationship with God and an overflow into social change based on Gospel values was also the foundation of the movement begun by Canon Cardijn in the 1920s (Young Christian Workers, Young Christian Students) and Catholic Action in the 1950s. In the 1960s and 1970s other movements, many of them international, picked up some of the same elements. We will note a few of the groups in which Columbans in the United States and elsewhere engaged and in some cases exercised national or international leadership.

Cursillo

A *Far East* article in 1965 indicated with reference to Chile, "Great as our material problems may be, our major problem is religious indifference. Men are the problem." [1355] To activate men's faith, ten *cursillistas*, who made a *cursillo* in

---

[1353]   When he was in the United States and living at Silver Creek after expulsion from China, Aedan McGrath gave a talk on the Legion of Mary to the St. Columban's Retreat League.

[1354]   "Statements and Recommendations of the 1972 Regional Convention," 14-1-4, p.13.

[1355]   *FE* (February 1965), 2–3.

Chile, formed the core of the Columban San Mateo mission in Lima. Who were *cursillistas*? The Spanish word, *cursillo*, means "short course" in Christianity. In 1944 on the Mediterranean island of Majorca, a group of people were preparing pilgrims to hike the famous *Camino de Santiago* located in northwest Spain. The shrine/cathedral of Saint James de Compostelo is said to contain the remains of St. James, an apostle of Jesus. A one week course given to the pilgrimage leaders of Catholic Action members led to Eugen Bonnin and other members devising a "method" for a "short course in Christianity" conducted over a three-day period. The *Cursillo* formed small groups which continued to meet regularly after their weekend together for prayer, study, action and mutual support. In 1949, the local bishop got involved and gave support and the movement spread quickly, especially to Spanish speaking countries. By 1955 *Cursillos* were being given in Latin America as noted above in the *Far East* article.[1356]

Cursillos were introduced to the United States in 1961. In 1968, Father James McCaslin, who was working with Columban probationers in Bristol, was invited by laity in the Bristol area to be part of a *Cursillo* weekend. He wrote that until that point, "I had never been a part of such a faith-filled dynamic movement, nor had I been associated with so many joyful, enthusiastic people willing to work for the spread of the Kingdom of God." While some clergy thought they would lose influence on the laity with such a movement, the experience "stirred up my own enthusiasm for my job of trying to form young men for the missionary priesthood and I welcomed it as a great gift of God for the Church."[1357]

Marriage Encounter and *Retrouvaille* (Rediscovery)

Another example of the focus on the spiritual life of laity emerged in Marriage Encounter. In 1952 Father Gabriel Calvo, a labor priest in Spain, gave conferences to married couples to assist them in developing honest and open relationships with each other and to live their marriage in service to others. A group of "marriage teams" over the next ten years went throughout Spain giving the talks to other married couples. In 1962, Calvo offered the talks in Barcelona over the course of a weekend for couples. Four years later, he did so in Caracas, Venezuela. In the United States a married couple and a priest presented a marriage encounter weekend to seven couples and a few priests in connection with the Christian Family Movement conference held at

---

[1356] For additional information on the *Cursillo*, see Marcene Marcoux, *Cursillo: Anatomy of a Movement: The Experience of a Spiritual Renewal* (New York: Lambeth Press, 1982).

[1357] James McCaslin, *It's Not My Fault. Everything is Gift* (Hong Kong, 2001), 110. McCaslin also wrote about the Charismatic Renewal, or Catholic Pentecostalism, which in U.S. Catholic history started in 1967. Ibid, 110–112. He had reservations about the movement, when he saw it as having deleterious effects historically in the Catholic Church.

Notre Dame in 1967. The Marriage Encounter grew and in 1969 a National
Board formed to coordinate the movement. Weekend conferences assist couples
in gaining new skills to benefit their relationship, especially in learning to
communicate better. The team was composed of several couples, a priest, and
sometimes a Sister or deacon.

Columbans were part of a Marriage Encounter weekend in Japan in 1977.[1358]
The next year Columban John J. Howe, bishop in Myanmar (1959–1976), made
a marriage encounter weekend in Omaha. Father Richard Steinhilber was
on the team with the group. In 1980 Father Charlie Coulter was appointed
Executive Team Priest for the Archdiocese of Omaha Marriage Encounter.
Some other Columbans involved in that movement in the United States were
Fathers Sean Conneely, Desmond Maguire, Thomas Cleary, Eugene Ryan, Otto
Imholte, Sal Caputo[1359] and Peter Cronin. Charlie Coulter along with Bill and
Mary Anne Boylan of Philadelphia were elected as part of the International
Coordinating Team for World Wide Marriage Encounter in 1995.

The program did not meet the needs of all couples, however. Some
marriages were at a breaking point. The World Wide Marriage Encounter
Board, through a WWME presenting team in Quebec drew attention to the
situations they noticed on the Marriage Encounter weekends. In 1977 they put
together a weekend for people in troubled or transition marriages. In 1980,
Bruce and Marg Bridger and Father John Vella assumed leadership and refined
the framework and developed a new program with follow-up session over three
months for the couples. *Retrouvaille* leaders came to see their work as a ministry
of marriage healing. A few Columbans, including Fathers Sean Conneely and
Colm Rafferty and participated in *Retrouvaille*. The weekend was patterned in
some ways after the Marriage Encounter weekends with follow-up sessions but
the experience was meant for a couple to recover their marriage.

Alcoholics Anonymous and Gamblers Anonymous

Given the huge stresses of cross-cultural mission, which involved learning
a new language, customs, and worldviews that Columbans met in their mission
situations, with men sometimes being shifted quickly from one kind of

---

[1358] Columbans named included Maurice Hogan, James Mulroney, Vincent Power,
who conducted the weekends with Maurice Moloney and Ron Kelso being readied
for the work in Japan. *Columban Intercom* (June 1977). Between 1987 and 1994
Father Leonard Lavallee also participated in the charismatic movement retreats
in Wakayama, Japan.

[1359] Columbans were aware of what was happening to family life by the1960s when many
people moved to Seoul from outlying areas of the country. See, Salvatore Caputo,
SSC, *The Resilient Nurturing Survivor: A Study of Women as the Prime Family Provider.*
Advanced Professional Diploma in Religion and Religious Education. Fordham
University, 1988. Sal Caputo, "Pressure Points in Korean Family Life," *CM* (February
1992), 4–8.

experience to another, it is not surprising that in such circumstances alcoholism manifested itself. It was not until 1956 that the American Medical Association identified alcoholism as a disease of mind, body, and emotions. Alcoholics Anonymous, while not a religious group, was a kind of fellowship support group with spiritual principles. A "Twelve Step" approach toward recovery was applied to other recovery groups, including Gamblers Anonymous. The "Serenity Prayer" put forth by theologian Reinhold Niebuhr in the 1930s was picked up in the recovery group. "God, grant me the serenity to accept the things I cannot change, courage to change the things I can, and wisdom to know the difference." Columbans offered excellent care and treatment for their men through engagement with Guest House in Minnesota and more long-term treatment in Lake Orion, Michigan. In 1977 the region had an Alcohol and Drug Dependence Advisory Group of three Columbans. Two years later a region policy on alcoholism and chemical dependencies was in place.

Father Paul White, a native of Fonda, Iowa, is the Columban known for his work with Gamblers Anonymous (GA), which also uses the Twelve-Step Program. The group began after two men met in January 1957. They realized they had the same obsession to gamble and the same results of broken relationships, misery, and loss of self-respect. After meeting regularly for support and using principles of honesty, humility, generosity and kindness, and experiencing abstinence from gambling, they thought it important to carry the message to other people who found their gambling obsessive and out of control with the same debilitating results in their personal lives and relationships. In the United States, the first meeting of Gamblers Anonymous took place in Los Angeles in September 1957. As Alcoholics Anonymous had grown, so, too, did Gamblers Anonymous.

After sixteen years in Korea, White returned to the United States, where he did a renewal course, was part of a marriage encounter weekend, and joined Gamblers Anonymous. Doing things in English rather than Korean was helpful to him. "It was a great year for me, I learned more that year than [I did] in a long, long time."[1360] When he went back to Korea, he worked with GA groups at the American army bases and among Koreans. Three couples who had attended the GA meetings in Seoul had stopped gambling. When they moved to Los Angeles they began a Gamblers Anonymous group. The group met at a parish where Columbans worked with Koreans and Korean Americans. Father Charlie O'Rourke, who had been missioned to Korea and was at one point superior of the Columban house in Los Angeles, had helped the group. When White arrived in the States, he was asked to give talks in the Chicago area, where a Korean GA group had started. White was interviewed for newspapers and often spoke to groups about the framework of gambling and other addictions. When

---

[1360] Unnamed interviewer, interview of Father Paul White, 2013.

asked by a Columban interviewer whether White's own addition to gambling was a plus in terms of inspiring people to come together and try to solve their own problems, Father Paul responded, "Yes. If I hadn't had the problem myself, I would not have been able to help anybody else."[1361]

Better World Movement

Perhaps not as well-known as the above groups, the Better World Movement was a precursor of many perspectives expressed in the Second Vatican Council. The founder of the movement, Father Riccardo Lombardi, SJ (1908–1979), was widely known for his preaching of personal and corporate conversion throughout Italy in the public square, at universities, and on the radio, starting in 1938. In 1945 he gathered a group of coworkers and formed a "Promoting Group of Movement for a Better World." They set out together to preach a "Crusade of Goodness." Lombardi's preaching led to a dissemination of the "Exercises for a Better World," from 1943–1956. Lombardi called for renewed structures in Catholic life to support laity, who in turn, could change the world. He was a friend of Pope Pius XII, who delivered a radio message to the Diocese of Rome in 1952, *Proclamation for a Better World*,[1362] in support of these ideas. The Pope addressed the Diocese of Rome because he wanted Rome to be the first area to be renewed. Lombardi's emphasis on the common priesthood of the faithful, the vocation of laity in every area of life, and the call of laity "to make the world conform better to the surpassing dignity of man and to strive for a more deeply rooted sense of universal brotherhood"[1363] found voice in the Second Vatican Council, especially in the Council document, *Gaudium et Spes*.[1364] The Better World Movement, as the group came to be known, began in 1952, a kind of reform of the church from below.[1365] On December 14, 1988, the Pontifical Council for the Laity gave recognition to the group as an international association of the faithful of Pontifical Right.[1366]

The movement spread to other countries in Europe. In 1950 Father Lombardi extended his talks and activities to several cities in the United States.

[1361]   Ibid.

[1362]   "*Proclama per un Mondo Migliore*," *Discorsi e Radiomessaggi di S.S.Pio XII*, XIII, 1952.

[1363]   *Discorsi e Radiomessaggi di S.S.Pio XII*, XIII, 471.

[1364]   www.communitybetterworld.org/node/80. "Making a Better World." Fiftieth Anniversary of the Better World Movement. 2002. Retrieved 9 November 2016.

[1365]   For other experiences in the Better World Movement, see, Robin Anderson, "The Movement for a Better World," *Life in the Spirit* Vol. 14, No 163 (January 1960), 306–314; Daniel Duffy, "Better World Movement of Father Lombardi: Reflections on a Retreat," *The Furrow* 17, No. 4 (April 1966), 236–240.

[1366]   The movement in 2014 had pastoral programs that involved more than fifty million people in about 100 dioceses around the world. *Agenzia Fides*, 13 December 2014. www.fides.org. Retrieved online 10 November 2016.

That year, Columban Father James Ryberg, born in Chicago, though his family moved to other cities in his growing up years, would have just finished the minor seminary at Silver Creek. But a year after his ordination in 1957, he studied Canon Law in Rome, where he remained until early 1960. Most likely, Ryberg met Lombardi there. Back in the United States he was assigned to promotion and vocation over the next years. In March 1967, Ryberg was appointed to the Philippines, but in November, the superior general gave permission for Ryberg to postpone his departure in order to join the Better World Movement. "Father Lombardi asked specially to have him on their international team." [1367] Between 1968 and 1972, Ryberg "gave retreats and established the Better World Movement in various countries of the Far East and in the Philippines."[1368]

Spiritual Life in Various Religious Traditions
        The section on Columban spirituality in the *Acts of the 1970 Chapter* focused on the development of a spirituality in keeping with the sense of the Second Vatican Council. One element was the recognition that the call to priesthood is one way to respond to mission that comes from one's baptism. Personal prayer to sustain one's union with Christ, the Divine Office, community prayer in Eucharist and other forms of common prayer were united with apostolic service and mission.[1369] The formulations from the 1976 Society Chapter included in the Society's "Aim and Nature" to "freely choose to situate ourselves . . . where Christians and non-Christians are in religious dialogue."[1370] The 1986 *Constitutions and Directory* of the Society characterized a missionary spirituality in part as "a sensitive listening to the Spirit speaking through peoples of other religions cultures and in history."[1371] One objective in relation to crossing

---

[1367]   Typed note on James Clifford Ryberg biography file card, CFA-USA. An article in the Omaha *Catholic Voice* on the occasion of Ryberg's Golden Anniversary of priesthood in 2007 noted that he was in Southeast Asia in 1967 with a return in 1972 to the United States. Retrieved 2 November 2016 from http://catholicvoiceomaha. com/anniversary-mass-set-father-ryberg. In September 1972 he was appointed on the Due Process Committee at headquarters in Ireland. He returned three months later to the United States. In February 1978 he was appointed pastor of the Catholic Church in Platte Center, Nebraska. He incardinated in the Archdiocese of Omaha in July 1981. He died March 26, 2014, and is buried in the priest section of Calvary Cemetery in Omaha.

[1368]   *Catholic Voice Omaha.com.*

[1369]   Missionary Society of St. Columban, *Acts of the Chapter* (1970), 91–99.

[1370]   Ibid., 35.

[1371]   Missionary Society of St. Columban, Constitutions and Directory (1986), C107, p. 12.

boundaries of country, language, race and culture is that Columbans "promote dialogue between Christianity and other religious traditions."[1372]

In several early issues of the *Far East,* Columbans featured the religious art of Asia, employing the work of Chinese artists, for example. Articles explained the practices and teachings of Confucianism, Buddhism and Shinto. The Columban Justice and Peace Office engaged in ecumenical cooperation through the Ecumenical Border Working Group (2001ff.), as well as participating with other Christian denominations to address issues related to the international debt, human rights and other justice concerns. Probably the two largest religious groups Columbans met in their missions were Muslims and Buddhists.

Columban Mission in 2011 featured *Interreligious Dialogue. A Quest for the Sacred* in each of the articles for the month. Grouped around that topic, the Columbans have a wealth of experience with people who live from religious perspectives other than Christianity in the Philippines, Fiji, Pakistan, and aboriginal experience. Father Patrick McCaffrey (1944–2010), who died suddenly of a heart attack in Pakistan, gave a tremendous witness in building bridges among various religious groups in that country. His ability to interact in significant ways (including his ability to converse with people in six languages) with Muslims, Hindus and Sikhs, as was witnessed in memorial services for him in Pakistan, England and elsewhere.[1373] In Mindanao, Philippines, Muslims and Christians had troubled relationships against the backdrop of Muslims who sought separation from the mainly Christian area of Mindanao. For twenty years, Father Michael Rufus Halley (1944–2001) was renowned for his work to bring peaceful relationships between Christians and Muslims. He learned two local languages, worked in a Muslim owned store, and had the ability to interact with both religious communities. Unfortunately Father Halley was waylaid by a Muslim extremist who executed him, as Halley road home from a meeting with Muslims. Hundreds of Muslims and Christians came to his funeral.

Some Columbans in Japan were conversant with the spiritual traditions they met there. In the 1970s, Father Kevin Flinn in Wakayama City became friends with Tibetan Buddhist monks, who fled from Tibet with the Dalai Lama. This was the beginning of some significant contact with Buddhists. One of the monks was recruited to teach Sanskrit at Koyasan University, which was founded on the principles of Shingon Buddhism. As the monks and Columbans got to know each other over time, they realized that what both groups had in common was that they were foreigners.[1374] This was an ecumenism of friendship

---

[1372] Ibid., C. 102, p. 11.

[1373] Two stories recount elements from McCaffrey's life in *Columban Mission* (February 2011), 12–16.

[1374] Information from Father John Burger to author, telephone interview, 1 February 2017. Fathers John Burger and David Padrnos engaged in conversation with an

based on the human level. *Columban Mission* readers learned of Japanese rituals surrounding funerals through a story about a ninety-three-year-old woman active in the Hodogay church.[1375]

Conclusion

Columban involvement in retreats and spiritual movements noted in the chapter were important in and of themselves. Columbans with mission experience in the Philippines, Japan, Fiji or elsewhere could provide specific examples of marriage life and spirituality elsewhere. With interreligious dialogue, Columbans brought insights from living among groups with religious traditions other than Catholic or Christian. Columban sensitivity toward the relationships with God, family life, society, and the environment were infused with mission. In other words, spirituality was not simply a "God/Jesus and me" experience. Spirituality was a holistic set of relationships with interacting societal consequences.

---

aikido master at the latter's home in the Chicago area around the spirituality of Aikido, a Japanese martial art, Judaism, Buddhism and Christianity. "Magnolia Avenue," *Columban Newsletter* (April 1992), 4.

[1375] Fr. Barry Cairns, "A Funeral in Japan, An Atmosphere of Peace," *Columban Mission* (August/September 2014), 5–6.

SEEN IN THE SEMINARIES

Benediction on Calvary Hill, St. Columban's, Bristol, at the close of the outdoor concert held on August 3

BRISTOL

WE CAN'T IMAGINE it! 2,000 people here? "It's true," said the Rector, Father Gilsenan, as we gathered around him for news that September opening day.

"We arranged an outdoor concert program for Sunday, August 3, 2,000 people came—from all New England, but mostly from Rhode Island and Massachusetts, of course. Through the perfect co-operation of friends, we had a fine concert, enjoyed by everybody. Most of our old friends came, met other old friends and made new ones. Then there was a taste-fully arranged Mission Exhibit where St. Columban Sisters displayed Chinese art work. We ended the day's program with Benediction on Calvary Hill." He paused a moment and then said suddenly:

"I tell you, boys, there are a lot of wonderful people in the world."

(Continued on page 18)

Blind retreatants and their guides, with Fathers J. P. O'Brien and Martin H. Marnon, at Silver Creek in July.

Far East October 1941 Page 17

First Retreat Photo, NE, 1929

CHAPTER 12

Columbans, the Earth and Water—From Saving Souls to Saving the Environment

Columban Seminaries and the Land

As the newly "planted" U.S. region of the Missionary Society of St. Columban started to build a seminary on a hill overlooking the Missouri River, they were immediately connected to the land in a way they had not foreseen. The construction crew discovered the burial site of Chief Big Elk and other Omaha people, whose remains had been buried there but without an indicating marker. The Native American remains were then reburied with ceremony on a hilltop in the Bellevue Cemetery overlooking the Missouri River.

This chapter plays forward the initial Columban interaction with "land" and environment at Omaha, Silver Creek, and Bristol to situate seminaries where there would be beauty—through nature itself or through human interaction with trees, crops, water, and animal care. In the midst of finding friends in the United States, donors, promotion of the *Far East*, and teaching young men at a fledgling seminary, the Society had other concerns. The initial efforts at Columban headquarters included responsibility for managing the farm, the nurture of the land and a meticulous itemization of the names of trees and bushes planted on the property, for example. Later, seminarians dug Victory Gardens during World War II and replanted trees affected by Dutch Elm disease in the early 1960s along the drive into headquarters. When the Society reflected on how to share the land they held in Omaha, they chose to share with elderly in need of a home. More recently care for and sharing the land includes the development of a community garden for neighbors to plant vegetables and flowers in a sunny section of Columban property and the development of the Columban Martyrs Memorial Garden, a place of beauty, prayer and remembrance.

With Lake Erie lapping the shore of Columban's Silver Creek property, the Society had a farm with chickens, pigs, an orchard, grape vines and vegetable rows. To buffet the strong north winds that bore down upon priests and seminarians in winter, a variety of deciduous and conifer trees were planted resulting in a small forest over the years. The land provided recreation for the seminarians, for the Buffalo Mercy Sisters who came for a week's vacation in summer, and for a pleasant space for annual fund-raising festivals. Eventually, a small plot of land was set aside as a burial site for Columbans. With the closing of the seminary, the Columbans turned over the Silver Creek property and buildings for the Columban Sisters' mission to people of retirement age.

The Columban property in Bristol, Rhode Island, initially used for promotion and as the location for the Probation Year, had the magnificent beauty of Narragansett Bay as a backdrop for the year of prayer, reflection, and decision making about one's call as a Columban missionary. The site was also fitting for the House of Prayer of the 1970s and as a Columban retirement home, which it remains to this day. The latest addition to the Bristol building highlighted the Bay view from the twelve bedrooms and the dining room. Since Father Victor Gaboury has resided in Bristol, he has enhanced the beauty of the land through cultivating large flower gardens especially at the entrance to the grounds. Neighbors stop in to admire what they see as they meander through the gardens. Local artists perch their easels to capture the beauty.[1376]

Taking care of the land at headquarters, Silver Creek and Bristol reflected good stewardship. Land had more than a mundane function (providing food, for example). The environment was appreciated for its beauty and reflected a spiritual topography for seminarians and priests. The Columbans more recently conducted a "carbon audit" at their headquarters.[1377] Columbans through mission education, the Justice, Peace and Integrity of Creation office in Washington and through other means provided resources for people in the United States to reflect upon their use of and attitudes toward creation.

Mission Education

[1376] Fr. Bill Sullivan, "The Green Thumb. Bringing About the Beauty of God's Creation," *CM* (June/July 2010), 11.

[1377] A carbon audit measures an organization's "carbon footprint." This is the total amount of greenhouse gases that are produced to directly and indirectly support human activities. The measurement is expressed in equivalent tons of carbon dioxide.

The Columban Mission Education Office over the years produced award-winning materials reflective of sensitivity toward land and water. "Care for Creation," the fourth grade teaching unit in the *Journey with Jesus* program, drew students to see and appreciate all creation as a gift from God. Through videos, conversations, art, scripture, and other means, students focused on the importance of water in people's lives and the responsibility people have to use God's resources wisely. The Columban audiovisual, "As Water in the Desert," evoked a powerful insight as viewers realized the contrast between the waters of baptism that joined people to Christ and to each other, and the waters of the Rio Grande flowing on both the U.S. and Mexican borders. The latter waters were dangerous and death dealing in current political practice and separated individuals from their families. *Columban Mission* portrayed the experience of "Earth, Wind, Sand, and Sea" as seen in various Columban locations. Father McFadden, chaplain in the Apostolate of the Sea ministry in Buenos Aires from 1952–1962, would probably have been amazed to learn how greatly the shipping industry has changed since his ministry there. He might also be surprised that Soon-Ho Kim, a Columban laywoman missionary, is engaged in that very same difficult ministry in the twenty-first century in the Port of Yokohama, Japan.[1378]

Speak, Write, Engage Civic and Religious Groups on Environment Issues

In the 1980s, some themes that Columbans used in Brazil for catechesis centered on the realities people faced daily: abandoned children, unemployment, hunger. Father John Wanaurny observed that in that decade, they had catechetical programs on "the situation of the land, and, a long time ago ecology." These topics "were probably the least popular topics because at the time it wasn't a world issue."[1379] Over time, a collective consciousness about land, water and environment began to develop. The common lands that Father Wanaurny's parish people determined were not good for farming were used by all the people for grazing their cattle. One day "people from the south showed up with deeds to the [common] land."[1380] Agribusiness came in with soybean production. Profits and product were exported and the people became poorer.

Columban awareness of environment issues grew from understanding the effects the World Bank policies and international debt had on the people

---

[1378] Soon-Ho Kim, "Apostleship of the Sea. Mass on Board," *CM* (June/July 2010), 18–20.

[1379] Interview with Father John Wanaurny, 1991. Unnamed interview. Transcript. Lines 114–117.

[1380] Ibid., lines 300–312.

with whom they worked.[1381] The Columban experience in the Philippines, an archipelago in the Northwest part of the Pacific Ocean, raised issues relative to the impact of agribusiness overuse of land/water, especially in fragile ecosystems.[1382] Father Vincent (Vinny) Busch, born in Buffalo, New York, a renowned "snowbelt" area of the United States, found himself in quite a different climate when he was missioned to the Philippines after ordination in 1974. He arrived two years after President Ferdinand Marcos declared martial law in the Philippines. After taking courses in television production in the United States in 1978, he returned to the Philippines to work with local artists to produce documentaries, movies, and other audiovisual materials about the life issues of tribal peoples in Mindanao.

Having listened for many years to the wisdom of tribal people, Busch's assessment of the realities in Mindanao evolved into broader understandings of the relationship of people to their habitat, especially the exploitation of the area's natural resources.[1383] Poverty had ecological consequences. Ecological consequences produced more poverty. The Filipino government allowed "the country's soils, seas and forests to be plundered and degraded by logging and mining companies, commercial fishing trawlers and huge, export-oriented agribusinesses."[1384] In other words, Filipinos were not experiencing the benefits of "development." Subsistence farmers and landless peasants were driven to uplands and ended up overworking the land.

Looking back on his experience in the Philippines to that point, Father Busch wrote in 1994,

---

[1381] One example of many on the point is, Christina Cobourn Herman, "Sustainable Development: Moving Toward a Livable World," *Columban Intercom* (May 1996), 87–89.

[1382] Letter of Concern Committee, "A Letter of Concern from U.S. Missioners in the Philippines to the Christian Churches of the United States." Davao City, Philippines (July 1986), CFA-USA. Two Columbans—Father Vincent Busch and Sister Glenda Struss—and two people from the Mennonite Central Committee were four of the ten members. Susan Cobourn Herman, who was hired by the Columban Justice and Peace office, had been involved with the Mennonite Central Committee in the Philippines. Patrick McMullan, ed., "Climate Change: The Agenda for Mission Today. Papers and Reports of the Columban International Climate Change Conference held in Manila, Philippines, 23–29, September 2007."

[1383] Interview of Father Vincent Busch. DVD. Unnamed interviewer, 1991. His information sheet from the Columbans, Philippines indicates that from 1984–1994, he was missioned at Catadman Video Pro., Justice and Peace, etc.; Studies in the USA 1994–1995. Between 1995 he is at Katipunan, 1997–2000 the Lay Mission Coordination in Mindanao, and from 2000–2008, the Catadman-Subanen Ministry.

[1384] Letter of Concern Committee, "A Letter of Concern from U.S. Missioners in the Philippines to the Christian Churches of the United States." Davao City, Philippines (July 1986), 7.

> Seventeen years ago I planted myself in Mindanao. I faced a new and wondrously diverse community of tropical animals and plants, mangroves and rain forest, reefs and rivers, volcanoes and earthquakes. In the beginning, the hungry, suffering people of this community led me, with the help of the exodus story, to hear the cry of oppressed human beings. More recently, the degraded seas, soils, and forest of this community have led me, with the help of creation stories in Genesis, to hear the cry of the dying earth.[1385]

He produced an award-winning video, "Voices of the Earth," wherein one community (Midsalip) learned from another group (Subanen) to care for the earth. Education, organic farming, basic health care service all tied in with the prayer life of the community and its relationship with the land. This was a holistic way to live as good neighbors with the earth, each other and with God.

Recognizing the skills of Subanen women in beadwork and woven baskets, Father Busch developed the Subanen Crafts Project, which honored the women's crafts. The women created Creation Mandalas that celebrate the earth and the creation story. Each mandala is accompanied with an illustrated booklet to explain people's understanding of the symbol. Since the start of the project, the women have expanded to creating jewelry and cards with creation and Christmas motifs. Sale of the items is a way for the women to contribute to the family income, receive an education, and better their living conditions.[1386]

The 1990s saw an upswing in public and Catholic response around environmental issues. The U.S. Catholic Bishops in their 1991 pastoral statement, "Renewing the Earth," began with the perspective, "At its core, the environmental crisis is a moral challenge. It calls us to examine how we use and share the goods of the earth, what we pass on to future generations, and how we live in harmony with God's creation."[1387] The bishops developed their ideas further in their 2001 statement, *Global Climate Change. A Plea for Dialogue, Prudence and the Common Good.*

[1385] Father Vinny Busch, "The Dying Earth," *Misyon*online.com. (January/February 1994).

[1386] The project began in 2001. Their story is told in several places, including, "Fr. Vincent Busch: A Ministry That Betters the Lives of Tribal Women," 15 February 2010. https://columban.org/61/missionaries/fr-vincnt-busch. The Columban Sisters and Fathers continue their efforts to stand with the Subanen group, even going to court to defend the rights of the tribe. See, for example, Father Sean Martin, SSC, Tweet, 7 February 2011, "When it rains it pours!"

[1387] U.S. Catholic Conference of Bishops, *Renewing the Earth. An Invitation to Reflection and Action on Environment in Light of Catholic Social Teaching* (USCCB, Washington DC, 1991), par. 1.

In the meantime, Columban Father Sean McDonagh had become well-known for alerting people to issues related to the environment. He provided biblical/theological reflections toward action about land and water abuses. His mission experience was also in Mindanao where he was missioned in 1972. Questions and issues he met there led him down a mission path he might not have anticipated when he was ordained. On his way back to Ireland in 1980, he stopped in New York to study under the tutelage of a Passionist priest, Thomas Berry.[1388] McDonagh's early writings, such as *To Care for the Earth: A Call to a New Theology* (1987) drew attention to what was happening to the earth/water/environment, as a result of a "throwaway culture," the imbalance between the disproportionate use of resources by people in the northern hemisphere and resulting negative effects on people in the southern hemisphere. He would go on to write many books and articles related to care for the earth, the environment, and climate change in a framework of reflection on experience and scripture. He has won numerous awards for his work.

Sponsored by the Columban Center for Advocacy and Outreach in Washington DC in March 2016, McDonagh made a ten-day trip through the Northeast, speaking to diverse groups about Pope Francis's encyclical, *Laudato, Sí*. McDonagh's *Care for Our Common Home* contained the encyclical *Laudato, Sí*, for which he was an adviser to the Vatican, along with the Columban's commentary.[1389] The Columbans in the U.S. region had earlier worked with the Archdiocese of Chicago to produce a study guide for the Latin American bishops' *Aparecida* document.[1390]

The Society drew up a "Columban Society Statement on Climate Change" in 2014.[1391] "We are Called to Right Relationship with all of Creation" synopsized the major issues undergirding the complex problems of climate change and

---

[1388]   Father Thomas Berry (1914–2009) was an historian of world religions and cultures. Influenced by the thinking of Teilhard de Chardin, he moved toward being a historian of the earth, or "geologian" as he called himself. An interesting connection with the Columbans is that at one point, Berry assisted in an educational program for the T'boli tribal people of South Cotabato, a province of Mindanao. Berry coined the term, Ecozoic, to describe the "geologic era that Earth is entering—when humans live in a mutually enhancing relationship with Earth and the Earth community." www.Ecozoictimes.com. Columbans have opened the "Columban Center for Ecozoic Living and Learning" in the Philippines.

[1389]   Sean McDonagh, *Care for Our Common Home* (Maryknoll, NY: Orbis Books, 2016). See also, "Eco-theologian Fr. Sean McDonagh: Don't let this 'Laudato Si' moment pass," *National Catholic Reporter*, 9 March 2016.

[1390]   The study guide can be found on the United States Catholic Mission Association website: www.uscatholicmission.org *Mission Update* (Spring 2015), 9–16.

[1391]   A 2012 preassembly gathering in the United States expressed the point that "Environmental concerns [become] the lens through which to prioritize mission activities."

indicated a Columban Response in each area. One category listed under "Ecological Conversion" was the role of education. "Columbans strive to help society and particularly the Catholic Church to understand the magnitude of the Climate Change issue, its consequences, and links with other issues."[1392] A possible action was then indicated. With the background of faith and Catholic Social teaching, "We develop and provide education materials utilizing a See-Judge-Act methodology for Catholic parishes, schools, institutions, individuals and families, as to what can be done to counteract global warming." Awareness raising, advocacy in the political and corporate spheres, lifestyle change and ideas for worship were included as proposed areas for action.

In Washington, the Columban Center for Advocacy and Outreach spotlights environmental justice issues in relation to current legislation, informing its constituencies of developments in Congress or elsewhere in the country. So it was fitting that in November 2016, the Catholic Climate Covenant people, joined by partners from the Columban Center for Advocacy, the U. S. Catholic Conference of Bishops and the Sisters of Mercy delivered a petition to Congressional leaders.[1393] The petition referenced the teachings of the recent popes (John Paul II, Benedict XVI) and Pope Francis, each of whom placed "climate change as a moral issue that society must address." [1394] The document noted among its points that the "Clean Power Plan and Green Climate Fund are two important ways to do that."[1395] Columbans brought to the table many examples of the international effects on vulnerable communities they serve.

The impact of climate change, the destruction of land, water and habitat became important to the Columbans because they saw what happened to people they served over the years. The Columbans paid attention to their "locations,"[1396]

[1392] Missionary Society of St. Columban, *Columban Society Statement on Climate Change*, 2014. https://columban.org/wp-content/uploads/2014/12/Prayer-Study-Action-for-MSSC-Climate-Change-Statement.pdf.

[1393] Senate Majority Leader, Mitch McConnell (Kentucky), Speaker of the House, Paul Ryan (Wisconsin), and Minority Leader, Nancy Pelosi (California).

[1394] "Catholics Deliver Climate Change Petition to Congressional Leadership." Catholic Climate Covenant Press Release, 16 November 2016. http://www.usccb.org/issues-and-action/human-life-and-dignity/environment/renewing-the-earth.cfm. The bishops have a webpage devoted to environmental issues. The representatives of Catholic Climate Covenant also gave every member of Congress a copy of "Legislative Response to Climate Change," published by the U.S. Conference of Catholic Bishops.

[1395] "Catholics Deliver Climate Change Petition to Congressional Leadership." Catholic Climate Covenant Press Release, 16 November 2016. http://www.usccb.org/issues-and-action/human-life-and-dignity/environment/renewing-the-earth.cfm.

[1396] While not a topic specifically focused from the U.S. region, an insightful Columban symposium, "The Ocean and Theology," was held in Seoul, Korea, in December 2015. A range of geographic areas where Columbans serve were featured, including the Indus River Delta and Brazil, as well as the tradition of Celtic monks in relation

contributed that knowledge to the U.S. congressional representatives and other key groups, and worked with interfaith communities to achieve goals that enhance the quality of life for all people, especially those impoverished through circumstances not of their doing. Columbans also experienced a darker, death-giving side of "development" in countries that provided gain and profit for big business while local resources became depleted. "Earth" had moved from being written as a common noun with a small "e" to a proper noun with a large "E."

Rather than through an extensive mission education program that for decades directly targeted teachers, parish religious education directors, as well as other adults, and students from kindergarten through high school and college, the Columban Center for Advocacy and Outreach now incorporates mission education as one of their functions directed to a diverse audience. People can respond to "Action Alerts" from the Center to make their voice heard in the appropriate venue. Given the increased number of Catholics of Hispanic background and the work of the Society in parishes and locations in the United States with Hispanic populations, Columbans have a website in Spanish: https://www.columbanos.org and publish *Columban Mission* in Spanish, so this large group of people in the United State can also become aware of the issues.

The Waters of Baptism and Waters in the Environment

How does an emphasis on environment relate to the idea that Edward Galvin had of converting the Chinese, bringing them into the Catholic Church and saving them from hell? His perspective was a prevailing mission theology when the Columbans were founded. Father John Blowick, who taught Columban seminarians in Ireland, thought long and hard about the idea and wrote about "the fate of the unbaptized."[1397] In practice, as Galvin and the early China missionaries, the Sisters of Loretto and the Sisters of St. Mary, Hanyang met the Chinese and went through many traumatic events with them, other facets of Christian life slowly came to the fore. The corporal and spiritual works of mercy, emphasis on Catholics themselves becoming evangelists through the Legion of Mary, and the message of God's love and care gave new dimensions to Catholic life.

---

to the ocean. Columbans with relevant education background or expertise on the topic gathered to pool their knowledge for a greater understanding of the issue. Symposium papers are available at www.koreannewsletter/ocean-symposium.html.

[1397] For an overview of John Blowick's perspective on the "pagans and the practice of idolatry," see Neil Collins, *The Splendid Cause. The Missionary Society of St. Columban 1916–1954* (Ireland: Columba Press, 2009), 36–38.

The "fate of the unbaptized" came from a theology that was based on Thomist philosophy, which was thought of at the time as a "scientific" way to do theology. If there were those who are saved through baptism, and those who are condemned to hell because of evil they chose to do, what about unbaptized babies? What about sincere unbelievers? Where do they "fit" into the philosophical system? "Limbo" became the theological "location" for unbaptized babies.

Actual experience with Chinese (or other non-Christian groups) raised questions for missionaries. An example from an American Sisters' community in China at the same time as Galvin provides an example of one Sister's experience of sincere but not Catholic believers. The Sister, who had a basic knowledge of Chinese, went with her Chinese teacher "to Huo Shan, the mountain on which there are many [Daoist] temples and which is devoted entirely to the worship of pagan gods. . . . Though I can't speak Chinese well yet, I can understand a great deal more, so when one of the pagan virgins explained the meaning of the things in the temple, I could get practically all she said."[1398] Perhaps surprising even herself, the Sister continued in her letter, "Believe me, it was worthwhile listening to that dear little old lady grown old in service to those heathen gods. That she sincerely believes, no one can doubt. When she explained one monstrosity, which I thought no intelligent human being could ever believe, I forgot myself and said right out loud: 'Do you really believe that?' She looked at me in mild surprise and said very gently: 'Why, indeed I do.' The simple faith with which she spoke those words told volumes."[1399]

The Second Vatican Council document, *Nostra Aetate* (1965), a short but key document for understanding the Catholic Church's relationship with other religions, began with a different premise than the "fate of the unbaptized." Instead of starting with the philosophical position of how something "fit into the system," the document began with what all people hold in common, then what other religions, Jews, and Catholics have in common. While the document had important consequences for interreligious dialogue, the principle applied elsewhere. The question *Nostra Aetate* raised is, how are we all connected?

As seen in the narrative of the U.S. region, Columban missionaries all along have been pastors of small or large parishes, have attended to the sick and dying, and prayed at other times with their congregations and with individuals, often traveling great distances and under difficult circumstances to do so. In this regard, they were doing what Father Pierre Charles, SJ, termed, "planting the church," which was a different way to view mission than John Blowick's

---

[1398]   Sister Mercedes Tintel to Dear Mother Superior, 12 August 1932. China Collection. Archives of the Sisters of St. Francis of Assisi, St. Francis, Wisconsin.

[1399]   Ibid.

theological expression.[1400] Columbans have seen to the medical, educational, and other daily needs of people, often inviting women religious to be part of the mission, as seen in chapters 9 and 10.

By the 1970s, as missionaries felt the effects of a more globalized economy and shared their insights with other missionaries, they saw larger connections. As seen in chapter 6, a major realization focused by the Columban Justice and Peace office was the negative effects on people when policies of the World Bank and the International Monetary Fund affected people Columbans served in Latin America and elsewhere. Not only did people in poor countries become less self-reliant, the effects of "development" showed up in degraded land and water.

A fundamental dynamic underlying the sacraments and a priest's role is the formation of a *community*. Privatizing the resources of the earth worked against the community bond. The sacraments are conveyed through the "ordinary stuff" of daily life—water, bread, light. Theologically we could say Catholics take seriously the Incarnation. Columbans noticed that the "ordinary stuff" had become a problem for many people they served. We all have need of common resources. The Columban Center for Advocacy and Outreach had pointed to that reality. In addition to water's environmental and geopolitical significance, "Water has profound religious symbolism. In the moment of our baptism, we are reborn and reconciled with the Divine through water."[1401] To learn more about the relationships between the elements of nature and spirituality, the Society offered its members a Spirituality workshop on "Creation-centered Spirituality," given by Joseph Holland from the Center of Concern in Washington DC as one way to find a spirituality "which can effect social change in a technological society."[1402]

Given that Columban Sean McDonagh was a consultant for Pope Francis's, *Laudato Sí*, "on care for our common home," it is fitting to end the chapter with the Pope's summary of the themes raised in his encyclical.

> I will point to the intimate relationship between the poor and the fragility of the planet, the conviction that everything in the world is connected, the critique of new paradigms and forms of power derived from technology, the call to seek other ways of understanding the economy and progress, the value proper

---

[1400] Joseph Masson, SJ, "Pierre Charles, SJ (1993–1954). Advocate of Acculturation," in Gerald H. Anderson, et al., eds., *Mission Legacies. Biographical Studies of Leaders of the Modern Missionary Movement* (Maryknoll, NY: Orbis Books, 1994), 410–415.

[1401] https://columban.org/469/columban-center-for-advocacy-and-outreach/water. Retrieved 5 January 2017.

[1402] *Columban Newsletter* (November 1984), 3.

to each creature, the human meaning of ecology, the need
for forthright and honest debate, the serious responsibility of
international and local policy, the throwaway culture and the
proposal of a new lifestyle.[1403]

But it is also fitting to close the chapter with a recent episode in the life
of Columban Sister Kathleen Melia, working for over thirty years with the
Subanen tribe in a remote part of the Philippines. She has helped them in an
ongoing fight against large-scale mining companies. People's land has been
ravaged with intense deforestation, as a step to the removal of gold and other
resources by overseas companies. Company practices undercut tribal people's
way of life and, as we saw earlier in the chapter, the land is taken from them.
Sister Kathleen's work includes translating documents and preparing legal
papers so the tribes can stand up in court for their rights. On March 1, 2017,
as she closed the convent windows (Midsalip), she was attacked and gagged
by a man, punched on her face and chest until she became unconscious, and
sustained a broken leg. It took days over rough terrain and a two and a half day
trip across rough seas from the remote region to get her to a Manila hospital.
The Irish Times quoted a "source familiar with the region: We don't know who
was behind the attack but the ones that stand to gain most from it are people
connected with the mining industry."[1404]

The Columban mission continues.

[1403]   Pope Francis, *Laudato Sí, On Care For Our Common Home* (Washington DC: United
        States Conference of Catholic Bishops, 2015), par.16. As noted in an earlier chapter,
        the Columban Center for Advocacy and Outreach was a leader in development of
        a study/action guide for *Laudato Sí*. Guide available at https://uscatholicmission.
        org. *USCMA Newsletter* (Spring 2015).

[1404]   "Irish Nun attacked in the Philippines waits days for surgery," *The Irish Times*, 15
        March 2017, retrieved online 23 March 2017.

St. Columbans Memorial Garden

CONCLUSION

"Moving On." Columbans as Pilgrims

In the 1970s and 1980s, a television commercial aired in the United States for the American stock brokerage firm, EF Hutton, thought of as the "quiet [but powerful] company." The scene depicted a party where well-dressed people spoke animatedly to each other. One young professional quietly remarked to the person next to him that his broker was EF Hutton. Immediately people stopped talking to hear what the young man had to say. The voice-over was, "When EF Hutton talks, people listen." While we do not want to compare the Columbans with the well-known brokerage firm, we could put it this way, "When the Columbans speak (not only with words but with their lives, actions, and spirit), people listen!" The Columbans had a lot to say, as we have seen. Several overarching themes surfaced in the history of the U.S. region of the Missionary Society of St. Columban over a century: the U.S. region's role in relation to the entire Society, the region's particular contributions within and beyond the Catholic Church in the United States, and a Columban spirit and style inflected through their words and actions.

The United States as a Region and the
Internationalization of the Columbans

The development of a region in the United States occurred quickly after the authorization of the Society in 1918. While Galvin might initially have thought of the priests who came first to the United States as a kind of appendage to Ireland, the immediate issues the men faced on the other side of the Atlantic became the first practical working out of what it meant to be a "region." A key element proved to be the value of "local knowledge" in decision making. Land and legal systems the men encountered in their first years in Omaha and Bellevue were different than Irish systems. E. J. McCarthy felt restricted in making decisions, given slow mail communication between Ireland and the States and costly cablegrams for a Society with limited funds. Patterns for the flow of money and the authorization for its use needed to be established. The Columbans worked out the parameters of "region" in the midst of internationalization—i.e., the changing political and national factors before and after the First World War.

In the context of globalization, "inculturation" has raised a different focus than the term "international." Inculturation examined the deeper nuanced interaction between local "cultures" and the transmission of the Gospel. Initially "inculturation" was thought of in relation to people in mission lands. A careful look at culture with its variations unfolded subtle nuances in how people approached their individual and common lives in relation to their habitat. Missionary observation would enable them to match better the Gospel message and the people. At the same time, the Columbans realized that they had their own national backgrounds and "cultures" as part of the mix. The process became more "colorful" with lay missionaries and seminarians from countries thought of as "mission countries" having roles in the Columban mission fold.

From the start of the region, the Columbans had to "adapt" their life in the United States. They realized that a name change of the Society for the United States was required for the group to attract donors and seminarians. Catholics would not give money to a "Maynooth Mission to China," even though donors might have Irish relatives. Another custom the region adopted was to add the initials "SSC" (Society of St. Columban) after their name. McCarthy told the Society in Ireland that the practice was a tradition in the United States as a way for people to identify religious orders and mission congregations.

The U.S. region was considered the "bread and butter" of the Society. This meant the region was expected to provide a substantial portion of funds for missions. Given the large Catholic population in relation to other Society regions, that seemed a realistic expectation. The United States also became a place of recuperation for missionaries, initially for those who went to China. A number of early missionaries had tuberculosis. Others were adversely affected by the stresses of mission. Mission was often lonely work among a people whose language and culture were unfamiliar. Missionaries typically had few resources, and life in local conditions over the years sometimes meant dealing with bandits, floods and war. As we have seen in the chapters which viewed Columbans in Korea, the Philippines, and Latin America, experiences of war, dictatorships, threats on one's life, feeling anxious about the level of one's language, and the insecurities of daily life continued to produce anxiety. The U.S. region very early on provided houses—first in California—for missionaries who had adverse effects from these stresses. If the Sisters of Mercy were in charge of hospitals in an area, the Columbans tended toward sending their men to those care centers, given that the men especially from Ireland would be knowledgeable about the fine nursing the Irish Sisters of Mercy provided the sick. Columban Sisters, first at Silver Creek, and then overseas, provided and still provide wonderful nursing care for the Columbans.

Administratively the configuration of the region evolved over the years. Sometimes the U.S. region became responsible for Latin America missions as a "pro-region" or was designated as the region of North and South America. The fact that the United States was a powerful international force was a key factor in the creation of a Justice and Peace office, not only for the region, but as a vehicle to make known Columban worldwide issues.

The region lived through the same significant events and realities Americans faced: the Great Depression, the effects of World War II in the country, an intense period of social upheaval of the 1960s, altercations related to the Vietnam War and then Central and South America in the 1970s and 1980s, the fall of the Berlin Wall and the collapse of Communism as it had been known, the Gulf War, environmental movements, terrorism in the United States, and the rise of international religious fundamentalists. These situations shaped some areas of Columban life and fashioned new ways to bring forth and live mission. Columbans addressed these realities through creative individuals, mission structures and thoughtful leadership.

Columbans and the Church in the United States

Fortuitously, when the Columbans arrived in the United States, several national Catholic organizations were starting to form in a post–World War I era. E. J. McCarthy's participation in the mission directors' meeting at the University of Notre Dame provided the Society an introduction to key church figures. The gathering, on the heels of Columban arrival in the country, gave the Nebraska Society personal contact with priests and bishops from the populous eastern states. The second regional director, Paul Waldron, who preached retreats to priests and laymen, had a different type of national contact with bishops and clergy.

Did the Columbans make a difference in the home church? As an elected delegate to the 1982 General Chapter in Lima, Peru, Michael O'Loughlin pondered a similar matter. "The role of the Society in the home regions will be one of the big questions for me. The Missionary task of the Church has a

broader and more flexible connotation today than in the past. Our manner
of collaboration with the Missionary Churches and function in the 'home'
Church demands more flexibility. The future with all its uncertainty must be
looked at in the light of our past performance and our present capabilities."[1405]
Looking back over a century, the Society has provided numerous gifts to the
"home church." One set of gifts can be thought of as "tools" and "structures"
for mission. The other set reflects the prevailing perspectives and spirit that
undergird the expression of Columban mission.

Tools and Structures

Tools are handy items with which to accomplish a task. What tools did
Columbans use to imbue a mission spirit and open people to the world of
mission life? The Society provided at least four ways to engage Catholics: a
mission magazine, an organized mission education program, retreats, and
various types of mission promotion.

The *Far East/Columban Mission* kept up with new technological production
over the years. An initial search to find an audience and scale the magazine to
that audience—should they have humor, cartoons, a page for women—settled
in to a publication that captured the attention of a diverse group of readers. In
the process, Columbans engaged and informed people from various walks of
life about mission, people, and cultures where Columbans worked. Readers in
the 1920s into the 1950s were introduced to the art of China and Korea with
images of the Madonna and Jesus rendered with Asian features. Magazine
articles made correlations between a Chinese man or Japanese woman, for
example, and the person in the United States reading the article. Readers
learned about courageous Asian people exercising mission among their own
people sometimes under difficult circumstances. The implication was, if the
women and men in so called "mission countries" are evangelizing their people,
I need to be doing so where I live.

Beginning with Father Ranaghan's film about China and with special
mention of decades of film production by Bill Chvala and Ron Chvala, brothers
whose Chvala and Company Productions (Omaha), filmed and produced
Columban mission materials, brought home what was happening on the
missions and how U.S. Catholics could become involved in mission. Films
provided something tangible for Columbans to show when parishes or schools
invited them to "give a talk on the missions." Films also gave a "you are here"
feeling to the viewer. Under the Chairmanship of New Jersey native, Father
William J. Carney (1924–1973), a mission education task force for 1971–72
proposed a program under the theme, "the pilgrim church is missionary by her

---

[1405] Michael O'Loughlin, quoted in *Columban Newsletter* (April 1982).

very nature."[1406] The mission education program grew in scope and sequence and was carried forth in more organized fashion in the 1980s through 2016. As we have seen in chapter 7, many laity, Sisters, and Columbans contributed to the robust, award-winning Columban mission education programs.

Alongside these two tools, Columbans engaged in various types of retreats to assist people in their faith growth and to have them reflect upon their call to mission as lay Catholics. Sometimes this was done through a specific talk on the missions. With retreats offered at headquarters and at Silver Creek, the location itself would evoke thoughts of mission. Among the various missionary societies in the United States, the consistent relationship between retreats and mission that the Columbans emphasized for laity and religious stands out as a unique feature of the Society up to the present. The emphasis might harken back to the experience of Jesuit-patterned retreats of Father Paul Waldron and other Columbans.

Promotion events held on Columban grounds could have the same effect of mission awareness. Columbans giving parish mission talks raised for some young men the possibility of becoming a missionary themselves. Missionaries had more engaging stories to tell than the parish priest did, according to several Columban missionaries who had been "young boys in the pews" when a Columban came to their parish. Even golf tournaments as a fund-raiser/ promotion event put laymen in contact with Columbans. Informal chatting on the links opened up all kinds of conversation starters with Columbans.

The promise that Regional Superior E. J. McCarthy made when the region was only a few years old rang true over the century. "In whatever was to be done to develop the missionary potential of the Church in America, we were determined to lend a hand."[1407] They not only "lent a hand." Columbans became leaders in the field.

Structures provide patterns of organization, design and form to something in order to have continuity and long-term growth in ideas, practices, or values. What structures did the Society put in place to promote a world view commensurate with the experience Columbans met in Fiji, the Philippines, or Brazil, for example? Beginning in the 1980s, the development of a Justice and Peace office in the nation's capital provided a dependable and plausible medium through which the Columbans drew on the vast experience of its members and conveyed to the U.S. government, the World Bank, and a variety

---

[1406]   *Ad gentes* ("On the Mission Activity of the Church"), 7 December 1965. Austin Flannery, OP, general editor, *Vatican Council II. The Conciliar and Post Conciliar Documents.* New Revised Edition (Northport, NY: Costello Publishing Company, 1992), Volume 1, 813, par. 2.

[1407]   E. J. McCarthy, *A Few Personal Reminiscences* (1916–1920), 14.

of international organizations the realities Columbans experienced in their mission areas.

The present form of the Justice and Peace office, the Columban Center for Advocacy and Outreach in Washington DC has recently become the main locus for most of mission education, the organization of mission immersion trips, and advocacy issues Columbans have been working on for decades.[1408] Internships at the CCAO provide an "insider" view of Columban experience and strengthen interns' faith-based understanding of issues. Interns learn ways of interaction and effectiveness with other groups aligned for migration, environmental justice, economic justice, peace, and reconciliation.

The CCAO staff has worked with others to provide a group study guide to explore the CELAM *Aparecida* document and Pope Francis's encyclical, *Laudato Sí*, both of which point clearly to Catholic life as mission oriented and interconnected with the community of humanity and the environment. AITECE, the Association for International Teaching, Educational and Curriculum Exchange is now "housed" in the Center. With a realization of the global shift from Europe and North America to the East, the Central Administration of the Missionary Society of St. Columban moved to Hong Kong in 2008. They are probably the first western missionary congregation to do so. The geographic location also keeps the Society remembering the origins of their mission group, provides experience navigating a China that remains complex and evolving, and keeps an international focus on primary evangelization.

Another structure for Columban mission has been the parish, especially in relation to ministry among immigrants. The Columbans were leaders in ministry to ethnic groups in the United States, particularly the Chinese, Filipino, Korean and Hispanic communities. Whether the group was designated a Center or a parish, Columbans helped people navigate a variety of cultures while nurturing people's faith. Columbans introduced a new generation to mission, especially in Korean/Korean American communities, through providing a cross-cultural experience at the U.S./Mexican border, for example. Given the political climate in the late-twenty-teens, the latter geographic location and similar points along the border might very well become even more prominent as a mission focus. Columbans have abundant experience to share on border issues.

Probably more so than other missionary congregations, the Columbans have reached out to the branches of the armed forces through chaplaincy as service members and auxiliary chaplains. The Society engaged the military men and women through mission literature beginning in the World War II and through allowance to do promotion work through the Archdiocese for the Military Services, USA.

[1408]   *Columban Mission* is still located at Columban headquarters, Nebraska.

Nationally, Columbans were at the beginnings of what became the U.S. Catholic Mission Association, the National Catholic Development Conference (NCDC, 1968), and NATRI (the National Association of Treasurers of Religious Institutes, now called ATRI).

Columban Perspective and Spirit

Through specific tangible "tools and structures" of Columban mission in the United States, some of which are reviewed above, we see demonstrated a Columban perspective and spirit. Here we get to the heart of the missionary, the energy that moves the Columban to engage with people in the process of proclamation of the message of Jesus in many ways: liturgically, as a witness, standing with people who are oppressed, or by advocating on their behalf.

The history of the U.S. region of the Columbans, especially in describing its perspective and spirit, unfolds a relationship between mission, hospitality, and pilgrimage.[1409] Saint Columban is pictured with a walking staff in hand to assist him as he traveled through difficult terrain (geographic, ecclesial and political) founding monasteries from Ireland to northern Italy.[1410]

Pilgrims depended upon the *hospitality* of shelter and care from others along the way. They told stories from their lives as they moved from one holy spot to another. The Columban tradition of a central house in their mission areas where the men could gather periodically was meant to be a source of fellowship and hospitality, time to recoup one's energies, and "a little bit of home," when missionaries came in from mission stations often in remote or challenging areas.

What other words might be carved on the Columban "walking staff" for the U.S. region? The answer lies partially in how people have depicted the Columban

---

[1409] On the relation between hospitality and mission, see Angelyn Dries, "Hospitality as a Life Stance in Mission. Elements from Catholic Mission Experience in the Twentieth Century," *International Bulletin of Mission Research* 39.4 (October 2015), 194–197.

[1410] Writing from China, Galvin congratulated McCarthy on his book on St. Columban. Galvin then proceeded in a two page typed letter to McCarthy with five theses Galvin derived from Columban's life and inquired, whether those five points could be defended regarding Columban. The first four points were, 1. "That from the time he left Bangor till his death in Bobbio he was a missionary and not a monk and that his great objective was Missions." 2. "That in Annegray and her two sister Mission houses he and his fellow missionaries lived as secular priests and not as monks." Their austerities were necessary "to attract the semipagan population and they recited the office in common." 3. It was never Columban's intention to write a rule. 4. What Columban did write for his priests "were the principles of the spiritual life including the saying of their office. . . . For the rest they were comparatively free and guided by the will of the Abbot." Everything about the life of the group was focused toward mission. E. J. Galvin to "Dear Mac" [E. J. McCarthy] 19 November 1929.

perspective and spirit they felt. Most frequently, Columban experience narrated *walking with others*, manifest in myriad ways. Sometimes that happened through actions initiated by their Justice and Peace office, retreat direction, pastoral care of ethnic communities, addressing the needs of missionaries, or simply listening to people's stories. Father Vinnie Busch noted, "People know the Columbans in the Philippines. The Society has been through it all with them: military, tidal waves, volcanic eruptions."[1411] Since Busch wrote that, we would add that Columbans have been with Filipinos in the struggles in southern Mindanao between Christians and Moslems, the murder of Columban Rufus Halley (2001) and capture of Father Michael Sinnott (2009), both happening to men deeply involved in working toward peaceful relationships between the two groups. "Walking *with*" is carved into the Columban staff. The perspective is a hallmark of Columbans in wherever they serve.

A second word carved on the staff is *making connections*. This strong *leitmotif* is found abundantly throughout the region's history, whether that was a reader of the mission magazine connecting with people in mission countries, a donor feeling a bond with Columbans, or Columbans feeling a strong responsibility to donors. One appeal for mission funds in the United States linked *Far East* readers both with the martyred Columbans and with the beleaguered Filipinos. "Wounds that show in shattered churches, as well as in bleeding bodies. . . . Wounds in stricken homes and broken hearts—these are the wounds of the Philippine people today. You bind some wound every time you help the work of the priests and Sisters." The appeal concluded, "The work of the six priests of St. Columban who have recently given their lives in the Philippines needs your help to continue. Wounds can't wait."[1412] Once again, the Columbans placed their service in the perspective of what people in their missions were enduring. Columbans consistently pointed to mission, to the people they serve, to donors, and to Christ.

Another key relationship focused on Columbans in the U.S. region and their fellow priests in the missions. Urging "utmost care in incurring expenses," Regional Director Timothy Connolly in 1950 reminded the men about the region's obligation "not to fail in its duty to our brothers in the missions, the poverty of whose lives as compared with ours is—or ought to be—well known to every priest in the region. It is relevant here to draw attention to the magnificent spirit of generosity which inspires these missionaries of ours to give, without a thought, their personal funds and what should be their personal leisure to the service of their missions." [1413] He added, "Thrift may not be a Columban

---

[1411]   Unnamed interviewer, interview of Father Vincent Busch. DVD, 1991.

[1412]   "Appeal for mission funds," *FE* (May 1945).

[1413]   Fr. Connolly to "All Columban Priests in the Region of America." Easter Week, 1950. 9-A-11.

charism but generosity and appreciation of the needs of the missions certainly are. So, too, are the spirit of self-sacrifice and hard work unaccompanied by the blare of trumpets, and, in most cases, unrewarded by any pat on the back."[1414]

Columbans made connections when they sought women religious from the United States to assist in the foundation of religious communities where Columbans served. The men then carried through to make the U.S women religious feel that they had a new "home" in a mission country. The fruit of these connections was the development of leadership in local churches.

A third perspective might be termed *quiet innovation* to make people "more missionary."[1415] Archbishop Hunthausen's request for Columbans to serve the Korean Catholics in the Seattle area held an additional invitation: to have a few Columbans take the place of his diocesan priests so the latter could take theology and scripture courses following Vatican II. Hunthausen particularly identified the "Columban approach and style in the parish," i.e., "having a mission view of ministry as an example of what can be accomplished if you are mission aware. People could gain a sense of a larger church and a mission spirit."[1416] Another instance was the Columban initiative in team ministry with a "mission mindedness," and an adult education focus for mission and ministry among Korean Catholics in Connecticut and the diocese of Providence, Rhode Island. These examples of mission awareness further point out an issue raised by the Society General Council in preparation for the 1988 Society General Chapter. The Council reminded the men not to be so involved in parish and diocesan responsibilities, that there "is little time or energy to pursue the missionary objectives we profess, especially those concerned with the international exchange of people, information, experience, solidarity linkages.[1417]

Some of the above perspectives were mentioned in various ways when Father James McCaslin, who, having asked whether there is a "Columban spirituality," decided to interview Columbans to see how each man described

---

[1414] Ibid.

[1415] General Council of the Missionary Society of St. Columban, "The Society and the Future," 21 December 1987. CFA-USA. The Council raised six issues, among which were Integrating Inculturation and Dialogue, Facilitating Laity in Mission, and Preparing for International Membership. On the point related to Columbans in parishes, the Council wrote that often the men were so involved in parish/diocesan responsibilities, there "is little time or energy to pursue with missionary objectives we profess, especially those concerned with the international exchange of people, information, experience, solidarity linkages. Ibid., 4.

[1416] Author telephone interview with Father Richard Parle, at the time Senior Priest at St. Edward Church, Shelton, Washington, 11 July 2014.

[1417] General Council of the Missionary Society of St. Columban, "The Society and the Future," p. 4. 21 December 1987. CFA-USA.

the experience. Father Leo Lyons (1917– 1988) of Providence, Rhode Island, was ordained in 1943 and missioned to the Philippines from 1945 to 1949. He spent the rest of his life in the Westminster and Los Angeles areas. McCaslin asked him if the experience in the Philippines, when Lyons was just learning about being a missionary, affected his work in California. Lyons responded,

> Oh, I don't know. Let me put it this way, overall I have heard it mentioned so many times . . . there is something different about Columbans. I don't think it was missionary experience or anything else, I think it was just being a Columban. We handle things in different ways. Maybe we are down to earth. We have a better relationship with people. People seem to be able to get close to us, they respect us. Maybe the work is *simpatico* to people. That doesn't come from the missions because some guys who have never been on the missions have it.[1418]

Father Joseph Murrin (1916–2002), from a farm family in Iowa, expressed the "ordinariness" of the Columbans. McCaslin asked Murrin whether in his various jobs, he felt free to do so without anyone "looking over your shoulder?" Murrin, who had overseen a good number of Columban construction projects in the United States and Korea, remarked,

> As far as knowing what I was doing, I always had a job that was above my abilities. I realized I had to get them done. I don't think ever in my life I experienced anyone checking up on me. Maybe they were but that's their problem, not mine! I was fortunate to be living with nice guys all the time. . . . My life was ordinary. Nothing startling, which I think is the way it's supposed to be. It's a learning process. I am definitely still learning, I know that." [1419]

[1418] James McCaslin interview of Father Leo Lyons, 16 June 1987, transcript. Lyons cited the example of Father Owen MacElroy (1903–1983), with whom Lyons worked for five years. Having developed tuberculosis after ordination and recovering his health somewhat, Owens came to the United States where he worked at Silver Creek, Columban headquarters in Nebraska, Milton and Westminster. For several years in the 1960s he edited the *Far East* (*Columban Mission*).

[1419] James McCaslin interview of Father Joseph Murrin, 18 March 1987, transcript. The pastor of the parish in Murrin's Iowa parish was Father Timothy Leahy. Leahy joined the Columbans in 1926 and was missioned to Hanyang until 1940, when he was unable to return because of the situation in China.

The Vatican II document on missionary activity, *Ad Gentes,* had stated that the "church on earth is by its very nature missionary." The other half of that sentence provided an answer to why that is true: Mission has its "origin in the mission of the Son and the Holy Spirit" and flows from "a 'fountain-like love,' the love of God the Father."[1420] Mission, therefore, is ultimately about relationships. Columbans, being priests of the people, came to understand the broader realities of the relationship people have with each other and with their habitat. A faith perspective identifies what is life giving in these events, difficult as they might be, and affirms what brings life, hope, and witness to that truth.

Father Chuck Lintz, with mission experience in Korea, on staff at the Columban Justice and Peace office in Washington, and then formator with the Korean Missionary Society remarked, "I am heartened because I know mission will continue. It will be different, but I am basically optimistic because of what I see happening with young people. A certain number of young people are interested in going abroad and connecting with people. I believe that the Spirit of the Lord is still with us and we will continue to do this kind of work."[1421]

Columbans will continue to examine questions that arise *internally* with respect to administration and the day-to-day life for the group. They will also approach the issues that are *raison d'être* for them: primary evangelization and the relationship between Gospel message, communities of people, especially migrants or marginalized in some manner, and the close connections with environmental issues. How is *priestly* mission envisioned by the Columbans who engage in these areas? Whether the Missionary Society of St. Columban will continue the next one hundred years is not the concern. Institutions come and go historically. The larger emphasis is mission. That will remain, though perhaps through lay missionaries, priest associates, the mission education materials the Society has produced and through people in Fiji, Latin America, Korea, Pakistan, Myanmar, China, the Philippines, the United States, and wherever Columbans have nurtured people in mission.

The Columban walking staff is emblazoned with *make connections, walk with others*, and *quiet innovation*. What Regional Superior Charlie Coulter said in 1978 is true still for today: "Changing, 'moving on,' has always been part of the witness and charisma of our Society, whose motto is *'Peregrinari pro Christo,'* and whose spirituality, it is suggested, is a 'Spirituality of the road."[1422] Throughout the history of the region of the United States, Columbans have deflected attention from themselves and toward the people they serve and love, drawing people to greater possibilities of love in God, of each other, and of the

---

[1420] *Ad Gentes*, par. 2.

[1421] Sean Dwan interview of Father Chuck Lintz, 12 June 2013.

[1422] Regional Superior Charles Coulter letter to Columban Fathers in the U.S. region, 15 March 1978.

earth and its environment. As Michael McLoughlin remarked, "Our experience today has taught us that we always work from the periphery rather than from the inside,"[1423] especially so with ethnic communities, people in impoverished situations, or people in transition/migration.

Quoting the Latin America and Caribbean Catholic bishops' *Aparecida* document (1988), Pope Francis in his apostolic exhortation, *The Joy of the Gospel*, wrote, "I hope that all communities will devote the necessary effort to advancing along the path of a pastoral and missionary conversion, which cannot leave things as they are presently. 'Mere administration can no longer be enough.' Throughout the world, let us be 'permanently in a state of mission.'"[1424] With wit, always with stories, and sometimes with song, the Columbans have been living for a century Saint Columban's motto, "Be centered in Christ and not in self."

[1423]   Regional Director Michael O'Loughlin to Frank Mannion 14 October 1991. 8-B-30-21. (Dallas, Texas file). CFA-USA.

[1424]   Pope Francis, *Joy of the Gospel* (*Evangelii Gaudium*), 14. (Washington DC: U.S. Conference of Catholic Bishops, 2013).

APPENDICES

List of Superiors General, U.S. Regional Directors (with photos)

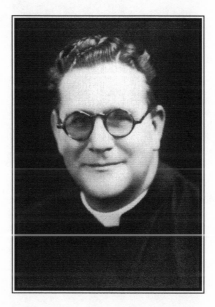

1919-1934 Father E J McCarthy

1934-1947 Father Paul Waldron

1947-1952 Father Timothy Connolly

1952-1962 Father Peter McPartland

1962-1967 Father Daniel Boland

1967-1970 Father Richard Steinhilber

1971-1976 Father Hugh (Hubert) O'Rourke

1977-1983 Father Charles (Cathal) P. Coulter

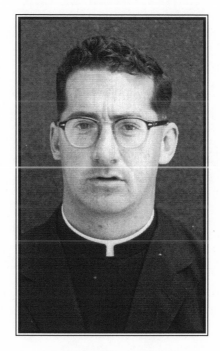

1983-1987 Father Peter J. Cronin

1987-1991 Father Edward V. Naughton

1991-1995 Father Michael J. O'Loughlin

1995-2000 Father Brendan O'Sullivan

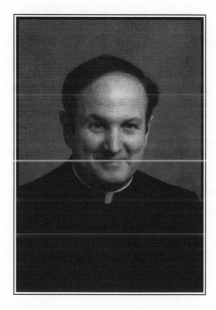

2000-2006 Father John E. Burger

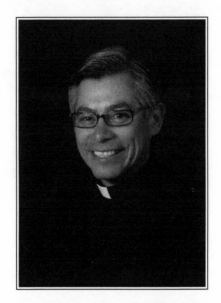

2006-2012 Father Arturo Aguilar Jr.

2013-2018 Father Timothy Mulroy

INDEX

Edwards Brothers Malloy
Ann Arbor MI. USA
August 15, 2017